M. Schlauch
U-25

THE ESSENTIAL ARTICLES SERIES

Bernard N. Schilling
University of Rochester
General Editor

Donald G. Adam
Chatham College
Assistant General Editor

Harry G. Rusche
Emory University
Assistant General Editor

Volumes Available

ESSENTIAL ARTICLES FOR THE STUDY OF ENGLISH
AUGUSTAN BACKGROUNDS

Ed. Bernard N. Schilling

ESSENTIAL ARTICLES FOR THE STUDY OF ALEXANDER
POPE. Revised and enlarged edition.

Ed. Maynard Mack

ESSENTIAL ARTICLES FOR THE STUDY OF JOHN DRYDEN

Ed. H. T. Swedenberg, Jr.

ESSENTIAL ARTICLES FOR THE STUDY OF OLD ENGLISH
POETRY

Ed. Jess Bessinger and Stanley J. Kahrl

ESSENTIAL ARTICLES FOR THE STUDY OF FRANCIS BACON

Ed. Brian Vickers

Essential Articles

for the study of
Old English Poetry

*Property of
Charles A. Owen, Jr.
Medieval Studies Library*

Edited by **Jess B. Bessinger, Jr.**
New York University

Stanley J. Kahrl
University of Rochester

ARCHON BOOKS   Hamden, Connecticut   **1968**

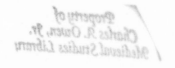

SBN: 208 00153 0
Library of Congress Catalog Card Number: 68-20087
Printed in the United States of America

CONTENTS

CONTENTS

IV. THREE METRICAL STUDIES

V. ORAL-FORMULAR ARGUMENTS

VI. PARTICULAR POETS AND POEMS

FOREWORD

Immense resources are now available for literary study in England and America. The contributions to scholarship and criticism are so numerous and often so valuable that the student preparing himself for a career in literary teaching and study may be embarrassed, not to say overwhelmed. Yet from this mass of commentary certain titles have emerged which seem to compel attention. If one offers a seminar in one of the standard areas or periods of English literature, the syllabus will show year after year some items which cannot be omitted, some pieces every serious student should know. And with each new offering of the course, one must face the task of compiling a list of these selections for the seminar's reserve shelf, of searching out and calling in the library's copies, and reserving space for the twenty or thirty or forty volumes the list may demand. As if this were not enough, one must also attempt to repair or replace the volumes whose popularity has had the unfortunate side effects of frequent circulation and the concomitant wear, abuse, and general deterioration.

We propose an alternative to this procedure. We propose to select from the many learned journals, scholarly studies, and critical books the best selections available, the selections which consistently reappear on graduate seminar shelves and on undergraduate honors program reading lists. Let us choose from those articles which time has sanctioned, those too from the best of more recent performances, and let us draw them into a single volume of convenient size. This offers a clear gain in simplicity and usefulness. The articles chosen make up a body of knowledge that cannot fail to be valuable, and they act as models of the kind of contributions to learning which we are training our students to make themselves. And if we can have ready to hand a concentration of such articles for each of the standard areas, and several individual authors, we may conduct the study of these subjects with greater confidence, knowing more fully the extent and kind of reading we can take for granted. And, while we benefit our classes and students, we can also allow the library to keep the original editions of the articles on its shelves and so fulfill its proper and usual function.

FOREWORD

We must add, finally, that each book in the series, and therefore the whole series, is the result of unselfish help from contributors and editors from all of Great Britain and the United States. We wish to acknowledge their help and the help of the Bowdoin College Research Fund in rendering this useful service.

B. N. S. Rochester, N. Y.
D. G. A. Pittsburgh, Pa.
H. G. R. Atlanta, Ga.

PREFACE

This collection began when the editors exchanged reading lists for their introductory courses in Old English literature, courses centered in poetry, but excluding Beowulf. Some articles were obviously important, and the outlines of some areas of general critical interest became apparent as well. However, it also became clear that the best efforts of at least three generations of scholars could not be confined in a single volume. We believe then that a selective anthology best serves the growing number of courses in Old English poetry—happily made up increasingly of volunteers rather than conscripts—by present ing as variously as possible the multiple approaches to Old English poetry available to the student. Thus the articles included here are meant to serve as stimulants to further efforts of like kind, and to act as signposts toward paths still needing clearing rather than as roadsigns on the highways of current fashion.

The sections into which the anthology is divided are in most cases suggestive rather than definitive. By and large the best examples of literary criticism of Old English poetry have dealt with general topics, which has at times made grouping difficult, particularly as regards those articles included in the first section. There variety itself seemed to be the sole organizing principle. Thereafter the approaches become more clearly defined. Rigorous analysis of single key terms or concepts in Old English poetry is still an essential task (cf. William Whallon's recent fruitful application of this technique to "The Idea of God in Beowulf," PMLA, LXXX (1965), 19–23). Here early studies have unquestioned relevance, as they do in the still largely unexplored area of stylistics.

The section on prosody can only be a gesture: we have provided the first English translation of Sievers' great study, together with Lewis' lively exposition, plus a sample of the metrical school that finds Sievers too metrical, but nothing of the imposing theory that finds Sievers unrhythmical. No such sample available to us would fit into our pages or seemed comprehensible without prior knowledge of John C. Pope's The Rhythm of Beowulf, fortunately now available in a new printing. Nor are the discussions of the oral-formulaic theory meant to be complete. Once again, we have included representative analyses, together with a carefully considered caveat.

We wish we had more articles dealing with individual poems. Once we had amassed the general articles, it was our intention to include in

PREFACE

a separate volume critical clusters on individual poems similar to the group devoted here to <u>The Wanderer</u> and <u>The Seafarer</u>. Few such clusters exist of the caliber attained in the discussion of those two poems. If this anthology does nothing more than to stimulate wider scholarly interest in the corpus of Old English poetry, we will consider our efforts rewarded.

We must express our gratitude both to the general editors of this series and to the authors and editors whose original labors made this collection possible. With their permission and assistance we have made factual corrections wherever we could, and have tried not to introduce new errors.

Jess B. Bessinger, Jr.   Stanley J. Kahrl
New York University   University of Rochester

I. GENERAL CRITICAL APPROACHES

THE LOST LITERATURE OF MEDIEVAL ENGLAND

R. W. Chambers

I have more than once heard the late W. P. Ker express surprise at the way in which students of Medieval English literature leave out of their calculation what has been lost. The same temptation does not beset the student of classical literature, or at any rate not in equal measure. Startling new discoveries are being made with more frequency, and serve to keep the classical student constantly reminded that "it is hard to say what the sands of Egypt still hide for us." These words were placed at the end of his narrative by a historian of Greek literature, writing in the year 1890, and he has been justified by a succession of finds, beginning with the announcement in the following January of the discovery of the treatise on the Constitution of Athens. Generally, too, in classical literature we have titles, and often a few odd lines preserved, to keep us reminded of what has been lost. With the names of well over a hundred vanished plays of Sophocles before us, we cannot think of him as the author of seven plays alone. And we know enough of the subject of many of the lost plays to stimulate our curiosity. A Gretna Green marriage, with papa upset at the critical moment, because his wicked minx of a daughter has bribed his charioteer to betray him, does not strike one as a very Sophoclean theme. We wonder how Sophocles treated it, and whether the lost Oenomaus would have modified our conception of Sophoclean tragedy.

The temptation is much greater to overlook the lost literature of the Middle Ages: for it has often left very little trace behind it. We do not get much light on the lost vernacular literature of the earlier Middle Ages from scrutinizing the catalogues of monastic libraries which have come down to us. A good deal of this lost literature, as we shall see, was very possibly never

Reprinted from The Library, 4th Series, Vol. 5, No. 4, March 1925, by permission of the publisher and University College, London.

written down at all: it may have depended entirely upon the memory of minstrels. Yet it is safe to say that if the lost poetry had been preserved, the whole history of English literature, prior to Chaucer and Langland, would appear to us in a different light. The homilies and lives of saints, which bulk so largely in Medieval English verse and prose, would subside till they occupied a just, and a small, proportion of our attention.

Bacon has put it that "Time is like a river, which carrieth down things which are light and blown up, and drowneth that which is sad and weighty." So far, however, as medieval literature is concerned, the serious works which Bacon would have characterized as "sad and weighty" have very largely been preserved. What has been lost is the legendary poetry written in honour of kings and heroes, many of whom did indeed actually exist, but whose exploits were perverted in a way which Bacon would have deplored as showing a "light and blown up" spirit of indifference to historical fact. The complaint we have really to make against the river of Time is the reverse of that which Bacon makes. It is that it has brought down masses of medieval literature which are sad, weighty, and dull, but has drowned so much which might in some senses be called light, but which was certainly cheering, romantic, and sometimes heroic in spirit. In England, we have to deplore the almost complete loss of two distinct schools of heroic poetry.

In marked contrast to this loss, is the security with which the tradition of English scholarship has come down to us. That tradition begins in the seventh century, when two streams of learning met in England, the one coming from Ireland and the other from Mediterranean lands. The tradition of learning which then started in England has, despite many set-backs, continued unbroken to the present day. One example of this continuity may be given.

Of all the scholars born in England in the seventh century, by far the greatest is the Venerable Bede: and his greatest work is the Ecclesiastical History of the English People. Bede himself tells us that he finished the work in 731; but he was apparently adding the finishing touches in the following year, for the book contains what seems an allusion to the great defeat of the Saracens by Charles Martel, which took place in 732. Now we have four manuscripts of the Ecclesiastical History which seem to have been transcribed before the close of the century; and one of these, the Moore manuscript at Cambridge, must have been transcribed in or before the year 737, since some chronological notes which must belong to that year have been entered on a blank page. The Moore manuscript, then, cannot have been copied more than five or six years after the completion of Bede's work, and it may have been copied within a few months of that completion.

Then, from the ninth century, we have at least 7 manuscripts surviving, from the tenth 7, from the eleventh 11, from the twelfth and very early thirteenth 23, from the thirteenth 15, from the fourteenth 18, from the fifteenth 9 manuscripts and four printed editions, beginning from about the year 1475.[1]

What is even more noteworthy than the fact that we possess a manuscript written only a few years, or even months, after the first publication of the Ecclesiastical History, is the fact that this manuscript, early as it is, is not the original of the rest. Only one manuscript of any importance has so far been proved to be derived from the Moore manuscript. The other oldest manuscripts are not derived from the Moore manuscript, nor from any other extant manuscript.

The continuity of this tradition affords a striking contrast to the fate of classics like Catullus or Lucretius, forgotten by the world until the end of the Middle Ages, and then discovered only in a single copy, or in transcripts which can all be traced back to some not very remote archetype. An equally striking contrast is supplied by the Annals of Tacitus, partly lost, partly dependent (so far at any rate as the first six books are concerned) upon a single manuscript, copied some nine hundred years after the Annals were composed. The Ecclesiastical History, on the other hand, has come down to us by distinct channels which can be proved, by many trifling divergencies, to have already become independent streams within half a dozen years, at most, of the publication of the book. That is to say, there has never been a time, since the Ecclesiastical History was fairly launched in the years after 731, when the destruction of one manuscript, or, for the matter of that, of a considerable number of manuscripts, would have endangered the transmission of the book.

As a matter of fact, such destruction did take place, and on an extensive scale. It is noteworthy that the overwhelming majority of the earliest manuscripts are foreign. Yet the subject, The Ecclesiastical History of the English People, is not

one which we should expect specially to interest the foreigner.
The reason for the preponderance of foreign manuscripts is
to be sought, partly in the amazing activity of English missionaries upon the Continent, but also in the overwhelming destruction of English manuscripts which took place in the eleven years
between 867 and 878. For generations before and after those
eleven years, monasteries and libraries were destroyed by the
Danes: but at no other period was there such universal destruction. "Everything," in the words of King Alfred, "was harried
and burnt up." That this wholesale conflagration could not en-
danger the continuous handing down of the Ecclesiastical History,
shows how strong, since the eighth century, has been the position
in England of any author who, writing in Latin, could make himself a European reputation.

A further fact emphasizes this. Bede is not only the father
of modern history: he is the father of English bibliography. Historians have drawn attention to the epoch-making fact that Bede
begins his History by giving a list of his sources and authorities.
It is even more important for us to note that he concludes it with
a bibliography of the works he had already published: Bede is
the first, and certainly the most venerable, of English bibliogra-
phers. The overwhelming majority of the forty or fifty[2] books
which he enumerates are still extant. Indeed, I would hazard
the guess that it is quite possible that a larger percentage of
late eighteenth-century novels is already lost, than of the works
of the Venerable Bede.

But when we come to composition in the English language,
the difference is marked. Every one knows the story of Bede's
death-bed: how he spent his last days in translating the Gospel
of St. John, and how he composed a short poem in English "being
skilled in English poetry." But the gospel-translation has vanished; nor have any English poems of Bede been preserved, except this five-line death-song, recorded by the piety of a disciple.
This serves to show how different has been the fate of the vernacular prose and verse from that of the Latin literature of the
Middle Ages.

To trace the beginnings of this English vernacular poetry
we must go back seven centuries behind Bede. Tacitus had
noted the poetry of the Germanic peoples as the one kind of
Annals prevalent among them: and when mentioning the death

of Arminius he had recorded how, nearly a century after, he was still remembered in the songs of his people. Centuries later we hear of lays commemorating the history of the Goths, when they had left their homes on the Baltic, and were wandering over the steppes of Russia to the Black Sea. The Emperor Julian heard the Barbarians beyond the Rhine singing their wild songs, which he thought like the croaking of harsh-voiced birds. Whatever may have been thought in orthodox circles of the other views of the Apostate, no one protested against this literary judgement. Indeed, it received in the course of the next century the endorsement of one who either was at the time, or was later to become, a bishop. At Clermont, Sidonius Apollinaris had to live in the immediate neighbourhood of the Germanic tribesmen settled in the South of France. "How can I write Latin verse," he asks, "when I live among the long-haired tribes, and am having to bear up under the weight of Germanic words, and am having to praise, albeit with a wry face, whatever the Burgundian, with his hair smeared with rancid butter, chooses to sing?"

It is much to be regretted that the cultivated Roman writers have not told us more of the productions of these "barbaric lyres." The words of Tacitus, and of the historian of the Goths, show the important part played in this poetry by traditional lays, dealing with the adventures of Germanic chiefs and tribes during the whole period in which they were warring, some in the pay of the Roman Empire, some against it, until finally they overthrew it. But this literature would doubtless also include charms, proverbs, mnemonic verses, formulas used in the service of the gods, out of which a ritual drama might later have developed. The only thing which, at this early stage, is definitely mentioned by our literary authorities is, however, the semi-historical lay dealing with the history of the race.

But such semi-historical lays passed freely from one tribe to another, so that any deed of valour, any tragic struggle of any Germanic chieftain might form the subject of a lay among any Germanic tribe. Professor Ker puts it: "If any one were to ask 'What does the old English literature prove?' the answer would be ready enough. It proves that the Germanic nations had a reciprocal free-trade in subjects for epic poems."

It is interesting to note how this fact, so important in the history of literature, has been appreciated by Charles Kingsley. Hard things have been said of Kingsley as a historian. It should be remembered to his credit how he perceived (what no one in these days would dispute) that the story, found in the Latin of Paul the Deacon, of the fight in which Woden gave victory to the Longobards, is simply one of these old lays of the period of the Germanic migrations. But when Kingsley puts this lay into the mouth of a Goth, supposed at the moment to be in Alexandria, and destined ultimately to settle in Spain, he illustrates exactly how these lays travelled from tribe to tribe of the Germanic race:

> Over the camp-fires
> Drank I with heroes,
> Under the Donau bank
> Warm in the snow-trench,
> Sagamen heard I there,
> Men of the Longbeards,
> Cunning and ancient,
> Honey-sweet-voiced.

Unless we get a clear perception of this "free-trade" in subject matter among the Germanic tribes, the whole history of their heroic legends will be a puzzle to us. And there is nothing to surprise us in the fact that the constant and cruel inter-tribal warfare did not prevent the Germanic tribes from having common literary ideas and traditions, and even taking an interest in each other's work.

The same was the case in Ancient Greece. At the end of the generation-long struggle between Sparta and Athens, whilst the victorious leaders were pondering whether they should utterly destroy the enemy city, it was nevertheless possible for a Phocian musician to sing a monody from the drama of an Athenian poet in the presence of the assembled enemies of Athens.[3]

There is therefore no reason to be surprised at what the documentary evidence definitely proves: that when the Angles and Saxons came to England, they brought with them a mass of heroic lays celebrating the heroes of many different Germanic tribes. These lays have all been lost, but allusions to the traditions they enshrined remain. Of course native heroes were not forgotten. A favourite hero was Offa, son of the blind king Wermund, who must have ruled over the Angles when they were

8

still on the Continent, about the end of the fourth century A. D.
Both in Beowulf and in Widsith we have enthusiastic praise of
the glory of Offa: but Beowulf is more concerned with Scandinavian kings, such as the Danish Hrothgar, of whom we also hear
in the Danish history of Saxo Grammaticus, or Ohthere, King of
Sweden in the sixth century, whose actual burial mound has been
opened by Swedish antiquaries within the last few years. Widsith,
curiously enough, is primarily concerned with the glory of
Eadgils, King of the Myrgingas: and Eadgils and the Myrgingas
are the very enemies against whom Wermund and Offa had to
defend their Anglian realm. Widsith is a very early poem, and
Eadgils was probably forgotten in England before the Norman
Conquest: the legends of Offa, on the other hand, reinforced by
other legends concerning the historic King Offa, who reigned in
Mercia twelve generations after his continental ancestor and
namesake, survived in the Midlands till at any rate about the
year 1200.

But the Angles and Saxons also brought over lays dealing
with Germanic peoples much more remote than the Scandinavian
peoples to the North, or the puzzling Myrgingas to the South,
or the Frisians to the West. One of the most familiar of all
these names in England was that of the great Gothic King
Ermanaric, whose kingdom, stretching almost from the Black
Sea to the Baltic, had been destroyed by the Huns about the year
A. D. 375. Sixty years later, the same adversaries had overthrown the Burgundian King Gundahari, ruling on the Rhine, and
his downfall came to be known to all people of Germanic speech
from Austria to Greenland. Corresponding to the Gunter of the
Nibelungen Lied, or the Gunnar of the "Greenland" lay, the English form of the name would be Guthhere: and the Burgundian
king is commemorated under this name twice in the scanty remains of Anglo-Saxon heroic poetry. In the same scanty remains
we have allusions to Attila (who died in 453), to Theodoric the
Great, whose magnanimous rule in Italy ended with his death
in 526, and to Alboin, who, after conquering Northern Italy, died
in 572 or 573. The way in which these names are introduced
show that they were household names in England. The historic
perspective has, however, been lost, and these chiefs have all
come to be regarded as living at about the same time; references
to the captivity of Theodoric among giants show us also how
legendary his story had become.

But with the later developments of these heroes we are not for the moment concerned. When, in the generation after the fall of the historic Gundahari, Sidonius was vexed at having to listen to the lays of his long-haired Burgundian neighbours, we may be fairly certain that these neighbours would not be silent about the last terrible battle in which their fathers had all fallen fighting around their King. But the story would be very different from what it had become seven or eight centuries later, in the form in which the story of the fall of the Niblungs has come down to us.

This first period of Germanic heroic poetry we may date from the first century A. D., when the traditions about Arminius must have had their origin, to the seventh, when this poetry was, in England, brought into touch with scholarship and booklearning, in a way which had noteworthy results. During the intervening centuries this poetry had doubtless spread wherever the barbarian conquerors of Rome went. It is just conceivable that a fragment of it might yet turn up amid the sands of Egypt, just as a fragment of a Gothic Bible recently did: or a piece of parchment might be found embedded in an old binding in some European library: or some very old manuscript in a Spanish monastery might be found to have had some verses written upon its blank pages by a Visigoth, who happened to combine ability to write with a love of the old poetry. But we may be fairly sure that most of this oldest Germanic poetry was never written down at all, although many millions of lines must have been composed during these six or seven centuries, when every chief had his attendant minstrel, and when the recitation of this poetry was the recognized accompaniment of the evening feast.

Of all these verses, historical, gnomic, magical, encomiastic, mnemonic, epigraphic—for, as Tacitus said, it was their one form of memorial and of history—two short inscriptions only survive, which were written down before the date when Christian and heathen tradition were brought face to face in seventh-century England. Both examples are of a sternly practical character. An alliterative (but not as a whole metrical) inscription in Southern Norway contains at least one distinctly metrical line:

Ek Wiwaz after Woðuriðe
witaða-halaiban worahto runoz.

"I Wiwaz in memory of Wothurithaz
Wrought the runes for my rightful comrade (or lord)."

This sixth-century inscription has been claimed as the earliest
example of Scandinavian verse. Even earlier is the inscription
on one of the golden horns found near Gallehus, in Southern Jutland, which has been attributed to a date as early as A. D. 300:

Ek Hlewagastiz Holtingaz horna tawiðo.

"I Hlewagastiz son of Holt (or of Holt) made the horn."

And the district where this horn was found is, as we know from
Bede, the region from which came the Jutish settlers of England.
There is of course nothing in the Gallehus inscription which we
can call specifically English: at this early period the dialects of
the dwellers on the North Sea coast, Frisians, Angles, Saxons,
Jutes, have not differentiated sufficiently for us to find any
phonological clue in this short inscription. But, when we "praise
famous men and our fathers that begat us," Hlewagastiz the goldsmith ought to be remembered among "such as found out musical tunes, and recited verses in writing." His verse is not as
musical as Milton's, nor his thought as subtle as Shakespeare's;
but at least it is metre, and it is sense; and since that is more
than can be said of much of the Georgian poetry which I have
read, it is not for us, in this century, to cast scorn on Hlewagastiz,
the first man known to have combined rime with reason in speech
which is the direct ancestor of the speech of Milton and of Shakespeare.

For the next step in the history of English poetry we have
to wait some three centuries. The conversion of the English
to Christianity seems to have been an easy one; there seems to
have been little fanatical adherence to the worship of Woden or
Thunor. But the love for the poetry connected with the old
heathen life was so real as to make the champions of Christendom uneasy. At a much later date, when one might suppose the
attachment to the old heroic poetry to be somewhat less intense,
Alcuin had to warn the very monks of Lindisfarne against it.
"Let the word of God," he says, "be read in the Refectory: there
it behooves the lector to be heard, and not the harper, the works

of the fathers, rather than the songs of the heathen. For what
has Ingeld to do with Christ?" Ingeld was the tragic hero of
heroic song, alluded to in Beowulf, who had to choose between
love of his wife, and the duty of revenging his father, whom his
wife's kinsfolk had slain. But, as Alcuin goes on to point out,
these pagan kings are now in Hell, and therefore it is wrong to
mention their names with that of the King of Heaven.

It is this antipathy between the monk and the minstrel
which explains the importance attached by Bede to the story
of the dream in which Caedmon was commanded to celebrate
the Creation of the World in the style of the old heathen lays.
Many learned ecclesiastics were assembled, to decide what
and whence such a vision might be. They decided that a divine
grace had been conferred upon the poet.

"Nothing," the late Sir Walter Raleigh once said, "is more
striking than the way the English people do not alter": and nothing could show better our typical English love of compromise
than do the Christian imitations of the old heathen poetry. Inconsistency does not matter to the English mind, if only a good
end is attained. This Christian epic is not afraid to tell us that
the twelve apostles were glorious heroes, whose might failed
not in battle when the banners clashed: and this discrepancy is
raised to noble poetry when the Crucifixion is described in terms
applicable to the last contest of a mighty young warrior. At the
same time that Caedmon was beginning this school of Christian
poetry in Northumbria, Aldhelm, Bishop of Sherborne, was doing
the same thing in the South. The account of Aldhelm's achievement, as given by King Alfred in his lost Handbook, has been
preserved by a later historian.

On the authority of Alfred's lost work,[4] William of Malmesbury tells us that the reason why Aldhelm composed the popular
poetry (carmen triviale) which in his time was still current, was
that his half-civilized flock used to depart to their homes as
soon as mass had been celebrated. So the holy man placed himself, in the guise of a minstrel, at the bridge which they had to
pass. When, after more than one performance, he had made
himself popular, he began gradually to mingle words of Scrip-
ture amid the more amusing matter (sensim inter ludicra verbis
scripturarum insertis, cives ad sanitatem reduxisse). Further,
William quotes the opinion of Alfred, that at no period had there
been any equal to Aldhelm as a writer of English verse, which
he could either sing or recite.

That so very little of this Christian poetry has come down to us in early manuscripts is probably to be attributed to the wholesale destruction of written documents between the years 867 and 878. Precisely as in the case of Bede's <u>Ecclesiastical History</u>, most of our records come from abroad; and we are justified in assuming that if English verses are found abroad, they would, but for untoward circumstances, have been found in greater numbers at home. Caedmon's first hymn—a nine-line poem, and the only one of his compositions certainly extant—is preserved on the top of what was a blank page of the Moore manuscript, which was written on the Continent, "perhaps at Epternach or at some Anglo-Saxon colony on the other side of the channel."[5] As the Moore manuscript did not come to England till the end of the seventeenth century, this hymn must have been written into the manuscript abroad. The lines must, however, have continued to be currently known in England, where we have other texts written down much later, so that this is one of the very few poems which have been preserved in more than one manuscript. Bede's Death Song,[6] a two-line proverb,[7] and a riddle[8] have also been preserved abroad.

There is one exception to this rule that all the early transcripts of English verse have been preserved on the Continent, and this one exception is of the kind which proves the rule. The only fragments of Anglo-Saxon religious verse of which we possess a very early transcript, certainly made in this island, are the lines engraved in runes upon the Ruthwell Cross: and this has doubtless been preserved only because it was an inscription too massive to be easily destroyed.

That "Saxon poems" <u>had</u> been written into books at a period before the great Danish destruction, is shown by the statement that Alfred, in his childhood, received such a volume as a gift from his mother. The statement that till he was twelve years old he could not read, but used to listen to the recitation of "Saxon poems" by day and night, till he had them by heart, shows what a large part memory still played in the preservation of this literature. Indeed, so far as we can interpret the rather obscure words of Asser, it would seem that the boy Alfred earned his prize, <u>quendam Saxonicum poematicae artis librum</u>, not by learning to read it, but by having it read to him till he had it all by heart, and was thus able to prove that he had "learnt" the book. It seems to have been rather the learning by heart than the reading of Saxonica carmina which Alfred enjoined upon his children, Edward and Ælfthryth, and which he recommended to his friends.[9]

Finally, about a hundred years after Alfred's time, and more than three hundred years after this school of vernacular religious poetry had been begun by Caedmon and Aldhelm, three books were transcribed, about the year 1000, to which we owe almost all our knowledge of this poetry.

The Exeter Book ("one great English book, on all sorts of subjects, wrought in verse," as it is called in the list of Bishop Leofric's donations to his Cathedral) contains about eight thousand lines of verse, almost exclusively religious and moral.[10] Junius 11, in the Bodleian, contains some five thousand lines: the Genesis and Exodus deserve special mention. The Vercelli Book, left on the Italian side of the Alps, apparently by some pilgrim on his way to or from Rome, contains between three and four thousand lines of verse.

There is reason to think that these three codices give us only a small proportion of the total body of old English religious poetry. The greatest of the poets was, according to Bede, Caedmon, and according to Alfred, Aldhelm. We have no evidence that the work of either is represented in these collections. It is true that Junius, when, in 1655, he printed the Bodleian manuscript, attributed the poems in it to Caedmon. But he had no evidence, and it is now quite certain that the Bodleian collection is a composite one. A school of religious heroic poetry, similar to that which had been founded by Caedmon in Northumbria, flourished among the Saxons on the Continent. As these Saxons had been christianized by English missionaries, it seems clear that these missionaries had carried with them their native institution of Christian heroic poetry.[11] But in 1875 Eduard Sievers showed that about six hundred lines of the Junian manuscript gave evidence, both in their metre and in their language, of being only an Anglo-Saxon transliteration of a Continental Saxon original. In 1894 long fragments of this hypothetical Continental Saxon original were discovered in the Vatican Library. The composite nature of the poems in the Junian manuscript was therefore finally demonstrated, though they all doubtless owe their ultimate inspiration to Caedmon.

Now, taking these three great collections, the Exeter, Vercelli, and Junian codices, we find extraordinarily little

repetition. Although they are all collections of poems very similar in character, all the portions common to any two of them are
75 lines which occur both in the Junian manuscript and the Exeter
Book (because a poem on Daniel runs parallel to a poem on
Azarias), and a short address of the Soul to the Body (129 lines)
which is common to the Vercelli and to the Exeter Books. It
might reasonably be argued that the total corpus of religious
verse must have been very great, to make it possible for three
collections to be written down about the same time, with so little
overlapping. For the writing and form of the three codices suf-
fices to prove that they are not merely the three volumes of one
collection, which have got separated. It cannot, of course, be
proved that they have no connexion. Indeed it might be suggested
that the Vercelli Book was formed by, or for, some man who
already possessed a collection similar to that from which the
Exeter Book was copied, and that repetition was therefore deliberately avoided. But even if we make assumptions like this,
there is further evidence that these three volumes contain only
a small portion of the religious poetry which was written in
Anglo-Saxon times. Outside these three great collections there
are about a score of pieces of religious and moral poetry, preserved in many different ways. In two cases only do these pieces
overlap the collections: the inscription on the Ruthwell cross
gives lines which also occur in the Vercelli Book, and the Northumbrian Riddle, preserved at Leiden, occurs in West-Saxon form
in the Exeter Book. The legitimate conclusion would seem to
be that the total body of religious and moral poetry must have
been very great, and that only a very small proportion of it is
preserved in our three extant collections.

Side by side with this religious epic, the old heroic poetry
lived on, as the poem of Beowulf proves. Beowulf shows how it
was possible to combine the Christian spirit and the wild heathen
legends; the author seems to be cherishing the same deliberate
purpose as Caedmon or as Aldhelm. He wished to show how much
the spirit of the old poetry could be brought into harmony with
the spirit of the new teaching. Albeit his theme is avowedly
heathen ("they knew not the Lord God, nor how to praise the
Guardian of the Heavens, the Ruler of the World") it is not treated
in the heathen spirit. The result is something very like the Idylls
of the King, where stories

15

Touch'd by the adulterous finger of a time
That hover'd between war and wantonness

are so treated as to be fit for reading in the garden of a Victorian rectory. Again we observe how the English people do not alter.

The fact that Beowulf approximates in spirit to the Christian heroic poetry may help to account for its preservation. Two fragments of heroic poems remain. A single leaf, dealing with the fight in Finn's Hall, survived in the Lambeth Library till the eighteenth century, although it has now been lost. Two leaves exist at Copenhagen, dealing with the fight of Waldere against Guthhere and Hagena (the Gunter and Hagen of the Nibelungen Lied, the Gunnar and Hogni of the Elder Edda). They seem to have come from the binding of a book, and were discovered in England by the Icelander Thorkelin, and carried by him to their present home.

Now, when we consider that King Alfred deliberately set to work to have the English laity educated, so that they could read and write their own language, it is reasonable to suppose that books like Beowulf or Waldere may have been not uncommon, in the houses of Anglo-Saxon gentlemen in the tenth or early eleventh centuries. But the Norman Conquest meant an entire change in the composition and outlook of the aristocracy. Unless such books had found their way into monastic libraries, they would not have survived. And their chances of doing so would be small; for whatever a layman might do, this literature was taboo to the clergy. It was one of the charges brought against Dunstan that in his youth he had learnt the vain songs of ancestral heathendom.[12] His biographer rebuts this charge indignantly, as scabiem mendacii. The Laws of King Edgar forbade a priest to sing these songs, even to himself. A competent and energetic librarian, who had found such manuscripts on his shelves, would probably have ejected them as summarily as a Sunday School superintendent would remove the works of Nat Gould from his library. Fortunately for literature, librarians have not invariably been competent and energetic. But the odds were heavily against such volumes surviving, even long enough to be cut up for binding other books in the fourteenth, fifteenth, or sixteenth centuries. That two remnants have thus survived renders it probable that, in the tenth and eleventh centuries, a considerable amount of this heroic poetry must have existed in written form. The "erroneous English books" of which Ælfric speaks may well have been of this kind.

The history of Old English prose literature is in marked contrast to that of the poetry. The prose literature seems to have been very limited in amount, and we do not seem to have lost very much. In spite of Bede's translation from the Gospel of St. John, there seems to have been practically no vernacular prose before the time of Alfred. The books of edification, kept in the churches, were all in Latin. We have the direct evidence of Alfred as to this. He is giving his reasons for translating into English the Pastoral Care of Gregory the Great. "I called to mind," he says, "how I saw, before it was all harried and burned up, how the churches throughout all England stood filled with treasures and books; there was a great company too of God's servants, but they could make very little use of the books, because they were not written in their own tongue, and they could in no wise understand them." This refusal to translate into English had been, Alfred thinks, the deliberate plan of the scholars of old time, who had hoped to keep up a high standard of scholarship by refusing to tolerate translation. But this method had proved a failure, and Alfred suggests, as a deliberate innovation, the formation of a collection of English translations. "And so," he says, addressing each of his bishops in turn by name, "it seems good to me, if it also seems good to you, that we should turn into the speech which we can all understand certain books which are most needful for all men to know." Such an apology for innovation makes it clear that Bede's example in translating from St. John had not been followed at all generally. Except, therefore, for a very exceptional translation, interlinear gloss, or vernacular charter, we have probably lost little English prose literature prior to Alfred, because there was little to lose. And the prose literature which Alfred created has come down to us in a pretty secure tradition. The first of these translations was apparently that of the Pastoral Care of Gregory; for it is in the Preface which he prefixes to this translation that Alfred gives his plan for a series of translations: "and so, among the other many and manifold cares of this kingdom, I began to turn into English the book which is called in Latin Pastoralis. . . . And I will send a copy to every bishopric in my kingdom." This

meant an immediate circulation, about the year 894, of some
ten copies throughout the kingdom: and it is interesting to note
what has been the fate of these copies. The Preface was per-
sonally addressed to each bishop: "King Alfred bids greet
Bishop — with words of love and friendship"; and according to
the name of the bishop we can tell from which diocese any extant copy has been derived.

Six copies have come down to modern times. The most
interesting of all, Cotton Tiberius B. xi, was lost in the Cottonian fire, but is known to us through a transcript made by
Junius. It seems to have been a copy used in the Scriptorium
of Winchester. A blank space is left for the name of the bishop
whom Alfred greets, and a note had been made that Archbishop
Plegmund had received his copy; so had Bishop Swithulf [of
Rochester] and Bishop Werferth [of Worcester].

It does not follow that this Cottonian MS. was the archetype
of the other extant copies; even if they were copied from it,
they may have received authoritative corrections giving them
independent value.

The copies sent to Canterbury and Rochester have been
lost. Presumably the great Canterbury fire of 1067 was responsible for the loss of Plegmund's copy: at any rate it is not to be
found in the catalogue of books in the Cathedral Priory of Christ
Church, made in the time of Prior Henry of Eastry (1330), although copies of four other English prose works issued by Alfred and his fellow workers are mentioned in that Catalogue.[13]

The copy actually sent to Bishop Werferth of Worcester is
extant. It is now in the Bodleian (Hatton 20). An eleventh-century copy of this Worcester book, glossed in what is known to
be a Worcester hand, is now Corpus Christi Coll. Camb. 12.
The other bishops' copies have all been lost, but two have left
descendants: Cotton Otho B. ii is a tenth-century transcript of
the copy sent to Hehstan, Bishop of London: Cambridge University ii. 11. 4 and Trin. Coll. Camb. 717 are eleventh-century
transcripts of the copy sent to Wulfsig, Bishop of Sherborne.
Our six copies therefore represent four distinct textual traditions, which diverged at the time of publication, about the year
894.

The translation of Bede is represented by five manuscripts
and a fragment, all belonging to the tenth or the eleventh centuries. The tradition of the other Alfredian translations is not

so good. The "Orosius" is extant in the contemporary Lauderdale MS.; the much later Cotton Tiberius B. i is apparently a
copy of Lauderdale.[14] The "Boethius" was preserved in the
tenth-century Cotton Otho A. vi, and in the early twelfth-century
Bodl. MS. 180; there is also a fragment of the first half of the
tenth century, Bodl. MS. 86; all three are independent copies of
one archetype. Finally, the translation of the "Soliloquies" of
St. Augustine has had a very narrow escape from destruction.
In the middle of the twelfth century a transcript of this was made.
It seems remarkable that at that date anybody should care to
transcribe books in a language which was so rapidly becoming
unintelligible as was the classical West-Saxon. To this tran-
scription (Cotton Vitellius A. xv) we owe our text: all earlier
copies are lost.

Alfred's Encheiridion or Handbook has been lost. This is
not surprising, for it was rather a personal commonplace-book
for the entry of noteworthy passages, than a properly published
book. It was, however, still extant when William of Malmesbury
wrote in the twelfth century.

Very similar has been the handing down of the other books
which owe their origin to Alfred's inspiration: The Anglo-Saxon
Chronicle, the Martyrology, Gregory's Dialogues. The Chronicle
was, as one might expect, the most widely copied of these.
Seven copies have come down to modern times. One of them,
the Parker MS., must have been transcribed "not much, if at all,
later than 892," the year in which the Chronicle seems to have
been launched. The other manuscripts are all much later, but
it is noteworthy that, as in the case of the Ecclesiastical History
of Bede, the contemporary manuscript is not the archetype of
the later ones; for these later manuscripts sometimes preserve
the correct tradition, even when the Parker MS. goes wrong.

Ælfric the homilist, writing a century after Alfred, tells us
that there were erroneous English books admired by the ignorant, but that Alfred's translations were the only reliable books
for those who did not know Latin.[15] The meagre way in which
the Chronicle was kept up suggests that prose was dormant during the first two-thirds of the tenth century.

When we come to the age of Ælfric, the abundance of manuscripts seems a sufficient guarantee that a fair proportion of
what was written remains. For example, when Prof. Napier
made his collection of the homilies which go under the name of

Wulfstan, he used 23 different manuscripts. Occasionally a homily is extant in one manuscript only, but more commonly in three, four, or five.

The catalogue of English books in the Cathedral Library of Christ Church, Canterbury, made in the days of Prior Eastry (c. 1330), leads to the same conclusion. It is difficult from the meagre titles to be certain in many cases what these books were: but most of them were Anglo-Saxon prose books of the school of Alfred and Ælfric: and most of the works have come down to us: in very many cases the actual volume which was in the Canterbury library has survived. Genesis anglice depicta, Dr. M. R. James thinks was a volume like the Bodleian Junius 11, and possibly identical with it. The Actus Apostolorum may be a lost translation of Acts, or legends of apostles in verse, like those in the Vercelli Book. Gregory's Dialogues, Boethius, and Bede are the Alfredian translations: and the Liber sermonum beati Augustini may be a misdescription (natural enough in the fourteenth century) of the Alfredian translation of the "Soliloquies." The three books of sermons in English, even if lost, would probably have contained little not extant in the many other collections of sermons; and the two Chronicles can be identified with extant manuscripts. The Herbarius Dr. James would identify with Vitellius C. iii, the Gospels with Royal 1. A. 14, and the Grammar with a copy of Ælfric's Grammar in the University Library, Cambridge. The Liber de ordine monastico, and the Regula Canonicorum, remain to be accounted for. They have apparently been lost, but we have similar books (e.g. the Rule of St. Benedict) in both Anglo-Saxon and Middle English. Finally, the Liber Edwini is apparently a lost book by the Eadwine whose Canterbury Psalter is mentioned just afterwards, and is still extant.

During the last century of the Anglo-Saxon period a new group of narrative poems seems to have sprung up. The heroes of these lays were the great kings of the house of Alfred: Athelstan and Edgar, their successors and their kinsfolk. We hear of these lays more especially in the Gesta Regum Anglorum of William of Malmesbury, who gives many stories which he has learnt "magis cantilenis per successiones temporum detritis, quam libris ad instructiones posterorum elucubratis." Such stories are those of the birth of Athelstan, of the wrong Athelstan did to his brother, and his penitence, of the adventures of

Edgar, "infamias quas resperserunt cantilenae." Another such tale was that of Gunhilda, daughter of Canute, who was married to Henry, emperor of Germany. "Celebris illa pompa nuptialis fuit, et nostro adhuc seculo etiam in triviis cantitata." Gunhilda was falsely accused of unchastity, and none could be found to face the gigantic champion whom her accusers put forward, till a small page whom she had brought from England triumphantly vindicated the honour of his mistress. A century later Matthew Paris refers to the same story, as told in conuiuiis et tabernis by histriones: and the fact that Matthew Paris gives the name of the page, Mimecan, seems to show that he knew more of the ballad than was merely to be derived from William of Malmesbury. Other chroniclers[16] give yet more of the story: the name of the gigantic champion, Roddyngar, overthrown by the page.

Many other tales, now extant only in Latin, are probably to be traced to similar cantilenae. Such are, for example, the stories told by a monk of St. Albans of the two Offas, one of whom is identical with the Continental Offa whose achievements had supplied material for the stories brought over by the invading Angles and Saxons, and which had got strangely blended with the deeds of the historic Offa II, King of Mercia. The secondary characters in the story are provided with a double set of names: "Hic Riganus binominis fuit: vocabatur enim alio nomine Aliel." The story was evidently known in two versions, which the Latin writer had to harmonize. Freeman has pointed to the same feature of a double name, indicating a double tradition, in a story which William of Malmesbury derives from ballad sources.

The tale of Gado is told by Walter Map, and is probably one of the "tales of Wade" to which Chaucer refers; in this tale of Gado Offa is also one of the principal characters.

As these cantilenae were already ancient per successiones temporum detritae, in the days of William of Malmesbury (c. 1125) they must have originated before the Norman Conquest. It is noteworthy that during the century before the Conquest a new kind of metre was becoming prevalent. In this new metre the structure of the lines seems to have been much more free than in the case of the strict alliterative measure, and in place of the alliteration, governed by very rigid laws, we have sometimes a loose alliteration, sometimes assonance or rhyme, sometimes nothing at all. This new, loose, measure is often spoken of as "ballad metre," and it is sometimes rather hastily assumed that the cantilenae or "ballads" spoken of by William of Malmesbury were necessarily in this free or loose measure, rather than in the stricter alliterative metre. Often, no doubt, they were: the six lines of a Tale of Wade discovered by Dr. M. R. James in a Latin sermon are of this free type. But one consideration makes it probable that the stricter alliterative verse was also well represented among these lost ballads. We find such alliterative verse surviving in the latest Anglo-Saxon times. The Chronicle contains not only the passages in loose verse, but poems like that in praise of Edward the Confessor and of King Harold (1065), which shows a very great command of the old technique. And the Battle of Maldon (991), although occasionally rather weak metrically, nevertheless on the whole shows a marked survival of the old art. Then, after the Conquest, we have, for nearly three centuries, nothing but the loosest kind of alliterative verse, and extraordinarily few examples of that. Suddenly, in the middle of the fourteenth century, the strict form of alliterative verse emerges again, preserving many rules of correct Anglo-Saxon alliteration, which appeared to have been quite forgotten. Now it is quite possible, even in the late Middle Ages, that a monk, interested in history or in the charters of his abbey, may have puzzled out some knowledge of Anglo-Saxon prose. But that any one in the fourteenth century, from a study of Anglo-Saxon manuscripts, could have recovered the rules of the old alliterative versification, if they had once been lost, is incredible. A continuous tradition, handing down these rules through a series of lost poems, is the only way of accounting for the phenomena.

The loss of these cantilenae of the eleventh and twelfth centuries, whether they were in "free" verse or in the stricter alliterative measure, is to be attributed to the neglect of popular literature by the learned, rather than to any deliberate Norman-French antipathy to the English tongue. Philological hatred is characteristic more of the twentieth century than of the eleventh. In monasteries under Norman rule Anglo-Saxon prose continued, though feebly. Of the seven manuscripts of the Chronicle which have come down to us, three had become barren stocks long before the Conquest; but of the remaining four, three were still receiving additions in English a full generation after the Conquest, though an accident of mutilation conceals this fact

in two cases. In the South of England a chronicle, now lost, was
being kept up till 1121.[17] This was borrowed by Peterborough
(presumably to replace a book destroyed there in the fire of 1116).
It was copied at Peterborough, and received additions there till
1154. Accident has preserved a single page of an English chronicle which was being continued in 1113, 1114: how much longer it
ran we cannot tell. But, with the close communication with the
Continent inevitable in Norman and Angevin days, it was natural
that the great historians of the twelfth century should write in
Latin. Nevertheless, the value of the vernacular for instructing
the ignorant was recognized, and the eight English manuscripts
of the Ancren Riwle, the seven of the Moral Ode prove that religious literature of merit written in the vernacular, even during
the early Middle English period, had a good chance of survival.
Orm's autograph of the Ormulum remained uncopied, but who
can wonder? Still less surprising is it that, at a later date, the
autograph of the Ayenbite of Inwit, which the author, Dan Michel,
presented with his Latin books to the library of St. Augustine's
Abbey, Canterbury, should have remained a barren stock.

There is nothing to surprise us in a town keeping one official
copy, and one only, of a cycle of Miracle Plays. In that case
the disappearance of the plays is easily accounted for, especially
if, at the Reformation, the volume fell into the hands of a puri-
tanically-minded prelate like Grindal. The elaborate details
given by Mr. E. K. Chambers in his Medieval Stage enable us
to form a good estimate of the proportion of lost plays to those
which have been preserved.

As in the case of so many miracle plays, the fact that it
was never "utterly published" may account for the loss of a version of Palamon and Arcyte in seven-line stanzas. For if such
a version ever existed, Chaucer may have refused to allow it
to be transcribed, which would account for its being "knowen
lyte." On the one hand, we have the Canterbury Tales, extant in
some sixty-eight manuscripts, and on the other, the loss of

Origenes upon the Maudeleyne

or

Of the wrecched Engendryng of Mankynde
As men may in pope Innocent y-fynde.

In the earlier Middle Ages it would have been otherwise. Religious works had then a better chance of survival than worldly
tales. It is surprising that Chaucer's many Balades, Roundels,
Virelayes, should be so poorly represented in his extant works.
Turning to the alliterative poetry, we have the 49 manuscripts of Piers Plowman, showing how widely copied a book
might be which, despite its rather provincial style, made an
appeal to the temper of the nation. On the other hand, the reference in Piers Plowman to

rymes of Robyn Hood and Randolf Erle of Chestre

reminds us again of a vanished body of popular poetry. And
poems like Sir Gawayne and the Green Knight, or the Alliterative
Morte D'Arthur, which should have appealed to every chivalrous
gentleman in England, have had the narrowest escape from destruction. Despite the very difficult dialect of Sir Gawayne,
which must have limited strictly the circle in which it could be
appreciated, it is strange that we should have only one manuscript, and no allusion to the writer anywhere. Whether the
Alliterative Morte D'Arthur is identical with the Gest Historiale
of Huchoun of the Awle Ryale, alluded to by Andrew of Wyntoun,
or whether that be yet another lost work, we need not inquire:
nor yet whether Huchoun be identical with the Sir Hugh of Eglin-
toun of Dunbar's Lament for the Makaris. That Lament shows
how many Scottish Medieval poets have perished.

In England, the rise of standard English in the early fifteenth
century, the disuse of dialect for literary work, and the introduction of printing, have done much; but they have not ensured the
survival of minor literary work. One example of this may suffice.
Miss Winifred Husbands, working at the minor novels written
between 1770 and 1800, found reviews or notices of publication
of 1,341; of these only 621 were in the British Museum: and when
the Bodleian, the Advocates Library, and the Picton Library,
Liverpool, had also been searched, all the novels forthcoming
were little more than half of those known to have been published.
I questioned on this subject the two pillars of English bibliography:
the one thought that most of these novels had vanished from the
earth, the other thought that most of them could probably still
be found in country towns and country houses. Amongst the
missing books is the Fair Syrian of Robert Bage, of which a

French translation, but no English copy, is forthcoming. Yet Scott thought Bage worthy of a place in his Lives of the Novelists. This paper will have served a useful purpose if it moves some one to find a copy of the Fair Syrian and present it to the British Museum. For perhaps future generations will think hardly of us, if we preserve in every important library a complete set of the publications of the Bibliographical Society, whilst we allow the Fair Syrian to perish. For, as Robert Louis Stevenson put it, "no man knoweth what he doth." Monastic scribes and librarians thought they were doing God service, in that they transcribed and preserved so many copies of Aldhelm's Epistola ad Acircium, sive liber de septenario et de metris, whilst they neglected the vernacular poetry of the same beloved bishop, although it was the joy alike of simple peasants and of King Ælfred Æthelwulfing.

NOTES

1 T. D. Hardy, Rolls Series 26 (London, 1862), Descriptive Catalogue of Materials relating to the History of Great Britain and Ireland, I. 1. 433–441. But as Hardy mentions many other manuscripts, of which he does not give the date, the totals for each century must be considerably in excess of those given above.

2 It is in many cases difficult to decide what exactly constitutes a separate work.

3 Plutarch, Life of Lysander, ch. 15.

4 William calls it Manualem librum regis Elfredi.

5 See the description by Bradshaw in the publications of the Palaeographical Society.

6 St. Gall MS., 254.

7 In Vienna MS. of Epistles of St. Boniface.

8 Leiden, MS. Voss, 106.

9 See Asser, ed. W. H. Stevenson (Oxford, 1904), §§ 22, 75, 76.

10 Riddles may be included under this head. The composition of riddles seems to have been a favourite pastime of the higher ecclesiastics of the Anglo-Saxon Church.

11 Cf. R. Priebsch, The Heliand Manuscript (Oxford, 1925), p. 37.

12 Vita Sancti Dunstani, in Memorials of St. Dunstan, ed. William Stubbs, Rolls Series 63 (London, 1874), p. 11.

13 M. R. James, The Ancient Libraries of Canterbury and Dover (Cambridge, 1903), p. 51.

14 There is said to be also a fragment in the Vatican.

15 Homilies, ed. B. Thorpe (London, 1844), 1, 2.

16 Radulphus de Diceto, Opera historica, ed. William Stubbs, Rolls Series 68 (London, 1876), I, 174.

17 Charles Plummer, Two of the Saxon Chronicles Parallel (Oxford, 1899), II, liii.

WIDSITH AND THE CRITIC

Kemp Malone

Mr. Ernest Newman, in a recent essay, writes as follows
about criticism and the critic:[1]

> Aesthetic judgments, as we are now beginning to
> recognize, are at bottom merely instinctive indi-
> vidual reactions of attraction or repulsion: we do
> not find this or that good in art because it complies
> with certain eternal and demonstrable canons of
> good, but we find it good because it happens to
> strike on our own box, whereupon we solemnly
> proceed to frame canons to dignify and justify
> our pleasurable reactions.

If this authority is right, those who urge an editor of a poem to
make "a general statement" of "critical principles"[2] are urging
him to a course of conduct scientifically indefensible. For such
an editor, the proper critical course is to tell the public in detail how the poem struck on his box, not to frame canons or set
up principles in the hope of lending spurious weight to his esthetic
reactions. Everyone will agree that the editor of a poem owes
it to his readers to tell them what he thinks of the poem as a
work of art. If esthetic judgments are worth giving at all, those
of an editor are especially worth giving, since he in the nature
of the case knows his text with an intimacy that nobody else can
hope to achieve. And Mr. Newman is right enough in thinking
that these judgments ought to be given as the editor's personal
opinions, not disguised in pseudo-objective canonical terms.
And yet this is far from being the whole critical story. Whatever the state of things in journalism, the philological critic

Reprinted from English Literary History, Vol. 5 (1938), pp. 49–66, by
permission of the author and the publisher.

(i.e. the editor of a literary text) has much work to do of an objective kind, work good in its own right, and worth doing, besides, not only because it "controls" in detail the critic's first esthetic impressions, but also (and chiefly) because it leads at last to ripeness of understanding and helps to precipitate that full esthetic experience upon which alone an esthetic judgment may properly be based. It is with this objective criticism that the present paper will deal. Here, at least, critical principles can be set up. The paragraphs which follow are devoted each to a critical question that an editor of Widsith must face. Let me preface them by summing up my own critical principles in three words: follow the text. It is the first duty of the critic to make clear the characteristics of the text under study. In so doing, he must take account of form and function, manner and matter, and his conclusions must be based on the text itself, not on preconceived notions about the text. The critical problems taken up below are presented in these terms.

1. Scribal errors. The only authoritative text of Widsith is that recorded in the Exeter Book, a MS of the tenth century. This text is not in holograph; on the contrary, it stands at many removes from the author. Such texts rarely if ever are free from mistakes. The scribal errors to be found in the inherited text of Widsith would presumably come under the following heads: omissions, repetitions, substitutions, misplacements and misspellings. In finding and righting such errors, the editor must be guided by his text as a whole (inclusive of its literary setting). At the points where he marks gaps or flaws in the textual pattern, he must suspect corruption and it becomes his duty to consider the possibilities in the way of emendation. In general, emendation is plausible if it makes sense out of nonsense, order out of disorder. Mere improvement of a text is hardly enough to justify emendation. In my edition of Widsith (hereafter referred to as MW), more than one passage might be made smoother by emendation, but it does not follow that the text is here corrupt; other explanations are possible, and wherever any explanation is possible the inherited text ought to be kept. Sometimes, it is true, we are confronted with a passage truly corrupt. Here we must set to work, in the hope that close study of the passage, in terms of the textual pattern, may lead to a plausible reconstruction of the original text. For such a study, see MW 27ff. All in all,

28

MW is notable for conservatism in emendation, as compared with earlier editions of the poem.

2. Interpolations. Passages in an inherited text may be rejected as interpolated only if they depart radically from the textual pattern in shape or thought (or both). The greater the incongruity, the stronger the case for rejection. Certainty is rarely attainable. In making my text of Widsith, I proceeded here with conservatism: I rejected only eight lines (14–17, 82–83, 114, 118) of the 143 found in the MS, and even these I printed in the text, following in this matter the traditional practice of editors of Widsith. My reasons for thinking these eight lines interpolated will be found in MW 5 ff.[3]

3. Divisions. An author often makes plain to reader or hearer, by changes in the textual pattern, the various parts into which he divides his text. Such is eminently the case with Widsith. The poem begins in the third person, but shifts to the first at the tenth line. In the first nine lines, moreover, which tell us something of a gleeman named Widsith, we are twice warned that a speech by this gleeman is to follow. It is therefore a legitimate inference (and one regularly made) that the shift to the first person marks the beginning of Widsith's speech. The end of the speech is less clearly marked, but since lines 131–134 are the last lines in the first person, they are commonly thought to be the last lines of the speech. The nine lines in the third person which follow them conclude the poem with some general observations on a gleeman's calling. The poem, then, is divisible into a prologue and an epilogue, of nine lines each, and a speech, of 125 lines. The fact that prologue and epilogue are of equal length may be accidental,[4] but it seems reasonable to interpret this equality as evidence of design on the part of the author, and this the more since there is a correspondence in theme as well: the prologue deals with a particular minstrel; the epilogue, with minstrels in general.

The speech of Widsith is itself divisible into parts in terms of the distinction between first and third persons. Here we may make a threefold division: (a) passages in the third person; (b) passages in which the first person is merely a conventional device; and (c) passages in which the first person has a didactic or a lyric function. The first person is twice used for didactic

purposes: in lines 10 and 131. In each case it is followed by a
passage of advice, and in each case the statement in the first
person serves to present the speaker's qualifications for giving
this advice. Moreover, the two passages (lines 10–13 and 131–
134) are of equal length, and deal with the same subject: king-
ship. The one introduces, the other concludes the speech of
Widsith. In his introduction, the speaker tells how to win a
throne; in his conclusion, how to keep one. If we consider these
two passages together (as we must), the case is overwhelming
(pace Souers) for design and against accidental correspondence.

The passages in which the first person has a lyric function
begin with line 50 and end with line 111. In 18 of the lines between these limits, however (in 20 if we include the interpolated
lines 82 f.), the first person is merely a conventional device:
the oft repeated formula ic wæs mid here serves as a frame
(the kunstgriff of Heusler) for a mnemonic metrical list of names
or thula. By virtue of this distinction, the lines 50–111 fall into
nine parts or sections, all marked by the use of the first person,
but alternately lyric and mnemonic in character. This repeated
alternation of sections points to design.[5] Again, the formula
sohte ic serves as a frame for a thula that begins with line 112
and ends with line 124, but does not include lines 119b–122 (nor
yet, of course, the interpolated lines 114 and 118). In line 126,
too, the first person is used conventionally enough, as part of a
formula (lines 125–126) that answers to the modern "last but
not least."

In the rest of the speech of Widsith, the third person is used:
the speaker gives us information, but not in terms of his own
experiences (I ignore the interpolated lines 14–17). Most of the
lines spoken in the third person come together: lines 18–49.
The other two passages in the third person, lines 119b–122 and
127–130, are tied to the sohte ic thula: the "last not least" formula links lines 127–130 with the thula, and lines 119b–122 are
imbedded in the thula. This analysis of the speech of Widsith
in terms of the distinction between first and third persons gives
us the following divisions:

Introduction: didactic first person	10–13
Interpolated passage: first person	14–17
First Fit: third person	18–49
Second Fit: first person, nine sections al- ternately lyric & mnemonic	50–111

It is worthy of special note that the digressive or episodic passages in the Third Fit, viz., lines 119b–122 and 127–130, are not given in terms of the speaker's own experiences. The poet might perfectly well have had Widsith sing before Wulfhere and Wyrmhere, Wudga and Hama (as he sang before the rulers named in the Second Fit), and receive gifts at their hands, but we are told nothing of the kind. Whatever the personal experiences of the widely faring scop at the many courts he visited, we know of them only from the Second Fit. This strict limitation can hardly be accidental. Moreover, each of the two didactic passages (lines 10–13 and 131–134) is more sharply defined thereby: its first person stands out in virtue of the contrast with the third person just before and after.

The divisions of the poem pointed out above are themselves divisible, in terms of other changes in the textual pattern. For further discussion, however, I must refer the reader to MW.

4. Units. A given division hangs together and can be said to make a unit in virtue of specific uniformities in the textual pattern. Thus, lines 10–134 of Widsith make a unit, complex though it be, because they are given to us as a set speech, put in the mouth of a specific speaker, the minstrel Widsith, and the poem as a whole can be said to make a unit because lines 1–9 lead up to the speech and lines 135–143 lead away from it— in other words, are subordinated to the speech as prologue and epilogue respectively. The speech itself, as we have seen, falls into five parts: an introduction, three fits, and a conclusion. Each of these parts makes a unit. Here I will discuss only one of them, the Second Fit, lines 50–111. Above (as in MW) I have made a distinction between the lyric and mnemonic passages of this fit. To the lyric passages, taken together, I have given the name yed; to the mnemonic passages, taken together, the name thula. That the lyric passages belong together is old doctrine. Thus, in 1906, W. W. Lawrence wrote of three of them (MP, IV (1906), 343 f.):

One would like to believe that the references to
Guðhere (ll. 64 [sic]–67) and to Ælfwine (ll. 70–
74) formed originally a part of the same story as
ll. 88 ff., as they are similar to it in style and
metre, and unlike the material in which they are
imbedded.

The story to which Lawrence refers is presumably the story of
the scop's personal experiences at the various courts which he
visited. I do not believe what Lawrence would like to believe,
viz., that this tale was told, originally, in consecutive lines,
without interruption by thula-material; certainly we have no
evidence that it was ever so told. But the unity of the yed (as
of the thula) is not dependent upon the immediate succession of
its lines. The likeness of the lyric passages in style and metre,
to which Lawrence justly calls our attention, is reinforced by a
likeness in theme, and these likenesses are enough to give to
the passages a true unity, as against the passages with which
they alternate. After all, the technic of alternation is no modern
invention. The Second Fit as it stands is divisible into five lyric
and four mnemonic sections, and these sections occur in the following order: lyric (50–56), mnemonic (57–64), lyric (65–67),
mnemonic (68–69), lyric (70–74), mnemonic (75), lyric (76–78),
mnemonic (79–87), lyric (88–111).[6] The alternation is regular,
and gives evidence of design. In the first lyric passage the scop
tells us that he has travelled much, served under many a king,
and received from his masters rich rewards. In the second lyric
passage he begins to particularize: Guðhere, the Burgundian king,
gave him a ring, as a reward for his singing. In the third lyric
passage, he gives another particular: he was in Italy with Ælfwine,
the most generous king he had ever heard of. In the fourth lyric
passage the specifications continue: we learn that he was with
the Emperor, ruler of "towns of revelry," etc. In the fifth and
last lyric passage, we are given the most important particulars
of all: he tells us a good deal about his relations with Ermanric,
Ealhhild, Eadgils and others. Throughout we have to do with
persons, and the scop tells us something of his impressions and
experiences. On the other hand, the four mnemonic passages
are bare lists of tribes. The contrast is striking, and the alternation correspondingly effective. The Second Fit, therefore, is
best described as made up of two units, a yed and a thula, two

themes used several times in alternation. And it was by virtue of this alternation of two themes in terms of the same person (the speaker, Widsith) that the poet was able to give to the fit the needful unity.

5. Links. The divisions of a work may be bound together, not only by uniformities of textual pattern, but also by links, that is, connective words or word-sequences at the points of junction. It is one of the duties of the critic to study and classify such links. The simplest of all links, of course, are the so-called conjunctive particles. The Widsith poet's use of the particle ond 'and' in lines 88 and 97 is noteworthy. In both passages ond begins the sentence. Thereby the particle is made emphatic, and it gains even greater emphasis if I am right in thinking that it is included in the alliterative pattern of these lines. I scan the lines as follows:

88   Ónd ic wǽs mid Éormanrìce   éalle þráge.
97   Ónd me þá Éalhhìld   óþerne forgéaf.

Here the acute marks full stress; the grave, half stress.[7] By weighting the connective the poet links the passage more firmly to the one before it. In line 88 the formula ic wæs mid reinforces ond as a link with the previous section of the poem. In line 65 the on-verse as a whole links the lyric section (65–67) to the preceding mnemonic section (57–64); see my discussion, in MW 33 f. The first line of a section may serve also as a link. Thus, line 76, which reads

Mid Creacum ic wæs ond mid Finnum   ond mid Casere,

begins the Casere section of the yed (lines 76–78), but, cast as it is in a pattern consonant with the ic wæs thula, serves also to link the section with the thula-section that precedes. That it does not belong to the thula is sufficiently obvious from the fact that it ends, not with a tribal but with a personal name. Now and then a whole passage serves as a link; thus, lines 109–111, and lines 125–126. Such passages are perhaps better called passages of transition. These and other links are duly discussed in MW. Links may be wanting in places where one might expect to find them. Thus, the shift from the Offa Episode (lines 36–44) to

the Heorot Episode (lines 45–49) is made without the help of any
link. For an explanation of this peculiarity, see MW 23.

6. Foreshadowing and echo. The devices so called may
serve (a) to hold a given unit together or (b) to connect one unit
with another. Thus, in the prologue of Widsith, line 9b echoes
line 1, or, if you will, line 1 foreshadows line 9b. The two, taken
together, mark the limits of the prologue and announce the speech
which begins with line 10. They have, therefore, a double function.
Again, the sohte ic of line 110 foreshadows the characteristic
frame or kunstgriff of the Third Thula and thus serves to connect
the Second Fit with the Third. An interesting example of echo
is line 45b, which reminds one of line 28 and thereby helps to tie
the Heorot Episode to an earlier part of the First Fit. Other
examples of foreshadowing and echo are pointed out in MW.

7. Variation and repetition. These are familiar stylistic
devices, of course. The former is referred to in the well known
critical passage of Beowulf as wordum wrixlan (874a); Klaeber
explains this as meaning "vary words in the customary manner
of Germanic poetry." Simple repetition (as distinguished from
variation) is a noteworthy feature of Widsith; we find it in many
parts of the poem; thus, Offa(n) occurs four times in lines 35–
44; song occurs twice in lines 104–108; and dom occurs twice
in the epilogue. These departures from the customary technic
of variation were presumably deliberate; the many repetitions
of Offa's name are especially striking, since they go with a consistent avoidance (within the limits of the passage) of the usual
technic of variation. Apart from this passage, however, and the
three thulas (where of course there was little occasion for such
a device), we find in the poem what may be called a normal use
of variation. Lines 2–3a, it must be added, may be reckoned a
variation of Widsith's name; if they are, we have here a variation
uncommonly elaborate. The threefold variation Hreðcyninges 7 /
Eormanrices 8 / wraþes wærlogan 9 is of interest in that the
true name appears in the middle; one would have expected to find
it either at the beginning or at the end.

8. Versification. The critic in studying a poem must of
course determine the formal characteristics of the verse. In
Widsith the most important distinction is that between the thulas

on the one hand and the rest of the poem on the other. The thulas
are marked by (a) set line patterns few in number and rigidly
followed, (b) exclusive use of end-stopt lines, and (c) avoidance
of the alliterative pattern abbc. In the rest of the poem we find
(a) no set line patterns, (b) frequent use of run-on lines, and (c)
frequent use of the alliterative pattern abbc alongside the other
two chief patterns, aaab and abac. The contrast, so far, is
striking enough. But we must go further. In the thulas, the lines
either (d) stand in isolation or (e) fall into couplets and stanzas.
Thus, in the First Thula the first 10 lines fall into a stanza, itself divisible into five couplets, and the six lines which follow
make up a second stanza, while the last line makes an isolated
unit; in the other two thulas we find no stanzas, and these thulas
are made up wholly of couplets and isolated lines.[8] Line 34 is
an isolated thula-fragment which, like each of the isolated lines
of the three thulas, is complete in itself. The metrical structure of the thula material is thus uniform enough. When we turn
to the rest of the poem, we find something markedly different:
no isolated lines, no couplets, no stanzas, but a stichic system
like that of Beowulf and West-Germanic poetry in general. The
poet has modified this stichic system in one particular only:
the various divisions of the poem regularly end at the end of a
line, not in the middle of a line (as would be possible in Beowulf).
This modification makes the stichic parts of the poem more
consonant with the thulas, although of course the fundamental
metrical contrast remains. For further discussion, see my
papers "Alliteration in Widsith" (ELH, II [1935], 291 ff.), and
"The Alliterative Pattern abbc in the þulur" (Saga-Book of the
Viking Society, XI [1934], 250 ff.).

9. Exegesis. It is the duty of an editor to explain in detail
what the author of the text means by what he says. This involves,
among other things, the determination (so far as possible) of the
exact sense in which each word and word-group of the text is
used. Here we shall confine ourselves to this aspect of exegesis.
In his attempt to determine the meaning of a given word or
phrase, the editor ought to proceed with conservatism. He must,
of course, consider all the possibilities, but he ought not to depart from the primary, original, literal meaning of a word unless the context compels him to do so. This principle of procedure is well illustrated in the wraþes wærlogan of Widsith 9a,

an on-verse which refers to the famous Ostrogothic king Ermanric. The primary, original, literal meaning of wærloga is "treaty-breaker." If now we look into the career of Ermanric, we find that in history and story alike he is represented as hostile to treaty-breakers. This hostility, indeed, is the outstanding and dominating feature of his character, and serves to motivate judicial sentences so ruthless that only a fanatical legalist could have brought himself to pronounce them. The epithet wraþes wærlogan which the poet applies to Ermanric therefore presumably means "hostile to treaty-breakers," and this interpretation makes no difficulties, grammatical or contextual (wærlogan may perfectly well be a late dat. pl. form; see MW 51). The alternative explanation, according to which wærlogan here is a gen. sg. and has a secondary, derivative, figurative, generalized sense, that of "wicked person, tyrant" or the like, cannot be reconciled with conservative treatment of the inherited text. This later meaning of wærloga arose out of the association of the term with the devil of Christian belief, the treaty-breaker par excellence, the rebel against God. The application of wærloga to Satan, and to the followers of Satan, is not inconsistent with its literal meaning, of course, and we have no reason to think that the literal meaning was ever lost sight of, in Saxon times. We have rather to do with a secular legal term, seized upon by Christian writers and made into a theological legal term as well. It seems unreasonable to suppose that the Widsith poet used it in this theological sense, so out of keeping with the context. If he did, we must further suppose that the secular sense of the word had faded completely from his mind (or was unknown to him), since otherwise he could not have been guilty of the gross blunder involved in calling Ermanric, of all people, a wærloga — Ermanric, known to fame as a stickler for his legal rights, at whatever cost to himself and his nearest and dearest. Ignorance of, or indifference to, secular usage is not characteristic of the Widsith poet, and cannot properly be attributed to him in this instance. See further MW 141 ff.

10.   Authorship and composition. It is the duty of the critic to determine, if possible, who composed the poem under study, and to recapture, so far as possible, the poet's method of procedure in composing the poem. Widsith is an anonymous poem, and we have no means of identifying its author. We can draw

some general conclusions about him, however, from the peculiarities of the text. For such conclusions, see MW 50 f. In
view of the striking differences, in manner and matter alike,
between the thulas on the one hand and the rest of the poem on
the other, we must also consider the possibility of multiple
authorship. In my opinion the Widsith poet did not himself compose the three thulas; he found them already in existence and
incorporated them in his poem, a poem which he wrote with this
incorporation constantly in mind. If so, the thulas are older than
the rest of Widsith. Certainly we have reason to think that composition in the thula kind is old. The only truly ancient Germanic
verse-fragments which have come down to us (in Latin or Greek
dress) belong, without exception, to the thula kind. Thus, if I
am right in reading unithones for the nuithones of the Tacitean
text (with its un-Germanic diphthong), the Nerthus tribal list of
the Germania (A. D. 98) falls into a thula-like couplet:

> Reudigni, Auiones, Anglii, Varini,
> Eudoses, Suardones, Unithones.

It is worthy of note that this couplet conforms to that rule of
thula-composition whereby the alliterative pattern abbc is allowed
in the first line (witness Widsith 57) but forbidden elsewhere.
The list of the sons of Mannus which Tacitus records earlier in
the Germania likewise makes a thula-fragment, an isolated line
not unlike the isolated lines of the thulas of Widsith. Again,
Ptolemy's list of Cimbric peninsular tribes in his Geography
(A. D. 150) makes a thula-like couplet:

> Σάξονες, Σιγούλωνες, Σαβαλίγγιοι, Κοβανδοί,
> Χάλοι, Φουνούσιοι, Χάρουδες.

The thulas of Widsith, then, exemplify a traditional kind of poetic
composition old indeed. We should be hasty, however, if we concluded at once that the Widsith poet could not himself have composed the thulas which we find in his poem. Here we must distinguish between thula-composition as such and the particular
thulas before us. The Widsith poet might well have composed
thulas, once he had learned (whether through teachers or by his
own delving) the rules that govern their composition. If he could
not have composed the particular thulas recorded in Widsith, it

was because he could not have chosen the matter of these thulas, much less put this matter together, as we have it. Widsith, apart from the thulas, belongs to the classical tradition of OE poetry, and this tradition took shape in the seventh century. Our author could hardly have flourished earlier than the Age of Bede. But the thulas in their matter reflect and reveal a different world, that of the English before their migration to Britain; see MW 14 ff., 30 ff., 42 ff. No English poet of the Age of Bede (or later), however learned, could have reconstructed and reproduced, in a thula or otherwise, this world of his forefathers.

The distinction in authorship which I have drawn between the thulas and the rest of the poem is not new. The considerations which I have presented above have, in the past, led various critics to conclude that the Widsith poet did not himself compose the thulas. This is the view of Sievers, Brandl and Heusler (to mention only a few names). That the thulas are much older than the rest of the poem is also a view widely held.[9] Schücking, in his Kleines ags. Dichterbuch (Cöthen, 1919), p. 62, describes as follows the poet and his procedure:

Auf alle fälle hat man doch wohl anzunehmen, dass
ein an der vorzeit interessierter dichter, der zeitlich
und künstlerisch dem Beowulf und namentlich der
lyrik nahestand, aus sehr altem material an über-
lieferten merkversen—das älteste wird der Königs-
katalog v. 17 [sic] ff. sein—seine auswahl traf,
vielleicht auch namen aus heldenliedern zusammentrug
und dafür den dichterisch anmutigen rahmen der
Widsith-erzählung schuf.

Heusler, in his Altgermanische Dichtung (Potsdam, 1926), p. 86, expresses himself similarly (though with important differences):

Zu der zeit nun, als in England auch geistliche die
heimische dichtkunst pflegten, verviel einer von
ihnen auf den gedanken, einen skop der alten zeit als
rahmenfigur hinzustellen, ihn von seinen höfischen
erlebnissen erzählen zu lassen und ihm, als kern
seines vortrags, drei vorhandene merkreihen in den
mund zu legen.

My own reconstruction of the process of composition, as set
forth in MW 3 ff., reads, in part, as follows:

> When the Widsith poet conceived the idea of making
> a poem about the Germanic heroic age, a poem to
> which the figure of a fictitious scop was to give the
> needful unity, he began his work of composition by
> putting into the scop's mouth these three thulas,
> and about the thulas he built up the rest of the poem.

These judgments reflect current critical opinion. For further
discussion, the reader is referred to MW.

11. Dates. The critic must determine, within limits as
narrow as may be, the date of the text under study. In MW, in
Anglia Beiblatt, XLVIII (1937), 351 f., and in Anglia, LXI (1938),
116, I have given my reasons for thinking that the poem was
composed in the second half of the seventh century. This date
is earlier than that set by most of the recent students of the
poem (but see Chambers 178). The three thulas, in my opinion,
were all composed in the sixth century. The First Thula is
generally reckoned the oldest of them; Heusler dates it "before
540." Since the thulaman included King Theodric of the Franks,
who reigned from 511 to 534, he must have composed the thula
after 511. But we can be more precise. King Theodric doubtless won inclusion in the thula (as he won fame in the North) by
virtue of his great victory over King Hygelac of the Geatas; if
so, the thula could hardly have been composed before about 520.
It is an odd feature of the thula, however, that Theodric appears
in it but not his opponent Hygelac. And Hygelac's absence cannot be due to metrical difficulties, since the thulaman, instead
of composing line 24 thus:

þeodric weold Froncum,   þyle Rondingum,

might perfectly well have composed it thus:

Hygelac weold Geatum,   Hugum þeodric.[10]

The line as we have it seems explicable, indeed, only on the
theory that the thulaman, though he had heard of Theodric's great

victory over the Scandinavian pirates, had not learned Hygelac's
name or tribe. Now þyle is best taken as the eponym of the þilir,
a well known Scandinavian tribe, inhabitants of the South Nor-
wegian shire of Telemark, and the tribe itself might well have
been referred to, in poetry at least, as Rondingas, i.e. inhabitants
of a mark or borderland. I conceive that the thulaman, knowing
nothing of the defeated pirates except that they were Scandinavians, and unable, in the circumstances, to couple Theodric with
a contemporary Scandinavian king, was inspired to couple him
with an eponymous Scandinavian king; the king chosen for that
purpose would naturally be one whose name began with þ, and
here King þyle filled the bill to perfection. It is possible enough,
besides (as I pointed out in MW 192), that a body of vikings from
Telemark were actually included in Hygelac's army; if so, the
thulaman would have had all the more reason to couple Theodric
with King þyle. If I have hit upon the right explanation of the
presence in the thula of þyle and his Rondings, then it would
seem to follow that the thula was composed shortly after Theodric's victory, at a time when little news had reached Sleswick
beyond the bare fact that Theodric had defeated a host of Scandinavian pirates. If so, one may date the First Thula at about
520. For further discussion, see MW 18.

The Second Thula is a list of tribes, and tribes cannot be
dated like persons.[11] Heusler, however, ventured to give this
thula an eighth century dating. In so doing, he was bravely taking
the consequences of his heterodox view that all the biblical and
oriental names in our inherited text belonged to the original thula.
I regard this view as untenable, and, with Chambers (7 f.) and many
others, reject such bookish material as interpolated. The number of bookish names, however, has been unduly swelled by the
critics. I find only five names of the kind in the thula, and these
all occur in a single passage, lines 82–83; if we set this passage
aside as interpolated, we have 49 tribal names left, and none of
these names can rightly be held out of place in a thula based on
Germanic oral tradition. These 49 tribes, moreover, reflect an
ethnological range to be expected of an English thulaman before,
not after the migration to Britain; see MW 30 ff., where I have
suggested 530 as a suitable date of composition for the thula.
It could hardly have been composed earlier, since in the Amo-
things it includes a tribe known to heroic story through an event
of 530 or thereabouts.[12] And it was hardly composed much later;

Heusler's reasons for dating the First Thula before 540 apply
also to the Second, though, as we have seen, Heusler failed to
make the application. The Third Thula could not have been
composed before about 550, since it includes King Eadwine of
the Langobards. And since it fails to include Ælfwine, the most
famous of all Langobardish kings, it was probably composed before that king's rise to fame in the years 565–572. Here again
one prefers a date of composition as early as possible, for after
the migration to Britain the English soon gave up that close
touch with their Continental kinsmen which they had maintained
as a matter of course while they lived in Sleswick. On all these
datings, nevertheless, my words of caution in MW 135 are worth
repeating:

> Such inferences, however, cannot be looked upon as
> certain: we have to do with indications rather than
> with determinations.

12. Identifications. The datings given above depend, in
part, on identifications of persons and tribes named in Widsith.
The critic, therefore, is concerned with such identifications, and
with the conclusions drawn from them. In MW an identification
is taken to be established if the names brought into connexion
show correspondence in (1) form, (2) function, and (3) setting,
and if (4) no plausible alternative connexions are to be had. Thus,
I accept the identification of Ætla with the Attila of history because the two names correspond in phonetic form,[13] designate
a king, and localize this king as ruler of the Huns, and because
no other plausible connexion can be found for Ætla. The etymology of the name is of course irrelevant to the identification;
whether Attila is a Germanic name and means "little father" or
is a Hunnish name of some other meaning, the identification stands.
Again, I accept the old identification of the Sweordweras with
the Suardones of Tacitus. As some students have found this
identification exceedingly dubious and hypothetical, I will take
it up here, under the four heads given above.

(1) The Sweord- of Widsith answers precisely to the Suard-
of Tacitus if we can derive the eo of the OE name-form from
Gmc a, and this of course we can do. Putting the Tacitean Suard-
into prehistoric English, we get *Swærd-, whence, with breaking,

41

the archaic *Swærd- > Sweord-. In a part of the Northumbrian area this eo was kept as late as the tenth century, but elsewhere it was unrounded to ea in the course of the seventh. The Sweord- of our text may therefore be explained either as an archaic spelling or as a Northumbrian dialectal spelling.[14] In MW 52 it is reckoned dialectal, but I should now prefer to classify it as archaic, a survival of the Widsith poet's own spelling, along with manna 36, Moidum 84, Amothingum 85 and Gislhere 123.[15] It escaped modernizing because the copyists (naturally enough) connected it with sweord 'sword' and therefore did not recognize it as archaic in spelling. Let me add that some MSS of the Germania read Suarines, not Suardones; connexion with Sweordweras is not possible, of course, if one follows the reading Suarines. Linguistic considerations, however, make Suarines an inacceptable reading; see Much, BGDSL, XVII (1893), 212 f., who makes out a plausible case for an original reading *Suardiones, out of which both the extant readings grew. For our present purposes, it is immaterial whether we adopt Much's reading or cling to the MS reading Suardones.

(2) The Suardones of Tacitus designates a Germanic tribe. The same may with confidence be said of the Sweordweras of Widsith. The Second Thula includes, it is true, a few non-Germanic tribes (nine out of a total of 49; see MW 30), but these are all readily identifiable as such, and no one, so far as I know, has ever suggested the addition of the Sweordweras to their number.[16]

(3) In Tacitus the Suardones belong to a group of seven tribes, localized (vaguely enough) in a region commonly identified as the Jutland peninsula. In Widsith the Sweordweras are mentioned in the following passage (lines 61–63):

Mid Englum ic wæs ond mid Swæfum ond mid Ænenum.
Mid Seaxum ic wæs ond mid Sycgum ond mid Sweordwerum.
Mid Hronum ic wæs ond mid Deanum ond mid Heaþoreamum.

These nine tribes, so far as they can with plausibility be localized, all belong to the Jutland peninsula and its immediate neighborhood. The Engle and Swæfe lived in Sleswick. The Seaxan lived in Holstein. The Sycgan are the Secgan of the Finnsburg Fragment; Chambers (199) put the name into (Latinized) Germanic as

*Sagiones; the only plausible connexion for this name is that
with the Sabro district of northeast Jutland (near Aarhus), the
Saghæ-brok heret of King Valdemar's Jordebog.[17] The Dean
lived in the southern part of the Scandinavian peninsula, if Chambers (210) was right in identifying them with the Dauciones of
Ptolemy; see further MW 131. The Heaþoreamas lived in southern Norway, over against the point of Jutland. The identity of
the Ænenas and the Hronan is too uncertain to throw light on
the habitat of the Sweordweras, although students of Widsith
commonly take it for granted that both tribes lived somewhere
in the North. On the whole, it seems clear that the geographical setting of the Sweordweras is in every way consistent with
their identification as the Suardones of Tacitus. It ought to be
added that the Anglii, Auiones and Varini, three tribes mentioned by Tacitus along with the Suardones, appear also in Widsith,
in the same section (lines 57–64) with the Sweordweras; see MW
141, 147 f., and 194 f.

(4) Neither Sweordweras nor Suardones can with plausibility be given other tribal connexions.

It needs to be emphasized that the identification of the
Sweordweras with the Suardones (like that of Ætla with Attila)
does not depend on any particular etymology of the tribal name.
And the localization of the Sweordweras in the Jutland region is
not dependent on etymology either. I have elsewhere advanced
an etymology of Suard(i)ones[18] which (if it is sound) enables us
to localize the tribe more narrowly still: in the Galten district
of Jutland, immediately adjoining the Sabro district where (in
all likelihood) lived the Sycgan; and this localization is of special
interest to students of Widsith, since in that poem the Sycgan and
the Sweordweras are named in the same line, and in immediate
sequence. But whatever the etymology, the identification must
be based on evidence of other kinds, as set forth above. In view
of this evidence, the identity of Sweordweras and Suardones may
be looked upon as reasonably well established.

13. Summary. In the paragraphs above, I have by no
means considered all the critic's duties. It would take a book,
indeed, to do the subject justice. The topics which I have taken
up, however, may serve to give the reader some idea of the
principles of criticism which one philologist, at least, strives

to follow. Let me conclude with a summary statement. In studying a work of art, the critic must seek to answer three questions, and to answer them in some detail. The first: what is the author trying to do? The second: how does the author go about his task? The third: how well has the author done his work? These are hard questions, not often to be answered with finality. But the editor who shirks them on that account, and limits himself to the certainties, stands revealed thereby as a literary mechanic, and turns his profession into a trade.

NOTES

1 Sunday Times, London, 19 September 1937. Cf. Stuart Chase, The Tyranny of Words (New York, 1938), p. 378.

2 P. W. Souers, in Speculum, XI (1936), 532–536.

3 Oddly enough, the reviewer in TLS (Feb. 22, 1936, p. 165) represented me, not as rejecting, but as keeping lines 14–17.

4 This seems to be the view of Souers, loc. cit.

5 Souers, loc. cit., seems to think otherwise. But here, at least, he surely strains to the breaking point his theory of unconscious art; so long a series of alternations was hardly composed in a mental fog.

6 Line 76 has a mnemonic look, but in its off-verse it departs from the thula pattern, and cannot have belonged to the original thula; see below, and cf. MW 34 f. and 130.

7 I did not venture, in MW, to suggest a scansion so heterodox; see p. 55. My present suggestion will be defended elsewhere.

8 On the isolated half-line 119a, see MW 39 ff.

9 The Second Thula, it is true, has commonly been thought to be late in date, and its author represented as a monkish would-be cosmographer, but this view is mistaken; see my discussion below.

10 On Hugas, a poetical name for the Franks, see Klaeber, Beowulf, glossary of proper names, s. v., with the references there given.

11 The Frumtings of line 68, it is true, can be dated precisely enough: 457–464. See my paper in ES, XIV (1932), 154 ff.

12 See cap. 29 of Snorri's Ynglingasaga, and cf. my comments in MLN, XLVII (1932), 367 ff.

13 In strictness, Ætla answers to a name-form Attala, but this form occurs in the historical records as a variant of Attila.

14 I pointed out these alternative explanations in Namn och Bygd, XXII (1934), 47, note 3.

15 If my reading Hehcan 112 holds, it reflects another archaic spelling, as does Frumtingum 68 if this is a scribal error for Framtingum. See MW 161 and 78, and cf. Anglia, LXI (1937), 116, note 2.

16 The alternative connexion which can be given to the tribal name, viz., the connexion with OE sweord 'sword,' carries with it the presumption that the tribal name is Germanic. Let me add that "Swordmen" would be an odd name for a tribe in that it would have no distinctive feature: the sword was in general use among all tribes. This etymology of Sweordweras therefore wants plausibility.

17 The tribal name Secgan has been connected with OE secg 'sword' (Holthausen), but it is hard to see how a weapon so generally used could have given rise to a tribal name (contrast Seaxan, derivable from the name of a distinctive tribal weapon). Connexion with OE secg 'man' is hardly more suitable, since a name meaning "men" would not be distinctive. Derivation from a district name is obviously to be preferred, and the Sabro district meets every requirement neatly enough. The j-suffix here presumably has its old meaning of "belonging to, pertaining to." The connexion of the Secgan with the Sabro district is here made for the first time. In MW 191 it was still needful to say, "the Sycgan have not been localized with plausibility." On the name Sabro see O. Nielsen, in Blandinger 1. 4 (1886), 229 (Universitets-Jubilæets danske Samfund, No. 35); I owe this reference to the kindness of Gunnar Knudsen.

18 In Namn och Bygd, XXII (1934), 46 f.

ANGLO-SAXON LITERATURE: "ATTIC" OR "ASIATIC"?
OLD ENGLISH POETRY AND ITS LATIN BACKGROUND

René Derolez

The question "Is Anglo-Saxon literature classic or non-classic, 'Attic' or 'Asiatic'?" was first suggested to me by the use which some scholars have made of the term "classic" (or, occasionally, "classical") with reference to certain aspects of OE literature. No complete survey of all instances where "classic" has been used in this connexion will be needed for defining the data of our problem, nor do we need a full discussion of the various shades of meaning the scholars in question have given to this word. In fact, some such definition as that in the Concise Oxford Dictionary provides us with a safe starting-point:

> Of the first class, of allowed excellence; of the standard ancient Latin and Greek authors, art, or culture; of Latin and Greek antiquity; in the — style, simple, harmonious, proportioned, and finished (cf. Romantic).

"Classic," then, not only serves to characterize a stylistic principle, but tends to represent that principle as a standard by which to measure the artistic and literary achievements of various cultures and periods. This implication of superiority stands in the way of a better understanding of mannerism as a phenomenon in its own right, as "a constant in European literature . . . the complementary phenomenon of the Classicism of all periods."[1] It was mainly to avoid the ambiguity inherent to "classic" that I did not use it in the title of this paper, and replaced it by the less engagé terms "Attic" and "Asiatic." If "Attic" stands for

Reprinted from English Studies Today, 2nd Series (1961), pp. 93–105, by permission of the author and the publisher.

"simple, harmonious, proportioned, finished" (cf. supra), then
"Asiatic" may roughly be equated to "preferring grandeur or
picturesqueness or passion or irregular beauty to finish and
proportion, subordinating whole to part or form to matter," i.e.
the terms by which the COD defines Romantic.[2]

I owe my first instance of the use of "classic," or, as happens to be the case, of "classical," to Professor Kemp Malone.
In his survey of OE literature,[3] he applies "classical" to a type
of poetry with a well-defined relationship between syntactical
and metrical patterns. A "pre-classical" style survives in the   (1)
mnemonic parts of Widsith, in the Leiden Riddle, and there are
also many instances in the Charms. This style is characterized
by every line ending with a syntactical pause, and every sentence
making up either one line or a couplet. The bulk of OE poetry,
however, shows a different structure. It is made up mainly of   (2)
plurilinear units, with a fair number of run-on links giving a
strengthened impression of continuity: sentences tend to go on
from one line to the next with little of a syntactical division, or
even no pause at all. Beowulf, e.g., has some plurilinear units
of great length, whilst single lines and couplets are infrequent.
Although Malone does not use the term "post-classical," some   (3)
such subdivision seems to be implied by his characterization of
Judith: not 5 per cent of the lines end with a full stop, most
sentences beginning in the middle of a line. As a result, "the
syntactical and alliterative patterns rarely coincide at any point."
"Classical" OE poetry, then, has neither the archaic stiffness
of the small-unit, end-stopped style, nor the disintegrating lack
of parallelism of the post-classical style. From the point of
view of OGmc poetry one might perhaps argue that Malone's
"classical" period was in some ways "post-classical." But there
is little cause for questioning the adequacy of his chronological
system, the more so as his use of "classical" hardly implies
greater artistry, and is founded entirely on internal criteria.

The latter can hardly be said of Kenneth Sisam's use of the
term "classic." In his Israel Gollancz Memorial Lecture on
Cynewulf, "classic" rather indicates a timeless, absolute quality.
In the oral delivery of OGmc verse, the abundant use of synonyms
had a special function:[4]

> they helped a primitive audience by diluting the sense and
> hammering it in with varied repetition. They also gave

an improviser an easy way of introducing words and
ideas into the alliterative frame.

The first Anglo-Saxon poets who tried to compose verse on
Christian subjects were confronted with two difficulties. There
was no stock of ready-made phrases for expressing Christian
ideas, and, hence, no traditional experience for their easy manip-
ulation in alliterative verse. But if, at first, "the struggle with
the mechanism of alliteration becomes too obvious," as soon as
the new practice is well established the very facility which resulted from it becomes a source of weakness: synonyms are
often multiplied in a way which, to us, seems purely mechanical.
Even in the best verse,

> synonyms are often used to introduce a new alliterative
> sequence, so that in the first half of the line the poet
> seems to mark time in order to change feet and take
> a step forward in the second half.

Sisam finds instances of such "padding" in Beowulf (e.g. l. 344 ff.)
and also, though very rarely, in Cynewulf's poems. Nearly half
of Caedmon's famous Hymn is taken up with synonyms for "God"—
there are eight of them in this poem of nine lines. Bede's Death
Song, on the other hand, "the only certain specimen of Anglo-
Saxon verse composed by an expert writer of Latin prose," is
remarkably free from "the doublings and circumlocutions of the
native style." It is to Bede's style, and to Cynewulf's, that Sisam
would apply the term "classic." From the extracts just quoted,
it seems clear that, in Sisam's opinion, Bede's training and experience as a Latin scholar must be reflected in the "classicism"
of his Death Song. In the case of Cynewulf, too, Sisam believes
that the poet's familiarity with Latin played an important part:
his is

> the style of a man trained to read and write Latin, to
> admire the orderly progress of a Latin sentence, and
> to prefer its clarity to the tangled profusion of the
> native style.

I am afraid I cannot follow Sisam in this attempt to measure
the value of native OE poetry by its conformity to an extraneous,

Latin, standard, or by its deviation from it. But Sisam is certainly right when he emphasizes the necessity of a knowledge of the Latin background for the understanding of OE literature.[5] There can be no doubt that Latin literary practice, and perhaps also the theories underlying it, had a profound influence on some types of vernacular literature, and probably, in the first place, on such works as stood the best chances of surviving. But Latin influence does not necessarily mean "classic" influence, at any rate not in seventh and eighth century England. In fact, to circumscribe the supposed Latin "models" or "ideals" is not an easy undertaking. In works on OE literature we usually find some simplified account of "currents" or "schools," e.g.:

> The see of Canterbury, largely because of the training and background of its first great occupant, Theodore of Tarsus, was given perhaps more than the see of York to the Christianity of Alexandria and the Levant rather than to the Christianity of Rome. Naturally there were no fundamental schisms in Britain; but the Oriental color of some writers like Aldhelm is in sharp contrast to the simple occidentalism of Bede, and what is true of the respective protagonists of the south and north is true in general of the two schools they represent.[6]

But in reality the situation was far more complicated; Aldhelm's very peculiar Latinity can hardly be adequately explained by pointing to his indebtedness to Theodore and Hadrian, nor is it sufficient to connect Bede's simplicity of style with a special cult of classical authors and ideals in Northumbria. If Aldhelm owed much of his training to Theodore and Hadrian, so did Ceolfrith, Bede's teacher and abbot; and even Benedict Biscop, the founder of Bede's spiritual home, spent some time under their direct guidance. Bede, on the other hand, had close relations with Nothelm, the later archbishop of Canterbury, and with abbot Albinus, Hadrian's successor, to whose encouragement we owe the Historia Ecclesiastica; and, vice versa, Aldhelm dedicated his treatise on metrics to King Aldfrith of Northumbria. There may have been something like an Aldhelmian school, whose influence is noticeable in Boniface and even in Alcuin, and perhaps much later still, but the evidence for a "school of Bede" is far less conclusive. Moreover, Aldhelm's style is not uniform; he wrote alternately a fairly straightforward prose (oratio simplex) and an ornate, highly artistic style (oratio perpetua). It was the latter which was much imitated, and also gave rise to severe criticism as early as William of Malmesbury's days.[7]

Without considering further questions, such as the very tricky problem of the impact of Irish art and scholarship on Anglo-Saxon England, we may safely conclude that Latin influence did not a priori have the effect described by Sisam. I hope to show that in some instances Latin models led OE poets to produce OE verse which was less classic both from the point of view of native poetics and from that of Latin classicism.

As to the question of the possible contacts between Latin and OE literature, the very climate of the period under discussion should warn us against all hasty conclusions. Hardly any period of English history saw such profound cultural changes as the second half of the seventh century. The death of Penda in 653 marked the end of what might be called the Germanic period of the Anglo-Saxons, and so, in many ways, did the Sutton Hoo cenotaph. Within a decade or so, the synod of Whitby convened and put an end to the Irish supremacy in ecclesiastical matters. In 669–670 Archbishop Theodore and abbot Hadrian took upon them the task of reorganizing Church and education in England. Benedict Biscop, who had been their guide on their journey from Rome to England, worked for some time under their supervision before returning to his native Northumbria there to found the monasteries of Wearmouth and Jarrow. At about the same time, Caedmon received divine inspiration and became the first great Christian poet of Anglo-Saxon England; a few years later, Aldhelm began his career as the first native Latin writer. Before the close of the century, Willibrord set out on his attempt to convert the Frisians, and Anglo-Saxon kings abdicated and left their country for Rome, there to devote the last years of their lives to the salvation of their souls. Within half a century, a country in which the fate of Christianity itself seemed to be hanging in the balance had become a centre of Christian learning and was beginning to play a part in the extension and organisation of the Church on the continent. It is not surprising, then, that our views on this period have been deeply modified during the last two or three decades. We have only to compare Girvan's discussion of the Beowulf-problem either with

Miss Whitelock's illuminating study of the audience of <u>Beowulf</u> and its implications, or with Wrenn's chapter on <u>Beowulf and Sutton Hoo</u> in his new edition of Chambers's introduction to the poem, to realize how radical these changes have been.[8] As a result, however, it has not become easier for us to visualize certain events of the period within their context, and this is especially true of the origin of OE literature. Broadly speaking, one may of course trace back its origin to the days of Tacitus and to the songs on Mannus, Arminius and the Germanic Hercules, or else to the inscription on the Golden Horn of Gallehus. For practical purposes, however, we cannot go beyond Caedmon's time, which means that the beginnings of OE literature in the sense of <u>litterae</u> or <u>ars litteraria,</u> a craft connected with letters and books, coincide with the beginnings of Latin literature in England. There may have been, and there probably was, a stream of OE poetry that kept clear of the scriptorium and stayed on its natural breeding ground, the banquet hall. The poems on Maldon and Brunanburh indicate that this stream only very gradually mingled with the literature that was meant to be written down from the very beginning; but the vast majority of surviving OE poems shows some traces of the atmosphere of the scriptorium. Unfortunately, the evidence on the contacts between writers of Latin and writers of English is very scarce, and instances of writers using the two languages are very rare and shed but little light on our problem.

With his fine description of Caedmon's vocation as a Christian poet, Bede may well have obscured the process through which OE literature came into being, at least for later historians of literature. Bede and his contemporaries looked upon this vocation as a miracle, and historians would perhaps have been wise to leave the matter there. The miracle was not that Caedmon should have succeeded in composing good English verse on hitherto untried Christian subjects, but that he should have done so without any training either as an Anglo-Saxon <u>scop</u> or as a theologian. Whether we accept Magoun's psychological account of the miracle or not, his general appreciation of the story should always be kept in mind:

> Bede's story tells one nothing about the birth of Anglo-Saxon poetry of any kind, not even of Christian narrative verse, and it makes no claim to furnish such information.[9]

Neither (and here I agree with Sisam) does the story point to any special influence of Latin literature on Caedmon's works, beyond providing the subject matter. But this will hardly have prevented a contemporary audience from enjoying them; and who knows whether the next generation did not call these poems something like "classic"?

As a native poet Bede achieved no great fame. If his pupil Cuthbert had not described his last days and, in doing so, preserved the short poem his master dictated on his death-bed, there would be no need for my mentioning him here at all. Bede's training as a native poet may have been no better than Caedmon's: he had entered monastic life at the age of seven; he was more inclined towards the pleasures of the study and the classroom than to those of the banquet-hall; and, finally, he seems to have had no strong feeling for poetry. His contemporaries may have shown less understanding for the classic restraint of his OE poetry than our time, but to Bede we owe one of the rare statements on the relationship of Latin and native poetic techniques. In describing the two basic types of Latin poetry, metrical and rhythmical, he points out that the technique of the latter is rather similar to that of the native poets[10] — a comparison to which I shall have to return in a moment.

The third poet I should like to mention in this connexion might have provided me with the ideal case-story, but he actually leaves me in a rather awkward position. We have nine lines of OE poetry ascribed to Caedmon and five presumably by Bede, but of Aldhelm's OE works not a single line survives. To William of Malmesbury we owe all our evidence on Aldhelm's activity as an English poet, but he held it from no mean source: in his Handbook King Alfred himself had highly praised Aldhelm's vernacular poems, some of which had remained popular to his days. Aldhelm may have been better versed in native poetic techniques than either Caedmon or Bede, but, things being as they are, we cannot even guess in what way his poems were superior to those of his contemporaries. We do, however, know what his Latin style was like: he left us a lengthy treatise on metrics, including a collection of riddles, and two treatises on virginity, one in prose and one in verse, besides a number of letters and minor poems.[11] His Latin has been almost universally denounced as "wholly artificial and completely without style" (L. Traube) or "utterly unpalatable to a modern taste" (M. L. W. Laistner); but since Professor Malone has bravely taken his defence, I may perhaps be allowed to point out a few peculiarities of his style which struck me when I was making a collection of Aldhelm glosses. Aldhelm is not without reason the author whose works contain the largest number of OE glosses. His Latin is full of difficult, abstruse words, most of which he must have picked up in glossaries. He is especially fond of Greek words, of which Ehwald lists some 700 in his edition. Whatever modern scholars may think of his tendency to avoid everyday words and to replace them by sonorous, colourful or rare terms, his contemporaries greatly admired this mannerism. Aldhelm may have looked upon this stock of precious words somewhat with the eyes of a <u>scop</u> surveying his traditional vocabulary, as an arsenal from which to draw as circumstances required. For it appears that Aldhelm's choice of words was not so wholly arbitrary or fanciful as has been supposed. He uses a great number of formulae, some very simple, such as <u>sacrosancta solemnitas</u>, which occurs four times:

Ehwald, p. 67, l. 19: <u>sacrosancta penticostes solemnitas</u>—
p. 269, l. 1: <u>sacrosancta palmarum solemnitate</u>—p. 289,
l. 16: <u>sacrosancta paschalis solemnitas</u>—p. 483, l. 15:
<u>in sacrosancta paschali solemnitate,</u>

and similarly he combines <u>solers</u> and <u>solertia</u> with <u>sagax</u> or <u>sagacitas</u>, <u>sapientia,</u> or <u>sollicitudo.</u>[12] In all these combinations there is a striking amount of <u>parhomoeon</u> or alliteration.[13] This stylistic device, which poets of previous centuries had been allowed to use only rarely, seems to have fascinated Aldhelm. It occurs in many of his favourite three-word groups:

p. 232, l. 8: <u>arta fenestrarum foramina</u>—ibid.: <u>angusta alvearii vestibula</u>—l. 9: <u>amoena arvorum prata</u>—l. 10: <u>memoriale mentis ingenium</u>—l. 11: <u>priscorum prophetarum oracula</u>—l. 13: <u>antiquarum arcana legum.</u>

At times Aldhelm alliterates three consecutive words, as in <u>cavatis consuta codicibus</u> (p. 233, l. 12) or even four, as in <u>sonantibus septem sacerdotum salpicibus</u> (p. 70, l. 11) and there is one instance, the initial sentence of his <u>Epistola ad Eahfridum,</u>

where out of 16 consecutive words fifteen have an initial p:
<u>Primitus pantorum procerum praetorumque pio potissimum
paternoque praesertim privilegio panagericum poemataque
passim prosatori sub polo promulgantes</u>, etc. (p. 488, l. 4 f.).
There is another feature of contemporary Latin poetics which
Aldhelm uses more sparingly, viz. the homoeoteleuton or
rhyme.[14] He uses it occasionally to link consecutive lines as
in ll. 2834 ff. of his <u>Carmen</u>: <u>loquentum . . . legentum . . .
canentum</u>—<u>tenebras</u> . . . <u>salebras</u>, but it is especially conspicuous where it serves to connect the two halves of a line.
This type appears in four lines appended to a charter of King
Ceadwalla (685–686):

> Pax cunctis [sit] legentibus | Consensumque praebentibus
> Sitque laus utentibus | Luxque perpes credentibus.
> Virtus vita faventibus | Rite constet senatibus
> Anglorum atque c[o]etibus | Qui dona firment nutibus.
> (p. 512, l. 5 ff.)

and also in a letter sent to him by his pupil Aethilwald:

> Sospitem tete sortibus | servet Herus ab omnibus,
> Tegat totum tutamine | truso hostis acumine,
> Mite reddens refugium | robustum per suffragium,
> Inque locet aethereum | caelestis sceptri gremium,
> Ubi semper consortium | perfruaris angelicum,
> Fine carens, caelestibus | vitam degens cespitibus.
> (p. 537, l. 67 ff.)

In this latter instance rhyme has been combined with alliteration,
a device which Aethilwald was to bring to perfection. His <u>Oratio
ad Deum</u> is a model application of this difficult technique:

> Summum satorem, solia | sedit qui per aethralia
> Alti olympi arcibus | obvallatus minacibus
> Cuncta cernens cacumine | caelorum summo lumine, etc.
> (p. 533, l. 1 ff.)

Each sixteen-syllable line consists of two half-lines linked by
rhyme and by alliteration. An Irish origin has been widely assumed for this type of Latin poetry, but the origin of some of

the supposed models is at best somewhat uncertain. The lines
of Aethilwald's Oratio remind us, to be sure, of the famous
Carmen ad Deum:[15]

> Sancte sator, suffragator,
> legum lator, largus dator,
> jure pollens, es qui potens,
> nunc in aethra firma petra,
> a quo creta cuncta freta,
> quae aplustra verrunt, flustra,
> quando celox currit velox:
> cujus numen crevit lumen,
> simul solum supra polum, etc.

which is sometimes quoted as formally the most perfect of Irish
Latin poems.[16] Some scholars, however, admit that its origin
may well have to be looked for in England, and in his study on
the OHG translation of the Carmen ad Deum Baesecke argues
that it may be ascribed to Aethilwald himself.[17] Although
Baesecke points out that a closer study of this and similar
poems is badly needed, his suggestion does not seem unlikely.
There seems to be no point, however, in pursuing this particular question any further, as long as the respective contributions
of the poetic systems of late Antiquity, of Celtic (especially Old
Irish) poetry, and of Germanic poetry, have not been clearly defined. Yet one may a priori assume that Anglo-Saxons were
favourably predisposed towards the use of alliteration: here at
least Latin and OE poetry had a common ground, although the
basic binding principle of the latter, alliteration, was no more
than a mannerism in the former. Latin rhythmical poetry, which
had given up the metrical patterns of classical antiquity for
syllable-counting, thus became more closely linked up with the
carmina vulgarium poetarum. The rhythmic pattern of the
Carmen ad Deum is so similar to that of OGmc verse, that it
can easily be read as such.[18]

It is true that the OE poets were rather reticent in their
adoption of that other device, homoeoteleuton or rhyme, but this
was probably due to the fundamental contradiction between initial
stresses and final rhymes as the binding elements of verse.[19]
Unlike the German poets, who abandoned their alliterating technique on a large scale as early as the ninth-century (Otfrid), En-

glish poets went on using it until long after the Conquest. When they resorted to rhyme, they did not look upon it as an alternative for alliteration, but rather as an additional ornament,[20] the result being rather like Aethilwald's Latin poems. A striking parallelism, e.g., may be discovered in the Latin-OE proverbs of Cotton MS. Faustina A. x and Royal MS. 2. B. V. :

> Ardor frigescit, nitor squalescit,
> amor abolescit, lux obtenebrescit.
> Hat acolað, hwit asolað,
> leof alaðaþ, leoht aðystrað,[21]

the OE version moreover having the same rhythmic pattern as the Carmen ad Deum. To become wholly effective, rhyme had to be combined with a regulation of the number of syllables, and here too the example of rhythmical Latin poetry could be followed. The Latin-OE proverbs clearly bear out this point. In the 15 rhyming lines which he inserted in his poem Elene (presumably to draw attention to his runic signature), Cynewulf did not yet reach this perfection:

```
1236   þus ic frod ond fus    þurh þæt fæcne hus
       wordcræftum wæf    ond wundrum læs,
       þragum þreodude    ond geþanc reodode,
       nihtes nearwe.    Nysse ic gearwe
1240   be ðære [rode] riht    ær me rumran geþeaht
       þurh ða mæran miht    on modes þeaht
       wisdom onwreah. Ic wæs weorcum fah,
       synnum asæled,    sorgum gewæled,
       bitrum gebunden,    bisgum beþrungen,
1245   ær me lare onlag    þurh leohtne had
       gamelum to geoce,    gife unscynde
       mægencyning amæt    ond on gemynd begeat,
       torht ontynde,    tidum gerymde,
       bancofan onband,    breostlocan onwand,
1250   leoðucræft onleac.    þæs ic lustum breac,
       willum in worlde.[22]
```

Yet, though the rhythm is not yet "regular," Cynewulf's use of rhyme serves the same purpose as Aethilwald's: it connects two half-lines which are also linked by alliteration. On the whole,

rhyme is perhaps not so rare in OE poetry as it seems at first
sight, even if we do not take into account all the types listed by
Kluge and Sievers.[23] Where rhyme occurs in a single line, as
in Beowulf 1014

> fylle gefægon, fægere geþægon,

it may at times be purely accidental, but there is no room for
doubt with the batches of two or more consecutive rhyming lines
in Christ (591–596, 1641–47), Andreas (867–870, 887–889),
Elene (114–115), Guthlac (828–830), and Phoenix (15–17, 53–55),
besides the many instances in Judith, and, of course, the Rhyming
Poem. The latter, unfortunately, remains one of the most puzzling
of all OE poems. Egill Skalagrimsson's Höfuðlausn has often been
cited as a possible model, but the editors of The Anglo-Saxon
Poetic Records[24] have proposed an earlier date for the English
poem, on account both of the metre and of the language. Their
suggestion that Egill may rather have modelled his poem after
OE rhymed verse (of which there may have been more examples
than the Rhyming Poem), has much in favour of it. OE rhymed
verse itself must owe its origin to Latin rhymed hymns.

In all probability Anglo-Saxon critics looked upon the use
of rhyme in their native verse as a mannerism, perhaps as an
interesting experiment, but one not to be encouraged in "classic"
OE poetry. Only at the very end of the OE period, in the chronicle
poem on the death of Alfred (1036), does rhyme take the place of
alliteration:

> Ac Godwine hine þa gelette   and hine on hæft sette,
> and his geferan he todraf,   and sume mislice ofsloh;
> sume hi man wið feo sealde,   sume hreowlice acwealde,
> sume hi man bende,   sume hi man blende,
> sume hamelode,   sume hættode,[25]

but the poem on the death of Edward, written about 30 years later
(1065), has no rhyme at all, apart from the homoeoptoton of l. 11:

> Englum and Sexum,   oretmægcum[26]

There were other mannerisms besides rhyme that attracted
Anglo-Saxon poets. The author of the poem Phoenix made up the

last eleven lines of his work out of alternating OE and Latin half-lines:

> 667 Hafað us alyfed   lucis auctor
> þæt we motun her   merueri,
> goddædum begietan   gaudia in celo,
> 670 þær we motun   maxima regna
> secan ond gesittan   sedibus altis,
> lifgan in lisse   lucis et pacis,
> agan eardinga   almae letitiæ,
> brucan blæddaga,   blandem et mitem
> 675 geseon sigora frean   sine fine,
> ond him lof singan   laude perenne,
> eadge mid englum.   Alleluia.[27]

This mixture of Latin and vernacular (also found e.g. in the OHG poem De Heinrico, where the first half-lines are Latin) assumes different proportions in a short OE poem preserved in MS. 326 of Corpus Christi College, Cambridge. It is a fragment of 17 lines in which the book addresses the reader:

> þus me gesette,   sanctus et iustus
> beorn boca gleaw,   bonus auctor
> Ealdhelm, æþele sceop,   etiam fuit
> ipselos on æðele   Angolsexna,
> 5 byscop on Bretene.   Biblos ic nu sceal,
> ponus et pondus   pleno cum sensu,
> geonges geanoðe   geomres iamiamque,
> secgan soð, nalles leas   þæt him symle wæs
> euthenia   oftor on fylste,
> 10 æne on eðle   ec ðon ðe se is
> yfel on gesæd.   Etiam nusquam
> ne sceal ladigan   labor quem tenet
> encratea,   ac he ealneg sceal
> boethia   biddan georne
> 15 þurh his modes gemind   micro in cosmo,
> þæt him drihten gyfe   dinams on eorðan
> fortis factor,   þæt he forð simle . . . .[28]

The Ealdhelm of line 3 is, of course, Aldhelm, whose prose treatise De laudibus virginitatis fills the bulk of this manuscript.

It can hardly be a coincidence that this tenth-century poem should present the same sort of linguistic ingenuity as Aldhelm's Latin works. Two centuries after his death the insertion of a number of Greek words (l. 4 ὑψηλός; l. 5 βίβλος; l. 9 εὐθενία; l. 10 æne = αἴνη? l. 13 ἐγκράτεια; l. 14 βοήθεια; l. 15 μικρῷ ἐν κόσμῳ; l. 16 dinams = δύναμις) was still felt to be a fit tribute to his verbosa garrulitas. Dobbie, in his introduction to the poem, ascribes it to the same "neo-Aldhelmian" movement to which we owe the Vita Ethelwoldi of Wulfstan of Winchester, the Vita Wilfridi of Fridegod (written at the request of Odo, archbishop of Canterbury 942–959), and the Vita S. Dunstani.[29] Whether the Aldhelmian features of these works and of the poem Ealdhelm are due to a tenth-century revival of older ideals,[30] or whether they point to an uninterrupted tradition going back to the days of Theodore and Hadrian—this is the explanation which Dobbie tentatively puts forward—is again a problem which we must leave for students of the Latin Middle Ages to solve for us.

More mannerisms are probably to be found in OE poetry. Perhaps the division of some poems into short stanzas may be mentioned in this connexion. It is striking, indeed, that, apart from the poems Seasons for Fasting and Deor's Lament, stanzaic structures only appear where they were suggested by a Latin original, as in the translations of the Pater Noster and of Psalms. Popular Gmc poetry did, to be sure, use such structures, e.g. in the Charms, but in the more literate genres they seem to be a late development, partly due at least to foreign examples. Riddle 28 uses a mannerism of a different kind:

> Biþ foldan dæl   fægre gegierwed
> mid þy heardestan   and mid þy scearpestan
> ond mid þy grimmestan   gumena gestreona,
> corfen, sworfen,   cyrred, þyrred,
> bunden, wunden,   blæced, wæced,
> frætwed, geatwed,   feorran læded
> to durum dryhta.   Dream bið in innan
> cwicra wihta . . . .[31]

The solution of the Riddle ("John Barleycorn," or "beer," or "a harp") need not occupy us at this moment; it is the peculiar structure of ll. 4–6 which calls for our attention. Here we have

an instance of "verse-filling asyndeton":[32] the poet has tried
to crowd in as many significant words as possible into each line,
leaving out the conjunctions to heighten the effect produced by
the sequence of past participles. His use of this stylistic device
would perhaps be less conspicuous if he had not emphasized it
by a copious use of rhyme (cf. ll. 1242–44 in the passage from
Elene quoted above).

There are two angles from which a stylistic appreciation of
OE poetry can be attempted. One may try to assess its permanent value by applying the standards of a twentieth-century critic;
or one may try to view it from the inside, as it were with the
eyes of an Anglo-Saxon critic. The present paper is an attempt
to clear the ground for the latter approach. I do not wish to
minimize the dangers of this procedure: it will always be very
difficult to decide what kind of poetry the Anglo-Saxons themselves considered as "classic" in the sense of "of the first
class, of allowed excellence."

Neither do I believe that this hurried tour of a vast territory is an altogether adequate introduction to our problem. I
am confident, however, that a further study of some of the questions raised in this paper may lead to a better understanding of
the poetic achievement of the OE period. We shall only reach
this aim if we succeed in viewing the literary production of
Anglo-Saxon England as a unit, and that is why I hope that Latin
scholars will join us in our effort.

NOTES

1   E. R. Curtius, Europäische Literatur und lateinisches
    Mittelalter (Bern, 1948), p. 278; English translation by W. R.
    Trask, European Literature and the Latin Middle Ages,
    Bollingen Series, XXXVI (New York, 1953), 273.

2   The definitions of Attic and Asiatic given by the NED, viz.
    "marked by simple and refined taste" and "formerly used
    to describe a florid and imaginative style," offer a less
    promising starting point: they do not reflect the original
    correlation between the two terms. A fuller discussion of
    "Atticism" and "Asianism" in relation to mediaeval esthetics
    will be found in E. De Bruyne, Etudes d'esthétique médiévale,
    Rijksuniversiteit te Gent. Werken uitgegeven door de Faculteit
    van de Letteren en Wijsbegeerte 97–99 (Bruges, 1946), I, 108 ff.

3 Kemp Malone, "The Old English Period," in A Literary
   History of England, ed. by A. C. Baugh (New York, 1948),
   I, 26 ff.

4 Kenneth Sisam, Cynewulf and his Poetry, reprinted in his
   Studies in the History of Old English Literature (Oxford,
   1953), esp. p. 16 f.

5 See e.g. R. Vleeskruyer, The Life of St. Chad. An Old English Homily (Amsterdam, 1953), p. 46 f.

6 G. K. Anderson, The Literature of the Anglo-Saxons (Princeton, 1949), p. 225.

7 J. W. H. Atkins, English Literary Criticism: The Medieval
   Phase (London, 1952), p. 92, and E. De Bruyne, op. cit., p. 142.

8 R. Girvan, Beowulf and the Seventh Century (London, 1935).
   — Dorothy Whitelock, The Audience of Beowulf (Oxford, 1951).
   — R. W. Chambers, Beowulf. An Introduction to the Study of
   the Poem . . . with a Supplement by C. L. Wrenn (Cambridge,
   1959), pp. 509—523.

9 F. P. Magoun Jr, "Bede's Story of Caedmon: the Case History
   of an Anglo-Saxon Oral Singer" in Speculum, XXX (1955), 62.

10 "Videtur autem rhythmus metris esse consimilis qui est
   verborum modulata compositio non metrica ratione sed
   numero syllabarum ad judicium aurium examinata, ut sunt
   carmina vulgarium poetarum." (De re metrica, ed. Keil,
   VII, 242). Cf. E. De Bruyne, op. cit., I, 151 ff., and
   W. P. Lehmann, The Development of Germanic Verse Form
   (Austin, 1956), p. 171 f.

11 Aldhelmi Opera, ed. R. Ehwald, MGH, Auct. Ant., XV (Berlin,
   1919).

12 Op. cit., p. 81, l. 3; p. 229, l. 12; p. 231, l. 1; p. 241, l. 17;
   p. 242, l. 10; p. 320, l. 7; p. 476, l. 8; p. 483, l. 18, etc.

13 "Paromoeon est multitudo verborum ex una littera inchoantium."
   Isidorus, Etymologiae, ed. W. M. Lindsay (Oxford, 1911), I,
   XXXVI, 14; cf. Bede, De schematibus et tropis sacrae scripturae,
   ed. J. P. Migne, P. L., XC, 178.

14 "Homoeon teleuton est, quum uno modo verba plurima
   finiuntur." Isidorus, Etymologiae, I, XXVI, 16; Isidorus lists

the homoeoptoton as a separate "schema," ibid. 15: "Homoeoptoton est, quum plurima nomina per unum casum de-
nuntiantur," whilst Bede defines homoeoteleuton quite generally as "similis terminatio," loc. cit.

15 Blume, Analecta Hymnica, LI, 229.   Note that the poem contains a number of Greek words (e.g. πέτρα in l. 5).

16 F. J. E. Raby, History of Secular Latin Poetry in the Middle
Ages (Oxford, 1934), I, 163.

17 G. Baesecke, Das lateinisch-althochdeutsche Reimgebet (Carmen
ad Deum) und das Rätsel vom Vogel federlos (Berlin, 1948),
p. 10 ff.

18 Ibid., p. 13.

19 W. P. Lehmann, op.cit., p. 3 f.

20 Ibid., pp. 73, 174, 177.

21 E. V. K. Dobbie, The Anglo-Saxon Minor Poems (New York,
1942), p. 109.

22 G. P. Krapp, The Vercelli Book (New York, 1932), p. 100.

23 F. Kluge, "Zur Geschichte des Reimes im Altgermanischen,"
BGDSL, IX (1884), 422 ff. — E. Sievers, Altgermanische
Metrik (Halle, 1893), p. 146 ff.

24 G. P. Krapp and E. V. K. Dobbie, The Exeter Book (New York,
1936), p. xlviii f.

25 E. V. K. Dobbie, The Anglo-Saxon Minor Poems (New York,
1942), p. 24.

26 Ibid., p. 25.

27 G. P. Krapp and E. V. K. Dobbie, Exeter Book, p. 112 f. Cf.
also A Summons to Prayer in A. S. Minor Poems, p. 69 f.

28 E. V. K. Dobbie, The Anglo-Saxon Minor Poems, p. 97 f.

29 Ibid., p. xci.

30 On a renewed interest in Aldhelm's works see ed. R. Ehwald,
p. 216.

31 G. P. Krapp and E. V. K. Dobbie, Exeter Book, p. 194 f.

32 E. R. Curtius, op.cit., p. 289 (Engl. trans. p. 285).

PATRISTICS AND OLD ENGLISH LITERATURE:
NOTES ON SOME POEMS

Morton W. Bloomfield

In recent years, because of various controversies about the
interpretation of mediaeval literature, the term patristics has
unfortunately come to be associated with only one aspect of
Patristic activity—biblical exegesis. However, the rich theological and philosophical fare which the Fathers offer moderns
comprises a great deal more than a method of hermeneutics
with an accompanying biblical symbolism, however important.
It is the purpose of this brief article to call attention to three
passages in OE literature which can be illuminated by the
writings of the Fathers whereby a sense of the meaning of the
whole poems of which they are a part can be suggested if not
completely attained. The interpretations here put forth will add
to the steadily growing body of scholarship which is pointing to
the connection between the ancient classical world, both Christian and pagan, and OE literature.

With a poem like Caedmon's Hymn, this connection is not
to be wondered at, as it is a Christian poem in every way and a
short example of a favorite ancient Christian literary genre, the
poetic biblical paraphrase of an hexaemeral cast. However, even
in poems not composed on Christian themes nor within Christian
literary genres, such as The Battle of Maldon and Beowulf, we
may find such connections which will not only explain particular
lines but clarify the background implicit in these works and help
identify the overall purpose of these poems. It has always been
recognized that these a-Christian poems of the OE corpus are
an amalgam of pagan and Christian elements, even though the
proportions of both have not always been agreed upon. At present,
the Germanizing interpretations, dominant for many years, seem

Reprinted from Comparative Literature, Vol. 14 (1962), pp. 36–43, by
permission of the author and the publisher.

to be on the wane and Christianizing interpretations are very common. Obviously both Christian and Germanic themes are present in these poems, but the exact determination of their relative weight is still to seek. Perhaps no general answer is possible; each poem presents a special union of the two traditions. In the last analysis, a subjective element in this task must always be present, but this factor should not blind us to whatever objective facts can be ascertained. Whatever the origin of these poems, it is clear that in their preserved and thus final form they were the products of Christians and written by Christian scribes. This does not preclude, of course, a basic heathen story. Inasmuch as the Germanic element has been extensively explored, often to the extent of claiming as Germanic dubious or even clearly erroneous themes,[1] the balance needs to be redressed. It is in the Fathers, the main literary material (along with the Bible) of the Christians who wrote or composed OE literature as it is preserved, that we can find the best sources for discovering the Christian materials in these poems. Even in avowedly Christian poems, like Caedmon's Hymn, we can still find new meanings and explanations when they are closely examined from the point of view of these basic sources. Three examples of the use of this material follow.

A. The Battle of Maldon, lines 175–180:

> Nu ic ah, milde Metod, mæste þearfe
> þæt þu minum gaste godes geunne,
> þæt min sawul to ðe siðian mote,
> on þin geweald, þeoden engla,
> mid friþe ferian; ic eom frymdi to þe
> þæt hi helsceaðan hynan ne moton.

Now I have, merciful Creator, great need that Thou grantest to my spirit grace so that my soul may be permitted to go to Thee, into Thy power, O Lord of angels, to fare in peace. I entreat Thee that devils may not be permitted to afflict it.

These last words of the hero Byrhtnoð as he is being hacked to death by the hæðene scealcas, the heathen warriors of the Vikings, take on a special poignancy[2] if we interpret his speech

much more literally than is usually done and if we understand
the Patristic and Christian concept of the passage of the soul *(also Egyptian)*
out of the body. What is in Byrhtnoð's mind at this moment is
the widespread belief that a struggle between the minions of the
Devil and angels takes place for the soul as it leaves the body.[3]
Byrhtnoð is not speaking figuratively when he speaks of the devils
afflicting the soul, but literally.

Gregory the Great puts it very well in a sermon:

> We must seriously consider how terrifying to us will
> be the hour of death . . . . Then the wicked spirits seek
> their works in the departing soul. Then they unfold
> the wickedness to which they have seduced it that they
> might draw the soul as a companion in torments. But
> why do we say this only of the wicked soul, when they
> come to the dying elect as well, and seek to prevail
> over them and to demand something in them as their
> own.[4]

This semi-physical struggle with the devil in death was the
expected fate of all men, but martyrs and saints could expect rapid
help from angels who would protect the soul and carry it off to
heaven. In the Passio Sancti Bonifatii, the martyr utters a similar prayer to God and asks him to send "angelum tuum, et impediat
me pestifer et interfector draco sua malignitate."[5]

No doubt as a fighter against the heathen and in the manner
of his death, Byrhtnoð had a religious dimension in the minds of
his compatriots, as the tradition of his life and death shows.[6]
In this poem written shortly after his death, such a speech would
suggest a consciousness of his martyrdom. And in the brutal
killing of Byrhtnoð by a mass of heathens, the poet (or perhaps
Byrhtnoð himself) saw the hordes of devils who were waiting for
his soul. By his prayer, the hero was asking, as a martyr might
ask, for special protection from God, and no doubt the poet and his
his audience felt he would obtain his wish.

B. Beowulf, line 2330:   *(2)*

> wende se wisa   þæt he Wealdende
> ofer ealde riht   ecean Dryhtne
> bitre gebulge.

> The wise one [Beowulf] supposed that he had bitterly
> offended the Eternal contrary to old law.

The phrase ealde riht is taken by most commentators on
Beowulf to be an allusion to Old Testament law, although apparently the phrase can also be used of what we might call customary
law. Klaeber, in his note on this line, writes that this phrase "is
here given a Christian interpretation' ;[7] Wrenn similarly writes,
"Here Beowulf's thoughts may be Christian, though they need
not necessarily be so. But the whole tone points to Christianity,
and the expression ofer ealde riht, 'contrary to ancient law,'
seems to refer to God's commandments."[8] Even Charles Dona-
hue is extremely cautious in discussing this line, although he has
pointed out how Irish tradition conceived of its pagan heroes (or
at least some of them) as saints under natural law or naturally
good rather than damned as outside the Judaeo-Christian tradition. He writes,

> When Beowulf heard that a dragon had destroyed his
> royal hall, he was troubled in his heart, the poet
> says, because "as a wise man, he believed that he
> had broken the ancient law . . . ." The contents of
> the ancient law, in so far as they can be deduced
> from the poem, seem to be the traditional precepts
> of Germanic morality.[9]

Whether the equation of pagan with Old Testament law is
due to Celtic influence or not or whether it be due to a general
consciousness of the "danger of celebrating a pagan hero,"[10]
it is clear that pre-Christian moral law of whatever origin
was considered something of a unity before the time of the
Beowulf poet. The tendency to assimilate the best part of paganism to the Old Testament is one way converted pagans could
accept the New Law and still maintain pride of ancestry.

The problem of the "Old Law" is complicated and it cannot
be solved here. The fact that the word "law" is used for a body
of moral obligations would argue for Patristic influence, for law
is the normal term for religious and moral obligations in the
Fathers. It is also true that the law of the Old Testament which
was considered binding on Christians—the moral laws—was
equated for the most part with natural law, although in general

this equation is later than the early Middle Ages — in St. Thomas, for instance.

But St. Thomas is discussing the Mosaic law, or the moral part of it. It is, however, often forgotten that figures like Cain to whom Grendel was assimilated lived before the promulgation of the "Old Law" on Mount Sinai and if he sinned, as he obviously did, he sinned against natural law. So did Lucifer and the rebellious angels. Subordinating pre-Mosaic Old Testament figures to pagan or natural law is not really difficult. Abel and Cain (and the devil) are the only Old Testament figures mentioned in Beowulf. They are Old Testament figures but not Jews, and to Christians and Jews they were the ancestors of the whole human race. Even a good man like Abraham, who lived before at least the full knowledge of the Mosaic law, was certainly saved by faith. These pre-Mosaic figures of the Old Testament provided, then, an opening of salvation for the pagan ancestors of the Germanic and Celtic peoples. If good men were saved before Sinai, then good pagans like Beowulf could be saved.[11] If bad men were damned before Sinai, then Grendel and his ilk could be damned without inconsistency.

All this is argued at length by Origen in his commentary on St. Paul's Epistle to the Romans, especially on Chapter VII in discussing passages like "Nay, I had not known sin, but by the law" (verse 7) and "For without the law sin was dead" (verse 8). Origen points out that there was sin in the period from Adam to Moses and that Paul was not referring merely to the Old Law but to natural law in Chapters IV and VII. To take one passage from his treatment of the subject,

> Magis ergo illud in hoc loco [one of the Pauline
> verses] debet intelligi esse . . . legem naturæ
> quæ "scripta" est "non in tabulis lapideis, sed
> in tabulis cordis" . . . quæ lex ab illo qui ab
> initio creavit hominem ita in principali cordis
> ejus ascripta est . . . .[12]

Thus Patristic thinking helps us to see why the Beowulf poet could, without qualms, mingle pagan and Old Testament elements. To him there was no mixing of incompatibles in this procedure, especially as he confined his Old Testament figures to pre-Mosaic personages. The ealde riht refers not to Old Testament (i.e., Sinaitic) law but natural law which was implanted even in the hearts of pagans, including the pre-Mosaic "pagans" of the Old Testament. All this helps us to solve the problem of the mingling of biblical and pagan elements in the poem.

C. Caedmon's Hymn:

> Nu we sculon herigean   heofonrices Weard,
> Meotodes meahte   ond his modgeþanc,
> weorc Wuldorfæder,   swa he wundra gehwæs,
> ece Drihten,   or onstealde.
> He ærest sceop   eorðan bearnum
> heofon to hrofe,   halig Scyppend;
> þa middangeard   monncynnes Weard,
> ece Drihten,   æfter teode
> firum foldan   Frea ælmihtig.

Now we shall praise the guardian of heaven, the power of the Creator and his thought [design], the work of the Father of glory, the eternal Ruler, as [how] he created the beginning of each wonder. He, the holy creator, first created for the children of the earth heaven as a covering; then the Guardian of mankind, the eternal Ruler, the almighty Lord, next created the world, the earth for men.

This poem of Caedmon's is an expanded version in the style of scriptural poetic paraphrase of the first verse of Genesis. Bernard Huppé has devoted a penetrating chapter of his recent book to elucidating the setting and meaning of this short poem.[13] He has shown how the Patristic tradition helps us to understand it and has quoted a number of useful parallels. The learning manifest in this poem by an unlettered peasant, not to speak of its pleasing form, is indeed a miracle.

Huppé suggests that the parallel phrases Meotodes meahte, his modgeþanc, and weorc Wuldorfæder may suggest the Trinity. There are difficulties in this interpretation, not the least of which is the fact that Bede translated this hymn into Latin in such a way as not to suggest the Trinity, particularly the Third Person,[14] but my purpose here is not to argue this one way or another, but rather to concentrate on the word modgeþanc

68

which can give some support to a Trinitarian interpretation.

Huppé translates modgeþanc as "wisdom," a possible
translation and obviously suitable as an epithet for the Son,[15]
but only by a great freedom can this word be so translated. I
believe, however, that the reference to the Son can still be found
cohering in this word if we take it in its more normal sense of
"thought" as revealed by Grein[16] and Bosworth-Toller in their
entries on this word. One is tempted to translate it as Logos, ?
a classical designation for the Son in his role as creator or
co-creator of the universe. Yet Bede in his Latin translates it
as consilium rather than verbum.

The Thesarus linguæ latinæ lists various meanings for
consilium, none of which can be unequivocally linked with the
meaning "wisdom," but there are examples to illustrate it in
the sense of cogitatio or deliberatio. Thus the natural sense of
modgeþanc-consilium is a "thought," but does this meaning remove it from any connection with the Second Person?

Not at all. Bede makes the point, following Augustine, in
his commentary on Genesis, that God created the world first
of all in His Son,[17] basing like him his proof on John 8 : 25 where
principium provides the bridge to Genesis 1 : 1. "Filius autem
ita Principium est," writes Augustine,[18] of "In principio fecit
Deus cœlum et terram."

What does Augustine mean by this? In what sense was the
world created in the Son? The answer to this question is provided in a recent article of Professor Wolfson's wherein he discusses the impact of Plato's Timaeus on Christian and Jewish
thought in antiquity.[19] Plato had left the location of his Ideas
vague and never clearly related them to God, sometimes placing
them in God as thoughts and at other times outside of God.

Philo attempted to solve this problem of divine exemplars
in his comments on creation, and his solution may be summed
up in Professor Wolfson's words:

> When God by His own good will decided to create this
> world of ours, He first, out of the ideas which had
> been in His thought from eternity, constructed an
> "intelligible" world and this intelligible world He
> placed in the Logos, which had likewise existed pre-
> viously from eternity in His thought. Then in the

likeness of this intelligible world of ideas, He
created this "visible" world of ours.[20]

The Christian step was taken by John who equated the Logos
with Jesus. These notions explain Augustine's and Bede's statement that the world was first created in Christ. The world here
is the divine exemplars by which God worked.[21] Hence, in
Caedmon's Hymn we praise God's power and his thought (or design) which, according to the Fathers, was externalized (from
the point of view of the Father) in the Son. Thus the Platonic
ideas could be both within and without God at the same time.
The dangers of extreme views could then be avoided. God had
no eternal rival in the form of Ideas and at the same time had
divine exemplars to work from to provide universals for particulars.

One further theological point. Both Augustine and Bede are
concerned with another problem in the first verse of Genesis:
the question of whether God needed time to create the whole
world. Augustine emphasized that everything was created at
once and not sequentially. Otherwise a limitation would be
placed on God. The six days are merely the realization of what
was already created from the beginning as Ideas.[22] This may
be the point of Caedmon's remark that we praise God for creat-
ing at the beginning the "beginning of each wonder."

If all this seems rather complicated and subtle for the
simple Caedmon, we may perhaps, if we do not wish to account
for the hymn, as Bede does, by a miracle, assume that these
current problems were being discussed in Caedmon's monastic
environment and that somehow they reached his ears and were
transmuted into poetry. In any case the "thought" of God can
only be understood even on the simplest level as a reference
to the divine exemplars, even if we refuse to see the Son therein.
This notion is complicated enough to make us wonder at the
source of Caedmon's sophistication. The adding of the notion
of the Son to the word does not increase very much the difficulty
of explaining it at all. We may say of this matter as was said
of St. Denis' walking two miles with his head in his hands, "it
is only the first step that counts."

NOTES

1 The widespread tendency to use the word "wyrd" as evidence
of Germanic paganism seems to be dangerously simplistic, for
wyrd was soon given a Christian meaning. After all, there is
a Christian meaning to fate well summed up in the term
"providence." On this subject, see Bertha S. Phillpotts,
"Wyrd and Providence in Anglo-Saxon Thought," E&S, XIII
(1928), 7–27, and especially B. J. Timmer, "Wyrd in Anglo-
Saxon Prose and Poetry," Neophil, XXVI (1940–41), 24–33,
213–28; see also his "Heathen and Christian Elements in
Old English Poetry," Neophil, XXIX (1944), 180–85.
  For a plea to use Patristics in interpreting mediaeval
literature, see J. M. Campbell, "Patristic Studies and the
Literature of Mediaeval England," Speculum, VIII (1933),
465–78.

2 I am indebted to Mr. Jerome Mandel, a student of mine, for
pointing out the relation of the manner of Byrhtnoð's death
to the point of his last remarks.

3 This concept is widespread in the writings of the Fathers
(and in early mediaeval literature and later). It is perhaps
most succinctly discussed in Alfred C. Rush, "An Echo of
Christian Antiquity: Death a Struggle with the Devil," Traditio,
III (1945), 369–80.

4 Quoted in Rush, p. 369 (from Hom. in Evan., lib. II, hom.
xxxix, §8; P. L., LXXVI, col. 1298.

5 Quoted in Rush, p. 375.

6 See the summary of what is known about Byrhtnoð in E. V.
Gordon's edition of The Battle of Maldon (London, 1937),
pp. 15–21.

7 Beowulf, 3rd ed. (Boston, 1950), p. 211.

8 Beowulf (London, etc., 1953), p. 220.

9 "Beowulf, Ireland and the Natural Good," Traditio, VII
(1949–51), 275.

10 As Margaret E. Goldsmith argues in "The Christian Theme
of Beowulf," Medium Ævum, XXIX (1960), 83. The purpose
of this article may be summed up in the author's words:

"I suggest that the Beowulf poet saw, in the legendary life of a heathen hero, an opportunity to write of this fight against the devil and the seed of Cain" (p. 101).

11 Beowulf must have been regarded by the author of the final form of Beowulf as a pagan, but, owing to a lack of true historical perspective, Christian sentiments of a general sort may sometimes have been attributed to him.

12 P. G., XIV, col. 1033. The whole sections of Books IV and V of this work discuss the problems involved in Paul's remarks. I owe this reference to the kindness of Mrs. Carol Kaske. Hrabanus Maurus, in Enn. in Epp. Pauli (P. L., CXI, col. 1422), says specifically that Cain sinned against natural law.

13 Bernard Huppé, Doctrine and Poetry, Augustine's Influence on Old English Poetry (New York, 1959), pp. 99 ff.

14 The beginning of the hymn ("the theme of praise" as Huppé says, p. 108) reads in Bede "Nunc laudare debemus auctorem regni cœlestis, potentiam creatoris, et consilium illius, facta Patris gloriæ . . ." The past participle facta hardly suggests the activating work of the Holy Ghost, but rather the completed work. Consilium we shall discuss below. Potentia is certainly traditionally connected with the Father.

15 Doctrine and Poetry, pp. 101, 108, and 111.

16 Sprachschatz der angelsächischen Dichter (Heidelberg, 1912), p. 477.

17 In lib. Genesis I, in J. A. Giles, ed., Works of The Venerable Bede (London, 1844), VII, p. 3.

18 De Genesi ad litteram, lib. imperfectus, c. iii; P. L., XXXIV, col. 222. Cf. his De Genesi contra Manichæos, lib. I, c. ii; P. L., XXXIV, col. 174, where he writes, "His [arguments of the Manichees] respondemus, Deum in principio fecisse cœlum et terram, non in principio temporis, sed in Christo, cum Verbum esset apud Patrem . . ."

19 Harry A. Wolfson, "Extradeical and Intradeical Interpretations of Platonic Ideas," JHI, XXII (1961), 3–32.

20 Ibid., p. 6.

21 See also Roger Miller Jones, "The Ideas as the Thoughts of God," CP, XXI (1926), 317–26.

22 Bede puts it: "Deus autem, cujus omnipotens manus est ad explendum opus suum, non equit mora temporum, quia scriptura est: omnia quæcumque voluit fecit" (In lib. Genesis I; Giles ed., VII, p. 3).

DIALECT ORIGINS OF THE EARLIER OLD ENGLISH VERSE

Kenneth Sisam

Do the linguistic tests now available enable us to determine
the dialect in which any longer piece of the earlier Old English
poetry was composed? There seems to be no recent general
treatment of this question, though it is customary for editors
to say something about the original dialect of the particular
poems they present. When reviewing a modern edition of exceptional interest,[1] I indicated some reasons for doubting the
view that practically all the early poetry is demonstrably of
Anglian origin:

> The method of approaching this problem which
> has become almost traditional is by no means se-
> curely based. It assumes that dialect colouring
> traceable to the original form of an Old English poem
> is evidence of the poet's natural dialect, though con-
> sideration of dialect conventions in Greek literature
> must raise doubts. From the fact that some early
> poems were composed in the Anglian dialect, it
> reaches the conclusion that no extant early poem
> was composed in the South, though practically all
> the surviving verse was preserved there. Yet, with-
> out early Southern texts, there is no sure distinction
> between words, forms and constructions unknown to
> Southern poets in early times, and those, once general,
> that survived in Anglian only.

A development of this summary criticism may help to distinguish
fact from opinion, and may encourage others to produce more
convincing arguments.

Reprinted from Studies in the History of Old English Literature, by
permission of the author and the Clarendon Press, Oxford.

DIALECT ORIGINS OF THE EARLIER OLD ENGLISH VERSE

The stock to which the poet belonged and the locality in which he composed may be left out of account: we are concerned only with the dialect he used. But at once a difficulty arises. A dialect is recognized by a combination of features in its sounds, vocabulary, accidence, or syntax. Within Anglo-Saxon England there were not many forbidding physical barriers, political boundaries seldom remained fixed, and the surviving texts that can be dated and localized with reasonable certainty are so few that we do not know the geographical limits within which any dialectal feature was current at a given time. A philologist, asked what were the characteristics of West Saxon about the year 800, and in what districts they prevailed, would have very little direct evidence on which to base an answer. So "West Saxon," "Mercian," "Anglian" in this connexion are vague terms.

If, in the attempt to be more precise, one of the principal dialects is closely defined as the language of a particular text or author, it ceases to be comparable with others more vaguely defined. Some not very critical studies of Anglian elements in Ælfric's vocabulary have raised doubts about the purity of his West Saxon; and to avoid these doubts there has been a tendency to rely chiefly on the prose works for which Alfred's authorship is generally accepted as the standard of pure West Saxon vocabulary. But if a poem has to be attributed to one or the other, "West Saxon" in such a narrow sense is at a disadvantage compared with "Anglian" in the vague sense, because differences from standard West Saxon will be relatively clear and certain.

A new difficulty appears when the definition of dialects by texts is carried through—if, for instance, "West Saxon" is defined as the language of Alfred and Ælfric, and "Mercian" as the language of the Vespasian Psalter and Royal Glosses, which correspond roughly in dates. In its regular characteristics the dialect of Alfred's prose was probably that of the districts around Winchester, the capital, and Wilton, a principal residence of the kings of his line. The regularity and widespread literary use of Ælfric's dialect is easiest explained if it was the language of Æthelwold's school—again at Winchester.[2] Similarly both the Vespasian Psalter and Royal Glosses[3] seem to represent the dialect of the district around Worcester. So large parts of the South and Midlands are not covered by these specimens of the late ninth and tenth centuries. For the period to which the earlier poetry is commonly assigned—the seventh, eighth, and early ninth centuries[4]—hardly any consecutive prose survives.

Nor is it safe to treat the few surviving specimens of local dialects as true samples for larger areas and earlier centuries. The work of historians and archaeologists does not suggest that the Anglo-Saxon invaders settled and remained in big homogeneous blocks, segregated according to their Continental homes, so that original differences of dialect would persist and new features develop uniformly. There are many indications of irregular conquest and subsequent advances or recessions as one Anglo-Saxon leader or group came into conflict with others. In the later period, when evidence is fuller, one century is enough to produce considerable differences between the standard West Saxon of Alfred and of Ælfric. We find Mercian influence at Canterbury, where the Mercian gloss seems to have been copied into the Vespasian Psalter; and West Saxon influence at Worcester, where the Royal Glosses, in the texts used and the script as well as the language, are an old-fashioned survival; contemporary Worcester charters leave no doubt that West Saxon had become the official language at Worcester by the end of the tenth century. In earlier times, when evidence is scarce, conditions were certainly simpler in one respect only—that dialect differences were less well marked—and this makes it harder to determine the original dialect of early poems.

So much preamble may help to explain why the question of origin is difficult, and why it is often reduced to the crude alternatives: Anglian or West Saxon? If the issue could be so simplified, there is a fair chance of getting a right or at least a defensible answer even if the methods used are faulty. But it is to the quality of the arguments, rather than to particular results, that I wish to call attention.

It is important to distinguish words and forms that could arise in the course of transmission from century to century, or from dialect to dialect, from those that are structural in the verse, i.e. necessary to the metre. Most of the poetry is preserved in single manuscripts of the late tenth or early eleventh century, and in a language that is predominantly West Saxon in forms, though it differs in many details from the standard Late West Saxon of Ælfric's prose. Then any reliance on words or forms that are not confirmed by the metre will tilt the balance against West Saxon origin. For all such forms that are regular

in West Saxon are naturally accounted for by the transmission.
Yet those that are irregular are often treated as evidence that
Anglian originals have been incompletely transposed into West
Saxon. This assumes that the history of the earlier poetry is
simply one of composition in Anglian with a one-way transmission ending in the Late West Saxon manuscripts: which is really
the thing to be proved.

It is true that any Anglian poem that survives in a late Anglo-
Saxon manuscript has passed into West Saxon. Yet whenever a
few facts are known, they do not suggest that transmission was
simple. The Dream of the Rood appears first in extracts on the
eighth-century Ruthwell Cross in Dumfriesshire. A complete
text, West-Saxonized and probably expanded from the original
poem, is preserved in the late-tenth-century manuscript at
Vercelli. There are echoes in the couplet inscribed on an Anglo-
Saxon reliquary of the eleventh century now at Brussels.[5] The
history that links these three survivals must be one of movement
and change that stretches the imagination. And there are no historical reasons why poems composed in the South should not
pass to the North and Midlands, assume an Anglian dress or
colouring there, and return to the South. The Northumbrian
version of the Mailcoat Riddle is found in a ninth-century manuscript at Leyden, together with Latin riddles by Aldhelm, who
wrote its Latin original. This would be good evidence that Latin
texts composed in the South came into Northumbrian hands in
early times, even if Aldhelm's dedicatory letter to the Northumbrian King Aldfrith ("Acircius") were not extant.[6] Had Aldhelm
himself made the English translation it might travel the same
way; and there is nothing in the Northumbrian version to prove
that it was not transposed from West Saxon. The Mailcoat Riddle,
wherever it was translated, is an example of literary or learned
communication. But in an age when recited verse was one of the
few means of popular instruction and amusement, and when travelling entertainers carried verse to all classes of society, the
chances are not great that poems, whether secular or religious,
would remain localized for long periods or would move uniformly
southwards. Obviously oral transmission at any point in the
chain would eliminate non-structural forms of the original, unless the reciter spoke the local dialect in which it was composed.

It is desirable then to confine attention to words and forms
that are confirmed by the metre. The doubt will remain whether

a poem preserved in one late manuscript has been interpolated or partly recomposed in a dialect different from that of the original; or whether the original itself contained things imitated from other dialects. But an inquiry that begins by accepting as original what is structural in the verse will not be overburdened with evidence.

The most important structural test that has been proposed concerns forms of the present indicative, which are so common that they are pretty certain to occur in any longer poem. It was formulated by Sievers in a classic study:[7] poems that have only uncontracted forms of the 2nd and 3rd person singular present indicative such as bindest, bindeð, are of Anglian origin, and poems that show some short forms such as binst, bint, are Saxon, or Kentish. In fact, the Anglian prose texts from the late ninth and the tenth century have uncontracted forms; the standard West Saxon of Alfred at the end of the ninth century normally has the short forms, which are regular in Ælfric a century later; the poems thought to be early have long forms with insignificant exceptions; and several poems from the South that are known to be later, e.g. Alfred's verse epilogue to the Pastoral Care, the verse Metres of Boethius, Menology, and Seasons of Fasting, have some short forms.

Yet there are wide gaps in the argument. Evidence is wanting that the short forms were characteristic of West Saxon in earlier times, say in the eighth century. Even in Alfred's day it is not clear that they were used all over the South—in Devon, for instance, or Surrey or Middlesex. Æthelwulf's charter of 847, which Sweet classes as Saxon,[8] has only long forms; so have the Surrey charter (871–89), and the Kentish charters of Oswulf (805–10) and Abba (833–39). These are perhaps the best witnesses for the South before Alfred's reign, and though the number of examples is small, their consensus carries weight. Many Southern prose texts also show a significant number of long forms.[9] Then again, the long forms may have been a feature of the old poetic diction, and the appearance of short forms in some late pieces may be part of the breakdown in the traditional verse technique of which there is other evidence. Sievers, who seems never to have regarded the test he proposed as decisive,[10] in his latest work is said to have preferred the view that the un-contracted forms belong properly to slow, dignified speech. This has been questioned.[11] But there is clear evidence that these forms were associated in the South with the language of verse. In the verse Metres of Boethius there are more long than short forms, and those who doubt Alfred's authorship[12] usually agree that this paraphrase comes from the South, and is based on a prose version containing only short forms. The evidence of Alfred's verse epilogue to the Pastoral Care in the contemporary manuscript Hatton 20 (H) is more precise. Here, as Sievers noted, the short form 469/7 werð is required by the metre: the prose text has contracted wierð, wirð, wyrð in some sixty-six places and only once 255/5 weorðeð (H and C).[13] But the epilogue contains two other examples, 469/4 and 469/6 tofloweð, both required by the metre. In the whole prose text H and C (where it is available) have only short forms, four of toflewð, three of the parallel grewð. So although Alfred admitted the short forms, normal in his prose, when they were metrically convenient, he associated the long forms with verse and did not use them to vary the rhythms of prose.

All the evidence is consistent with the view that the uncontracted endings were general Old English in early centuries, and were regarded as appropriate to verse, at least till the end of the tenth century, by writers for whom the short forms were normal in prose. It is possible that the short forms, which most philologists[14] explain as by-forms derived from the inverted bindis þu, bindið he, had become generalized by the late ninth century in the spoken language of the districts around Winchester; that the rapid development of prose under Alfred established them as the standard literary prose forms in the South; and that they were extended to verse by prose-writers like Alfred and other late composers of prosaic verse.[15] But it is unnecessary for the present purpose to establish this last hypothesis. The considerations that have been mentioned are enough to show that the consistent use of long forms in a poem presumed to be early, say before 850, is not good evidence of Anglian origin. No other test from inflexion or phonology is so widely applicable or so much respected.

On the usefulness of vocabulary for determining the dialectal origin of early verse there is some difference of opinion. Jordan, whose Eigentümlichkeiten des anglischen Wortschatzes is distinguished by its strict method, uses the poetry only when it supports the evidence from prose.[16] On the other hand, the late Professor Menner, who faced the difficulties with characteristic fair-minded-ness, concluded that vocabulary supplies "striking testimony to the provenience of a [poetical] text."[17] The chief difficulty lies in the artificial, often archaic vocabulary of Anglo-Saxon alliterative poems, whatever may be the period or dialect which produced them. The technique and style of the verse kept the poet hunting for synonyms or variant expressions, and encouraged the persistence of set phrases. Hence many poetic words are not found in prose at all, and many compounds are hardly conceivable except in poetic diction. If then some words of an early poem occur in the prose of one dialect only, it cannot safely be argued that the poem was composed in that dialect. For words that were once general Old English may survive into the comparatively late prose period in one local dialect after they have become obsolete in others. Or again, a local dialect may adopt for use in elevated prose words that belonged only to the poetic dialect in earlier centuries. Two examples will make the problem more concrete: —

Mēce 'sword' is notable for its phonology. From the cognates Gothic mēki, Old Norse mǣkir, Old Saxon māki, it should be standard West Saxon mǣce, but in Southern manuscripts of the later tenth and the eleventh centuries it is regularly spelt mēce, which is the form to be expected in Kent and a large part of the Anglian area. It appears mostly in poems in which there is a good deal of fighting, for instance Beowulf, Waldere, Exodus, but not in Genesis, the Riddles, or the signed poems of Cynewulf. It is not always required by the alliteration; it makes the second half of poetic compounds like beadumece; and it occurs in a fair variety of half-lines, with one stock phrase meces ecgum (cf. Heliand 2807, 4877), and one recurring pattern bradne (scirne, scearpne) mece. There is no indication that, like the adjective weird in modern English, it spread from one famous passage. Most West Saxon scribes of the later period seem to have known the word,[18] but only in the non-West-Saxon form; that is to say, as a borrowing from a dialect other than standard West Saxon. This has been treated as evidence that the poetic vocabulary, and consequently the earlier poetry, was Anglian.

But there are complications. Mece is used in several late poems connected with the South: in the Metres of Boethius, Brunanburh, Maldon, and last in Layamon's Brut. Again, the Anglian prose evidence for it is slight. It renders mucro once in the Corpus Glossary (ca. 800), a composite word-list which has

Mercian elements. It renders machaera in the influential Vespasian Psalter (lvi. 5), whence it passes unchanged into the West-Saxonized copies Junius 27 (Winchester ca. 925) and Cambridge University Ff. 1.23 (before 1050); and from the Junius tradition it was transferred by a corrector to another Winchester Psalter, Vitellius E XVIII, about the middle of the eleventh century. But mece also occurs several times in eleventh-century glosses to Aldhelm;[19] and once in the early-twelfth-century Eadwine Psalter xvi. 13 frameam = (sword) vel meche.[20] Even if it is coincidence that the Corpus Glossary, the Vespasian Psalter, the Eadwine Psalter were all Canterbury books, and that the Aldhelm glosses bear the marks of a Kentish ancestry,[21] we have here an illustration of the importance of Canterbury in the transmission of certain texts. There is one more vagary in the record of this word: mecefisc is used to render mugil(is) 'mullet' in Ælfric's Grammar and its appended list of the names of well-known fishes.[22] Yet this book may be taken to represent what was taught in Æthelwold's school at Winchester, the stronghold of West Saxon; and the mullet, which is more common in the South, is not likely to have a name borrowed from the North or Midlands.

In sum: Mece is an old word in Germanic poetry which survives very late in Southern England. All the prose examples belong to the artificial and often unpredictable language of glosses to hard words. West Saxons seem to have known it in the tenth and eleventh centuries, and even used it in the name of a fish; but they wrote it regularly in the exceptional, presumably borrowed form mece, which is Kentish as well as Anglian. The occurrence of mece is not evidence for the Anglian origin of particular poems; and it should be noted that evidence of this rare kind could never be used to establish West Saxon origin: if any word were borrowed into the general vocabulary of Old English poetry in a specifically West Saxon form, there would be no way of detecting it in the late manuscripts.

The second specimen word is leoran 'to go,' hence 'die,' with its compounds be-, forð-, ge-, ofer-, þurh-leoran, and derivatives like geleor(ed)nes. Jordan, who assembles prose examples,[23] calls it the most important distinguishing mark of the Anglian vocabulary. The occurrences of most distinctive words are generally too few to give a just idea of the boundaries within which they were current, and there is no reason to think that the natural use of many words stopped short at political boundaries. But the evidence for leoran is full. It is common in the Northumbrian Gospels (Lindisfarne, Rushworth), and Durham Ritual; in the Mercian Rushworth Matthew and the Vespasian Psalter; common, too, in the early prose texts that preserve Mercian features — Martyrology, Old English Bede, Gregory's Dialogues; and it survives in the Blickling and Vercelli Homilies. On the other hand, it is replaced by feran, wendan, &c., in some West Saxon copies of the Martyrology, Bede, and Dialogues, and in others it is confused with leornian 'to learn' often enough to show that some scribes of the tenth or early eleventh century did not understand it.[24] There is no example in Alfred. The apparent instances in Ælfric distinguish pieces that are not by him.[25] A few in the West Saxon Gospels (Matt. i) probably derive from a gloss. A better-attested Anglian and non-West-Saxon word could hardly be expected.

Yet this outstanding Anglian word, whose meanings 'go (away),' 'die,' made it usable whatever the subject-matter might be, is rare in verse. In poems that can be reckoned fairly early it occurs twice in Andreas: lungre leorde (leordan), once in Guthlac A 726 oferleordun; otherwise twice in a Prayer in the Exeter Book and once in the late Southern Menology 208 geleorde: this last is the only place where it is not held by alliteration.[26] The inference to be drawn is not that Beowulf, Genesis, the signed poems of Cynewulf, and the rest are non-Anglian, but that vocabulary is a tricky guide to the original dialect of verse.

The late Professor Menner suggested a method which seemed to him to meet objections. Referring to the review quoted at the beginning of this paper, he wrote:

> According to Sisam, Solomon and Saturn II, for instance, if of Early West Saxon composition, might possibly have preserved Common Old English words or meanings, used in early but lost Saxon poetry, which have died out in West Saxon, but not in Anglian prose. That is, gēna 'yet,' 241; (eormen)strynd '(mighty) race,' 322; þecele 'torch,' 410; gewesan 'converse,' 'debate,' 172 — recorded in Anglian but not in West Saxon prose — might have been part of a common poetic vocabulary cultivated in the South as well as in Anglia in early times. This contingency seems highly un-

likely in itself. But, if it were true, we should then
certainly expect that some words which became restricted to West Saxon prose (as opposed to Anglian)
would be found in the poem, just as we have in ad-
mittedly Anglian poems words which became restricted
to Anglian prose (as opposed to West Saxon). Such
words, with one doubtful exception, clūd 'rock' 185,
we do not find.[27]

Since he used "West Saxon" in the strict sense, excluding texts
that are not pure, "Anglian prose" should be similarly defined.
Then several words in Salomon and Saturn II that are (I believe)
lacking in Anglian prose are found in Alfred's West Saxon prose,
e.g. gielpen 'boastful,' leoftæl 'well-liked,' getigan 'to tie,'
weorðgeorn 'desiring honour'; indeed, Bosworth–Toller records gielpen only from the poem and from four places in Alfred's Pastoral Care. These words are not put forward as evidence that the poem is a West Saxon composition. They can be
disposed of by good arguments. But arguments as good can be
turned against the words used to show its Anglian origin. To
take one as a sample: — From the parallel passages (in Studies
in the History of Old English Literature, p. 31 ff.) and the Old
Saxon lines corresponding to the end of Genesis B, it appears
that the alliterating sounds are fairly stable; they are usually
preserved even though the wording is altered in transmission.
Of the four words mentioned by Professor Menner, only the
very rare gewesan (ymb) lit. 'be together,' is held by the alliteration; and the evidence is insufficient to show that it is
Anglian.[28] The other three are not structural in the verse,
and so might be substituted if a poem composed in standard
West Saxon were adapted to Anglian use, and if none of them
belonged to the traditional language of poetry.
    In the present state of the investigation, vocabulary remains
unsatisfactory or inconclusive as evidence of the original dialect
of poems presumed to be early; and too many favourable hypotheses
are used to produce the result that all the earlier poetry is Anglian.
No doubt some of it is, if only because more than half the country
and perhaps more than half of the population were under Anglian
rule for most of the early period. Still, it is safer to work with
no prepossession against West Saxon or Kentish origin. Where
there is enough decisive evidence, a prepossession is soon cor-

rected. But where, as in this case, much depends on the selection and interpretation of tangled or fragmentary evidence, a bias at the outset is likely to influence the result. The example of the series of investigations which gave Cynewulf most of the early poetry is comparatively recent.

It may be said that what I have called a prepossession is a reasonable presumption; that the background of history makes decisive for Anglian linguistic symptoms which are inconclusive when taken by themselves. A short survey of non-linguistic considerations may therefore be useful.

From the beginning of the study of Anglo-Saxon poetry, Northumbria has always been favoured. Her early eminence in Latin learning and the arts, the advantage of Bede's historical record, above all the story of Cædmon, gave Northumbria the first claim to the early poetry. On a simplified view, catastrophic Danish invasions made the ninth century a blank in literary production. As the attributions to Cædmon broke down under closer examination, the vagueness of these considerations became generally admitted. Critics still feel the fascination of Bede's Northumbria as a setting for poetry, but the pieces for which there is specific evidence are very few, though they are historically precious. Two short poems that were certainly composed in Northumbria are preserved by quotation in Latin texts: Cædmon's Hymn and the verses Bede made on his deathbed. The inscriptions on the Franks Casket are probably of Northumbrian origin.[29] The inscriptions on the Ruthwell Cross make it reasonable to claim the Dream of the Rood for Northumbria: not the whole text that appears centuries later in the Vercelli Book, but the best of it, which is the best of Anglo-Saxon religious poetry. Of these pieces, which have been preserved by exceptional chances, only the Dream of the Rood survives in the West Saxon collections; and it is to be expected that Northumbrian poetry would suffer most losses in transmission, owing to the misfortunes that came on the Northern kingdom and the consequent weakening of contact with the South in the ninth and tenth centuries.

When the Mercian dialect was recognized[30] and studied, the difficulty of distinguishing West-Saxonized copies of Northumbrian from similar copies of Mercian poems became evident. The term "Anglian" was conveniently used to cover both dialects, and though Northumbrian origins were favoured, Mercian was

often admitted as a second string. But the historical claims of
the Mercian kingdom are better than secondary. Even after
Sir Frank Stenton's <u>Anglo-Saxon England</u>, their importance for
literary history needs to be emphasized. Mercia was a formidable power in the critical period 650–850, coming into prominence under Penda and reaching its zenith under Offa, who seems
to have had all the attributes of a great ruler except a contemporary historian. When he died in 796 he had attained an authority
unequalled by any other English king before Athelstan. Outside
his Midland kingdom he had the overlordship of Kent and Wessex
and a powerful influence in Northumbria. He dealt firmly with
Charlemagne; the Pope treated him with deference; his new arch-
bishopric of Lichfield challenged Canterbury's leadership of the
English Church; Alcuin praised his encouragement of learning.[31]
The production of verse was favoured throughout the period of
Mercian predominance because prose was not yet a serious com-
petitor in vernacular literature.[32] For transmission Mercia had
the advantage over Northumbria of a central position, close
political relations with Kent and Wessex, and—what was particularly important for written transmission—an area in the South
and West Midlands which escaped the Danish attacks and linked
Alfred's revival of education to the earlier English tradition.

No extant verse is proved to be Mercian by external evidence. But we are dealing with presumptions, and the two long
poems on Guthlac, the hermit of Crowland in the Lincolnshire
fens, are presumptively Mercian, probably from East Mercia
like Felix's Latin <u>Life</u> (ca. 740) on which they depend. Such
compositions are signs of an active cult, and there is no evidence that Guthlac was popular outside Mercia before the late
ninth century.[33] These poems, especially <u>Guthlac B</u>, are remarkably like the signed poems of Cynewulf in language and
style. It may be inferred either that the Anglian dialect[34] of
Cynewulf was Mercian, which fits the available data very well;
or that in his time Northumbrian poetry and the poetry of Guthlac's
country, cut off by the Humber and the fens, were uniform: in
which case little is to be hoped for from stylistic and linguistic
studies.

Mercian claims extend to secular poetry. Interest in a
royal house can be as significant as interest in a local saint;
and the episode of Offa's Continental namesake and ancestor,
with a fragment of the Mercian royal genealogy, is loosely in-

serted in Beowulf in a way that is hard to account for unless it
was a compliment to his great Mercian namesake. Those who
believe that Beowulf is the work of one man, in the sense that
one man made all its verses, should see in this episode an indication that the poem was composed in Mercia in the late
eighth century. But it is a safer inference that Mercia had a
share in the transmission of Beowulf and the moulding of it into its extant form.[35] Signs of Mercian transmission at a fairly
late period have been noted in an earlier chapter.[36]

For the dialect of the Kentish kingdom there is very little
evidence — some early charters, the Glosses from the end of
the tenth century, a colouring in many texts that are predominantly West Saxon. Perhaps for that reason orthodox modern
criticism allows Kent no part in the making of extant Anglo-
Saxon verse: the so-called Kentish Hymn and Kentish Psalm
are preserved with the Kentish Glosses in the St. Augustine's
MS. Vespasian D VI, and may owe their dialectal colouring to
that chance. Yet, historically, Kent should not be barren ground.
In the seventh and eighth centuries the Kentish kingdom had a
considerable though diminishing importance, and it maintained
some coherence through the ninth century. Its population was
perhaps not greatly less than that of Northumbria. It was the
main gateway to the Continent from which Northumbria drew
so much inspiration. In so far as learning favoured the writing
of religious verse, Kent with the primacy of the English Church
was always favourably placed. In so far as an unbroken tradition
from the earliest centuries to the latest favoured the preservation of what was written, no Anglo-Saxon centre compared with
Canterbury.

Even if religious verse is discounted as a secondary growth,
Kent has a specific claim to consideration. Hengest was the ancestor of the Kentish kings, and in Bede's time Horsa's tomb
was shown in Kent, so that the story of Hengest and Horsa, mentioned in Bede, Nennius, the Anglo-Saxon Chronicle, and the very
late list of popular legends which Imelmann discovered,[37] has its
natural origin there. No verse fragment of it survives; but some
good authorities identify this royal ancestor with Hengest of the
Finn story. Whether they are historically the same hardly matters, because there is no reason to think that poets of later centuries could distinguish two legendary heroes of that name. In
the Finnsburh Fragment Hengest is in the background, but a
special interest in him is clear in the expression:

And <u>Hengest sylf</u>   hwearf him on laste.

Sympathy with his dilemma and gentleness towards his treaty-breaking are features of the Finn episode in <u>Beowulf</u>. There is a presumption that these stories, though not necessarily the extant forms of them, were told to his successors at the Kentish court, and were favoured (if secular stories found favour at all) in the many South-Eastern religious foundations that were associated with the families of the early kings of Kent.[38]

There remains the Saxon kingdom, with its stablest territories in the western and middle South. It too had influential rulers in early centuries: Ælle and Ceawlin are in Bede's list of overlords; Cædwalla and Ine were no petty kings. From the beginning of the ninth century the West Saxon kingdom was usually the strongest. It had learned men too—Aldhelm of Malmesbury, Bede's correspondent Daniel of Winchester, and Boniface, a Devon man, the greatest of Anglo-Saxon missionaries. After all, Aldhelm, not a Northumbrian, was the first Englishman to practise classical metres, and he is credibly reported to have been Alfred's favourite poet in the vernacular.[39] The correspondence of Boniface's circle, which is remarkable for the literary interests it reveals, preserves the earliest recorded couplet of secular verse.[40] Aldhelm, Boniface, and Tatwine, a Mercian from the Worcester district who became archbishop of Canterbury, are the three chief English writers of Latin verse riddles, so that it would be strange if all the English riddles are Anglian. Still, <u>Ruin</u> is the only surviving poem presumed to be early which has a specific claim to be West Saxon, if, as is most probable, it describes the ruins of Bath; and even here an Anglian poet visiting Somerset might be invoked.[41]

But there is a compelling reason why West Saxon claims to a share in the production of early verse should not be discounted as unlikely. For at least four generations their royal house showed a remarkable interest in English poetry, and gave it an honourable place in education. Alfred's mother Osburh, who came of Jutish, not of Anglian stock, offered a book of English poems to whichever of her sons could read it first. As a boy, before he could read, Alfred listened day and night to English poetry.[42] Later he delighted to read English poems and learn them by heart.[43] His children, the future King Edward and Ælfthryth, were taught the psalms, English books, and above all English poetry;[44] and no doubt the schooling of promising young men[43] was similar. Edward's son Athelstan followed in the same tradition. "Nemo literatius rempublicam administravit," says William of Malmesbury. English and Latin panegyrics survive to show his interest in verse.[45]

At a critical period, the example of the royal house was an important factor, perhaps the decisive factor, in securing that so much early verse was handed on to the late tenth century. Alfred's praise of Aldhelm as the best English poet is evidence that some old West Saxon verse was known at the West Saxon court. According to William of Malmesbury, Alfred also explained in his Handbook that a carmen triviale quod adhuc cantitatur (perhaps a riddle) was composed by Aldhelm in order to attract people to his serious teaching.[46] It is of course possible that by some chance all West Saxon poetry was lost in the following century of West Saxon predominance; but that would be one more doubtful hypothesis necessary to maintain the Anglian origin of the older verse.

This survey does not support a presumption that the extant earlier poetry is Northumbrian or Anglian. Rather it suggests that while verse was the medium of vernacular literature, it was produced in all the Anglo-Saxon kingdoms. As we go farther back in time, the grammarian's conception of poetry, classified according to the local dialects spoken by its makers, becomes less useful and creates many difficulties. More attention should be given to the probability that there was a body of verse, anonymous and independent of local interest, which was the common stock for the entertainment or instruction of the English peoples. A poem, wherever composed, might win its way into the common stock. The native metre, based primarily on the alliteration of stressed syllables, carried well because in this essential the usage of seventh-century Northumbria and tenth-century Wessex was the same; but any local dialect forms that affected the verse-structure were a handicap to circulation. A poet might prefer to take his models from the common stock rather than from the less-known work of his own district. In this way poems could be produced that do not belong to any local dialect, but to a general Old English poetic dialect, artificial, archaic, and perhaps mixed in its vocabulary, conservative in inflexions that affect the verse-structure, and indifferent to non-structural irregularities, which were perhaps tolerated as part of the colouring of the language of verse.

DIALECT ORIGINS OF THE EARLIER OLD ENGLISH VERSE

Once produced, the prospects of any one poem surviving are very much a matter of chance. On the whole, the opportunities of transmission were most favourable for the survival of Southern poems into the late collections, and least favourable to Northumbrian. Because the requisites for making books were always limited, and were mostly at the disposal of the Church, religious verse had the advantage in transmission over secular stories. Most of them would not be written down at all if sound churchmen like Alcuin and Ælfric had their way; and the chances are small that any of them would be made into fine books, which have the best prospect of survival to modern times.

NOTES

1 The Poetical Dialogues of Solomon and Saturn, ed. R. J. Menner (New York, 1941), reviewed in Medium Ævum, XIII (1944), 31 ff.

2 See Sisam, Studies in the History of Old English Literature (Oxford, 1953), p. 153.

3 For non-linguistic evidence that MS. Royal 2 A XX was a Worcester book, see I. Atkins and N. R. Ker, Catalogus Librorum MSS. Bibliothecae Wigorniensis (Oxford, 1944), pp. 18, 67.

4 The eighth century is favoured by most critics, and the ninth tends to be a blank. By "earlier poetry" I mean poetry generally thought to be of the period specified above.

5 First printed by H. Logeman, L'Inscription anglo-saxonne du Reliquaire de la Vraie Croix (Brussels, 1891).

6 Aldhelmi Opera (Mon. Germ. Hist.), ed. R. Ehwald (Berlin, 1919), p. 61.

7 BGDSL, X (1885), 464 ff.

8 The Oldest English Texts (Oxford, 1885), p. 433 f. The other three are at pp. 451, 443, 447. An instance of limpð occurs in Æthelberht's charter dated 858, p. 438/25.

9 J. Hedberg, The Syncope of the Old English Present Endings (Lund, 1945), aims at collecting all the examples from

printed texts, but does not undertake the critical study of
each text that is needed to show the significance of this
great body of materials.

10 In the article cited, p. 473 and note, he attributed Exodus
to Kent though it has only uncontracted forms: 282 (bis),
540 (restored), 543, 544, 555.

11 A number of long forms in Ine's Laws (MS. CCCC 173,
circa 925, from Winchester) may be archaisms. Alfred's
formal Ælfred kyning hateð gretan has often been noted,
and a good late example is Dunstan's letter of 980–8: þis
gewrit sendeþ se arcebisceop (A. S. Napier and W. H. Stevenson, The Crawford Collection of Early Charters [Oxford,
1895], p. 18).

12 On this question see Note D, Sisam, Studies in the History
of Old English Literature, p. 293 ff.

13 P. J. Cosijn, Altwestsächsische Grammatik (Den Haag,
1883–88), II, 149. Long forms usually have the unmutated
vowel, restored by analogy.

14 Since A. Walde, Die germanischen Auslautgesetze (Halle,
1900), p. 125 n.

15 The occurrence of short forms beside the long as a test of
Southern origin does not concern the earlier poetry, because
all poems containing a significant number of short forms
are known to be of Alfred's time or later. Generally there
are grounds other than linguistic for associating them with
the South, though R. Jordan, Eigentümlichkeiten des anglischen
Wortschatzes (Heidelberg, 1906), p. 67 n., inclines to Imelmann's view that the Menology is of Anglian origin. The
particular case is unconvincing, but it brings to mind a possibility that deserves attention. In the tenth and eleventh
centuries West Saxon had a position as the literary and
official language of England which no dialect had previously
attained (see Sisam, Studies, p. 94 f.). A good deal of work
has been done on borrowing in this period from Anglian into
West Saxon, which is to be expected. But borrowing by An-
glians from West Saxon, which was almost inevitable, has
not been much considered; and it is important, at least
theoretically, when the distribution of words in Middle En-

lish is used as evidence for Old English, or when the preference in Modern English for West Saxon words, rather than
the Anglian prose alternatives, has to be explained (see Jordan,
op. cit., p. 108 ff.). It should be considered before the presence of West Saxon words or forms in the structure of late
verse is treated as decisive against Anglian authorship.

16 See his Introduction, p. 3.

17 "The Vocabulary of the Old English Poems on Judgment Day,"
PMLA, LXII (1947), 588.

18 The Winchester scribe who copied Brunanburh into the
Parker Chronicle has mecum 24, but mæcan gemanan 40,
a bungling of the difficult phrase mec(e)a gemanan B, C;
D reads mecga in this phrase but mecum 24.

19 See A. S. Napier, Old English Glosses (Oxford, 1900). Mece
renders machaera, framea, romphea, once in the phrase
mid awendenlicum mece (Digby gloss 1151).

20 There is no means of telling whether this particular rendering is a recent addition to the complex gloss, which in parts
may go back to the ninth-century period of Mercian influence
at Canterbury. The spelling is late, and a thorough contemporary corrector allowed the word to stand here.

21 For the relations of the extant MSS. see Napier, op. cit.,
p. xxiv f.

22 Ed. J. Zupitza (Berlin, 1880), pp. 39/1, 308/5. One MS.
(Julius A II) has the spelling mæce, but though it was copied
rather before than after 1050 it has irregular spellings elsewhere, e.g. 155/10 mælce for the verb melce: so it is not
good evidence for the true West Saxon form. For the compound Bosworth–Toller compares garfish, which is not really
apt: the grey mullet could be likened to a sword; the garfish
has a gar on its snout.

23 Op. cit., p. 44 ff.

24 For Bede see T. Miller's edition (EETS, Oxford, 1890),
p. xlix f. In MS. Otho C 1 of the Dialogues, ed. Hecht
(Leipzig, 1900), the confusion appears, e.g. at 136/5, 138/29.

25 Lives of Saints, ed. W. W. Skeat, II (London, 1900), xxiii B. 752, 761, 804; xxxiii. 285. On xxiii see Jordan, p. 45 n.; on xxxiii see Sisam, Studies, p. 185, n. 1.

26 Geleorene rhyming with forweorone in Ruin 7 is taken to represent a related strong verb: Sievers, Grammar (transl. Cook [Boston, 1903]), §384, n. 3.

27 "The Vocabulary of the Old English Poems on Judgment Day," PMLA, LXII (1947), 585 f.

28 On gewesan see Jordan, p. 56. The details are worth examining as an example of the kindness shown to Anglian claims. The verb gewesan is recorded in English only at Salomon and Saturn 172, where the collocation with geflitan indicates the meaning 'to dispute' (not necessarily 'to quarrel'). This is the text whose provenance is to be determined: —
　　(a) In the Late Northumbrian gloss to the Durham Ritual an unexplained giwosa thrice glosses conversatio; but grammar, meaning, and the occurrence of simple wosa twice to render the same word, make the relation with gewesan 'to dispute' uncertain; the parallel with to-wesnis translating di-vortium is worth noting, and all these compounds of wesan may be translator's compounds.
　　(b) In Miller's edition of the OE Bede 274/5 gewesnis ond unsibb translates dissensio, and gewesnis is not otherwise recorded. The argument from this seems to be: "The OE Bede, though attributed to Alfred in early times, bears marks of Mercian origin; so gewesnis implies that gewesan 'to dispute' was used in Anglian, and it was not used in West Saxon." The unsupported tail of this argument is its effective part. But was gewesnis used by the translator? The relationship of the MSS. of the OE Bede needs more study in detail, but broadly: T (a good MS.) and B (sophisticated, but not derived from T) form one branch of the tradition against C, O (not derived from C), and Ca (essentially derived from O). At 274/5 gewesnis is the reading of T only: B, C (in Nowell's transcript B. M. Addit. 43703), O, and Ca have spellings of towesnis which in the sense dissensio 'quarrel' is a natural development from unrecorded to-wesan 'to be divided.' But dissensio is translated again at 300/3 where T, C, O, Ca read, effectively, towesnis ond unsibb: T has towestnis altered from towæstnis, and B, which often smooths out difficulties,

omits the word, so that it was probably disguised in the common source of T, B. From this evidence, the natural inference is that the translator rendered dissensio by towesnis ond unsibb in both places, and that gewesnis in T is a variation introduced at some place indeterminable: purely graphic confusion of to-: ge- is possible. In that case, so far from gewesan 'to dispute' being an Anglian peculiarity, evidence is needed that it was used in Anglian.

There are no late OE examples of towesnis, which seems to have gone out of use early in the tenth century; but its distribution does not suggest that it was limited to any one dialect. Besides the examples from the OE Bede, Bosworth–Toller records four in the sense 'quarrel' from Alfred's Pastoral Care, the standard of Early West Saxon. Among glosses to Bede, thought to be Kentish, it renders divortium (Sweet O.E.T., 181/41); and among glosses from the West Country (?) MS. Harley 3376 which have a dialectal element, it renders dissolutio (Wright-Wülker, Vocabularies, i. 224/11). All these uses develop naturally from *to-wesan.

29 See Napier in An English Miscellany presented to Dr. Furnivall (Oxford, 1901), pp. 379 ff., who shows that the forms are Anglian and regards the loss of inflexional -n in sefu(n) as decisive for Northumbrian. This test is properly used where we have the original. As a curiosity, I note Sweet's remark on the Hatton MS. of the Pastoral Care in the Introduction to his edition, p. xxxii: "Dropping of final—generally inflectional—n is very frequent in H. The n is frequently added above the line, but often the correction is neglected, especially towards the end of the MS. It is the n of the infinitive, weak adj. inflection and subjunctive that most frequently suffers this apocope." Yet the author was Alfred, the MS. was sent out from Winchester, and the handwriting tells against Northumbrian tendencies in the scribe.

30 In 1875 J. A. H. Murray suggested that the gloss to the Rushworth Gospel of Matthew was Mercian. By 1889, when Zupitza published the Royal Glosses, the characteristics of the dialect were established.

31 M. G. H., Epist. Karol. Aevi, II, 107.

32 A rich Mercian religious prose before Alfred is sometimes
assumed without good evidence; cf. Menner, art. cit., p. 585.
The poverty of the Mercian "Register" which is incorporated
into some texts of the Chronicle is notable. From Alfred's
Prose Preface to his Pastoral Care, it appears that he knew
no English versions of the classics of Church literature
earlier than those he made or promoted. No doubt prose
was used for sermons and other necessary purposes; but
the extant Mercian glossaries, and interlinear versions of
psalters and Matthew's Gospel, are rather tools for education than prose literature.

33 Guthlac, who died in 714, is not mentioned in Bede; in the
York Poetical Calendar ca. 800; in the Northern calendar
of the late ninth century in MS. Digby 63; or in the metrical
calendar of Athelstan's Psalter composed at Winchester
ca. 900. The language of the Anglo-Saxon prose version of
Felix's Life shows signs of Mercian origin (Jordan, p. 11).
In a classic article, Anglia, X (1888), 131 ff., Napier
proved that the prose life of the Lichfield saint Chad is also
Mercian.

34 For the rhyming passage in Elene as evidence of Anglian
dialect, see Sisam, Studies, p. 2.

35 Cf. Miss Whitelock's discussion, The Audience of Beowulf
(Oxford, 1951), pp. 57 ff. Similar considerations apply to
the less striking but still excrescent account of the Continental Offa in Widsith, 37 ff. Sir Cyril Fox, "The Boundary
Line of Cymru," PBA, XXVI (1940), 21, has suggested
that when Offa built Offa's Dyke against the Welsh he had
in mind his namesake's fame as a marker of lasting boundaries. This is not fanciful. Beowulf contains plenty of
evidence that heroic poetry was much occupied with examples
to follow or avoid. The confused Vitae Duorum Offarum,
written in the twelfth century at St. Albans in old Mercian
territory, is evidence that parallels were drawn between
the two Offas.

36 See Sisam, Studies, p. 94 ff.

37 In MS. Vespasian D IV, f. 139b; see Deutsche Literaturzeitung,
XXX (1909), 999.

38 See the first part of the text edited by Liebermann as Die Heiligen Englands (Hannover, 1889), which is a unique record of the early ramifications of the royal family.

39 By William of Malmesbury, Gesta Pontificum, ed. Hamilton, p. 336: "nativae quoque linguae non negligebat carmina; adeo ut, teste libro Elfredi, de quo superius dixi, nulla umquam aetate par ei fuerit quisquam." The book referred to is Alfred's lost Handbook.

40 The Saxonicum verbum beginning Oft daedlata, ed. with bibliography in Dobbie, The Anglo-Saxon Minor Poems (New York, 1942), p. 57. The name of the monk who quoted it is still a puzzle: see W. Levison, England and the Continent in the Eighth Century (Oxford, 1946), p. 130 n.

41 Miss C. A. Hotchner's Wessex and Old English Poetry, with special consideration of The Ruin (New York, 1939), deserves mention. Miss Hotchner, a champion of Wessex, assembles many interesting facts and opinions bearing on dialect in the early poetry, but the arguments are uneven in quality.

42 Asser, ch. 22–23.

43 Op. cit., ch. 76.

44 Op. cit., ch. 75.

45 On the verses beginning Carta dirige gressus see W. H. Stevenson, EHR, XXVI (1911), p. 482 ff. When Dunstan's detractors tried to deprive him of Athelstan's favour by reporting him avitae gentilitatis vanissima didicisse carmina (Memorials of St. Dunstan, p. 11), they meant heathen charms and incantations, not ancient poetry.

46 Historia Pontificum, ed. Hamilton, p. 336. From the same source William learnt how Aldhelm was related to the royal family; op. cit., p. 333.

II. CONCEPTUAL ANALYSIS

OLD ENGLISH BEOT AND OLD ICELANDIC HEITSTRENGING

Stefán Einarsson

I

In his "Introduction" to Beowulf (p. lvii) Klaeber makes the following remark:

> That some of the speeches follow conventional lines
> of heroic tradition need not be doubted. This applies
> to the type of the gylpcwide before the combat (675 ff.,
> 1392 ff., 2510 ff.), the "comitatus" speech or exhorta-
> tion of the retainers (2633 ff., cp. Bjarkamál [Par. § 7:
> Saxo ii.59 ff.], Maldon 212 ff., 246 ff., Finnsburg 37 ff.).

Let us begin by looking at two of these passages. Beowulf 675 ff. contains Beowulf's speech before his fight with Grendel:

> Gespræc þa se goda gylpworda sum,
> Beowulf Geata, ær he on bed stige.

Then follows the speech defined as gylpword. The hero does not consider himself less strong than the formidable Grendel; there-fore he is not going to use his sword against him, but as Grendel fights without weapons, he is going to do likewise; God may de-cide the issue. At 2510 we read:

> Beowulf maðelode, beotwordum spræc
> niehstan siðe.

And here follows Beowulf's last speech before his fight with the dragon. First he lets his mind wander back to the victorious

Reprinted by permission of the Modern Language Association and the author from PMLA, Vol. XLIX (1934), pp. 975–93.

fights of his youth: once more he is going to gain glory by fighting.
He would not bear a sword now any more than he did when he
fought Grendel if he knew how to attack the dragon without it.
As it is, he is going to meet him with sword, shield, and coat
of mail. But not a foot is he going to retreat, and nobody's help
will he have; alone he intends to fight it out and win the gold, or
else lose his life in the battle. In both instances we have to do
with a solemn promise to carry out a feat—a fight—under very
difficult circumstances, partly self-imposed to add glory. In
the first encounter he is going to fight without a sword; in the
second, without help.

The words gylpword and beotword thus seem to mean the
same thing, but it is probable that gielp- stresses the glory of
the adventure, something to boast of, whereas beot- stresses
the fact that it is a promise, a vow. Both words with their derivatives recur again and again, at least in the heroic poetry,
in similar situations. Going through Beowulf we find beot for
the first time in v. 80:

> He beot ne aleh, beagas dælde,
> sinc æt symle . . . .

"He (Hroðgar) did not belie his promise, but distributed rings,
treasures at the banquet." We are not told exactly that he promised or vowed to build the hall Heorot in order that he might
therein shower his gifts upon his faithful retainers, but we are
told (67 ff.) that he got the idea to do so.

When king Hroðgar is telling Beowulf about the ravages of
Grendel he tells him among other things (480 ff.):

> Ful oft gebeotedon beore druncne
> ofer ealowæge oretmecgas,
> þæt hie in beorsele bidan woldon
> Grendles guþe mid gryrum ecga.

The men fulfilled their vows, but were defeated. This passage
introduces us to more than a few passing incidents; it shows us
what the custom was among the retainers in the mead-hall.[1]
When their spirits were running high over the beer-cups, they
could make a vow to carry out some difficult but glorious deed,
usually at the risk of their lives. Needless to say, such vows

were not always carefully thought out beforehand, hence the warning we read in the <u>Wanderer</u> (70 ff.):

> Beorn sceal gebidan, þonne he beot spriceð,
> oð þæt collenferð cunne gearwe
> hwider hreðra gehygd hweorfan wille,

"When an impetuous warrior is making a vow, he ought to pause
until he knows full well the issue whither the impulse of his heart
will lead" (Kershaw's translation).

In <u>Beowulf</u> 628 ff. we have another great example of the making of solemn vows over the beer-cup. Wealhþeow, Hroðgar's
queen, carries the cup around and comes at last to Beowulf:

> He þæt ful geþeah,
> wælreow wiga æt Wealhþeon,
> ond þa gyddode guþe gefysed;
> Beowulf maþelode, bearn Ecgþeowes:
> "Ic þæt hogode, þa ic on holm gestah,
> sæbat gesæt mid minra secga gedriht,
> þæt ic anunga eowra leoda
> willan geworhte, oððe on wæl crunge
> feondgrapum fæst. Ic gefremman sceal
> eorlic ellen, oððe endedæg
> on þisse meoduhealle minne gebidan!"
> Ðam wife ða word wel licodon,
> gilpcwide Geates . . . .

Beowulf's speech is thus a <u>gilpcwide</u>, a solemn vow just like
<u>gylpword</u> and <u>beotword</u>. Probably <u>þryðword</u>, in the following
lines, means something similar. Beowulf reiterates his vow
in line 675 (see the beginning of the present paper), and when
he actually has carried out his promise, he is said to have fulfilled his <u>gilp</u> (828):

> Hæfde East-Denum
> Geatmecga leod gilp gelæsted.

There are still some more instances of vows made in the
mead-hall, presumably over the cup of beer. In the famous
speech of Wiglaf exhorting his fellow-retainers to stand by

Beowulf in his fight against the dragon, he reminds them of their
vows in the banquet-hall (2633 ff.):

> Ic þæt mæl geman, þær we medu þegun,
> þonne we geheton ussum hlaforde
> in biorsele, þe us þas beagas geaf,
> þæt we him ða guðgeatwa gyldan woldon,
> gif him þyslicu þearf gelumpe,
> helmas ond heard sweord . . . .
> . . . Nu is se dæg cumen . . . .

We find the same situation in the Battle of Maldon, especially
in Ælfwine's speech (211 ff.):

> Ælfwine þa cwæð, he on ellen spræc:
> "Gemunað þa mæla, þe we oft æt meodo spræcon,
> þonne we on bence beot ahofon,
> hæleð on healle, ymbe heard gewinn:
> nu mæg cunnian hwa cene sy."

And it is more than possible that the vows of Eadric and Offa
(Maldon 15, 288 ff.) were made in the mead-hall also; at any rate
one can see that they have been made before:

> (Eadric) . . . beot he gelæste ("he fulfilled his promise"),
> ða he ætforan his frean feohtan sceolde.
> . . . .
> [h]raðe wearð æt hilde Offa forheawen;
> he hæfde þeah geforþod ðæt he his frean gehet,
> swa he beotode ær wið his beahgifan,
> ðæt hi sceoldon begen on burh ridan,
> hale to hame, oððe on here cringan,
> on wælstowe wundum sweltan;
> he læg þegenlice þeodne gehende.

We have seen from the Wanderer's comment that the ale must
have been instrumental in many a vow. But the last examples
show that it was considered shameful not to stand by one's guns.
E. Budde in Die Bedeutung der Trinksitten in der Kultur der
Angelsachsen (diss. Jena, 1906), pp. 49–50, stresses this fact
and adds an example from William of Malmesbury. We shall

see later that the Englishmen were not at all exceptional in re-
specting the word spoken at drink. In fact it is even likely that
the drink was considered to add weight and authority to the spoken
word. It is important to notice that not only on such an important
occasion as the buying of a bride, but also in the case of minor
commercial transactions, the bargain had to be fortified with a
cup of ale or wine (cf. Budde, p. 9).[2]

We have now seen a good many instances of a vow in the
banquet-hall over the beer-cup. But, naturally, that was not the
only occasion when a vow could and would be made. Thus Beowulf
(2510) makes his vow immediately before he attacks the dragon.
Likewise the speeches of exhortation, e.g., in the Battle of Maldon
usually contain a vow:

Ne sceolon me on þære þeode þegenas ætwitan,
þæt ic of ðisse fyrde feran wille,
eard gesecan, nu min ealdor ligeð
forheawen æt hilde, . . . (Ælfwine's words) (220 ff.)

Leofsunu gemælde, and his linde ahof,
bord to gebeorge, he þam beorne oncwæð:
"Ic þæt gehate, þæt ic heonon nelle
fleon fotes trym, ac wille furðor gan,
wrecan on gewinne minne winedryhten.
Ne þurfon me embe Sturmere stedefæste hæleð
wordum ætwitan, nu min wine gecranc,
þæt ic hlafordleas ham siðie,
wende fram wige; ac me sceal wæpen niman,
ord and iren."— (244 ff.)

Ða gyt on orde stod Eadweard se langa,
gearo and geornful; gylpwordum spræc,
þæt he nolde fleogan fotmæl landes,
ofer bæc bugan, þa his betera læg. (273 ff.)

In all these instances the adventure has meant life or death.
But the adventure might be dangerous enough without ending in
these two extremes, the alternatives being victory or defeat. Such
was the stake in the case of the fallen angels, Genesis 69 ff. Such
are also the alternatives in the more friendly contest related in
the Breca-episode, Beowulf 499 ff. So Unferð greets Beowulf by

twitting him for his dolgilp, the foolish boast, and his defeat
at the hands of Breca the son of Beanstan:

> Beot eal wið þe
> sunu Beanstanes soðe gelæste.

What sort of beot it was, Beowulf explains in his answer (535 ff.):

> Wit þæt gecwædon cnihtwesende
> ond gebeotedon — wæron begen þa git
> on geogoðfeore — þæt wit on garsecg ut
> aldrum neðdon, ond þæt geæfndon swa.

Then he describes the swimming contest in detail showing that
he won the victory and winding up by a malicious hint to Unferð,
saying that Grendel would not be ravaging the hall now if he
(Unferð) had been so doughty a warrior as he was a speaker.

We come across a similar beot in Orosius, Book II, ch. 4
(Sweet's ed., EETS 79 [London, 1883], p. 72). When Cyrus king
of the Persians had led his forces to Babylon, he was at first
prevented from taking the city by the great river Gandes:

> þa gebeotode an his ðegna þæt he mid sunde þa
> ea oferfaran wolde mid twam tyncenum; ac hiene se
> stream fordraf. Ða gebeotode Cirus ðæt he his ðegn
> on hire swa gewrecan wolde, þa he swa grom wearð
> on his mode ond wið þa ea gebolgen, þæt hie mehte
> wifmonn be hire cneowe oferwadan, þær heo ær wæs
> nigon mila brad þonne heo fledu wæs. He þæt mid
> dædum gelæste.

There is no direct correspondence to be found in the Latin
original to gebeotede in these two places. But the self-reliance
of the thane who vows to swim the river is perhaps indicated
by the fiducia of the original, and the vow of the king lies in
the words: Rex . . . statuit, contestans . . . . In both instances
we have to do with a boasting promise or vow which will add
to the glory of the man who fulfills it.

One more example is found in Orosius, Book II, ch. 11
(Sweet, p. 144):

Æfter þæm Antigones and Perðica gebeotedan þæt
hie woldon him betweonum gefeohtan, and longe ymb
þæt siredon hwær hie hie gemetan wolden, and monig
igland awestan on þæm geflite hwæðer hiera mehte
maran fultum to geteon.

Here there is nothing in the Latin original to correspond, but
the meaning "promised boastingly, vowed" seems obvious enough
and may be compared with the instances in Beowulf.

Attention must, however, be called to the fact that the word
beot, etc., is used in many other circumstances than the ones
just discussed, which I think exemplify a peculiar custom. Thus
we cannot here consider the vows of the lovers (The Wife's Complaint 21 f., The Husband's Message 14, 47) or the vows of the
Roman Vestal maidens (Orosius, Book III, ch. 6.). For these and
other instances of different meaning see the dictionaries. They
give three chief meanings: (1) a threatening, menace; (2) danger;
and (3) boasting promise. It seems that the third one is the most
usual, and logically the meanings would seem to have developed
in the order: promise — boasting — threatening — danger. This
is supported by etymology, if the word comes from bihat (so NED,
Sievers, Altenglische Grammatik, ed. Brunner [Halle, 1951], §43,
and H. Paul, BGDSL, VII [1871], 122).

II

We noted in the beginning that Klaeber compares Wiglaf's
speech to Bjarkamál, Saxo II, 59 ff. According to Bugge ("Studien
über das Beowulf-epos," BGDSL, XII (1876), 45 ff.), Kemble
(Beowulf, appendix to v. 5262) had already noted the similarities
between the words of Wiglaf and Hialto in Saxo's work, but Bugge
goes on to compare also the Icelandic Hrólfs saga kraka, which
he thinks contains traditional elements from the same lost poem,
Bjarkamál, which Saxo gives in a Latin version.

Corresponding to Wiglaf's speech, quoted above, we find in
Saxo among other things:

Omnia quae poti temulento prompsimus ore,
fortibus edamus animis, et vota sequamur
per summum jurata Jovem, superosque potentes.

(Saxo, ed. Holder, p. 60.)

105

(Whatever we promised with drunken mouths over the
drink, we shall fulfil with stout hearts, and we shall
carry out the vows which we swore by the highest
Jupiter and the mighty ones.)

To this A. Olrik (Danmarks Heltedigtning, I (Copenhagen, 1903),
48) compares the Danish proverb: "Hvad drukken mand gör,
skal ædru mand forsvare." In Hrólfs saga the corresponding
lines are:

efnum nú vel heitstrengingar várar, at vér verjum
vel enn frægasta konung, sem nú er á ǫllum
Norðurlǫndum, ok látum þat á hvert land spyrjast
mega, ok launum hánum nú vápn ok herklæði ok
margt eptirlæti annat [Hrólfs s., ch. 48, Fornaldarsögur, Reykjavik ed., I, 76], (i.e. let us now carry
out our vows that we defend well the most renowned
king now in the whole realm of the North, and let
the fame of this fly to every country, and thus let
us reward him for weapons and armour and many
other goodly things).[3]

What concern us here are simply the parallels: geheton
ussum hlaforde/in beorsele, omnia vota.... sequamur, and
efnum nú vel heitstrengingar várar. For heitstrenging is a
rather common custom and is well defined in Old Icelandic
literature. Although others have noticed the similarity long
before me—especially in the example above, the Old English
and the Old Norse material never have been treated in detail
together, and I have not found evidence that Anglicists know
of the chief study on the subject.[4]

An article by Kr. Nyrop, "En middelalderlig skik" in Nordisk
tidskrift för vetenskap, konst och industri, NF. II (1889), 312–
32, discusses the Scandinavian custom in detail, as known from
Icelandic literature, and calls attention to some of the parallels
in Beowulf. Thus according to him ll. 633 ff. (quoted above) may
be interpreted as a heitstrenging, and he notes that "such vows
are called in Anglo-Saxon: gilp, gilpcwide, gilpspræc, gilpword,
dolgilp; one finds also beot in the same sense." That it was a
common custom he judges from the word gilphlæden, originally
"laden with vows," hence—as such a man must have fought many

a fight—"highly esteemed, glorious," etc. Apart from Scandinavia Nyrop chiefly studies the custom in France with hasty glances at other localities and literatures, such as those of Medieval England, Germany, and Russia.[5]

The term <u>strengja heit</u> occurs for the first time in a verse (if genuine) by Þormóðr Bessason Kolbrúnarskáld, a well-known poet who fell with his lord king Ólafr of Norway (later called Saint) in the battle at Stiklastaðr in 1030. Þormóðr is said to have awakened the army on the morning before the battle by reciting the old <u>Bjarkamál</u> at the request of the king. But the verse in question would be of a little earlier date—some five years perhaps — Þormóðr had succeeded in slaying Þorgrímr trǫlli, the killer of his foster-brother. As the deed takes place in a crowd, he is not found out; but he listens to the vows of Þorgrímr's stepson and describes them in the verse:

> Strengði þess á þingi   Nær stóð ek randa rýri
> þarflyndr, ef mik fyndi,   — rekkr lézk ei mik þekkja—
> hǫldr at hǫggva skyldi   gott er þat at huldar hetti
> heit lofgerðar veiti   hefir haldit smiðr stefja.

(<u>Flateyjarbók</u>, ed. Unger, II, 212, F. Jónsson, <u>Skjaldedigtning</u>, I, A, 283.)

> (The doughty yeoman vowed at the meeting that if he
> found me he would hew the poet [i.e. me] down. I
> stood near by the warrior—he acted as if he knew
> me not—good it was that the verse-smith [i.e. I]
> kept his mask.)

It is unfortunate that this verse is preserved in only one of the two representative texts of our saga, and that one the worse of the two: <u>Flateyjarbók</u> (the famous manuscript dating from 1370–80. The text of <u>Fóstbrœðrasaga</u> is not supposed to be older than the fourteenth century by Finnur Jónsson, <u>Den Oldnorske og Oldislendske Litteraturs Historie</u> [Copenhagen, 1923], II, 458 ff.). Yet the authenticity of the verse has not been doubted by critics, as far as I know (cf. Jónsson, loc. cit., and Gaertner, <u>BGDSL</u>, XXXII [1896], 417), until now that it is attacked by Jónsson in the article "Þormóðr Kolbrúnarskáld," <u>APS</u>, VII (1933), 60. In enumerating the different things which, in his opinion, make the verse doubtful, Jónsson does not mention the term strengja heit although it does not appear again in any Scaldic verse or any Old Norse text whatever until about a hundred and seventy years later. It should not be overlooked, however, that Þormóðr knew Bjarkamál, which must have contained some sort of heitstrengingar even if that term was not used to express it.

Next we find the term in Bishop Bjarni Kolbeinsson's Jómsvíkingadrápa, dating from ca. 1200. It is not definitely known when the poem was composed, but Bjarni became bishop of the Orkneys shortly before 1190 and died in 1222.

> 11: En vildu þá einkum ok haukligar hefja
>   ǫldurmenn at skyldu heitstrengingar tóku;
>   — slíkt eru yrkisefni — eigi segik at ýta
>   ágæta sér leita, ǫlteiti var lítil.
>
> 12: Heitstrenging frá ek hefja Búi var ǫrr at efla
>   heiptmildan Sigvalda; órœkinn, þrek slíkan.
>
> 14: þá réð heit til hvítrar hri(n)ga meiðr at strengja.
>
>   (F. Jónsson, Skjaldedigtning, II, A, 3–4.)

> (But the chiefs then especially wished that men should engage in something bringing glory — that is stuff for the poet! — and they began to make proud vows; I submit that there was no small mirth among the men over the ale.
> I heard that the bellicose Sigvaldi made a vow; Búi was quick, reckless as he was, to indulge in such a show of strength.
> Then the man [i.e. Vagn] vowed to obtain the fair [woman].)

It is interesting to notice that, in commenting upon verse 12, E. A. Kock (Notationes Norrœnæ [Lund, 1923], I, 177) seizes upon the Old English parallel: "beot ahofon ymbe heard gewinn" (Maldon 213). The heitstrengingar referred to are the famous ones described in detail in Jómsvíkinga saga, Fagrskinna, and Heimskringla. These words are practically contemporary with Bjarni Kolbeinsson, all of them dating from the first quarter of the 13th century. Jómsvíkinga saga is perhaps the oldest in its original

108

form (see F. Jónsson, Litt. Hist., II, 653), and Fagrskinna is
slightly older than Heimskringla.

I shall here first give Heimskringla's account[6] in the Morris-
Magnússon's translation and then compare it with Fagrskinna and
the one and a half century later account of Flateyjarbók.

> King Svein held a famous feast, and bade to him all
> lords of his realm, for he would hold his grave-ale (erfi)
> after king Harald his father; and a little before had died
> Strut-Harald in Skaney; and Veseti of Borgundholm, the
> father of Bui and Sigured. So King Svein sent word to the
> Jomsburgers, bidding Earl Sigvaldi and Bui, and the
> brethren of each, come hold the grave-ale of their fathers
> (erfa feðr sína) at this same feast which the king was
> arraying. So to the feast fared the Jomsburgers with
> all the valiantest of their folk; eleven ships from Joms-
> burg had they and twenty from Skaney. So thither was
> come together a full great company. The first day of
> the feast, before king Svein stepped into the high seat of
> his father, he drank the cup of memory to him (minni
> hans), swearing therewith (ok strengði heit) that before
> three winters were outworn he would bring an host to
> England, and slay king Æthelred, or drive him from his
> realm. And that cup of memory must all drink who were
> at the feast.
>
> Thereupon was poured forth to those lords of Joms-
> burg; and ever was borne to them brimming, and of the
> strongest. But when this cup was drunk off, then must
> all men drink a cup to Christ. And then were borne to
> the Jomsburgers the biggest horns of the mightiest
> drink that was there. The third cup was Michael's mem-
> ory, and that also must all drink. But thereafter drank
> Earl Sigvaldi the memory of his father, swearing oath
> therewith that before three winters were worn away he
> would come into Norway and slay Earl Hakon or else
> drive him from the land.
>
> Then swore Thorkel the High, the brother of Sigvaldi,
> that he would follow his brother to Norway, nor ever flee
> from battle leaving Sigvaldi fighting (cf. Battle of Maldon
> and Wiglaf's speech).

Then swore Bui the Thick that he would fare to Norway with them, and in no battle flee before Earl Hakon.

Then swore Sigurd his brother that he would fare to Norway, and not flee while the more part of the Jomsburgers fought.

Then swore Vagn Akison that he would fare with them to Norway, and not come back till he had slain Thorkel Leira, and lain a-bed by his daughter Ingibiorg without the leave of her kin.

Many other lords also swore oath on sundry matters. So that day men drunk the heirship-feast.

But the morrow's morn, when men were no more drunken, the Jomsburgers thought they had spoken big words enough; so they met together and took counsel how they should bring this journey about, and the end of it was that they determined to set about it as speedily as may be. So they arrayed their ships and their company; and wide about the land went the fame of this.

Fagrskinna (F. Jónsson's ed., pp. 83–87) describes the ceremony:

On the first eve of the grave-ale (er menn komu til erfis) many cups (full) should be poured forth, in such a way as now are the cups of memory (minni), and those cups they devoted (eignuðu) to their most powerful kinsmen, or to Thor or to other Gods of theirs while they were yet heathen (þá er heiðni var). But last of all should be poured forth the Bragi-cup (braga full) and then should he, who celebrated the grave-ale, make a vow over the Bragi-cup (strengja heit at bragafulli), and similarly all the partakers of the grave-ale, and after that he was to step into the high seat of the dead one (þess er erfðr var).

It looks as if Snorri is so sparing in his comment at this place because in Ynglinga saga ch. 40 (see Morris-Magnússon's transl., I, 57 ff.) he has almost the very same description that we find here in Fagrskinna.

In Flateyjarbók I, 179–181 we find the corresponding story, but here the old formula is omitted or forgotten:

The king (Sveinn) answers: I know that men have used
to do this at good feasts where there is a great body
of select men assembled, that they have made vows for
the fun and glory of it (menn hafa strengt heit sér til
skemtanar ok til ágætis), and I am for it that we try
this game.

Obviously the old heitstrenging has here lost some of its old
severity.

Before we leave the Sagas of the Kings of Norway we must
mention the oath of Harald Hairfair never to cut his hair (or
comb it) until he has won the whole of Norway with scat and dues
thereof (or else he will die). He was led to make this vow after
he had been rejected by a fair maiden who said that she would
not waste her maidenhood for the sake of a man without a realm
(cf. Heimskringla, Morris-Magnússon, I, 93–95). To swear by
one's hair is known from other sources, and on the importance
of the hair see Grǫnbech, Vor Folkeæt III, 157–58, 190.

Next in time after the Noregs konunga sǫgur discussed above
and belonging to the first quarter of the thirteenth century comes
the prose of the Elder Edda, which according to Bugge (Norrœn
Fornkvæði, p. lxvii), is hardly later than 1240 but may be much
earlier in parts. Here we find our term in the prose of Sigrdrífumál (Edda Saemundar, ed. S. Bugge [Christiania, 1867], p. 229):
Odin, wishing to punish the valkyrja, condemns her among other
things to be married; "but I told him that against this I vowed to
marry no man who knew fear" (en ek sagðak hánum, at ek
strengðak heit þar í mót, at giptaz ǫngum þeim manni er hræðaz
kynni). A later version of this may be read in Vǫlsungasaga ch.
20 (M. Schlauch's translation [London, 1930], p. 104). But nothing
corresponding is in the verses of Sigrdrífumál.

In Helga kviða Hjǫrvarðssonar we find our term again—in
the prose only, it is true—but here the verses have at least
something corresponding, and these verses are considered by
some critics to date from the latter half of the tenth century
(B. Sijmons, F. Jónsson), while others (e.g., Boer, Edda, II, 155)
put them as late as 1100. The prose has also generally been
regarded as older than the collection of the poems itself; it might
thus belong to the twelfth century. We shall see that it resembles
the instances we had from Heimskringla and Fagrskinna above
in that it describes an old custom apparently discontinued. But
here we find additional features.[7]

Helgi was a mighty warrior. He fared to King Eylimi
and asked for the hand of his daughter. Helgi and
Sváva sware oaths to each other and their love was
great. Sváva stayed at home with her father, but Helgi
was in the wars, yet was Sváva a valkyrie as before.
Hethin was at home with his father, King Hiorvarth,
in Norway. One time Hethin was coming home alone
from the forest on Yule eve. He met a trollwoman
riding on a wolf, with snakes as reins. She asked him
leave to keep him company, but he would not. She said:
"That shalt thou rue when drinking from the hallowed
cup" (þess skaltu gjalda at bragarfulli). In the evening vows were made (váru heitstrengingar): the sacrificial boar was led in (var fram leiddr sonargǫltr),
men laid their hands on him and sware dear oaths as
they drank from the hallowed cup (ok strengðu menn
þá heit at bragarfulli). Hethin made a vow that he
would have Sváva (strengði heit til Svávu), Eylimi's
daughter, the maiden beloved by Helgi, his brother;
but he forthwith rued it so greatly that he hastened
South on wild ways till he found his brother Helgi.

Helgi asks news from him. Hethin said (v. 32):

Mik hefir miklu glœpr	A wretched wrong
meiri sóttan,	I wrought on thee,
ek hefi kǫrna	(far greater, brother,
ena konungbornu	than good I can make):
brúði þína	on holy beaker
at bragarfulli	in banquet hall
	thy bride I chose me,
	the child of kings.

And this transaction is referred to as ǫlmál "things spoken over
the ale" in verse 33:

Sakask eigi þú!	Taunt thee no more
sǫnn munu verða	for true will come
ǫlmál, Heðinn,	thy vow on beaker
okkur beggja	for both of us.

OLD ENGLISH BEOT AND OLD ICELANDIC HEITSTRENGING

Thus if we may depend upon the literary critics, the custom of an oath over the Bragi cup[8] may be on record from the second half of the tenth century or at any rate not later than ca. 1100. And we find it combined in the prose with another very old looking custom of swearing over a sacrificial boar, the sonargǫltr (an extremely old-fashioned animal) which has its parallels— besides some other instances in the Edda and Hervarar saga ok Heiðreks—in the sonorpair of some Longobardian laws (see Sievers, BGDSL, XII [1876], 177 note, and XVI [1871], 540 ff.).

It is interesting to note that we find in Hervarar saga ok Heiðreks—a fornaldarsaga of the thirteenth century—two parallels to the case in Helga kviða Hjǫrvarðssonar, the first is heitstrenging at bragafulli and the second is a heitstrenging over the sonargǫltr. In Hervarar saga, ch. 3 (Fornaldarsögur Norðurlanda, Vladimir Ásmundarson, compiler [Reykjavík, 1885–89], I, 311–12), we read:

> Einn jólaaptan í Bólm, þá strengði Angantýr heit at
> bragarfulli sem siðvenja var til, at hann skyldi eiga
> dóttur Yngva (v. l. Ingjalds) konungs at Uppsǫlum,
> Ingibjǫrgu, þá mey er fegrst var ok vitrust á danska
> tungu, eða falla at ǫðrum kosti. (One Yule even in
> Bólm Angantýr swore at the Bragi cup, as then was
> customary, that he should get the daughter of Yngvi
> . . . king at Uppsalir, Ingibjǫrg by name, the fairest
> and wisest maiden within the Danish-speaking world,
> or else fall [in battle].)

And in Hervarar saga, ch. 10 (p. 328):

> Heiðrekr konungr blótaði Frey; þann gǫlt er mestan
> fekk, skyldi hann gefa Frey; kǫlluðu þeir hann svá
> helgan, at yfir hans burst skyldi sverja um ǫll stór
> mál, ok skyldi þeim gelti blóta at sonarblóti; jólaaptan
> skyldi leiða sonargǫltinn í hǫll fyrir konung; lǫgðu
> menn þá hendr yfir burst hans ok strengja heit.
> Heiðrekr konungr strengði þess heit, at engi maðr
> skyldi svá mikit hafa af gert við hann, ef á vald hans
> kœmi, at eigi skyldi kost eiga at hafa dóm spekinga
> hans. (King H. sacrificed to Freyr; the biggest boar
> available was to be given to Freyr; they considered

113

it so holy that over its bristles should be sworn all
oaths of great import; and that boar was to be sacrificed at the boar-sacrifice; at Yule eve the boar was
to be led into the hall before the king, then the men
laid hands on its bristles and swore oaths. King H.
swore an oath that nobody should have injured him
to such an extent that he would not grant him, if he
came in his power, the judgement of his wise men.)

This description almost looks like an expansion of the one found
in Helga kviða. That the oath over the boar is old, although not
mentioned in the verses of Helga kviða, is made probable not
only by the Longobardian parallel but also by similar oath-pro-
cedures in many different nations (cf. Encyclopedia Britannica,
s. v. oath), among which also the English and the French in the
Middle Ages (cf. Nyrop's article). But the content of the king's
vow seems to be late. As to the custom of choosing a bride over
the cup cf. Jómsvíkingadrápa above, and especially a line in
Málsháttakvæði (v. 25: fljóðin verða at ǫlðrum kǫrin, "the maidens
are chosen over the ale."). Málsháttakvæði has been attributed
to the author of Jómsvíkingadrápa and it dates at any rate from
about 1200. For other parallels see Detter and Heinzel's commentary to their Edda edition.

It is perhaps not without significance that Helga kviða
Hjǫrvarðssonar shares with these two Scaldic poems composed
by an Orkney bishop of the second half of the twelfth century
the major interest in a love theme. Whatever this means in the
case of the Eddic poem (cp. the comment by B. S. Phillpotts,
The Elder Edda and Ancient Scandinavian Drama [Cambridge,
1920], pp. 80, 114), the conclusion seems not unreasonable that
the Orkney bishop had been touched by the first stirrings of the
romantic spirit in England or Scotland. And in this connection
it should not be forgotten that G. Vigfússon found the Helgi-
poems "most distinctly southern in character," and both he and
S. Bugge (Helgedigtene i den ældre Edda) believed that they
originated in the British Isles. But if there is a real connection
between these poems we have to admit the possibility that the
custom of heitstrenging also came from the South, since this
is the first uncontested appearance of the term. We shall come
back to this.

OLD ENGLISH <u>BEOT</u> AND OLD ICELANDIC <u>HEITSTRENGING</u>

But since we have already been led into the Fornaldarsǫgur in search for heitstrenging, it is best here to adduce the remaining examples found in that type of literature. There are only two of them. The first is from Hrólfs saga kraka (Fornaldarsögur I, ch. 42, p. 68) in addition to the one mentioned in the beginning of this chapter. It is the story of Vǫggr who is said to have given the nickname <u>kraki</u> to king Hrólfr. The king gave him a ring on this occasion, at which Vǫggr was so delighted that "he stepped upon a log with one foot (sté á stokk ǫðrum fœti) saying: 'I vow that I shall avenge you if I live longer than you, and you are overcome by men'"(<u>þess strengi ek heit, et ek skal þín hefna ef ek lifi lengr, ef þú verðr af mǫnnum sigraðr</u>). Although the saga is late (fourteenth century) it has venerable ancestors in Saxo and Skjǫldungasaga (Snorra Edda), for a discussion of which see A. Olrik, <u>Danmarks Heltedigtning</u>, I, 127 ff. The second example if from Ragnars saga loðbrókar (Fornaldarsögur I, 178), according to F. Jónsson from the first half of the fourteenth century. þóra, daughter of Earl Herrauðr in Gautland, is enclosed in a bower surrounded by a serpent. The Earl thinks this is a great pity, "and he vows that he will give his daughter to the man who kills the serpent" (<u>ok strengir þess heit, at hann mun þeim manni gefa dóttur sína . . . ef at bana yrði orminum</u>). This example is not of course very illuminating as to the age of the custom, but it goes to show how popular it became in the later romantic or fantastic literature as a motif.

As yet we have not mentioned any instance from the Icelandic family sagas, and it is fitting to begin by quoting Landnámabók (ed. F. Jónsson, 1900, p. 4). The history of Iceland begins, so to speak, with a heitstrenging:

> The foster-brothers Ingólfr and Leifr went on a viking-expedition with the sons of Atli the Slender, Earl of Gaular: Hásteinn, Hersteinn, and Hólmsteinn. They were of good agreement, and when they came home they planned to go together next summer. But in the winter the foster-brothers gave a feast in the honor of the Earl's sons. At that feast Hólmsteinn vowed (<u>strengði heit</u>) that he should marry Helga, the daughter of Qrn (Ingólfr's sister), or else no other woman. People were silent at this vow, but Leifr reddened in the face,

and few words were wasted between him and Hólmsteinn
when they parted after the feast.

The matter ended with the killing of Hólmsteinn, but after that
the foster-brothers had to leave their lands and then went out to
Iceland as the first settlers—in the seventies of the ninth century.
     The same heitstrenging is retold with interesting additions
in the late Flóamanna saga, ed. V. Ásmundarson (Reykjavík,
1898), p. 4 (see F. Jónsson, Litt. Hist., II, 750 ff.). In the saga it
is Hersteinn who vows to marry Helga, and after that follow
other heitstrengingar: Hallsteinn vows that he shall not deviate
from just judgment, if people will confide in him (ek skal eigi
halla réttum dómi, ef mér er trúat til dygðar um); Ingólfr vows
not to share his inheritance with anybody except Leifr, and
Leifr vows not to be worse than his father (at vera eigi
verrfeðrungr). These additions reveal the taste of later times
(cf. Hervarar saga above).
     Next to Landnáma we shall look at Hrafnkels saga Freysgoða,
ed. F. S. Cawley (Cambridge, Mass., 1932). It starts off with
this motif (ch. 3, p. 5): Hrafnkell had a horse of which he was
very fond, and which he shared with Frey, "this horse he loved
so much that he vowed (strengði þess heit) that he would kill the
man who rode on it without his leave." When this actually happens he has to kill the man against his will because of the belief
that no good befalls those who break their oath, and he comments
upon his vow in words decidedly reminiscent of the Wanderer:
"Often we shall repent when we speak too much but seldom we
would rue it if we had spoken less" (p. 10). Similarly Heðinn in
Helga kviða Hjǫrvarðssonar is made desperate after his vow
because he cannot break it without becoming a níðingr, as
Grǫnbech would say.
     Hrafnkels saga is one of the best among the sagas and so it
is put by critics in the first half of the thirteenth century. All
the other sagas which I shall consider are late, belonging to the
second half of that century or even still later times. They are:
Harðar saga ok Hólmverja (ch. 14, Íslendinga sögur, II [Copen-
hagen, 1847], 42–43), Hœnsna-þóris saga (ch. 12, ibid., pp. 165–
67), Svarfdœla saga (ch. 19, ed. F. Jónsson [Copenhagen, 1883],
pp. 57–58), and Flóamanna saga, already mentioned and discussed.

OLD ENGLISH BEOT AND OLD ICELANDIC HEITSTRENGING

In Harðar saga the young men make vows at the Yule feast. Hróarr rises and says: "Here I step on the log and make a vow (hér stíg ek á stokk ok strengi þess heit) that I shall have broken the grave-mound of Sóti the Viking before next Yule." Then Hǫrðr vows to accompany him into the mound of Sóti and not to depart before him. Similarly a third one vows to follow Hǫrðr and never to part with him without his leave, etc. The formula is also found in Hrólfs saga kraka. 9

In Hœnsna-þóris saga we find ourselves at a bridal feast.

And as the tables had been set and all men were seated,
Hersteinn the bridegroom steps forth from the table
and walks thither where a certain stone10 was placed.
He stepped on the stone with one foot and said: This vow
I make (þess strengi ek heit) that I shall have fully out-
lawed (fullsektat) Arngrim godi before the end of Althing
this summer, or else he shall have had to accept my
own judgement in the case.

He goes to his seat and another man comes forth to make a simi-lar vow.

In Svarfdœla saga (not earlier than 1400 [Jónsson]) we have another bridal feast where heitstrengingar 'vows,' are combined with mannjafnaðr 'manpairing.'11

Karl the Red began this sport, and took as his mate
(jafnaðarmaðr) Ljótólfr godi, and made the vow that
within three winters he should have branded him as
a coward (skyldi hafa heimilat ragmælit á hendr
honum, i.e., Ljótólfi goða). Gríss named Skíði as his
mate, and vowed that he should be sure to pick the
harbour he wanted, wherever he sailed abroad (between lands). Klaufi took for his mate O— and vowed
that he should go into bed with Yngvildr fǫgrkinn (fair-
cheek) against the will of Ljótólfr godi.

In all these instances the man vows to do some deed which his mate (jafnaðarmaðr) either could not do equally well (so Gríss' vow, cp. the contest of Beowulf and Breca), or which in itself is an insult to the mate, and so leaves him a lesser man if he does not prevent or avenge it.

117

We have now traced the custom through Scaldic and Eddic poetry, through the "historical" Noregs konunga and Íslendinga sǫgur, and through the "unhistorical" Fornaldarsǫgur. One thing all these sources have in common: it is open to doubt what is historical truth in them and what is fiction. But there can be no doubt that the following passage from the Sturlunga saga (ed. Kr. Kålund's [Copenhagen, 1904], II, 41; G. Vigfússon's ed. [Oxford, 1878], II, 36), a contemporary chronicle of the second half of the thirteenth century, reflects an actual happening of the day:

> Fór þórðr (kakali Sigvatsson) nú heim á Mýrar. Sat
> hann þá heima um vetrinn alt um jól fram. En at
> jólum bauð hann til sín ǫllum beztum mǫnnum ór Vest-
> fjǫrðum; hafði hann þá veizlu mikla á Mýrum. Strengði
> þórðr þá heit ok allir hans menn. þórðr strengði þess
> heit at láta aldri taka mann ór kirkju, hverjar sakir sem
> sá hefði til við hann, ok þat efndi hann. En er menn fóru
> í brott, veitti hann mǫrgum mǫnnum gjafir; váru þá allir
> meiri vinir hans en áðr.

This is an important locus for the history of the heitstrenging. We know the date: it was at Christmas in the year before the famous Flóabardagi (Battle of the Bay), which took place at Easter 1244. þórðr kakali is one of the chieftains or warlords of the troubled Sturlunga-age; he

> is sitting at home during the winter up to Christmas.
> But at Christmas he invites all the best men of the
> West firths, and he gave a great feast at Mýrar.
> þórðr then made the vow never to capture a man in
> a church, no matter how much that man might have
> offended him, and this vow he kept.

Historians writing about this time have remarked that of all the warlords of the Sturlunga-age, þórðr seems to have been the one most touched by the chivalrous ideals of the time. Thus, on another occasion, it is stated that he warned his men to spare women and churches.

It was Nyrop's opinion, expressed in his first article, that the heitstrenging among the Norsemen was an old custom which died out with heathendom. However, in his second article, he believes that he has found in a French poem of the thirteenth century: Sone de Nansai, edited by Moritz Goldschmidt (Tübingen, 1899), lines 3265–3302, a description of heitstrenging as performed at a feast in the hall of the king of Norway. The case from Sturlunga saga removes all doubts as to the existence of the custom in the thirteenth century. In fact it is much more certain than its existence in older times, for since we cannot trust þormóðr's verse, which would take us back to ca. 1025, we find the word first in poetry and prose dating from the beginning of the thirteenth century. It is rather astonishing that it should not be preserved somewhere in the great bulk of Scaldic and Eddic poetry if it was old, and we have in connection with Helga kviða Hjǫrvarðssonar and Jómsvíkingadrápa mentioned the possibility that it was of southern origin introduced with the romantic spirit in the twelfth century. Moreover, it is singular that two of the oldest instances should be associated with English sources, viz. the Hrólfs saga tradition, whose Danish and Icelandic branches have near parallels in Beowulf, and the Jómsvíkinga tradition, with striking parallels to be found in the Battle of Maldon, a contemporary poem celebrating a battle in which some Jómsvíkingar in all probability took part. This goes far to prove the existence of the custom in Denmark of ca. 1000, and, in view of that, one can probably agree with Nyrop and Grønbech (Vor Folkeæt, IV, 69–73) that the custom is ancient in Scandinavia. It follows that the instances of heitstrenging in Landnáma, Hrafnkels saga, etc., might be old, although they could just as well be explained on the theory of the twelfth-century romantic influence, mentioned above.

III

I shall now give a short résumé of Nyrop's article in so far as it treats the custom outside of Scandinavia. As far as Germany is concerned Nyrop is able to adduce only one example, from Ekkehard's Waltharius de Aquitania (tenth century): Before he starts fighting with twelve of Gunther's picked men he says: "This I promise proudly that no Frank shall return to tell my wife that he has, unpunished, dared to take anything of my dear treasure." Hardly has he spoken these words before he throws himself on the earth and asks God's forgiveness quia talia dixit. "This," says Nyrop, "can hardly mean anything else than that he has suddenly discovered that he has sinned against God by keeping an old heathen custom."

In France the custom is well known, but Nyrop is of opinion that it is not autochthonous there, as neither the Romans nor the Celts knew it. He therefore believes that it was introduced by the Germanic Francs. Nyrop cites instances from the Chanson de Roland (eleventh cent.; Marsilie's nephew vows to kill Roland, Roland vows to fall foremost of his men), and the Lay of Gaydon (thirteenth cent.; vows in the hall). The French words for strengja heit are: vouer, faire veu, and se vanter, the vow itself is vœu, vantance, vantise, but vanter and its derivatives are used not only of future deeds, but also of things past. Thus it corresponds to OE gilp, 'boast.'

Besides these words there also occurs in Old French the word gaber used about comical vows and boasts (gabs), these gabs occur e.g. in Pèlerinage Charlemagne, and they are not translated into ON by heitstrenging but by geipun, geiplur, the verb geipa 'to use big words, boast.'

In the later romances of chivalry one finds the motif in Méraugis, Perceforest, Lancelot du Lac, Tirant le blanc, and other works. The living custom has developed into an empty literary motif. Later on, however, there are attempts to re-introduce it into real life.

In Les Vœux du Paon (ca. 1300) the knights make vows over a peacock. The peacock—a highly esteemed bird in the Middle Ages—was sent around for everybody to make a vow on it, whereupon it was carved by the most valiant knight and everybody received his share. This poem became very popular; it is copied in Le Restor du Paon and Le Parfait du Paon, and translated into other languages. The motif becomes not only a "lieu commun" in the literature but is sometimes actually introduced into chivalrous feasts. Thus Oliver de la Marche describes a feast celebrated by the Duke of Burgundy, Philippe le Bon, in 1454, in which vows are made on a pheasant. Nyrop believes that this bird ceremonial is of English origin, where the motif of vowing is found in the older romances: The Avowinge of King Arthur, Sir Gawan, Sir Kaye, and Sir Bauvdewyn of Bretan. See J. Robson, Three Early English Metrical Romances (London, 1842).

For later examples of vowing over birds Nyrop cites the Chronicle of Matthæus of Westminster (cp. Canterbury Tales,

OLD ENGLISH <u>BEOT</u> AND OLD ICELANDIC <u>HEITSTRENGING</u>

VII. 872, ed. Robinson [Cambridge, Mass., 1957], n.): In 1306 King Edward I swears by two swans to go to Scotland and avenge Johan Comyn's death. Cp. also <u>Les Vœux du Héron</u> from ca. 1340, a sort of prelude to the Hundred Years' War between the English and the French.

In addition Nyrop adduces some examples of the motif from See p. 106 Spanish and Italian sources, but he looks upon them as introduced from France.

His résumé of the custom's history is as follows:

> Among the Germanic tribes it was customary in heathen times that the warriors in the evening after a party under the influence of the wine should praise themselves in different ways, either by vowing to do great deeds, or by boasting of deeds they already had performed, or else of some treasured things of their own. This can, however, be proved only indirectly. The first form of this social custom is represented by the Norsemen's <u>heitstrenging</u>, which exclusively consists in vowing to perform great deeds in the future; in the French heroic poetry we find both forms combined. Among the Scandinavians the custom is linked with many heathen ceremonies, of which we find no trace in France, where a certain ceremonial is introduced only later from England. Among the Scandinavians and the Germans the custom died out with heathendom and never degenerated into a "survival"; in France it persisted after the introduction of Christianity in a modified form, but soon lost its hold in real life, but as a part of French culture the knowledge of the custom, in the form of a literary motif, was spread to England, Italy, and Spain.

This conclusion now needs to be modified. We meet the custom first among the English, and there in its original form, devoid as yet of any ceremony. It is of considerable interest that there we also find it—as later in France—with its two faces, one to the past or present, and one to the future; <u>gilp</u> has both these aspects, and <u>beot</u> seems to acquire them too. In the Icelandic sources we find it also perhaps in a primitive stage, but forms of it occur in which it is strengthened with all sorts of ceremony. Nor is it quite right to say that the custom died away with Christendom in the North, or if so, the custom must have been reintroduced through southern influence: witness the vows of Þórðr kakali at Christmas 1243, and Nyrop's article in Aarböger.

Nyrop mentions the fact that a similar custom is well known in Old Russia,[12] judging by the Old Russian bylini; and he quotes Rambaud, La Russie épique (Paris, 1876), pp. 83, 135, 258. He believes that the custom is autochthonous in Russia, not introduced by the Væringjar. As in France the custom there seems reduced to a conventional epic motif, and in Russia it tends to be boasting of past deeds (cf. the Scandinavian manpairing), whereas in France it is rather of future deeds.

Nyrop says that he was not able to find parallels in the epic poetry of other nations, although "the custom is in itself so natural that it should be able to originate in any warlike society." The only further example he draws from a book on the Nicobar Islands: Dictionary of the Nancowry Dialect of the Nicobarese language, by Mrs. de Roepstorff (Calcutta, 1884). He seems thus to have overlooked the existence of the example in the Iliad (XX, 83 ff.) quoted by Klaeber (Beowulf, p. 143) as a parallel to Beowulf 480 ff.

NOTES

1 Cp. Wilh. Pfändler, "Die Vergnügungen der Angelsachsen," Anglia, XXIX (1907), 463, and F. B. Gummere, Founders of England, 2d ed. by F. P. Magoun, Jr. (New York, 1930), p. 76. Klaeber, Beowulf, p. 143, comments: "A kind of gylpcwide . . . cp. 2633 ff.; Iliad XX, 83 ff."

2 On the potency of the drink and its mystic quality see V. Grønbech, Vor Folkeæt i Oldtiden, IV (Copenhagen, 1912), 17 ff.

3 For further comparison see Axel Olrik, Danmarks Heltedigtning I (Copenhagen, 1903), 47–48, and his interesting reconstruction of Bjarkamál.

4 Gummere, Pfändler, and Budde make no allusion to the Old Norse custom.

5 He came back to the subject in another article: "Norske Forhold i det 13. Arhundrede efter en samtidig fransk Kilde,"

in Aarböger for nordisk Oldkyndighed og Historie, II, Række 22, 1–18. Of equal interest is the penetrating, if not so detailed study of heitstrenging and cognate forms in V. Grønbech, Vor Folkeæt i Oldtiden, III (Copenhagen, 1912), 143 and especially 159 with the notes on pp. 186 and 191; cf. also IV, 69 with notes p. 126 on OE gilp.

6 Heimskringla, Morris-Magnússon, I (London, 1893), 271–73 (cf. F. Jónsson's ed. [Copenhagen, 1911], pp. 129–30. Codex Frisianus [Christiania, 1869–71], pp. 119–20, and Jómsvíkinga saga, ed. C. Petersen [Lund, 1879], pp. 92–98).

7 Helga kviða Hjǫrvarðssonar, Prose IV, Hollander's translation, p. 206.

8 On braga(r)full see M. Cahen, Études sur le vocabulaire religieux du vieux-scandinave: La libation (Paris, 1921), p. 174.

9 For other parallels see Grønbech, Vor Folkeæt, III, 159, with notes on p. 191.

10 Oaths sworn by a stone are mentioned in Helga kviða Hundingsbana II, 31, Guðrúnar kviða III, 3, and Atlakviða 30.

11 For that custom see the classical example in Heimskringla, Morris-Magnússon, III, 279–83; cf. also I, 210–11; II, 296; III, 186, and Eyrbyggja, Morris-Magnússon, p. 95 ff.

12 The Russian custom is also discussed briefly by O. B. Briem, "Germanische und Russische Heldendichtung," Germ.-Rom. Monatschrift XVII, 346 ff., where Beowulf is also compared (the Unferð episode). Note: Pertinent literature partly coming to my notice after this article was written: Sofus Larsen, "Jómsborg," Aarböger f. nord. Oldk. III Række 17: 1–138; 18: 1–128; 21: 1–106; see esp. 17: 54. B. S. Phillpotts, "The Battle of Maldon," MLR, XXVII (1929), 172–90. Marie Ashdown, English and Norse Documents relating to the Reign of Ethelred the Unready (Cambridge, 1930). John R. Reinhard, "Some Illustrations of the Mediaeval gab," Essays and Studies in English Comparative Literature (Ann Arbor, 1933), pp. 27–57. Levin L. Schücking, Heldenstoltz und Würde im Angelsächsischen (Leipzig, 1933) [= Abhandl. der phil.-hist. Kl. der Sächsischen Akademie der Wissenschaften XLII, No. V] contains a most important study of beot.

WYRD IN ANGLO-SAXON PROSE AND POETRY

þios wandriende wyrd þe we wyrd hatað.

B.J. Timmer

I

There can hardly be any doubt that the outlook on life of the Germanic peoples was fatalistic. In all the Old-Germanic dialects words and expressions occur representing an original belief in Fate, still visible even after the actual words had lost much of their original meaning. Such a word, common to all the Germanic languages, is the Anglo-Saxon wyrd, Old-Saxon wurd, Old-High German wurt, Old Norse urðr (which also occurs as a proper name for one of the Norns—cp. Völuspá 20³ and Hugo Gering and Barend Sijmons, Kommentar zu den Lidern der Edda, I [Halle, 1927], 25). The meaning of these words in the various languages is the same and they have all had a similar development: from the abstract use (= Latin fatum) they develop the meaning of death.[1]

In Anglo-Saxon literature the idea represented by wyrd has a special interest, because after the conversion of the Anglo-Saxons to Christianity the word continued to be used. As Brandl remarks (Paul's Grundriss II², p. 950): "Die bedeutsamste unter den Nornen, den weird sisters der spezifisch schottischen Volkskunde, empfahl sich unter ihrem gut Westgerm. Namen Wyrd d.h. 'Vergangenheit' sogar den Christlichen Schriftstellern, die sie als eine Verkörperung des Weltlaufs, des Schicksals oder der Vorsehung in mancherlei Gedichten verwendeten." The new creed had no use for a belief in a superhuman, blind and hostile Fate ruling men's lives, for it is God who governs the lives of men. Thus the idea of wyrd, the blindly ruling Fate, disappeared or, when a sense of the inevitability of the events of a man's fate remained, this inevitability, represented by wyrd, was made sub-

Reprinted from Neophilologus, Vol. XXVI (1940), pp. 24–33, (1941), pp. 213–28, by permission of the publisher.

ject to God (see Alfred's translation of Boethius, De Consolatione Philosophiae, XXXIX). In this way the word wyrd passed
from heathen into Christian times and continued to be used long
after people had ceased to believe in a blindly ruling Fate.

At this point the question arises: what exactly does the word
wyrd represent at this stage in its history? It should be noted
that the texts as they are handed down to us show the word only
at this stage, viz. after it had passed into the Christian atmosphere, for no unequivocally heathen poetry is extant. When,
for instance, we read in Elene 1046 "wyrd gescreaf," it should
be asked: what did this expression convey to the Anglo-Saxons
of the eighth century? Again, when "wyrda Waldend," a term for
God, occurs in poems that are fully Christian in atmosphere,
does this mean that the poet still thought of God as the Ruler of
the Fates, i.e. the three Sisters? In connection with these questions two currents are distinguishable in the contending opinions
as regards the proper interpretation of wyrd. The majority of
scholars hold that wyrd, even when used in otherwise Christian
texts, still has some more or less remote associations with the
heathen belief in Fate and they find a strong support for this view
in the fact that Beowulf, though predominantly Christian in its atmosphere, still contains references to heathen beliefs and practises.
This view is represented e.g. by Klaeber, who says in the Introduction to his edition (3d. ed. [Boston, 1936], p. xlix): "By the side
of the heathen fate is seen the almighty God," and further down:
"Yet God is said to control fate" (see also Klaeber's articles on
"Die christlichen Elemente im Beowulf," Anglia, XXXV [1911];
XXXVI [1912]). It is further supported by Ehrismann ("Religions-
geschichtliche Beiträge zum germanischen Frühchristentum,"
BGDSL, XXXV [1900], 205–239), who sees God and Wyrd as ethical contrasts; R. Jente ("Die mythologischen Ausdrücke im altenglischen Wortschatz," Anglistische Forschungen, XLI [1921]); E. A.
Philipsson ("Germanisches Heidentum bei den Angelsachsen,"
Kölner Anglistische Arbeiten, IV [1929]). To this group also belongs Brandl, who in his article "Zur Vorgeschichte der Weird
Sisters im Macbeth" (dating from 1921, but reprinted in a collection of some of Brandl's articles called Forschungen und Fortschritte) says about the use of wyrd in Beowulf: "Dem Beowulf-
dichter als einem vorwiegend weltlich orientierten Manne, dem
der heidnische Hain- und Verbrennungskult noch vertraut war,
ist ein entsprechend altertümlicher Begriff der Wyrd noch eigen."
(Forschungen und Fortschritte, p. 82).

The alternative opinion concerning the meaning of wyrd we find already expressed in Bosworth-Toller's Anglo-Saxon Dictionary, where s.v. wyrd it was first pointed out that wyrd had weakened its sense in the course of time. Under section IV the meaning is registered as follows: "an event 1) with the special idea of that which happens by the determination of Providence or fate, 2) in a general sense." Bosworth-Toller's Dictionary was followed by most of the editors of Anglo-Saxon eighth-century poetical texts, who in their Glossaries give the meaning "fate, destiny" by the side of "event," for singular and plural alike (Klaeber gives "event" only for the plural use in Beowulf 3030). This view was for the first time fully elaborated by Enrico Pizzi in his article "Zur Frage der ästhetischen Einheit des Beowulf," Anglia, XXXIX (1916), 1–15, in which he contends that wyrd "ganz in den Dienst der christlichen Weltanschauung getreten ist" (p. 11). The use of wyrd in poetry was examined by A. Wolf in his dissertation Die Bezeichnungen für Schicksal in der ags. Dichtersprache (Breslau, 1919), in which he attempted to prove that nowhere in Anglo-Saxon poetry wyrd occurs in the meaning of fatum or as a goddess of Fate or death. Wolf's views tend in the same direction as those of Pizzi, only he does not carry the argument to the point of saying that wyrd has become a fully Christian idea.

The situation is, therefore, at present thus, that by some wyrd and God are considered as ethical contrasts, whereas others consider them as practically identical phenomena, which means that some stick to the mythological idea behind the word, whereas others admit a development of meaning which led to a complete weakening of its sense. This situation is far from satisfactory and would in itself provide enough justification for attempting a new investigation of the use of wyrd. But when I found that Miss E. E. Wardale, in her Old English Literature (London, 1935), uses the plural of wyrd as an argument in favour of the early date of the Wanderer (p. 30, note 1, in which she says that in the phrase "wyrda gesceaft" the plural seems to point to the three goddesses of fate), and moreover that G. Neckel also explained the plural in this phrase as a reference to the three norns (Die altgermanische Kultur [Leipzig, 1934], pp. 26 f.), I started to try and ascertain what exactly the meaning of wyrd is in the texts as we have them, which is the object of the following pages. No allusions are made in the following to the mythological side of the question.

WYRD IN ANGLO-SAXON PROSE AND POETRY

In details my explanation of certain passages is sometimes the same as that of others, e.g. B.-T. or Wolf,[2] but the matter is approached from a different point of view and leads to a result that is partly at least different from that of other writers on the subject as regards the general development of meaning of wyrd. I am conscious, however, of laying myself open to the charge of wishful thinking, but that is unavoidable, because the whole question is more a matter for conjecture than for decision. Further, it may be added that my list of occurrences of wyrd does not claim to be exhaustive. I left out of discussion the three instances of wyrd in the Riddles (ed. Frederick Tupper [Boston, 1910]), because the Riddles are strongly influenced by Latin, and the Metra of Boethius, because the use of wyrd is here the same as in the corresponding prose.

Finally, I wish to stress the fact that I have everywhere in the translation of passages avoided the use of modern English fate. This word can express "lot, destiny," but I wanted to remove any suggestion of the existence of something inevitable outside the relation of man to God, which still clings to the word fate.

II

WYRD IN PROSE

In Alfred's translation of Boethius' De Consolatione Philosophiae (ed. W. J. Sedgefield [Oxford, 1899]) wyrd occurs many times, but chiefly in five different groups of passages, viz. Ch. IV, V; X, XI; XX; XXXIX; XL. In each of these 5 groups wyrd forms the subject of the chapters.

In the chapters X and XI Boethius discusses the subject of happiness or unhappiness. Wisdom says (Sedgefield, pp. 21, 19 ff.): "Ne meaht þu no mid soðe getælan þine wyrd and þine gesælða, swa swa þu wenst, for þā leasū ungesælþū þe þu ðrowast." (Latin text fortuna). Here wyrd, which is used on the same level with gesælða, means: your fate = destiny = lot. There are no associations with a heathen fate, because, as appears from a passage inserted by Alfred later on (p. 131, 8–12), it is not Fate, but the divine predestination which governs the happiness or unhappiness of man.

At the end of this chapter the same subject is referred to in the words (p. 23, 2 f.): "Ne meaht ðu nu giet þinre wyrde nauht oðwitan ne þin lif no getælan, ne eart þu no eallunga to nauhte gedon swa swa þu wenst" (Lat. fortuna). In this passage wyrd is used synonymously with lif, in the same way as we can use lot and life synonymously. Similarly, p. 24, 14 f.: "Forþā ne mæg nan man on þys andweardan life eallunga gerad beon wið his wyrd" (Lat. fortuna). Wyrd, again preceded by the possessive pronoun, expresses: what happens to man, his lot.

Used in the general sense, the word is found later on in the same chapter (p. 25, 24): "Ne sio wyrd þe on geniman ne meahte" (Lat. fortuna). Again, the passage means "which the lot (now in the general sense, but corresponding to his lot) cannot take away from him." Cp. p. 39, 10, "Be eallum þā woruld-gesælðum þe seo wyrd brengð" (Lat. fortuna), where the meaning is clearly lot in general, almost "life."

In this group of passages (Ch. X and XI), wyrd therefore expresses "that which happens to man, the events of his life or his lot." No heathen associations are possible.

The next group (Ch. XX) deals with the question what should be one's attitude to an adverse lot. We find the word used in the general sense and preceded by an adjective. The first passage runs (p. 47, 4 f.): "Ne wen ðu no þ ic to anwillice winne wið ða wyrd" (Lat. fortuna), which expresses that man should not obstinately struggle against his lot because, whether favourable or unfavourable, it is ordained by God's Providence. Here, too, the meaning of wyrd borders on life (used in the general sense). The other examples in this chapter are in accordance with this meaning: 1. 6 "sio lease wyrd," 1. 13 "sio wiðerwearde wyrd" and p. 48, 13 "and þe þuhte þ seo wyrd swiðost on þinne willan wode." In all these cases the Latin text has fortuna (cp. p. 54, 11 "seo lease wyrd" = Lat. fortuna).

Thus we see that here, too, the word wyrd no longer represents the heathen blind and hostile fate. This is further illustrated by the next group of passages, Ch. XL., where wyrd occurs preceded by an adjective expressing a favourable meaning. It appears, therefore, that wyrd does not represent an unfavourable lot only, but that the word itself is neutral in meaning, because it can be preceded by an adjective both of a favourable and of an unfavourable sense. The subject discussed in this chapter is indicated by the title: "Hu ælc wyrd beoð god, sam heo mannū god þince, sam heo him yfel þince." All the occurrences of <u>wyrd</u> in this chapter correspond to <u>fortuna</u> in the Latin text (except p. 140, 21, where the Latin text has <u>fatalis catena</u>, because it refers to the use of <u>wyrd</u> in Ch. XXXIX). Note ælc wyrd in the title and on p. 137, 3.

A similar meaning of <u>wyrd</u> is found in a passage inserted by Alfred, p. 102, 21–25: "Ða eode he furður, oð he gemette ða graman metena ðe folcisce men hatað Parcas, ða hi secgað ðæt on nanum men nyton nane are, ac ælcū men wrecen be his gewyrhtū; ða hi secgað ðæt walden ælces mannes wyrde" (who are said to govern the <u>lot</u> [life] of each man). Here the Parcae are not called Wyrda, as e.g. in Wright-Wülcker's <u>Vocabularies</u> (see B.-T., loc. cit., s.v. <u>Wyrd</u>, III, also the examples given by Jente, para. 55), but <u>wyrd</u> is used in the sense of (each man's) lot.

In another group of passages, Ch. IV and V, the discussion is about the fact that our lot as it befalls us, is not mere accident, that it is not chance which governs the world, but God. Thus the word <u>wyrd</u> assumes the meaning of chance, accidental happenings. P. 10, 17 f.: "Hwy þu la Drihten æfre woldest þ seo wyrd swa hwyrfan sceolde? heo þreat þa unscildigan and nauht ne ðreaþ þam scildigū." The Latin text has (<u>Metra</u> 5. 28) "Nam cur tantas lubrica versat Fortuna vices?" The meaning of <u>wyrd</u> is clearly "chance." Similarly, p. 11, 5 ff., a passage which is not in the Latin original: "And wendest þ seo weord [wyrd] þas woruld wende heore agenes ðonces buton Godes geþeahte and his þafunge and monna gewyrhtū," and p. 11, 31 "þa woon wyrd" (Lat. <u>fortuna</u>). That not Fate, Latin <u>fatum</u>, is meant in these passages, is clear from the Anglo-Saxon text and its Latin original in the following examples of the same chapter: p. 12, 16 "Gelefst ðu þ sio wyrd wealde þisse worulde, oððe auht godes swa geweorðan mæge butan þæm wyrhtan" (Lat. <u>fortuitis casibus</u>); p. 13, 24 "þ þios sliðne wyrd ðas woruld wende buton Godes geþeahte" (Lat. has <u>fortunarum vices</u>); p. 13, 31 "þ sio wyrd þurh hie selfe butan Godes geþeahte þas weoruld wendan ne mæge" (Lat. <u>casuum temeritati</u>).

In these groups of passages, therefore, and in the occasional use of <u>wyrd</u> outside them, we see that <u>wyrd</u> mostly translates Lat. <u>fortuna</u> to express "that which happens to us in our life," the events of our lot, life (so our <u>lot</u>), except in Ch. IV and V, where the secondary meaning of chance (the events of our life which happen <u>accidentally</u>) is found (Lat. <u>fortuna</u>, <u>vices</u>, <u>casus</u>).

There remains one group (Ch. XXXIX) in which the subject of wyrd = Lat. fatum = Fate is discussed. Naturally the Latin text here has fatum.

In Ch. XXXIX Boethius discusses the relation of Fate to God's Providence. He attempts to prove that, as long as something is in God's mind, it is his Providence, but as soon as it is accomplished, it is called wyrd (= fatum). Thus he makes Fate subject to God, in that it comes from the Providence of God. It is especially this passage (Sedgefield, pp. 127 ff.) which forms the "bridge between the ancient philosophy of the Nordic peoples and their new religion" (Dame Bertha S. Phillpotts, "Wyrd and Providence in Anglo-Saxon Thought," E&S, XIII [1928], 25) and which is of the utmost importance for the proper understanding of wyrd and its transition into Christian terminology.

We shall first discuss the passage in the Anglo-Saxon translation on p. 128, 10 ff., which in the Latin original runs as follows:

> Qui modus cum in ipsa divinae intellegentiae
> puritate conspicitur, providentia nominatur; cum vero
> ad ea, quae movet atque disponit, refertur, fatum a
> veteribus appellatum est. Quae diversa esse facile
> liquebit, si quis utriusque vim mente conspexerit;
> nam providentia est ipsa illa divina ratio in summo
> omnium principe constituta, quae cuncta disponit,
> fatum vero inhaerens rebus mobilibus dispositio, per
> quam providentia suis quaeque nectit ordinibus.
> Providentia namque cuncta pariter quamvis diversa,
> quamvis infinita complectitur, fatum vero singula
> digerit in motum locis, formis ac temporibus dis-
> tributa, ut haec temporalis ordinis explicatio in dininae
> mentis adunata prospectum providentia sit, eadem vero
> adunatio digesta atque explicata temporibus fatum vocetur.
>
> Quae licet diversa sint, alterum tamen pendet ex
> altero; ordo namque fatalis ex providentiae simplicitate
> procedit.

Alfred's translation runs (p. 128, 10 ff):

> 1) Ac ðæt ðætte we hatað Godes foreþonc and his
> foresceawung, þæt bið þa hwile þe hit ðær mid him
> bið on his mode, ærðæm þe hit gefremed weorðe, þa

hwile ðe hit geþoht bið; ac siððan hit fullfremed bið,
þonne hatað we hit wyrd. Be þy mæg ælc mon witan
þæt hit sint ægþer ge twegen naman ge twa þincg,
foreþonc and wyrd. 2) Se foreþonc is sio godcunde
gesceadwisnes; sio is fæst on þæm hean sceppende
þe eall fore wat hu hit geweorðan sceall ær ær hit
geweorðe. 3) Ac þæt þæt we wyrd hatað, þæt bið
Godes weorc þæt he ælce dæg wyrcð, ægþer ge þæs
ðe we gesioð ge þæs þe us ungesewenlic bið. Ac se
godcunda foreþonc heaðerað ealle gesceafta, þæt hi
ne moton toslupan of hiora endebyrdnesse. 4) Sio
wyrd þonne dælð eallum gesceaftum anwlitan and
stowa and sida and gemetgunga; ac sio wyrd cymð
of ðæm gewitte and of ðæm foreþonce þæs ælmihtegan
Godes. Se wyrcð æfter his unasecgendlicum foreþonce
þonne swa hwæt swa he wile.

From the passage marked 1) we see then, that Providence
is that which is still in God's Mind, His forethought, but when
carried out, it is called wyrd. Now we call God's plans carried
out in relation to us, human beings, that which happens to us,
our lot. The second passage is an elaboration of what is meant
by Providence, the divine intelligence; God knows beforehand
how everything must become before it has been carried out.
In the third passage it is explained that wyrd is God's work that
he works every day, whether we see it or not, which means that
part of what happens to us is the result of measures taken by
God that we do not see. The last passage, which is a very free
translation of the corresponding Latin text, shows without doubt
that wyrd = lot: wyrd gives to all things created by God's providence (i.e. to that which happens to us), faces, place, time and
regulation. So what we see as the results of God's forethought
in place, form and time ("locis, formis ac temporibus distributa"),
that is what happens to us, our lot.

These theses are worked out in the next section of Alfred's
text: just as every skilful man first thinks and designs his work
in his mind, before he carries it out, "þios wandriende wyrd þe
we wyrd hatað færð æfter his forþonce" (p. 128, 29), so this
varying wyrd that we call wyrd goes according to His forethought
and according to His thought, as He designs that it should be.

"þios wandriende wyrd," what else can it be here but a reference to the <u>varying</u> character of our <u>lot</u>?

Then follows the elaborate simile of the wheel and the axis (p. 129, 19 ff.) to illustrate the relation of Providence to our lot: just as the nave of the wheel is always sound and secure, whatever the fellies may strike against, so the best men are free from care "and læs reccað hu sio wyrd wandrige, oððe hwæt hio brenge" (p. 130, 18; cp. p. 39, 10 "be eallum þā woruldgesælðum þe seo wyrd brengð"), which means that they care less how their lot should vary, or whatever it should bring.

Thus it will be clear that here, as elsewhere in <u>Boethius</u>, <u>wyrd</u> (= <u>fatum</u>) is used with reference to that which happens to us, our lot. <u>Wyrd</u> is subject to God: what happens to us comes ultimately from God. But, as we have already seen from the passages in Ch. IV and V, our lot was by some considered as happening quite accidentally, so that <u>wyrd</u> may mean Chance. It is therefore not to be wondered at that in this passage about the relation of <u>Providence</u> and <u>Wyrd</u> Alfred should seize the opportunity of taking up the subject of <u>chance</u> once more and of reminding his readers that God's Providence governs the world. This passage (p. 131, 8–12) is an addition of Alfred's: "Sume uðwiotan þeah secgað þ sio wyrd wealde ægþer ge gesælða ge ungesælða ælces monnes. Ic þonne secge, swa swa ealle cristene men secgað, þ sio godcunde foretiohhung his walde, næs sio wyrd." Here <u>wyrd</u> expresses <u>chance</u>, as in Ch. IV and V. This passage is quoted by Jente (loc. cit., p. 197) as a direct witness of a heathen belief, together with Hom. Th. I, 110–114, but it does not refer to a heathen belief in Fate, the goddess, any more than Hom. Th. I, 110–114 does, which alludes to astrology. Both these passages imply that the old-Germanic heathen belief had decayed and that some people, who had lost the old faith and did not yet accept the new Christian creed, in this period of transition, seized the idea of chance or astrology as substitutes.

From the above it will be clear that in <u>Boethius</u>, <u>wyrd</u> had lost all associations with the heathen belief in a superhuman, blind and hostile power which destines the lot of men. It has come to assume the neutral meaning of <u>lot</u>, that which happens to us, with the secondary meaning of chance, that which happens accidentally. I do not agree, therefore, with Jente (loc. cit.) who ranges the passages from <u>Boethius</u> under the heading "Schicksal; die übermenschliche Macht, die das Menschengeschick bestimmt."

In Boethius it is only God who through his Providence destines the lot of man.

We now pass on to the prose texts of Alfred's time and later prose.

In Orosius (ed. H. Sweet, EETS, LXXIX [London, 1883]) there are two passages in which wyrd occurs. In the first the word is used in the singular, in the second it is plural.

Orosius 60. 23 (not 69. 23, as given in B.-T. s.v. wyrd): "Ðæt wille ic gecyþan, þæt þa ricu of nanes monnes mihtum swa gecræftgade [ne] wurdon, ne for nanre wurde buton from Godes gestihtunge." Lat. "Ut omnia haec profundissimis Dei judiciis disposita, non autem humanis viribus, aut incertis casibus accidisse perdoceam." The incerti casus of the Latin text point to the meaning chance, accident, also given to wyrd in this passage in B.-T. (cp. wyrd in Boethius above, p. 129). The general meaning "lot" that which happens to man, can easily shift to the more concrete sense of the actual events that happen to man in his lot (Cp. D. lot > lotgeval, gebeurtenis = event). This is the meaning of the plural of wyrd in the second passage from Orosius, 62. 10 "Giet scæl ic, cwæð Orosius, monigfealdlicor sprecan wiþ ða ðe secgað ðæt ða anwaldas sien of wyrda mægenum gewordene, nales of godes gestihtunge" (no Latin). The idea of accidental event is probably meant here, as may be inferred from the contrast of wyrda mægenum to godes gestihtunge. B.-T. register this passage also under the heading chance, accident, but the plural makes it necessary to specify and so we get accidental event (also Jente, loc. cit., who gives for this passage "zufälliges Ereignis").

The word wyrd occurs in another shade of meaning in Wærferth's Dialogues of Gregory the Great (ed. H. Hecht, Bibliothek der ags. Prosa, V [Cassel, 1900]).

227. 25–228. 1 (MS C): "And forðon full oft þonne þæt mænnisce mod byð gelæded ofer hit self hwæthwylces to geseonne, hit sceall nyde þæt licumlice fæt beon getydrod, þonne hit ne mæg aberan þa byrðene swa mycelre wyrde." (Latin text ed. U. Moricca, Fonti per la Storia d'Italia, LVII [Rome, 1924], 194. 12–14). Gregory, pointing to the story of Daniel, who became ill after miraculous things had happened to him, explains this in the passage just quoted. Thus we may assume for wyrd a further development of meaning, viz. miraculous event (very common

in the religious poetry of the seventh and eighth centuries, see below). Similarly,

59. 25–30 (MS C): "and he him þæt ondredde, þæt he scolde innan þanon atydrian, þanon he utan wære mannum mycel æteowed, gif he o wære gecnyssed mid mænniscre herenesse fram þam mægne þyssere wyrde" (MS H: "on þæs weorces mægene"). Lat. 52. 5–7 — "in virtute facti" —. A miracle has happened and the bishop to whom it has happened fears that he may become weak through human favour being shown him on account of the miraculous happening. So here, too, wyrd means a miraculous event (the meaning event is shown too by the Latin word factum).

In another passage Gregory tells about a priest who could heal sick people by laying on his hands. He concludes (248. 4–6 MS C): "Of þære wyrde þæs arwyrðan weres we geleornodon, þæt we gelyfdon eallra oþra weorca, þe we gehyrdon be him secgan." Lat. 215. 24 f.: "ex quo eius uno facto dedicimus. . . ." Here we see the meaning of wyrd shifted from "miraculous event" to something miraculous done in his life = miraculous deed (Latin factum). The same holds good for the following two passages:

91. 18–21 (MS C): "Ac forðon þa wundru, þe þonne geweorðað, bringað symble þa gewitnysse þæs godan lifes, þy ic bidde gyt, gif hwylce syn þe cuþe þara haligra wyrda, þæt þu secge to þon þæt þu me hingriende fede and trymme þurh þa bysene godra weorca" (Lat. 70. 15 diff.).

Wyrd = (miraculous) deed.

188. 5 (MS C): "Ac nu, þa þa ic sæde þa wyrda haligra wera, færinga me becom to gemynde." (Lat. 148. 1 "Sedecce, dum facta fortium virorum narro, repente ad memoriam venit".)

In this, as in the other passages, the wyrda have nothing to do with the lot or fate of these holy men; they refer to their holy deeds. Cp. also 185. 19 (MS C): "þæt we sume hwile ge-swigian be þam ærran wyrdum and dædum, and us is to cumene to þam wundrum" (Lat. 144. 22); and also 223. 20 (MS C): "gelice þy wyrde" (MS O has worde) "þære soþfæstnesse" (Lat. 189. 21 facta). The text of the Dialogues, then, shows another side-de-velopment of meaning of the word wyrd: from the neutral sense of lot, plural: events in a man's lot = events (mostly with the idea miraculous event), the stress shifts to the meaning of some-thing miraculous done in a man's life, deed (also with the idea of miraculous deed).

In the Blickling Homilies (ed. R. Morris, EETS, LVIII, LXIII [London, 1874–76]) the word occurs in the following passages.

135. 31 "Him ne wæs nænig earfoþe ðæt lichomlice gedal on ðære neowan wyrde." Here we must start from the meaning lot, but the preceding adjective shows that the word is used in a slightly different shade of meaning; their new lot = their new condition (as B.-T. translate; cp. Gospel According to St. John, ed. W.W. Skeat [Cambridge, 1887], p. 5. 10 under wyrd = sub condicione).

In the other examples from the Blickling Homilies, wyrd refers to a miraculous event, with the special idea of the end of the world. 83. 10 "Nænigne tweogean ne þearf, ðæt seo wyrd on ðæs andweardan tid geweorþan sceal, ðæt se Scyppend gesittan wile on his domsetle."

The wyrd explained in the dependent clause is a miraculous event. Similarly, 91. 22 "On ðæm ðæge gewiteþ heofon and eorþe. . . . Swa eac for ðære ilcan wyrd gewiteþ sunne and mona."

109. 32 "He wyrde bideþ, hwonne God wille ðisse worlde ende gewyricean."

Here, too, the dependent clause shows that a miraculous event is meant. As regards "wyrde bidan," cp. Genesis 2570, below in part III.

217. 37 "ða gesawon hie wundorlic wyrd—ðone man lifgendne, ðone ðe hie ær deadne forleton.

Similarly, 221. 11 "Ða gelamp wundorlic wyrd, ðæt se leg ongan slean ongean ðone wind."

As will be seen later on, in poetry wyrd can be used parallel with wundor (cp. the examples from Daniel, below in part III).

The late text of the Epistle of Alexander (ed. O. Cockayne, Narratiunculae Anglice conscriptae [London, 1861]), contains two examples of the use of wyrd which do not give rise to special remarks: 7. 20 f. "Ac swa hit oft gesæleð on þæm selran þingum and on þæm gesundnum þæt seo wyrd and sio hiow hie ofton cyrreð." Lat. "Sed ut aliquid plerumque in secundis rebus fortuna obstrepit" (Cockayne, loc. cit., p. 53). Wyrd = fortuna.

31. 20 ff. "Gif ic þe þone [dæg] gesecge þines feores yþelice þu ða wyrde oncyrrest and his hond befehst. . . ."

Lat. (Cockayne, loc. cit., p. 62): "Sublato eo facile instantia fata mutabis mihique tres irascent[ur] sorores . . . clotos. lachesis. atropos." Evidently strongly under the influence of mythology.

In the Regius Psalter (ed. F. Roeder, Studien zur englischen Philologie [1904]) the word occurs in the meaning of death (cp. below, in poetry): 106. 20 "He nerede hy of wyrde heora." Lat. "Eripuit eos de interitu eorum."

Summing up, it may be said that wyrd occurs in the prose of Alfred's time and after in a much weakened sense and without any associations with a heathen conception of Fate. The general meaning of the word as it occurs in prose is lot, i.e. that which happens to a man in his life. From this general meaning is developed its reference to a special lot: wyrd preceded by a possessive pronoun (þine wyrd, his wyrd), or to a special kind of lot: wyrd preceded by an adjective (gōd, wiðerweard etc. wyrd, ælc wyrd). Sometimes (e.g. Boethius, Ch. IV and V) it may express what happens accidentally in our lot, accidental lot, chance. Further, what happens to saints may be miraculous events. From this meaning a side-development may be traced in the meaning: something miraculous done, (miraculous) deed. Finally, when the sense of lot becomes paled, wyrd may assume the meaning of condition of life, condition.

III

WYRD IN POETRY

Poetry being more archaic in its terminology than prose, expressions may occur which seemingly are still heathen in meaning and which must certainly have been taken over from heathen times. Such an expression is e.g. Elene 1046 "wyrd gescreaf" (cp. Beowulf 2572). But it must be remembered that no genuinely heathen poetry in Anglo-Saxon has come down to us. Either the poems have been Christianized (but to what extent is entirely unknown to us) or they are fully Christian in tone and atmosphere. We can only say that in poetry words are used which originally belonged to heathen terminology and which through representing ideas common to both the old and the new faith have become adapted to Christian terminology.

The idea of Fate and the unalterable course of events in life is one which is common property both of the heathen and of the Christian faith, as A. E. Schönbach (Das Christentum in der altdeutschen Heldendichtung [Graz, 1897], p. 30) pointed out: "Denn an sich sind Blutrache und Schicksalsfügung zwar Ideen, die nicht aus dem Christentum aufsteigen konnten, sie sind jedoch ganz allgemein menschlich und finden sich in allen christlichen Zeiten und Ländern." We saw already in Part I how the idea of wyrd = Fate, Chance, could be made subject to God's Providence in the prose of the ninth century. Just as the idea of wyrd was adapted to Christian conceptions in prose, words and expressions that were originally heathen received a Christian meaning in poetry too. Thus we find, by the side of "wyrd ne gescraf" in Beowulf 2574 the entirely Christian expression (979) "hu him scir Metod scrifan wille."

Both metod and wyrd are originally heathen words, but in the case of metod there is less doubt as to its Christian meaning in Anglo-Saxon than in that of wyrd. Apart from four alliterative passages in Aelfric's Homilies, in which metod is either a weak noun or an adjective (according to B.-T. Supplement, s.v. metod) the word occurs only in poetry. It is now generally assumed that the word as it occurs in our texts has lost its heathen character (see e.g. Klaeber, Anglia, XXXV [1911], 124; B.-T.). Only Kauffmann ("Über den Schicksalsglauben der Germanen," ZDP, L [1926], 394), and Jente (loc. cit., para. 55) hold that the word has sometimes retained its pre-Christian meaning. Now among the places in which Jente would see a heathen meaning of metod are Christ 716, Andreas 1207, 1513, Hymns 63, Daniel 235 (all these places have the expression "meotud meahtum swið," except Dan. 235, "mihtig metodes weard") and how could the word be used in a pre-Christian meaning in poems like these which are fully Christian in tone? There is only one place in which the meaning is doubtful, viz. Waldere I, 19 (ed. F. Norman [London, 1933], p. 37, note).

It will be clear that the word metod could more easily assume a Christian meaning than wyrd, because it was applied directly to God, whereas wyrd was used for something that was subject to God, but so closely connected with God that it cannot surprise us when we find the word now and again used in a function parallel to that of God (cp. J. R. R. Tolkien, "Beowulf: The Monsters and the Critics," PBA, XXXII [1936], 52, note 35).

We shall now examine the use of wyrd in poetry.

> We þæt spell magon,
> wælgrimme wyrd wope cwiðan,
> nales holunge.   (Genesis 995 ff.)

This passage refers to the killing of **Abel** by **Cain**. The words "þæt spell" are specified by "wælgrimme wyrd" = "this dire event." There can therefore be no question here of "unbarmherzige Wyrd" as Philippson (loc. cit., p. 129) translates the words; moreover the poem is entirely Christian in atmosphere.

> þa seo wyrd gewearð, þæt þæt wif geseah
> for Abrahame Ismahel plegan. (2778 f.)

Here the same meaning is to be assumed: the event happened, it came about.

> þe sceal wintrum frod on woruld bringan
> Sarra sunu, soð forð gan
> wyrd æfter þissum wordgemearcum. (2355 ff.)

God announces to Abraham that Sarah will bear him a son. "This miraculous event" will take place according to these terms. Here we find <u>wyrd</u> referring to something like a miracle, just as in some prose texts. Closely connected with this is the passage a few lines further down:

> Ne wille Sarran soð gelyfan
> wordum minum: sceal seo wyrd swa þeah
> forð steallian, swa ic þe æt frymðe gehet. (2390 ff.)

This miraculous event will take place. In neither of these passages is there any reason to see in <u>wyrd</u> anything like Fate: the word refers to a specific event, which will take place.

In the following example, too, we find <u>wyrd</u> referring to a "miraculous" event:

> þæt is mæro wyrd. (1399)

The word refers to the Flood. Just as the word <u>wundur</u> is preceded by the adjective <u>mære</u> in the <u>Psalms</u> (ed. Thorpe [London, 1835], p. 110, 3) we find here "mære wyrd" = "a tremendous event," as B.-T. translate it (s.v. <u>mære</u>).

> Nu sceal heard and steap

> on þam wicum wyrde bidan,
> drihtnes domes, hwonne dogora rim
> woruld gewite.   (2571 ff.)

This is a reference to Lot's wife being changed into a pillar
of salt. Here wyrde is parallel with drihtnes domes, which makes
any association with a pre-Christian fate impossible. The words
express that she will have to stay there like that till the end of
the world. Cp. Crist 1021: "Bidað beofiende beorhte gesceafte,
dryhtnes domes," and Dream of the Rood 50f., also Bl. Hom.,
above p. 135, etc. This meaning is connected with that of wyrd =
"death," only here it is applied to the whole world, the end of
the world. The meaning "death" is supplied by the next example,
from Exodus.

> . . . ne ðær ænig becwom
> herges to hame, ac behindan beleac
> wyrd mid wæge.   (456 ff.)

The reference is to the passing through the Red Sea. B.-T.
mention this example under the heading "fate, fortune, as a personification," which according to them is closely connected with
the meaning "death" (see B.-T., s.v. wyrd, V a).

But as the next lines (458f.) refer to the drowning of the
army:

> þær ær wegas lagon,
> mere modgode, mægen wæs adrenced,

it seems preferable to assume for wyrd the meaning "death."
At any rate, Fate, as a personification, would remind too strongly
of the heathen fate: what the poet means to express was no doubt
wyrd = drihtnes dom.

> wyrda waldend.   (433)

This is a very common way of referring to God. It has very
often been said that God, being superior to Fate, is therefore
called "wyrda waldend," see e.g. Kauffmann (loc. cit., p. 368):
"Desgleichen in der ags. Genesis und den verwandten Dichtungen
ist gott herr des schicksals, das der mensch zu gewärtigen

hat . . . und heisst darum wyrda waldend . . . ." (Cp. also Wardale, loc. cit., p. 30, note 1) and below p.146). Kauffmann and
Miss Wardale start from the idea that the plural wyrda refers
to the three goddesses of Fate, but neither in prose nor in poetry
is there any proof for this contention,[3] because this plural
wyrda occurs elsewhere, as we shall see below, in such a way
that any association with the goddesses of Fate is impossible.
It may suffice to refer to Beowulf 3030, "wyrda ne worda." For
this reason the translation given by B.-T. (IV, 1) is to be preferred: "an event, with the special idea of that which happens
by the determination of Providence or fate," and here the special
idea will be that of Providence. Similarly Andreas 1058; Elene
80.

The same use of wyrd is found in Daniel 132 ("wyrda
gesceaft"), 149 ("wyrda gerynu," cp. Elene 280 "dryhtnes
geryno"), 546 ("wyrda geþingu"). Cp. Elene 1124, 1255, 589,
813, Wanderer 107;

> Wyrd wæs geworden, wundor gecyðed,
> swefn geseðed, susl awunnen,
> dom gedemed, swa ær Daniel cwæð. (652 ff.)

A forecast has come true, so that we may assume the meaning "miraculous event." Moreover the word is parallel with
"wundor gecyðed." Cp. above p. 133–134, and p. 135. Similarly,

> wyrd gewordene and wundor godes. (470)

Again, wyrd is parallel with wundor.

In the three poems discussed above, therefore, we find the
word wyrd used in the meaning of "event," sometimes with direct reference to a "miraculous event," also referring to the
end of a person or of the world, while all through Anglo-Saxon
poetry the term "wyrda Waldend" is found in which wyrda, the
plural, is used with reference to the events as determined by
Providence. These uses are essentially the same as those found
for the prose of the ninth century. There is no justification in
these texts for the assumption that wyrd was still associated with
a pre-Christian conception.

We now pass on to the group of religion poems from the
eighth century.

WYRD IN ANGLO-SAXON PROSE AND POETRY

Apart from the phrase "wyrda Waldend" (Andreas 1056),
already discussed above, wyrd occurs in Andreas in the following passages:

> Hie seo wyrd beswac,
> forleolc ond forlærde.   (613 f.)

Here seo wyrd expresses "the events as they happened."
In how far the word still had a fatalistic connotation is, of course,
impossible to decide, but in connection with the text and its Christian atmosphere and also with the use of wyrd in the other places
of the poem, it is very doubtful that wyrd ought to be written with
a capital, as e.g. Grein does in his Bibliothek der ags. Poesie:
it is not used as a personification.

> Hwæt frinest ðu me, frea leofesta,
> wordum wrætlicum ond þe wyrda gehwære
> þurh snyttra cræft soð oncnawest? (629 ff.)

Here, too, the meaning is "events," as Krapp translates it
in the Glossary to his edition (Boston, 1906).

> Is seo wyrd mid eow
> open, orgete, magan eagum nu
> geseon sigores god, swegles agend.   (758 ff.)

From the context it appears that "seo wyrd" here refers to
"a miraculous event." Krapp translates "event," also B.-T.

> Hwæt! ic hwile nu haliges lare,
> leoðgiddinga lof þæs þe worhte,
> wordum wemde, wyrd undyrne,
> ofer min gemet.   (1479 ff.)

The reference is here to miracles done, so that the meaning seems to be "miraculous deeds." Krapp translates event,
but adds "the word seems to bear reference to a plural idea, so
to speak collective." This is true: wyrd refers to the miraculous events that have been told of the man, so that it approaches
the meaning of a collective word ("series of miraculous deeds").

A similar use of wyrd is found in the Fates of the Apostles 42, "Huru wide wearð wurd undyrne," where it refers to the fame of Bartholameus which became widely known, his miraculous deeds (cp. above p. 134, wyrd in Dialogues).

> Us seo wyrd scyðeð
> heard ond hetegrim: þæt is her swa cuð! (1561 f.)

Andreas is in fetters and a storm rages. One of the men says that it is not right to keep Andreas fettered. "These miraculous happenings," hard and cruel, harm us (1563 f.) and then he goes on to say that it is much better to release Andreas. Wyrd here refers to the storm and the binding of Andreas connected with it. Just as in Genesis 996 "wælgrimme wyrd" referred to the killing of Abel, so here "wyrd heard ond hetegrim" refers to the storm and the binding of Andreas.

A miraculous event is also expressed by wyrd in Christ 81.

> . . . ne we þære wyrde wenan þurfon
> toweard in tide.

The reference is to the Immaculate Conception: such a "miraculous event" we cannot expect any more.

In Juliana the word occurs twice:

> . . . wyrd ne ful cuþe
> freondrædenne hu heo from hogde,
> geong on gæste.   (33 ff.)

Heliseus did not yet fully know that Juliana despised his affection, that this would be part of his lot. Wyrd here expresses lot. B.-T. (s.v. wyrd) translate: "He did not fully know this circumstance, how her heart was turned from loving him," but the meaning "circumstance" is rather too vague for the word in a poem of the eighth century. W. Strunk (in the Glossary to his edition [Boston, 1904]) gives "event, situation," neither of which seems to do full justice to wyrd. As the word is used here, there is still a connotation of something outside human control, which is rendered by the word lot. It is this meaning, too, which should be assumed for the other example from Juliana:

Ongan þa hreowcearig
siðfæt seofian, sar cwanian,
wyrd wanian, wordum mælde.   (536 ff.)

B.-T. register this place under their heading V: "What happens to a person, fate, fortune, lot, condition." Strunk translates
"fate," which had better be avoided by taking the word lot: she
bewails her lot.

Apart from the places mentioned above (p. 140), in which
wyrda refers to "events," the word occurs in Elene in six other
passages:

. . . þegn oðerne þyslic cuþan
ymb swa dygle wyrd.   (540 f.)

"Never yet did we hear anybody speak about such miraculous
events, concealed from our knowledge." From the context it is
clear that this is meant. Similarly:

ymb þa mæran wyrd,   (1063)

where the reference is to the nails through Christ's hands and
feet; cp. 1070 wundorwyrd; also

. . . bæd him engla weard
geopenigean uncuðe wyrd
niwan on nearwe.   (1100 ff.)

Here, too, the reference is to a wonder, a miraculous event. In
the following instance wyrd expresses a grievous event:

. . . ond wæs Iudeum gnornsorga mæst,
werum wansæligum wyrda laðost.   (976 f.)

This refers to ll. 972 f.:

þæt Cristes rod,
fyrn foldan begræfen, funden wære.

Therefore the translation in B.-T. does not seem to be quite
right: "most grievous of fates." That the Cross is buried, is

143

not a fate, but an event. In this context it seems to mean "grievous event."

> . . . ne magon ge þa wyrd bemiðan,
> bedyrnan þa deopan mihte.　　(583 f.)

Elene says that they cannot avoid this lot; that they have to
go to hell. So wyrd expresses "lot."

With Elene 977 may be compared the two instances of wyrd
in the Dream of the Rood:

> Feala ic on þam beorge gebiden hæfde
> wraðra wyrda.

The addition of the adjective and the lines that follow make
it clear that wyrda here means "terrible events." Similarly
73 f.:

> þa us man fyllan ongan
> ealle to eorðan; þæt wæs egeslic wyrd!

The direct reference to the felling of the tree makes the
translation "that was a terrible event" preferable to "that was
a terrible fate." Bruce Dickens and Alan S. C. Ross in the Glossary to their edition (London, 1934) t ranslate in both cases "experience." But, like the translations "circumstance, situation"
mentioned above for Juliana 33, this wanders too far from the
idea represented by wyrd, viz. "event that must happen, that
forms part of one's lot." Cp. Ruin 1, "wyrde gebræcon" = "the
terrible events of its lot (events > lot)."

> Huru wyrd gescreaf,
> þæt he swa geleaffull ond swa leof gode
> in woruldrice weorðan sceolde,
> Criste gecweme: þæt gecyðed wearð. . . .　　(1046 ff.)

The expression "wyrd gescreaf" illustrates very clearly
how wyrd was adapted to Christian terminology. Originally it
must have been a heathen expression, just as e.g. wyrd itself
and metod. But at the time when the Anglo-Saxon religious poems
were written, in the seventh and eighth century, no heathen as-

sociations will have been connected with this expression, certainly not in these entirely Christian poems. Wyrd has here lost its original meaning and the whole expression simply means,"it was ordained." Consequently, because in the seventh and eighth century poems it is God who ordains the course of events, it could happen that God took the place of wyrd in this expression, as e.g. already in Beowulf 106, "siþðan him Scyppend forscrifen hæfde," and Beowulf 979, "hu him scir Metod scrifan wille" (for other examples see B.-T. s.v. scrifan). Here we see for the first time how wyrd and God come to be used in parallel functions (other examples below). From this point of view it is not right to say, as Ehrismann (loc. cit., p. 237) does, that God and Wyrd are ethical contrasts. This does not hold good for the time in which the extant religious poems were written down. God and wyrd necessarily become parallel, as soon as wyrd is weakened in sense, as in the expression "wyrd gescreaf," and it is not at all strange that in one and the same poem both wyrd and God are used with scrifan, e.g. in Beowulf 106 and 979 by the side of 2574, "swa him wyrd ne gescraf hreð æt hilde."

As regards the last example Kauffmann (loc. cit., p. 400) remarks: "Von den römischen parzen gieng er [the Beowulf-poet] dagegen aus, wenn er die tätigkeit des schreibens sogar der Wyrd zumutete. Ein ags. poet der christlichen epoche durfte es also wagen, wyrd und metod mit ein und derselben, einem latinismus zu verdankende amtshandlung zu betrauen und mit literarischen erbgut auf so seltsame art zu wuchern, dass altgerm. metod-wyrd und lat. scribere sich zusammenfanden." This combination of wyrd-metod-scrifan (scribere) is indeed very curious, when one starts, as Kauffmann does, from the mythological figure of Wyrd the goddess of Fate, but it is quite natural when one bears in mind how wyrd is actually used in the Anglo-Saxon texts as we have them. Cp. Juliana 726 ff. (quoted by Kauffmann), where "seo þrynis scrifeð."

For the use of wyrd in Guthlac (1030; 1319) see below.

We now come to the Gnomic Verses in the Cotton and the Exeter MSS. It is generally assumed that these verses originally date from pre-Christian days and that Christian references were inserted later on by a Christian poet. A. Brandl (H. Paul, Grundriss der germanischen Philologie, II [1901], 960) says of the verses in the Cotton MS: "Im ganzen Gedicht sind ersichtlich zweierlei Elemente zusammengeflossen: ein heidnisch-höfischer

Kern und christlich-fromme Zutaten eines Überarbeiters, der sich vor dem inneren Widerspruch nicht scheute eine Übersicht der Natur- und Menschenordnung mit einer Klage über allgemeine Unordnung im irdischen Jammertal abzurunden." However this may be, we have here only to do with the poem as it stands and it will be clear that any direct allusion to the goddess <u>Wyrd</u> by the side of the Christian additions is impossible: if the poet who inserted or made the additions still thought of <u>wyrd</u> only as a goddess of Fate, he would have struck out the word. If the insertion therefore stands by the side of <u>wyrd</u>, the adapter must have felt <u>wyrd</u> as weakened in sense.

The word occurs in the beginning of the verses in the Cotton MS. in this passage:

> Wind byð on lyfte swiftust,
> þunar byð þragum hludast.   þrymmas syndan Cristes myccle,
> wyrd byd swiðost.

Apart from what has been said above, there is another reason why <u>wyrd</u> must have had the more weakened sense of later times for the adapter: if Fate were meant here, it would appear that Fate is even stronger than the powers of Christ. This is the view taken by Miss Wardale (loc. cit., p. 23), as her translation shows, but it is highly improbable. The adapter probably read in the word: "However great the powers of Christ may be, the order of events as ordained by God's Providence is mightiest." At the same time it may be admitted that, if the words "wyrd byð swiðost" actually belonged to the poem in its pre-Christian form, they must have referred to Fate.

The combination of <u>wyrd</u> and a form of the adjective <u>swiþ</u> occurs elsewhere, e.g. in the homiletic addition to the <u>Seafarer</u> and in <u>The Ruin</u>. <u>Seafarer</u> 115: "Wyrd biþ swiþre, / Meotud meahtigra." This is another example of how <u>God</u> and <u>Wyrd</u> occur in parallel positions. In this unequivocally Christian addition to the <u>Seafarer</u>, <u>wyrd</u> can only express "the order of events as ordained by God," so that <u>meotud</u> can be used as a variant. <u>Ruin</u> 25: "Oþ þæt þæt onwende wyrd seo swiþe."

As this is probably not a very early poem, and as <u>wyrde</u> in line 1 may be considered as expressing "terrible events as part of its lot," there is no reason to assume that here the word is used in a pre-Christian sense, although it seems certain that the expression itself dates from heathen times (cp. Salomon and Saturn 442, "wyrd seo swiðe").[4] It is here used archaically and has a collective meaning: "the powerful (unalterable) course of events."

In the Gnomic Verses of the Exeter MS. the word occurs in the plural:

God us ece biþ:
ne wendað hine wyrda ne hine wiht dreceþ,
adl ne yldo ælmihtigne.

The meaning is the usual one for the plural, viz. the events (as they happen or have to happen) of our lot cannot change Him; our lot depends on Him.

Before discussing the occurrences of wyrd in the Wanderer, it is necessary to explain our conception of the poem. The two main questions arising in connection with this poem are: Does it form a unity? Is it essentially heathen, with Christian additions? As to the first question, that of the unity of the poem, it was at one time supposed by Boer (ZDP, XXXV [1902], 1 ff.) that several scribes had been at work on the poem. This theory, dating from a time when the interpolation theory was still in vogue, has now been abandoned. All the more remarkable, therefore, that Miss Wardale (p. 59) should seem to return to it. On one point, however, opinions still differ: it is assumed by many that some lines at the beginning and the last five are additions made by a Christian scribe. Miss Wardale (p. 58), e.g. says: "One is at once struck with the difference in spirit between the opening lines and final passages which are clearly Christian, and the rest which is essentially heathen in its unrelieved gloom and its belief in fate, in spite of a Christian term interpolated here and there." Let us examine the five opening lines and the final passage. To me the general idea expressed by these lines seems to be that the solitary one, the exile, lives to see grace, Mercy of God, although he has to undergo all kinds of troubles. He cannot avoid these troubles, for his lot is appointed by God.

I take gebidan (l. 1) in the same sense as that of Beowulf 1060.

Fela sceal gebidan

> leofes ond laþes se þe longe her
> on ðyssum windagum worolde bruceð (cp. also 1386 f.).

These lines really express the same idea as Wanderer 1–5. The difficulty is in aræd, l. 5. Sweet (Anglo-Saxon Reader) gives "inexorable," which is taken over by Miss Wardale in the translation of these lines. B.-T. translate "resolute" (with a question-mark). But when we think of the meaning of the passage, it seems obvious to assume aræd to be the past-participle of arædan "to appoint, determine": man's lot is determined. This view is also taken by Schücking in the Glossary to his Kleines ags. Dichter-buch, Sedgefield in his Anglo-Saxon Book of Verse and Prose, and by Klaeber, Anglia Beiblatt, XL (1930), 30.

Now in the final passage the words "are gebideð" of the first line are taken up again in l. 114. "Wel bið þam þe him are seceð" and the last line (115) "frofre to Fæder on heofonum, þær us eall seo fæstnung stondeð" seems to point back to ll. 108–110:

> Her bið feoh læne, her bið freond læne,
> her bið monn læne, her bið mæg læne:
> eall þis eorþan gesteall idel weorþeð.

The lines 112–115 seem to contain an admonition (through their special reference to the Wanderer) to those who are inclined to lose faith owing to accumulation of hardships. Indeed, the whole poem seems to me to express that, in spite of misfortunes and hardships, one should not lose hope, but remain faithful to God: in Heaven one finds the security one cannot find on earth.

Another objection made by Miss Wardale (p. 58) is that "the beginning lines do not agree with what follows in another way. They speak of the hardships endured by one who is long tossed about on a stormy sea, while the rest of the poem is on the sorrows of exile and solitude. It is true that a sea journey is mentioned, but not as one of the causes of suffering, and it is not dwelt upon." But in the opening lines the sea journey is not mentioned as one of the causes of suffering either. It is meant as a kind of background, to stress the loneliness of the Wanderer. The introduction sets the atmosphere. For that reason there are two more references to the sea in the poem, just to keep up the atmosphere created by the background. The first describes how

the Wanderer after the death of his chief went across the sea
(ll. 23, 24) in search of some new chief. Further, in ll. 46–
48 the poet describes how the "wineleas guma" feels the pain
of remembering happier times and how he sees before him
the grey waves, sea birds that are bathing with outspread wings
(ll. 46–48). Thus the impression of the atmosphere is now and
then strengthened by references to the loneliness of life at sea.

As regards the second question, that of the supposedly
heathen or Christian character of the poem, it may first be
pointed out that its general theme is the transitoriness of life
and of the world and the insignificance of time (ll. 57 ff., especially ll. 108–110 with their stressing of the idea læne).
These themes are typical of the Christian poem and the unrelieved gloom of the poem, to which Miss Wardale refers, is certainly not "essentially heathen," but purely Christian.

As the use of wyrd is closely connected with this question,
we shall first examine how the word is used in the Wanderer.

> Wyrd biỗ ful aræd. (5)

This passage has already been explained above. Man's
wyrd = "his lot is determined." These words clinch the meaning of the opening lines: in spite of misfortunes, man will often
live to see the grace of God; he himself cannot alter his lot, it
is determined by God. No heathen sentiment is expressed in
this line (see below, p. 150 note). Wyrd (= his wyrd) is here used
in the same meaning as e.g. in Juliana 33 and 538 (see above).

> Ne mæg werigmod wyrde wiỗstondan
> ne se hreo hyge helpe gefremman. (15–16)

This passage is a variation on the same theme as is expressed
in l. 5: when a man is weary in spirit, he cannot resist his lot and
the disturbed mind cannot give help. The last line varies the preceding, so that "helpe gefremman" is parallel with "wyrde
wiỗstondan."

> eorlas fornomon æsca þryþe,
> wæpen wælgifru, wyrd seo mære. (100–101)

"Wyrd seo mære" here expresses "the glorious lot of dying on the battle-field." This use differs, therefore, from "mæro wyrd" in <u>Genesis</u> 1399 and <u>Elene</u> 1064 (see above), where it referred to a miraculous event.

> onwendeð wyrda gesceaft weoruld under heofonum. (107)

See above p. 135 for similar expressions with <u>wyrda</u>. Miss Wardale (p. 30, note 1) says that the use of the plural suggests an early date, at which the older belief had not quite died out. But we know now from the preceding that this cannot be true at all. Miss Wardale seems to accept only one meaning of <u>wyrd</u>, viz. a heathen meaning. The preceding pages have already shown that this view is entirely incompatible with the use of <u>wyrd</u> in the Christian poetry of the seventh and eighth centuries. "Wyrda gesceaft" means the course of events as ordained by God and also occurs in an undoubtedly Christian poem, <u>Daniel</u> 132.

Thus we see that <u>wyrd</u> is not used in a pre-Christian sense in the <u>Wanderer</u>. So neither of the two reasons assigned by Miss Wardale for calling the bulk of the poem "essentially heathen" in its unrelieved gloom and its belief in Fate holds good. Our general conclusion then as regards the sentiment and the unity of this poem is that it undoubtedly forms a unity as it stands and that the tone and the subject of the poem are purely Christian.[5] The use of <u>wyrd</u> does not differ from that in the other poetry of the seventh and eighth centuries. If there are no strong reasons for rejecting parts of poems as later additions (e.g. the homiletic addition to the <u>Seafarer</u>), we had better judge the poems as they stand and there is no justification at all for assuming that "any Christian touches which appear in either [<u>Wanderer</u> and <u>Seafarer</u>] are quite out of character and must be looked upon as later insertions, probably due to the scribe who added the continuation of the <u>Seafarer</u>" (Wardale, loc. cit., p. 61).

Our view of the unity of the poem corresponds to a large extent with that of Lawrence, <u>JEGP</u>, IV [1902], 460 ff.), except that he still sees "a mingling of Christian and heathen material" in the <u>Wanderer</u>, especially in l. 5, of which he says that it expresses a pagan sentiment.

Finally, I come to <u>Beowulf</u> and here I find myself, as will be seen, in disagreement with Prof. Klaeber. However I take

courage from the challenge contained in his own words at the
end of the Introduction to his edition (3rd ed. [Boston, 1936],
p. cxx): "It is hoped that [the student] will feel encouraged to
form his own judgement as occasion arises— 'nullius addictus
iurare in verba magistri.'"

Although there are clear references to heathen practices
in Beowulf, besides many supernatural elements associated
with heathendom, it is generally admitted that the tone of the
poem is Christian, as Klaeber remarks (loc. cit., p. xlix):
"We almost seem to move in normal Christian surroundings."
It is true, that these Christian passages have now and again
been considered as interpolations, but the most generally accepted view is that expressed by Chambers (Beowulf: An Introduction [Cambridge, 1932], p. 128): "We are justified in regarding the poem as homogeneous: as a production of the Germanic
world enlightened by the new faith" (see also pp. 488 f. and cp.
Tolkien, pp. 20 f.).

The date usually assigned to Beowulf, viz. the beginning of
the eighth century (see Klaeber, pp. xciv and cxiii; cp. p. cxxiii)
does not lead us to expect a use of wyrd greatly different from
that in the group of religious poems of the seventh and eighth
centuries discussed above. The word occurs twelve times in
Beowulf, eleven times in the singular (Klaeber "fate, destiny")
and once in the plural (Klaeber "event, fact").

Gæð a wyrd swa hio scel. (455)

These words occur at the end of Beowulf's speech to
Hrothgar, after he has arrived to fight Grendel. In this speech
Beowulf has already alluded to God in a Christian way: 440 f.
"Ðær gelyfan sceal / Dryhtnes dome se þe hine deað nimeð."

For that reason alone it would already be improbable that
Beowulf should suddenly refer to a heathen wyrd, or that the
word should here be used with heathen associations. Even if
these words actually form part of a heathen proverbial saying,
for which we have no proof, the word wyrd will have been used
here in the weakened sense of "events of life," so that the line
would mean: "The events of our lot go as they must go (as ordained by God's Providence)." As regards the combination
wyrd and "going," cp. Genesis 2355; as to the meaning of wyrd,
cp. Andreas 613.

Hoops (Kommentar zum Beowulf [Heidelberg, 1932], p. 71) remarks to this passage: "Der altgermanische Schicksalsglaube tritt im Beowulf trotz der im übrigen christlichen Grundfärbung der Weltanschauung des Dichters noch an zahlreichen Stellen zutage." Hoops starts from the idea that wyrd is still a heathen conception. As we shall see from the discussion of the other occurrences of wyrd in Beowulf, this is not the case, any more than in the rest of Anglo-Saxon poetry. What comes out in Beowulf is not the Old-Germanic belief in Fate, but a Christian resignation to the inevitability of the course of events as they are ordained by God's Providence.

In the following four examples wyrd represents the meaning "death" (< the destined end).

> Hie wyrd forsweop
> on Grendles gryre. God eaþe mæg
> þone dolsceaðan dæda getwæfan.   (477)

Here, too, we find wyrd in the immediate neighborhood of a Christian passage. As Hoops (loc. cit., p. 73) remarks, "dæda getwæfan" is a kenning for "to kill." In ll. 477 f. the same idea is expressed as in ll. 478 f. So wyrd here means "death." Similarly 2814 and cp. 1205, "hyne wyrd fornam."

> Him wæs geomorsefa,
> wæfre ond wælfus, wyrd ungemete neah,
> se ðone gomelan gretan sceolde,
> secean sawle hord, sundur gedælan
> lif wið lice.   (2419 ff.)

Beowulf's heart is full of gloomy forebodings of his approaching death ("wyrd ungemete neah"). A similar use of wyrd is found in Guthlac 1319: "He ða wyrd ne mað, fæges forðsið."

The word fæge also belongs to the originally heathen words which were adapted to Christianity: "doomed (by God) to die." The word is very common to Christian poetry (see B.-T. s.v. fæge). Another example of wyrd "death" is given by B.-T. s.v. wyrd, Va.

Another shade of meaning is illustrated by the following three passages:

> Ne wæs þæt wyrd þa gen,
> þæt he ma moste manna cynnes
> ðicgean ofer þa niht.   (734)

Klaeber's translation (in the Glossary to his ed.) is right:
"it was not destined." Wyrd expresses here, that it did not fall
to his lot. In prose it would have been: "ne was þæt his wyrd"
(cp. other examples with wyrd + possessive pron. above. Similarly:

> . . . swa he hyra ma wolde
> nefne him witig God wyrd forstode
> ond ðæs mannes mod. Meotud eallum weold
> gumena cynnes, swa he nu git deð.   (1055 ff.)

Both Klaeber (note to 1056) and Hoops (loc. cit., p. 131) read
in this passage that God is superior to Fate, because He can
control Fate. Hoops adds, however, "Der Ausdruck wyrd hat
allerdings hier mehr appellative als persönliche Geltung," and
also Klaeber ("Introduction," p. xlix, note 2) states that in general wyrd is not felt to be a personal being. But there is here
no question of a heathen idea of Fate, whether a person or not.
As in the preceding example we may complete wyrd by adding
the possessive pronoun and then the sense is: God withstands
Grendel's lot, i.e. it was not given him, it did not fall to his lot.
"God (his) wyrd forstode" is, therefore, synonymous with: "ne
wæs þæt his wyrd þa gen" (l. 734).

> Wyrd ne cuþon,
> geosceaft grimme, swa hit agangen wearð
> eorla manegum. . . .   (1233 ff.)

With this example may be compared Juliana 33, "wyrd ne
ful cuþe." Here, as there, the word expresses "lot." Again
the possessive pronoun may be added in thought (they did not
know their lot). Compare "geosceaft grimme" (or, with the
MS. and B.-T. Supp. s.v. geosceaft: grimne) with Genesis 996
"wælgrimme wyrd."

In the following three passages wyrd is somehow connected
with the functions of God.

Wyrd oft nereð
unfægne eorl, þonne his ellen deah.   (572 f.)

It has already been pointed out how wyrd and God could come
to be used in parallel functions. This passage is another illustration of this fact. Moreover, a few lines before the poet speaks of
"beorht beacen Godes" (l. 570), which makes it difficult to see
in wyrd an expression for a heathen conception of Fate. Now the
fact remains that the above passage must have been a very old
saying, as Klaeber points out in his note to this passage: "A proverbial saying (Fortune favors the brave)." Hoops (loc. cit., p.
82) compares Lat. "Fortes fortuna adiuvat." It must, however,
be pointed out that, as in the case of Beowulf 455, "Gæð a wyrd
swa hio scel," which may also have been a proverbial saying,
the idea expressed by ll. 572 f. is both heathen and Christian.
Thus it came to survive in a Christian poem, but this does not
mean that wyrd here still has any pre-Christian associations.
The meaning may be rendered in this way: "(the lot as ordained
by) God often saves him who is not doomed, when his courage
avails."

Both Klaeber and Hoops point out that very often "God is
substituted for fate," (cp. Klaeber, Anglia, XXXVI [1912], 174
and note 3); "Introduction" to ed., p. xlix), but the passages
which they mention as illustrations of this statement are just
ordinary Christian passages (ll. 669 f., 1270 ff., 1552 ff.; 2291
ff., cp. also 696 ff.). Both Klaeber and Hoops start from a
heathen conception of wyrd. As has been explained above the
juxtaposition of wyrd and God is a logical result of the weakening of the sense of wyrd. Klaeber (Anglia, p. 174, note 1) draws
attention to Andreas 459 f.:

. . . þæt næfre forlæteð lifgende god
eorl on eorðan, gif his ellen deah.

Klaeber calls this passage "das christliche gegenstück zu
B. 572 f.," but there is hardly any difference between these two
passages, with our conception of wyrd; they are both equally
Christian. A similar use of wyrd may be seen in Beowulf 2574,
"swa him wyrd ne gescraf."

> swa unc wyrd geteoð,
> Metod manna gehwæs.   (2526 f.)

Here, as in Seafarer 115, wyrd and Metod actually occur
side by side in one passage. The meaning is practically: "as
God assigns us, Metod of all men"; wyrd and Metod are here
used synonymously. There is therefore no reason to alter the
punctuation, as Grein and B.-T. do, who take wyrd as the object
of geteon, although this too makes good sense (then wyrd would
be "lot").

With this use of wyrd may be compared Guthlac 1030:

> Wyrd ne meahte
> in fægum leng feorg gehealdan,
> deore frætwe, þonne him gedemed wæs.

This passage seems to form a transition to the use of wyrd
as a synonym of God. In Guthlac 1030, wyrd is still something
different from God. As the text is purely Christian, this must
be considered as an archaic use of wyrd, in which the word is
no longer felt as something separate in the sentence (cp. "wyrd
gescraf"), but the sense of the passage is that he could not live
longer than had been determined for him by God. The word
wyrd has here too lost its heathen associations. The juxtaposition of wyrd and God became possible via such an archaic use
of wyrd as we see here.

Finally, wyrd occurs in the plural in l. 3030 in the formula
"wyrda ne worda." The word expresses events (as Klaeber also
translates it) and it is not a very old meaning preserved in this
formula, as Hoops (loc. cit., p. 314) considers it, but the common meaning of wyrd in the plural in the seventh century and
later.

IV

The general development of meaning of wyrd is then something like this: wyrd, originally the name for the power that
ruled men's lives, the blind and hostile Fate, and at one time
a proper name for the goddess of Fate, came to be used for the
events as they happened according to Fate. In the period of
transition from the heathen to the Christian belief and also after

that time the word was used by the astrologers with reference
to the course of men's lives as predetermined by the stars (see
Blickling Homilies, I, 110–114) and by those who believed that
this world was governed by chance. Then the word continued
to be used in the Christian texts with reference to the lot as ordained by God's Providence, so that it came to mean lot, both
in the general sense and in the special sense of one man's lot
("þine wyrd") and kind of lot ("wiðerwearde wyrd," "god wyrd").
From this the word developed the meaning of events (in a collective sense in the singular, but also in the plural, e.g. "wyrda
Waldend," "wyrda gesceaft"), but often with reference to a special
kind of event in man's life, a miraculous, wondrous event, or a
terrible, grievous event. In the prose of the ninth century wyrd
was also used for the miraculous deeds of saints and priests.
From the general sense of lot may be traced the development
of meaning represented by wyrd = "end of the world" ("wyrde
gebidan"; wyrd = "Drihtnes dom") or the end of a person's life =
"death."

Thus the originally heathen word passed into Christian
terminology and was adapted to Christian ideas. Here lies the
cause of the difference in conceptions as regards the meaning
of wyrd, to which I referred in my introduction: the idea originally represented by wyrd was in the Christian period no longer in
accordance with the actual meaning of the word as used in the
texts. It has not always been fully taken into account that the
heathen meaning of wyrd had lost much of its mythological value
to the Anglo-Saxons of the Christian period. Yet this made it
possible for wyrd to pass from heathen into Christian times and
to form a bridge between the old and the new creed: the idea of
unalterability of the events of our life, at one time expressed by
the heathen word wyrd, is also common to the Christian faith,
so that wyrd then expresses the course of events as ordained
by God's Providence.

This development of the word, which may be seen in the
texts of the seventh and eighth centuries, was philosophically
established in Alfred's translation of Boethius, De consolatione
Philisophiae, where it is shown how wyrd is made subject to
God's Providence and thus becomes really a Christian idea.

If the conception of wyrd expounded in the above pages should
be plausible, there is nothing strange in the occasional juxtaposition of wyrd and God in the poetical texts of the seventh and

eighth centuries. Just as in Beowulf 734 "Ne wæs þæt wyrd þa gen" simply expresses "it was not destined," the expression "wyrd gescreaf" in Elene 1046 shows a weakening of the sense of wyrd from "Fate decreed" into "it was decreed." Now as it was considered in those days that it was God who decreed men's lives, it is quite natural that by the side of "wyrd gescreaf" we find "hu him scir Metod scrifan wille" (Beowulf 979) or "siþðan him Scyppend forscrifen hæfde"(Beowulf 106). In this way God and wyrd are no longer ethical contrasts, but the functions of God and wyrd become parallel; but this is only possible at a time when wyrd had no longer any heathen associations.

Further, it may be pointed out that the idea of wyrd was a powerful instrument in the conversion of the Anglo-Saxons, who always had a strong sense of the unalterability of things and the transitoriness of earthly life. Is this perhaps due to the many wars they had to fight before their society was consolidated? The Anglo-Saxons were converted to a large extent by means of a stressing of the transitoriness of life and the consequent feeling of resignation to what is inevitable (as well as by stories about miracles, see e.g. Gregory's Dialogues). Gordon's view, therefore, of Beowulf as "an elegy on the common Old English theme lif islæne" (suggested in his edition of Maldon [London, 1937], p. 24, note 1; cp. also Wanderer 108–110) seems very attractive; cp. also Tolkien, loc. cit., pp. 23, 33. Here, too, it seems to me, lies the explanation for the elegiac spirit in Anglo-Saxon literature, which Dame Bertha S. Phillpotts (loc. cit., p. 23) explains "as a result of the clash between the pagan philosophy of life and the new doctrine, so readily accepted." In connection with the preceding it seems doubtful that there was much of a clash between the pagan and the Christian outlook on life, for such a powerful idea as wyrd formed as important a factor in the Christian belief as it did in the heathen faith.

NOTES

1 Fatalism is common in other literatures as well, e.g. in Greek, Russian and Indian heroic legends; see Sidhanta, The Heroic Age of India (London, 1929), pp. 83 f.

2 In many cases, however, I do not agree with Wolf's explanation of passages.

3 See, however, Corpus Glossaries s.v. <u>Parcae</u>, wyrde.

4 As Saturn is a heathen who is going to be converted by Salomon, it is to be expected that in this tenth-century poem the word <u>wyrd</u> actually refers to the heathen goddess of Fate. This poem will not be discussed here, owing to its intentional use of <u>wyrd</u> in a pre-Christian meaning. I may only point out that the plural <u>wyrda</u> occurs in it in the usual meaning of events (310, 332, 438).

5 Miss Wardale's discussion of <u>Wanderer</u> 5b, "wyrd biδ ful aræd"(p. 59, note 1) shows typically how one conjecture leads to another, if one works with the interpolation theory: "It may be suggested that the second half of verse 5 . . . must belong to the original poem. The sentiment is purely heathen and the scribe's object in his addition was to introduce some Christian element. The poem cannot, however, have begun in the middle of a line. The scribe may have worked over an existing passage, leaving, in a surprising way, this definitely heathen half-line."

COLOUR WORDS IN ANGLO-SAXON

L. D. Lerner

The aim of this article is to suggest a more exact meaning
for some of the Anglo-Saxon colour words than those given in
most dictionaries and translations. No satisfactory explanation
of the colour vocabulary of Anglo-Saxon, or indeed of most early
European languages, has yet been advanced; and an adequate
theory of their meanings would have to compare the development
of cognate words in all European languages. The present aim
is more modest; and the discussion is confined to the colour
words of Anglo-Saxon and the significance of some of the contexts where they occur.

Colour vision is one of the most controversial topics in
modern psychology, and no adequate account of it can be given
with which many psychologists would not disagree. The one
essential fact for our purposes, however, would probably be
disputed by none: that the complex sensation known as "colour"
is made up of four different sensations. These are hue, which
is determined by wave-length; admixture with white, which
makes a colour pale or intense; admixture with black, which
makes it dark or intense; and brightness, determined by the
amount of light falling on or emanating from it. The first three
can be conveniently represented diagrammatically by a double
pyramid. The base represents all hues at their most intense:
as they mingle with one another they tend towards the grey of
the centre. Moving up towards a white apex, we find each hue
becoming paler and at the same time more like its neighbor;
moving down towards a black apex we find them becoming
darker and more alike. Brightness is not represented on the
pyramid; for the same object can appear bright at one moment,
dull at another.

Reprinted from the Modern Language Review, Vol. 46 (1951), pp. 246−9,
by permission of the Modern Humanities Research Association and of
the Editors and the author.

Modern colour words refer almost exclusively to hue, and the other qualities have to be indicated by adverbs placed before them: dark green, pale lemon yellow, brilliant white light, etc. As a result, we tend to assume that hue and colour are identical, though a moment's thought will show that the sensation of pale lemon yellow is very different from that of bright lemon yellow. This specialization of our colour vocabulary has enabled us to achieve remarkable precision when referring to hue, and artists and dress designers can often draw distinctions at least as fine as those between burgundy, plum and claret. It has, however, rather blunted our perception of the other elements of colour sensation. We tend not to realize the great similarity between a very pale yellow and a very pale green, hues which would be very different if more intense; and, more important, we tend not to notice that different hues of a similar brightness may give very similar sensations. A piece of green corduroy, well rubbed and caught by the sun at the right angle, will be almost indistinguishable from a similar piece of yellow, orange or even red material. (They are all, in fact, <u>fealu</u>.)

In this fact may lie the clue to the understanding of Anglo-Saxon colour words. If this concentration on hue is a comparatively modern tendency, we should hardly be surprised to find earlier languages using words which describe the whole complex sensation of colour. When four Latin words are translated in a dictionary as "a dark murky hue," "chestnut colour," "brown with a touch of gold," "something between red and black" (<u>fuscus</u>, <u>spadix</u>, <u>fulvus</u>, <u>rubidus</u>) and no word is found for "brown," it is clear that our words do not describe the same things as the Romans'. It is not necessary to suggest, as has been done of Homer, that they were colour-blind. It is we who are colour-blind. They were hue-blind.

A study of Anglo-Saxon colour words in their contexts will show, I think, that the authors were much more interested in brightness than we are. The most valuable passage is probably the <u>Phoenix</u>, ll. 291–313, which describes the appearance of the bird. It has almost as many references to brightness and shining as to "colour."

> ond þæt nebb lixeð
> swa glæs oððe gim   (ll. 299–300)
> geaflas scyne   (l. 300)

>   is seo eaggebyrd
>   stearc ond hiwe stane gelicast
>   gladum gimme   (ll. 301–3)

(This passage, incidentally, shows that whatever the meaning of
hiw it is not "hue.")

>   beaga beorhtast   (1. 306)
>   scir ond scyne   (1. 308)

In Beowulf, too, passages such as the description of the monster's
lake-dwelling have an impression of gleaming lights and lowering
shadows rather than of reds, yellows or greens.

This importance of brightness helps to explain why our
modern words for hues cannot adequately translate Old English
colour words. The following are a few of the most puzzling of
these:

(i) brun is used of a helmet, a sword-edge, the waves of the
sea, the feathers of the Phoenix and an Ethiopian (brune leode).
It obviously cannot mean brown: the only thing in common between
these objects is that they flash in the sunlight. Brun would seem
to indicate brilliance; and so of course to be particularly applicable to metals.

The application to the skin of an Ethiopian suggests that the
meaning may have been more complicated. The skin of a Negro
may shine, and this quality is perhaps as notable as its dark hue:
yet if brun was beginning to be applied to dark hues in preference
to light, we should understand better the reference to night as
brunwann in Andreas, 1. 1306. The blackness of night sometimes
gives, by its very intensity, the impression of brightness; and
there is no need to imagine that brun has yet lost its primary
signification, or has gone very far towards its modern meaning,
in some respects the complete opposite of the original.

(ii) The meaning of fealu has already been suggested. The
hue can range from green through yellow to a reddish brown; it
seems generally to be intense rather than pale or dark. But the
essential quality of anything fealu is that peculiar brightness
which almost obscures hue. Brightness being largely the product
of circumstances, the word would apply to all objects only in certain contexts. It should not be difficult to realize the resemblance
between a well-groomed horse, a polished shield, a flame, and

waves in the sunlight. The <u>fealwe wegas</u> of the <u>Wanderer</u>, l. 46, are definitely not seen in the sunshine, but this is not a great difficulty. It might easily be an example of the generalizing of meaning and conventionalizing of epithets so common in alliterative poetry; <u>fealu</u>, being so common an adjective for the sea, would easily become a stock epithet to be applied in all circumstances: much as <u>wang</u>, originally meaning "plain," is watered down to mean "land" and finally "a place."

(iii) <u>wann</u> is a word whose meaning has very little connexion with hue. In so far as it has, it indicates something close to the centre, closer to grey than to anything else—any intensity except very pale (i.e. approaching white); this latter meaning is a modern development. Most important, however, is the fact that it always refers to a dull colour—the raven, waves (presumably on a dull day), night, armour (chain-mail, not a polished surface), a height above the sea. It does not mean "pale"; and this modern meaning is very apt to mislead us when reading Anglo-Saxon. Something very like the old meaning is found in Coleridge's "her neck that made the white robe wan." "Wan" is one of the three colour words now left in the language which do not refer primarily to hue; the others, of course, are "dun" and "sallow"; and of these "wan" is already archaic. Most users of these words use them fairly accurately, but they would be hard put to define them. This fact suggests the advantages of the modern system of describing colour. The modern method makes precision easier—by splitting up the sensation into its component parts and reserving our vocabulary for hue, the most diverse and perhaps the most important of these, we obtain an exact terminology that makes possible the scientific study of colour vision. Yet at the same time we have moved further from experience. Anglo-Saxon colour words probably describe more truly what are actually the commonest colour sensations, simply because they were not concerned with their analysis and classification.

W. E. Mead, in a very painstaking article,[1] has collected and classified all the colour words used in Anglo-Saxon. His material is invaluable, but he has shown a singular reluctance to draw conclusions from it. If the theory I have outlined above is more or less correct, many of the points which puzzled him will be explained. He complains, for example, that black and dark are not adequately differentiated. But this is surely a misapprehension caused by the limitations of our vocabulary. Black is usually contrasted with red, yellow or blue, and may be called a hue-word; dark is contrasted with bright and may be called a brightness-word; yet the sensation they refer to is much the same. It is possible to find uses of one word where the other could not be substituted (e.g. a bright black metal surface), but these are rare: in the great majority of cases the words are interchangeable. Is it surprising then that the Anglo-Saxons, who did not have separate hue-words and brightness-words, did not draw this distinction?

Under the heading "grey" Mead declares that Old English is fond of mixed neutral colours. This is a priori unlikely; those in a less sophisticated and less urbanized state of culture (as the Anglo-Saxons certainly are in relation to us) tend to have more finely developed senses. It would be surprising then if on the question of colours they were so unobservant as to run most of them together into a neutral grey. Wann and fealu have meanings quite as precise as our modern colour words. Here again, Mead has not been able to free himself from the preconceptions imposed by our language.

A study of medieval and Renaissance colour words in English might reveal something of the process by which our modern hue-vocabulary developed. Some words, like grēne, seem to have taken on their modern meanings in the Old English period. Read, which is often used of gold and a shining sword-edge, is applied in the Ruin to patches of colour on a stone wall that have been fading for centuries. This suggests that it already tended to be used of one hue in particular.

A more thorough investigation might, in fact, show that a transitional stage had already been reached in the Old English period, and that many of the colour words which seem to have something like their modern senses did indeed have that. The transition, which is almost complete to-day, will not be finally over until "wan," "dun," and "sallow" join hasu among obsolete words, or like har change their meaning completely.

NOTE

1 "Colour in Old English Poetry," PMLA, XIV (1898), 169 ff.

THE DEVIL IN OLD ENGLISH POETRY

Rosemary Woolf

The view that the heroic convention was never satisfactorily adapted to Christian themes has become a commonplace in the critical theory of Old English poetry. It is, moreover, a just opinion, for, even when allowance has been made for a different and more receptive response from a ninth-century audience than from one of the present day, it must be admitted that the presentation of subject-matter from conflicting standpoints cannot at any date be entirely convincing. The heroic formulae were, however, usually merely decorative, for any more integral use of the old style would have resulted in a deep-rooted incongruity; but, nevertheless, even this superficial usage is unsatisfactory: the apostles, for instance, even though they are the apostles of Apocryphal tradition, rather than of the New Testament, are ill at ease in their disguise of Germanic retainers, Cristes þegnas.

To this generalization the devil is an exception. Because of the characteristics already attributed to him by the Church Fathers, he had natural affinities with characters in both northern mythology and northern literature. Christ triumphant and his disciples and saints must have seemed foreign to a people whose ancestors had worshipped boastful, quarrelling gods, themselves doomed by fate to be destroyed. But there was a counterpart to the devil, not only in Loki of northern mythology, "vársinna ok sessa Óðins ok ása," "goða dólgr,"[1] but also in certain characters native to Germanic literature: the devil's common role of tempter was paralleled in the part played by the wicked counsellor who incited his master to evil-doing; whilst by an almost metaphorical treatment the terms used of persons and situations derived from heroic society could be applied to Satan, for his disobedience to God had an intrinsic like-

Reprinted from the Review of English Studies, Vol. 4 (1953), by permission of the author and the Clarendon Press, Oxford.

ness to the revolt of a þegn from his lord, and his subsequent
punishment of being an outcast from heaven was a fate of which
the exile of a þegn from his natural place in his lord's hall
might well appear the earthly shadow.

Now whilst there is no evidence that at any historical date
the Anglo-Saxons knew of Loki,[2] the similarities between him
and the devil are undoubtedly sufficiently marked to deserve
comment; in fact, according to the investigations of Grimm,
Loki was at one time popularly associated with the devil.[3] Moreover, in accordance with patristic tradition, the devil is generally
identified with heathen gods in Old English poetry.[4] Idols are
never mere wood and stone, but evil and deceitful objects, ani-
mated by the devil. In some points, too, Christian tradition about
Satan and northern tradition about Loki coincided: Loki so en-
raged the gods by his evil deeds which culminated in the death
of Baldr, that, after capturing him, they placed him in a cave,
where he was to lie bound until Ragnarøkr, just as Satan, on the
authority of Revelation xx. 2, and elsewhere, was said to lie
bound in hell, until he should be loosed before the Day of Judgement. Loki, moreover, like many of the Norse gods and heroes
who were shape-shifters, could alter his appearance, as, for
instance, when he transforms himself into a mare in order to
lure away the giant's horse Svaðilfari: and so in Solomon and
Saturn the devil appears as a bird, dragon, and wolf, the latter two
derived no doubt respectively from the dragon of Revelation and the
wolf of the parable; in Guþlac the devils assailing the saint turn
themselves into human and serpent shape,[5] whilst in Juliana and,
presumably, in Genesis B,[6] the devil disguises himself as an
angel of light in order to make his temptation more convincing,
a hypocritical device, to which Eve through credulity succumbs,
whereas Juliana's faith is so strong that she remains undeceived
and unshaken by the insinuating persuasiveness of her tempter.
This power of self-transformation is therefore common to both
mythology and Christian belief, although the angel-of-light disguise is of specifically Christian origin, as it appears, for instance, in the Vita Adae et Evae and the Apocalypse of Moses,
and is stated as a doctrine with biblical support by Gregory I
in his Moralia (Lib. xxix, Cap. xxx): "Transfigurat enim se velut
angelum lucis (ii Cor. xi, 14), et callida deceptionis ante plerumque proponit laudabilia, ut ad illicita pertrahat."

The devil in Old English poetry is twice referred to as the
hobbler.[7] Loki himself was not lame, but the semi-divine smith

Weland was, possibly because a man, strong but crippled in the leg, would be likely to take up the occupation of a smith, or possibly because he had been hamstrung in order to prevent his escape from bondage. The devil's lameness, however, was more probably caused by his fall from heaven, just as was Hephæstus', who had been "thrown by angry Jove/Sheer o'er the crystal battlements." Fable told how he had alighted on the island of Lemnos, but Milton, preserving the orthodox identification of heathen gods with devils, maintained that he had dropped long before with Satan to hell.

There are two pieces of mythological property associated with the devil, which seem to have no origin in Christian history or legend: a feðerhama[8] and a helmet of invisibility.[9] The former has been compared to the fjaðrhamr of Weland, by Mr. Timmer, who claims that the poet "has given some of the features [of the Weland story] to Satan's helper."[10] But the only other resemblance stated is the motive of vengeance. Now although, in the þiðrikssaga af Bern,[11] the fjaðrhamr is used by Weland to accomplish his mission of revenge, in the Vǫlundar-kviða[12] it is probably used instead for his escape. Furthermore, the types of vengeance are quite dissimilar: Weland's on Niðhad is of a real and terrible kind, whilst the devil's, directed at man, is only a malicious pin-prick at the Almighty. The resemblance to Loki is in fact much more marked. Detachable wings or shoes were, of course, common features of both Germanic and classical myth; in the latter there were the winged shoes of Hermes, and the wings of Icarus, although these were not made of feathers; whilst in the former, there was the fjaðrhamr of Freyja lent, at Þorr's request, to Loki in order that he might journey to Jǫtun-heim to recover the hammer Mjollnir; and Loki also possessed shoes which enabled him to fly through the air. The hæleðhelm, though clearly of mythological origin, is not associated with Loki. It is, however, reminiscent of Pluto's helmet, forged by the Cyclops, and, in Germanic mythology, of the tarnkappe won by Siegfried from the dwarf Alberich in the Niebelungenlied,[13] and of the head-covering used by the elves for the same purpose of rendering the wearer invisible.

Yet too much stress must not be laid on these mythological trimmings; it is not, for instance, the fact that both Loki and the devil make use of a feðerhama which is chiefly interesting, but a more fundamental similarity. That is, on broad grounds,

that Loki too is the "foe of the gods," in other words Satan (derived from the Hebrew for "adversary"), Godes andsaca, he who
is to lead the forces of evil at the end of the world, whilst, more
specifically, it is that he also delighted in giving evil advice for
evil's sake. When the gods, according to Snorri, asked each
other in their consultation who had advised them to make their
disastrous bargain with the jǫtunn, whereby they were in danger
of losing Freyja, and with her the sun and moon, "en þat kom
ásamt með ǫllum, at þessu myndi ráðit hafa sá er flestu illa
ræðr, Loki Laufeyjarson."[14]

But Loki was not the only person sá er flestu illa ræðr in
Germanic story. There were human beings of this type too:
Bikki,[15] Sibeck,[16] and Bolviss,[17] and in Old English literature
probably Unferð. Attempts have, of course, been made to clear
Unferð's name from the charge of malicious scheming at the
Danish court, but these attempts at whitewashing do not convince. Unferð's ambiguous position at Heorot, his former
fratricide, and his significant association with prophetic references to later treachery in the Scylding dynasty, together suggest overwhelmingly that, in some version of the story of Hroðgar
and Hroðulf, Unferð took the same part as did Bikki at the court
of Eormenric. For the purpose of comparison with the devil,
however, the behaviour of Unferð is too hypothetical, and it is
better therefore to make use of the most famous of all Germanic
wicked counsellors, Bikki, whose history was almost certainly
known to the Anglo-Saxons, for they knew of the evil deeds of
his master Eormenric, as both Beowulf[18] and Widsiþ[19] testify,
and they knew his name, for it appears in place-names, such as
Biccanhlew, Biccanpol, and others.

The devil is clearly the counterpart to, or rather the archetype of, those who, to quote Coleridge's well-known comment on
Iago, act out of "motiveless malignity," who commit, according
to common belief, the sin against the Holy Ghost which will not
be forgiven. It is therefore possible to trace parallels between
their courses of behaviour. Bikki is notorious for the evil advice which he gave to Randver, son of Eormenric, that he should
take Swanhild, his father's destined bride, for himself, and for
his evil advice to Eormenric that he should have Swanhild tram-
pled to death by wild horses; whilst, according to the author of
the Vǫlsunga Saga, this latter incitement to a brutal vengeance
was only the worst of many bad counsels, for "marg ill ráð hafde

hann honum áðr kent."[20] In the same way Satan is remembered
for his disastrous advice to Eve, but is also portrayed in Old
English poetry as the constant giver of bad advice. His evil
suggestions range from the encouraging of men drunk with beer
to renew old grudges[21] to the occasion when he

> forlærde ligesearwum, leode fortyhte,
> Iudea cyn, þæt hie god sylfne
> ahengon, herga fruman.[22]

Both the devil and Bikki show an equal resourcefulness when their
immediate plans go astray. Thus when the wild horses will not
harm Swanhild because of her beauty, before Eormenric can in-
tervene, Bikki swiftly devises the method of covering her face;
whilst in the same way, when the first method of killing Juliana
has failed, the devil, before Heliseus has time to relent or fear
the angelic intervention, advises him to try again to put the saint
to death, this time by means of burning oil.

 It is interesting to notice how Bikki's love of evil for its own
sake puzzled later writers. In Saxo's version of the story, therefore, Bikki is given a motive, although it is briefly and uncon-
vincingly stated.[23] It is, moreover, generally agreed that the
incident alluded to, the slaying of Bikki's brothers by Eormenric,
is a later addition to the story, a mere repetition of Eormenric's
other crimes, such as the slaying of his nephews the Harlungs:
whilst, according to Chambers, the enmity between Eormenric
and Bikki, who is said to be the son of the Livonian king, reflects
racial quarrels of a later age.[24] The same effort to rationalize
this type of evil-doing may be seen again in the medieval treatment of Judas. Unable to accept the Gospel narrative, which
assigns to Judas no motive for his betrayal of Christ, except,
by implication, an evil delight in betraying for evil's sake, for
"Satan had entered into him," men of the Middle Ages found in
John xii. 3–6[25] the basis of an explanation, which was apparently
popular and is to be found, for instance, in the thirteenth-century
ballad of Judas and in the York Mystery plays. Judas as bearer
of the money-bag felt himself cheated over what seemed to him
the waste of the pot of precious ointment, since this might have
been sold for 300 pieces of silver, of which he could rightfully
have claimed a tithe, hence his willingness to sell Christ for
thirty pieces of silver. This is a trivial excuse, but one which

would leave him with some shred of motive. In the same tradition of villainy, Iago in his soliloquies makes an ineffectual attempt through his pretended jealousy of Othello to justify his logically motiveless actions to himself; Bradley, unable to accept this diabolical state of mind, labours to find some rationality in him.

The character of the devil is precisely similar. At the beginning, before he has been damned for innumerable centuries, he deludes himself, as in <u>Genesis B</u>, that he will be happier if he can bring about the downfall of man. However, in the poems which describe him after the coming of Christ, that is in the second period defined by Gregory I,[26] no justification for his actions is suggested. The devil tempts because it is his nature to tempt. There is no possibility of any relief from torment, any more than for Marlowe's Mephistopheles or Milton's Satan, for "fyr biþ ymbutan/ on æghwilcum, þæh he uppe seo,"[27] in other words, whichever way he flies, he carries hell-fire with him.

From the human point of view, then, Satan is the wicked counsellor, a supernatural manifestation of a type of evil-doer, already familiar to the Anglo-Saxons. But from the divine point of view he is the rebel and outcast or, by an almost inevitable form of imagery, the faithless retainer and eternal exile. It has already been pointed out how superficial and unsatisfactory is the treatment of the apostles as retainers of the Lord: from one aspect alone are they <u>milites Christi</u>. The application of the heroic code to the devil in <u>Genesis B</u>, however, is extremely interesting because it is integral. The Anglo-Saxons were, of course, familiar with the Augustinian doctrine that the devil had fallen through pride, the <u>engles oferhygd</u>,[28] and yet pride was a prominent characteristic of Germanic heroes: not the pride of Guþlac, over which the fiends taunt him, which depends upon a complete reliance on God, but the pride of Beowulf who "strenge getruwode, / mundgripe mægenes,"[29] and who, despite a pious acknowledgement of God's assistance, would scarcely have been content to ascribe to him the glory of his victories.[30] This poetic dilemma is solved in <u>Genesis B</u> by the use of the lord-retainer relationship with reference to God and Satan. The Anglo-Saxons clearly had quite as rigid a conception of a hierarchic system as had the Elizabethans, but whereas in the sixteenth century, under the influence of the Neoplatonists who had spread the Aristotelian idea of a universal order, a chain of being was imagined which stretched "from the foot of God's throne to the meanest of inanimate objects,"[31] in Anglo-Saxon times it was not extended above or below human society, and the idea could therefore only be applied to the supernatural world by analogy. In other words, whilst Milton could depend upon his readers recognizing Satan's rebellion as a violation of the natural order, an Anglo-Saxon poet could only arouse this comprehension in his audience by the use of imagery drawn from contemporary society.

The Anglo-Saxon emphasis on a fixed and ordered relationship may be seen in Beowulf itself. Beowulf after his fight with Grendel was already great enough to bring to the minstrel's mind a famous hero such as Sigemund, and by his complete cleansing of Heorot, he won for himself measureless fame. Were a man's social honour to depend only on personal achievements, there would be no need or point for Beowulf's payment to Hygelac of such elaborate homage on his return home to the land of the Geatas. When he professes Hygelac to be his superior, this sentiment must spring from a courteous aknowledgement that, although he has achieved braver deeds than Hygelac, the King is rightfully his lord. Now the use of the lord-retainer relationship in Genesis B enables the poet to show that Satan's pride is illegitimate. His rebellion is based on two mistakes: firstly that he "mæg swa fela wundra gewyrcean"[32] as God, which is an error of fact; and secondly that, even if he could, he would therefore be equal with God, a proposition of which the comparison with Beowulf exposes the falseness and absurdity.

This distinction between legitimate and illegitimate pride may be further illustrated by a comparison with the Battle of Maldon. The epithet ofermod is used of both Satan and Byrhtnoþ, but whereas this excessive pride in Satan is the greatest of sins, in Byrhtnoþ it is shown as a "last infirmity of noble mind." The reason for this is again that Satan's pride violates the natural order, being therefore at once evil and preposterous:

> ne meahte he æt his hige findan
> þæt he gode wolde geongerdome
> þeodne þeowian.[33]

How different is this from Byrhtnoþ, whose allegiance to King Æþelred is twice mentioned, once when Byrhtnoþ refers to Æþelred

as his ealdor, and the other time when the phrase Æþelredes
þegn is used as a synonym for him. The result of Byrhtnoþ's
pride is therefore neither evil nor unreasonable, but a splendid
and generous gesture, though, from the point of view of practical strategy, misguided. His granting of permission to the
Vikings to cross the ford is of the same kind as Beowulf's refusal to fight Grendel with weapons: they both spring from an
unwillingness to profit from an advantage over the enemy gained
by fortunate circumstances, not by personal achievement. That
the outcome of Byrhtnoþ's decision was less happy than Beowulf's is, from the moral aspect, irrelevant.

It is ironical that Satan, in Genesis B, who had denied the
proper þegnscipe to God, yet expects from his followers in hell
the loyal service in return for previous generosity which it was
the duty of men in the meadhall to give to their lord. This appeal to a code of behaviour does not, however, long survive the
Fall. Despite Satan's optimistic promise to his messenger, in
Genesis B, there is nothing of value in hell to be given, all that
he can dispense is evil, and he therefore becomes morþres brytta,
not the familiar sinces brytta. The miserable devil in Juliana
is only slightly less terrified of his fæder in hell than he is of the
saint herself. The clear implication is that punishment in hell
is not restricted to men who have failed to satisfy God, but is
also inflicted on devils who have failed to satisfy Satan. The
leader of the devils had not acted in such a way that, after the
passage of years, loyal companions would still voluntarily stand
by him.

The devil by his own sin had put himself into the position of
a faithless retainer, and his punishment is therefore that of a
faithless retainer: the deprivation of a lord and a meadhall. He
is by his own actions self-condemned to be eternally hlafordleas.
That is why the devil in Old English poetry, with the exception
of Satan in Genesis B, who is still flushed with the exhilaration
of defiance, is always miserable, skulking wretchedly round the
outskirts of the world. Fah ond freondleas, he is doomed per-
petually to wadan wræclastas. The last lines of the fiend's lament in Christ and Satan sum up his position:

> sceal nu wreclastas
> settan sorhgcearig, siðas wide.[34]

Although the Wanderer never stoops to the whining self-pity of
the devil in some Old English poetry, there is yet in the speeches
of both the Wanderer and the devil the same weariness and
abandonment of hope, the same yearning for what has been lost
for ever.[35] The resemblance is carried a step farther by the
frequent description of heaven in terms of the meadhall. There
was, of course, some biblical authority for this conception and
for the language used. The beorhte burhweallas,[36] for instance,
might so well belong either to Heorot or the New Jerusalem.
The idea of life in heaven as a banquet, the symbel of the Dream
of the Rood, may owe something to the parable of the marriage
of the king's son, whilst the traditional association of harps and
singing with celestial rejoicing might easily recall the minstrelsy
at great feasts. But such a phrase as wloncra winsele[37] seems
rather to suggest a Germanic hall, or even Valhǫll, where the
einherjar, the chosen heroes of the dead, feasted until the time of
their last fight in support of Oðin.

The symbolical portrayal of heaven as a meadhall, the place
where the greatest of men received the best of entertainment,
does not then require any explanation. But, in view of the customary association of a hall with happiness and rejoicing, it is
somewhat surprising to find that this idea is also sometimes applied to hell. Apart from passages in such poems as the Phoenix,
strongly influenced by Latin thought, heaven is never clearly
described in religious terms. The description of hell, however,
is usually orthodox: it is a place of darkness (this primitive,
mythological, and biblical equation of light = goodness, darkness = evil is very pronounced in Old English poetry) and of
flames, which, in the same tradition as Milton was later to follow,
are sweart and do not illuminate the blackness around; heat and
cold alternate to increase the torment of the damned, and the
place is infested with wurmas, sometimes used to mean snakes
and sometimes worms, either the undying worm of Isaiah, or
from contemporary graveyards, for such poems as the Soul and
Body show that the Old English poets were as much horrified by
the idea of bodily corruption as Donne or Webster. In contrast
to this type of description, the customs of the meadhall are
twice used with reference to hell: once in Genesis B, where its
ironic force has already been noted, and once in Juliana,[38] where
after the statement of the fact that Heliseus and his followers
were drowned and went to hell, the poet adds the curious comment

that there, on the benches of the winehall, the men would have
no need to look for gold rings from their lord: a typical example of Old English litotes, but unexpected and grimly incongruous in its place.

There is yet one aspect of the relationship between Satan
and man, interpreted in the light of Germanic thought, which
is so far unmentioned, because the evidence for it is by no
means as certain and widespread as it is for the others. It is
the aspect in which the devil is seen as the bringer of evil, one
which is emphasized, for instance, in the confession of the devil
to Juliana, in which he enumerates to the saint all the disasters
which he has brought about—in particular, deaths by drowning,
burning, and crucifixion,[39] and these were not caused by the
incitement of human beings to wrong-doing, but by direct and
supernatural intervention. The precise theological doctrine
behind this is not made clear, but it might be suggested that it
sprang from a belief in a divine permission to the devil to afflict the good, such as was granted to Satan when he tormented
Job, and in a divine commission of the evil into the hands of
Satan. But although this may be logically deduced, from the
literary point of view Satan is simply one who has power to
bring misfortune to mankind. This is probably the reason for
the surprising identification, found twice, of the devil with wyrd.
So startling at first sight does it seem, that, were it not that
this identification is incontrovertible in Solomon and Saturn,[40]
and that good sense and the laws of syntax undoubtedly demand
it in the Andreas,[41] its acceptance might still be disputed.

But wyrd in Old English poetry is also shown as the bringer
of disaster; not with any regularity, for it was naturally in conflict with the philosophical reconciliation, which had been made
between the new theological system and the old pagan concept of
fate, whereby wyrd was defined as the active, pre-ordaining will
of God. Such a formulation is given by Alfred in his translation
of the De Consolatione Philosophiae of Boethius:

Ac ðæt ðætte we hatað Godes foreðonc ond his fore-
sceawung, þæt bið þa hwile þe hit ðær mid him bið
on his mode, ærðæm þe hit gefremed weorðe. þa
hwile ðe hit geþoht bið; ac siððan hit fullfremed
bið, þonne hatað we hit wyrd.[42]

and an identification is sometimes found in poetry; in the Andreas itself, for example, in a passage which appears to be a deliberate reminiscence of the now famous lines in Beowulf,[43] the poet, using god instead of wyrd, as the author of the former poem had done, writes:

> Forþan ic eow to soðe secgan wille,
> þæt næfre forlæteð lifgende god
> eorl on eorðan, gif his ellen deah.[44]

This logical compromise, however, was comparatively rare. Because of the poetical fluctuations between Christian belief and the heathen, heroic ways of thought, wyrd, which in Norse mythology had brought about the downfall and death of the gods, more often in Old English poetry was still shown as a power which afflicted the world. In Beowulf, for example, it is wyrd who has swept off so many of Hroðgar's band into Grendel's power, wyrd who carried off Hygelac when he fought the Frisians, wyrd who had deprived Beowulf of his kinsmen. The philosophical inconsistency, however, and the erratic treatment of wyrd make this adoption of the devil yet farther into the pre-Christian Germanic system far less happy than the other methods already noticed. It is deserving of interest but not of praise.

For the ease with which the devil was fitted into already existing tradition there remains one final, but important, reason, which is of a different kind from these identifications based on fundamental resemblances. This reason may provide the solution to the question of why Genesis B is a remarkable exception to the almost general mediocre standard of extant religious poetry in Old English.[45] The weakness in this verse seems to spring from the fact that the Germanic inspiration was essentially tragic, whilst Christianity left little room for tragedy: there could be no final sadness, as Professor Una Ellis-Fermor has pointed out with reference to later drama,[46] in a scheme of things where tribulation was restricted to this world, and was not worthy to be compared with the joys of the next: in other words, there was no longer room for the great type figure of the hero defiant in defeat, defeat that was eternal and absolute. But there yet remained one exception: the devil could still be the first and greatest tragic figure, not for the simple medieval reason which makes his story head the Monk's list of tragedies, but because for him, as well of course as for the damned, there could be no remission of unhappiness. He could be viewed against the background of eternity as well as of time and yet arouse that sense of pity which is an essential element of tragedy: a sense of pity, which is not theologically justified, but which human sensibility stirred by great art cannot withhold from Dr. Faustus, Macbeth, and others who share the plight of Satan.

Therefore, whilst bearing in mind the simple possibility that Genesis B is better than the works of the Cædmonian and Cynewulfian schools because its author[47] was a greater poet than Cynewulf and these other nameless writers, one may still suggest that part of the explanation may plausibly be that the subject was more manageable. Satan, of course, degenerated, passed into the second phase defined by Gregory, and could no longer be a powerful central figure. But, immediately after his fall, his situation and behaviour, as recounted by the Fathers, gave scope for a typically Old English treatment, for his situation was hopeless, but his courage remained. This situation was exploited in Genesis B, not to the full, of course — it remained for Milton to express, though no doubt unconsciously, the old heroic position from the mouth of Satan, with his "unconquerable will" and "courage never to submit or yield" — but, considering the apparent lack of precedent for this new blending, with extraordinary skill.

By the above approach it may be possible to discover subtleties undreamed of by the poet. Frequently, it may be argued, some heroic phrase may be used of the devil because it was a familiar fragment of the common poetic stock, or some heroic word may be used because it was convenient for the alliteration. But this does not affect the general proposition that the heroic formulae, when applied to Christ and his apostles and saints, always remained separate from the fundamental conception, whereas, when applied to the devil, they became fused with the Christian idea and produced a deeper meaning. That this felicitous method may have been used by a conventional habit and not by deliberate poetic purpose need in no way invalidate an appreciation of its result.

NOTES

1 Skáldskaparmál, 16. "The evil companion and bench-mate of Oðin and the gods," "the enemy of the gods."

2 The total absence of reference to heathen gods by proper names in Old English literature makes it impossible to determine clearly what mythological figures were known to the Anglo-Saxons, or had been worshipped by them. That some tradition remained seems certain from the mention of the feðerhama and hæleðhelm, which must be of mythological origin. It is beyond the scope of this essay, however, to pursue mythological speculation. I intend only to point out interesting resemblances between Loki and the devil, without insisting on any actual influence.

3 Grimm, Teutonic Mythology, trans. J. S. Stallybrass (London, 1882–88), p. xii.

4 Cf. F. Klaeber, "Die christlichen Elemente im Beowulf," Anglia, XXXV (1912), 249.

5 Guþlac, 907 ff. In the Vita S. Guthlaci of Felix, from which Guþlac II is almost certainly derived, the devils transform themselves into many terrifying animal shapes, a lion, a bear, a bull, &c.

6 The poet is apparently following two different traditions here. In l. 491 the devil "wearp hine þa on wyrmes lic," whereas at ll. 656 f. Eve refers to him as "þes boda sciene, / godes engel god." This confusion occurs also in the Apocalypse of Moses.

7 Hellehinca, Andreas, 1171; adloma, Guþlac, 912. Both words have been disputed. But the difficulty of supplying plausible emendations together with their mutual corroboration seems sufficient to substantiate them.

8 Genesis B, 417.

9 Hæleðhelm, Genesis B, 444; heoloþhelm, The Whale, 45.

10 The Later Genesis, ed. B. J. Timmer (Oxford, 1948), note to l. 417.

11 Chs. 57–90. This is a later version of the Weland story.

12 Cf. Die Edda, ed. R. C. Boer (Haarlem, 1922), note to the Vǫlundarkviða, stanza 27.

13 Aventiure iii. 97, and ibid. vi. 337.

14 Gylfaginning, ch. xlii: "And they all agreed that he must have advised this, who gives most evil counsels, Loki Laufeyjarson."

15 Vǫlsunga Saga, ch. xli.

16 þiðrikssaga af Bern. The name in its Old English form, Sifeca, appears in Widsiþ, 116.

17 Saxo Grammaticus, Gesta Danorum, bk. vii.

18 Line 1201.

19 Line 88, &c.

20 Vǫlsunga Saga, ch. xli: "Many evil counsels had he given him previously."

21 Juliana, 483 ff.

22 Elene, 208 ff.

23 Gesta Danorum, bk. viii.

24 Widsith, ed. R. W. Chambers (Cambridge, 1912), p. 20.

25 3. Maria ergo accepit libram unguenti nardi pistici pretiosi, et unxit pedes Jesu, et extersit pedes ejus capillis suis; et domus impleta est ex odore unguenti.
4. Dixit ergo unus ex discipulis ejus, Judas Iscariotes, qui erat eum traditurus:
5. Quare hoc unguentum non veniit trecentis denariis, et datum est egenis?
6. Dixit autem hoc, non quia de egenis pertinebat ad eum, sed quia fur erat, et loculos habens, ea quae mittebantur, portabat. (Biblia Sacra Vulgatae Editionis.)

26 Gregory I had classified the devil's life into three periods. For a detailed study of this see C. Abbetmeyer, Old English Poetical Motives derived from the Doctrine of Sin (Minneapolis, 1903).

27 Christ and Satan, 263 f.

28 Genesis B, 328. Dr. Sisam in "Notes on Old English Poetry," RES, XX (1946), 257 f. has suggested that engles should be emended to egle. I quote here, however, from the manuscript as its reading is by no means inadmissible.

29 Lines 1533 f.

30 Cf. <u>Beowulf</u>, 1384 ff. It might be argued, however, that at
11. 1657 ff. Beowulf acknowledges assistance from God.
But such a passage as this seems out of keeping with the
general tone of the poem, and anyway does not contradict
the fact that Beowulf was, in the word of the dirge, <u>lofgeornost</u>

31 E. M. W. Tillyard, <u>The Elizabethan World Picture</u> (London,
1943), ch. iv, p. 25.

32 <u>Genesis B</u>, 279 f.

33 Ibid., 266 ff.

34 <u>Christ and Satan</u>, 187 f.

35 Despite the poet's comment on the Wanderer's attitude in
the first line of the poem, and also, perhaps, in the concluding lines, there is nothing in the Wanderer's monologue
to suggest that he hoped for or expected any relief from his
distress through the benevolence of God.

36 <u>Christ and Satan</u>, 294.

37 Lines 683 ff.

38 Ibid., 93.

39 <u>Juliana</u>, 468 ff.

40 Lines 434 ff.

41   Deofles larum
    hæleð hynfuse hyrdon to georne,
    wraðum wærlogan. Hie seo wyrd beswac,
    forleolc ond forlærde.   (611 ff.)

Mr. Timmer in his article "<u>Wyrd</u> in Anglo-Saxon Prose and
Poetry," <u>Neophilologus</u>, XXVI (1941), by only quoting the
second half of the passage, ignores the necessary relationship of the whole.

42 Ch. xxxix. The Latin reads: "Qui modus cum in ipsa divinae
intellengentiae puritate conspicitur, providentia nominatur;
cum vero ad ea, quae movet atque disponit, refertur, fatum
a veteribus appellatum est."

43 Lines 572 f.

44 Andreas, 458 ff.

45 This generalization does not, of course, apply to the Dream
    of the Rood. But the devotional tone and the absence of ex-
    plicit heroic formulae exclude its consideration from the
    scope of this essay.

46 The Frontiers of Drama (London, 1946), pp. 146 ff. Profes-
    sor Ellis-Fermor does not, however, recognize characters
    such as Dr. Faustus as tragic heroes.

47 Whether the merit is to be ascribed to the Old Saxon or Old
    English poet is irrelevant to this point. It would be difficult
    to prove that the exploitation of this situation in Genesis B
    is of a specifically Old Saxon character. The use of the lord-
    retainer relationship is found, though not so fully developed,
    elsewhere, e.g. Elene, 766, "he þinum wiðsoc aldordome."

III. STYLISTICS

DICTION AND IMAGERY IN ANGLO-SAXON POETRY

Henry Cecil Wyld

If in the following pages I have been too often lured away
from the path I set out to pursue — a slight study of part of the
poet's machinery — into expressing opinions upon what he made
with it, in other words, into some sort of literary criticism, I
ought to apologize to my readers. I have not the slightest pretensions to the art of the critic, my occupations having led me
in quite other directions. I cannot expect to have avoided the
pitfalls that await a trespasser on unfamiliar ground. My
justification must be that in my excursions I may have gathered
several flowers from the garden of Anglo-Saxon poetry which
did not grow on the straight path I had originally marked out
for myself.

I owe a deep debt of gratitude to Mr. Kenneth Sisam, who
most kindly offered to read this article in proof. He sent me
a number of very valuable suggestions on textual and interpre-
tative questions, by far the larger number of which I accepted
and incorporated in the article to its great advantage. In a few
cases where more than one interpretation seemed possible, I
have given, as an alternative, that proposed by Mr. Sisam. It
is a pleasure to acknowledge help so generously given.

I

The considerable body of poetical literature, belonging to
the earliest period of our history, that has come down to us is
a remarkable expression of national and racial genius. The
date of the composition of most of this poetry is a question of
controversy, and it is safest to be content with round figures.
We may say that most of it is from a thousand to twelve hundred

Reprinted from Essays and Studies, Vol. XI, published for the English
Association by the Clarendon Press, Oxford, and reprinted by Messrs.
Wm. Dawson & Sons Ltd., by permission of the publisher.

years old, while some may incorporate, not merely stories and
legends, and names of heroes whose memory might be preserved
by tradition from the remotest ages, but even actual lines of
verse which may have been shaped before our ancestors came
to these islands. Without insisting upon this, we are perfectly
safe in asserting that the most important remains of Anglo-Saxon
poetry are more than a thousand years old. Not only does this
ancient literature, the creation of a people formerly regarded
as barbarous, exhibit arresting qualities of elevation of thought,
and a sustained intensity of poetic emotion, together with great
delicacy and tenderness of feeling, but the form in which it is
couched is often wrought to the last pitch of elaboration, with a
wealth of ornament in the shape of metaphor and pictorial phrase.
Here is a vocabulary of great richness and variety, of which many
elements are reserved exclusively for poetry, as being remote
from everyday familiar usage, and deliberately employed to
beautify and lend dignity to the style. This usage, which appears
in the oldest poems, is clearly based upon a long-descended
literary tradition, while the general tone of thought and emotion,
which is everywhere perceptible, must imply an ancient cultiva-
tion of the mind and of the heart. How far removed in the dim
past of our race must that age be, in which the words that already
twelve hundred years ago had become archaic, and had passed
into the sacred treasury of the poet, belonged to the language of
common life.

Such a collection of poetry must always possess a high
archaeological interest, and hold an important place in the history of European culture, but for students of English poetry,
that of the Anglo-Saxons has, apart from its intrinsic value as
poetry, a peculiar claim on their attention.

I think that the more one reads this poetry the more one
feels the community of spirit between it and our greatest poetry
of every succeeding age. My friend, Sir Arthur Quiller-Couch,
has said, "in words that admit of no misunderstanding," so he
puts it: "From Anglo-Saxon Prose, from Anglo-Saxon Poetry,
our living Prose and Poetry have, save linguistically, no derivation." The saving clause, we may note in passing, is a comprehensive one. If the statement simply means that there is not an
unbroken literary tradition between the Anglo-Saxons and Chaucer
and his successors, in the sense that the later poets did not draw
their inspiration either direct, or through linking generations of

singers, from the actual poems of the Anglo-Saxons, then I suppose that no one will question it seriously. But between the old
native poets and those of much later days there is, nevertheless,
a continuity, not of conscious inheritance, but "of something far
more deeply interfused," namely, of national genius. It may be
said that in Chaucer and his successors there is a gaiety, an
urbanity, a winning sweetness and grace of nature, a lightness
of touch—a thousand other qualities for which you will look in
vain in Cynewulf, or Cædmon (or whoever wrote the poems once
attributed to the latter), or anywhere else in Anglo-Saxon poetry.
We have derived these qualities, if you will, from France, or
Italy, or Greece, but something remains, without which we could
have made nothing of the gifts of the Greeks and the Celts and
the Latins, and that is that strange thing, the English mind.
This has, no doubt, developed new qualities and convolutions in
a thousand years, but it still remains essentially the same.

There are three aspects of modern poetry which are, perhaps, most characteristically English. First, that which appeals (1)
to the more massive, solid, and serious sides of our character.
These find their highest expression in Milton, in whose work
this is raised to grandeur and sublimity. Secondly, often closely (2)
related to this, there is the love of the romantic, the mysterious,
the vague, the half-expressed; a preference for those manifesta-
tions of nature which are but partially revealed to the senses,
and seen dimly emerging from the mountain mists, or glimmer-
ing through a cloud of spray. Upon these shadowy forms, suspected rather than fully perceived, the mind dwells and the imagination works, often contriving from them visions of unearthly
beauty. All our greatest poets abound in images of this suggestive kind, and it is from such passages that we should generally
select, if we wished to illustrate a poet's peculiar magic. We
should perhaps find this mysterious, suggestive beauty super-
abundantly in Peele, Keats, Wordsworth, and Tennyson—but
when one begins to pick out names one wants to include them all. (3)
The third quality which I take to be engrained in the blood and
fibre of our poetry is a wealth of human sympathy, and a tenderness which embraces all living things, which

> Maintains a deep and reverential care
> For the unoffending creatures whom it loves.

These three qualities, a feeling for the mysterious in the loveliness of nature, a sense of the solemn and sublime, sympathy with the impulses of the human heart, pervade the whole of Anglo-Saxon poetry, and through them it establishes its kinship with that of later times. In all periods, too, our poets have found in the sights and sounds of the external world the mirror and symbol of spiritual experience, and have for ever gone to nature for their images and similes.

A striking example of this identity of feeling, treatment, and expression exists in the close resemblance of certain passages in Paradise Lost, dealing with the surroundings of Satan and his infernal peers after their rout by the heavenly host, and with the Temptation and Fall of Man, with corresponding passages in the Anglo-Saxon Genesis, formerly attributed to Cædmon, and also with some in another poem, known as Christ and Satan. It is not impossible, though no direct evidence is forthcoming, that Milton may have become acquainted with the Anglo-Saxon poems through Junius. If he had, he evidently at once felt the spiritual affinity between himself and the old poet, and wrought much of the former's work into his own poem. If Milton knew nothing of these poems, the coincidence in feeling, treatment, and general atmosphere between them and Paradise Lost is the more astonishing. In either case, the fact remains that nine hundred years before Milton England produced a poet who was capable of conceiving work on a great and majestic scale, one whose style, allowing for differences of language, reminds us so much of Milton's that the "great language" of Paradise Lost would seem the only fitting form of Modern English into which to translate it. The grandeur and the peculiar impressiveness of the Anglo-Saxon Genesis are nearer, perhaps, to Milton than to any other English poet, and the emotional effect made on the reader by both seems identical. The writer of the Genesis also shares with Milton that love of the mysterious in nature, and the tender humanity which we take to be characteristic traits of English poetry. The latter quality is particularly notable in the attitude of both poets to Eve, both before and after the Fall. It must be mentioned that Genesis B, or the "later Genesis," as it is called, that is the portion of the poem which is so strongly Miltonic in character, is believed by many scholars, including the late Dr. Henry Bradley to have been based upon an Old Saxon original, and indeed a fragment of MS. in this language was discovered in the Vatican Library in which twenty-five lines correspond almost word for word with the Anglo-Saxon. While many scholars consider this conclusive proof that the Anglo-Saxon version is a translation from Old Saxon, others hold it more probable, seeing that the Old Saxons derived their Christianity and culture from the English, that the poem was of English origin, and was translated into Old Saxon, the version we possess being, so it is suggested, a retranslation from the latter.[1]

I pass now to the more immediate purpose of these pages, namely, to discuss some of the leading features of Anglo-Saxon poetic diction.

It will be convenient to deal with these under three heads: (1) the use of distinctively "poetical" words and phrases, that is, words and phrases which are either peculiar to poetry, and which evidently have traditionally a definitely poetical association and value; or words which are traditionally used in poetry with a different meaning from that which they have in prose. (2) The figurative or metaphorical use of words, to express natural, material objects such as the sea, ships, swords, the sun, the body, the tomb, etc.; ways of expressing Death and Dying; and typical epithets, etc. used in connexion with these. (3) What appears to be a more or less individual use of words and phrases with striking poetic effect. Under this head I shall indicate some original poetic touches which are to be distinguished from the more conventional use of words and phrases as part of the traditional stock-in-trade of the poet.

It will appear, I believe, that although a word or phrase may occur in several passages, and must therefore be considered as conventional or traditional, this fact does not necessarily destroy its poetical value, nor detract from our estimate of the poet who uses it. Such clichés, although traditional, may be, and often are, expressive of a genuine emotion, and produce delight in the mind of the reader.

The use of words or phrases deliberately chosen because they differ from those used in everyday life is common in later English poetry. The justification of the practice depends upon the poetical effect in each passage where the "poetical" word is used. It is certainly possible to employ such words without any poetical gain; it is also possible so to employ them that they are felt as appropriate to the context, and as adding beauty to the passage. Such gems of late poetic diction as the following have perhaps rarely a value superior to that attaching to more familiar words:

> hoary pile ' old house,' or 'building'; zephyr, gale, for 'breeze'; swain 'man, youth'; tincture (of the skies) for ' colour,' or 'tint'; nectareous for 'delicious'; briny main ' sea'; courser, steed, 'horse'; garbs succint 'tucked up skirts'; respire 'breathe,' and so on.

Corresponding to these, in some degree, in Anglo-Saxon, we have:

> hæleþ, beorn, freca, rinc, secg, ' hero, warrior, man'; þengel, fengel, þeoden, aldor, brego, eodor, þeod-cyning, land-fruma, ord-fruma, ræswa, ' prince, king'; ides ' lady, woman,' used of Eve, and of Queen Wealhþeow in Beowulf, but also of Grendel's mother, therefore also = ' hag'; bill, mæl, ' sword'; fyrgen- ' mountain,' in such compounds as fyrgen-holt, -wudu, ' mountain wood'; fyrgen-stream ' mountain stream'; tungol ' star, heavenly body'; up-rodor 'heavens, sky'; swegl 'sky, sun'; hador 'brightness, radiance' (of the sky); bune 'wine cup'; geofon 'ocean,' etc.; wær 'sea'; holm 'ocean, sea, mere'; wielm, wylm, etc., 'that which boils, surges,' of of the tossing waves, and of fire; gar-secg 'ocean'; eagorstream, lagostream, 'sea-stream'; yð 'wave, waves collectively, the sea'; lagu 'sea, water.'

We should be glad to know the exact meaning of some of these different words for "sea," and to be certain which of the ever-changing aspects and conditions of the ocean each represents. Thus holm, though it appears often to be used in a perfectly general sense, probably originally meant ' the high, lofty sea; the billowy, wave-broken sea'; it may also have referred to the 'crest' or ' summit' of a wave. (Professor Chambers gives ' billowy sea' for wægholm, Beowulf 317.) It is the same word as the Norse holmr 'sea island.' In English place-names it often means 'rising land near, or surrounded by, water.' The basal meaning was almost certainly 'something high, lofty'; whence 'mound, slope.' 'Island' appears to be a secondary meaning derived from the idea of something standing up above lower surroundings. The Gmc. base *hulm- is no doubt cognate with Lat. celsus 'lofty, high,' with collis 'hill,' and is related more closely still to the almost exactly equivalent culmen 'top, summit.' I have taken the liberty of occasionally translating holm as 'crest, wave-crest,' in some of the passages quoted below.

It is difficult for us to-day to reach back through the centuries and grasp the precise shade of meaning which each of these apparent synonyms once expressed, to recapture the mood or emotion which they called up, or to be fully alive to the grace or glamour with which, for our forefathers, this or that word may have lighted up a line. It may be possible in many cases to discover the remote origin of words by the light of etymology. But even when this is reliable for one particular purpose, it may be but a misleading guide to the poetical and emotional value of a word in the mouth of a poet. It is likely that the old poets often used words whose ancient, precise meaning they did not know; it is certain that many etymological relationships quite escaped them, and as Professor Tolkien well says in his admirable "Contributions to Middle English Lexicography" in the Review of English Studies, I (1925), 211, speaking in particular of the poetical synonyms for 'man': "the original meanings were so far forgotten . . . as to be more apparent to the modern Germanic philologist than to the Old English poet himself." This is a depressing thought, but, after all, the position of the old poet had its compensations. If he did not know the etymology of the words he used, he had at least a feeling for them, and a direct tradition which the modern Germanic scholar can scarcely recover. The path of etymology is but rarely the path to poetry. The origin of a word may be lost in the misty past, but the succeeding generations of men, and in particular the poets, can give it new life and fresh power of beauty. The specifically "poetical" elements in diction derive their value partly from their remoteness from common life and everyday usage, but chiefly from association. In fact, such words come from ancient habit to be regarded as essential elements in a poetic whole, and are felt to lend loftiness and distinction to the style of poetry because they are a kind of speech of the gods. But still more of their quality comes from their surroundings. They occur habitually in close union with lovely and gracious images, with serene and elevated thoughts; they are found in the grave utterances of great kings and heroes; they may depict scenes of strange and impossible beauty, or the throes of majestic terror; they tell of deeds that no human powers could accomplish. These words, then, become ennobled by the company they keep, and at last, their mere presence, in a line or a passage, by the half-sleeping memories which it evokes, by the various images of beauty or sublimity, which by some subtle power of association it conjures up, is often sufficient to invest a commonplace idea with dignity and charm, just as the appearance of some great and imposing figure on a public platform may sometimes serve to lift what promise to be dull proceedings above the level of vulgarity.

These "poetical" words then are a vital element in the poet's properties, an important means for obtaining his effects, we might say his atmospheric effects. But these words depend for their value upon their history in poetry. Etymology may put us moderns on the track of their primary meaning, but it will not take us far. The real life of all words is made by usage; that of such as we are now considering has been made by a long line of poets, and so exuberant is that life, that at last these words may almost be said, in their turn, to make poetry.

We can only go about our business of interpretation patiently and humbly, and hope to learn, by constant and sympathetic study of our old poetry, gradually to group poetic associations round these ancient words till they become for us the symbols of particular moods and emotions.

II

I pass on now to consider another aspect of Anglo-Saxon poetical diction, the habit namely of metaphorical expressions, the use of figurative phrases to denote things and actions. This is what Sir Arthur Quiller-Couch calls "the besetting sin of the Anglo-Saxon gleeman—the pretentious trick of calling things 'out of their right names' for the sake of literary effect." Now the Anglo-Saxon poet undoubtedly does very often avoid calling a spade a spade. The question therefore arises whether a spade is, under all possible circumstances, the best name for a spade, or whether in a particular passage a poet does or does not secure a better poetical result by calling it something else.

DICTION AND IMAGERY IN ANGLO-SAXON POETRY

Such figurative expressions as we now have in view may indeed be merely "pretentious" and bombastic, or merely vulgar, as, for instance, when the sea is called "the briny," or when men speak of "lifting the light fantastic" instead of plain "dancing." Many readers nowadays condemn, and affect to despise, the eighteenth-century poets for artificiality of diction, as if this w..s all that, say, Mr. Pope had to his credit; others, more sympathetic, may smile indulgently, and not without enjoyment at certain fantastic gambols, as at the harmless and endearing foibles of a beloved friend. Here are a few choice phrases from eighteenth-century poetry:

> nectared urn 'wine cup'; watery plains 'sea';
> finny prey 'fish'; a lion's yellow spoils 'lion's skin';
> balmy blessings of the night 'sleep'; restored the
> pleasing burden to her arms 'handed the baby back
> to her'; fuming liquor 'hot coffee'; fleecy breed,
> care, wealth 'sheep'; briny torrent 'tears'; thunder-
> ing tube 'shot-gun.'

Such fanciful phrases as these, which were formerly regarded as giving variety and elegance to the diction of poetry, are not a permanent enrichment of the language. They express no emotion, they add nothing to our stock of vivid and beautiful images, they reveal no justness of observation or insight. They do not strike the imagination and set the mind "voyaging on strange seas of thought." They contain, indeed, nothing of the essence of true poetry. While it is certainly true that Anglo-Saxon poetry has many set phrases no more vital than these, it is none the less so that it exhibits also many others which possess qualities of a very different kind, and which are impressive by reason of their truth and beauty.

The sea is referred to in a large number of phrases of both classes. Of the former class we may recall the following:

> swanrad 'swan's road' Juliana 675; hranrad
> 'whale road' Andreas 634; fisces bæþ 'fish's bath'
> Andr. 293; ganotes bæþ 'gannet's bath' Beowulf
> 1861; hwæles eþel 'country of the whale' Andr. 274;
> mæwes eþel 'country, home, of the (sea)-mew'
> Husband's Message 25; seolhpæð 'seal path' Andr.

1714; flotweg 'sea way' H.M. 41; egorstreamas ' sea
streams' Genesis 1374, and Andr. 379; ȳða ful
'cup, beaker of the waves' Beow. 1208.

Of quite a different order are the following:

ofer holmes hring 'across the circle of the sea'
Gen. 1393; wægholm 'the wave (-covered) sea'
Beow. 217; þurh wæges wylm 'upon the wave surge'
Jul. 680; flodes wylm 'the boiling, surging of the
flood' Andr. 367; ȳða swengas 'blows of the waves'
Elene 239; ȳða geþring 'tumult of the waves' Andr.
368; sealtyȳða geswing 'the swing, roll, of the salt
waves' Panther 8; ȳða gewealc 'rolling, heaving,
of the waves' Chronicles A. D. 975, 25; sealtyȳða
gelac 'leaping of the waves' Seafarer 35; mere-
streama gemeotu 'the clashing, meeting, of the sea
currents' Andr. 454; argeblond 'mingling of the
waves' Andr. 383, and Beow. 239; flodes fæðm 'the
embrace of the flood' Andr. 252; lagufæsten 'sea
fastness' Andr. 398; waðema gebind, Wanderer 24,
usually translated 'frozen waves,' but meaning
literally 'the binding together, conglomeration,
of the waves,' which are here thought of as frozen
into a solid mass.

The epithets applied to the sea, and the expressions used
concerning it by the Anglo-Saxon poets, show that they had
really felt and seen, by actual observation, many aspects of it;
they do not merely repeat, parrot-like, conventional commonplaces, but record a genuine emotion in words that evoke it in
the reader.

Of the more general epithets may be mentioned:

sidne sæ 'the broad, spacious sea' Beow. 507,
Christ 853; sæs sidne fæðm 'sea's broad bosom' El.
728; sæs sidne grund 'sea's spacious depths' or
'floor' Wonders of Creation 40; is-caldne wæg 'the
ice-cold wave' Seaf. 19; sincalda sæ sealtum ȳðum
'the sea for ever cold, with its salt waves' Exodus
472. The noun sincieldu 'enduring cold' occurs in

the description of the Land of the Blessed in the
poem on the Phoenix. The prefix sin- meaning
'long-lasting, ever-enduring' is a very ancient
Germanic word or base, and is found in the Gothic
sin-teins 'daily' and sin-teino 'ever, continually,'
also in sin-eigs 'old' which is cognate with Lat.
senex. Other aspects of the sea are expressed in
such phrases as ofer hreone hrycg 'across its
rough (rugged) back' Chr. 859 (cp. Wordsworth's
"The main flood roughened into hill and valley"
Egyptian Maid 42); gyllende gryre 'the yelling
terror' Ex. 489; garsecg wedde 'the ocean raged
(grew mad)' Ex. 489; famig sæ 'the foamy sea'
Gen. 1452; famige flodas 'the foamy floods' Gen.
2213; famige walcan 'the foamy rollers' Andr.
1524; flod famgode 'the flood foamed' Ex. 481;
windige holmas 'the windy crests, waves' Chr.
856; ofer heanne holm 'across the towering (lofty,
mounting) wave' El. 983 and Wand. 82.

The colour of the sea is variously described:

> wonne wægas 'the dark waves'; wonne wælstreamas
> 'dark and deadly streams (currents)' Gen. 119, 1301;
> sweart wæter 'black water' Gen. 1300; brune yða 'the
> brown waves' Andr. 519; on fealone flod, Brunanburg
> 36; on fealone wæg, Gifts of Men 53

The word fealu is given in OE Glossaries as equivalent to
Lat. gilvus, flavus, fulvus, and even to rubicundus. It is applied
in OE to things as different as withered leaves and blossoms,
fire, horses, and the horn of an ox. The word apparently expresses various shades of yellow, from pale to ruddy, and may
probably be best translated 'dun' or 'tawny' when applied to the
sea. The word wann, wonn, our wan, has undergone considerable
change of meaning. It is used several times in Anglo-Saxon
poetry and we shall return to it again.

A forcible and vivid image of toppling waves is called up in
the passage in Exodus describing the catastrophe of the piled-
up waters of the Red Sea, just in time to overwhelm Pharaoh
and his host:

> Lagu land gefeol, lyft wæs onhrered,
> wicon weallfæsten, wægas burston,
> multon meretorras. . . . (482–484)

'The sea fell back upon the land, the very air was stirred, the
battlements crumbled, the waves were riven asunder, the sea-
towers melted away.' The use of the word <u>weallfæsten</u> to describe the walls of water between which the Israelites had passed,
and the phrase <u>meretorras multon</u> are touches of true poetic
genius. This, surely, is the real thing. The whole episode of
the flight and pursuit is presented in this poem with infinite
spirit and gusto.

The Anglo-Saxon poet uses the word <u>fæðm</u> 'the bosom, lap,
or embrace' of the sea, but he does not forget "the deep, un-
fathomed caves of ocean." In the poem known as the <u>Wonders of
Creation</u> or <u>The Order of the World</u>, the poet, speaking of the
setting sun, tells how it

> on æfenne utgarsecges
> grundas pæþeð, (70–71)

'traverses at eve the abyss of furthest ocean,' and then

> gescyndeð in gesceaft godes
> under foldan fæþm, (74–75)

'plunges, according to God's decree, beneath the lap of earth.'

'No man of his own wit can tell —

> hu geond grund færeð gold torht sunne
> in þæt wonne genip under wætra geþring,
> oþþe hwa þæs leohtes londbuende
> brucan mote siþþan heo ofer brim hweorfeð (78–81)

'how the sun, all glorious with gold, flashes across the ocean-bed,
in that dim shade beneath the tumult of the waters, nor what in-
habitant of earth enjoys its light, when once it sinks below the
verge.' In the poem on the Whale, the plunging of the monster
into the depths of the sea, carrying with him the weary seamen,
who, mistaking it for an island, have imprudently landed and en-
camped upon his back, is likened to the overwhelming of an evil

man's soul in hell, when the devil seizes and carries it away—

> mid þam he færinga
> heoloþhelme beþeaht helle seceð
> gode geasne, grundleasne wylm
> under mistglome. Whale 44–47.

'Suddenly, enshrouded in darkness, stripped of his possessions, he seeks hell, visits the bottomless surge beneath the misty gloom.' It is evident from the context that the poet has really conjured up in his mind the journey of the whale itself to the ocean bed, although he is actually speaking of the passing of the soul to hell. We have in these passages a cluster of words which call up romantic and mysterious images:

> grundas 'depths'; under foldan fæðm 'below earth's bosom'; wonne genip 'dim darkness'; wætra geþring 'tumult of waters'; heoloþhelm 'dusky covering'; grundleasne wylm 'bottomless surge' — wylm 'boiling, raging, swirl' is used in A-S. both of fire and of water—; mistglom 'misty gloom.'

As might be expected, the ship is very often mentioned in Anglo-Saxon poetry, and it has many names. I am not inclined to dispute with those who find nothing of great poetic value in most of the following:

> wægflota 'wave-floater' El. 246, Andr. 487; hringed-stefna 'curved prow' Beow. 32; heahstefn naca 'high-prowed ship' Andr. 266; sægenga 'sea goer' Beow. 1882; brimwudu 'sea wood' El. 244; merehus 'sea house' (of the Ark) Gen. 1364; sæmearh 'sea horse' El. 228, 245, Andr. 267; sæhengest 'sea-stallion' Andr. 488; fearoðhengestas El. 226; wæghengestas 'wave stallions' El. 236, and Guthlac 1303; yðmearas Chr. 864; sundhengestas Chr. 863; wægþel 'wave plank' Gen. 1358; brimþisa 'sea monster' El. 238; wæterþisa Guthl. 1303; brontstefn 'steep-prowed' Andr. 504.

The epithets, however, applied to the ship, and of some of
the passages concerning voyages are often of singular beauty.
The ship is famig scip 'foamy ship' Genesis 1417; isig ond utfus
'icy and eager to be gone' Beowulf 33, of a ship standing in port;
men are said neþan on nacan tealtum 'to venture upon the heaving (unsteady, lit. tilting) ship,' Runic Poem 64. It is impossible
not to recognize the vivid imagery of

> Streamwelm hwileð
> beateþ brimstæðo: is se bat ful scrid,
> færeð famigheals   fugole gelicost,
> glideð on geofone.   Andr. 495–498.

'The eddying surge roars loud; it beats the shore.
The boat with all sails set (literally, full shrouded, or
clothed, or, simply "very swift") flits foamy-throated,
likest to a bird; glides across the sea.'

The same beautiful phrase had already been twice used in
Beowulf:

> gewat þa ofer wægholm   winde gefysed
> flota famig-heals   fugle gelicost.
>> (217–218, cp. 1909)

'Departed then across the wave-crests, driven by
the wind, the foamy-throated ship most like to a bird.'

In Wanderer 81, a ship is not said to be like a bird, but becomes the bird itself — fugel. [2]
We cannot deny to the poet who could write like this, qualities of a very high order. We may get rather tired of the
brimhengestas and so forth, but when we find the poet saying se
brimhengest bridles ne gymeð (Runic Poem 66), 'the sea-stallion
heeds not the bridle,' it is evident that the poet by a swift flash
of imagination is identifying the thing with the image called up
by the metaphor — he really sees the ship as a restive, uncontrollable steed. A similar vivification of the ship as a living
thing is suggested by the verb plegean in Elene 245, 'he who was
looking on might behold' sæmearh plegean 'the sea-horse play
(gambol, frolic).' The noun is also used in reference to a ship's

journey, which is called <u>sundplega</u> 'sea play, sea frolic, or sport,'
Guthlac 1308.

A common verb in connexion with a ship, used both transitively and intransitively, is <u>drifan</u>:

> þeah þe he ne meahte   on mere drifan
> hringedstefnan: holm storme weol,
> won wiδ winde;   winter yþe beleac
> isgebinde.   <u>Beow</u>. 1130–33.

'But he could not drive his curved ship forth
upon the sea; the billows raged fiercely, contended
with the wind; winter locked the waves in icy fetters.'

Or again—

> Sum mæg fromlice
> ofer sealtne sæ   sundwudu drifan.
> <u>Chr</u>. 676–677.

'One may vigorously drive his ship (sea-wood)
across the salt sea.'

Beowulf with his dying breath commands that a lofty beacon
shall be raised on the headland to his memory, which seafarers
shall call Beowulf's cairn (2807–08):

> þa δe brentingas
> ofer floda genipu   feorran drifaδ.

'Those who drive the high ships from afar
through the darkness of the flood.'

Another pregnant word is <u>brecan</u>:

> Oft þæt gesæleδ   þæt we on sælade
> .   .   .   .   .   .
> brecaδ ofer bæδweg   brimhengestum.

'Often it betides that in our voyaging we . . .
break forth across the sea (bathway) on our sea-
stallions.' <u>Andr</u>. 513.

It must be confessed that the effect is marred here by the fussy insistence on variety of phrase—bæðweg is almost as bad as the 'briny deep.'

Again, in Elene 244, the "sea horse" is said to brecan ofer bæðweg.

But it is time to leave the sea and ships—a whole article might easily be devoted to the Anglo-Saxon poets' treatment of them—and with two characteristic passages I must conclude this part of my remarks. The first describes the homeward voyage of Beowulf from Heorot. I follow the text of Professor Chambers:

>   . . . gewat him on naca
> drefan deop wæter,   Denaland ofgeaf.
> þa wæs be mæste   mere-hrægla sum,
> segl sale fæst;   sund-wudu þunede;
> no þær weg-flotan   wind ofer yðum
> siðes getwæfde;   sægenga for,
> fleat famig-heals   forð ofer yðe
> bunden-stefna   ofer brim-streamas,
> þæt hie Geata clifu   ongitan meahton,
> cuþe næssas;   ceol up geþrang
> lyft-geswenced,   on lande stod.
>   Beow. 1903–13.

'And so the ship departed, and churned up the deep water, left the land of the Danes. The sea-garment was upon the mast, the sail held fast by its ropes; the sea-wood creaked. In no wise did the wind (blowing) across the billows impede the journey of the wave-floater; the sea-goer sped on, scudded foamy-throated forth across the main, the vessel, trim and taut (passed) through the ocean currents, till they could see the cliffs of the Gauts, the well-known headlands. The ship rose, wind-impelled, and came to rest upon the land.'

This passage, which the translation but poorly renders, illustrates nearly every feature and quality of Anglo-Saxon poetry: the extraordinary variety of phrase and word; the repetition of the same idea in different terms; the highly pictorial and vivid

forms of expression; the beautiful epithet <u>famig-heals</u>, and finally
the engaging human touch of the <u>cuþe næssas</u>, winding up a piece
of description in which every word throbs with life, calls up an
image or a sound, and has a true poetic value both from its character and its associations.

The second passage is equally typical, though very different
in character, and expresses another and more solemn aspect of
the Anglo-Saxon spirit. It is pervaded by an atmosphere of serene
yet wistful melancholy. This is probably the most elaborate
simile in our old poetry, and is characteristic on the one hand
from its moralization of experience drawn from actual life, and
on the other, from the way in which the poet turns to Nature for
images to enforce his moral.

> Nu is þon gelicost,   swa we on laguflode
> ofer cald wæter   ceolum liðan,
> geond sidne sæ   sundhengestum,
> flodwudu fergen: is þæt frecne stream,
> yða ofermæta,   þe we her on lacað
> geond þas wacan woruld,   windge holmas
> ofer deop gelad.   Wæs se drohtað strong,
> ær þon we to lande   geliden hæfdon
> ofer hreone hrycg: þa us help bicwom,
> þæt us to hælo   hyþe gelædde
> godes gæstsunu   ond us giefe sealde,
> þæt we oncnawan magun   ofer ceoles bord,
> hwær we sælan sceolon   sundhengestas,
> ealde yðmearas   ancrum fæste.   <u>Chr</u>. 851–864.

I must here, as in other passages, only attempt a more or
less free translation which shall render as faithfully as I can
the spirit of the original, but does not always abide by the actual
words.

> 'Our life is most like a journey in a ship across
> the sea-flood; when we sail upon the chill water, put
> forth on sea-stallions, upon the spacious ocean steer
> our bark.

> That is a dangerous stream, its waves are huge,
> On which in this frail life a while we toss,

On windy crests, across a plumbless track.
Our life was harsh ere we had come to land,
Brought safe to port o'er ocean's rugged back.
God's blessed Son gave us the grace to know,
While still aboard the ship, where we at last,
The journey done, should tie our horses up,
Tether the trusty coursers of the sea.'

I have had to alter the last line slightly in translation, as
the metaphor of tying a horse to an anchor is rather more than
the modern reader can stand. In this passage the old poet is
using the favourite sundhengestas, and yōmearas simply as
picturesque variants for 'ship,' and appears to have lost sight
of the literal sense altogether, so that what in Modern English
would be a rather ludicrous mixture of metaphors was almost
certainly not felt as such by those who heard this line when it
was composed.

The treatment of landscape and the ever-changing face of
nature in the Anglo-Saxon poets is pervaded with a gentle, placid
beauty when exhibiting the milder phases, but is less interesting
here, than when the more sombre and mysterious aspects are
revealed. No single poem, probably, has so much of sunlight,
and of the sweetness of woods and rills as the Phoenix. The first
84 lines are well known to all beginners in Anglo-Saxon, from
Sweet's Anglo-Saxon Reader. In this passage occurs the famous
description of the Land of the Blest, parallels to which are
pointed out in Homer, in Tennyson, and in Swinburne, to mention
no other poets. There are other passages throughout the poem
scarcely inferior in poetic quality, though none of the same sustained beauty. Although the subject of the poem is the fabulous
phoenix which occasionally lends a kind of unreality to the descriptions, we feel that most of it could only have been written
by a poet who knew and loved nature.

The poets make use of fewer metaphorical clichés in referring to earth and sky than when writing of the sea and ships.
Still we have, for the sun:

wuldres gim 'gem of glory' Ph. 117; heofones
gim 'heaven's gem' Ph. 183, and Beow. 2072; gimma
gladost 'gladdest of gems' Ph. 289; swegles tapur
'taper of the sky' Ph. 114; heofon-condel 'candle of

heaven' Andr. 243, Ex. 115, and Chr. 608; swegl-condel 'sky candle' Ph. 108; wyn-condel 'joy candle' Guthl. 1186; godes condel Ph. 91 and Brunanb. 15; heofon-tungol 'heaven's luminary' (tungol means 'heavenly body, luminary,' and is used of the sun, stars, and planets); forðmære tungol 'most glorious star'; swegles leoma 'ray, brilliance, of the sky' Ph. 103; wedertacen wearm 'warm weather-token' Guthl. 1267; torht tacen Godes 'glorious token of God' Ph. 96; beorht beacen Godes 'bright beacon of God' Beow. 570; se æðela glæm 'the noble gleam' Guthl. 1252.

The epithets applied to the sun, apart from those occurring in some of the above phrases, are few in number, and not particularly interesting. Gold-torht 'glorious with gold' Wonders of Creation 78, morgen-torht 'morning-glorious' Andreas 241, are, I believe, the most striking. The rising of the sun over land and sea is constantly referred to, often with much felicity of phrase: glad ofer grundas 'glided across the earth' Beowulf 2073 and Brunanburg 15. The same verb is used of the departure of darkness nihthelm toglad 'the night shadows glided apart,' or 'parted' Elene 78.

> þa com morgen-torht,
> beacna beorhtost   ofer breomo sneowan
> halig of heolstre,   heofoncandel blac
> ofer laguflodas.   Andr. 241–244.

'Then all glorious with morning, the brightest of beacons came hastening over the sea; the holy thing from its secret place, the candle of heaven (came hastening), pale, across the sea-floods.'

The epithet blac 'pale' (which glosses pallidus, Napier, OE Glosses, 11, 145) is a good touch to describe the newly-risen sun. It is, however, equally possible, and Mr. Sisam thinks it more probable, that blac here is the preterite of blican, in which case I should render it 'glimmered.' The idea of the rapid coming on of day when once the sun rises above the horizon is again expressed, and by the same verb sneowan in Wonders of Creation 59–63:

> . . . and þis leohte beorht
> cymeð morgna gehwam   ofer misthleoþu
> wadan ofer wægas   wundrum gegierwed,
> and mid ærdæge   eastan snoweð
> wlitig and wynsum   wera cneorissum.

'And this bright being comes with its light each
morning over the misty slopes, traverses the waves,
adorned with spendour, and with the dawn hastens
from the East, radiant, and delightful for the races
of men.'

The Anglo-Saxon poet is perhaps even happier in describing
the coming on of night. He revels in shadows, in mists and darkness and strange half-lights. For instance:

> swearc norðrodor
> won under wolcnum,   woruld miste oferteah
> þystrum beþeahte,   þrong niht ofer tiht
> londes frætwa.   Guthl. 1253–56.

'The northern sky grew dark, black beneath its
cloudy canopy, it curtained the world in mist, covered
it with darkness; night pressed on and blotted out the
beauty of the land.'

The latter portion of the passage is ambiguous in construction
and meaning. The text is apparently corrupt. I have, however,
rendered what appears to be the general meaning. The fine
phrase woruld miste oferteah, with its picture of 'drawing over'
as it were a curtain or veil of mist, recalls Collins's

> and marks o'er all
> Thy dewy fingers draw
> The gradual dusky veil.

Here is the kind of picture which the poet loves:

> Sunne gewat   to sete glidan
> under niflan næs;   niht helmade,
> brunwann oferbræd   beorgas steape.
>   Andr. 1304–10.

'The sun departed, sinking to its bed, (dropped)
below the lofty headland; night dark and dun covered
up, enshrouded, the steep hills.'

Or again, nap nihtscua, norðan sniwde 'the shadow of night grew
dark, and from the north it snowed' Seafarer 31.

There is a vagueness in the lines which tell how Hrothgar
half expected the monster to come on the night when Beowulf
was waiting for him, which is in keeping with the atmosphere of
mystery which the poet wishes to create:

Wiste þæm ahlæcan
to þæm heah-sele   hilde geþinged,
siððan hie sunnan leoht   geseon ne meahton,
oððe nipende   niht ofer ealle,
scadu-helma gesceapu   scriþan cwoman.
                                              Beow. 646–650.

'He (Hrothgar) knew that battle was in store for
the monster in the high hall, so soon as they could
no longer see the light of the sun, when darkening
night was over all things, and shadowy shapes would
come stealing under the dusky sky!'

This appears to mean that in the dark, when strange creatures
of the shadows are abroad, anything might happen. It is not
actually suggested or specifically implied that Grendel will be
among these creeping shadows,—unless indeed, as is just possible, that scadu-helma refers to him and his mother—but he
may be. Well, let him come, and he will meet his match to-
night!

The old poets are fond of using the processes of nature as
symbols of moods; it might indeed almost be said that for them

the meanest flower that blows can give
Thoughts that do often lie too deep for tears.

Hu seo þrag gewat,

exclaims the Recluse,

> genaþ under niht-helm   swa heo no wære.
> > Wand. 95–96.

'How that time'—that is, time of happiness—
'has fled, grown dark beneath the helm of night, as
though it had never been.'

> > Nu synt geardagas
> æfter fyrstmearce   forðgewitene,
> lifwynne geliden.   El. 1266–68.

> > Landes frætwa
> gewitaþ under wolcnum   winde geliccost.
> > Ibid. 1270–71.

'Now in due time, the good old days have passed
away, life's joys are fled. The loveliness of earth
shall flee away beneath the clouds like the wind.'

The cuckoo for the Anglo-Saxon is not usually a 'blithe new-
comer,' but

> > Geac monað   geomran reorde,
> > singeð sumeres weard,   sorge beodeð
> > bittre in breosthord,   Seaf. 53–55.

'The cuckoo admonishes, summer's guardian
sings with lamentable voice, tells of bitter sorrow
to come';

or, again:

> > þu gehyrde   in hliþes oran
> > galan geormorne   geac on bearwe,
> > > H. M. 21–22.

'Thou hast heard from the hillside the mournful
cuckoo singing in the grove.'

But more cheerful is

> fæger fugla reord   folde geblowen
> geacas gear budon.   Guthl. 714–715.

'Sweet were the notes of birds, the fields ablow,
and cuckoos ushered in the year.'

The vocabulary for describing the milder aspects of nature
is rich enough, but it cannot be said that these pictures are very
convincing. They resemble too much a stage landscape, bathed
in eternal sunshine, with trim cottages nestling by pastures for
ever green, woodlands which "never bid the spring adieu," and
gleaming brooks meandering through the fields and groves.
Brade sind on worulde/grene geardas (Gen. 510–511) 'spacious upon the earth are the green enclosures'; þæt is wynsum
wong, wealdas grene (Ph. 13) 'that is a gracious plain, its woods
are green'; wudu sceal on /foldan blædum blowan; beorh sceal
on eorðan /grene stondan (Cotton Gnomes 33–35) 'a wood shall
be blowing with flowers and fruit in the land, a hill shall stand
green upon the earth'; geseah he geblowene bearwas standan,
blædum gehrodene (Andr. 1448–49) 'he saw the blossoming
groves all gay with fruitage stand.'
Or take a couple of longer passages from the Phoenix:

> . . . ac þær lagustreamas
> wundrum wrætlice   wyllan onspringað,
> fægrum flodwylmum   foldan leccaþ,
> wæter wynsumu   of þæs wuda midle,
> þa monþa gehwam   of þære moldan tyrf
> brimcald brecað,   bearo ealne geondfarað
> þragum þrymlice.   (62–68)

'There springing from their source, smooth-flowing streams
With gentle, eddying flood the champaign lave;
Those waters fair, in some far woodland glade,
Break through the turfy soil, cold as the sea,
And sweep in stately windings through the grove.'

The style of this passage in the original is so elaborate and highly
wrought, every word being chosen to give variety and wealth of
imagery, that it seems permissible to use a corresponding flower-
iness of language in translating it. No impression equivalent to

that produced by the Anglo-Saxon can possibly be gathered from
a bald and literal rendering. Among the chief features of the
diction we may note the following: the variety of words for water,
stream, spring, etc.: lagustreamas, wyllan 'well, spring, fount,'
wæter, flodwylmum literally 'flood-bubblings, eddyings,' etc.;
the use of the words onspringað 'spring forth, issue, gush out,'
etc., brecað 'break forth, burst out,' leccaþ 'to water, irrigate,
lave,' etc., geondfarað 'flow through, traverse, wind through,'
and so on; to describe the movements of the water the adverbs
wundrum 'marvellously,' wrætlice 'splendidly, with pomp and
dignity,' etc., þrymlice 'gloriously, splendidly, in a stately manner' from þrymm 'might, splendour, magnificence' and so on;
the adjectives wynsumu (on which see below, pp. 208–209),
fægrum, with the same poetical significance as its modern descendant 'fair,' and brimcald 'sea-cold.' This is indeed one of
those passages which abound in Anglo-Saxon poetry, on which
the writer has lavished the treasures of his art, and piled word
upon word, each pregnant with meaning and rich in poetical associations.

The other passage I propose to quote has the same smooth
beauty, but from the nature of the scene described its atmosphere is more unreal.

> Smylte is se sigewong   sun-bearo lixeð,
> wuduholt wynlic: wæstmas ne dreosaþ
> beorhte blede,   ac þa beamas a
> grene stondað   swa him god bibead;
> wintres and sumeres   wudu bið gelice
> bledum gehongen;   næfre brosniað
> leaf under lyfte.   Ph. 33–39.

'Serene the plain, its sunny woodland gleams;
Fair wood whose foison ne'er declines, whose flowers
Eternal glow, on boughs for ever green.
So God ordained; and whatsoe'er the time,
Winter or summer, still the grove shall stand
All hung with fruit, and 'neath that placid sky
No leaf decays, no petal flutters down.'

(Cp. also various other passages throughout the poem, notably
lines 71–82, where the same unfading wood is further described.)

DICTION AND IMAGERY IN ANGLO-SAXON POETRY

This is assuredly no English wood; it has no more substance than

> Those Hesperian gardens famed of old
> Fortunate fields and groves and happy vales;

it is indeed the wood in which the Phoenix built his nest.

This poem of the Phoenix, in spite of the unreality of the world which it depicts, is full of beauties; the whole of the diction is sweet and varied. It deserves to be studied as a whole, and not merely in the short passage found in Sweet's and other Readers. We may take leave here of this fortunate island, where for ever the marvellous bird lives, perishes, and rises, refreshed and more brilliant from its own ashes, by quoting a brief reference to a genuine English Harvest Home to which there is no parallel in the Latin of Lactantius, of which the poem is a paraphrase:

> Swa mon to andleofne eorðan wæstmas
> on hærfeste ham gelædeð,
> wiste wynsume, ær wintres cyme
> on rypes timan, þy læs hi renes scur
> awyrde under wolcnum: þær hi wraðe metað
> fodorþege gefean, þonne forst and snaw
> mid ofermægne eorðan þeccað
> wintergewædum.   Ph. 243–250.

> 'So at the harvest in the time of reaping, men carry home the fruits of the earth, for their sustenance, a pleasant feast, ere the coming of winter, lest storms of rain from the clouds should injure them; herein men find nourishment; they rejoice over their banquet when frost and snow cover the earth abundantly, with a wintry mantle.'

This glimpse of reality is, however, only introduced to give the poet the chance of comparing the reproduction of fresh corn from the old, with the rise of a new phoenix from the ashes of the old.

There are several passages here and there in Anglo-Saxon poetry where the coming of Spring is alluded to with real feeling and with great delicacy of phrase; for instance:

Bearwas blostmum nimað,   byrig fægriað,
wongas wlitigað,   woruld onetteð.   Seaf. 48–49.

'Groves put forth their blossoms, cities grow
fair; the plains are jocund; all nature stirs.'

I take woruld onetteð here to mean, as we should now say,
'things are moving,' 'all Nature is quickening.' 'The world hastens onward,' the literal translation, is meaningless in this passage.

A picturesque phrase occurs in Beowulf 1135–36, oþer com/
gear in geardas . . . þa wæs winter scacen,/ fæger foldan bearm;
that is, 'another year came into the courts (dwellings of men);
winter was driven away, the bosom of the earth was fair.' Note
the use of scacen here. I shall return later to this word. I conclude these instances of the old poets' treatment of the milder
moods of Nature by a passage full of sweetness from the poem
on Daniel, which is (or ought to be) often quoted by those who
write and lecture on Anglo-Saxon literature, because it contains
one of the rare similes in this poetry. The reference is to the
coming of the angel to deliver Daniel and his companions from
the burning fiery furnace:

þa wæs on þam ofne,   þær se engel becwom,
windig and wynsum,   wedere gelicost
þonne hit on sumeres tid   sended weorðeð
dropena dreorung   on dæges hwile,
wearmlic wolcna scur: swylc bið wedera cyst,
swylc wæs on þam fyre   frean mihtum
halgum to helpe.   Dan. 346–52.

'Then was it in the furnace, when the angel
appeared, breezy and delightful, most like the weather
when in the summer time, there comes from heaven
a fall of drops, in the daytime, a genial shower of
rain: just as is that best of weather, so was it in the
fire, by God's might, for the succour of his saints.'

It is difficult to find fit equivalents for windig and wynsum, a
beautiful phrase in the original, the charm of which vanishes if
it be rendered, as I have heard it, 'windy and winsome.' The

former word may refer in OE equally to the gusts of a tempest (e.g. windige weallas 'windy walls,' said of cliffs facing the sea, Beowulf 572), or to the sighings of a gentle breeze, which latter is what is intended here. Wynsum is full of agreeable suggestiveness. It means 'pleasant, delightful, sweet, charming, gracious, graceful, comely,' and it has a tinge also of gaiety and liveliness. In Professor Napier's OE Glosses it is variously used to gloss dulcis, suavis, venustus, egregius, jocundus, lepidus, amoenus. It is much used in Anglo-Saxon poetry as an epithet for almost anything of which the poet approves. It is not always easy to find a suitable equivalent in Modern English having regard to the character of the passage as a whole. Milton's phrase jocund and boon would express it pretty well.

I turn now to the treatment of the mysterious and sombre in Nature. It is noteworthy that many of the words expressing storm, mist, dark(ness), gloom, and the like, survive and still retain for us the old poetic association.

In Beowulf, everything relating to the home of the monsters, its surroundings, the stealthy comings and goings of Grendel and his avenging Mother, is dark and terrible. Of Grendel, it is said, sin-nihte heold / mistige moras (161–162) 'during the long night he held the misty moors.' Com on wanre niht, scriþan sceadu-genga (702–703) 'the shadow-lurker came stealing on, in the dark night'; of more under mist-hleoþum (710) 'from the moor, beneath the misty slopes'; the Mother returns ofer myrcan mor 'across the dark (murky) moor' (1405), carrying the body of the murdered Æschere. After this last outrage the hunt is up, and Beowulf and Hrothgar track the monster to her lair guided by a trail of blood. They pass over

        steap stanhliðo,   stige nearwe,
        enge an-paðas,   uncuð gelad,
        neowle næssas,   nicor-husa fela.
                        (1409–11)

        Oþ þæt he færinga   fyrgen-beamas
        ofer harne stan   hleonian funde,
        wyn-leasne wudu;   wæter under stod
        dreorig und gedrefed.   (1414–17)

'Steep rocky slopes, toilsome upward tracks,
narrow paths where only one can go, ways hard to
find, towering headlands, and many a place where
goblins dwell.'

'Till of a sudden he descried some mountain
trees, which arched over a hoary rock, a joyless
wood; below it stood a water, blood-stained and
turbid.'

This horrible lake, in whose depths Grendel hid, had already
been more particularly described by Hrothgar in a passage
which is famous now, and which was still well known centuries
after it was written, since a picture of the abode of lost souls
in a Blickling Homily written in the last quarter of the tenth
century is based upon it.

I must content myself with giving only a translation; for the
original, most readers of Anglo-Saxon poetry know it by heart.
The reference is <u>Beowulf</u> 1357–76.

That is a secret place in which they dwell:
Wolf-haunted slopes and windy promontories;
A treacherous fenny track; the mountain streams
Fall sheer adown the headland's shadowy side,
The flood sinks under ground. 'Tis not far hence,
Bosomed in rimy thickets stands the mere—
Deep-rooted trees that make a vault above.
There every night an eerie sight is seen,
A portent strange, a fire upon the flood.
None lives so wise, of all the sons of men,
That he may reckon out how deep it be.
And the heath-rover, the strong-antlered stag,
Though he may seek the wood when driven afar,
And by the pack hard-pressed, yet will he rather
Yield up his breath, his life, upon the bank,
Ere he within those depths will hide his head.
That is a dismal place; the leaping wave
Thence rises black, wind-driven, towards the sky;
Fierce tempests stir, and in the darkening air
The very heavens weep.

DICTION AND IMAGERY IN ANGLO-SAXON POETRY

The Anglo-Saxon poets know how to produce an atmosphere of gloom and mystery by the use of one or two words, as in this exclamation of the sorrowful lady in the Wife's Lament, 30–32:

> Sindon den dimme,   dun up-hea,
> bittre burg-tunas   brerum beweaxne,
> wic wynna leas.

'Dim are the valleys, the hills exceeding high,[3]
the cities are desolate, overgrown with briars, the
dwellings emptied of delight.'

Note dimme, wynna leas, and the unexpected transference of meaning shown in the use of bittre 'bitter, grievous,' here meaning 'causing bitterness of heart.' There is perhaps also a side glance at the cruel, trailing briars. Our phrase 'a dismal sight' would render the idea pretty well.

The poet of the Creation and the Fall has plenty of scope for descriptions of the sombre, the mysterious, and the terrible. He pictures the Creator in high heaven, looking out upon Chaos. Nothing was there as yet, i.e. where the earth was to be, but heolstorsceado 'enveloping shadow' (Genesis 103); the wide abyss stod deop and dim (Genesis 105). God gazed, and saw that place dreama lease 'void of joys';

> geseah deorc gesweorc,
> semian sinniht,   sweart under roderum
> wonn and weste.   Gen. 108–110.

'He saw dusky cloud, and eternal night brooding,
black beneath the heavens, dark and desolate.'

The rebellious angels are cast on þa deopan dala 'into the deep dales' (of hell). Here, for every fiend the fire is ever renewed.

> þonne cymð on uhtan   easterne wind
> forst fyrnum cald,   symble fyr oððe gar.
>   Gen. 315–316.

'Then comes from the east a wind in the morning, frost with fearful cold; ever either fire or the
stab of frost.'

We read of hatne heaðowelm 'hot battle-surge' (Genesis 324);
brand and brade ligas swilce eac þa biteran recas, / þrosm and
þystro (Genesis 325–326) 'burning, and broad flames, likewise
bitter smoke, vapour, and darkness.' Satan exclaims in rage
and agony:

> Ac licgað me ymbe   irenbendas,
> rideð racentan sal.   Gen. 371–372.

> 'Bonds of iron lie about me,
> A chain of fetters rides me.'

> Ic a ne geseah
> laðran landscipe.   Ibid. 375–376.

> 'I never saw a loathlier region.'

Here is a passage which will go word for word into Modern
English:

> hafað us god sylfa
> forswapen on þas sweartan mistas. Gen. 31.

> 'God himself has swept us away into these black
> (swart) mists.'

The words and expressions for the human body, human death,
and the tomb are very varied. The body is:

þæt earme flæsc Run. P. 62; flæsc-homa 'fleshly
covering' Beow. 1568; ban-cofa 'bony case' Guthl. 927;
banfæt 'bony vessel' Ph. 229 (of the body of the Phoenix);
ban-loca 'bony enclosure' Chr. 769; lic-hord 'body
treasure' Guthl. 1003; feorh-hus 'life, spirit's house'
Maldon 297; sawel-hus 'soul's house' Guthl. 1003, 1114;
cp. Waller's the soul's dark cottage; þæt fæcne hus El.
1236 'treacherous house (of the spirit)'; lamfæt 'clay

(lit. 'loam') vessel.' In <u>Fates of the Apostles</u>, the
poet speaks of leaving behind him at death, 'my
body, that portion of earth, that garment of mortality,' <u>lic, eorþan dæl, wælreaf</u>, 94–95. Human
life is <u>þis deade lif læne on londe</u> <u>Seaf</u>. 64–65,
'this dead, this transitory life upon the land' (cp.
Vaughan's 'this dead and dark abode,' i.e. life
here, contrasted with that hereafter); <u>þis wace lif</u>,
<u>þis læne</u> <u>Death of Edgar</u> 3–4, 'this frail, this tran-
sitory life'; <u>fyrst is æt ende lænes lifes</u> 'the period
of transitory life is at an end' <u>Ex</u>. 267–268; <u>oflet</u>
<u>lifdagas, and þas lænan gesceaft</u> (<u>Beow</u>. 1622) 'he
forsook his life-days, and this transitory being
(existence)'; <u>hæfde ende gefered lænan lifes</u> (<u>Beow</u>.
2844–45) 'he had reached (journeyed to) the end of
this fleeting life.'

Death is <u>feorh-gedal</u> 'severance, cutting off, of life' <u>Andreas</u>
181, <u>Guthlac</u> 1173; <u>sawel gedal</u> <u>Guthlac</u> 1008; the soul is said to
be 'hurried away on its outward journey' <u>afysed on forðsið</u>
<u>Guthlac</u> 1911; <u>æfter hinsiþe</u> 'after the going hence' <u>Judith</u> 117.
Death is called <u>deaþ se bitera</u> 'bitter death' <u>Death of Edward</u> 26;
<u>hæleþa hryre</u> 'fall of heroes' <u>Beowulf</u> 3005; <u>swyltdæge</u> 'the day
of death' <u>Beowulf</u> 2798.

The tomb is <u>deaþreced</u> (<u>Phoenix</u> 48) 'death chamber';
<u>hæleþa heolstorcofa</u> (<u>Phoenix</u> 49) 'the dark retreat, secret cham-
ber, of men (heroes).' In <u>Juliana</u> 683 the phrase <u>in þam þystran</u>
<u>ham</u> 'in that dark home,' is applied to the place in which wicked
men who have been drowned remain, and in the following line,
<u>in þam neolan scræfe</u> 'in that deep cavern,' it being evident from
the context that, in a typically Anglo-Saxon manner, both expressions are used at once of the depths of ocean which hold their
bodies, and of the abyss of Hell to which their souls have fled.

In the passage in <u>Judith</u> 105–121 which describes the death
of Holofernes at the hands of the savage heroine, there is a similar identification of the fate of the body and soul; or rather the
figurative language which is used of each appears to be applied
almost indistinguishably to both at once. The "foul carcass"
lies gaping, and the spirit "goes elsewhere"—<u>gæst ellor hwearf</u>,
<u>under neowelne næs</u> (112–113) 'his spirit went elsewhere, be-·
neath the steep promontory' (i.e. 'into the abyss'), and is said

to be 'held fast in torment, encompassed with worms' (115); þystrum forðylmed 'girt about with darkness' (118); he need not hope, we are told, ever to escape from the 'wormy abode' of ðam wyrmsele, but must remain eternally 'in that dark home,' in ðam heolstran ham (121). It appears that the poet is speaking of the grave and of the place of the wicked soul, in the same breath, and in identical terms. In a moving passage at the end of the Fates of the Apostles, the poet asks those who love his song to pray for him after his death, that he may have peace and consolation. "How much," he exclaims, "shall I have need of friends, and loving ones, upon my journey, when I shall seek my long home, my unfamiliar dwelling-place, alone."

> Hu ic freonda beþearf
> liðra on lade, þonne ic langne ham
> eardwic uncuð ana gesece. F. of A. 91–93.

Mr. Tolkien, in his article in RES cited above, points out that the phrase 'long home,' so familiar to us now in the well-known chapter of Ecclesiastes, occurs not only in the above passage (as is recorded by Toller in the Supplement to Bosworth), and in Handlyng Synne (as indicated by the Oxford Dictionary), but is also found in another place in OE, namely, in the Vision of Leofric (Napier [TPS, 1908]). Mr. Tolkien quotes this last passage: he sceolde cuman to cofantreo to his langan hame, þær he on restet, which, he says, proves that the phrase means 'grave' and not 'future life.' It is quite certain that it means 'grave' in this instance, but it is, I think, equally certain that in the passage just quoted from the Fates of the Apostles, the expression refers not only to the grave in which the body lies, but to the future life of the spirit as well. Here, as in the passages from Juliana and Judith, the poet, in speaking of death, has simultaneously in his mind the physical and the spiritual aspects; he blends them inextricably in thought, and uses his words, at the same time, both literally and metaphorically. Cp. also to þam langan gefean, Juliana 670, quoted below.

We have already mentioned several phrases used to express the act or process of dying, but one or two others call for mention. The commonest phrase, of a figurative character, though this is not confined to poetry, is gewitan 'to depart, go hence.' More strictly belonging to poetical usage is on weg hweorfan

'to go away,' though hweorfan is much less colourless than 'go,'
meaning originally 'to turn, change, wander.' The word is used
in Beowulf 264–265:

> . . . ær he on weg hwurfe,
> gamol of geardum,

'ere he went away, an old man, from his dwellings.'

Feorh ofgefon 'they gave up (relinquished) their lives,' Fates
of the Apostles 12, is commonplace, but sume wig fornam, ferede
in forðwege 'some war has taken away, has carried them upon
their outward journey,' Wanderer 80–81, has that touch of mystery which is so frequent in this poetry. We get this note again
in the last words of Beowulf (2814–16):

> Ealle wyrd forsweop
> mine magas   to metod-sceafte,
> eorlas on elne;   ic him æfter sceal.

'Fate has swept them all away, my kinsmen, to
their appointed doom—earls in their pride; I must
after them.'

In Brunanburg 28–30, five young kings are said to lie low
sweordum aswefede 'put to sleep by swords.'

A word several times used of dying is cringan (also gringan),
which means apparently in the first instance 'to give way, yield,
sink down, crumple up.' It is used of men falling in battle, but
has also a more extended use. For instance, on here cringan
(Maldon 292) 'to fall among the troops,' i.e. in the midst of battle;
wigend cruncon 'warriors fell' (ibid. 302); he on hilde gecranc
'he sank down in the battle,' (ibid. 324); he æt wige gecrang
Beowulf 1337 (of Grendel) 'he has fallen in war'; heo on flet
gecrong Beowulf 1568, of Grendel's Mother under the blows of
Beowulf, 'she sank down upon the floor'; he (Dæghrefn) . . .
in campe gecrong (Beowulf 2505) 'he sank down in the fight.'
The word is used less specifically in the Wanderer, of the Prince
and his retainers who have died, and left the mead-hall empty
and ruinous: duguð eal gecrong wlonc bi wealle 'the doughty ones
have all sunk down, the proud by the wall' (79–80).

The death of Beowulf himself is thus simply described: <u>him</u>
of hreðre / gewat sawol secean soðfæstra dom 'his soul departed
from his bosom to seek the reward of the faithful' (2819-20).
Of King Edgar it is said that he ended the joys of earth, and <u>geceas</u>
him oþer leoht 'chose him another light.' <u>Leoht</u> is often used
for the 'light of day, of life,' and hence comes to mean simply
'life,' but it is impossible not to feel that at least a suggestion
of the literal meaning 'light' was present in the poet's mind,
and not to be reminded of Hood's

> Her tired eyelids closed, she had
> Another morn than ours.

The phrase <u>geceas ecne ræd (Beowulf</u> 1201) 'he sought eternal
counsel,' is thought by many to refer to death, though Professor
Chambers is rather inclined to a different view. The use of
<u>ceosan</u> 'to choose,' in the sense 'seek, find' occurs also in
<u>Maldon</u> 113 ælræste geceas 'he sought (or found) a bed of death.'
The soul of Juliana is said to be alæded of lice to þam langan
gefean 'led (conducted) from her body to long (enduring) joy'
(<u>Juliana</u> 669-670). Of Edward the Confessor the poet says that,

> Englas feredon
> soþfæste sawle   innan swegles leoht.
>
> <u>Dth. of Edw.</u> 27-28.

'Angels bore his faithful soul into the light of heaven.'

Perhaps one of the most felicitous phrases used of the deatʰ
of princes and nobles is that in <u>Wanderer</u> 61. The poet, pondering upon the passing away of earthly spendour, and of those who
once enjoyed it, remembers <u>hu hi færlice flet ofgeafon</u> 'how they
(earls) suddenly gave up the floor' (of the hall). This exactly
corresponds to the expression 'quit the stage,' than which it has
an even greater appropriateness, because the floor of the mead-
hall was indeed the stage upon which the drama of life was enacted by our ancestors, when they were not hunting or fighting.
<u>Flet</u> occurs a good many times in <u>Beowulf</u>, and nearly always
in connexion with some important action or event. Wealhtheo,
the noble queen, goes all along the floor (<u>flet</u>) bringing the cup
to the guests. Hrothgar's daughter Freawaru ('so I heard those

sitting in the hall, fletsittende, call her'), 'young and gold-adorned' was betrothed to 'the genial son of Froda,' and the poet speaks (2034) of the prince of the Hathobards 'walking with his bride across the floor' (flet). Across the floor (flet), too, were led the eight horses with gold-plated bits which Hrothgar gave to the hero (1035–36). In 1085–86 the Frisians are described as making a bargain that Hengest's followers shall prepare for them oðer flet 'another floor,' and the implication of this is shown by the echoing phrase healle ond heah-setl 'hall and throne' which immediately follows. It is said of Widsith that 'he often had received (standing) upon the floor, the lovely treasure' (Widsith 3–4); on flette geþah, an expression identical with Beowulf geþah ful on flette (Beowulf 1024–25) 'received the cup on the floor,' otherwise, 'in the hall.'

I bring to an end this somewhat lengthy list illustrating the various ways in which the old poets called things 'out of their right names' with some instances of metaphorical expressions for king, sword, and arrow. As we should expect, the old heroic poetry, and the later imitations of this, have a great variety of phrases for king, prince, chief, lord, etc. The following are chiefly from Beowulf. The list makes no pretensions at completeness. The words have merely an associational poetic value, and are mainly interesting as exhibiting a particular and very ancient phase of culture.

The first group expresses that sovereign virtue of princes, generosity:

> beaga brytta 'ring distributor' Beow. 35, 352;
> sinces brytta 'distributor of treasure' Beow. 1170;
> sinc-gifa 'treasure giver' Beow.1012, 1342, etc.,
> and Mald. 278; beah-gifa 'ring giver' Beow. 1102;
> goldwine gumena 'gold friend of men' Beow. 1171.
> The next group refers to the no less essential
> kingly qualities of leadership, and power to pro-
> tect dependants: folces hyrde 'shepherd of the people'
> Beow. 610; heria hildfruma 'battle chief of hosts' El.
> 101; winia baldor 'leader, bold one, of friends' Beow.
> 2567; aðelinga hleo 'protector of princes' El. 99;
> wigendra hleo 'protector of warriors' Beow. 899;
> helm Scyldinga (of Hrothgar) 'helm, covering, pro-
> tection, of the Scyldings' (his people), Beow. 371,

456; frea-drihten 'lord and master' Beow. 796; ealdor
þegna 'ruler of thanes' Beow. 1644; folces aldor
'ruler of the people' El. 157. Finally, a few phrases
expressive of the graciousness and friendliness of
bearing which characterize a good prince: freawine
folca 'lordly friend of peoples' Beow. 2429; freowine
'gracious friend' Beow. 2438; freowine folca 'gracious
friend of peoples' Beow. 430.

A sword is beadu-leoma 'battle ray, gleam, flash'(Beowulf
1523); guð-wine 'battle friend' Beowulf 1810, 2735; homera laf
'leaving of hammers' Beowulf 2829, in reference to the blows
struck in forging it, though laf alone is sometimes used for a
sword, as in Beowulf 454, Hrædlan laf, where it is generally
rendered 'heirloom.' It is possible that the other association
also existed here. Another designation for a sword is drihtlic
iren 'noble, lordly, iron,' Beowulf 892. A phrase for weapons
generally is ord and ecg 'point and edge,' that is, 'spears and
swords,' e.g. Beowulf 1549, Maldon 60. A sword is said to
bitan 'bite in' Beowulf 1454, 1522. Another word, used of a
spear, is wadan þurh 'go through, penetrate,' our 'wade,'
Maldon 140. Arrows (or darts) are hildenædran 'battle adders'
Elene 119, and we read of flana scuras 'showers, storms, of
arrows' Elene 117. A picturesque phrase is hwinende fleah
giellende gar 'whining flew the yelling javelin' Widsith 127–128.
In OE the verb giellan implies a shriller cry than does its
modern descendant 'yell'; it is used, for instance, Seafarer 24,
for the cry of the eagle.
    Battle is lind-plega 'shield play' Beowulf 1073; hand-plega
'hand play' Brunanburg 25; grim guð-plega 'grim war play'
Maldon 61; garmitting gumena 'spear-meeting of men' Brunanburg 50.

III

    We have now examined a considerable number of the meta-
phorical circumlocutions which the Anglo-Saxon poets make use
of in their efforts to avoid calling a spade a spade. It would be
wrong, I think, to regard this habit as a mere mannerism, though
it easily degenerates into one, and the "kennings" too often seem
to be dragged in where a simple and direct expression would be

better. It seems sometimes as if the poet were trying to live up to his responsibilities, to show that he had learnt his lesson, and mastered the technique of his craft. It must be confessed that many of the metaphorical phrases become tedious from iteration and are mere frozen lifeless things. On the other hand, that is not an exhaustive criticism of them. Many of these phrases are full of life, and were certainly composed with the eye on the object. They appear to arise naturally and inevitably to the poet's lips, and at their best they are the creations of a lively and true imagination. It will be noticed how few are the similes in this poetry. We have referred to nearly all that occur, except that in Beowulf 1608, which describes the sword melting away like ice; from the virulence of the monster's blood hit eal gemealt ise gelicost 'it melted all away, most like to ice.' Here the word mealt, a typical metaphorical expression, was quite enough to suggest the ice; indeed "to melt away like ice" may already have been a proverbial phrase. Simile, then, is a very rare ornament of our old poetry. The poet does not merely feel that things are like something else, his mind bridges the gulf, and he sees the two things as identical. We have seen several instances of the intermingling of the symbol and the thing symbolized. This habit of mind is very characteristic of English poets, and it is a habit foreign to the genius of many other peoples, such, for instance, as the French. To turn the daring metaphors of Shakespeare literally into French would probably be to render him unintelligible to French readers. When Shakespeare calls the leafless trees 'Bare ruined choirs where late the sweet birds sang'; when Milton desires to hear the lark 'singing and startle the dull night From his watch-tower in the skies'; when Wordsworth hears 'The cataracts blow their trumpets from the steep'; are they not following the natural bent of the English genius, and doing just what the Anglo-Saxon poet did? I fancy that it would be found difficult to translate into French the passages just quoted, and hundreds of others, whether from Anglo-Saxon poetry, or from later English poets, without turning the metaphors into similes. The speech of ordinary life teems with metaphor, though this is often obscured by the fact that the original, etymological, sense of words is forgotten and only the secondary meaning survives. Again, many metaphors are so familiar that, although a moment's reflection reveals them as such, they cease to delight or surprise.

WYLD

The noblest metaphors are new and fresh creations of poetic imagination. A sense of their truth, "the moment that it is perceived, grows, and continues to grow, upon the mind." Others, often delightful and exciting, are more transient in their effect, they belong to fancy, and have not the "indestructible dominion" of those framed by the imagination. In this greatest of poetic acts, the imaginative creation, working in "the plastic, the pliant, and the indefinite," "the images," as a great poet says, "invariably modify each other."

Of this quality, often imparted by the use of a single word, are Vaughan's

> all the way
> Primros'd and <u>hung</u> with shade,

or,

> Happy are the dead!
> What peace doth now
> <u>Rock him asleep</u> below?

Or Milton's

> Anon out of the earth a fabric huge
> <u>Rose like an exhalation.</u>

Or Peele's

> Now comes my lover tripping like the roe,
> And brings my longings <u>tangled in her hair.</u>

Or Keats's

> But here there is no light,
> Save what from heaven is <u>with the breezes blown.</u>

The reader will not, perhaps, have failed to perceive something of this imaginative quality in many of the phrases from Anglo-Saxon poetry quoted in the foregoing pages.

The examples given in the preceding section, however, were not as a rule chosen primarily for their outstanding quality or originality, but were brought together to illustrate in a general way certain habits of diction as applied to a variety of objects or processes.

I want, in the present section, to illustrate some of the more individual touches of poetic imagination in Anglo-Saxon poetry. Limitations of space permit only a very brief, and, I fear, a rather desultory treatment here, and I have grouped my remarks chiefly, though not entirely, round the use of particular words.

SCACAN. This word has some very interesting uses in poetry. It is the ancestor of the modern shake, which has itself been used with striking effect by modern poets. In OE the word is both intransitive and transitive. It has the general sense of 'shake, agitate,' and of rapid movement or action generally. When used intransitively of immaterial things, time, life, etc., the dictionaries say it means simply 'depart, pass away, hasten on,' and so forth; used transitively of these, it is said to mean 'to dispatch, hasten (departure of).' The question is whether in poetry the word has not a more specific, image-creating force.

The best way of bringing this point before the reader will be to cite a number of passages in which scacan is used of time, life, prosperity, light. I translate in the first instance by a colourless word which I italicize.

(1) intrans. (a) þa seo tid gewat ofer timber scacan mid-dangeardes 'now time passed hastening over the fabric of the earth' Gen. 135–136.

(b) þa com beorht scacan [scima æfter sceaduwe]. (The last words have been supplied by editors to fill a gap in the text; they are pretty generally accepted, but whether the suggestion be right or wrong is immaterial to our present purpose, as it is certain that something to this effect is necessary, and the essential words are there.) 'Then came hastening the bright beam after darkness' Beow. 1802–03.

(c) oþþæt eal sceaceð, / leoht and lif somod 'till all passes away, life and light together' Wids. 141–142.

(d) þonne min sceaceþ / lif of lice 'when my life departs from my body' Beow. 2742–43.

(e) duguð ellor scoc 'my trusty retainers have all departed elsewhere' (i.e. 'have died') Beow. 2254.

(2) trans. (a) þa wæs winter scacen 'now winter had been sent away' Beow. 1136.

(b) þa wæs dæg sceacen 'day had been sent away' Beow.
2306. (With this may be compared Ða wæs morgen-leoht /
scofen and scynded 'Now the morning-light had been thrust
forth and hastened on' Beow. 917–918.)

(c)   Wisse he gearwe
  þæt he dæg-hwila gedrogen hæfde
  eorðan wynne; ða wæs eall sceacen
  dogor-gerimes; deað ungemete neah.
           Beow. 2725–28.

'Well he knew that he had lived out his hours
of life, his earthly joy; now the span of his days
was all run out; death was exceeding near.'

(d) bið his lif scæcen 'his life is departed' Fates of Men 39.

(e) Hu mæg ic þæt findan þæt swa fyrn gewearð
  wintra gangum? Is nu worn sceacen
  c.c. oððe ma geteled rimes. El. 632–634.

'How shall I find that which with the flight of
winters has become so remote? The number of
them now passed is two hundred or more.

(f)   Lig ealle forswealg,
  gæsta gifrost, þara þe þær guð fornam
  bega folces; wæs hira blæd scacen.
           Beow. 1122–24.

'Fire, that most ravenous of spirits, devoured
all those of both peoples whom war had snatched
away; their glory had departed.'

Now as regards the passages in group 1, in several cases perhaps 'hurry, hasten,' etc., are good enough, but in others, if we
can preserve some of the ideas associated with 'shaking' the
effect is distinctly enhanced. Thus in (1) (b) may not the idea
be 'diffusing itself' or 'coming on by leaps and bounds'? In (1)
(c) and (d) may we not believe that the poet in using sceaceþ had
at the back of his mind an idea of 'scattering, flinging out, dis-

persing, jerking'? We might almost use Vaughan's 'packs away,'
or 'is sent packing,' if either of these were now consistent with
serious poetry.

In group (2) it can hardly be doubted that the idea of 'shaking
off, shaking out,' and so on, is present. There is a phrase in
Vaughan which is closely parallel to (2) (a) and (b): 'The whole
Creation shakes off night' (The Dawning); and another passage
in the same writer which contains a figure such as I believe the
old poet intended in (1) (b):

> Awake! awake!
> The sun doth shake
> Light from his locks.   Christ's Nativity.

In the former of these passages the image of nature shaking off
darkness, scattering it, shaking free from it, will cover, with
certain amplifications or modifications, a number of figurative
uses of scacan in OE; that in the latter, of the sun scattering as
in largesse, the light, flinging it broadcast in profuse distribution, underlies others. A third sense, applicable to (1) (c) and
(2) (c) (d) and (f), is "to render, or become, unsteady, to rock,
totter; to upset, shatter," etc., which we still apply to action
affecting immaterial as well as material things, e.g. to shake
one's confidence, resolution, etc.

BLÆD. The phrase in (2) (f) wæs hire blæd scacen is doubly
figurative. As blæd, generally rendered 'prosperity, fame,' and
so on, is a poetical word, a few remarks on it will be in place
here. The word is etymologically connected with blawan 'to
blow' (of wind), and is apparently often confused with an originally
different word bled from blowan 'to blow as a flower, flourish.'
The two verbs, which are identical in all parts except the infinitive and present indicative, are ultimately from the same base.
The noun means 'a blowing, that which blows or flourishes,'
hence 'shoot of a plant, flower, fruit.' In a figurative sense it
means 'period of flourishing, prosperity, fame'; it is equivalent
to the German blütezeit. It also undoubtedly has the sense of
'flower of age, beauty,' and so on. In the passage (2) (f) we might
legitimately translate 'the flower of their life was shattered.'
Vaughan again has the very phrase required to interpret blæd:

> Let my youth, my <u>bloom of days</u>
> Be my comfort and thy praise.

The word is found in at least two other passages in <u>Beowulf</u>—
blæd is aræred <u>geond widwegas</u> 'thy fame is raised high, over
far-lying ways' 1703–04; again, <u>nu is þines mægnes blæd ane</u>
<u>hwile</u> 'now is the very flower of thy might, for a time' 1761–62.
Of the angels' hosts it is said, <u>wæs heora blæd micel</u> 'great was
their glory' <u>Genesis</u> 14. The word occurs again in a beautiful
passage in <u>Juliana</u>:

> Min se swetesta   sunnan scima
> Juliana!   hwæt þu glæm hafast,
> ginfæste giefe,   geoguðes <u>blæd</u>.   (166–168)

> My Juliana, sunlight's sweetest ray!
> Thou hast a bounteous dower, the gleam, the bloom
>   of youth.

The last passage contains another word, GLÆM 'gleam,' etc.,
which is several times used in a figurative sense in Anglo-Saxon
poetry. In a physical sense the word, as now, means 'a gleam,
flash, of light.' Thus in <u>Guthlac</u> 122 <u>se æþela glæm</u> 'noble gleam,'
and in 123 <u>se leohta glæm</u> 'bright gleam' is applied to the sun.
In the passage quoted from <u>Juliana</u> the word has the sense of
'radiant beauty, charm, glamour.' It is used in the same sense
in the phrase <u>geoguðhades glæm</u> 'gleam of youth' in <u>Elene</u> 1266.
Both <u>Juliana</u> and <u>Elene</u> are by the same poet—Cynewulf. The
last expression is the exact equivalent of Wordsworth's "youth's
golden gleam."

The word MIST, which has ever been used by English poets
to call up a picture of sombre and shadowy beauty, has appeared
already in several of the phrases and passages quoted in the preceding section. It is worth noting a rather new use of it applied
to an exhalation or emanation which is not visible. In the <u>Fates</u>
<u>of Men</u>, not the least vivid lines in a graphic and terrible de-
scription of a dead man hanging on the gallows are these:

> Blac on beame   bideð wyrde
> bewegen wælmiste.   (41–42)

> 'Livid upon the gibbet he abides his fate, en-
> veloped in a deadly mist.'

WAN(N), WON(N). This word is usually, and no doubt rightly, rendered 'dark, dusky,' and so on, and I believe in all the passages hitherto noted in which it occurs, this is the proper rendering. But se wonna leg (Christ and Satan 713) can hardly mean 'dark fire.' Cp. also: Nu sceal gled fretan, / weaxan wonna leg (Beowulf 3114–15): 'Now must fire devour him, the wan flame wrap him round.' As a matter of fact, the word is recorded in Napier's OE Glosses 23.34 as a gloss for pallidus, which shows evidently that already in OE it had acquired something like its present sense. It apparently denoted a rather vague shade neither very dark nor very bright, sometimes tending to one, sometimes to the other, a livid, pallid hue. It is interesting to note that in Prelude XIV. 11–12, Wordsworth appears to use the word with a suggestion of something rather darker than is implied by the ordinary modern use:

> It was a close, warm, breezeless summer night,
> Wan, dull and glaring, with a dripping fog.

Truly a detestable kind of night!

ÐICCE, ÐICLICE 'thick, thickly.' These words are used in Genesis of the eager, excited speech of Eve to Adam when she is urging him on 'to that dim deed' on þa dimman dæd, which had such unfortunate results for all of us. Hio spræc him þicce to (Gen. 684); and again heo spræc ða to Adame idesa sceonost ful þiclice (Gen. 704–705). Sweet gives 'frequent(ly)' in his Dictionary, evidently with an eye to this passage. But is not the phrase far more vivid than that? Does it not rather mean, and did not the poet intend, 'her words came thick and fast, thickly, one after the other,' or something of that kind? This would be admirably suggestive of a panting rush of words.

SLITAN 'to tear, slit up,' etc. After the Fall Adam, in his despair for their future now that they have disobeyed God and will certainly lose Paradise, cries out:

> Slit me hunger and þurst,
> bittre on breostum.   Gen. 802–803.

'Hunger and thirst <u>tear</u> me grievously in my bosom.'

It is worth mentioning, perhaps, that what some consider the
Old Saxon <u>original</u>, in the Vatican fragment, has the much
feebler word <u>thwingit</u> 'torments, oppresses.' The same expressive phrase is used by another Anglo-Saxon poet in the <u>Seafarer</u>:
<u>hungor innan slat / merewerges mod</u> (11–12) 'hunger within
<u>tore</u> the heart of the sea-weary man.'

SWINGAN 'to strike,' also 'to swing.' The word is used
with fine effect in <u>Beowulf</u>, in a passage in which the last survivor of a band of noble kinsmen deplores the death of the others,
and contemplates the ruined hall:

> Nis hearpan wyn,
> gomen gleo-beames, ne god hafoc
> geond sæl swingeð, ne se swifta mearh
> burh-stede beateð.   (2262–65)

> 'There is
> No joyous harp, no mirthful sound of lyre;
> Nor through the hall the gallant falcon swings;
> Nor the fleet charger beats the court-yard now.'

This seems to me at once to call up a vision of the powerful
flight of the hawk wheeling and swooping backwards and forwards
through the hall in short, rapid bursts, constantly brought up by
the walls.

But the Anglo-Saxon poet is perhaps at his best when he
presents a poignant situation in the simplest words. To illustrate this quality I select, as a final example, the passage from
<u>Beowulf</u> which describes the hero and his retainers preparing
to spend their first night in Hrothgar's hall, where they fully
expect to be attacked by the blood-thirsty monster Grendel.
The translation conveys but a feeble idea of the simple and
serene dignity of the original. Beowulf himself has already
stripped off his armour and thrown himself upon his bed:

>   . . . ond hine ymb monig
> snellic særinc selereste gebeah.
> Nænig heora þohte þæt he þanon scolde
> eft eardlufan æfre gesecean,

folc oþðe freo-burh þær he afeded wæs.
Ac hie hæfdon gefrunen þæt hie ær to fela micles
in þæm win-sele wæl-deaþ fornam
Denigea leode.   (689–696)

'Around him many a seaman, young and bold,
Had stretched him on a bed within the hall.
Not one had hope that he should e'er again
Win out, or see once more his own dear land,
His kin, or the fair house where he was bred.
For they had heard, how in that banquet-hall,
Grim death had snatched full many a Dane away.'

In conclusion, I would appeal to students of English poetry to devote more attention to our oldest verse than they have been in the habit of giving. The more closely and sympathetically it is studied, the more clearly do the all-pervading qualities of imagination and sensibility in Anglo-Saxon poetry appear, the more overwhelming becomes the conviction that our ancient writers are in the true great line of English poets. The spiritual affinity between these and the later poets is no less indubitable than is their kinship in blood.

NOTES

1 Those unfamiliar with the story may consult Dr. Bradley's article: "The 'Cædmonian' Genesis," ES, VI (1920), 7–29.

2 Mr. Sisam suggests 'bird of prey' here, and if the phrase sumne fugel oþbær ofer heanne holm means 'one, the bird of prey carried off (that is, tore him to shreds when dead) far away, across the lofty wave,' or something of the kind, it would indeed be parallel to the following phrase — sumne se hara wulf deaðe gedælde, but I am inclined all the same to Sweet's view that fugel in the context means 'ship,' which was first suggested by Thorpe and supported also by Wulker.

3 Mr. Sisam would render burg-tunas by 'walls,' referring to the sides of the valley, and thus an echoing phrase to dun up-hea. This would also require wic wynna leas to be rendered — 'mine,' or 'this, is a joyless abode.'

UNDERSTATEMENT IN OLD ENGLISH POETRY

Frederick Bracher

One of the most striking features of the style of Old English poetry is the frequent use of rhetorical understatement. A. H. Tolman[1] was apparently the first to point out this stylistic trait, and more recently passing references to it have been frequent.[2] The following article attempts an investigation of its origin, occurrence, and uses.

A common type of understatement in modern English is achieved by the use of a weaker word than the context calls for; e.g., a schoolboy's remark that it was "slightly decent" of Father Damien to live and die with the Molokai lepers. The recognition of understatement of this kind depends upon a knowledge of the full connotation and exact force of words; and although our lack of knowledge of the precise shades of meaning in Old English would probably prevent us from recognizing such understatement if it occurred in the poetry, there is very little evidence that it did occur. The common type of understatement in Old English is achieved by the use of a negation: the denial of the opposite; and this type is easily recognizable. For example, it is not necessary to know the exact force of <u>sarlic</u> in the passage describing the rejoicing of the Danes over Grendel's death (<u>Beowulf</u> 841 f., "No his lifgedal / sarlic þuhte secga ænegum")[3] in order to feel the understatement. <u>Sarlic</u> might mean anything from "mildly unpleasant" to "extremely painful," but the passage would still be understatement, for neither "not painful" nor "not unpleasant" is equivalent to "joyful," which is what the context demands.

The denial of the opposite does not necessarily require a specifically negative word. O. Jespersen[4] has pointed out what he calls "implied negation," and "incomplete negation." Both

Reprinted by permission of the Modern Language Association and the author from <u>PMLA</u>, Vol. LII (1937), pp. 915–34.

are used to achieve understatement in Old English verse: the first only occasionally (cf. Juliana 109 f.); the second, which makes use of such words as lyt and fea, very frequently. An example is Beowulf 2897 f., "Lyt swigode / niwra spella se ðe næs gerad." In a sense, such constructions contain double understatement; that is, "he little kept silent" is understatement (by incomplete negation) for "he did not keep silent," which is understatement for "he spoke," the true import of the passage, as indicated unmistakably here by the second half of the antithesis, "ac he soðlice sægde ofer ealle."

But although all examples of understatement which I have found are formed from negations, not all negations are understatement. The context of the passage determines what is intended. When the Beowulf poet says (1071 f.), "Ne huru Hildeburh herian þorfte / Eotena treowe," the context clearly shows he meant that she had good reason to denounce them, and the passage is, consequently, understatement. But when, in Beowulf 2124 f., the poet says of the slain warrior, "Noðer hy hine ne moston . . . bronde forbærnan," he is simply stating a fact, and he gives the reason: Grendel's mother had carried the body away. Of course, not all instances are as clear as these; often it is impossible to determine what the author intended. It is the clear cases, rather than the borderline cases, with which I shall be chiefly concerned.

Words formed with a negative affix occur frequently in Old English poetry, and these have sometimes been taken as examples of understatement. T. B. Haber[5] cites, among other examples, Beowulf 126 f. "Ða wæs on uhtan mid ærdæge / Grendles guðcræft gumum undyrne," as "emphasis by understatement." W. J. Sedgefield[6] also considers this understatement; and if one translates undyrne literally as "not hidden," he would have to agree. Are we justified in translating such words literally? In some cases we certainly are: e.g., Beowulf 2548, unbyrnende, or Prose Guthlac, x, 6, unforhtlice, used in reference to the birds who sat on Guthlac's shoulder, a translation of the Latin non hæsitantes.

But we have numerous instances, in other languages as well as in Old English, of words with a negative affix becoming positive terms. If taken literally, Modern English unhappy would mean merely "not happy"; actually it has a positive meaning, "miserable." So with disgrace, impertinent, insipid, etc.

Undyrne is used twice in Beowulf (150, 410: undyrne cuð) in contexts which indicate pretty clearly that it meant "plainly, manifestly." Unrot appears to mean "sad" rather than "not joyful" in Guthlac 1037: "Ne beo þu unrot"; and the use of the comparative of unspedig, unswiðe, and sorgleas (Genesis 962, "eard ond eðyl unspedigran"; Beowulf 2578, "bat unswiðor"; Elene 96, "þy bliðra ond þy sorgleasra") would seem to indicate that they had more positive meanings than "not rich," "not strongly," and "without sorrow."

More conclusive evidence that such words did not always have their literal meanings and hence did not necessarily produce understatement may be found by an examination of Old English prose. When we find words formed with a negative affix used in prose contexts which demand positive meanings, we can be reasonably sure that the words had positive meanings and are not examples of understatement, for understatement (as I shall show later) is no feature of Old English prose style.

> Prose Guthlac (Gonser's edition, Anglistische Forschungen, XXVII [1909]), V, 99 and III, 41: unmanige [few] dagas. Cf. the Latin originals: paucis intervenientibus dierum cursibus and aliquot itaque diebus.
> Boethius (Sedgefield's edition [Oxford, 1899], p. 103, 9 f.), Ac ða lufe mon mæg swiðe uneaðe oððe na forbeodan 'with much difficulty or not at all.'
> Blickling Homily (J. W. Bright, Anglo-Saxon Reader [New York, 1894], p. 70, 21): laþlico ond unfæger.
> Voyage of Ohthere and Wulfstan (ibid., p. 39, 5 f.): "Ne dorston forþ bi þære ea siglan for unfriþe."

Since we cannot tell to what extent such words had acquired positive meanings, and since we have consequently no good reason for assuming that they were intended as understatement,[7] I have omitted them from the following discussion.

The most common and most striking type of understatement might be called adjectival—not that it necessarily involves adjectives—in the sense that it expresses certain kinds of qualities: a moral attitude, a value judgment, an intellectual or moral attribute, etc.

Beowulf 1575, "næs seo ecg fracod" (the sword with which Beowulf slays Grendel's mother).

Widsith 67, "næs þæt sæne cyning" (said of Guðhere, who "me . . . forgeaf glædlicne maþþum/songes to leane").

Genesis 610, "nalles he hie freme lærde" (the devil tempting Eve).

Juliana 605 f., "Hine se cwealm ne þeah/siþþan he þone fintan furþor cuþe" (the judge who sentenced Juliana to death).[8]

Understatement is also used, though not so commonly, to indicate action; and on occasion to express quantity, measure, and degree:

Beowulf 2489, "feorhsweng ne ofteah" (Wulf gives Ongentheow his deathblow).

Elene 1098, "hygerune ne mað" (Cyriacus prays).

Christ 1275, "On him dryhten gesihð/nales feara sum firenbealu laðlic."

Beowulf 660, "Ne bið þe wilna gad."

Beowulf 1455 f., "Næs þæt þonne mætost mægenfultuma/þæt him on ðearfe lah ðyle Hroðgares."

In a few instances the understatement is exaggerated almost to the point of the ludicrous by denying a proposition which is highly improbable or absurd:

Exeter Gnomes 151 f., "Ne huru wæl wepeð wulf se græga/morþorcwealm mæcga, ac hit a mare wille."

Juliana 117 f., "Hyre þa þurh yrre ageaf andsware/fæder feondlice, nales frætwe onheht." (Rather, her father promised to have her torn by wild animals if she persisted in her refusal.)[9]

That understatement of the kind illustrated above is a definite characteristic of Old English poetic style is indicated by the fact that it occurs, with varying degrees of frequency but usually oftener than is normal for poetry in other languages, in nearly all extant Old English poetry; whereas it occurs rarely, if at all, in Old English prose. Furthermore, in at least two cases we are able to compare prose and poetic versions of the same

231

material, and in both cases, understatement is found in the
poetic version and is absent in the prose.

The Alfredian Boethius exists in two manuscripts: Cotton
MS. Otho A. vi, and Bodleian MS. 180. The prose portions of
Boethius' work are done into Old English prose in both manuscripts, and the texts are practically the same. But whereas
in the Bodleian manuscript Boethius' Latin metra have been
translated into Old English prose, in the Cotton MS these same
metra have been done into alliterative verse. The prose version of the metra contains one or two passages which might con-
ceivably be taken as understatement, but no clear cases; the
metrical version contains ten fairly certain instances, including such unmistakable understatements as[10] Metrum I, 42 f.,
"Het Iohannes godne papan / heafde beheawon; næs ðæt hærlic
dæd"; and Metrum XX, 187 f. (in a discussion of the three
Platonic properties of the soul), "Is sio þridde gecynd þæm
twæm betere, / sio gesceadwisnes. Nis ðæt scandlic cræft."[11]
None of the understatements occur in the original Latin nor in
the prose translation; they are purely Old English additions to
the metrical translation.

The Latin life of St. Guthlac, Hermit of Crowland, served
as a source for two Old English accounts of the Mercian saint:
the prose legend in the Cotton MS. Vespasian D. xxi, and the
poems (Guthlac A and B) in the Exeter Book. Although the
poetic versions omit some of the episodes found in the prose
account, these texts enable us to make another comparison of
a prose and a poetic version of approximately the same material;
and again we find a difference as regards the use of understatement. The Guthlac poet uses understatement almost as frequently
as does the poet of Beowulf (on the average, once in 38 lines).
Some striking examples are the following:

> 209, "þa þe for his life lyt sorgedon."
> 392, "no þær þa feondas gefeon þorfton."
> 783 f., "him þæt ne hreoweð æfter hingonge/
> ðone hy hweorfað in þa halgan burg."
> 1330, "huru ic swiðe ne þearf hinsið behlehhan."[12]

The Prose Guthlac has no clear cases of understatement at all,
and the few passages which in any way suggest the figure are
shown, by a comparison with the Latin original, to be attempts

at a literal rendering of Latin constructions; for example 3, 2, 'naht feor fram þære cestre' (haud procul a castello).[13] That the translator of the <u>Prose Guthlac</u> was not interested in understatement is further demonstrated by his failure to render adequately such litotes as occurs in Felix's florid Latin. In 17, 1, the translator writes "swylce nys eac mid idele to forlætenne" for "non est praetereundem silentio." In both Latin and Old English this expression is little more than a conventional introduction to a new paragraph, with nothing of the effect of rhetorical understatement; yet in 19, 1, the translator uses the same Old English phrase to translate the striking litotes "Non me quoque supramemorati viri Guthlaci vatidico pectore quoddam spiritale praesagium narrare piget."

Whereas understatement appears only occasionally, if at all, in Old English prose, we find it in all the longer poems except the <u>Physiologus</u> and <u>Be Domes Daege</u>. Although it is probably impossible to establish an absolute norm for determining whether the frequency of occurrence is normal or excessive, the figure occurs often enough, it seems to me, to justify the assertion that understatement is a definite characteristic of Old English poetic style. The following table indicates the frequency of occurrence of understatement in the various poems.

	No. of lines	Examples	Ratio
Riming Poem	87	5	17
Battle of Brunanburh	73	4	18
Waldhere	61	3	20
Doomsday (Exeter)	119	6	20
Debate of the Body and the Soul	169	8	21
Battle of Maldon	325	12	27
Exeter Gnomes	206	7	29
Wanderer	115	4	29
The Fates of Men	98	3	33
Beowulf	3182	94	34
The Wonders of Creation	102	3	34
Guthlac A	790	21	38
Deor	42	1	42
Andreas	1722	39	44
Fates of the Apostles	95	2	47
Runic Poem	94	2	47
Widsith	143	3	48

Finnsburh Fragment	50	1	50
Guthlac B	563	11	51
The Husband's Message	52	1	52
Dream of the Rood	156	3	52
Juliana	731	14	52
The Wife's Lament	53	1	53
Salomon and Saturn	504	8	63
Genesis B	617	9	68
Metra of Boethius	1752	22	79
Genesis A	2318	29	80
The Minds of Men	84	1	84
Daniel	765	9	85
Elene	1320	14	94
A Father's Instructions	94	1	94
Prayers	194	2	97
Exodus	589	6	98
Christ and Satan	733	6	122
The Seafarer	124	1	124
Riddles	c. 1243	10	124
Verses from the A. S. Chronicle	128	1	128
Christ	1694	13	130
The Harrowing of Hell	137	1	137
Judith	350	2	175
Azarias	191	1	191
Phoenix	677	2	338
Charms	20	0	
Gloria and Creed	109	0	
The Gifts of Men	113	0	
Pater Noster	170	0	
Physiologus	176	0	
Be Domes Dæge	305	0	

It should be noted that, roughly speaking, understatement occurs most frequently in the early pagan and heroic poems (Waldhere, Exeter Gnomes, Beowulf, etc.), in later imitations of these (Maldon and Brunanburh), and in Christian epic (Andreas, Fates of the Apostles, Guthlac, etc.). It occurs least frequently in the later Christian poems, both narrative and didactic. An analogous difference is apparent if one considers the effectiveness with which the figure is used. The poems which use understatement most frequently use it, on the whole, most effectively—

for definite purposes and with striking rhetorical effect. In most of the later poems, the use of understatement seems mechanical and conventional, as though the poets used it merely out of stylistic habit, or for convenience in meeting the demands of alliterative verse form. These differences suggest that understatement as a stylistic trait was most characteristic of the unwritten pagan poetry of which most of the Old English poems we now possess are decadent descendants.[14]

There is considerable disagreement among the critics as to the effects intended and achieved by the use of understatement in Old English poetry. John Earle[15] speaks of "the derisive, bitter, mocking irony of hatred and aversion." L. Cazamian[16] thinks that understatement was primarily humorous, whereas Fr. Klaeber[17] asserts that "in such a gloomy atmosphere there can be no room for levity, fun, or humor. Passages which to modern readers might seem to be humorous were certainly not so meant by the Anglo-Saxon author." B. Haeuschkel[18] while admitting that understatement sometimes gives greater emphasis, thinks that on the whole it is "ungeschickt und schwerfällig."

Such disagreement is no doubt normal enough, in view of the impossibility of knowing for certain how the Anglo-Saxons felt about their poetry. Granting that understatement may have as many different "effects" as there are readers to be affected, our best method of approach would seem to be an attempt to discover the author's purpose in using the figure. The critics quoted above have mentioned three of the commonest uses of understatement: the "mocking irony of hatred and aversion," humor, and emphasis. To these I would add a fourth: moderation, or tempering, of an expression. These categories are by no means exhaustive (a good many cases of understatement in Old English, for example, seem to have no rhetorical purpose at all, but to be the product of stylistic habit or convention) nor are they mutually exclusive. Ironic sarcasm may be humorous, and any instance of understatement is apt to be emphatic. In considering each example of understatement, I have tried to disregard the incidental effects of the figure in order to discover the chief reason for its use.

The first class, which includes most of the striking cases, is chiefly distinguished by a hostile intent; it is mocking, exulting, or scornful. Such understatement is usually directed against the villains of the poems: in the <u>Beowulf</u>, against Grendel, his mother, the Hetware, etc.; in the Christian poems, against Judas, Cain, the devil, etc.

> Battle of Brunanburh 39 f., "Har hilderinc hreman ne þorfte/mecea gemanan" (the defeated King Constantine).
> Beowulf 2006 f., "Swa begylpan [ne] þearf Grendeles maga/(ænig) ofer eorðan uhthlem þone."
> Beowulf 109, "Ne gefeah he þære fæhðe" (Cain is punished).
> Christ and Satan 79, "Ne bið swelc fæger dream" (Satan suffers in Hell).
> Andreas 1702 f., "þ(æt) þam banan ne wearð/ hleahtre behworfen" (the murderer of St. Andrew).
> Genesis 72 f., "Ne þorfton hlude hlihhan" (the fallen angels in hell).[19]

The Old Norse sagas very frequently use understatement for a similar purpose; in Grettis Saga, an exchange of taunts and insults is a prelude to almost every fight:

> (Boer's edition [Halle, 1900]) 36, 2 f., þa mælti þorbjorn ferðalangr: "þat var bæði," sagði hann, "at ek sa hann Gretti ekki til frægðar vinna . . . ok þvi ætla ek aldri hug i honum, ef hann hefir eigi nogan liðsafla." Gerði þorbjorn at þessu et mesta gabb.
> [Then Thorbjorn Slowcoach said: "What I saw of Grettir's fighting was not famous; . . . I do not believe there is much heart in him, except when he has a sufficient force behind him." Thorbjorn went on jeering at him in this way.]

Grettir's speech is full of understatement, and the author remarks[20] that he had a habit of "making verses and ditties which were always a little ironical." The irritating effect of such behavior on his associates is shown in Chapter 17. Grettir took passage for Norway, but when the weather became bad and all hands were desperately needed to bail ship, Grettir refused to help. Instead he lay in the shelter of the ship's boat, amusing himself with the mate's wife, and made lampoons and ironic comments on the sailors and their troubles. When the sailors finally complained to the leader of the expedition, it was not Grettir's mutiny which they objected to, but his intolerable lampoons.

We should expect to find feelings of hatred, scorn, and exultation expressed, not only in saga, but in heroic poetry, the main purpose of which is to celebrate prowess in battle. The scop would express the exultation of a victorious tribe by praising the chief and reviling the enemy. Such poetry probably also served to whip up the courage of the warriors and to spur them on to greater deeds.[21] Bitterly sarcastic understatement is an effective device for the expression of all such feelings, and was probably a characteristic of the heroic poetry from which developed the Old English poetry we know today.

By humorous understatement, I mean those instances which seem to be used out of a kind of waggishness, to make friends laugh instead of to make enemies wince. There seem to be relatively few instances of primarily humorous understatement in Old English verse; and when one considers how much the appreciation of humor depends on a knowledge of the full connotations of words and how little we can know of the exact flavor of Old English, he has grounds for distrusting his own feeling for humorous effects in Old English poetry. Nevertheless, I see no a priori reason for assuming, as Klaeber does, that "in such a gloomy atmosphere there can be no room for levity, fun, or humor." One might as well say there can be no room for humor in Shakespeare's tragedies. It is true that Old English poetry is not notable for humor and that its subject-matter is not such as would call forth humorous effects, but it certainly does not follow because the poems are generally solemn, or even gloomy, in tone that we must regard as certainly unwarranted any humorous effects we may feel. Indeed, it is difficult to conceive of the frame of mind of a person who would perceive the incongruity of understatement with perfect solemnity or gloom and not the least tendency to smile. There is a possibility for some degree of humor of some kind—merry, wry, or bitter—in every passage which is felt as understatement at all; that is, which is not so stereotyped through use that the incongruity is no longer perceived; and we have no right to assume that the Anglo-Saxons always missed the point.

Beowulf 3126 f., "Næs ða on hlytme, hwa þæt hord strude/syððan orwearde." (Lots were often cast to determine which men should undertake dangerous ventures; the implication here is that, the dragon being dead, the men were very eager to plunder his hoard.)

Beowulf 3129 f., "Lyt ænig mearn, /þæt hi ofostlic(e) ut geferedon /dyre maðmas."

Beowulf 841 f., "No his lifgedal /sarlic þuhte secga ænegum" (Grendel's death).

The cases quoted above seem to have been used as a kind of humorous relief, appropriately expressing the feeling of relaxed tension after danger.

Beowulf 791 f., "Nolde eorla hleo ænige þinga/ þone cwealmcuman cwicne forlætan, /ne his lifdagas leoda ænigum/nytte tealde."

Beowulf 138 f., "þa wæs eaðfynde þe him elles hwær/gerumlicor ræste [sohte], /bed æfter burum, ða him gebeacnod wæs, /gesægd soðlice sweotolan tacne/healðegnes hete; heold hyne syðþan/fyr ond fæstor se þæm feonde ætwand."

Andreas 1534 f., "þær wæs ælcum genog/fram dæges orde drync sona gearu." (St. Andrew has caused the stone image to flood the city of the Mermedonians and drown the people.)

This is, to be sure, a long way from that "complete detachment from one's self, and the expert playing with one's own frame of mind, which full-grown humour requires." By and large, Old English poetry is almost childishly single-minded and earnest, and we seldom find that degree of disinterestedness which makes for geniality and humor in the modern sense of the term. But humor of a grim and simple sort there certainly is, and understatement appears to be its characteristic form.

The most common use of understatement, paradoxically enough, is to secure emphasis. Modern English slang provides good examples: "not half bad," "not so dumb," etc. St. Paul's "a citizen of no mean city" is well-known; and C. Weyman[22] cites examples from Latin, Greek, Sanskrit, Syrian, Old Persian, and Bohemian. Emphatic understatement is very common in Old English poetry.

> Beowulf 1811 f., "nales wordum log/meces ecge" (Beowulf praises the sword which Unferth has given him).
> Beowulf 249 f., "nis þæt seldguma/wæpnum geweorðad" (the coast-guard is favorably impressed with Beowulf's appearance).
> Fates of the Apostles 75, "Næron ða twegen tohtan sæne" (emphasizing the zeal of Simon and Thaddeus).
> Guthlac 741, "Nis þæt huru læsast, þæt seo lufu cyþeð" (the gift of spiritual grace).
> Christ 1275 f., "On him dryhten gesihð/nales feara sum firenbealu laðlic."
> Andreas 233, "heard and higerof, nalas hildlata."[23]

In the examples cited above, understatement is used to give greater emphasis. But understatement can be put to more subtle uses than this; it can express a less degree, or a precise shade, of emphasis. In modern English we often take advantage of its two levels of meaning to imply what we do not wish to state with blunt explicitness: "I am not unaware of the honor that has been done me, and it is not without a certain pride that . . . etc." Understatement of this sort is apt to strike us as a relatively late, sophisticated development of the figure; but there is some reason to suppose, on the contrary, that it is a natural expression of a very primitive attitude. According to J. A. K. Thomson[24] irony originated in the belief, among the primitive Greeks, in "the Jealousy of the Gods." The feeling that any good fortune to a mortal is apt to be resented by the Gods if it comes to their attention and that the wise thing to do is to "lie low" in action and speech, is at the heart of primitive religions. The gods were created in the image of the Old Man of the Tribe, greedy and jealous of the success of others. Modern, civilized man knocks on wood or adds "God willing" when he speaks of his good fortune or his plans for the future. Primitive man tried to propitiate the jealous gods with burnt offerings, euphemistic names like "the Eumenides," and other disingenuous evidences of affection; and he avoided their unfavorable notice as much as he could by minimizing his own virtues and successes.

Certain examples of understatement in Germanic poetry may have contained some element of this primitive "selbstgeringschätzung."

> Beowulf 2738 f., "ne me swor fela/aða on unriht
> . . . /forðam me witan ne ðearf Waldend fira/
> morðorbealo maga."
> Andreas 1289 f., "þæt ic, meotud, þinum/larum
> leofwendum lyt geswice."
> Lokasenna 142, "þa-ek mǫg gat, þann es mangi
> fiar." "I have begot a son whom no ones hates."
> (Njorðr speaks of his son, who is "best of the Anses.")
> Sonatorrek 57 f., "Veit ek þat sialfr at i syni
> minom/vasat illz þegns emni vaxit." "I know very
> well that in my son no ill thegn was growing up."

For the most part, however, understatement used to temper or moderate expressions seems to have been motivated by a regard for politeness and decorum. Among warlike and highly individualistic peoples, decorum is often closely related to precautionary self-interest. A remark in Hrafnkels Saga,[25] possibly a gnome, comments on the value of tempered speech:

> En ver munom opt þess iðraz er ver rom of
> malger, ok sialdnar mundom ver þess iðraz þo at
> ver mæltem færra en fleira. [We must often re-
> pent making too big vows, and we shall seldom re-
> pent speaking less than we meant.]

The virtue of moderation in all things, and particularly in speech, is pointed out several times in the gnomic passages of the Wanderer. In one instance, restraint in speech is cited as a noble quality (11 f., "Ic to soþe wat / þæt biþ in eorle indryhten þeaw / þæt he his ferðlocan fæste binde, / healde his hordcofan, hycge swa he wille.") But two other passages suggest the practical value of restraint:

> 65 f., "Wita sceal geþyldig, /ne sceal no to
> hatheort ne to hrædwyrde /. . . ne næfre gielpes
> to georn, ær he geare cunne."

UNDERSTATEMENT IN OLD ENGLISH POETRY

> 112 f., "Ne sceal næfre his torn to rycene /
> beorn of his breostum acyþan, nemþe he ær þa
> bote cunne, / eorl mid elne gefremman!"

The terms of the treaty between Finn and Hengest give additional evidence of the social importance attributed by Germanic warriors to circumspect behavior and careful speech. Throughout Germanic poetry, and particularly in the Old Norse Sagas, we find scattered examples of understatement seemingly used out of a kind of wary politeness.

> Njals Saga 41, 5, "Sva er mer fra honum sagt,"
> sagði Gunnarr, "at hann se þer engi skapbœtir."
> [I have been so told about him (Sigmund's servant)
> that he is no betterer of thy temper.] (Gunnar re-
> luctantly grants Sigmund's request that his servant
> also be given lodging at Lithend.)
> Andreas 317 f., "Ne gedafenað þe . . . ðaet ðu
> andsware mid oferhygdum / sece sarcwide." (St.
> Andrew reproaches the ship's captain in moderate
> words, as becomes a man who is under an obliga-
> tion.)

However, not all politeness in Germanic literature is to be attributed to such ignoble motives as craven self-interest. Old English understatement sometimes is motivated by a disinterested regard for due modesty and decorum which we are too apt to think of as peculiarly modern.

> Beowulf 2432 f., "næs ic him to life laðra owihte /
> beorn in burgum, þonne his bearna hwylc." (Beowulf
> comments on King Hrethel's affection for him).
> Genesis 2823 f., "Gyld me mid hyldo, þæt ic þe
> hneaw ne wæs / landes and lissa." (Abimelech asks
> a favor in return for the kindness he has shown
> Abraham).

Understatement may also serve as a kind of euphemism, and is so used for a variety of reasons.

> Andreas 271 f., and 476 f., "þeh ic þe beaga
> lyt, / sincweorðunga syllan meahte" (St. Andrew

is trying to secure passage to Mermedonia without
paying his fare, and instead of saying bluntly that
he has no money, he uses understatement).

Juliana 70, "þæt heo mæglufan minre ne gyme."
(The saint has spurned the love of Eleusius and has
let him know in plain language that she scorns him.
Eleusius, complaining to her father, apparently cannot bring himself to say frankly that Juliana de-
spises him.)

At the feast celebrating Beowulf's victory, Unferth's somewhat
shady past is referred to euphemistically: 1167 f., "Gehwylc
hiora his ferhþe treowde, / þæt he hæfde mod micel, þeah þe
he his magum nære / arfæst æt ecga gelacum." And the allusion
to Beowulf's youthful lack of promise is expressed through understatement: 2184, "Swa hyne Geata bearn godne ne tealdon."
    Where did the Old English poets get this stylistic manner-
ism? Did they develop it themselves? Was it an inheritance,
along with alliteration, variation, the kenning, etc., from an
earlier, possibly common-Germanic, poetic tradition? Or is it
the result of borrowing from the Latin literature which came
into England along with Christianity? I shall attempt to answer
the last question first.
    Classical literature, existing side by side in Anglo-Saxon
England with the native literature, affords a tempting field for
comparative study with a view to showing "influence" of one
on the other.[26] While it cannot be denied that Latin literature
may have influenced Old English poetry in some respects, there
is considerable indirect evidence that understatement is not a
borrowing from Latin style. The Old English verse translation
of the metra of Boethius uses understatement where the original
does not. The Old English poems on Guthlac, where they cover
the same material as the Latin original, use understatement
much more frequently than does the Latin, and the Prose Guthlac
even fails to render striking understatement occurring in the
Latin. Furthermore, Old English understatement appears most
frequently and is used most effectively in the early, "heroic"
poetry, which presumably was least subject to Latin influence.
In the later, more explicitly Christian, poems, understatement
occurs less frequently and suggests by its use that it was mechanically conventional. And while Latin influence on the literature

increases as we approach the Middle English period, understatement as a characteristic of poetic style decreases and finally disappears.[27]

Furthermore, it must be remembered that the style of Old
English poetry is, basically and for the most part, Germanic;
and the burden of proof is with those who would show Latin influence. It is not enough to point out similarities in style in Old
English and Latin verse; it must be demonstrated further that
the stylistic traits in question are not part of the native tradition. T. B. Haber (op. cit.) attempts to do this; his third chapter
is entitled "Indications of Non-Germanic Influence in the Beowulf"; in it (p. 34) he states that "the marked preference ex-
hibited by both epics [i.e., Beowulf and Aeneid] for this figure
[i.e., litotes] is one of the most important rhetorical features
which they have in common." The implication is that understatement is one of those non-Germanic traits which he finds
throughout the Beowulf and which he suggests "may find explanation in references to the Aeneid." But is understatement a
non-Germanic trait? This question can best be answered by
finding out whether or not understatement is common to the alliterative poetry of the other Germanic peoples—a poetry which,
together with the Old English, apparently represents offshoots
from a common Germanic tradition going back to the heroic age
of the migrations.[28]

Aside from Old English, the earliest surviving examples
of Germanic heroic poetry are found in Old High German, but
these are unsatisfactory as sources of evidence. The Hildebrandslied fragment, for example, is brief; we have only sixty-
eight lines of the poem. When one considers that in the Beowulf,
which uses understatement relatively very frequently, we find
examples on the average once in every thirty-four lines and that
there are passages of more than one hundred lines containing
no examples at all, it is plain that we should not expect to find
many instances of understatement in the fragment of the Hildebrandslied and that we should not be surprised if we found none
at all. A further difficulty arises from the lacunae within the
fragment and the lack of context; we cannot be sure of the import and bearing of any passage.

There are, however, two possible cases of understatement
in the Hildebrandslied. The first is in 46 f.: "Wela gisihu ih in
dinem hrustim / dat du habes heme herron goten / dat du noh bi

desemo riche reccheo ni wurti." This may be interpreted as
follows: Hildebrand remarks that he sees by his garb that Hadubrand has a generous lord, that he is no exile in the kingdom;
i.e., that he is a favorite of his lord.[29] But this may have been
a literal negative statement; Hildebrand had himself been a
"reccheo," and he may be merely contrasting Hadubrand's obviously happy situation with his own youthful hardships. One
other possible instance may be mentioned, although there is disagreement as to how it should be translated. In line 67 f., the
poet says that they fought "unti im iro lintun luttilo wurtun /
giwigan miti wabnu(m)." If "luttilo wurtun" means "were of
little use"[30] it may be understatement for "destroyed."

The Muspilli fragment, although thoroughly Christian in
content, keeps the old alliterative verse form. The Ludwigslied,
on the other hand, while its material suggests the old Germanic
preislied (with, however, Christian coloring), is in rhymed
couplets. Neither has any clear cases of understatement, but
both contain passages employing the denial of the opposite, the
outstanding syntactical feature of Old English understatement.

> Muspilli 65, "Ni darf er sorgen, denne er ze deru
> suono quimit." (This is said in reference to the
> righteous man, who, in sharp contrast to the wicked,
> may rejoice at the last judgment.[31])

Later Old High German Poetry affords numerous examples
of understatement of a kind similar to that found in Old English.
E. Lörcher[32] gives a number of references to what he calls
"litotes" in Otfrid's Evangelienbuch:

> 3, 16, 31, "Thoh sie nan nieretin." "They did not
> honor him." (The Jews were angry with Christ and
> "ihn töten wollten.")
> 1, 3, 9, "Niuuas Noe . . . in then thaz minnista deil."
> "Nor was Noah the least among them" (Lorcher: "er
> war das wichtigste").
> 2, 19, 6, "Nirgeit imo iz zi guate." "It will not turn
> out well for him." (Said of a man who looks on a
> woman to lust after her in his heart; Lörcher takes
> it as equivalent to "er muss strafe leiden.")[33]

The style of the Middle High German epics has been studied in detail by many different writers. Most of them mention (not always by this name) the occurrence of understatement as a notable characteristic of the style.[34] D. Zeeman[35] has made a study of litotes in Rudolf von Ems' Weltchronik. He points out that types of litotes depending on the use of a weaker word than the context calls for are rare; the typical cases involve a negation. Of constructions like "darnach gie do niht ze lanc" Zeeman says (p. 106), "Es sind alte epische Wendungen, die schon im Althochdeutschen vorkamen." He cites a number of examples of rhetorical understatement from Rudolf, e.g.:

> 16399, "sie waren niht ze snel."
> 438, "der niht grozer schulde truoc wan daz
> Got sin opfer nam" (In reference to Abel's innocence).
> 1627, "der im vil kleine iht schaden hat."

In conclusion Zeeman says (p. 110), "Es kommen bei ihm die allgemein üblichen Fälle vor, die wir durch die ganze mittel-hochdeutsche Literatur finden können." We can now add to his summary: Understatement by means of the denial of the opposite can be traced in High German poetry from the earliest examples down to the thirteenth century.

Understatement similar to that found in Old English poetry occurs also in the Old Saxon Heliand; in 1300 lines chosen at random from different parts of the poem I counted 20 cases, an average of one every 65 lines. I list a few typical examples.[36]

> 3818 f., "Ni skal iu that te frumu werðan." "That will not turn out to your profit." (Christ rebukes and threatens the Pharisees. Cf. Juliana 218, Genesis 610, Maldon 48.)
> 5156, "so ik wet that it mi ni thihit." (Heyne: "dass mir das Blutgeld keinen Segen bringt." Judas attempts to return the thirty pieces of silver to the Jews.)
> 3194 f., "Ni skal that likon wel / minumu herron." "That will not please my lord." (The king's emissary comments on Christ's refusal to pay the poll-tax.)
> 752 f., "No biskribun giowiht / thea man umbi menwerk." "The men did not trouble themselves over their crime."

245

741 f., "Menes si sahun /wities thie wam-skaðon."
"The evil-doers did not reck of their sins." (These
last two comments refer to Herod's soldiers, who are
slaughtering the innocents. Cf. Andreas 154, Beowulf
136, Guthlac 101, Andreas 1227.)

4333 f., "Nis that minnista /thero witeo an thesaru
weroldi, the her giwerðan skulun /er domes dage."
"That is not the least of the punishments which shall
befall the world ere Doomsday." (This refers to a
great famine, "meti-gedeono mest." Cf. Guthlac
741, Beowulf 2354.)

3054 f., "Tho te lat ni warð /Simon Petrus."
"Simon Peter was no laggard." (Cf. Beowulf 1529,
Fates of the Apostles 33, Juliana 573, Andreas 46.)

726, "That he gio oðar thesaro erðu ald ni wirðit."
"That he shall never become old on this earth."
(Herod speaks of his plan to kill the infant Jesus.
Cf. Atlamal 278.)[37]

Understatement occurs throughout Old Norse poetry, Eddic
and Scaldic, and the figure is similar in form and use to that
found in Old English, Old Saxon, Old and Middle High German.
Some typical examples are the following:[38]

The Guest's Wisdom 212, "at hann esa vamma
vanr." "That he has no lack of faults." (VP)

Hamðismal 29, "glyja þu ne gaðir" "thou hadst
no mind for joy" (VP), says Hamðir to his mother,
referring to the death of Sigurd.

Hamðismal 83, "Titt vasat biða." "It was not
pleasant to stay there" (VP). Hamðir and Sorli pass
by the gallows-tree.

The Lay of Weyland 64, "Esa sa nu hyrr es or
holti ferr." "He does not look blithe that is coming
out of the wood" (VP), says Cynwig, taunting the
captured Weyland.

Grottasongr 60, "Vasa kyrr-seta aðr Knui felli."
"We were not sitting at rest when Knui fell"; i.e.,
we were fighting.

The Lay of Gripi 193 f., "Muna fyr reiði rik bruðr
við þik /ne af of-trega all-vel skipa." "The mighty

maid (Brunhild), in wrath and despair, shall not
deal well with thee." Gripi prophecies Sigurd's
death.

Atlamal 53, "Ykkr mun ast-kynni eigi i sinn
þetta." "It will not be a friendly meeting this time."
(VP) Hogni's wife warns him that the runes hint
at his death if he goes to Atli's court.

Glum's Grafeldardrapa 36, "Reðat oss til auðr
. . . Haraldz dauði." "Harold's death was no blessing to me" (VP). Cf. Guthlac 1330, Juliana 526.[39]

A prominent characteristic of understatement in Old Norse
is the very frequent use of "incomplete negation," constructions
in which far, 'few'; litt, 'little'; and a variety of other terms are
used in place of a negative.

Woden's Love Lessons 32, "Fatt gat-ek þegjandi
þar." "I got little there by keeping silent"; i.e., I
spake many words to my profit, "morgom orðom
mælta-ek i minn frama."

Harbardslioð 91, "Gagni urðo þeir þo litt fegnir."
"They got little joy of victory." (Thor defeated
them.)

Hromund and His Sons 27 f., "Enn ek . . . hugða
. . . at gæfim grið-bitom frið litinn." "For I know we
gave the truce-breakers little grace." (VP)

Satires by Icelanders 42, "Litt hygg ek Goð gætti
Gylva hreins it eina." "God, I ween, kept little watch
over the sea-king's reindeer." (VP) The heathen
Steinunn taunts the missionary, Thangbrand.

Grimnismal 43 f., "A þvi landi es ek liggja veit /
fæsta feikn-stafi." "The land in which the fewest
curses lie (the most blessed of lands)." (VP)

The Christian's Wisdom 99 f., "Enn soko-dolgar
hygg-ek siðla muno / kallaðir fra kvolom." "But I
think the murderers will late be called from their
torments [in Hell]."[40]

The Old Norse poets exercise a good deal of ingenuity in
using and developing the figure of understatement. Whereas
Anglo-Saxon understatement is characteristically blunt and

terse (often being confined to a single half-line of verse), in Old
Norse the figure soon loses the vigorous simplicity which
characterizes its use in the Eddic poems, and in the court poetry
is elaborated and exaggerated in much the same way as the kenning is strained and tortured by the scalds. The elaborate, self-
conscious exaggeration characteristic of scaldic understatement
is shown in the following examples:

> Tind-Hallkelsson: Fragment 1 f., "Varða gims
> sem gœrði Gerðr biug-limom herða /. . . farlig
> sæing iarli: / þa es hring-fǫm hanga hryn-serk
> Viðorr brynjo /. . . varð at kasta." "It was not as
> if the damsel were making a bed for the Earl in her
> arms when he had to throw off his ring-stripped
> mail coat." (VP)
> Cormac's Improvisations 158 f., "Vasa sem
> flioð i faðmi þa es fangremi 'mœtask' /við streng-
> mara styri Steingerði mer hefðak." "It was not as if
> I had my lady Steingerd in my arms when I grappled
> with the champion, the sea-steed's steerer." (VP)
> St. Olaf's Court, Minor Fragments 51 f., "Vasa
> Sunno-dag, svanni . . . /morgun þann sem manni
> mær lauk eða ǫl bæri." "That Sunday morning it was
> not as when the maid is serving men with leeks or
> ale." (VP)
> Sighvat: Nesja-visor 23 f., þagi vas sem þessom
> þengils a io strengjar /miǫð fyrir malma kveðjo
> mær heið-þegom bæri." "On board the prince's ship
> in the fight it was not at all as when the damsel is
> bearing mead to the henchmen." (VP)[41]

Constructions like these are, in a sense, inverted metaphors
and similes; the poet describes things by telling at some length
what they are not like. They are also, however, clear cases of
understatement, and there seems to me no doubt that they are
elaborations, in the characteristic manner of the scalds, of the
simpler understatement common to all Germanic poetry.

The frequency of understatement varies in the different Old
Norse poems, as it does in Old English; one may say generally
that in the Eddic poems it occurs about as frequently as in Old
English, in the Scaldic poems somewhat less. It occurs most

frequently in the pagan heroic poems — Hamðismal, Atlakviða, Atlamal, the Helgi trilogy. There are many cases in the bitter Lokasenna, but few in the later Scaldic "flytings." In the early Christian poems it occurs about as frequently as in the corresponding Old English Christian poetry. It dies out of the Scaldic poetry when the courts became Christianized; after the time of Eric the Good of Denmark (c. 1130) and Magnus Bareleg of Norway (1093–1103), "the last king of the real old type" (VP), not much understatement occurs in the court poetry of the scalds. The fact that in Old Norse, as in Old English, understatement occurs most frequently in the early pagan poetry, and dies out after the introduction of Christianity is additional evidence that this figure has its roots in a common Germanic poetic tradition.

Understatement in Old Norse is not, however, confined to the poetry. It occurs in most of the sagas, and in some of them it occurs very frequently. E. E. Kellett[42] speaks of "a noteworthy love of what grammarians call 'litotes' — that is, the figure of speech by which much less is said than is meant." In general, understatement occurs most frequently in those sagas which show most evidence of conscious artistry — that is, in those which combine and elaborate, or embroider with folk-lore and fiction, already-existing stories —, and least frequently in the earlier, more strictly historical sagas. For example, the Brennu-Njals Saga, which is apparently a thirteenth century version and combination of two or three earlier pieces, uses understatement very frequently and for a variety of effects. The Laxdæla Saga and Egils Saga, which belong to the same class, also use rhetorical understatement frequently. On the other hand, Hrafnkels Saga — "one of the best examples of the historical saga; . . . its text is probably very near to the original taken from oral tradition"[43] — uses almost no understatement at all.

Different parts of Grettis Saga illustrate this same difference. The first dozen chapters or so are primarily historical, recording the establishment of Grettir's family in Iceland, and are probably quite close to oral tradition. In this historical introduction practically no understatement occurs. The remainder of the saga, including the supernatural elements which play so important a part in the characterization and plot, is rather a historical novel than history, giving evidence of considerable literary skill; and here understatement occurs on almost every page. J. Sephton[44] notes this same contrast in his comparison of the Great Olaf Tryggvason Saga and the same story as told in the Heimskringla. "He [the author of the saga] avoids positiveness in his statements, using 'many' where the Heimskringla has 'all,' 'very often' instead of 'always,' 'slowish' instead of 'slow'; and he makes more frequent use of the figure of speech, litotes." In short, understatement in Old Norse seems to have been felt as a decorative, or embellishing, rhetorical device, traditionally proper to poetry, but used also in "artistic," as distinguished from more practical prose.

Since understatement is found in the early poetry of all the Germanic peoples, there is reason to assume that it was characteristic of that common Germanic poetry from which, presumably, the alliterative verse we know has descended. It would be a remarkable coincidence if four related peoples developed such a usage independently, and even more remarkable in view of its occurrence along with the other stylistic characteristics (such as the verse structure, kenningar, variation, epithets used in place of pronouns, noun-compounds, etc.), which are common to early Germanic poetry. It is possible, of course, that understatement was a relatively late development, which spread from one Germanic people to another; the close connection between the Old English Genesis and the fragment of the Old Saxon Genesis is evidence of literary interchange as late as the ninth century. But if we assume, as seems likely, that the stylistic devices found in all Germanic poetry are descended from a common-Germanic poetic tradition going back probably to the period of the migrations, in the absence of positive evidence for late borrowing there is no reason to make an exception in the case of understatement. It occurs, along with the other stylistic traits, in the earliest extant poetry of the different Germanic peoples, and supplies additional evidence for the theory of a common stylistic tradition.

NOTES

1 "The Style of Anglo-Saxon Poetry," PMLA, III (1887), 32.

2 R. W. Chambers, Introduction to A. Strong's translation of Beowulf (London, 1925), p. xlvi; F. B. Gummere, The Oldest English Epic (New York, 1925), p. 19; W. J. Sedgefield, Beowulf (Manchester, 1913), p. xxiii; Fr. Klaeber, Beowulf

(Boston, 1928), p. lxvi; J. R. C. Hall, Beowulf (London, 1911), p. xxviii; R. Schuchardt, "Die Negation im Beowulf," Berliner Beiträge zur Germ. und Rom. Phil., Germanische Abteilung, XXV (1910), 120 f.

3 My references are to line numbers in Klaeber's edition of Beowulf (1928), and for the rest of the poetry, unless otherwise stated, to line numbers in the Grein-Wülcker Bibliothek der Angelsächsischen Poesie (Kassel, 1881).

4 "Negation in English and Other Languages," in Kungl. Danske Videnskabernes selskab, Historisk-filologiske meddelelser (Copenhagen, 1917), I, 5, 22 f.

5 A Comparative Study of the Beowulf and the Æneid (Princeton, 1931), p. 34.

6 Beowulf (Manchester, 1913), p. 112.

7 An exception might be made in the case of certain words compounded with leas. An indication that such words may have been taken in a literal sense and so have given an effect of understatement (e.g. Christ 1628, "þæt is dreamleas hus" in reference to hell—although the relative infrequency of understatement in the Christ might argue against this particular case) is the not infrequent occurrence of such phrases as Beowulf 850, "dreama leas"; Elene 693, "duguða leas"; Andreas 1314, "duguðum bereafod"; etc. These would almost certainly be taken literally. Cf. MnE words with -less: painless, useless, joyless.

8 Cf. also Beowulf 109, 793 f., 1304, 2687; Andreas 1702 f.; Maldon 192; Christ and Satan 576 f.; Elene 910; Exodus 42; Guthlac 783 f.

9 The fairly common practice among Old English poets of borrowing or adapting a half line of verse, often irrelevant or inappropriate, merely to get the proper alliteration (cf., for example, the modifications of the formula ". . . ne gymdon" in Andreas 139, Genesis 2459, Exodus 140, Christ 706, Maldon 192, Beowulf 1757) may explain this passage.

Compare Beowulf 2919 f., "feoll on feðan; nalles frætwe geaf / ealdor dugoðe," in which context the negation is quite appropriate.

10 My references are to W. J. Sedgefield's edition (Oxford, 1899).

11 Cf. also Metrum IX, 18; XIII, 23 f.; XIII, 33 f.; XX, 117; XXVIII, 35; VIII, 36 f.; XV, 10 f.; Proem, 7 f.

12 Cf. also 88, 172 f., 210 f., 283 f., 297 f., 362 f., 696 f., 741, 746 f., 1319 f.

13 References are to chapter and line of Gonser's edition, Anglistische Forschungen, XXVII (1909).

14 On the general decline of the Old English heroic style, cf. W. W. Lawrence, Beowulf and Epic Tradition (Cambridge, Mass., 1928), p. 4.

15 The Deeds of Beowulf (Oxford, 1892), p. 107.

16 The Development of English Humour (New York, 1930), Ch. I.

17 Beowulf (Boston, 1928), p. lxi.

18 Die Technik der Erzählung im Beowulfliede (Breslau, 1904), p. 29.

19 Cf. also Juliana 605 f.; Maldon 46 f.; Beowulf 562, 595 f., 756 f., 972 f., 1071 f., 2363 f., 2873 f.; Guthlac A 392; Christ and Satan 576 f.; Brunanburh 47 f.; Judith 117 f.

20 XIV, 24 "Orti hann jafnan visur ok kviðlinga ok þotti heldr niðskældinn."

21 Cf. Priscus' account of the effect of heroic verse on the warrior at Attila's court. K. W. Müller, Fragmenta historicorum Græcorum (Paris, 1851), IV, 92.

22 "Studien über die Figur der Litotes," Neue Jahrbücher für Philologie und Pädagogik, Supplement, XV (1886), 451.

23 Cf. also Beowulf, 1025 f., 1455, 2354 f., 2541, 2995 f.; Genesis 2327; Juliana 328 f.; Guthlac 783 f., 1330 f.; Maldon 268, 249 f.

24 Irony, an Historical Introduction (London, 1926).

25 G. Vigfusson and F. Y. Powell, Origines Islandicae (Oxford, 1905), II, 500, 14 f.

26 Cf. T. B. Haber, A Comparative Study of the Beowulf and the Æneid (Princeton, 1931); J. W. Rankin, "A Study of the

Kennings in Anglo-Saxon Poetry," JEGP, VIII (1904), 357 f.,
IX, 49 f.; A. Keiser, The Influence of Christianity on the
Vocabulary of Old English Poetry (Urbana, 1919).

27 Cf. J. S. P. Tatlock, "Laȝamon's Poetic Style and Its Relations," The Manly Anniversary Studies in Language and
Literature (Chicago, 1923), pp. 3 f.

28 R. Heinzel, "Ueber den Stil der altgermanischen Poesie,"
QF, X (1875); E. Sievers, Altgermanische Metrik (Halle,
1893), Abschnitt 2 and 7; L. Wolff, "Ueber den Stil der
altgermanischen Poesie," Deutsche Vierteljahrsschrift, I
(1923), 214 f.; W. Paetzel, Die Variationen in der altgermanischen Alliterationspoesie (Berlin, 1913), pp. 1 f.,
and passim; H. v. d. Merwe Scholtz, The Kenning in Anglo-
Saxon and Old Norse Poetry (Utrecht, 1927), pp. 176 f. and
passim; A. Heusler, Die altgermanische Dichtung (Berlin,
1923), pp. 134 f., 161 f.

29 Cf. Beowulf 249 f., "nis þæt seldguma / wæpnum geweorðad."

30 B. Dickins, in Runic & Heroic Poems (Cambridge, 1915),
p. 85, translates "were of none avail."

31 Cf. Muspilli 99, Ludwigslied 35, Guthlac A 783, Debate of the
Body and the Soul 163.

32 "Die unechte Negation bei Otfrid und im Heliand," BGDSL,
XXV (1900), 544.

33 Cf. also 2, 5, 20; 2, 14, 38; 2, 16, 40; 3, 1, 20; 4, 15, 35;
5, 23, 152; etc.

34 J. Wiegand, "Stilistische Untersuchungen zum König Rother,"
Germanistische Abhandlungen, XXII (1904), 57; J. Schmedes,
Untersuchungen über den Stil der Epen Rother, Nibelungen-
lied und Gudrun (Kiel, 1893), p. 36; H. Timm, Das Nibelungen-
lied nach Darstellung und Sprache ein Urbild Deutsches
Poesie (Halle, 1852), p. 201 f.; K. Kinzel, "Zum Charakter-
istik des Wolframschen Stils," ZDP, V (1874), 3; C. Borch-
ling, Der jüngere Titurel und sein Verhältnis zu Wolfram
von Eschenbach (Göttingen, 1897), p. 168; S. Singer, Wolframs
Stil und der Stoff des Parzival (Vienna, 1916), p. 15.

35 Stilistische Untersuchungen über Rudolf von Ems' Weltchronik
und seine beiden Meister Gottfried und Wolfram (Amsterdam,
1927).

36 Some of these are noted by Lörcher, op. cit., p. 544. My
    references are to M. Heyne's edition (Paderborn, 1905).

37 Cf. also, 83 f., 243, 263 f., 320, 538 f., 1094, 1855 f., 3818 f.,
    4194 f., 4595.

38 My references are to line numbers in Vigfusson and Powell's
    Corpus poeticum boreale (Oxford, 1888). I have, however,
    used their final corrected readings, which appear sometimes
    in the notes and sometimes in the list on pp. cxxiv–cxxx of
    Volume I. I have also used their translations, indicated by
    VP, except where these are not sufficiently literal to bring
    out the understatement.

39 Cf. also The Old Play of the Wolsungs 19, Lokasenna 121,
    Hakonarmal 20, Hofuðlausn 58, Sonatorrek 19 f., The Long
    Lay of Brunhild 280, Thiodwulf's Haustlong 12, Satires 44.

40 Cf. also Hamðismal 23 f., The Old Play of the Wolsungs
    35 f., Hyndlolioð 176, Eywind's Improvisations 2, Haleygia-
    tal 43 f., Atlamal 2, Havamal 117 f., The Christian's Wis-
    dom 71 f.

41 Cf. Cormac's Improvisations 162 f.: Sighvat; Dirge on
    Erling 29 f., Bersoglis Visor 15 f.

42 The Northern Saga (London, 1929), p. 66.

43 E. V. Gordon, An Introduction to Old Norse (Oxford, 1927),
    p. li.

44 The Saga of King Olaf Tryggvason (London, 1895), p. ix.

ANALYSIS OF STYLISTIC DEVICES AND EFFECTS
IN ANGLO-SAXON LITERATURE

R. F. Leslie

In this paper I shall attempt to illustrate how style and structure are intimately related in Anglo-Saxon poetry. Although it is true that the relationship is often a highly formal one, a concern with form has often obscured the profound effect of the poetic theme upon the style of individual passages or complete poems. The result of concentration on the primarily formal features of Old English poetry has been the widespread belief that it contains ornate and rigid stylistic elements, into which have been fitted—sometimes felicitously, sometimes incongruously—all sorts of poetic material. I hope to give some indication that the stylistic devices of the Anglo-Saxons were far from being mechanically applied.

As recently as 1935 it was possible for Miss Bartlett in The Larger Rhetorical Patterns in Anglo-Saxon Poetry to write that many of the studies of style had been confined either to one text or to one figure, usually the kenning, that little had been written on Anglo-Saxon poetry as a relatively homogeneous and independent body of verse, and even less that was concerned primarily with its style. But in her work also, there remained the belief that the poet was, as she said, "more interested in the elaborate detail than the composition of the whole."[1]

The view that many of the stylistic features of Old English were superimposed on, or arbitrarily inserted into, the flow of the verse, was one which could remain dominant largely because the study of syntax had fallen far behind the study of figures such as the "kenning." It is perhaps significant that, two years after Marquardt's definitive work on kennings, it was necessary for S. O. Andrew in Syntax and Style in Old English (Cambridge, 1940)

Reprinted from Stil- und Formprobleme in der Literatur, Proceedings of the Seventh Congress of the International Federation for Modern Language and Literature (Heidelberg, 1959), pp. 129–36, by permission of Walter de Guyter & Co. (formerly Karl J. Trüber) and the author.

to explain in his preface that his study was "an attempt to drive
a few main lines through the almost unexplored tract of Old English syntax." Both in this work, and in its successor Postscript
on Beowulf, Andrew has — by and large — shown that sense units
in Old English are more thoroughly integrated than the traditional
punctation of texts leads us to suppose, that there is in fact more
hypotaxis and less parataxis in the literature than has previously
been admitted. Perhaps he has gone too far in some of his
claims, and laid himself open to the criticism that he has "in
all probability unconsciously been a slave to his modern linguistic instincts," which Alarik Rynell made in his Lund mono-
graph entitled Parataxis and Hypotaxis as a Criterion of Syntax
and Style, especially in Old English Poetry.[2] Nevertheless, I
believe that enough cases can be made out on the objective
grounds of textual harmony to justify us in assuming a much
closer texture to Old English verse than has usually been allowed;
e.g. in The Wife's Lament 36–38, the woman must walk alone

> under actreo geond þas eorðscrafu,
> þær ic sittan mot sumorlangne dæg,
> þær ic wepan mæg mine wræcsiþas.

Editors generally begin a new sentence with the first þær, whereas the demonstrative adjective "these" before eorðscrafu indicates that þær is to be taken as a conjunction, not an adverb.
  Linked with this syntactical approach to the question of style
and structure has been a reappraisal of many passages that had
been held, because of their digressionary or repetitive or didactic nature, to be stylistically inept. M. Adrien Bonjour's work
on The Digressions in Beowulf[3] shows, as he says, that "each
digression brings its distinctive contribution to the organic
structure and the artistic value of the poem"; and in an article
on the technique of parallel descriptions in Beowulf (in RES,
XXVII [1951]) he compares the return of the Danes from the
lake where Beowulf fights Grendel's mother with the return of
the Geats from the same spot, pointing out how the poet made
use of parallel parts of the same plot to effect a simple and
telling contrast. In his comment on this article in YWES, XXXV
(1954), R. M. Wilson concludes: "when considering the art of the
poet we must take into account the parallelism of parts and other
structural features to a greater extent than has previously been
the custom."

STYLISTIC DEVICES AND EFFECTS

I turn to examine how these larger structural features echo, use, or grow from the various stylistic devices frequently used in minor contexts, devices which in their turn are related to the antithetical interlacing patterns of the alliterative verse medium itself, on which so much has been written. From a structural point of view, probably the most widespread stylistic feature is "variation," a term not always unambiguously used, but by which I mean simply the repetition of an idea in a different word or words. Basically the device adds emphasis to a word or group of words, and can be used in a number of different ways. Claes Schaar in Critical Studies in the Cynewulf Group (Lund, 1949) devotes a long chapter to listing and analysing examples from the Cynewulfian and related poems. You may recall that he makes a division between "close" and "loose" variation. In the first, the variant word or group of words corresponds syntactically to its correlative; e.g. in Elene 460–1, where Christ is described as:

> cyning on roderum,
> soð sunu meotudes, sawla nergend.

and with chiasmus in The Wanderer 13–14:

> þæt he his ferðlocan fæste binde,
> healde his hordcofan, hycge swa he wille.

In "loose" variation the variant expression corresponds semantically, but not formally, to its correlative, as in The Wanderer 99–100:

> Eorlas fornoman asca þryþe,
> wæpen wælgifru, wyrd seo mære.

The arrangement is frequently chiastic, as in Christ 677–8:

> ofer sealtne sæ sundwudu drifan,
> hreran holmþræce.

Schaar would confine his definition of "loose" variation to variants where nothing is added to the sense. Although such a definition often holds good for the Cynewulfian poems, with their

257

ornate and rather leisurely style, it does not apply so well to
Beowulf, and rarely to the elegiac lyrical poems, where something is almost always added in the variant expressions. While
I concur with Schaar in having two categories of variation, I
would extend the scope of his "loose" variation, calling it for
comparative stylistic purposes, conceptual variation, in contrast
to "close," or formal variation, where the variants are syntactically equivalent, and—in their simplest form—include most
kennings.

There is a distinct similarity between the stylistic employment of formal variation in minor contexts, encompassing only
a few phrases, and the use of conceptual variations which en-
compass whole passages, and sometimes whole poems. Sometimes the variant passages are interlaced with other matter in
a distinct pattern, often in the form ABA which has been called
an envelope pattern. Sometimes the effect of this interlacing is
heightened by conscious antithesis with the passage or passages
between the conceptual variants. These larger patterns appear
to have grown out of an expansion of the chiastic arrangement
of formal variants, of the kind that I have already quoted. We
can see this expansion with the chiastic arrangement of relatively simple conceptual variants in the following passage from
The Phoenix 34–41:

> Wæstmas ne dreosað,
> beorhte blede, ac þa beamas a
> grene stondað, swa him god bibead.
> Wintres ond sumeres wudu bið gelice
> bledum gehongen; næfre brosniað
> leaf under lyfte, ne him lig sceþeð
> æfre to ealdre, ærþon edwenden
> worulde geweorðe.

A negative statement is followed by a positive one; then follows another positive variant, followed by a negative one. It is
notable that we find nothing of this configuration in the Latin
source, the poem by Lactantius, which simply has: "Here is the
grove of the Sun, a holy wood thickly planted with trees, green
with the glory of never-failing foliage."

Chiasmus as a stylistic device in Old English poetry would
not have been possible without the development of what Kemp

Malone calls "plurilinear" units, in his article in RES, XIX (1943), 201–204. Within the bounds of the presumably early end-stopped lines a certain amount of straightforward variation was possible, but the development of chiastic phrases and patterns would require a syntactical pause in the middle of a line and would stimulate, or be stimulated by, the development of multi-linear sentences as in the Phoenix passage just quoted. The increasing importance of the medial pause led to many sentences beginning in the middle of the line, and in later poetry most of the sentences begin and end in the middle of the line. Malone says of Judith that "the verses give the effect of a never-ending flow, but this continuous effect is gained at a heavy structural cost." In this swift narrative poem perhaps we should not expect major structural patterns, but there are ample effective local uses of chiasmus and variation which give form to the narrative and provide contrast and vivid description, without holding up the flow of the verse, e.g. in lines 253–256:

> Mynton ealle
> þæt se beorna brego and seo beorhte mægð
> in ðam wlitegan træfe wæron ætsomne,
> Iudith seo æðele ond se galmoda.

—a neat use of variation and inversion, the variants being separated by a line of other matter.

I should like to turn now to two other stylistic devices which are used effectively, not only in minor contexts, but in large-scale patterns, where—like variation—they may have a pronounced bearing on the structure of a passage or poem. The first of these is "antithesis," which can be either implicit or explicit. In implicit antitheses contrast is obtained by the mere juxtaposition of phrases, without conjunctions, by adversative asyndeton. Schaar regards it as stylistically primitive and accuses the Andreas poet of using the device indiscriminately. A simple example occurs in Andreas 505–506:

> Ðu eart seolfa geong,
> wigendra hleo, nalas wintrum frod.

It is true that this appears rather artless beside the polished balanced phrasing in The Wanderer 32–33, where the poet says of the exile:

> waraঠ hine wræclast nales wunden gold,
> ferঠloca freorig nalæs foldan blæd.

Explicit antitheses, with adversative conjunctions, appear to be
most common with <u>ac</u>, as in <u>Christ</u> 1049:

> Ne sindon him dæda dyrne, ac þær biঠ dryhtne cuঠ.

A sustained use of antithesis effectively culminates Wiglaf's long
speech in <u>Beowulf</u> 3007–27. Here is the final vivid contrast of
life and death for the warrior:

>   Forঠon sceall gar wesan
> monig, morgenceald, mundum bewunden,
> hæfen on handa, nalles hearpan sweg
> wigend weccean, ac se wonna hrefn
> fus ofer fægum fela reordian,
> earne secgan, hu him æt æte speow,
> þenden he wiঠ wulf wæl reafode.

This sentence repeats a figure which occurs several times in
the preceding 19 lines, the sandwiching of the negative element
in the antithesis between two positive ones, forming an envelope
pattern.

Interlacing of this kind is carried still further in <u>The Sea-
farer</u>, where it comprises a major structural element in the
poem. The early part falls into two distinct sections—the
speaker's past experiences of coastal voyages, and his projected
experience of an ocean voyage. The predominant tone of each
is different, the first being concretely descriptive, the second
reflective and imaginative. Yet they are linked by a contrast
which runs through both.

In the first section the speaker describes the hardships of
sailing in wintry weather, then in line 12 comes the contrast:

>   þæt se mon ne wat
> þe him on foldan fægrost limpeঠ,
> hu ic earmcearig iscealdne sæ
> winter wunade, wræccan lastum.

STYLISTIC DEVICES AND EFFECTS

His distress is reinforced by the terse glimpse of the storm, hægl scurum fleag. The next passage indicates not physical but mental suffering, and in line 27 comes the contrast:

> Forþon him gelyfeð lyt, se þe ah lifes wyn
> gebiden in burgum bealosiþa hwon,
> wlonc ond wingal, hu ic werig oft
> in brimlade bidan sceolde.

Again the poet reinforces his sufferings by a graphic description of the elements, in terse asyndetic clauses, contrasting in verse texture, as well as in content, with the complex sentence just quoted:

> Nap nihtscua, norþan sniwde,
> hrim hrusan bond, hagl feol on eorþan,
> corna caldast.

In both passages we have the ABA sandwich pattern which we found in the Beowulf passage discussed above.

In the second voyage section the speaker describes his longing for the high seas, and the signs that urge him on to the ocean. The tone of the passage is exalted, and builds up towards a climax through two anaphoric series, with repetition of the negative particle ne, the second culminating in an antithesis with the conjunction ac (lines 39–43, and 44–47). There follows the lovely lyrical passage on the signs of spring—and how poignant are the Anglo-Saxons on this theme—then the contrasting motif of the fortunate landdweller is repeated, this time formally parallel to its first introduction in line 12:

> þæt se beorn ne wat,
> sefteadig secg, hwæt þa sume dreogað
> þe þa wræclastas widost lecgað.

The antitheses themselves, we see, are subject to variation, forming an ABA pattern, and to anaphora or repetition of words or phrases—a device to which I now turn.

Like variation, anaphora can be either formal and compact, or intimately woven into the structure of a poem. The formal

expression may be relatively simple, as in The Wife's
Lament:

> under actreo in þam eorðscræfe (28)

and

> under actreo geond þas eorðscrafu (36)

where the repetition links a descriptive and reflective passage
with a preceding narrative one, emphasising at the same time
the potency of the woman's environment.

The device of repetition can be built up into a powerful
rhetorical pattern, a purpose for which the negative particle
ne is frequently employed. The structure of The Phoenix 14–
21 is a good illustration, and—with its culminating ac clause
—it is very similar in structure to The Seafarer 44–47, referred to above.

> Ne mæg þær ren ne snaw,
> ne forstes fnæst, ne fyres blæst,
> ne hægles hryre, ne hrimes dryre,
> ne sunnan hætu, ne sincaldu,
> ne wearm weder, ne winterscur
> wihte gewyrdan, ac se wong seomað
> eadig ond onsund.

Other adverbs and the pronoun sum are used in the same way.

Repetition is more closely woven into the texture of the poem
in Beowulf 702–731, in the tense and vivid description of the approach of Grendel to Heorot. The echoed words and phrases,
each some seven or eight lines apart, mark decisive stages in
Grendel's advance, while the intervening lines flash back and
forward to events before and after. The technique is almost
that of the film camera. The relevant phrases are:

> Com on wanre niht scriðan sceadugenga . . . .
> Ða com of more under misthleoþum Grendel gongan . . . .
> Com þa to recede rinc siðian . . . .
> Geseah he in recede rinca manige . . . .

Atmosphere is built up in calculated phases.

STYLISTIC DEVICES AND EFFECTS

I should like in conclusion to refer to the lines which follow this passage in Beowulf. They contain several antitheses with hints of the outcome of Grendel's expedition; then follows an accumulation of short sharp paratactical clauses, with no links, indicative of swift action:

> . . . slat unwearnum,
> bat banlocan, blod edrum dranc,
> synsnædum swealh.

These bring a considerable change to the texture of the verse, and constitute what Schaar calls a "compound series," which is reserved for incidents and actions important to the plot, and for vivid description. Passages with a predominance of subordinate clauses he calls "complex series," and claims that they serve primarily a reflective and explanatory function, giving the result or consequence of what precedes.

It will be seen, then, that the stylistic features of Old English poetry are not merely decorative, but have an important functional part in the total structure, and that the syntactical constructions in their turn are diversified to suit the requirements of the style.

NOTES

1   Adelaide C. Bartlett, The Larger Rhetorical Patterns in Anglo-Saxon Poetry (New York, 1935), p. 7.

2   (Lund, 1952), p. 22.

3   (Oxford, 1950).

IV. THREE METRICAL STUDIES

OLD GERMANIC METRICS AND OLD ENGLISH METRICS

Eduard Sievers[1]

Introduction

The form of verse common to all Germanic poetry is confidently thought to be the alliterative line or verse (AV). If the verses chanced also to rime, this would be considered an unessential further embellishment. (Rimed verse [RV], which occurs as a separate art form, will not be treated in the following study of Old English metrics, except as under Section D below.)

We have large quantities of AV in the Old Norse and Old English literatures; in Old Low German there are only two works, the Heliand and the Genesis, both of which are of considerable importance by virtue of their length; only short fragments are preserved in Old High German. The remaining Germanic tribes have left behind no pertinent source material.

The underlying principles of the verse are evidently the same in all the above cases, but a considerable variety is to be noticed in the individual treatments of these, namely in the way each builds upon or fills in the basic pattern: how long the average single line is, or how many syllables are allowed in it. ON verse-lines are the shortest: the predominating verse-line has four syllables. Next comes OE verse, with a large number of such tetrasyllabic verses, yet not so many as in ON. German verse is completely different. The rule here is a longer verse, tetrasyllabic ones being the exception. In the Heliand the lines are expanded often to unwieldy length. As a result one can divide Old Germanic verse into two main groups: ON together with OE as against the German, the essential difference being the way in which each "fills" the verse (concisely on the one hand, diffusely on the other).

Reprinted from Grundriss der Germanischen Philologie, II, 2 (1905), pp. 1–38, by permission of the publishers.

One cannot say from the form alone which of the two groups represents the more original state. A comparative historical study shows, however, that the original Germanic verse probably held the mean between them.

The individual forms of the AV show such manifold variety that a theory has not yet been propounded upon which all scholars can find agreement. Instead of this, and over a period of years, there has developed a series of different theories, each with its greater or lesser train of followers.

I. Old Germanic Metrics

The whole of the poetry of the Scandinavians is stanzaic, a form which was virtually unknown to the West Germans; that is, if we go only by the works which have been preserved. Beginnings of a stanza formation can be found at best in the gnomic verse and also perhaps in the learned church poetry which borrowed from foreign models. The epic, however, which surpasses all other literary forms in length and importance, is exclusively stichic. Attempts have been made to uncover stanzaic foundations under the stichic forms of the epic, but they have failed. Such an attempt to "peel off" the layers can only be done at all by applying the most subjective arbitrariness and ignoring the most obvious stylistic characteristics of the West Germanic epic.

We cannot conclude from this state of affairs, as has often happened, that the whole of Germanic poetry before the time of the separation into the various tribes must have been stanzaic and hence must have been sung. We know of course that old, amply-documented choral songs had a stanzaic form and were sung, but at the same time it is very probable that with the rise of the epic, which was intended to be performed by a single individual, the stichic form and its characteristic style developed. This development could already have taken place in a very early period. Hence for the general Germanic period we must reckon with the coexistence of rhythmically bound and prose-like poetry, of stanzaic and stichic verse, and parallel with this the coexistence of sung and recited poetry.

Then later, in a period devoted mainly to epic poetry, the West Germans cultivated the epic-stichic form and with it the recitative in contrast to the sung delivery. This was done so exclusively that literature has preserved works composed only in this form. In the North, the opposite is the case: the stanzaic form was generalized. But even here the recitative delivery finally won out. The older, more popular poems of the North do not yet have the stanzaic regularity which was later to become the leading principle of the professional artist, presumably because they were composed in the afterglow of an older time and practice. They are often divided into long declamatory passages, and in this they approach much closer to the form of stichic poetry.

Against this point of view, that as a result of the flourishing of epic poetry sung delivery yielded to recitative, and regardless of the meaningless objection that all "old" poetry must have been sung, it has been customary to bring up the argument that the Greeks and Romans, whenever they speak of Germanic songs, use such expressions as <u>carmen, cantus, modulatio, canere, cantare, psallere</u> or ἇσμα, ἀείδειν. There are two holes in this argument. On the one hand such expressions frequently refer to those old choral songs for which a sung delivery can be accepted without question, and on the other they are not strictly a proof, since the terms themselves could denote both a freer rhythmic recitation and a song with a fixed melody. They prove even less in a period when the Germanic words for "sing" and "say" or "speak" had become so confused that the concepts "vocal music" and "solemn elevated speech" were not strictly differentiated any longer. But this was only possible if the songs, i.e. "poems," were spoken in a solemn and ceremonious manner, i.e. recited. What is remarkable is that the term <u>kveða</u> 'to recite,' and no other, is used to refer to the delivery of the strophic poetry of the North. Only the poems in the so-called <u>ljóðaháttr</u> stanza appear perhaps to have been sung for a longer period.

Positive evidence against the existence of fixed melodies and against the supremacy of a special sung delivery, at least in West Germanic poetry, is the special relationship between verse and sentence arrangement which arises naturally when sentences and rhythmic-musical units do not run parallel, but essentially overlap each other. There is evidence of this overlapping even in the North. What is more, it would be difficult to account for the peculiar development of the characteristic five-type system unless we accept that it came about as a result of the transition from sung to spoken delivery. The Germanic verse, then, judged from what has been preserved in the literature, is in fact to be regarded as a spoken verse, unless special reasons exist in an individual case for accepting a sung delivery. The attempts of Möller, Heusler, and others to force a definite kind of rhythm and a smooth, even series of bars upon the whole of the AV are simply not tenable.

This does not deny in any way that the AV had a rhythmic structure. All I contend is that the AV is subject to the rules of the spoken verse (irrational rhythm), which is essentially different from sung verse in that it does not have an invariable rhythm. It is founded rather upon the principle of free rhythmic alternation expressed through the five-type system. Again, this applies only to the AV preserved into historical times. The forerunner of this, even according to my view, was a sung verse based on a regular bar system. The five types developed out of it as a consequence of the transition from vocal music to recitation.

Ordinarily in alliterative poetry there are two so-called short lines or half-lines per verse which are connected by alliteration to form the so-called long line. In West Germanic and also more frequently and regularly in the Norse ljóðaháttr there appear also unpaired lines without a caesura which have only inner alliteration and which can be called full lines. But these are an exception.

The two half-lines of a long line (to be called I and II) are not always constructed alike: certain forms are limited to the one or the other, or, if not limited, at least preferred in certain positions.

As to the length or extent of the verse, West Germanic has in general only two kinds of verse, the shorter standard or normal verse with two rises, and a longer expanded verse with three rises. The two also appear in North Germanic but in a modified form: the West Germanic standard verse corresponds to the popular verse of the so-called fornyrðislag and the expanded verse to certain forms of the ljóðaháttr. The remaining verse forms in North Germanic, especially in the professional poetry of the scalds, are the result of secondary developments. The standard verse is the most widespread of these two kinds. The characteristics of its construction are also common to the longer verses, and hence it seems expedient to begin here and deal with the standard verse separately.

270

OLD GERMANIC METRICS AND OLD ENGLISH METRICS

A. The Construction of the Standard Verse

The standard half-line falls into four, more rarely five, segments, two of which are given special emphasis and raised above the rest of the verse, the syllables of which receive only weak emphasis.

1. These raised syllables or rises (shown as ´) are usually syllables bearing primary stress (including stem syllables of the second members of compounds) and more rarely may be derivative and final syllables which have strong secondary stress.

2. The segments which carry a weaker stress are either grammatically and metrically unstressed or unaccented (shown as ×), forming light depressions or falls in the verse (or "dips" in the strict sense of the word), or else they bear a grammatical secondary stress (shown as ˋ). In the latter case, these syllables do not lose their secondary stress in the verse. Their position in the verse, however, determines how this will be realized. If a grammatical secondary stress stands alone in a two-part foot next to a rise, it is overshadowed by it and functions as a fall. The only difference is that the contrast between a rise and a fall of this kind is not as great as that which occurs when a rise with primary stress and a grammatically unstressed fall syllable are juxtaposed. Compare here such OE verses as wísfæst ǀ wórdum, fáh ond ǀ fýrhèard, gúðrìnc ǀ góldwlànc with such as wísra wórda. We are contrasting here then the two kinds of fall, the strong one consisting of a syllable bearing secondary stress, and the other a light one, based on an unstressed syllable. The metrical value of grammatical stress can hence be seen to be relative. In the three-part foot the interaction is again different. Here the syllable carrying a grammatical secondary stress forms a necessary link between the rise with primary stress and a grammatically unstressed fall syllable. See again such OE verses as wís ǀ wélpùngen, fýrst ǀ fórð gewàt, héalærna ǀ mæst. In this case the syllable bearing secondary stress is felt as a kind of weaker rise in contrast to the unstressed fall. Hence it will be called here secondary rise.

The syllables which carry the rises are as a rule long syllables. This length ⌣̄ can however be replaced or represented by the sequence ⌣×, that is, a short plus an unstressed syllable of any length. This substitution will be called here "resolution." Characteristic of it is an acceleration of the tempo of the speech

271

which is itself shortened, since the two syllables are compressed approximately into the measure of a single long syllable. This is called slurring.

If two syllables with grammatical stress appear in succession, then it is possible for the second, even if a single short one, to carry the rise.

The two rises in a half-line are not necessarily of equal strength in the delivery, but are most usually gradated according to what is to be emphasized. It would hence be possible that a stronger and a weaker rise could stand together in a half-line without the latter losing any of the character of full rise.

A syllable of any quantity which is grammatically unstressed (shown as ×) is sufficient to constitute a light fall, but several of such syllables may also occur together (e.g. ××, ×××). Every such series of grammatically unstressed syllables which is not broken by a stronger grammatical secondary stress is counted as a single fall. (Note: The necessary falling syllables will henceforth be shown by ×; permitted syllables in excess of this will be marked when necessary by periods: the pattern -́× . . .| -× shows that verses of the form -́× | -́×, -́×× | -́×, -́××× | -́× and -́×××× | -́× are all permitted variants of the basic form.)

Members bearing secondary stress in the verse (i.e. those functioning as either a secondary rise or a secondary fall) are as a rule monosyllabic and long. Resolution is permitted, and also the appearance of a linguistically short syllable whenever the member bearing secondary stress follows directly after a rise. In the verse of four members, these fall into two parts, either in pairs to a 2 + 2 pattern or to a 1 + 3 — alternatively 3 + 1 — pattern. These parts could be called metrical feet, and as seen, they may be made up of an even or uneven number of members. A foot with only one member consists simply of a rise, -́; one with two members consists of a rise and a fall, -́×, alternatively of a fall and rise, ×-́; and one with three members consists either of rise + secondary rise + fall, -́ -́×, or of rise + fall + secondary rise, -́ × -́. Combinations of feet with falling and rising characteristics can be formed thus: -́× | -́×, × -́ | × -́ and × -́ | -́×.

According to the above there occur the following five very simple basic forms of the AV:

OLD GERMANIC METRICS AND OLD ENGLISH METRICS

   a) Types with equal feet, pattern 2 + 2.

1. A ´× | ´×, double falling type
2. B ×´ | ×´, double rising type
3. C ×´ | ´×, rising-falling type

   b) Types with unequal feet.

4. D $\left\{ \begin{matrix} ´ | ´ ~ ´× \\ ´ | ´× ´ \end{matrix} \right\}$ pattern 1 + 3

5. E $\left\{ \begin{matrix} ´ ~ ´× | ´ \\ ´× ´ | ´ \end{matrix} \right\}$ pattern 3 + 1

A special falling-rising type ´× | ×´ was not developed, since the syllable series ´××´ can only count as three members (rise + fall + rise). Those variant forms of the simple types (which contain a fall with secondary instead of weak stress) are said to be intensified. In contrast to the normal A verse such as hýran scólde, ´× | ´×, there are also verses such as wísfæst wórdum, ´ ´| ´×, and fáh ond fýrhèard, ´× | ´ ´, with a single intensification, and gúðrinc góldwlànc, ´ ´| ´ ´, with a double one.

Alongside the verses with four members there also occur with greater or lesser frequency verses with five members (according to the usual way of reckoning them). This may be due to an additional fall or to a member with secondary stress within the actual verse. In this case, the patterns 2 + 3 and 3 + 2 arise. They are called extended forms because they extend beyond the average measure of four members, and will be indicated by an asterisk following the symbol of the schematic type, thus A*, B* and so on.

Those verses which have an introductory beat before an otherwise complete rhythmic series are, strictly speaking, also composed of five members, such as × ‖ ´× | ´×. However, because of the special position of this introductory beat such verses are kept apart from the extended ones where the additional matter appears within the actual body of the verse. The introductory beat will be indicated by the symbol "a" before the symbol for the schematic type, such as "aA" and so on, and the individual syllables of the introductory beat will be shown as "×, ××" (and when necessary by "×. . .").

Variations on the types include resolution and shortening of the rises; intensification of the fall by secondary stresses; and differing numbers of syllables in the falls. Of less importance

273

are the changing position of the alliteration and the use of introductory beats. The latter can hardly be considered sufficient cause for setting up special sub-categories: the types with this introduction will be taken simply as parallels to the forms occurring without it. But even the other methods of variation were not used with equal regularity. Instead of this, a number of distinct sub-varieties of the individual types were developed, which make a special schematic representation necessary.

1. The basic type A has three sub-varieties:

A 1. The normal form of the type with alliteration on the first rise (in the first half-verse the second may also alliterate) and grammatically unstressed syllables in the falls. Resolution of the rises is permitted more or less in all positions.

A 2 (or A n, that is A with secondary stress). This is type A with alliteration on the first rise and unlimited resolution. It is intensified by having grammatical secondary stresses in the falls. Sub-types of this are:

A 2 a, with secondary stress in the first fall. Since here the second rise may be long or short, this sub-type may be split into two patterns, A 2 a l and A 2 a s or for the sake of brevity A 2 l and A 2 s, i.e. A 2 with a <u>long</u> second rise as wísfǽst wórdum, $\acute{-} \stackrel{.}{-} | \acute{-} \times$, and A 2 with a <u>short</u> second rise as gúðrìnc mónig, $\acute{-} \stackrel{.}{-} | \smile \times$.

A 2 b, i.e. A 2 with a secondary grammatical stress in the second fall, as for example <u>Gréndles gúðcrǽft</u>, $\acute{-} \times | \acute{-} \stackrel{.}{-}$.

A 2 a b, i.e. A 2 with secondary stress in both falls, as for example gúðrìnc góldwlànc, $\acute{-} \stackrel{.}{-} | \acute{-} \stackrel{.}{-}$ (A with double intensification).

A 3. This is A with alliteration on the second rise only. This form is restricted almost completely to the first half-verse. Secondary stresses occur only in the second fall. This augmented A 3 will be indicated whenever necessary as A 3b.

2. The basic type B is more or less uniform. Resolution of th rises is permitted. The second fall fluctuates in general between one and two syllables, which can be designated if need be as B 1 an B2. For the very rare cases of B with alliteration of the second rise only, the label B 3 will be used by analogy with A 3.

3. The basic type C shows again three clearly pronounced forms.

C 1. The normal type $\times \acute{-} | \acute{-} \times$ without resolution as <u>oft Scýld Scéfing</u>.

C 2. Same as above with resolution of the first rise, ×◡̇×ǀ-́×,
as in wórold wócun.

C 3. The type C with shortening of the second rise, ×-́ǀ◡̇×,
as of féorwégum.

Note: Secondary stresses appear only in the second fall and are
rare. They can be indicated by the addition of an n, for example
C 1n as in ON troða hálir hélvèg ××◡̇×ǀ -̣ -̇.

4. The basic type D has four sub-varieties:

D 1. -́ǀ-́ -̇× along with its possible resolutions, as in
féond máncỳnnes, fǽder álwàlda.

D 2. -́ǀ-̇◡̇× with shortening of the secondary rise and
possible resolutions, as béarn Héalfdènes, súnu Héalfdènes.

D 3. -́ǀ◡̇-́× with shortening of the second rise and possible
resolutions, as éorðcýnìnges, wóroldcýnìnga.

D 4. -́ǀ-́×-̇ with secondary rise in final position and possible resolutions, as flét ínnanwèard, dráca mórðre swèalt.

5. The basic type E has two sub-varieties, differentiated by
the position of the secondary rise:

E 1. -́◡̇×ǀ-́ as wéorðmỳndum þáh, Scédelàndum ín (resolution), Súðdèna fólc (shortening of the secondary rise).

E 2. -́×-̇ǀ-́ as mórðorbèd stréd.

Some details of the extended forms (those having five members) should now be noted. In the popular Germanic poetry including the North Germanic málaháttr, the following forms occur:

1. Extended form A* with its sub-varieties A*1 -́ -́×ǀ-́×
as ON ǫlvǽrir urðu and A*2 -́×-́ǀ-́× as ON séndimènn Atla.

Note: Strictly speaking this type should be designated as an extended A 2 form, as it contains one more member with secondary stress than the simple A 2. It is unlikely however that
this will be misunderstood, even with the abbreviated terminology. I earlier called this type an extended E form.

2. Extended B* -́×-́ǀ×-́ as ON þàrs þū blǽju sátt.

3. Extended C* with the same sub-varieties as the simple
C group, hence C*1 -́×-́ǀ-́× as ON fèldi stóð stóra, C*2
-́×◡̇×ǀ-́× as ON èlla hèðan bíðìð, and C*3 -́×-́ǀ◡̇× as ON
vǫrum þrír tígir.

Note 2: B* and C* can be regarded as typically developed forms only in the North Germanic málaháttr with any certainty. It remains to be seen whether or not in other verses such as ON leika Míms sýnir the first syllable was pronounced with a definite secondary stress.

4. Extended D* had three sub-varieties.
   a) D*1 $\stackrel{\_}{-}\times$ | $\stackrel{\_}{-}$ $\stackrel{\_}{-}\times$ as áldres órwēna.
   b) D*2 $\stackrel{\_}{-}\times$ | $\stackrel{\_}{-}\stackrel{\smile}{-}\times$ as mǽre méarcstàpa.
   c) D*4 $\stackrel{\_}{-}\times$ | $\stackrel{\_}{-}\times\stackrel{\_}{-}$ as grḗtte Gḗata lēod.

The corresponding form to D 3 of course is lacking.

A (1). Alliteration

Two half-lines are bound together by alliteration to form a long line, i.e. of the two syllables in each half-line bearing a rise, at least one in each half-line should have the same initial sound. The following rules obtain for the details:

1) All vowels alliterate with each other. In North Germanic the normal syllabic vowels alliterate also with the [j] of the diphthongs ja, jǫ, já, jǫ́, jó, jú, which developed out of the original falling diphthongs ea, eo, etc. In old songs, although it is rare, it was even possible to alliterate [v] with vowels. In this case, we must assume that [v] was still felt as a semi-vowel [u̯].

2) All consonants alliterate whether they stand alone before a vowel or before another consonant: k alliterates with qu [ku̯]; a simple h alliterates with the clusters hl, hn, hr, hw. The clusters sk, st, sp may be alliterated only with themselves, i.e. sk- only with sk- and so on, and not with other s- groups or a single s. In OE and OS etymological g also alliterates with etymological j (and z in foreign words, pronounced however as simple s, was alliterated with s).

The position of alliteration:

1) Those initial sounds of words in a verse which alliterate are normally called staves (ON hljóðstafir): the stave in the second half-line is called the head-stave (ON hǫfuðstafir), and that or those of the first half-line the supports (ON stuðill, pl. stuðlar).

2) The head-stave occupies its alloted position on the
first rise of the second half-line. Exceptions to this rule in
favour of the second rise are rare and are mainly a symptom
of a declining art.

3) The first half-verse can have one or two supports.
In the latter case the supports form the initial sound of both
rises, in the former the alliteration falls on the stronger rise.
This is usually the first; only in A 3 is it the second; B 3 is very
rare. The remaining types do not have this kind of alliteration
at all. What is more, it follows that double alliteration is more
likely wherever the degree of stress on the two rises is equal.
But of course double alliteration is not precluded even where
the stress on the two rises is uneven.

Intensified or augmented alliteration:
Some scholars have considered this to be a special art
form, but this is rather improbable. A number of examples
drawn up to support this contention are based on a completely
wrong stress pattern: syllables in the falls, the initial sounds
of which have nothing to do with the alliteration, have been mis-
takenly taken for rises. It would be safer to say that apart from
a few isolated and certainly unintentional exceptions, a threefold
alliteration in I and a double one in II was not at all popular. So-
called "crossed alliteration" is more frequent, i.e. alliteration
to the pattern a b | a b as for example fóhēm uuórtum | huer sín
fáter uuári (Hildebrandslied 9). In some instances this could
probably be shown to be intentional, especially in North Germanic,
but in general it appears much more rarely than one would expect
if, with a simple main alliteration in I, the initial sound of the
second rise were in fact of no consequence. One can say then
that crossed alliteration was avoided rather than sought after,
the more so when it clashed with the function of the head-stave.

Alliteration and syntactic stress:
Alliteration gives extra emphasis to those words in the
verse bearing heaviest stress. The degree of stress however is
dependent on two main factors: a) the importance arbitrarily
attached to the meaning of a word in each particular case; b) a
traditional scale of grades of emphasis which was evolved for
the individual parts of speech. This scale is given preference
as long as there is no reason to make an exception.

1) When words of different degrees of emphasis appear in the two rises, the stronger one must alliterate. In II this is always the first, and in I usually the first. The weaker word in I may also alliterate.

2) Of two words having the same degree of emphasis, the first as a rule alliterates, but the second may also alliterate wherever double alliteration is permitted.

3) On the scale of emphasis, nouns, including verbal nouns (infinitive and participles), occupy first place.

    a) When a single nominal form stands along with other parts of speech in a half-line, it usually participates in the alliteration.

    b) When two nouns appear in a half-line, the first one practically always alliterates. Exceptions to this are rare, namely those where the second noun actually receives heavier stress. Most cases should be regarded as flaws in the poetic art.

    c) Three nouns can stand in a half-line only when one of them is bound to another in such a way that the stress on the second is weakened relative to that of the first, as for example OS fágar fólcgòdes 'fair people of God' or grŏtkràft godes 'omnipotence of God.' The two nouns form a so-called "noun formula," which is treated exactly the same as a simple noun.

4) The finite verb is weaker than the noun and hence may precede or follow it when not alliterated. It is of course not precluded from alliterating in I. A typical exception to this is the regular alliteration of the finite verb in II in descriptions, whenever more emphasis lies in the content of the verb than in that of its subject (see for example Heliand 2908 ff.). When two finite verbs stand in a dependent relationship the governing one receives a weaker stress than the dependent one. Hence the latter takes precedence over the former in regard to alliteration. On the other hand in case of a distinct coordination, rule 2 above becomes effective.

5) Adverbs.

    a) Simple adverbs of degree such as "very, much" are in principal weakly stressed, relative to the adjectives and adverbs which they modify: they

are alliterated in exceptional circumstances, as
they mainly appear in a fall when they precede
the stronger word.
b) Defining adverbs which precede and modify the
meaning of the following adjective or adverb have
preference over the latter.
c) Adverbial prepositions draw the stress and alliteration over to themselves when they stand before
the verb, whereas the verb alliterates when they
follow it. The same applies for nominal adverbs.
On the other hand pronominal adverbs of place
and time and a few semantically colourless words
such as "often, rarely, soon, always" are treated
as enclitics.

6) Pronouns and pronominal adjectives ("some, all, many,"
etc.) are properly enclitic, but can in certain circumstances receive a heavier stress than even a noun.

7) Prepositions, conjunctions and particles which are enclitic are not involved in the rises, nor, by definition, in the alliteration; prepositions, at any rate, only when they are made
fully stressed by a pronominal enclitic.

In the older West Germanic poetry these rules were followed
most rigorously, but they gradually degenerated later. The
Norse scalds for example were deviating a great deal from the
old practice when they paid more attention to the formal position of the alliteration in the verse than to its semantic significance.

A (2) Verse and Sentence Arrangement

Each half-line must be a grammatical unit, i.e. it must contain a free separable clause (possible en- and proclitics not in-
cluded). Divisions such as <u>dat Hiltibrant</u> hætti | mîn <u>fater</u>: ih
<u>heittu Hadubrant</u> (<u>Hildebrandslied</u> 17) are hence inadmissible.
On the other hand it is not only permitted but even very desirable to extend the construction beyond the limits of a verse.
This applies to the cæsura dividing the two halves of a long line
and also particularly to the division between one long line and
the next. In West Germanic it is quite usual to introduce a new
idea or aspect of an idea at the cæsura and to extend it further
beyond the end of the long line into the following one. In the

stanzaic poetry of the Scandinavians there are certainly still some traces of this, but in general the long line is already pre-eminent there, i.e. long line and sentence unit usually coincide. This is also true of the OHG <u>Muspilli</u>.

B. The Expanded Verse

The name "expanded verse" refers to those longer verses which appear usually grouped together in solemn or emotional speeches. It is a form peculiar to West Germanic. Individually they are not always easy to distinguish from the normal verses, for the shortest forms of the expanded verse coincide with the longest forms of the normal verse, at least superficially, if not in their true rhythmic pattern. Until now they have not been shown to be present in North Germanic, but, as will be shown below, they play an essential role in the formation of the ljóðaháttr stanza.

In contrast to the normal verse, the expanded verse appar-ently has three rises, but it is closely related to the former in its inner construction. This relationship is most easily recog-nized if one agrees with Karl Luick (<u>BGDSL</u>, XIII [1888], 388–392) and understands the expanded verse roughly as a blending together of two normal verses in such a way that a sequence be-gins at the second rise, which is treated as though it were the first rise of one of the five types. In this way the existing forms of the expanded verse can be described by combining the symbols of the five types:

A A: ´× ´× ´×		A 2 A: ´ ´ ´× ´×
A B: ´× ´× ´		A A 2 s: ´× ´ ´ ⌣ ×
A C: ´× ´ ´×		B A: × ´× ´× ´×
A D: ´× ´ ´ ´×		C A: × ´ ´× ´×
A E: ´× ´ ´× ´		C C: × ´ ´ ´×

—and so on. All possible combinations were not developed how-ever, and those which were developed do not appear with equal frequency. Variations on the above follow the normal pattern: resolution of the rises, variation in the number of syllables in the falls and possible subsequent apocope. The particulars belong to a more detailed special study. The three rises are to be sure of equal value, that is, they are full rises, but they are not necessarily stressed to the same degree, one of them receiving a lighter stress than the two others. This is shown very clearly in the rules for alliteration:

1) The first half-verse (and the full line of the ljóðaháttr which is considered on a par with it) may have a threefold alliteration, but has in fact only one. This may fall as a rule on any two of the three occurring rises. Single alliteration is very rare and probably not allowed on principle.

2) The head-stave usually falls on the second rise of the second half-verse, whereby a rising-falling rhythm is realized. Only rarely does the first rise carry the main emphasis and hence the alliteration.

II. Old English Metrics

The sources of our knowledge of Old English metrics, if one includes its very beginnings, extend from the end of the seventh into the tenth century. Most of the OE poetry, however, has come down to us in manuscripts of the tenth and eleventh centuries, for the most part transcribed into a common West Saxon dialect of that period. Original dialect forms have been eliminated from the manuscripts, and a number of later speech forms have been added. The result is that the metrics have often been sadly interfered with, the more so the further the original poetry lies in time and space from the date and dialect of the respective manuscripts. The material preserved from the classical period of the seventh and eighth centuries can hence not really be called metrically good. At the same time, however, the old prose manuscripts furnish information on the development of the language, with the aid of which most of the corruptions in the poetry can be safely identified and corrected.

Stress:

1) The stem syllables of the second members of nominal compounds which are still clearly felt as such bear a strong secondary stress. Examples of this are gūðrinc, gārholt, hringnet. This kind of secondary stress counts almost without exception as a separate member in the verse. The second members of proper names, as Bēowulf, Hygelāc, on the other hand, have only a weaker secondary stress which can be used at the poet's discretion: it can either stand as a separate member or

be ignored. The final syllables of compounds which are not felt
as compounds any longer are as a rule unstressed. Apart from
one or two exceptions, adjectives ending in -lic and -sum belong
to this category.

2) Other syllables which bore a heavy secondary stress
in the older language are the middle syllables of words with the
form $\acute{-} - \times$ such as ēhtènde, sémnìnga, éntìscne, which corresponds to the form $\smile \times - \times$ as in æðelìnga. In the old poetry such
syllables always stood as a separate member in the poetry, although later it was permissible to ignore the secondary stress.

3) Short middle syllables in words of the form $\acute{-} \smile \times$ are
variously treated. They usually show the stress pattern $\acute{-} \smile \times$
as bōcère, wīsìge, dénòde; less frequently they have just one
stress, as in fúndode wrécca (Beowulf 1137). It seems as though
they originally had a lighter secondary stress, which could also
be ignored.

4) All final syllables count as unstressed, irrespective
of their quantity. The poets seem to have treated especially heavy
final syllables as bearing secondary stress.

Number of syllables:

Apart from determining the purely linguistic and dialectic
differences in the number of syllables in individual forms of
words, two other characteristics of the poets' practice should
be especially noted:

1) The treatment of originally syllabic l, m, n, r, or
respectively the -ol, -or, -er, etc., which developed from them:

a) After a short root syllable, in such forms as setl,
fæðm, ðegn (or meðel, fugol, pronounced meðl, fugl) the l, m, n
function (as in Norse) not as extra syllables, but are measured
$\acute{-}$ rather than $\smile \times$. On the other hand the -er, -or which developed from r can be treated as independent syllables: words such
as wæter, leger are measured as $\smile \times$ wherever the metre demands two syllables.

b) Following a long stem syllable, these sounds normally count as separate syllables, although words like súsl, tungl,
bósm, béac(e)n, tác(e)n, frōf(o)r, wuld(o)r are not infrequently
treated as monosyllabic and measured $\acute{-}$ alongside $\acute{-} \times$.

2) Hiatus is perfectly normal, although before unstressed
syllables there was undoubtedly some elision. It is impossible
to formulate any definite rules about this, however, as the falls
do not consist of a definite number of syllables, as in North Germanic.

282

OLD GERMANIC METRICS AND OLD ENGLISH METRICS

Kinds of verse:

As pointed out above, Old English poetry possesses only two kinds of verse: the normal and the expanded verse, which are usually linked together in pairs. For exceptions to the latter rule, see below, Section D, concerning occasional inner and end-rime.

A. The Standard Verse

1. A is the most frequent of the five types, followed by types B, C, D, in varying frequency. E is in general the least frequent.

2. The falling types A and D appear more frequently in the first half-verse than in the second, where the rising types B and C are preferred. On an average E is more frequent in II than in I.

3. Of the sub-varieties of A, the most frequent is A 1, with A 2 the least frequent; the sub-type A 2 s $\doteq \doteq | \smile \times$ occurs more often in II than in I; the form $\doteq \times | \doteq \doteq$ with heavy secondary stress at the end is somewhat avoided in II. According to the laws of alliteration A 3 is limited to I; B 3 appears quite sporadically in I; the distribution of the sub-varieties of C fluctuates. Of the D varieties, the rarest is D 3 $\doteq | \smile \doteq \times$ (it occurs almost exclusively with compounds such as þéodcýnìnga and only exceptionally with two separate words in a half-verse, such as féorh cýnìnges followed by D 4, $\doteq | \doteq \times \doteq$. Of the form E, almost the only form which appears is $\doteq \doteq \times | \doteq$.

4. Of the extended types, D*1.2 $\doteq \times | \doteq \smile \times$ is frequent in I, sometimes even more so than the normal D; D 4 $\doteq \times | \doteq \times \doteq$ is not nearly so well represented as D 1.2. In addition in I, though rather rarely, there occurs the type A*, $\doteq \doteq \times | \doteq \times$, and with secondary stress on the final syllable: $\doteq \doteq \times | \doteq \doteq$. The secondary stresses in the extended feet are relatively light. What is more, a rather large proportion of the verses in this category cannot really be classified, since they contain an originally syllabic l, m, n, or r in either the first or second foot, the treatment of which is ambiguous. The extended types are all but completely lacking in II.

Note: Anomalous verse forms such as $\doteq \times (\times) \smile \times$ occur sometimes, i.e. an A type with foreshortening of the second rise, even

when not preceded by secondary stress, or the form ´ ⌣ ⌣ × as
andswarode (if we do not assume here an older *ándswòrode), or
´ × × (×) ´ without a definite secondary stress. Apart from
the form ´ × (×) ⌣ ×, most of the cases are probably the result
of a faulty tradition.

Resolutions:

1) Resolution of the first rise is rather widespread; the
least usual is B, next is A and most popular are types C, D and
E. Resolution is completely avoided only in type C 3, × ´| ⌣ ×.

2) The second rise of the normal types undergoes resolu-
tion less frequently. The form × ´| ⌣× × is an exception to C,
where the form × ⌣×| ⌣ ×× is preferred. On the other hand
this resolution is rather popular again in the extended D type
´ ×| ⌣× ´ ×. Even the final rise in E is not too infrequently
resolved ´ ´ ×| ⌣ ×.

3) Resolution of members bearing secondary stress is
permitted but not frequent.

Falls:

1) The falls normally consist of grammatically unstressed
syllables, except in the case of the augmented A 2. In B there is
occasionally a secondary stress following the first rise × × ´| ´ ´.
Secondary stress is much rarer in the final fall of C, × ⌣ ×| ´ ´
or in the extended D*, ´ ´| ´ × ´. They are totally lacking in
the simple D and E forms.

2) The introductory fall in B and C is composed usually
of two syllables. Then come the introductory falls with three,
one and four syllables, in that order of frequency. The extremely
rare fall of five and six syllables sets the maximum number.

3) With the normal A and A 2 b, the first fall comprises
one syllable, followed in order of frequency by two, more rarely
three and only in exceptional cases four to five syllables. The
figures for A 3 are the above increased by one: a monosyllabic
fall was avoided here if possible.

4) The inner fall of B is monosyllabic as a rule, much
more rarely disyllabic. A trisyllabic fall is an exception in
this position.

5) Again with D 4, ´| ´ × ´, and E 1, ´ ´ ×| ´, the fall
is only rarely disyllabic, as is the first fall of the extended D*,
´ ×| ´ ´ ×.

6) The three-part feet of types D, D* and E are a complete exception. Here an extra fall has been incorporated into the respective patterns. The foot is extended to ⌃ × ⌃ × as for example E 1, ⌃ × ⌃ × | ⌃ míddangèardes wéard. However most extant examples of this are doubtful.

7) The final falls of the types A, C and D are strictly monosyllabic. This rule is broken only when later forms are inserted during manuscript transmission.

The introductory beat rarely exceeds one syllable and only very exceptionally is it longer than two syllables. Alliteration follows the general rules set forth in Section A (1) above.

B. The Expanded Verse

Alliteration:

I usually has a double alliteration on the first and second, more rarely on the second and third, occasionally on the first and third rise. The exceptions are mainly of three kinds: triple alliteration, a single alliteration on the second rise only, or more rarely on the first rise only. The head-stave usually falls on the middle rise in II, and more rarely on the first if this happens to be especially stressed.

Types of verse:

1) By far the most numerous forms are AA ⌃ × ⌃ × ⌃ × and BA × ⌃ × ⌃ × ⌃ ×: all others are relatively infrequent. The following table indicates the number of times each form occurs.

	AA	A2A	A*A	BA	CA	AA2s	BA2s	AA21	BA21
I	250	20	16	53	7	3	1	1	1?
II	275	—	—	68	8	1	2	—	5

	AB	BB	AC	BC	CC	AD	BD	CD	AE	BE	CE
I	15	7	17	7	3	12	7	—	8	1	—
II	16	2	9	1	6	—	9	2(?)	12	2	1(?)

According to this the cadence A ⌃ × | ⌃ ×, including that of A 2 s ⌃ ⌃ | ⌣ ×, is completely typical for OE: it is found in approximately 85% of all expanded verses. Hence OE with its "ringing" cadences is a clear contrast to the full line of the Norse ljóðaháttr, which shows a preference for the "dull" cadences $\doteq \times \doteq$, $\doteq \times \smile \times$ and $\doteq \doteq$.

2) In OE as in Norse, there also appear occasional verses where three rises must be reckoned with. These are of course exceptions: in many cases it is very difficult to determine whether the verse should be measured as having three or even four rises.

Falls:

1) In AA, $\doteq \times \ldots \ldots \doteq \times(.) \doteq \times$, the first fall contains one to six syllables; likewise in AB, $\doteq \times \ldots - \times . \doteq$, AC $\doteq \times \ldots \doteq \doteq \times$, etc., and also in BA, $\times . \doteq \times . \ldots \doteq \times . \doteq \times$, BB, $\times . \doteq \times \ldots \doteq \times . \doteq$ and BC, $\times . . \doteq \times \ldots \doteq \smile \times$, and so on. The first inner fall is hence about as prone to lengthening as the first fall of the normal A. On the other hand it is striking that the introductory fall of the types listed here as BA, BB, etc., only rarely exceeds the measure of <u>one</u> syllable and scarcely ever exceeds two, whereas in B and C of the normal verse the first fall is especially prone to lengthening. As a result the symbols BA, BB, etc., are meaningful only as a guiding pattern. It would probably be more correct from a historical point of view to use the symbols aAA, aAB, etc.

2) The remaining inner falls are occasionally disyllabic, very rarely trisyllabic, but this is open to some doubt. The general rule of monosyllabicity obtains for the final falls.

C. Formation of Stanzas

Stanzaic forms are unknown to the OE epic. The Psalms and Hymns contain short sections separated from each other by general meaning, as do the <u>Runic Poem</u> and <u>Deor</u>, but there are no stanzas in the technical sense of the word. The most one may be allowed is a general comparison of the above cases with the French <u>tirades</u>. In the Exeter Book <u>Maxims</u> and in <u>Wolf and Eadwacer</u> on the other hand, the regular series of long lines is sometimes broken by full (unpaired) lines without a caesura, pointing to the first beginnings of a stanzaic form. Unfortunately, however, the fragments which have been preserved are too meager for us to derive definite rules about stanzaic formation in OE. It is nevertheless noteworthy that here, as in the Norse ljóðaháttr, the speeches are usually given inner form by inserting an unpaired full line at intervals to set off the rest. From this one may conclude that the first beginnings of a stanzaic form like that of the ljóðaháttr were already in existence in Germanic times.

D. Rime

OE poets occasionally used rime as well as alliteration to set off their verse, although not according to any strict rules. Only in the Riming Poem is end-rime carried through completely, but there are also longish sections with end-rime in Christ 591 ff., 1644 ff.; Andreas 867 ff.; Elene 1236 ff. According to position, the rime falls into two main classes:

1. Rime within the verse, such as hond rond gefeng (Beowulf 2609). This type of rime is especially popular in compounds such as wordhord, waroðfaroða; in copulative formulas such as sǽl ond mǽl, fród ond gód, and also in "grammatical rime" such as láð wið láðum, bearn æfter bearne.

2. End-rime, and specifically the two sub-classes:

   a. Linking the two halves of a long line as fylle gefǽgon, fǽgere geþǽgon (Beowulf 1014).

   b. Between the ends of corresponding half-lines in contiguous verses, as in Beowulf 465 f., 890 f.

Note: Occasionally there is a combination of end-rime and rime within the verse, e.g. wrenceþ hé ond blenceþ, worn geþenceþ (Vainglory 33). In cases such as góda geasne, grundléasne wylm (The Whale 46), it is doubtful whether the rime is intentional. In the Runic Poem the two kinds occur sporadically alongside each other. Internal rime is occasionally spread over two long lines also, such as sondlond gespearn, | grond wið gréote (Guthlac 1334–35), but here too there is doubtless much which is accidental.

The following degrees in the quality of the rime may be noted:

1) rime proper: wordhord, wordum and bordum.

2) internal rime in the same sense as the North Germanic hendingar: eardgearde, láð wið láðum.

3) assonance, which appears sometimes in the place of pure rime, apparently quite intentionally: wǽf : lǽs, gebunden : beþrungen in the rimed section of Elene 1236 ff.

4) probably also analogies to the North Germanic <u>skot-hending</u>, especially in compounds such as <u>holmwylm</u>, <u>sundgeblond</u> and the like. All the same one must be very careful in regarding these half-rimes as an intentional attempt to write ornately.

Note: Suffixal rime, which Kluge and others think to be rather widespread, can hardly be established as a special art form, as it concerns only those syllables in the verse which are always unstressed.

The rime has a limited number of syllabic forms. The most common are the "dull" cadence such as <u>fús</u> : <u>hús</u> (<u>Elene</u> 1236), extended as <u>præce</u> : <u>wræce</u> (<u>Christ</u> 593); and the "ringing" cadence such as <u>ásæled</u> : <u>gewæled</u> (<u>Elene</u> 1243), extended as <u>þreodude</u> : <u>reodode</u> (<u>Elene</u> 1238). In the <u>Riming Poem</u> there also appear trisyllabic rimes such as <u>flódàde</u> : <u>gódàde</u>.

NOTE

1   Translated for this volume by Gawaina D. Luster from H. Paul's <u>Grundriss der germanischen Philologie</u>, II.2 (Strassburg, 1905), pp. 1–38. Only the most important of Sievers' bibliographical notes have been retained, and sections on Old Norse, Old Saxon, Old High German and primitive Indo-European metrics have been omitted; for ease of reference to the German text, Sievers' paragraph numbers have been kept.

OLD ENGLISH VERSE AND ENGLISH SPEECH RHYTHM

Marjorie Daunt

It is with considerable diffidence that this paper is offered to suggest an entirely new approach to the vexed question of Old English "versification." So much has been written, from the time of Sievers and his (later repudiated) "five types" down to the recent contributions of J. C. Pope and Kemp Malone, that a revolutionary suggestion needs careful consideration.

All the previous commentators have made (often unconsciously) a fundamental assumption, namely, that in Old English poetry we are dealing with a "poetic metre," a definite artistic medium which needed to be acquired, of the same nature as later verse forms, though quite different in shape. J. C. Pope, the latest and most daring investigator of Old English verse since Sievers, says "a hitherto unexploited device— one that is altogether natural under the circumstances yet hardly to be discovered except by accident— has proved of amazing efficacy in producing the metrical order and expressiveness which we associate with competent poetry."

In one way or another this assumption that a metrical order or regularity, that we can recognize as such, must be produced, lest our ancestors be revealed as devoid of musical sense, underlies all the work in this field. It is not necessary to recapitulate all the theories of earlier writers, which are excellently summed up in the first thirty-seven pages of J. C. Pope's book, The Rhythm of Beowulf, and well known to all readers of Beowulf.

One simple oversight seems to have distorted much of this work, and that is the failure to recognize the importance, in relation to certain kinds of poetry, of the spoken language. All the talk which has gone on, and still goes on, about "literary language," "poetic diction," etc., has obscured the fundamental

Reprinted from the Transactions of the Philological Society (1946), pp. 56–72, by permission of the author and the publisher.

fact that the foundation of poetry was what is often called contemptuously "colloquial speech." In later and more sophisticated periods it is just conceivable that a poet might compose with pen and paper, but for poetry such as Anglo-Saxon, or Chaucer's longer poems, or Shakespeare's plays, the contemporary spoken language is never far away.

Germanic poetry, like that of any other Heroic Age, dates from a period when "prose" was non-existent and there was only a spoken language and spoken language arranged for remembrance. Whether the "remembrance" required was for instruction or pleasure, it would be achieved, one imagines, better if the shape of the spoken language was kept than if it was much distorted into "metre."

This point is plainly to be seen in the nursery rhymes which represent the spoken language so well that they are used to teach English babies English, and probably Chinese babies Chinese. The late Professor Lloyd James recommended "This is the House that Jack built" to foreigners studying English. Rhythm certainly helps remembrance, but it must be rhythm within the framework of the spoken language. Old English poetry, as we have it, represents a very much developed form with high artistic merit. Such poetic trappings as diction, kennings, compound words, etc., should not be allowed to obscure a basis of what at present may be called language with alliteration which is common to all kinds of Old English verse.

Alliteration is a feature found in the earliest poetry of several countries. It appears to provide the rim-ram-ruf which helps remembrance. Its purpose originally was both rhythmic and utilitarian, but only very faintly artistic. This leads on to the theory which it is the aim of this article to put forward. Old English verse is really conditioned prose, i.e. the spoken language specially arranged with alliteration, but arranged in a way that does no violence to the spoken words. It is true that the vocabulary of the extant Old English poems contains many words apparently confined to poetry and not "colloquial," but they are presented in a framework of ordinary words and they are native in origin, not artistic importations. And here we are up against our first difficulty. We do not know much about spoken Old English, but we do know a little; we have the recorded conversation of Cædmon and the Angel, which is admirably colloquial though too brief. We also have Alfred's conscientious record of

his conversations with Ohthere and Wulfstan, which, in brevity
of sentence and word order, differ markedly from such work as
the Preface to the Cura Pastoralis, and suggest a careful and
exact reproduction of what the travellers said; such a reproduction as Alfred, with his desire for truth, might be expected to
make. Then there are the glosses, which have not been sufficiently explored for colloquial forms. In the gloss to the Lindisfarne Gospels (Skeat, p. 18) there occurs the gloss ad patrem =
tom fæder, a form which is extremely valuable as it shows that
the English at that early date were telescoping unstressed forms
and had a use exactly parallel to the German zum Vater. It
seems that formal writing, then, as now, wrote out in full many
unstressed forms, but even when that very text was being read
the shortened form may have been used. To take a modern example, The Importance of Being Earnest is usually printed with
have not, shall not, is not written in full, but no actor ever says
his lines like that. So that it is probable that the relationship
of the spoken to the written word in Old English was not as rigid
as has often been supposed.

It is, of course, difficult to say how far poetry influenced
the spoken word in a period when everyone listened to it and was
expected to make it, but the influence of the Bible in later times
would suggest that, made out of the spoken language at its best,
it helped to keep it at its best.

The very best work that has been done on Anglo-Saxon verse
is unquestionably that of Sievers. His careful descriptive
method has resulted in the establishment of certain types of
word grouping which remain real even though he himself later
denied them as metre. When Sievers formulated his "five types"
he did so by methods of classification, and A is A because it is
the most frequent. For the purposes of this paper the basis of
Sievers' groupings is accepted as sound, though details may not
always be acceptable. "The descriptive portion of Sievers' work
is sound and must always be of service," says Pope.[1] What
neither Sievers nor any other writers, to my knowledge, have
ever pointed out, is that the "five types" are language patterns,
not metrical patterns. They are pieces of language and within
the piece the word order is usually normal, while the poetic effect is achieved by repetition and alternation of pieces. A may
be A because it is the most frequent, but it is most frequent because it is the shape of nouns and adjectives grouped together,

and nouns and adjectives occur most frequently in the spoken language. So A is A also because it is the shape nouns and adjectives were then. The pattern / x / x (or / x x / x etc.), is likely to appear in a language with root accent and a large number of dissyllabic forms in noun and adjective.

The recognition of this "language grouping" is so important that an analysis of 100 lines of Beowulf is not waste of time. The lines have been taken at random, ll. 1255 swylt æfter synnum . . . 1354 Grendel nemdon. This represents 200 "half-lines" of which A = 94, B = 32, C = 41, D = 21, E = 10, and doubtful lines = 2. The ninety-four A-type groups can be further classified, and the proportions are significant. The largest group is that of adjective (including past participle) and noun which amounts to thirty-two, such pieces as yldra broþor, cealde streamas, heardecg togen, dreame bedæled, which could not be any different in prose; with this group is allied that of noun and noun (including infinitive), which is 19, e.g. Grendles modor, moras healdan, wyrpe gefremman; 16 is the next largest group, of noun (subject or object), and finite verb, e.g. Grendel nemdon, deadne wisse, helm ne gemunde, cearu wæs geniwod, these again are completely prose-like (not prosaic) in form. A group of 8 represents finite verb with prepositional phrase, such as lifde æfter laþum, heo wæs on ofste, com þa to Heorote; clauses and half-clauses amount to 6, ne frin þu æfter sælum, hwæþre he gemunde. The remaining oddments are: noun and preposition and noun = 4; finite verb and infinitive = 3; adverb and past participle = 2; and one each of adjective and adjective; finite verb and finite verb, adjective and finite verb, and adverb and finite verb. What is of main importance is that of 93 groups 67 are formed by combinations of nouns and adjectives. It is not necessary here to give the exact statistics of the whole 100 lines, but it is important to point out the proportions of the various grammatical units. B as a whole produces 32 groups, of which 20 are whole or part sentences or clauses, all ending with a preterite singular of a strong verb; and nu oþer cwom, heo þa fæhþe wræc, þa heo to fenne gang. This is an exceedingly high proportion.

The group of 41 C-types is largely composed of 16 prepositional groups such as æfter neodlaþe, æfter weaspelle, on weres wæstmum, and 18 part or whole sentences or clauses (only one of which contains a strong preterite singular), e.g. ðe him God sealde, þanon woc fela, for þan he to lange. Turning to the D-types we find very few finite verbs; is and wæs occur once each, and gehnægde and eode appear, but 15 of the 21 D-groups end with a trisyllabic noun or adjective, e.g. Ingwina, hilderinc, Hroþgare, Scyldinga, and most of these are noun + noun or adjective + noun. E groups 10 in all, all begin with a trisyllabic noun or adjective, and as might be expected sometimes end with a strong preterite singular, but only 3 times as against 7 noun endings. It is not suggested that the results of this analysis would be exactly the same all through Beowulf, but this result is striking enough to suggest that these groups or patterns are the shape they are because the language itself is that shape and not because the poet arranged them.

The reasonable conclusion surely is that poetry, at that time, was made with pieces of language, groups of spoken language arranged to run easily and not monotonously, on the breath.

It is a fact that if an audience is to listen for any length of time to a recited narrative (or even to acted dialogue), the medium must not be an artificial verse form, but must follow the natural language. Can one imagine a greater form of torture than to listen, night after night, to a story set in the metre of Hiawatha? The dramatists of the sixteenth century very soon broke away from regularity of verse and undeniably approximated considerably to the spoken word — culminating in Shakespeare, who, as C. L. Wrenn maintains, brought colloquial language on to the stage to a much greater degree than has always been realized.

It is immaterial whether Beowulf itself was actually read aloud or not, the vehicle was definitely used in many poems which did provide the main entertainment of men who lived hard out-door lives, ate and drank well — and then listened. Nothing artificial or difficult would have been accepted as a pleasure, the tale must have been easy to understand.

If it is true that the A-E types (as it is convenient still to call them) represent shapes of spoken language, then it ought to be possible to find them, or something like them in any existing Anglo-Saxon which can be considered in any way colloquial, and as possible examples, the works already mentioned may be taken. It must, however, be remembered that even in poetry the half-lines do not necessarily stand apart, but, as Kemp Malone has shown, not only is the unit a half-line or a line, but the sense is often run on. þa wæs on healle heardecg togen, in the special connection in which it is used, the men waking in horror to find

Grendel's mother in the hall, can hardly have been said with
much pause in the middle. This has a bearing on the arrangement of the shapes. Such a line as <u>se þe wæteregesan wunian
scolde</u> is really x x / / x / x / x.

A very important link in the argument is provided by the
"extended types" of Old English. Here the line shows an increased number of stresses and the "pattern" can be regarded
as an enlargement of one type or a mixture of two, as the case
may be.

<u>Arfæst æt ecga gelacum</u> = / x x / x x / x = A + A or
/ \ x / x x / x = E + A. Whichever way it be taken it is the
bridge from prose to "verse," for the <u>shape</u> of Old English, with
many dissyllables, monosyllables, and few polysyllabic words,
except compounds, ensures a regularity of stress by sheer statistical necessity.

Even at the risk of repetition it is perhaps as well to emphasize once more that dissyllabic words such as most nouns,
adjectives, and finite verbs were in Old English, naturally combine into A groups, while prepositional phrases, beginning as
they do with an unstressed word followed by a stressed and inflected form, would naturally shape C, important monosyllables
would be the foundation of B and three-syllable words the basis
of D and E, and this must happen to a large extent quite independently of the poet's art.

If we turn now to such Old English prose as has already been
suggested as colloquial or near it, we find a very definite rhythmic
shape. Cædmon's talk with the Angel, if it is given the sentence
stress which seems natural to the situation, comes out like this:—

Angel.   Cǣdmon! Sing mḗ hwǣtwḗgu = D.

Cædmon. { Nē cónn ĭc nŏht sĭngán = A.

or   { Nē cónn ĭc nŏht sĭngán = C.

Ănd ĭc for þón | of þĭssum gĕbéorscĭpĕ | út ĕódĕ | = ½B
+ D + ½D.

Ŏnd hĭder gĕwát = B.

for þŏn ĭc nóht cúþĕ = C.

Angel.   Hwǣþerḗ þŭ mḗaht mḗ sĭngán = A + D.

OLD ENGLISH VERSE AND ENGLISH SPEECH RHYTHM

Cædmon. Hwæt sceal ic singan? = A.

Angel. Sing me Frumsceaft = A.

This is surely rather a remarkable result, for the syntactical sense has been carefully respected and still the "pattern" stands out.

The opening lines of Alfred's account of his conversation with Ohthere can very easily be reconstructed into a dialogue. The repetition of he sæde or he cwæþ shows where Alfred's opening questions must have come, and as Ohthere warmed to his tale he sæde is less frequent; but it comes where a new branch of the subject is opened, for example, turning from the tribute paid by the Lapps to the size and character of the land of the Norwegians, or from Norway in general to the particular district of Halgeland.

Ohthere sæde = A.

his hlaforde = C.

Ælfrede cyn(in)ge = A.

þæt he | ealra Norþmonna = D with upbeat.

norþmest bude = A.

He | cwæþ þæt he bude = A with upbeat.

on þæm | lande norþweardum = D with upbeat.

wiþ þa westsæ = A.

He sæde þeah = B.

þæt þæt | land sie swiþe = A with upbeat. ⎫ forming

lang norþ þonan = D. ⎬ a line

⎭ unit.

Ac hit is eall weste = C.

buton on feawum stowum = C.

Styccemælum = A.

wiciaþ Finnas = A.

295

DAUNT

These extracts have been taken at random, with no intention of "special pleading." If there is any truth in the thesis of this paper, that Old English verse is really the spoken language rather tidied up, then we should expect to find the rhythm a little more ragged in ordinary colloquial use, but on the contrary, the irregularities are strangely few.

If it be admitted that when all is said colloquial Old English is almost x, the unknown, there still remains one colloquial English about which we can know something (though we seldom do), namely our own. It is obvious that unless making a speech, or drunk, the ordinary Englishman talks in a series of short "pieces of language," linked syntactically into longer groups. Putting aside very short units of one, two, or three syllables, such as "yes," "why not?" or "He's gone out," which must have formed part of the Saxon's conversation also, we may consider the four (or more) syllable groups.

The sentence "The man has done that" can be said in a number of ways, with different stress and intonation and a change of significance: —

(1) ðə mӕnz dʌn ðӕt = B.

(2) ðə mӕn əz dʌn ðӕt = E.

In each of these the implication is on "man," either it is a special man, or not a woman, etc. There is also a strong emphasis on the thing he has done.

(3) ðə mӕnz dʌn ðӕt = C.
(i.e. 'He has finished his job, what shall he do next?')

(4) ðə mӕn əz dʌn ðӕt = A with up beat.
(The sense is much like (3).)

Or again, "Why don't you go?" can be stressed as A, B, C, E, or even D, or

wai! dount ju gou? Where the sense is somewhat changed.

It has been pointed out by several writers on the subject that modern English parallels can be found for what they call "Old English metre," e.g. "Tom's sending it" = D, "I'll come

to-day" = B, etc., but no one seems to consider this anything
more than an interesting coincidence. It is never suggested
that the living language still flows in its ancient channels in
spite of loss of inflexions and foreign influence. The changes in
sentence rhythm, following change of stress, from one " type"
to another in a short language group seem to the present writer
highly significant, and of the greatest importance.

Foreign loanwords or new coinings of words mould themselves in the same way. Vegetables, secretary, melancholy to
take three examples each have two distinct pronunciations,
['vedʒi'təblz] ['sekri'teri] ['melən'kɔli] are the forms heard
from less educated speakers while ['vedʒtəb`lz] ['sekrətr`i]
['melənkl`i] are the usual pronunciations of the better educated.

A small but interesting point adds emphasis to this continuity of speech rhythm. In April, 1941, Dr. Hugh Dalton, in a
BBC broadcast, said, "Bad news bluntly told, braces our people,"
which, complete with three alliterating stresses, might well be
a line from Beowulf. Dr. Dalton's reading is so extensive that
it is possible that he has read Beowulf, but, at that moment of
our war-time life, anything he said must be taken as entirely
natural and unself-conscious.

If this thesis is true, namely that modern spoken English
has preserved much of the pre-Conquest speech rhythm, it should
be traceable in colloquial written English, in language which is
really the spoken word recorded, or language which is intended
to be memorized easily, and to impress people and carry a message. Advertisements are seldom intended primarily for the
highly educated; they are intended to stick in the mind till the
weak moment comes. Take this example from The Evening
News, 4th April, 1939: —

Get your Easter shoes = B.

at Abbots now. = B.

Wherever you go for Easter = A with upbeat.

go in comfort, in style. = B.

Go in Abbots shoes. = B.

There are only two days left = E with upbeat.

to get a pair = B.

DAUNT

of the smartest shoes in London. = A with upbeat.

Hundreds of pairs to choose from. = A + A.

Sports shoes, promenade shoes. = A + E.

High fashion shoes for town. = E + B.

Come and be fitted = A.

by our expert staff = B.

and you needn't give your feet = B.

another thought. = B.

This is really a striking tour-de-force. The composer of the advertisement wrote quite as much of a poem as many of those embalmed in the Saxon Chronicle.

Political catchwords are meant to lodge in the mind of the unwary listener and influence his vote. A whole list is given by Lord Oxford[2] of the catchwords of his time. Here is a sample:—

Conspicuous by absence = A with upbeat.

Bag and Baggage = A.

A Leap in the Dark = B.

The Grand Old Man = B.

Mother of Parliaments = D.

Six Omnibuses through Temple Bar = D + B.

The reporters who jot down the day's happenings at break-neck speed for the evening papers seldom have time to polish their work. From The Evening Standard (9th February, 1944) comes this:—

Summonses were heard = E.

at | Guildhall to-day = E with upbeat.

against William (Charles) Foyle = B.
  (He would be William Foyle.)

charging him with making = A.

298

statements to obtain tea = E.

which he knew to be false. = B.

The alleged statements = C.

con | cerned the total number = A + A with upbeat.

of tea permits = C.

he | had in his possession. = A with upbeat.

He was a|ccused of procuring = A with long upbeat.

quantities of tea = E.

otherwise than under = A.

buying permits. = A.

One last example, out of many that have been collected, is provided by the late Lord Oxford. It is well known that he was a great scholar and that his public speeches go, without any difficulty, into Ciceronian prose. It is the more startling that his letters to Margot Tennant Asquith[3] are totally different in vocabulary, rhythm, and (naturally) style. Moved by real feeling he wrote as if he were speaking and the proportion of Latinate words is very small. The result is a poem.

Looking back on our talk yesterday = $\frac{1}{2}$ E or D.

I find of course = B.

that I left many = C.

things unspoken. = A.

The one that I should most = B.

like to have said, = E.

if I could have found = E. ⎱
                            ⎰ taken as a unit.
words, you can guess. = E.

It was better = A.

to be business like, = B.

matter-of-fact, = E.

even frigid, = **A.**

as I think I was, = **B.**

for how could I = **C.**

ever tell you = **A.**

what you have been to me? = **E.**

At once the hope = **B.**

and despair of my life. = **B.**

So near and so far, = **B.**

revealing to me = **E** (or A).

the unseen and unattained, = **B.**

now opening = **D.**

and now seeming to shut = **B.**

the Gate of Paradise. = **D** with upbeat.

This, as contrasted with his usual epistolary style, is quite amazing. The conclusion drawn here is that in so-called Old English "verse" we are faced with a tidied form of the spoken language, i.e. prose, and that the "pattern" is the pattern of the natural language shapes, that this rhythm has survived for centuries and is still largely the mould in which we cast our speech, unless a Latinate rhythm is superimposed by a special education, and even then the native swing often emerges. It is possible that the preserving medium has been stress and intonation, but this is a field awaiting exploration, and no more is intended here than to draw attention to the facts.

As an epilogue to the theory presented above may be added the suggestion that it is the presence of these particular rhythm-shapes that makes the verse of Shakespeare and Chaucer so time-less in its appeal and so easy to listen to. The monotonous regu-larity of Gorboduc did not survive, and quite soon the dramatists were swinging, across the pulse of their five-beat blank-verse line, a kind of rhythmic prose. This is exactly what Chaucer did before them. Regularity to a metrical pattern can be delight-ful for a line or so, or in a short poem, but could not be listened

to for hours on end. A few odd lines from Chaucer can illustrate
the point: —

> In listes thryes = A.
> and ay slayn his fo. = D with upbeat.

This line could never, with any sense, be made into a regular
"five-beat iambic" line.

> Singinge he was = E.
> or floyting all the day. = B + B.
> Faireste of fair, = E.
> O lady myn Venus. = B.

The last two examples are the same rhythmic shape.

In the line he who most felingly speketh of love the regular
five-beat would put no stress on "most," which in this context
seems to demand it.

> Ne who most felingly = B + D.
> speketh of love. = E.

Is this what Hamlet meant when he said "Speak the speech,
I pray you, as I pronounced it to you, trippingly on the tongue?"
In that very speech

> trippingly on the tongue = E.

Certainly his own speech fits his own requirements.

Angels and ministers of grace defend us seems to have a
natural pause at grace.

> Angels and Ministers of Grace = D.
> defend us. = ½ A, with upbeat.

or

> Be thou a spirit of health or goblin damned seems to run

> Be thou a spirit of health = E + B.

or Goblin damned. = B.

Bring with thee airs from Heaven = E + B.

or blasts from Hell. = B.

Be thy intents = E.

wicked or charitable = D.

thou comest in such = B.

a questionable shape = E.

(Or this line might be regarded as A with upbeat + E.)

that I will speak to thee.

This clause could be given only one stress, on speak, but more probably Hamlet gave it two stresses, will and speak.

that I will speak to thee = D.

I'll call thee Hamlet = A with upbeat.

King, Father, Royal Dane. O answer me.

The epithets naturally stand out separately, but

O answer me = D.

let me not burst = E.

in ignorance but tell = E.

Here it may be wise to repeat that there is no intention of breaking the line at burst, and that E + E is the formula of the line taken as a whole.

Why thy canonized bones, hearsed in death

If "canonized" is canonized then

Why thy canonized bones = A + B.

if Shakespeare used the modern pronunciation

Why thy canonized bones = A + E.

hearsed in death = E.

have burst their cerements. = D.

The fact that Shakespeare's verse approximated to natural speech has been accepted for a very long time, but it looks as if the dominance of the dissyllabic units iamb and trochee obscured the rhythmic and metrical importance of the three-syllable units such as / \ x or / x \. A phrase like most felingly does not need to be forced into x / x / to make poetry, / / \ x gives and probably always has given just as much rhythmic pleasure. Once this pleasure in the interweaving of rhythmic groups of two with rhythmic groups of three is recognized the line between "verse" and prose becomes misty.

In conclusion it is to be remembered that this paper is only concerned with the "verse" medium of work that was originally intended to be read or recited aloud for long periods for the pleasure of an ordinary audience, where the sense had to be conveyed to hearers quickly, and the word order could not be very greatly distorted. It is probable that many shorter and more formal poems of a definite metrical pattern show the same rhythm-shapes here and there, but that is too large a question to open here.

As to Old English "verse" the key to unlock its music lies hidden in the spoken language of the time, so that any attempt to "formulate" it, whether in terms of musical notation or metrical feet is likely to go astray. The only thing that can be safely done is to describe it, as Sievers so ably did, remembering that he himself was trying in his old age for some more living and elastic description.

You never know

the world aright

till the sea itself,

floweth in your veins,

till you are clothed with the heavens

and crowned with the stars

DAUNT

x   ´ x   ´
you never know
x   ´   x ´
the world aright.

Is this verse or prose?

Note.—Since writing this article, I have read for the first time "The Fifteenth-Century Heroic Line" by C. S. Lewis (English Association, Essays and Studies, 1938.) Mr. Lewis comes near to the line of my argument in noting the similarity of some of the "half-lines" of Beowulf with certain fifteenth-century lines. He recognizes the importance of D and E types, but to him they are still "metre." The types are "sharply divided." "A half-line of Anglo-Saxon verse, once metrically understood, can hardly be heard, even by the inner ear, as anything but what it is." I am not sure that I understand this remark, but it seems to attribute to "metre" an inevitability which I hold to rest on the authenticity of spoken language.

NOTES

1   Rhythm, p. 6.

2   Herbert Henry Asquith, Fifty Years of British Parliament, 2 vols. (Boston, 1926).

3   The Autobiography of Margot Asquith, 2 vols. (London, 1922).

THE ALLITERATIVE METRE

C. S. Lewis

In the general reaction which has set in against the long reign of foreign, syllabic metres in English, it is a little remarkable that few have yet suggested a return to our own ancient system, the alliterative line. Mr. Auden, however, has revived some of its stylistic features; Professor Tolkien will soon, I hope, be ready to publish an alliterative poem;[1] and the moment seems propitious for expounding the principles of this metre to a larger public than those Anglo-Saxon and Old Norse specialists who know it already.

1. Alliteration is no more the whole secret of this verse than rhyme is the whole secret of syllabic verse. It has, in addition, a metrical structure, which could stand alone, and which would then be to this system as blank verse is to the syllabic.

2. Latin verse is based on quantity (= the length of time taken to pronounce a syllable). Modern English is based on stress-accent (= the loudness with which a syllable is pronounced). Alliterative verse involves both.

3. In order to write Alliterative verse it is therefore necessary to learn to distinguish not only accented from unaccented syllables, but also long from short syllables. This is rendered difficult by our classical education which allows boys to pronounce ille so that it rhymes with silly, and nevertheless to call the first syllable long, which, in their pronunciation, it is not. In dealing with English quantity the reader must learn to attend entirely to sounds, and to ignore spelling.

Definition.

A long syllable is one which contains either a long vowel (as fath(er), fame, seek, pile, home, do); or, a vowel followed by more than one consonant (as punt, wind, helm, pelt).[2]

Reprinted from Rehabilitations and Other Essays (Oxford University Press, 1939), pp. 119–32, by permission of the author and the publisher.

[Caution. 1. It is here that the trouble from spelling occurs. In modern English spelling, for reasons which need not be discussed here, such words as <u>silly, pretty, merry, sorrow, attraction</u>, show a double consonant in spelling where there is no shadow of a double consonant in pronunciation. The reader can convince himself of this by comparing the pretended double T in <u>pretty</u> with the real double T in <u>hot toast</u>: and he will then hear how a real double consonant renders the first syllable of <u>hot toast</u> long, while that of <u>pretty</u>, though accented, is short. So, in <u>distiller</u> the pretended two L's are one, while in <u>still life</u> we have a real double L, disguised as a triple L. True double consonants can be heard in <u>palely</u> (cf. <u>Paley</u>), <u>fish-shop</u> (cf. <u>bishop</u>), <u>unnamed</u> (cf. <u>unaimed</u>), <u>midday</u> (cf. <u>middy</u>), <u>solely</u> (cf. <u>holy</u>).[3]

2. In modern English many words, chiefly monosyllables, which end in a single consonant are pronounced differently according to their position in the sentence. If they come at the end of a sentence or other speech-group—that is, if there is a pause after them—the final consonant is so dwelled upon that the syllable becomes long. If the reader listens carefully he will find that the syllable <u>man</u> is short in

> Manifold and great mercies,
> or   The man of property,

but long in

> The Invisible Man,
> or   The Descent of Man.

With this caution, the reader will be glad to hear, the serious difficulties in the re-education of our ear are over.]

4. Each line consists of two half-lines, which are independent metrical organisms, connected only by the alliteration.

5. The half-line consists of <u>Lifts</u> and <u>Dips</u>.

Definitions.

A Lift = either (a) one syllable both long and accented (as the first syllable of <u>ogre, mountain, Repton</u>),

or (b) Two syllables whereof the first is short but accented, and the second unaccented (as the first <u>two</u> syllables of <u>merrily, vigorous, melancholy, evident</u>).

(Thus in <u>vary</u> the first syllable is a Lift: in <u>very</u> the whole word is a Lift.)

A Dip = any reasonable number of unaccented syllables whether long or short.

In the following sentences the syllables printed in Capitals are Lifts, the rest Dips.

> Of COURSE we aSSUME.
> When a phiLOLOGist is a FOOL.
> RhadaMANTHus in his MISERy.

6. Every half-line must contain neither more nor less than two Lifts. (The ancient poetry sometimes introduces a three-lift type which stands to this metre much as the Alexandrine stands to decasyllabics: but the beginner will be wise to neglect it.)

The five different types of half-line depend on the five ways in which Lifts and Dips are combined. Before learning these, however, the reader should "work his ear in" with the following:

> We were TALKing of DRAGONS, | TOLkien and I
> In a BERKshire BAR. | The BIG WORKman
> Who had SAT SILent | and SUCKED his PIPE
> ALL the EVEning, | from his EMPTy MUG
> with GLEAMing EYE | GLANCED toWARDS us;
> 'I SEEN 'em mySELF,' | he SAID FIERCEly.

7. The "A" type of half-line is arranged Lift-dip, Lift-dip.

> e.g. GREEN and GROWing: MERRY were the
> MINSTrels: COME from the COUNTry.

<u>Licence</u>. One or two unaccented syllables may be added before the first Lift, forming what is technically known as an Anacrusis.

> e.g. And green and growing: and so merry were
> the minstrels: he came from the country.

<u>Warning</u>. But this licence should be very seldom used in the second half-line. In the first half-line (i.e. at the beginning of the whole line) it may be used freely.

8. B type = dip-Lift, dip-Lift.

> e.g. and NUMBED with NIGHT: where MAIDS are
> MERRY: and to the PALACE of PRIDE.

Warning. The first dip may contain "any reasonable number" of unaccented syllables: but the second should normally consist of a single unaccented syllable. In all circumstances a predominantly "anapaestic" movement is to be avoided.

9. C = dip-Lift, Lift-dip.
(Note: — Here we reach a rhythm of daily occurrence in our speech (e.g. 'I can't stand him') which has been allowed no metrical recognition for centuries.)

> e.g. The MERRY MASTer: In the DARK DUNGeon:
> Through CLOUDS CLEAVing: It is EVER-OPen:
> And with GOD'S BENISon.

Licence. In this type a single short, accented syllable may serve as the second Lift, giving us:

> A cold kipper: but they're hard-headed: a proud palace.

10. D = Lift, Lift-dip.
Here there is only one dip, whereas A, B, and C have two. To compensate for this, in D types the dip must be strengthened by a syllable[4] nearly (but not quite) as strong as the Lifts.
(Note: — This again rescues a genuine English speech rhythm from metrical non-existence.)

> e.g. HARD HAYmaking.

It will be heard that the syllable mak is as long as, but just less accented than, hard and hay.

> e.g. BRIGHT QUICKsilver: MAD MERRYmaking:
> SHODDY SHIPbuilders: GRIM GLADIator:
> HELL'S HOUSEkeeper.

In all these examples the strengthening element of the dip stands first in the dip: e.g. in "Hell's housekeeper," keep- comes before -er. Obviously the reverse order may be used, giving us:

> ALL UNDerclothes: MAD MULTitude: EATS ARTi-
> chokes: POOR DESTitute.

Licence 1. In D, as in C, a single short, accented syllable may serve as the second Lift, giving us, instead of Hard haymaking, such forms as:

> SHEER SHOTover: PURE PALimpsest.

Licence 2. The compensating element in the dip may also be a single short, accented syllable, giving us:

> MAD MELANCHoly: HEAV'N's WAR-office: BORN
> BOOTlegger.

Licence 3. The sub-type Mad multitude may be extended by inserting a single unaccented (and preferably short) syllable between the two Lifts, so as to give:

> MAD the MULTitude: EATing ARTichokes.

11. E = Lift-dip-Lift.
Here again we have only one dip, and again the dip must contain a compensating element. E, in fact, is a rearrangement of D.

> e.g. HAYmakers HEARD: SHIPbuilders SHOW: GLAD-
> Iator GRIM.

Licence. The compensating element in the dip may be a single short, accented syllable, giving us:

> NEW College KNOWS.

12. For the reader's convenience, I add a recapitulation of the five types.

A. 1. Green and growing.
    2. (With Anacrusis) The grass is growing.

B. And life runs low.
C. 1. A dark dungeon.
   2. (With single short for 2nd Lift) The gray gravel.
D. 1. Hell's housekeeper.
   2. (With compensating element last in dip) Earth's anti-
      dote.
   3. (With single short for 2nd Lift) East Abingdon.
   4. (With single short for compensating element in dip)
      Heav'n's war-office.
   5. (Extended) Evil antidote.
E. 1. Shipbuilders show.
   2. (With single short for compensating element in dip)
      New-College knows.

13. In every line both the Lifts of the first half-line may,
and one must, alliterate with the first Lift of the second half-
line. As

> In a Berkshire Bar; the Big workman

(both Lifts in the first half alliterating with the first of the second) or,

> We were Talking of dragons, Tolkien and I

(one Lift of the first half alliterating with the first of the second).
An alliteration on all four Lifts as in

> And walks by the waves, as winds warble

is regarded not as an added beauty, but as a deformity. (Its use
in Middle English, it will be found, radically alters the character
of the metre.)

14. Where only one Lift in the first half-line alliterates, it
should normally be the first.

15. All vowels alliterate with one another.
Warning. Do not be deceived by spelling. Union alliterates with
yeast, yellow, &c., not with uncle.

16. No half-line of any type should end in a pure dactyl.
Noble Norbury, with trash and trumpery, glancing gloomily, &c.,
are unmetrical.

17. <u>Structure</u>.

(1) The medial pause which divides the first from the second half of the line must be strictly observed, so that the two halves fall apart as separate speech-groups.

[By speech-groups I mean those units — rhythmical, rhetorical, emotional, and to some extent syntactical, units — out of which our actual conversation is built up. Thus if the reader says "The big workman who had sat silent and sucked his pipe all the evening," he will (I hope) find that the speech-groups coincide with the half-lines in the example given under para. 6. A good deal of re-education is here necessary, for the chief beauty of syllabic verse lies in a deliberate clash or contradiction between the speech-groups and the "feet," whereas in alliterative verse the speech-group is both the metrical, and the aesthetic, unit. See below, para. 18.]

> <u>Examples</u>. Thus, <u>he will stand as a stone till the stars crumble</u>, is metrically good. <u>The laugh of the lovely lady is silent</u> is bad. But <u>Lost is the laugh of the lovely damsel</u> is not a line at all: for it pretends metrically to be
>
> LOST is the LAUGH of | the LOVEly DAMsel

(A-type + A with anacrusis): and in this the first half is so impossible as a speech-group that a poet could have written it only because he was really still thinking in feet and syllables, and not in speech-groups and half-lines.

(2) But while we cannot run across the medial break, we can run across the end of a line. In other words, the last half of a given line and the first half of the next are more intimately connected than the two halves of a single line. Hence we may write

> There stands a stone. Still'd is the Lady's
> Peerless laughter.

<u>Corollary</u>. Hence, though the poem begins and ends with a full line, yet within the poem a new paragraph or sentence should usually begin in the second half of a line.

18. Aesthetics.

It follows that whereas syllabic poetry primarily uses the evocative qualities of words (and only secondarily those of phrases), alliterative poetry reverses the procedure. The phrase, coinciding with the half-line, is the poetic unit. In any English country tap-room the student may hear from the lips of labourers speech-groups which have a certain race and resonance in isolation. These are the elements of our native metre.

Such are the rules. Where no tradition—at least no modern tradition—exists it is rash to offer advice, but perhaps two counsels may be given. In the first place, if any one is attracted by the metre in general, but disposed to omit the rules of quantity and produce a merely accentual adaptation, I would like to save him disappointment by warning him that he will almost certainly produce rubbish. Torture the language, or the thought, as he will, the result will be thin. The thing to aim at is richness and fullness of sound, and this cannot be attained without quantity: with quantity, the metre opens possibilities of resonance which have not been exploited for a thousand years. In the second place, I would advise him to be on his guard against too many B types. His iambic training will probably be tempting him to them at every turn: but if he yields his poem will sound like octosyllabics. And lastly, I would advocate to all who have a taste for such things some serious contention with the difficulties of this metre. A few successful specimens would be an excellent answer to the type of critic (by no means extinct) who accuses the moderns of choosing vers libre because they are not men enough for metre. For if syllabic verse is like carving in wood and vers libre like working with a brush, this is like carving in granite.

A man who preaches a metre must sooner or later risk his case by showing a specimen: and if the fate of Gabriel Harvey deters me, that of Campion invites. In order to avoid misunderstanding I must say that the subject of the following poem was not chosen under the influence of any antiquarian fancy that a medieval metre demanded medieval matter, but because the characters of the planets, as conceived by medieval astrology, seem to me to have a permanent value as spiritual symbols— to provide a Phänomenologie des Geistes which is specially worth while in our own generation. Of Saturn we know more than enough. But who does not need to be reminded of Jove?

THE PLANETS

Lady LUNA, in light canoe,	A:B
By friths and shallows of fretted cloudland	B:C
Cruises monthly; with chrism of dews	A:B
And drench of dream, a drizzling glamour,	B:B
Enchants us—the cheat! changing sometime	B:A
A mind to madness, melancholy pale,	A 2:E 2
Bleached with gazing on her blank count'nance	A:C
Orb'd and ageless. In earth's bosom	A:C 2
The shower of her rays, sharp-feathered light	B:E 2
Reaching downward, ripens silver,	A:A
Forming and fashioning female brightness,	A:A
—Metal maidenlike. Her moist circle	D 2:C
Is nearest earth. Next beyond her	B:A
MERCURY marches;—madcap rover,	A:A
Patron of pilf'rers. Pert quicksilver	A:D
His gaze begets, goblin mineral,	B:A
Merry multitude of meeting selves,	D 2:B
Same but sundered. From the soul's darkness,	A:C
With wreathèd wand,[5] words he marshals,	B:A
Guides and gathers them—gay bellwether	A:D 4
Of flocking fancies. His flint has struck	C:B
The spark of speech from spirit's tinder,	B:C
Lord of language! He leads forever	A:B
The spangle and splendour, sport that mingles	A 2:A
Sound with senses, in subtle pattern,	A:C 2
Words in wedlock, and wedding also	A:C
Of thing with thought. In the third region	B:C
VENUS voyages . . . but my voice falters;	A:C
Rude rime-making wrongs her beauty,	D:A
Whose breasts and brow, and her breath's sweet-	
ness	B:C
Bewitch the worlds. Wide-spread the reign	B:E
Of her secret sceptre, in the sea's caverns,	A 2:C 2
In grass growing, and grain bursting,	C:C
Flower unfolding, and flesh longing,	A:C
And shower falling sharp in April.	C:A
The metal of copper in the mine reddens	B:C 2
With muffled brightness, like muted gold,	C:B
By her finger form'd. Far beyond her	B:A

The heaven's highway hums and trembles,	C:A
Drums and dindles,[6] to the driv'n thunder	A:C
Of SOL'S chariot, whose sword of light	C:B
Hurts and humbles; beheld only	A:C
Of eagle's eye. When his arrow glances	B:C
Through mortal mind, mists are parted	B:A
And mild as morning the mellow wisdom	A 2:C
Breathes o'er the breast, broadening eastward	E:A
Clear and cloudless. In a clos'd garden	A:C
(Unbound her burden) his beams foster	A 2:C
Soul in secret, where the soil puts forth	A:B
Paradisal palm, and pure fountains	E:C
Turn and re-temper, touching coolly	A:A
The uncomely common to cordial gold;	B:B
Whose ore also, in earth's matrix,	C:C
Is print and pressure of his proud signet	B:C
On the wax of the world. He is the worshipp'd	
male,	B:B
The earth's husband, all-beholding,	C:A
Arch-chemic eye. But other country	E 2:C
Dark with discord dins beyond him,	A:A
With noise of nakers, neighing of horses,	B:A
Hammering of harness. A haughty god	A:B
MARS mercenary,[7] makes there his camp	D 2:E
And flies his flag; flaunts laughingly	B:D
The graceless beauty, grey-eyed and keen,	A 2:E
—Blond insolence— of his blithe visage	D 2:C 2
Which is hard and happy. He hews the act,	B:B
The indifferent deed with dint of his mallet	B:B
And his chisel of choice; achievement comes not	B:A 2
Unhelped by him; —hired gladiator	B:D
Of evil and good. All's one to Mars,	B:E
The wrong righted, rescued meekness,	C:A
Or trouble in trenches, with trees splintered	A:C
And birds banished, banks fill'd with gold	C 2:E
And the liar made lord. Like handiwork	B:D 2
He offers to all—earns his wages	B:A
And whistles the while. White-featured dread	B:E
Mars has mastered. His metal's iron	A:C
That was hammered through hands into holy	
cross,	B:B

Cruel carpentry. He is cold and strong,	D 5:B
Necessity's son.[8] Soft breathes the air	B:E
Mild, and meadowy, as we mount further	A:C
Where rippled radiance rolls about us	C:A
Moved with music—measureless the waves'	A:E
Joy and jubilee. It is JOVE'S orbit,	D 5:C
Filled and festal, faster turning	A:A
With arc ampler. From the Isles of Tin	C:B
Tyrian traders, in trouble steering	A:C
Came with his cargoes; the Cornish treasure	A:B
That his ray ripens. Of wrath ended	C:C
And woes mended, of winter passed	C:B
And guilt forgiven, and good fortune	B:C
Jove is master; and of jocund revel,	A:C 2
Laughter of ladies. The lion-hearted,	A:A 2
The myriad-minded, men like the gods	A 2:E
Helps and heroes, helms of nations	A:A
Just and gentle, are Jove's children,	A:C
Work his wonders. On his wide forehead[9]	A:C 2
Calm and kingly, no care darkens	A:C
Nor wrath wrinkles: but righteous power	C:B
And leisure and largess their loose splendours	A 2:C
Have wrapped around him—a rich mantle	A 2:C
Of ease and empire. Up far beyond	A 2:E
Goes SATURN silent in the seventh region,	C:C
The skirts of the sky. Scant grows the light,	B:E
Sickly, uncertain (the Sun's finger	A:C
Daunted with darkness). Distance hurts us,	A:A
And the vault severe of vast silence;	B:C
Where fancy fails us, and fair language,	A 2:C
And love leaves us, and light fails us	C:C
And Mars fails us, and the mirth of Jove	C:B
Is as tin tinkling. In tattered garment,	C:C
Weak with winters, he walks forever	A:B
A weary way, wide round the heav'n,	B:E
Stoop'd and stumbling, with staff groping,	A:C
The lord of lead. He is the last planet	B:C 2
Old and ugly. His eye fathers	A:C
Pale pesilence, pain of envy,	D 2:A
Remorse and murder. Melancholy drink	A:E 2
(For bane or blessing) of bitter wisdom	B:C

LEWIS

> He pours for his people, a perilous draught A 2:B
> That the lip loves not. We leave all things C:C
> To reach the rim of the round welkin, B:C
> Heaven's hermitage, high and lonely. D 2:A

NOTES

1 [Subsequently published as J. R. R. Tolkien, "The Homecoming of Beorhtnoth Beorhthelm's Son," E&S, VI (1953), 1–18.]

2 That two or more consonants make the syllable long is not a metrical rule but a phonetic fact; that they make the preceding vowel long, as some say, is neither a rule nor a fact, but false.

3 -NG in English usually represents a single consonant (G nasalized), but sometimes it represents this consonant followed by a pure G in addition. Hence the first syllable is short in singer, ringer: long in linger, finger.

4 Or, of course, two syllables whereof the first is short. The rules for "compensating elements" are, in this respect, identical with the rules for Lifts.

5 Alliteration on second lift of the first half. The orthographic w in wreathèd has, of course, no metrical function.

6 Cf. Malory, V, cap. 8.

7 -ARY being the compensating element in the Dip.

8 The c in necessity, being an s in pronunciation, carries the first alliteration.

9 This is C 2 in my pronunciation because I pronounce forehead so as to rhyme with horrid. In the alternative pronunciation (which is now heard even among educated speakers) it would be C 1.

V. ORAL-FORMULAR ARGUMENTS

THE ORAL-FORMULAIC CHARACTER OF ANGLO-SAXON NARRATIVE POETRY

Francis P. Magoun, Jr.

In the course of the last quarter-century much has been discovered about the techniques employed by unlettered singers in their composition of narrative verse. Whereas a lettered poet of any time or place, composing (as he does and must) with the aid of writing materials and with deliberation, creates his own language as he proceeds, the unlettered singer, ordinarily composing rapidly and extempore before a live audience, must and does call upon ready-made language, upon a vast reservoir of formulas filling just measures of verse. These formulas develop over a long period of time; they are the creation of countless generations of singers and can express all the ideas a singer will need in order to tell his story, itself usually traditional. This progress is primarily due to the work of two men, the late Milman Parry[1] and his former pupil and successor in this field, Professor Albert Bates Lord of Harvard University.[2] First in connection with Homeric language, later as a result of field-work in Yugoslavia, chiefly among unlettered Muslim singers, Parry, aided by Lord, demonstrated that the characteristic feature of all orally composed poetry is its totally formulaic character. From this a second point emerged, namely, that the recurrence in a given poem of an appreciable number of formulas or formulaic phrases brands the latter as oral, just as a lack of such repetitions marks a poem as composed in a lettered tradition. Oral poetry, it may be safely said, is composed entirely of formulas, large and small, while lettered poetry is never formulaic, though lettered poets occasionally consciously repeat themselves or quote verbatim from other poets in order to produce a specific rhetorical or literary effect. Finally, it is clear that an oral

Reprinted from Speculum, Vol. 28 (1953), pp. 446–67, by permission of the author and the publisher.

poem until written down has not and cannot have a fixed text, a concept difficult for lettered persons; its text, like the text of an orally circulating anecdote, will vary in greater or lesser degree with each telling. The oral singer does not memorize either the songs of singers from whom he learns nor later does he memorize in our sense of the word songs of his own making. His apprenticeship involves the learning of thematic material, plots, proper names, and formulas with which he will gradually become able to compose in regular verse songs of his own. A good singer is one able to make better use of the common fund of formulas than the indifferent or poor singer, though all will be drawing upon essentially the same body of material. The length of a song or, better, the length of a given performance (since there is no fixed text) will largely depend upon the audience-factor, on how much time an audience has to give to the singer on any given occasion. A good singer can go on as long as an audience will listen to him, be it persons assembled in a Bosnian coffee-house, or in the presence of a tape-recorder or a stenographer. The analogies with musical improvisation will be evident.

The present paper is essentially an extension into the realm of Anglo-Saxon narrative poetry of the work of Parry and Lord, to whom it is indebted at every turn and in more ways than can easily be expressed. Indeed, without the stimulation of Parry's published works and the works and spoken words of Albert Lord, the present paper or, indeed, anything like it, would not have been written.

When one first reads of the existence of Anglo-Saxon poetry in the seventh century in Bede's account of Cædman (H. E., IV, 22 [24]), there is every reason to believe that already behind this lay a long tradition, running back to the Continental homeland and into a distant common Germanic heritage, a tradition of at least seven centuries and probably more. Toward the end of the first century A.D. Cornelius Tacitus comments on the art of poetry among the Germanic peoples of his day, and from that time on there are allusions by authors from late antiquity to the singing of songs among various Germanic tribes. Since these ancient Germanic singers were unlettered, their poetry must have been oral, and its diction, accordingly, must have been formulaic and traditional. The birth of this diction must have taken place in a very distant past and, like the birth of any diction, is beyond observation. As Parry observes of Homeric language:

A single man or even a whole group of men who
set out in the most careful way could not make even
a beginning at such an oral diction. It must be the
work of many poets over many generations. When
one singer . . . has hit upon a phrase which is pleasing and easily used, other singers will hear it, and
then, when faced at the same (metrical) point in the
line with the need of expressing the same idea, they
will recall it and use it. If the phrase is so good
poetically and so useful metrically that it becomes
in time the one best way to express a certain idea in
a given length of verse, and as such is passed on from
one generation of poets to another, it has won a place
for itself in the oral diction as a formula. But if it
does not suit in every way, or if a better way of fitting
the idea into the verse and sentence is found, it is
straightway forgotten or lives only for a short time,
since with each new poet and with each new generation
of poets it must undergo the twofold test of being found
pleasing and useful. In time the needed number of such
phrases is made up: each idea to be expressed in the
poetry has its formula for each metrical need, and the
poet, who would not think of trying to express ideas
outside the traditional field of thought of poetry, can
make his verses easily by means of a diction which
time has proved to be the best.[3]

At this late date speculation about origins is rather idle, but
one may perhaps imagine that in its earliest beginnings isochro-
nous utterances in Old Germanic, almost surely based on the
rhythmic beat of some instrument, involved short sequences of
verse at first almost accidentally arrived at and consisting, say,
of a maxim of a few verses or a protective charm or encomiastic
song of similarly modest dimensions. By the time of Tacitus it
would seem that more ambitious compositions were possible and
the order of the day. In his Germania (ch. 2) he says of the Germanic peoples:

In ancient songs (carminibus antiquis), which is the
sole kind of record (memoria) or history (annales)
among them, they celebrate the god Twisto, begotten

of the earth, and his son Mannus, as the beginning
and founder of their people. To Mannus they ascribe
three sons from whose names those tribes nearest
the Ocean are called Ingvaeones [North Sea Germans],
the central Erminones [Elbe Germans?], and the rest
Istvaeones [Western Rhine Germans?].

This suggests possibly rather elaborate narrative and there
seems to be little reason to assume that the apparently more or
less mythological or cult songs of the North Sea and Inland Germans were merely mnemonic verses on the order of the þular
in Widsith or in the Old-Norse Hervarar saga (ch. 12, Stanza
69).4 In the Annales (Book II, §88, ad fin.) Tacitus further re-
ports that songs about Arminius, who had died nearly a century
earlier, were still being sung by Germans of his day. These
familiar statements are adduced only to emphasize the presumably high antiquity of Old-Germanic poetry and the length of tradition behind it. Furthermore, in order to suggest the antiquity
not merely of the art of Germanic poetry in general but specifically the antiquity of the metrical-rhythmical forms of Anglo-
Saxon poetry as we know it, one may point to the fact that Anglo-
Saxon verse is cast in a form to all intents and purposes identical with all Old-Germanic poetry—Old-Norse, Old-Saxon, Old-
High-German—in a word, identical with everything except the
later skaldic vísur of Norway and Iceland. Since any theory of
independent origins for the five basic metrical-rhythmical patterns,
the "Sievers Five Types," is so exceedingly unlikely, one is
forced to assume that something very close to the later preserved
forms and patterns had been established and was in good running
order before the Anglo-Saxons began to colonize Britain.

In the nature of the case we do not have and cannot have any
record of Anglo-Saxon poetry before the introduction of the art
of reading and writing by Christian missionaries from Rome and
from Iona in the Hebrides; indeed, we have no poetical text which
can in exactly the form preserved be thought of as having been
put together very early at all. Consequently, it has been natural
to think of the preserved poems as composed as we compose
poetry, i.e., by lettered persons making use of writing materials,
and until the time of Parry and Lord there was no available technique permitting one to decide on the basis of internal evidence
alone to which tradition a given text might belong—to the oral

or to the lettered. The recurrence of verses and verse-pairs in Anglo-Saxon poetry, the <u>Parallelstellen</u> of German scholars, has been much noted and commented upon, and cross-references accumulated and often cited by editors of individual poems, with the main conclusion drawn from this phenomenon being that those parallels might constitute evidence of the direct influence of one poem upon another (see p. 337, below). But with the discovery of the dominant rôle of the formula in the composition of oral poetry and of the non-existence of metrical formulas in the poetry of lettered authors, we have suddenly acquired a touchstone with which it is now possible to determine to which of the two great categories of poetry a recorded text belongs—to the oral or to the lettered tradition.

As a first test I have analyzed the first twenty-five lines or, better, the first fifty verses or twenty-five typographical lines of <u>Béowulf</u>, chosen because they deal with highly specialized thematic material not represented elsewhere in the poetry, for the presentation of which in verse one might suppose that a poet would need to create his own language if he would ever have to do so. The formulaic character of the verse is demonstrated by Chart I (pp. 339–341, below).[5] A word-group of any size or importance which appears elsewhere in <u>Béowulf</u> or other Anglo-Saxon poems unchanged or virtually unchanged is marked with solid underlining and is a formula according to Parry's definition that a formula is "a group of words which is regularly employed under the same metrical conditions to express a given essential idea."[6] A word-group marked with solid and broken underlining, or with broken underlining only, may be called a formulaic phrase or system; such groups are of the same type and conform to the same verbal and grammatical pattern as the various other verses associated with them and cited in the supporting evidence. For verses which are unmarked I have found no supporting evidence. Following the marked text on the chart comes the supporting evidence assembled under numbers answering to the a and b parts of the respective typographical lines.

Looking at Chart I one notes first that of the fifty verses only some thirteen, or twenty-six per cent, are not matched wholly or in part elsewhere in Anglo-Saxon poetry. In a word, despite the relatively limited corpus of some 30,000 lines— a little more than the two Homeric poems—in which to find corresponding phrases, some seventy per cent of the text of this passage does occur elsewhere. Were the surviving corpus,

say, twice as big, and if, above all, we had other songs of any
extent dealing with anything like the same thematic material,
there well might be almost nothing in the language here used
that could not be demonstrated as traditional.

Though usefulness, rather than mere repetition, is what
makes a formula, it is instructive to look at the repeated formulas first, since it is easier to recognize a formula as such
when it occurs a second or third time,[7] and from this regular
use in various songs one readily sees how it helps this and that
singer to compose his verses. Verses 1b, 3a, 3b, 4b, 5a, 5b,
8a, 10b, 11b, 13a, 14a, 15a, 16a, 17a, 23a, and 25a are of this
sort. They occur exactly the same elsewhere or with only some
insignificant change in inflection about which a singer would
scarcely have to devote conscious thought in order to fit them
into some different context or slightly different grammatical
situation. The very fact of their recurrence in and/or outside
of this poem bears witness to their usefulness not only to the
singer of Béowulf but to singers of many other songs dealing
with quite different themes.

A number of these formulas are something more than mere
repeats and form part of larger formulaic systems used to express the same, or almost the same, idea, or used to fit some
larger rhythmical-grammatical pattern. As Perry observes of
such formulas in Homer, "any group of two or more such like
formulas makes up a system, and the system may be defined in
turn as a group of phrases which have the same metrical value
and which are enough alike in the thought and words to leave no
doubt that the poet who used them knew them not only as a single
formula, but also as formulas of a certain type."[8] Here belong
verses 1b, 6b, 11b, 16a, and 19a.

1b. on géar-dagum is one phase of a system on x-dagum
used to express the idea "long ago" and occurs twice elsewhere
in Béowulf and in other poems as well. Either alone or with one
or two preceding unstressed words it forms a complete C-verse.
With the substitution for géar, with the sense "of yore," of ǽr,
eald, or fyrn, the formula remains unchanged in meaning and
meter, though the variant first elements of the compound are
patently more than useful in meeting the exigencies of alliteration, a restrictive and technical problem with which neither
Homeric nor Yugoslav verse, for instance, have to contend. The
degree of thrift that marks the use of formulas in Homeric verse[9]

is scarcely conceivable in the construction of the much more restrictive alliterative Germanic verse.

6b. siþþan ǽrest wearþ shows us three words repeated as a
formula in Béowulf where it serves to express the general idea
"after something or other has happened"; it must have often been
used by singers to express this same idea in a complete D-
verse. But siþþan ǽrest (or furðum) can be followed by any
monosyllabic verb-form in the past tense and in the recorded
instance with wéox expresses a closely related idea.

11b. þæt wæs gód cyning! is a formula that may well have
come into being in connection with encomiastic verse, of which
we hear so much and have so little. Stylistically this and related
formulas stop the narrative for a moment and thus serve as a
kind of emphatic punctuation. It is used twice in Béowulf, and
elsewhere with unfavorable adjectives it serves as a parallel
phrase of disapprobation. The system is þæt wæs (is) x cyning.
There are other more distantly related formulas noted in the
supporting evidence, all referring to persons.

16a. lange hwíle is part of a large system expressing the
idea "for a long time" and is closely related to a similar system
with þráge, equally popular with the Béowulf singer. This formula or formulaic system occurs with ealle, góde, and micele
substituting for lange, alternates which affect neither sense nor
meter; here alliteration must dictate the singer's choice.
Whether he uses hwíle or þráge is surely a matter of accident
or indifference, since both words fill the same measure of verse
and here will not enter into the alliteration.

19a. Scieldes eafora is not repeated elsewhere in the poetic
corpus, for nowhere else does the need exist to use this particular patronymic. The value of this system, whereby an A-verse
can be constructed with the genitive of any monosyllabic personal
name, is obvious from the supporting evidence. For patronymics
involving the numerous dithematic names it may be observed
that sunu is the favorite keyword and automatically forms a D-
or E-verse, as do the somewhat less common maga and magu.

The present passage includes three nominal compounds
which I have underlined as formulas not merely because they
are repeated elsewhere to make up whole verses but because
their second elements constitute the core of many small systems
of formulas. These are þéod-cyninga (2a), ymbsittendra (9b),
and will-gesíðas (23a).[10] If these words did not make up entire

325

verses, one might perhaps be inclined to view them merely as repeated words, and just as formulas need not be mere repetitions, so mere repetitions need not constitute a formula.

þéod-cyninga (2a) is one of a large number of compounds with inflected forms of cyning, usually in the genitive singular, which express the idea "king" within the limits of a D3-verse. In most cases the first element merely emphasizes in one way or another the importance of the king or kings in question, as here where the Danish þéod-cyningas are tacitly opposed, as it were, to smákonungar 'roitelets' of ancient Scandinavia. Occasionally the first element will be more functional and will define or locate a king. In the on-verse position Béowulf 2795 has Wuldor-cyninge and in the off-verse position eorþ-, héah-, þéod-cyninges, also Frís-cyninge and sǽ-cyninga; of the same general order is weorold-cyninga. Except for Frís-, used to place geographically Dæghrǽfn's overlord, the first elements add little to the thought and were presumably chosen for alliterative convenience.[11]

ymbsittendra (9b), a compound present participle forming a D1-verse, presents a somewhat similar situation; it handily expresses the idea of "persons residing round about." Very close is ymbstandendra. In a broader way ymbsittendra is to be associated with a large number of verses consisting of a compound present participle, of which there are many in Béowulf, which tend in turn to break down into various semantic systems such as the idea of "sea-farer" expressed by brim- and sǽ-líðende in Béowulf, and in other songs with the substitution of éa-, mere-, and wǽg- as the first element but with no change in thought.

will-gesíðas (23a) is but one of a largish formulaic system centering on gesíþ to express in a complete A-verse the idea of "follower(s)," "retainer(s)," the large variety of available first elements being highly useful to the singers in connection with alliteration. Thus are found compounds with dryht-, eald-, folc-, wéa-, and wynn-.[12]

Within the first fifty verses of Béowulf occur three so-called kennings, two Christian: Líf-fréa (16b), varied by wuldres Wealdend (17a), and one non-Christian: hran-ráde (10a). Reserving the Christian formulas for later discussion in connection with the special diction of the Christian songs (pp. 331 ff. below), we may examine here the formulaic character of the C-verse ofer hran-ráde and some closely related expressions by the aid of

which the singers were able to place people on the sea or to get
them over it. Much has been written about Anglo-Saxon kennings
by themselves and as part of Old-Germanic poetical technique,
but there is one particular aspect of this problem which can
probably support further thought and investigation, namely, the
formulaic character of the kenning. Like the rest of the language
of oral poetry kennings must have developed over a long period
of time and must be traditional and formulaic. An examination
of the phrase ofer hran-ráde will tend to bear out this view. The
feminine accusative singular hran-ráde, combined with the prepositions geond, ofer, and on, forms a complete C-verse, whose repeated use marks it as formulaic. Yet it is more than that, in
that it is also one phrase of a formulaic system on (ofer, geond)
x-ráde, where for x one can substitute any appropriate monosyllabic first element. With the substitution of swan one finds
ofer swan-ráde in Béowulf and Elene, on swan-ráde in Juliana,
while on segl-ráde appears in Béowulf with little or no real
difference in meaning, and none in meter, from the other combinations. The singers are presumably concerned not primarily
with some refinement of imagery produced by varying the first
elements hran, segl, and swan—something for which an oral
singer could scarcely have time—but with recalling a formula
expressing the fundamental idea in question with availability for
different alliterative situations. It is hard to believe that they
had much concern with possible connotative effects produced by
passing mention of sails, swans, or whales.

There is another aspect of this general problem that semantically at least is related to the ofer hran-ráde verse in Béowulf.
Now this particular formula and related formulaic systems were
obviously useful to Anglo-Saxon singers and provided them with
a C-verse with the aid of which they could get their characters
onto or across the sea. Nevertheless, this system imposed certain limitations, including the fact that a verse based on this
formula cannot well contain a verb; yet the need for composing
such verses was felt and was met in more than one way. A fair
example centers on a parallel to rád, f., namely, weg, m. In
the accusative singular of weg there will be no ending; hence
any compound of weg in this grammatical case, where ending a
verse, must be fitted into a metrical pattern other than C, one
in which there will be place for a verb or some other important
alliterating word at the beginning. The pertinent compounds of

327

weg are bæþ-, flód-, flot-, and hwæl-, of which bæþ-weg is the most frequent combination. Ofer bæþ-weg occurs three times, always with some form of brecan in the sense 'pressing on across the sea': thus, brecan ofer bæþ-weg (And 223, Ele 244) and brecaþ ofer bæþ-weg (And 513), where the phrase ofer bæþ-weg combines with the alliterating verb to make a formula. The two f-compounds, flód- and flot-weg, serve their purpose in combination with faran. Flód-weg appears in an instrumental construction fóron flód-wege (Exo 106) '[the sailors] journeyed on or over the sea'; while in the accusative plural there is Fór flód-wegas (Rid 36, 9) '[it, probably a ship] traversed the seas.' With on the combination flot-weg appears in faran on flot-weg (HbM 42) '[was fated] to journey on the sea.' Finally comes hwæl-weg, in meaning identical with hran-rád of Bwf 10a and occurring in hweteþ on hwæl-weg (Sea 63a) 'impels on [to?] the whale's route.' Beside offering various alliterative alternates this cluster of weg-formulas permits the inclusion of a verb in a single D-verse, an opportunity of which the singers were obviously glad to avail themselves.

I shall conclude this discussion of the formulaic character of the first 50 verses of Béowulf with a brief word on the first five verses (1a–3a) of the poem, where the singer appears to have adjusted, combined, and recombined a number of formulas. He begins with a formula much used to start songs or to introduce an important new section of a song, a formula built around the weakly exclamatory hwæt plus a personal pronoun. This is in effect a sort of filler-in, something to let the singer get going; the phrase, ordinarily metrically unstressed, opens the way to a B- or C-verse. The total system, embracing all personal pronouns in the nominative and a few in oblique cases, is vast and cannot be presented here, but looking at all instances of the subvariety Hwæt, wé (1a), collected on Chart I, one is struck by two points: (1) that in each case the singer includes his audience in assuming familiarity with the thematic material of his song,[13] and (2), more important, the fact that he is saying "we have all heard or learned about something or other," at times adding that the events took place long ago. Híeran is the verb favored in preserved song, with frignan of Béowulf running (perhaps by chance), a poor second. It will be noticed that the singers ordinarily work in the important verbal idea "hearing about," "learning about" in the course of the first two verses, but the Béowulf singer introduced mention of the Spear-Danes (Gár-Dena) before proceeding farther. This apparently spoiled his chance of getting in a verb in what appears to be the favored or ordinary position in the first verse. Comparable to Cynewulf in Ele 397b, he might in some fashion have worked in a suitable verb in 1b, had there been such a one capable of g-alliteration, but at all events he next called upon one of the several available formulas expressing the idea "long ago," already discussed (p. 324, above) under on géar-dagum (1b). Thus gefrugnon is put off to the fourth verse (2b), while the hú of the total phrase wé gefrugnon hú has to wait for the fifth (3a). The basic formula is all there and the singer has used every scrap of it, though not in what would appear to be the usual way. One might interpret this exceptional treatment as an example of a first-rate singer coping quickly and deftly with an almost awkward situation into which he had got himself, even though the resulting order of words is perhaps not quite natural. To suggest that this order of words is in any sense "literary" is virtually to deny oral technique in the composition of the poem, a technique demonstrated in the preceding analysis of the first fifty verses of the poem. The traditional character of the recorded text is further borne out by the fact that at least fifteen per cent of the verses of the poem are to all intents and purposes repeated within the poem,[14] a phenomenon unthinkable in lettered tradition.

In the opening lines of Béowulf are two formulas which must be called Christian: Líf-fréa (16b) and wuldres Wealdend (17a). Neither of these so-called kennings could well refer to anything but the Deity and hence could not have formed part of the traditional language of pre-Christian poetry. They must be relatively young and their presence in Béowulf raises the general question of the relation of the language of Christian narrative poetry — by far the largest genre in the corpus — to the older traditional poetic language. There are no means of knowing when first a singer or singers started making songs based on such novel thematic material as that found in the Old Testament, Apocrypha, saints' lives, and homilies, but it cannot well have been before the arrival of Augustine in Kent in 597 and Paulinus in York in 625, an influence fortified by the settlement of Aidan on Lindisfarne (Holy Island) off the Northumberland coast in 635. Yet somewhere in the neighborhood of 675 St Aldhelm was quite possibly singing religious verse, interspersed among diverting secular songs, in public at Malmesbury in Wiltshire in order to get the local populace to stay on after mass for the sermon,[15] and sometime between 658 and 680, the years during which Hild ruled as abbess of Whitby in the North Riding, the unlettered Cædman, farm-hand on the monastic estate, is said on first-rate authority[16] to have been successfully composing all sorts of songs based on Christian story. There is no way of learning more about Aldhelm's compositions but, as I hope to show elsewhere, Cædman was probably the father of nothing but his own songs and composed these against the background of a developed tradition.

In talking or thinking about the chronology, real or relative, of Anglo-Saxon poems one is notoriously treading on very swampy ground, but if one adopts the conservative view that a B_eowulf song in form fairly close to the preserved performance had come into being not far from, say 730 or even somewhat later, it is clear that by that time Christian poetry was a commonplace and that its recitation was a familiar form of entertainment not only in monasteries but in lay circles. Were this not the case, the recitation in Heorot of a song about the Creation (Bwf 90–98) would, as Dr Whitelock has recently pointed out, "surely have been incongruous, or even ludicrous, if minstrels never sang on such themes to lay audiences."[17] As it is, the Creation song seems to enjoy a status no different from that of songs sung about Sigemund and Fitela or the tragedy of Finn's stronghold in the same hall on another occasion. Indeed, apart from this, the entire fabric of B_eowulf is shot through with the language and thought of Christianity and must be viewed as a Christian poem though of an unusual sort.[18]

Now, as Parry emphasizes, the traditional language of unlettered singers develops very, very slowly and over a long period of time and is created to deal only with traditional themes with which singers and audiences are in the main familiar. On his visits to Yugoslavia in 1950 and 1951 Professor Lord noted that the traditional singers were proving unable to cope with such radically new themes of a social-political nature as Marxism and related matters, for the simple reason that they lacked formulas necessary to express these new ideas in just measures of verse. Except for rather obvious substitutions of key-words in an old formula (e.g. engla Dryhten for eorla dryhten), no one singer ever creates many new formulas and most of them never create any at all. Thus, standing on the threshold, so to speak, of the year 600, one might well have wondered whether and how Anglo-Saxon singers would be able to meet the challenge of adapting their traditional verses to the needs of singing about themes so different as Christian material would seem to be. In actual fact they did rise to this occasion and often magnificently.

A glance of Chart II (pp. 342–344) analyzing ll. 512–535 of <u>Christ and Satan</u>, a poem of appreciably later date than <u>Béowulf</u> and mainly telling a story of Christ's harrowing of hell, exhibits plainly the formulaic character of the language. If not as many verses are underlined as in Chart I, this can, in the case of the unmarked verses, only mean that the surviving corpus of Anglo-Saxon poetry does not happen to contain verses which furnish supporting evidence, that is, either exactly similar verses or, equally significant, verses constructed on closely similar formulaic patterns.

It will be unnecessary to take up the text of this chart in detail, for the supporting evidence will now be telling its own story. There are, however, two matters, quite different from one another, which the present passage brings to one's attention. The first concerns the "Christianity" of the language of this and perhaps any other Christian poem, while the second concerns the possibility of occasionally making use of an understanding of the nature and function of the formula in textual criticism.

The prime point of interest in the sample of verse analyzed on Chart II lies in the fact that it is from a Christian poem. It is a passage treating a most central event in Christian belief, the Ascension of Jesus Christ, and in that sense at least could scarcely be more Christian as opposed to the opening verses of <u>Béowulf</u>. What, as far as the language is concerned, is Christian about it? Very largely references to God, specifically Jesus Christ. This passage of forty-six verses includes thirteen such references, more than one for every four verses: <u>wuldres Weard</u> (512a), <u>Meotod mann-cynnes</u> (513a), <u>Dryhten God</u> (514a), <u>engla Dryhten</u> (518b), <u>God</u> (522b), <u>Godes Sunu</u> (526b), <u>Sunu Meotodes</u> (527b), <u>se Éca</u> (530b), <u>þeodne</u> (532a), <u>Scieppend engla</u> (533b), and <u>Dryhten</u> (535a). These are all in one way or another different from one another. In addition there are ten other "Christian" words, that is, words which would normally only appear in a Christian context: Galilee is mentioned twice (522a, 529a), Simon called Peter twice (521b, 536b); there is one reference to the

Holy Spirit (525b), two to the disciples (520b, 529b), and three
to angels (518b, 520a, 533b), of which two occur as parts of
kennings designating the Deity. In all, these forty-six verses
include twenty-three Christian words, or words used in a Christian way; thus there is one Christian word for every other verse
or one for each typographical line. It might be hard to find a
more "Christian" passage, and for these words and formulas
used in a Christian way only giengran lacks supporting evidence.
This is no doubt due to the limits of the surviving corpus and,
had the singer happened to have preferred formulas with the
much more frequent equivalent of "disciple," namely þegn, it
would probably be possible to collect no little supporting evidence.

In this so very Christian passage there may be a hint and
more as to how Anglo-Saxon singers were able, apparently from
early on, to sing in a slightly adjusted traditional language songs
based on these novel and untraditional themes. In the first place
and stated in most general terms, the Christian themes that
the singers apparently liked best to sing about are in the main
stories involving extraordinary and exciting adventures and events,
such as the stories on which center Andreas, Azarias, Daniel,
Elene, Exodus, Judith, and Juliana. To the ear of Anglo-Saxons not
yet fully initiated in this new development most immediately striking and strange were no doubt the presence of non-Germanic proper
nouns, names of persons such as Simon Peter and places such
as Galilee. These could be and were, however, readily fitted
into older formulas created to embody Germanic proper names,
and since these strange new names were all but invariably accented on the first syllable, regardless of the stress in the original tongues, they offered few, if any, metrical problems to the
singer. Some of them must have been awkwardly long and more
than queer sounding, such as Nabochodonossar, used five times
in Daniel (48, 411, 497, 618, 663) and once in Azarias (183) to
form a complete A-type on-verse, yet the singers made do with
them. Aside from the pre-Christian word God and elsewhere
Críst, to be viewed as ordinary personal names, the singers had
available from pre-Christian tradition, already evidently rich
in words and kennings to express the idea of "ruler," a large
number of expressions ready to take off the rack, available as
substitutory epithets for the Deity. As a result of new formations
on the analogy of the old, e.g., the weaving into compounds of
such characteristically Christian word-elements as heofon and

wuldor, the number of epithets for the Deity was increased to a point where this is by all odds the largest single group of kennings in the poetical corpus.[19] The frequency and hence importance of this group can scarcely be overestimated. The concept "angel" is new as is the loan-word engel, an idea also capable of being expressed by the old word gāst. The Latin titles Sanctus and Beatus were easily handled by the old words hālig (originally 'inviolate') and ēadig ('favored by fortune,' 'prosperous'). Expression of general conceptions of theology, dogma, and Christian doctrine is notably rare in the Christian songs,[20] as it is in Béowulf, where action predominates, and even in that most beautiful song of meditation or devotion, The Dream of the Rood. This lack is surely due neither to mere accident nor to ignorance or indifference, but to a lack of formulas capable of adaptation to such ideas. The lyrically keyed poem on the Advent (Christ I) and the song on the Ascension (Christ II), based on the latter part of Pope Gregory the Great's Ascension homily, are both traditional in diction and adhere pretty strictly to narrative.[21]

It would be wrong to suggest that the adaptation of the traditional language of the ancient poetry to this new and different thematic material did not take doing on the part of the singers or to withhold from them full credit for the successful exercise of what at the outset particularly must have called for skill and ingenuity. It is, however, fair to point out, in view of the obviously traditional language of the Christian poems — a matter that in essence has long since been noticed and stressed — that the singers did not make things unnecessarily hard for themselves by attempting to sing about matters for the expression of which the old diction would have been inadequate. As it was, singers and audience probably felt little difference between the general style and narrative technique of, say, Béowulf and Christ and Satan, to mention two poems of very different thematic backgrounds. This marked uniformness or unity of style is largely to be accounted for by the continuity of the traditional formulaic language of the Anglo-Saxon singers, a continuity that seems to live until the Norman Conquest.

Many factors, political and social as well as linguistic, probably contributed to the death of the traditional poetry after the Conquest, and one must also reckon with the difficulties, probably insuperable, which the relatively swift introduction of ideas and activities incidental to the advent of the feudal age brought in their train, ideas which could not easily be sidestepped by singers trying to sing in the old tradition and for which they had no formulas.

Quite by chance the present passage from Christ and Satan offers an opportunity to consider the general possibility of the use of an understanding of the role of the formula in occasional matters of textual criticism. Verse 513b, with the manuscript reading ǽr on morgen (A), 'early in the morning,' technically violates a basic principle of alliteration in that the first down-beat or ictus in the off-verse does not here alliterate with the preceding on-verse where the alliteration is m. Acting on a suggestion of Professor Holthausen, Professor M. D. Clubb emended this verse in his edition of 1925 to read on morgen ǽr, thus producing which he rightly described as a normal (B) verse. Nevertheless, in the light of the supporting evidence which demonstrates the existence of a formula ǽr on morgen, taken together with the phrase on ǽr-morgen, with which may also be compared mid ǽr-dǽge of similar meaning, one may wonder whether the singer did not himself violate the usual procedures of alliteration in order to make use of a formula that he needed, a formula or system in which ǽr preceded the word it modified. Consequently, one might do well, not only here but in other similar situations, to test such alliteratively defective verses for their formulaic character before embarking on a course of emendation, however much better emendation may make, or may seem to make, matters. If given time to think his verse over, in a word, to compose at a more leisurely pace, a singer might well agree with what a modern editor was proposing to do; on the other hand, such an emendation might produce a sequence of words which would strike him as stranger than the technical de-fect in versification.

If this discussion of manuscript ǽr on morgen suggests that it should be left regardless of the technical imperfection that its use and retention produces, the case of manuscript on þǽm fæstenne (519a) would seem to speak in favor of emendation to of þǽm fæstenne, 'from, out of the tomb,' an emendation adopted by certain earlier editors, though not by Clubb or Krapp, last to edit the poem. The supporting evidence on Chart II exhibits two expressions, one with fram or of, meaning "from or out of the prison, stronghold or tomb," the other with on, always ex-

334

cept here with the obvious meaning "in the prison, stronghold or tomb." Now it is true that Old-English uses expressions with on which are convenient to render by "from," generally in connection with removing something from a surface on which the object in question is lying or reposing (see B.-T. s.v. "on," III, 2). From the Anglo-Saxon point of view on is in these cases entirely appropriate, though the approach to the act is different from ours. It is as if one said "he took the pencil on the table," that is, "he took the pencil which was lying on the table," in the sense that he took it from the table. When Grendel assails Béowulf, it is said that the troll nam . . . rinc on ræste (ll. 746–747), 'took the warrior from his resting place.' This is, however, far from saying that OE on means "from"; it is simply to say that the image of the action is different. In the verse in Christ and Satan such an image would in the nature of things be highly unlikely if not out of the question altogether. The singer must be trying to say that Our Lord went out of the tomb and thus it is all but certain that the manuscript on does not go back to the words of the singer or to anybody who was giving attention to the thought but to a miscopying by a scribe somewhere along the line of written transmission. If this is so, then in the small verbal matter of the preposition, manuscript on, the supporting evidence involving on's does not support the manuscript reading, but rejects it rather.

The future is full of many problems involving a reappraisal of certain aspects of Anglo-Saxon poetical style and compositional technique, and what these are, or at present seem likely to be, can here by merely adumbrated. First of all let it be said that, if further study of the formulaic character of the poetry is to be conducted in a thoroughgoing way, the first and most crying need is the construction of a concordance of the entire poetical corpus; without this the collecting of supporting evidence to test the formulaic character of a given verse or group of verses will prove to be incredibly laborious and often uncertain.[22]

More sample analyses of narrative verse are certainly desirable, though it seems doubtful that any narrative poem will be found to be non-traditional in language. Particularly interesting will be a study from this point of view of the diction of the rather small body of lyrical-elegiac poetry. One might suspect that lyrical composition would call for formulas not else-

where used and that for many of the verses there would be little
or no supporting evidence of their formulaic character, due to the
limited size of the body of lyric-elegiac verse. The same may
be said of the literary Riddles of the Exeter Book, a genre new
to the Anglo-Saxons and a direct imitation of Latin enigmas,
specifically those (685–705?) of Aldhelm, of which two are translated into Old English. At least some of the language of the
Riddles is traditional, since verses from these appear in the
support-evidence in the charts above, but it may turn out that
many riddles, often very short compositions, were composed
word by word. And what of the verses that embody runes other
than isolated logograms (e.g. éðel and mann), notably Cynewulf's
signature passages? [23]

Mention of Cynewulf raises a question concerning the relation between lettered persons and orally composed poetry.
Not all Anglo-Saxon Christian poetry needs to have been composed by lettered singers—witness the story of Cædman. Any
good unlettered singer who had translated for, or expounded to,
him the Apocryphal Gospel of St Matthew and St Andrew could
easily have composed Andreas. But Cynewulf was surely a
lettered person, else how could he have conceived a plan to as-
sure mention of his name in prayers by means of runic signatures which depend on a knowledge of spelling and reading for
their efficacy? [24] If, however, the narrative parts of his poems
prove on testing to be formulaic, one must assume that those
parts at least he composed in the traditional way. That he sub-
sequently got them written down, whether dictating to himself,
as it were, or to another person—possibly a more convenient
procedure—is beside the point. In any event there would be no
conflict with, or contradiction to, tradition. [25]

A different view will, I think, have to be taken of the significance or lack of significance of phrasal similarities between
this and that poem and poems than has prevailed up to now. [26]
Certain verbal similarities among poems may in a sense represent borrowing from one poem to another, for traditional singers
perforce learn from other singers. But one verbal similarity or
even a number of verbal similarities in themselves prove nothing
beyond suggesting that given singers have found the same formulas useful to express a certain idea in a similar measure of
verse. To quote Parry, "Plagiarism is not possible in traditional
literature. One oral poet is better than another not because he

has by himself found a more striking way of expressing his thought, but because he has been better able to make use of the tradition."[27] When by the aid of a concordance we gradually get to know what the Anglo-Saxon formulas are and what, indeed, constitute their dimensions[28] and the like, it will perhaps be possible to begin to detect individual styles. Apart from general over-all organization of material, the broad architectonics of a given poem, a singer's individuality will, as in other traditional poetry, presumably emerge in rather small matters,[29] verbal and stylistic, and will not be revealed by the large and rather obvious components known to all or almost all singers.

Lack of truly early material will preclude our ever knowing much about the relative age of the formulas encountered in the preserved poems, but perhaps something can be done with verses containing words which in earlier times had suffered contraction, either from the simple contraction of two vowels (as dón<dó-an) or as a secondary result of the loss of intervolcalic h (as héan< héahan).[30] The poetry abounds in such verses as héan landes (Gen 2854b) which, if pronounced as they almost surely were pronounced in later times, were metrically deficient though at the time created they formed metrically regular verses: héahan landes (A). The becoming unmetrical of such a verse would have been a gradual process and singers would naturally have hung on to it as long as possible, down, in fact, to the time when the contraction-process had long since been completed. This would suggest that later-day singers and their audiences became habituated to such metrical irregularities and accepted these "deficient" verses as traditional.[31] This matter might profitably be further explored.

Just as the half-hexameter is the basis of most Homeric formulas, so is the single verse that of Old-Germanic poetry. But in the Homeric poems there are also whole-line formulas[32] answering in a sense apparently to such Anglo-Saxon verse-pair formulas as on þæm dæge þisses lífes (Bwf 197, 790, 806), þæs oferéode: þisse swá mæg (Déo 7, 13, 17, 20, 42), and siþþan of líc-haman læded wære (Vercelli SlB 21) with which cp. Bwf 3177, where of líc-hamen læded weorðan is almost surely the right reading (cp. Jul 670a).

Oral singers are often faced with situations where enjambement is required,[33] and the Anglo-Saxon singers appear to be no exception. Béowulf offers at least one interesting example

337

where enjambement is accomplished with the aid of a two-verse formula: ende gebídan / weorolde lífes (Bwf 1386b–87a, 2342b–43a); Dr Whitelock has already pointed out how the formula God éaðe mæg (Bwf 478b, And 425b, Chr 173b) operates in this situation.[34]

There is perhaps much that will never be known about the origin and special function, if any, of the expanded or hypermetric verses, but a casual survey suggests that, whereas the second measure of each such verse seems to be formulaic and out of its context would form a complete verse, the organization of the first measure would appear to be somewhat different, perhaps somewhat less rigid in structure, thus perhaps allowing the singer certain freedoms not available in a normal verse. Here, too, a concordance will be necessary for further study of the character of these first measures.[35]

At the end of these rather miscellaneous remarks on possible problems of the future, problems which will require the thought of many persons to test and solve, I should like to comment on the possible relation of one aspect of the physical preservation of our Anglo-Saxon poems that may reflect their oral background, namely, the fact of their all being written out as prose. It is a not uncommon view that this method was employed as a measure of economy, that the vernacular poetry was perhaps felt not quite worth, or worthy of, as much parchment as writing the poetry out as we today print it would require. I find it hard to believe this to be the case and suspect it was written as prose merely because neither scribes nor singers understood in a formal sense the metrics of the verse, even when they may have had an understanding of Latin verse studied in monastic schools. That tenth- or eleventh-century scribes at times separate verses (not our typographical lines) by dots may merely reflect a feeling for the basic rhythm, the onset of a down-beat, comparable to a musically unschooled person's tapping time with foot or finger though knowing nothing of the writing of music or of musical composition.

CHART I

(Béowulf, ll. 1–25)

Hwæt, wé Gár-Dena   on géar-dagum
þéod-cyninga   þrymm gefrugnon,
hú þá æðelingas   ellen fremedon.
Oft Scield Scéafing   sceaðena þréatum,
5   manigum mǽgðum   medu-setla oftéah,
egesode Eorle,   siþþan ǽrest wearþ
féasceaft funden; hé þæs frófre gebád,
wéox under wolcnum,   weorþ-myndum þáh,
oþ-þæt him ǽghwelć   ymbsittendra
10   ofer hran-ráde   híeran scolde,
gamban gieldan;   þæt wæs gód cyning!
þǽm eafora wæs   æfter cenned
geong on geardum,   þone God sende
folce to frófre;   firen-þearfe ongeat
15   þe híe ǽr drugon   ealdorléase
lange hwíle;   him þæs Líf-fréà,
wuldres Wealdend   weorold-áre forgeaf
Béow wæs bréme   —blǽd wíde sprang—
Scieldes eafora   Sceden-landum on.
20   Swá sceal geong guma   góde gewyrćan
framum feoh-giftum   on fæder bearme
þæt hine on ielde   eft gewunien
will-gesíðas   þanne wíg cume,
léode gelǽsten;   lof-dǽdum sceal
25   on mǽgða gehwǽm   man geþéòn.

SUPPORTING EVIDENCE

1a–2b Hwæt, wé feorr and néah / gefrigen habbaþ (Exo 1);
Hwæt, wé gefrugnon / on fyrn dagum (And 1); Hwæt, wé þæt
gehíerdon / þurh hálge béc (FAp 63, Ele 364, 852); Hwæt, wé
éac gehíerdon / be Ióhanne (FAp 23); Hwæt, wé nú gehíerdon /
hú þæt Hǽlubearn (Chr 586, with whose gehíerdon cp. Bwf 2b–
3a gefrugnon hú); Hwæt, wé hierdon oft / þæt se hálige wer (Glc
108); Hwæt, wé þæt gehíerdon /hǽleþ eahtian (Jul 1); Hwæt, wé
Ebréisce ǽ leornodon / þá on fyrn-dagum fæderas cúðon (Ele
397–98). 1b XSt 367, Wan 44. Cp. Chr 251 þe on géar-dagum;
Bwf 1354 þone on géar-dagum, 2233 swá híe on géar-dagum.

Note also instrum. use without on: And 1519 giefum géar-dagum; Ele 290 þæt gé géar-dagum, 834 swá hie géar-dagum (also Bwf 2233). Note closely related formulas: on fyrn-dagum, on ær-dagum, and on eald-dagum (Chr 303, SFt 1). 2a Nom. pl. Gen 1965 þéod-cyningas / þrymme micele; gen. sg. Bwf 2694 þá ic æt þearfe gefrægn / þéod-cyninges; FAp 18 Ne þréodode hé fore þrymme / þéod-cyninges; Edw 34 þæs-þe þearf wæs / þæs þéod-cyninges. 2b See 1–2 above for combination of formulas to express the idea of "having heard or learned long ago." 3a FAp 3 hú þá æðelingas / ellen cýðdon, 85 þus þá æðelingas; Rid 49, 7 þá æðelingas. Cp. without def. art. but with a preceding word, usually of light stress Gen 1059 þára-þe æðelingas, 1647 þá nu æðelingas, 1868 ellor æðelingas; Dan 689, And 805 þær æðelingas, 857 Him þá æðelingas. 3b And 1208 Scealt þú, Andréas, / ellen fremman. 4b Jul 672 sceaðena þréate; cp. Glc 902 féonda þréatum.

5a Bwf 75 manigre mægðe, 1771 manigum mægða. 6b Bwf 1947; cp. 1775 siþþan Grendel wearþ; Ele 913 siþþan furðum wéox. Note the more general metrical scheme involving siþþan plus a two- or three-syllable word plus verb: And 1223 siþþan ge-ypped wæs; Ele 18 siþþan wæpen ahóf, 841 siþþan béacen geseah; Bwf 1077, 2124 siþþan morgen (mergen) cóm, 1233 siþþan æfen cóm, 1689 siþþan flód ofslóg. 7a Cp. And 181 onfindaþ féasceaftne. 8a Gen 1702 wéox þá under wolcnum; cp. Bwf 714 Wód under wolcnum; Phx 27 wrídaþ under wolcnum; Gen 1438 wære under wolcnum; Phx 247 awierde under wolcnum. 8b Exo 258 weorþ-myndum spræc. 9a Ele 865 oþ-þæt him gecýðde, 885 oþ-þæt him uppan. 9b Bwf 2734, Ele 33. Cp. other inflections: dat. pl. ymbsittendum PPs 78, 4; 88, 35; fem. acc. pl. Met 35, 14 ymbsitten-da. Cp. closely related Gen 2490 ymbstandendra; PPs 140, 4 ymbstandende.

10a Gen 205 geond hran-ráde; And 266, 821 on hran-ráde. Cp. Bwf 200, Ele 996 ofer swan-ráde; Jul 675 on swan-ráde; Bwf 1429 on segl-ráde. 10b Dan 135; Ele 367; Met 9, 45; Met 1, 31 híeran scoldon. 11a Gen 1977b–78a níede scoldon, / gamban gieldan. 11b Bwf 863, 2390. Cp. Bwf 1885 þæt wæs án cyning; Jul 224 þæt is sóþ cyning; Déo 23 þæt wæs grimm cyning; Wíd 67 Næs þæt sæne cyning, and further Bwf 1075 þæt wæs geómru ides, 1812 þæt wæs módig secg; Met 26, 35 (?) þæt wæs geó cyning, etc. 12a Gen 1188 Se eafora wæs / Énoc háten. Note and cp. Bwf 12a–b eafora . . . cenned with Gen 1159 þá wearþ on eðle / eafora féded, 2394 of idese biþ / eafora wæcned. 12b Cp. Cæd

8 æfter téode; Rid 40, 44 and ić giestran geong cenned. 13a Phx 355, 647; Chr 201 geongre on geardum. Cp. Jul 35 geong on gáste; Bwf 2446 geong on gealgan. 13b Dan 525 þe þider God sende; cp. Gen 1371 Dryhten sende. 14a Exo 88; And 606; Ele 1142; Men 228 folcum to frófre; Ele 502 folca to frófre; Rid 39, 19 manigum to frófre; Men 57, Ps 50 148 mannum to frófre.

15a Bwf 831, 1875; Chr 615 þe wé ǽr drugon; Jud 158 þe gé lange drugon. 15b Cp. Bwf 2935; And 405 hláfordléase. Ealdorléas is ordinarily used in the sense "lifeless." 16a Bwf 2159, 2780; Dan 660; DrR 24; Jul 674; Rid 28, 9; Met 4, 46. For numerous formulas to express a 'long' or 'short time' cp. DrR 70 góde hwíle, also mićele, lýtle, sume hwíle, and with þráge: ealle, lýtle, lange, sume, also ǽnige stunde. 16b Cp. Exo 271 and éow Lif-fréa; Chr 27 hwanne ís Líf-fréa. 17a Bwf 183, 1752; Dan 14; And 193, 539. 18a Sol 182 Saloman wæs brémra; Dan 104 þá wæs bréme; Sol 238 béć sind bréme. 18b FAp 6 Lof wíde sprang; cp. Bwf 1588 hráw wíde sprang; Jul Léad wíde sprang; also Max I 194 wíde gesprungen. 19a Bwf 897 Wælses eafora; 1847 Hréðles eaforan; Gen 1133 Séthes eafora, 2054 þáres eafora; Met 26, 36 Ióbes ('Jove's') eafora; Men 136 Zebedes eafora. Cp. also Gen 1578 eafora Nóes, 2834 eafora þáres. 19b Bwf 2357 Frís-landum on; Gen 1052 éast-landum on. Cp. Jul 83 wín-(wynn?) burgum on.

20a Bwf 1172, 1534 Swá sceal man dôn; cp. 2066 Swá sceal mǽg dôn, 2590 swá sceal ǽghwelć mann. 21b Cp. Bwf 35, Exo 375 on bearm scipes, 896 bær on bearm scipes, 214 on bearm nacan. Note related formula with fæðm: Bwf 188 and to Fæder fæðmum; Max II 661 on Fæder fæðm; And 616 on banan fæðme; Ele 765 on dracan fæðme. 22a-b Cp. FoM 60 and on ielde eft / éadig weorðan. 22b See 22a-b, also Phx 481 lang gewunien. 23a Gen 2003. 25a Pre 74 þá-þe hér on mǽgðe gehwǽm.

CHART II

(Christ and Satan, ll. 512–35)

Swá wuldres Weard   wordum sægde,
Meotod mann-cynnes,   ǽr on morgen,
þæs-þe Dryhten God   of déaðe arás.
515 Næs nán þæs strangliće   stán gefæstnod,
þéah hé wǽre mid írne   eall ymbfangen
þæt meahte þǽm mićelan   mægene wiþhabban,
ac Hé út éode,   engla Dryhten
on þǽm fæstenne.   And gefetian hét
520 englas eall-beorhte   endleofan giengran,
and húru secgan hét   Símon Pétre
þæt hé móste on Galiléam   God sćeawian,
éćne and trumne,   swá hé ǽr dyde.
þá ić gangan gefrægn   giengran ætsamne
525 ealle to Galiléam;   hǽfdon Gástes blǽd,
(ongéaton) háligne   Godes Sunu
swá híe gesáwon,   hwǽr Sunu Meotodes
þá on upp (a-?) stód,   éće Dryhten,
God on Galiléam.   To þæs giengran þider
530 ealle urnon,   þǽr se Éća wæs.
Féollon on foldan,   to fótum hnigon;
þancodon þéodne   þæt hit þus gelamp
þæt híe sćéawodon   Sćieppend engla.
þá sóna spræc   Símon Pétrus:
"Eart þú þis, Dryhten,   dómes geweorðod?"

SUPPORTING EVIDENCE

512a XSt 659. Cp. Gen 941 Híe þá wuldres Weard; And 596 hú
ús wuldres Weard; Ele 84 (beseoh) on wuldres Weard; Chr 527
þá wæs wuldres Weard. 512b Gen 707, 2053, 2704, Glc 451. Cp.
Exo 377, Phx 425 wordum secgaþ; And 624 wordum gesecgan;
Chr 64 wordum sægdon; Bwf wordum secge. 513a Sat 457, Gen
459, And 172, 357, 446. 513b Frag. Ps 5, 3; also cp. PPs 107, 2,
118, 148 on ǽrmergen, PPs 62, 7 and on ǽrmergen; Met 28, 37;
PPs 56, 10 and ić on ǽrmergene. 514a XSt 313 mid Dryhtne Gode;
And 1281 Geseoh nú Dryhten God, 1462 þá cóm Dryhten God;
Pan 55 Swá is Dryhten God; Bwf 181 ne wisson híe Dryhten God;
Jud 300 him féng Dryhten God; LPr 3 18 Críst, Dryhten God.
Cp. God Dryhten in And 897 Nú ić God Dryhten, Ele 759 þæs þú,

God Dryhten; also Dryhten Críst in Glc 592 gief éow Dryhten Críst; Sol 337 Dryhtne Críste. 514b Ele 187; FAp 56 þæt hé of déaðe arás; Chr 467 fram déaðe arás.

515a Cp. Chr 241 for-þon n'is ǽnig þæs horsc; GfM 8 Ne biþ ǽnig þæs / earfoþ-sǽlig; Sea 39 For-þon n'is þæs mód-wlanc. 515b Cp. Jul 499 folde (subj.) gefæstnod. 516b XSt 143b (cp. 145a selfe mid sange); cp. Bwf 2691 heals eallne ymbeféng. 518b Exo 559; XSt 395; Sol 462. 519a Wha 71; And 1034 fram þæm fæstenne, 1177 of fæstenne; cp. Gen 2536, And 1068 to þæm fæstenne; Sol 320 on fæstenne; Met 1, 79 né on þæm fæstenne. 519b Gen 525 and mec hér standan hét; XSt 521 and húru secgan hét; And 330 and ús féran hét, 587 and wendan hét; Bwf 3095 and éowic grétan hét. Cp. with subordination: Gen 1865 oþ-þæt hé lǽdan hét; And 823 þá gelǽdan hét, 931 swá ic þec féran hét; Ele 863 ǽr hé asettan hét, also 129 arǽran hét. With finite verb first: Gen 2667 hét him fetian tó; Ele 1160, Jul 60 hét þá gefetian; Bwf 2190a-b hét . . . inn fetian.

520a Chr 880; Aza 52 engel ealle-beorhta; Dan 336 engel eall-beorht. For this formula used to connect a verse-pair of consecutive off- and on-verses see Chr 506 Gesáwon híe eall-beorhte / englas twégen, 548 þæt him eall-beorhte / englas togéanes. 521a see 519b, above. 521b XSt 534b Símon Pétrus. 522a-b Cp. 529a. 522b For sceawian with preceding object entering into the alliteration: see Gen 979 (tiber), 1679 (weorc), 1780, 1920 (land), 2595 (wíc), Chr 1136 (weorod), 1206 (dolg), Rid 59, 2 (menn); Bwf 840, 3032 (wundor), 1391 (gang), 1413 (wang), 2402 (dracan), 2744 (hord). 523a Cp. Chr 1071 éce and edgeong. 523b Gen 1840; XSt 116, 278. Cp. Chr 1233 swá híe geworhton ǽr, 161 þá þu geworhtest ǽr. 524a Gen 2060 þá ic néðan gefrægn; And 1706 þá ic lǽdan gefrægn; cp. Sol 179 Hwæt, ic flítan gefrægn.

525b Cp. Phx 549 þurh gástes blǽd; XSt 644 gemunan Gástes blǽd; 526b Gen 1163 Enoses sunu; XSt 118 Wealdendes Sunu; Bwf 1009 Healf-Denes sunu; 2602, 2862, 3076 Wéoh-stánes sunu; Wal I, 11 Ælf-heres sunu. For the closely parallel and more common patronymic formula sunu X's see 527b. 527b XSt 142 þær Sunu Meotodes, 172 Sunu Meotodes; And 881 Swelce wé gesáwon / for Sunu Meotodes; Ele 1318 and to Suna Meotodes, 461, 564 sóþ Sunu Meotodes, 474 hú híe Sunu Meotodes, 686 þurh Sunu Meotodes. Cp. XSt Sunu Wealdendes. With the substitution of various personal names cp.: Gen 1064 (Enoses), 1081, 1086

(Lámeches), 1240 (Nóes), 2465 (Arones); Bwf 524 (Béan-stánes), 590 (Ecg-láfes), 645, 1040 (Healf-Denes), etc. For a patronymic formula centering on eafora see Chart I, 19b. 528a Cp. And 443 Hwilum upp astód, and note other combinations of upp and astandan in Grein-Holthausen-Köhler, suggesting the XSt 530a Ms. stód should, perhaps be emended to astód vs. gestód of the editors. 528b Frag. Ps. 5, 1, 3; PPs 53, 4; 70, 18, 20; 71, 19; 73, 17, 78, 1, etc.; Cæd 4; and in inflected cases as follows: gen. sg. Bru 16 Men 12 éces Dryhtnes; Gen 7, 1885; Chr 396, 711; Phx 600; PPs 67, 3, 9; 68, 29 écan Dryhtnes; dat. sig. Bwf 2796 écum Dryhtne, 1779, 2330 écan Dryhtne; acc. sg. PPs 55, 9; 65, 1, 3, 7 écne Dryhten; Bwf 1692 écan Dryhten.

530a Cp. PPs 61, 4 wide urnon. 531a XSt 544 féolon to foldan, And 918 Féoll þá to foldan; Bwf 2975 féoll on foldan. Cp. Phx 74 Ne feallaþ þær on foldan; Sol 298 afielleþ hine on foldan. 531b Cp. Gen 2441 þá to fótum [féoll / on foldan] Loth; Mal 119 þæt him æt fótum féoll. 532a Glc 778, and cp. with object (usually God) first: Dan 86, And 1011, Ele 1138, Bwf 1397 Gode þancode; Bwf 227, 1626 Gode þancodon. Note the combined formulas of Ele 961–62, Bwf 625–26 Bode þancode . . . þæs(-þe) hire se willa gelamp (see 532b, below). 532b XSt 568 þá hit þus gelamp, and cp. Ele 961–62 and Bwf 625–26 under 532a, above. 533b And 434; And 119, XSt 562 engla Scieppend. 534a Cp. Gen 862 þá sóna ongann, 1589 and þá sóna ongeat; Chr 233 And þá sóna gelamp; Bwf 1280 þá þær sóna warþ; Fin 46 þá hine sóna frægn. 534b XSt 522 Símon Pétre. 535a Bwf 506 Eart þú sé Béo-wulf.

NOTES

1 For a complete bibliography of the writings of Milman Parry,
see A. B. Lord, "Homer, Parry, and Huso," American Journal
of Archaeology, LII (1948), 43–44. Two of Parry's papers
may be specially noted as representing the full development
of this thought: "Studies in the Epic Technique of Oral Verse-
Making, I: Homer and Homeric Style," Harvard Studies in
Classical Philology, XLI (1930), 73–147, esp. pp. 118–121
for charts exposing the formulaic character of ll. 1–25 of
the Iliad and the Odessey respectively; and "II: The Homeric
Language as the Language of Oral Poetry," ibid., XLIII
(1932), 1–50, esp. pp. 12–17 ("The Art of Oral Poetry").
These papers are cited here as Parry I and II and by page.

2 Parry in the summer of 1933, and Parry and Lord in the
years 1934–35, studied the production of the oral epic style
in Yugoslavia and collected some 12,500 texts, "The Parry
Collection of South-Slavic Texts," now deposited in the
Harvard College Library. Following Parry's lead and working with this opulent material Lord submitted in 1949 a Ph.D.
thesis (Harvard, unpublished), "The Singer of Tales: A Study
in the Process of Yugoslav, Greek, and Germanic Oral
Poetry." Lord revisited Yugoslavia in 1950 and 1951; for
his report on the collecting trip of 1950 see "Yugloslav Epic
Folk Poetry," Journal of the International Folk Music Coun-
cil, III (1951), 57–61. His thesis, revised and expanded, has
been published by the Harvard University Press as The Singer
of Tales in the series "Harvard Studies in Comparative
Literature."
 The work of Parry and Lord and the rich material preserved at Harvard were very familar to Sir Cecil Maurice
Bowra and utilized by him in his Heroic Poetry (London,
1952). This distinguished work appeared too late for me
to use in preparing my London lectures or in preparing
this paper, though I am happy to be able to add a specific
reference or two in the footnotes below. For an excellent
review of Sir Maurice's book see TLS, Friday, 12 December
1952, p. 824.

3 Parry II, 7–8.

4 E.g., Rudolf Much, Die Germania des Tacitus (Heidelberg, 1937), pp. 21–22.

5 Quotations and line-references from Béowulf are based on Fr. Klaeber's third edition with First and Second Supplements (Boston, 1950), those from Judith on the edition of Benno J. Timmer (London, 1952); all others on The Anglo-Saxon Poetic Records (New York, 1931–42). Spellings are normalized on the basis of early W.S. as set forth in Les Langues modernes, XLV (1951), 63–69. Title-abbreviations, coded in three letters, are based on the titles used in The Anglo-Saxon Poetic Records.

6 Parry I, 80.

7 Parry I, 122.

8 Parry I, 85 and ff.

9 Parry I, 86.

10 For further instances of words of similar structure, and thus with similar rhythmical patterns, in Béowulf see John Collins Pope, The Rhythm of Béowulf (New Haven, Conn., 1942), pp. 300, 358 (type D1, No. 1) and 248 (type A1, No. 2a). Examples from other poems and with other first elements can be found in Christian W. M. Grein—Ferd. Holthausen—J. J. Köhler, Sprachschatz der angelsächsischen Dichter (Heidelberg, 1912).

11 See further ibid., p. 106, col. 1, under cyning.

12 Ibid., p. 608, under gesíþ.

13 See Dorothy Whitelock, The Audience of Béowulf (London, 1950), pp. 34–44 ff. passim on audience-familiarity in gross and detail with the Béowulf stories and substories introduced for purposes of embellishment; the latter are not in any ordinary sense "digressions."

14 Communicated orally by Professor Robert P. Creed, who is presently studying the oral style in Béowulf.

15 Reported by William of Malmesbury (d. 1125) in his De Gestis Pontificum Anglorum, ed. N. E. S. A. Hamilton, Rolls Ser., No. 52 (London, 1870), Bk. V, Pt. 1 ("Life of Aldhelm"),

p. 336, based on Alfred the Great's lost Handbóc (William's Manuale, ed. cit., pp. 332–333):

"Litteris itaque ad plenum instructus nativae quoque linguae non negligebat carmina, adeo ut, teste libro Elfredi de quo superius dixi, nulla umquam aetate par ei fuerit quisquam. Poesim Anglicam posse facere, cantum componere, eadem apposite vel canere vel dicere. Denique commemorat Elfredus carmen triviale adhuc vulgo canitatur Aldelmum fecisse . . . Populum eo tempore semibarbarum, parum divinis sermonibus intentum, statim cantatis missis domos cursitare solitum. Ideo sanctum virum super pontem qui rura et urbem continuat abeuntibus se opposuisse obicem quasi artem cantandi professum. Eo plus quam semel favorem et concursum emeritum. Hoc commento, sensim inter ludicra verbis Scripturarum insertis, cives ad sanitatem reduxisse."

"And thus fully instructed in [Latin] literature he also did not neglect the songs of his native tongue, so that, according to Alfred's book of which I spoke above, at no time was anybody ever his equal. He was able to make English poetry, compose a melody, and properly sing or recite the same. Finally, Alfred remarks that Aldhelm composed a light song which was still [i.e., in Alfred's day] being commonly sung . . . The people, at that time [about 675] semibarbarous and too little intent on divine discourses, were in the habit of hurrying to their homes after masses had been sung. Therefore, the holy man stationed himself on a bridge [over the Avon] which connects the town [of Malmesbury] and the countryside as an obstacle to those going away, as though professing the art of song. After he had done this several times [lit. 'more than once'] he gained the good-will and the attendance of the common people. By this device, gradually working in words of the Scriptures among entertaining words, he led the people back to right reason."

It may be remarked that the Scriptural words introduced in the course of the recitation of secular poems need not have been

in verse, though this is a reasonable inference. It should
also be noted that nothing is said about writing despite the
rendering "write a poem" (Poesim . . . facere) of George
F. Browne, St. Aldhelm: His Life and Times (London, 1903),
p. 79.

16 I refer not merely to Bede himself but to the tradition of
the Whitby community on which Bede drew, surely completely reliable in this local matter, unless one assumes
a monstrous conspiracy of falsification.

17 Whitelock, op. cit., p. 9; on pp. 9–11 she is on the verge of
suggesting what I suggest here.

18 Idem, pp. 3–4; Klaeber, ed. cit., p. xlix, ad fin.

19 See Hendrik van der Merwe Scholtz, The Kenning in Anglo-
Saxon and Old-Norse Poetry (Utrecht-Nijmegen, 1929), pp.
92–98, and Hertha Marquardt, Die altenglischen Kenningar,
etc., Schriften der Königsberger gelehrten Gesellschaft,
XIV, 3 (Halle, 1938), 269–292, and cp. ibid., pp. 266 ff.
passim (§ D "Christliche Begriffe").

20 Cp. Klaeber, ed. cit., p. xlix, ad init.

21 Mr Robert E. Diamond, presently engaged in the study of
"The Diction of the Signed Poems of Cynewulf" [subsequent-
ly published under this title in PQ, XXXVIII (1959), 228–
241] tells me (30 April 1953) that 20 per cent of the 5194
verses (i.e., 2598 numbered typographic lines of the editions)
in the signed poems of Cynewulf are repeated in the signed
poems themselves. A series of samples, amounting to 581
verses (including the entire Fates of the Apostles, the runic
passages in the other three poems, and several 15–20 line
samples chosen at random from the other three poems),
checked against the entire Anglo-Saxon poetical corpus,
shows 30.8 per cent of repeated verses, and 61.1 per cent
of verses, of which parts, by virtue of recurrence elsewhere,
demonstrate themselves to be formulaic.

22 For any comparative study of Old-Germanic formulaic diction
concordances are equally needed for the Old-Norse Edda-
type verse (Eddukvæði of Modern Icelandic parlance) and for
the Old-Saxon corpus (see n. 26, below).

Efficient techniques for concordance-making have been worked out by Professor Emeritus Lane Cooper of Cornell University and are set forth in considerable detail in "The Making and the Use of a Verbal Concordance," Sewanee Review, XXVII (1919), 188–206, esp. pp. 191–195, reprinted in his Evolution and Repentance (Ithaca, N.Y., 1935), esp. pp. 24–33. See also his "Instructions for preparing the Slips," three pages, inserted in A Concordance to the Works of Horace (Washington, D.C., 1916). No concordance should ever be attempted without consulting these writings.

23 Mr Diamond further informs me that the four verse paragraphs which include the runic signatures (72 typographic lines in all), checked against the entire Anglo-Saxon poetical corpus, show 25.6 per cent of repeated verses and 52.7 per cent of verses, of which parts, by virtue of recurrence elsewhere, show themselves to be formulaic.

24 From Juliana 718b–722 it is clear that the poem was intended for recitation (þe þis giedd wrece) and that a prayer was hoped for from a singer rather than some indefinite reading public. Does this suggest that Anglo-Saxon poems got put on written record primarily for memorization by a class of later, memorizing entertainers, answering somewhat to the Greek rhapsodes of post-oral times? One thinks here of Asser's familiar ch. 23 (ed. W. H. Stevenson, p. 20, notes on p. 221) where we are told that Alfred learned by heart native poems read aloud to him by his mother.

25 On oral-formulaic verse-making by lettered persons see Parry II, 29, and Bowra, op. cit., esp. pp. 370–372.

26 E.g., Klaeber, ed. cit., pp. cx–cxiii. For a competent survey of thought on "the testimony of the parallels" see Claes Schaar, Critical Studies in the Cynewulf Group, Lund Studies in English, XVII (Lund, 1949), pp. 235 ff. Over sixty years ago J. Kail, "Über die Parallelstellen in der angelsächsischen Poesie," Anglia, XII (1889–90), 21–40, was clearly nearer right than he lived to know. In the case of Old-Saxon poetry a start was made by Eduard Sievers in his ed. of the Hêliand (Halle, 1878) through his very comprehensive though inconveniently arranged "Formelverzeichnis," pp. 391–463, a reference for which I am most grateful to Professor Fernand Mossé of the Collège de France.

27 Parry II, 13.

28 Parry I, 84–85, n. 3, would for Homeric verse regard as
a formula or a possible formula nothing less than four words
or five syllables, a restriction that could not be applied to
Anglo-Saxon verse.

29 I am thinking of such small points as the þe of the formula
þe hit riht ne wæs (Mal 190) contrasted to the swá's of the
parallel formula in Gen 901, Vainglory 61, with gerisne
(Gen 1564), gedéfe (PPs 105, 22; Met 26, 90), geþiewe (Bwf
2331), references for which I am grateful to Dr Randolph
Quirk of University College, London. Without the negative
cp. Bwf 561, 1670 (with gedéfe).

30 For a somewhat analogous phenomenon see Parry II, 10,
30–31, and idem, "Traces of the Digamma in Ionic and Les-
bian Greek," Language, X (1934), 130–144, esp. p. 131 and
n. 6, for reference to Béowulf. See also Whitelock, op. cit.,
p. 27 and n. 1, for general observations on intervocalic h
and for references. Since the formulas in which contracted
forms occur are, like the rest of the diction, traditional,
their occurrence can tell us little about the age of a text in
which they appear.
    In his splendid and welcome edition Béowulf with the
Finnesburg Fragment (Boston, 1953) Professor C. L. Wrenn
has taken the revolutionary step of decontracting the various
contracted forms over which previous editors have placed a
circumflex (see pp. 31–32), e.g., fré⌈ge⌋a (16b) for manuscript fréa, dó⌈a⌋n (1116b) for manuscript dón. Were there
any evidence that such words (discussed in Luick, §§242–
249, pp. 218–226) were pronounced as if uncontracted at the
time when the text was first committed to writing, one would
welcome such a procedure, however daring, as restoring the
meter of otherwise metrically deficient verses (for literature
see Luick §242, nn. 2–3, p. 219). But the phenomena of contraction had almost surely quite run their course by, say, 650.
(See Luick, §249, pp. 225–226: after the working of i-umlaut;
for a few exceptional survivals of sorts see Sievers-Brunner,
2d ed., §218, 3, p. 197; Northumbrian dóan's and the like are
late and are analogical restorations comparable to Modern Icelandic smáum for smám of the old language and do not help here

350

31 See Parry II, 22–23, n. 1, for instances in Homeric verse where the retention of a formula leads to a violation of meter.

32 Parry, "Whole Formulaic Verses in Greek and Southslavic Heroic Song," Transactions of the American Philological Association, LXIV (1933), 179–197.

33 See Lord, "Homer and Huso III: Enjambement in Greek and Southslavic Song," ibid., LXXXIX (1948), 113–124.

34 Op. cit., p. 10. This formula is a phase of the system x éaðe mæg; cp. B 2764 sinc éaðe mæg. There are other systems with forms of magan to express the idea of the possibility of something happening or being done.

35 An impetus to a revaluation of the expanded verses has recently been given by Benno J. Timmer, "Expanded Lines in Old-English Poetry," Neophilologus, XXXV (1951), 226–230.

THE FORMULAIC EXPRESSION OF THE THEME OF "EXILE" IN ANGLO-SAXON POETRY

Stanley B. Greenfield

The study of the conventional qualities of Anglo-Saxon poetic diction has received a much-needed stimulus in Francis P. Magoun, Jr.'s "Oral-Formulaic Character in Anglo-Saxon Narrative Poetry."[1] In this article, Mr. Magoun examines the first twenty-five lines of Béowulf and twenty-four lines (512–535) of Christ and Satan for words and phrases which, by virtue of their repetition in the same grammatical-metrical patterns in the same or other poems, may be termed formulas. The large percentage of such expressions in these lines suggests that a good part of Old English narrative poetry is traditional and formulaic in nature, and hence of oral rather than lettered composition. Of the many provocative considerations this analysis leads to, I should like to quote the following:

> A different view will, I think, have to be taken of
> the significance or lack of significance of phrasal
> similarities between this and that poem and poems
> than has prevailed up to now. Certain verbal simi-
> larities among poems may in a sense represent
> borrowing from one poem to another, for traditional
> singers perforce learn from other singers. But one
> verbal similarity or even a number of verbal simi-
> larities in themselves prove nothing beyond suggest-
> ing that given singers have found the same formulas
> useful to express a certain idea in a similar measure
> of verse. . . . When by the aid of a concordance we
> gradually get to know what the Anglo-Saxon formulas
> are and what, indeed, constitute their dimensions and

Reprinted from Speculum, Vol. 30 (1955), pp. 200–6, by permission of the author and the publisher.

the like, it will perhaps be possible to begin to detect
individual styles. Apart from general over-all organization of material, the broad architectonics of a given
poem, a singer's individuality will, as in other traditional poetry, presumably emerge in rather small
matters, verbal and stylistic, and will not be revealed
by the large and rather obvious components known to
all or almost all singers.[2]

The concordance Mr. Magoun desires is not, alas, yet with
us, but further exploration of the formulaic dimensions of Old
English poetry is still possible. In particular, it is feasible to
investigate verbal formulas by analyzing the poetic expression
of certain themes of Old English thought, rather than a given
number of lines.[3] By the use of such an approach, I wish in the
following pages to establish the dimensions of the poetic convention for the theme of "exile," as a further contribution to the
study of convention and originality in Anglo-Saxon poetry.

To begin, we may look at several typical exile "images."[4]

A. 1. þá ić mé féran gewát   folgaþ sécan,
    winĕléas wrećća.   [WLa 9–10a]
  2.   Him þá Cain gewát
    gangan geómor-mód,   Gode of gesihþe,
    winĕléas wrećća.   [Gen 1049b–51a]
B. 1. Wæs á blíðe-mód   bealuléas cyning,
    þéah hé lange ǽr,   lande beréafod,
    wunode wræc-lástum   wíde geond eorðan. [Edw 15–17]
  2. For-þon ić sceal héan and earm hweorfan þý wídor,
    wadan wræc-lástas,   wuldra benœmed,
    duguðum bedǽled.   [XSt 119–121a]
  3. hú ić earm-ćearig   ís-ćealdne sæ
    winter wunode   wreććan lástum,
    wine-mágum bedroren.   [Sea 14–16]
C. 1.   ić sceal feorr þanan
    héan-mód hweorfan,   hróðra bedǽled. [Jul 389b–390]
  2.   Hé sceal héan þanan
    geómor hweorfan.   [Glc 1353b–54a]
  3.   þæt ić feorr hinan
    ell-þéodigra   eard geséće.   [Sea 37b–38]

4.   Íc sceal feorr hinan,
    án' elles forþ,   eardes néosan,
    síþ asettan.   [FAp 109b–111a]

Despite the fact that the exile figures are so different in kind
and character (I shall return to this point later)—a woman, Cain,
an historical king, Satan, a seafarer, a devil, a lordless thane,
a peregrinus,[5] a traveller to the unknown bourne—the expressions of their plights are clearly cast in similar molds. The
patterns in each of the above groups (A, B, and C) are quite distinct; yet there are noticeable overlappings between the groups.
Analysis of these images reveals that the Anglo-Saxon singer was
concerned primarily with four aspects or concomitants of the
exile state:

1. status (e.g., wineléas wrecca, A1 and A2)
2. deprivation (e.g., lande beréafod, B1; hróðra bedæled,
   C1)
3. state of mind (e.g., héan and earm, B2; héan-mód, C1)
4. movement in or into exile (e.g., wunode wræc-lástum,
   B1).

Not that other aspects of this unhappy condition were neglected
by the poets; there are, for example, formulas for the lamentation of the victim (one may compare the opening lines of The
Seafarer and The Wife's Lament). But the four features I have
named seem to have received the greatest emphasis in Old English exile images. They will, therefore, be the proper subject
of this paper.

STATUS

The key phrases designating the status of excommunication
are wineléas wrecca, an A-verse, and earm án-haga, a D-verse.
The former may be seen in WLa 10a, Res 91a, Gen 1051a; the
latter in Wan 40a, Max II 19a (of the wolf), Bwf 2368a (on Béowulf
as the lone survivor of Hygelac's Frankish raid). When a singer
wished to use the A-verse formula in the second half of a line,
he could substitute such words as guma (Wan 45b) and hæle (FoM
32b) for wrecca and thus avoid alliteration in the off-verse. In
the on-verse, on the other hand, he could alter the alliterating

modifier to fit the more specific nature of certain exiles: e.g., wundorlíc wrecċa (Dan 633a, of Nebuchadnezzar) and wérigum wreċċan (Chr 264a, of the wretched sinners, exiles from Heaven, awaiting Advent).

Án-haga is used with greater freedom in exile contexts. In addition to the distinctive D-verse formula, we find such verses as Oft him án-haga (Wan 1a), where the accompanying adjective has been omitted (though it appears in line 2b as mód-ċearig), and Ne mæg þæs án-haga (Res 89b)—here a B-verse—with earm transferred to the first verse of the line and used in conjunction with the idea of expulsion.

DEPRIVATION

The chief formula for the exile's deprivations is an A-verse consisting of the instr. or gen., sg. or pl., of the "property" removed together with the pp. of a verb of deprivation. The properties range from the physical ones of gold and land to abstract concepts of comforts and joys. In order of their frequency, the verbs employed are: bedǽlan, bescierian, beréafian, bedréosan, benǽman. The following list will amply demonstrate the richness and pervasiveness of this aspect of exilic imagery:[6]

cnosle bedǽled—Wid 52b—(of a wandering scop)
dréame bedǽled—Bwf 1275a—(of Grendel)
duguðum bedǽled—Gen 930a, XSt 121a—(of Adam, Satan)
eallum bedǽled / duguðum and dréamum—Chr 1407b–
    08a—(of sinners)
éðle bedǽled—Wan 20b—(of a lordless thane)
éðle bescierede—Chr 32b—(of mankind through Adam
    and Eve)
eorlum bedroren—Gen 2099a—(of the King of Sodom)
góda bedǽled—XSt 185a—(of Satan)
golde beréafod—Bwf 3018b—(of a captured maiden)
háma beréafod—Edg 28b—(of the earl Óslác)
hróðra bedǽled—Jul 390b—(of a devil)
lande beréafod—Edw 16b—(of King Edward)
wuldre benǿmed—XSt 120b—(of Satan)
wuldres bescierede, / dréamum bedǽlde—XSt 342b–
    343a—(of God's adversaries).

Identical with the above pattern, save that it is an E- rather than an A-verse, is the wine-mágum bedroren of Sea 16. For double alliteration in the first half of a line, with the "property" fréo-mæg, the adverb feorr is sometimes substituted for the pp. of the verb, making an E-verse, as in Wan 21a and Wid 53a. In Res 90a the adjective léas is substituted in the phrase léod-wynna léas. In Gen 2481a the adjective féascæft occurs in the phrase fréonda féascæft, here an A-verse, as in the main deprivative formula.

The suffix -léas occurs in combination with wine-, ár-, and hám- in exilic contexts. It is part of the convention, but not a formula, since the words to which it attaches never constitute by themselves a verse of poetry. The compounds with -léas are used, however, in recognizable patterns with other features of exile: to complete the status formula wineléas wrecca, for instance.

STATE OF MIND

Expressions of the state of mind accompanying exile cannot so readily be isolated into verse-formulas. While indisputably part of the exile convention, the exile's state of mind rarely occurs as a verse by itself. Rather, it combines chiefly with "motion" in various formulas, and even when the word for "state of mind" is found occupying a verse, it must be considered in connection with the idea of motion expressed in a following verse. However, certain words may be noted as forming the nucleus of this feature of exile: héan, earm, geómor, compounds of these adjectives, and compounds of -cearig. The passages cited above as A2, B2, and B3, C1 and C2 reveal both the variety of ways in which they are employed as well as the conventionality of their employment.[7]

MOVEMENT IN OR INTO EXILE

The many facets of this aspect of the convention can conveniently be divided into five major categories: (1) a sense of direction away from the "homeland" or "beloved"; (2) departure (initiative movement); (3) turning (initiative-continuative movement); (4) endurance of hardships (continuative movement in exile); (5) seeking.[8] Sometimes these facets supplement one another, especially that of "seeking"; sometimes, with the exception of the first category, they stand alone.

The first verses of the images in Group C above (i.e., ic sceal feorr þanan[9]) demonstrate the formula for the sense of direction away from native land or lord, whether in a literal or figurative sense. In every instance this C-verse formula occurs in the second half-line and depends for the completion of its meaning upon some following verb of motion. It seems that the Anglo-Saxon singer had his choice of either the state-of-mind adjective héan or the adverb feorr, as the exigencies of alliteration demanded, and a choice of þanan or hinan, as the context required.

Departure or initiative movement into exile is expressed by a B- or C-verse formula utilizing the verb gewitan in the final or initial position, respectively. The two images in Group A above illustrate the former (found also in Bwf 1274b). Gewát him fréa léoda, Gen 2098b, illustrates the latter (cf., also, Dan 631a, Gen 1039b, and Phx 554b, the last instance, gewite héan þanan, offering a synthesis with the "direction" facet of movement).

Turning, that is, the sense of departure into and consequent movement in exile, is accounted for by an A-verse formula with the verb hweorfan. See, for example, C1 and C2, above. An adjective for the state of mind usually precedes the verb (cf. Glc 1379a, Jul 703b, and Gen 1018b), though Rid 39, describing the moon as a wandering exile, offers us hámléas instead (9a), and Chr 31 expands the formula into a full line: þá wé héanlíce hweorfan scoldan (cf., also, XSt 119, Group B).

The most colorful facet of the movement aspect is that which expresses the continuative motion of the exile in his state of excommunication. The words employed connote the endurance of hardships, the difficulties encountered in the exile-track.[10] Several formulas are involved, though they are really only variations on the basic A-verse formula "in the track(s) of an exile": wreccan láste (-um) (Gen 2823b, 2480b; Rid 39, 8b; Sea 15b). This phrase depends, of course, upon a verb in either a preceding or following verse. One variation on this formula combines the idea of the "track" and the verbal expression of movement into a D-verse: wadan wræc-lástas (XSt 120a, Wan 5a) or wadaþ wíd-lástas (And 677a), or tredan úrig-lást (FoM 29a); another, for the same combination, into an A-verse: wíd-lást wrecan

(Gen 1021a) and el-land tredan (Bwf 3019b), or an E-verse: wræc-lástas træd (Bwf 1352b). Still another variation emphasizes the "laying" of tracks and utilizes two verses—in one instance with an intervening half-line—to express the idea: sceal nú wræc-lástas / settan sorg-ćearig (XSt 187b–188a); þe þá wræc-lástas wídost lecgaþ (Sea 57); for-þon ić lástas sceal / . . . wíde lecgan (Gen 1026b–27b).

The final phase of the idea of motion to be considered, that of seeking, finds expression in an A-verse formula consisting of the object of search together with the verb of seeking, the latter usually in the infinitive form. C3 and C4 provide illustrations of this.[11] Usually this formula completes some other phase of movement in an exile image.

That the formulas and formulaic systems outlined in this paper do indeed constitute a poetic convention is attested not only by their overlapping use in different images but by the variety of exile figures which Anglo-Saxon poets clothed in their dress. Historical figures like Edward and Óslác, Biblical figures like Abraham on the one hand and Cain and Satan on the other, creatures of the Teutonic supernatural world like Grendel, the soul departing this earth, riddle figures like the moon, and sundry anonymous literal or allegorical exiles (those of the lyrics especially)—all of these are in part at least formulaically accoutered. Further evidence that the poets had at hand a useful convention is furnished by translations of Latin texts, where the Old English elaborates upon, or even adds, the concept of exile. For example, Phx 554–555a renders the word moriar (Job, xxix, 18), as (Ić) hæle hráw-wérig, gewíte héan þanan / on langne síþ. God's pronouncement of exile on Cain as a vagus et profugus becomes, in Gen 1018b ff.:

> þú scealt geómor hweorfan
> árléas of earde þínum . . . .
> for-þon þú flíema scealt
> wíd-lást wrecan, wine-mágum láþ.

Abraham, simply an advena in Genesis, xxi, 23, is addressed by Abimilech in the Old English:

> siþþan þú féascæft feorran cóme
> on þás wer-þéode wreććan láste. [Gen 2822–23]

And Lot is similarly exhorted in <u>Gen</u> 2480–82a, despite the fact that the corresponding Latin of Genesis, xix, 9, in no way envisages him in this manner.

The importance of ascertaining conventional patterns in Old English poetry lies, of course, in the basis such patterns establish for the further investigation of the aesthetic values of individual poems. Which leads us back to the conclusion of the quotation from Mr. Magoun's article.[12] Though such a study is not my present design, I should like to make a few suggestions in that direction.

A highly stylized poetry like Anglo-Saxon, with its many formulas and presumably many verbal conventions, has certain advantages in comparison with a less traditional type of poetry. The most notable advantage is that the very traditions it employs lend extra-emotional meaning to individual words and phrases. That is, the associations with other contexts using a similar formula will inevitably color a particular instance of a formula so that a whole host of overtones springs into action to support the aesthetic response. Thus, by use of the formula <u>dréame(-um)</u> <u>bedǽled</u> in <u>Bwf</u> 721a and 1275a, twice applied to Grendel, the <u>Béowulf</u> poet is able to suggest Grendel's kinship with all other exiles, especially with the devils, indicating the monster's deprivation of both human joys and eternal blessedness.[13] The chief disadvantage of a conventional poetry is that its very virtue, the extra-emotional meanings, may supplant the denotation that should inhere in a specific situation, and the words and phrases become "conventional" in the pejorative sense of the word. For example, in the <u>Chronicle</u> elegy on <u>The Death of Edward</u>, the image of Edward as an exile (B1 above) seems to lack specificity of meaning; the pleasurable recognition it gives is chiefly that of its general exilic overtones. In the largest sense, therefore, originality in the handling of conventional formulas may be defined as the degree of tension achieved between the inherited body of meanings in which a particular formula participates and the specific meaning of that formula in its individual context.

We may turn briefly to some of the Old English lyrics, in which exile imagery plays such a large role. In addition to the more obvious differences in theme and structure between <u>The Wanderer</u>, <u>The Seafarer</u>, and <u>The Wife's Lament</u>, it is in the poems' specific development of the conventional imagery of exile that a large measure of their poetic individuality lies. <u>The Wanderer</u> begins with a general or impersonal image of an <u>án-haga</u>:

> Oft him án-haga   áre gebídeþ,
> Metodes miltse,   þéah-þe hé mód-ćearig
> geond lagu-láde   lange scolde
> hréran mid handum   hrím-ćealde sǽ,
> wadan wræc-lástas.

In the eard-stapa's recital, in the following lines, other conventional formulas are employed, specifying the speaker's personal position:

> oft earm-ćearig,   éðle bedǽled,
> fréo-mágum feorr   . . . .
> . . . . . .   and ić héan þanan
> wód winter-ćearig   ofer waðuma gebind,
> sóhte sele dréorig   sinces bryttan.   [20–25]

We have here almost every concomitant of exile. While there is no mere repetition, still the phrases reflect the features of the opening án-haga image. Notice especially the mód-ćearig, earm-ćearig, winter-ćearig sequence. It is perhaps no accident of textual transmission that the last of these words is a hapax legomenon. It catches up both the ideas of "state of mind" and the hrím-ćealde sǽ. Further, when the speaker resorts to an impersonal image to emphasize his own previous predicament, he returns to the status formula of the opening image (earmne án-hagan, 40a and winéléas guma, 45b).

A quite different effect is secured in The Seafarer, where the exile imagery underlines the ambivalence of attitude of the prospective peregrinus.[14] In describing his past experiences, so depressing in nature, the speaker formulates his ideas thus:

> hú ić earm-ćearig   ís-ćealdne sǽ
> winter wunode   wreććan lástum,
> wine-mágum bedroren.   [14–16]

To express his newly-resolved desire to seek exile, he uses a different set of formulas:

>   þæt ić feorr hinan
> ell-þéodigra   eard geséće.   [37b–38a]

But then, to express the doubts he still entertains about his projected voyage, he returns to a variation of his first formulaic group, saying that those people know the miseries an exile must endure, those þe þá wræc-lástas wídost lecgaþ (57).

In recent articles, I have endeavored to show how the imagery of exile in The Wife's Lament and Christ I has been individually developed in those poems for thematic and structural purposes, and I shall not repeat that material here.[15] It has been my chief concern in this essay to extend Mr. Magoun's investigations into the subject of conventionality in Old English poetry, with the hope that still further studies will blossom forth and enlarge our understanding and appreciation of the aesthetic values of that poetry.

NOTES

1 Speculum, XXVIII (1953), 446–467.

2 Ibid., pp. 460–461.

3 Albert B. Lord, in discussing Homer and oral poetry, defines theme as ". . . a subject unit, a group of ideas, regularly employed by a singer, not merely in any given poem, but in the poetry as a whole." He goes on to say, ". . . the themes in the repertory of any singer tend to become more or less fixed in content in proportion to the frequency of their use, although they never reach the rigidity of any written document. . . . The theme comes to be a unit unto itself, and habit tends to preserve this unity which it has itself built up over a long period." "Homer and Huso II: Narrative Inconsistencies in Homer and Oral Poetry," Transactions and Proceedings of the American Philological Association, LXIX (1938), 440–441. It is in this sense that I employ the word theme in this paper.

4 Quotations and line references throughout this paper are from The Anglo-Saxon Poetic Records, edd. Krapp and Dobbie (New York, 1931–53). Spelling has been normalized, however, on the basis of classical West Saxon and quantity marks have been added.

5 The seafarer and the peregrinus are, of course, the same man, but in different capacities. See note 14.

6   The deprivative formula does occur in other than exile con-
    texts, but its chief use is in the exile convention. It might
    be well to point out here that theme and formula do not nec-
    essarily coincide. Cf. Albert B. Lord, "Composition by
    Theme in Homer and Southslavic Epos," Transactions of
    the American Philological Association, LXXXII (1951), 71–
    80. I am indebted to Mr. Magoun for calling the two articles
    by Mr. Lord (see note 3) to my attention.

7   Cf., also Bwf 3018a, 2368a, 1274b, 1351b; Gen 1018b; Dan
    631a; XSt 188a; And 406a; Chr 31a, 1406a; Glc 1379a; Phx
    554b; Jul 703b; Wan 2b, 20a, 24a, 40a; Max II 19a.

8   Such facets as expulsion and yielding have been omitted.

9   Cf. Phx 415b; Wan 23b.

10 Cf. Bertil Weman, Old English Semantic Analysis and Theory
    (Lund, 1933), p. 121.

11 Cf. Phx 416b; W La 9b; Bwf 1275b; Gen 2099b.

12 See above, pp. 352–353.

13 Cf. Marie P. Hamilton, "The Religious Principle in Beowulf,"
    PMLA, LXI (1946), 320.

14 See my article, "Attitudes and Values in The Seafarer," SP,
    LI (1954), 15–20.

15 "The Wife's Lament Reconsidered," PMLA, LXVIII (1953),
    907–912; "The Theme of Spiritual Exile in Christ I," PQ,
    XXXII (1953), 321–328.

THE MAKING OF AN ANGLO-SAXON POEM

Robert P. Creed

I

The diction of <u>Beowulf</u> is schematized to an extraordinary degree.[1] Roughly every fifth verse is repeated intact at least once elsewhere in the poem. An essential part of about every second verse—such a part as a whole measure, or a phrase which straddles both measures, or one which encloses the two measures of the verse—is repeated elsewhere in the poem. Many of these verses or essential parts of verses bear such a resemblance to certain others as to suggest that the singer "knew them"—in the late Milman Parry's words—"not only as single formulas, but also as formulas of a certain type."[2] In composing a line containing any one of these verses, therefore, he was guided by the rhythm, sound, and sense of other verses belonging to this type or "system."[3]

The degree of the schematization of his diction suggests that the singer of <u>Beowulf</u> did not need to pause in his reciting or writing to consider what word to put next. His diction was one which, in Goethe's words, did his thinking and his poetizing for him, at least when he had completely mastered that diction and its ways. Precisely <u>how</u> that diction might have done his poetizing for the Anglo-Saxon singer is the subject of the present paper.

I cannot attempt to deal in so brief a study with the way in which the singer puts together the larger elements of his poem. I shall therefore take only a very small portion of <u>Beowulf</u>, eight verses (four lines), and attempt, by means of references to similar verses and lines in the rest of the poem and in other surviving Anglo-Saxon poems, to illustrate the thesis that the making

Reprinted from English Literary History, Vol. 26 (1959), pp. 445–54, by permission of the author and the publisher.

of any Anglo-Saxon poem was a process of choosing rapidly and largely on the basis of alliterative needs not between individual words but between formulas.

A formula may be as large as those whole verses repeated intact to which I referred earlier, or even larger. There are whole lines and even lines-and-a-half repeated within Beowulf. At the other extreme a formula may be as small as those tri-syllabic prepositional phrases which end certain A-verses, or even as small as a single monosyllabic adverb, if the adverb makes the whole spoken portion[4] of the measures and thus makes it possible for the singer to compose rapidly.

This last fact is important. The essential quality of the formula is not its memorable sound—although some formulas are, even for us, memorable—but its usefulness to the singer. To be useful to a singer as he composes rapidly a phrase or word must suggest to him that it belongs at only one point, or possibly only two points, in his verse or line; that is, it must be a significant segment of his rhythm. To be useful to the singer every phrase or word which is metrically significant should also be a syntactic entity, that is, if it is not a polysyllable which by itself makes a whole verse or whole "crowded" measure, it should at least be a phrasal group or a clause. It should be, for example, an article and its noun, or a noun or pronoun and its verb, or a verb and its object, or a preposition and its noun, not such syntactically meaningless groups as, for example, an adverb and a preposition.

The formula in Anglo-Saxon poetry is, then, to paraphrase and somewhat emend Milman Parry's definition of the formula in Homer, a word or group of words regularly employed under certain strictly determined metrical conditions to express a given essential idea.[5]

In a formulaic or traditional poem we are frequently able, because of this schematization of the diction, not only to examine the formula which the singer chose, but also to guess at with some measure of assurance, and to examine, the system or en-tire group of formulas from among which he chose at a given point in his poem. When we have studied his tradition with care we are able to appreciate his poetry in a unique way, because we can perform in slow motion the very process which he of necessity performed rapidly: we can unmake, and make in new fashion, each line according to the rules of the game, and thus

approximate what the singer himself might have done in a different performance of the same tale.

II

At line 356 of his poem the singer has got Beowulf safely
across the sea from Geatland to Denmark, and has placed him
outside the hall Heorot. Wulfgar, Hrothgar's herald, has just
learned from Beowulf who he is and what his mission is at
Hrothgar's court.

> Hwearf þá hrædlíce   þǽr Hróþ-gár sæt,
> eald and unhár,   mid his eorla ȝedryht;
> éode ellen-róf   þæt hé for eaxlum ȝestód
> Deniȝa fréan;   cúðe hé duguðe þéaw.[6]

Then he [that is, Wulfgar] turned quickly to where Hrothgar sat,
old and very hoary, with his troop of men; famous for his courage [he, Wulfgar] went until he stood before the shoulders of the
lord of the Danes; he knew the custom of the comitatus.

There are several different ways by which the singer could,
in good formulas, have got Wulfgar or anyone else from one
place to another. Not many lines before this passage the singer
has got Beowulf out of Geatland with the following verse: ȝewát
þá ofer wǽȝ-holm. At line 720 the singer will get Grendel to
Heorot with the following verse: cóm þá to recede. At line 1232
he will get Wealhtheow to her seat with éode þá to setle.
We can be sure that each one of the verb-adverb groups
(ȝewát þá, cóm þá, éode þá) which begins these lines is a formula
not only because it fits the conditions of usefulness and significance, but also because the singer has used each of these phrases
in this same position more than once.
But at our point in the story the singer chose to say hwearf
þá, like these other verb-adverb groups a demonstrable formula
since it appears at the beginning of lines 1188, 1210 and 1573.
We can find good reasons for his choice of hwearf þá in this
passage. Gewát þá suggests a journey longer than the length of
a hall, cóm þá suggests a new arrival rather than a return. The
singer might then have said éode þá as he will do at 1232 and
1626 (éodon . . . þá), or simply éode as he does at eight other

365

places in his poem. That he said hwearf þá here suggests that he had already thought ahead not only to the adverb with which hwearf incidentally alliterates, but to Hróþ-gár in the second verse of the line, which is the excuse for the adverb itself. The singer had no particular need to get Wulfgar from Beowulf to Hrothgar with haste; he did need to get him to Hrothgar with alliteration.[7]

In Beowulf 356, then, the singer has correctly established his alliterative bridge-head with hrædlíce for an assault on the second verse of the line. That verse, þær Hróþ-gár sæt, does not divide neatly into two formulas each of which makes a single measure as does 356a. Verse 356b belongs to a type the pattern of which can be expressed by þær x sæt, where x equals the subject of sæt. Eight hundred lines after this passage, at line 1190, the singer has composed another verse of this type, þær se góda sæt, in which the substitution for the sake of alliteration is perfectly straightforward. Just seventy lines before our passage, however, the singer has apparently used the same container, þær . . . sæt, with a different kind of alliterating content: þær on wicge sæt. Apparently the singer does not restrict himself to employing the same kind of substituting element within the framework of this simple substitution system. Or perhaps it would be more correct to say that he shows signs at such points as these of thinking in terms of two complementary types of formula which he can readily combine to make a single verse.

This verse, þær Hróþ-gár sæt, completes a line, and might, had the singer so chosen, have completed a thought. He does not so choose; he amplifies in the following line this brief mention of Hrothgar seated into a noble picture of the aged king surrounded by his retainers. But before we turn our attention to this picture in the next line of this passage, let us first observe how this line as a whole has helped to prepare the singer to make another whole line later in his poem.

Some eight hundred lines after this passage the singer moved Wealhtheow not into but across the hall with the following line: hwearf þá be bence / þær hire byre wæron . . . (1188). The design of this line is very similar to that of the one we have just studied. Both lines begin with the same formula; the second verse of both lines is enclosed by a similar phrase (þær . . . sæt, þær . . . wæron). The singer requires, however, a different alliteration in each line: he wishes to name Hrothgar in the first

and to refer to Wealhtheow's sons in the second, consequently
he uses a different second measure (hrædlíce, be bence). We
shall return to this later passage in a moment to indicate how
the earlier passage has influenced even further the construction
of the later.

To sum up my rather extensive remarks on this single line:
the singer appears to have composed his line of at least three
separate formulas, hwearf þá, hrædlíce, and þær x sæt. He
seems to have chosen the second formula, which carries the
important alliteration of the first verse, in order that he might
name Hrothgar in the second verse. He was, finally, guided in
the shaping of the line as a whole by the association in his mind
of these three formulas, as his later line 1188 seems to prove.

Line 357 presents fewer problems. The first verse, eald
and unhár, belongs to a type long recognized as a formula, the
so-called reim-formel. Formulas of this kind have sometimes
been regarded as a particularly characteristic kind of formula
in Anglo-Saxon poetry or elsewhere.[8] Such formulas are indeed distinctive and decidedly ornamental; in fact, so far as getting any real work done is concerned, they are more ornamental
than useful. For this very reason they can hardly claim to be
the type of formula par excellence.

In making this verse the singer was guided by its simple
and rather pleasing A-rhythm. At three other places in his
poem the singer was guided by the same play of sound and rhythm
to link eald with another alliterating word (eald and infród, 2449,
for example).

The vowel-alliteration of eald gets him easily to the second
verse of this line. Had he wished to name Hrothgar in the first
verse of this line, or, for any other reason to employ h-alliteration or even s-alliteration he would have been faced with no
problem in making the second half of the line. Mid his eorla
ʒedryht is an even better example than verse 356b of the simple
substitution system. For h-alliteration the singer replaces
eorla with hæleða, as he does at line 662; for s-alliteration he
replaces eorla with secga as he does in line 633 and 1672.

The noble picture is complete with this fourth verse; the
singer pauses momentarily, and editors punctuate accordingly.
If, during that pause, we turn again to that later picture of
Wealhtheow at which we have already glanced, we shall see
even further similarities between these two passages. Line 1188,

like 356, is followed by a reim-formula, Hrœþ-ríc and Hróþ-mund, in this case a reim-formula which, like 357a, amplifies the alliterating core of the previous verse. Again like 357a, and probably to some degree because of 357a, 1189a is followed by the mention of the troop of warriors, "sons of heroes," seated around the two princes: and hæleða bearn. But this later passage does not end with the fourth verse; hæleða bearn itself is amplified by the following verse, ȝeoguþ ætgædere. Thus the two passages are alike but not identical. We can only with increasing difficulty deny, however, that the rhythms and ideas which governed the making of the first passage played some part in the making of the second when we note that ȝeoguþ ætgædere is followed by the paradigm of 356b: þær se góda sæt. Se góda in verse 1190b refers not to Hrothgar but to Beowulf, whose name and whose location be þæm ȝebróðrum twæm completes in eight verses a reflection of the noble picture we have seen condensed into four.

But perhaps it is not quite correct to say that the earlier picture is yet complete, since, in verse 358a, the singer returns to the idea contained in the first measure of 356a. The singer has made the second measure of the later verse not out of a single adverb but a single substantive, ellen-róf. Eighteen lines before this he has made the entire second measure of a B-verse out of this word; twenty-eight hundred lines later in his poem he will again make ellen-róf the second measure of a D-verse.

But to stop with these observations of the other appearances of this compound as a compound is to ignore an important and interesting point of the singer's technique. That point may be expressed as a kind of rule-of-thumb which runs something like this: the first element of any compound noun or adjective will *again* more often than not exist for the sake of alliteration rather than for the sake of a more precise denotation. We can demonstrate the operation of this rule in the present case by noting that the singer has elsewhere combined hiȝe- with róf to mean something synonymous with ellen-róf but having a different alliteration and a different metrical value. He has also combined beadu-, brego-, gúþ-, heaðu- and siȝe- with this same adjective róf to obtain slightly different meanings and three more different alliterations.

Verse 358b, þæt hé for eaxlum ȝestód, appears to be made of two such complementary formulas as appear in 356b. The NB container, þæt hé . . . ȝestód, is made in the same fashion as the container of 356b. Again, the container does the real work of the verse, that is, it functions syntactically as a complete clause with its subject pronoun and verb. The easily replaceable contained element, for eaxlum, both carries the alliteration and delimits the action of the verb.

This verse might indeed be spoken of as a delimiting formula, or as a formula for indicating distance. Once the singer has learned to isolate the container from the alliterating content of the verse, as we have just done, he has learned a most useful technique. That the singer of Beowulf had so isolated the container is evident from the following verses in which he indicates, at various points in his poem, different distances travelled by inserting a different prepositional phrase into this same container:

> þæt hé on héorðe ȝestód (404)
> þæt hit on wealle ætstód (891)
> þæt hit on hafolan stód (2679)

Compare also

> þæt him on ealdre stód (1434)

The problem of indicating before whose shoulders it was that Wulfgar came to a stop caused the singer little difficulty. He knew several kinds of whole verse formulas for referring to Hrothgar. The most numerous group of these formulas, or, to express it properly, the most useful group, is the x Scieldinga group, to which belong wine Scieldinga, which he employs in the poem seven times, fréa Scieldinga, which he employs four times, helm (three times), eodor, léod, þéoden (each twice). This group alone provides him with six different alliterative possibilities.

But before speaking 359a, the singer must have thought ahead to the duguðe with its d-alliteration in 359b. Hence he provided himself here with a d-alliterating epithet, Deniga fréan, as he had done at line 271 and was to do at 1680.

359b, cúðe hé duguðe þéaw, has no very close analogues in Beowulf. If, however, we compare it with verse 1940b, ne biþ swelc cwénlíc þéaw, we can observe some similarity between the second measures of these two verses.

If the two second measures are derived from the same play of sounds and ideas, the two first measures which accompany them are not. Cúðe hé, which appears nowhere else in Beowulf, is quite unlike ne biþ swelć in 1940b, which appears again in line 2541. It has been suggested that, in such lightly stressed first measures as these, the singer has a kind of escape valve, or a measure into which he can cram, without worrying about alliteration, needed but metrically annoying words and phrases. Perhaps this is so, but it is also true that the singer composed many of these lightly stressed measures out of formulas.[9]

III

At the beginning of this paper I noted that we can both un-make and make again each of the singer's lines if we are care-ful to follow the same rules which seem to have guided the singer. It might be amusing, and perhaps even instructive then, for such a novice singer as I—who have, however ridiculous this idea seems, been training myself and the careful reader to be a singer, and in a way not unlike that by which the singer trained himself—to attempt to do just that: to remake this passage from Beowulf which we have just unmade, attempting to say as closely as pos-sible but with other formulas what the singer has said:

> Éode þá ofostlíće   þǽr se ealdor sǽt
> hár and hiȝe-fród   mid his hæleða ȝedryht;
> éode hilde-déor   þæt hé on héorðe ȝestód
> fréan Scieldinga;   cúðe hé þæs folces þéaw.

There is my poem. If you analyze it properly you will find every single formula elsewhere in Beowulf or in other poems in the Anglo-Saxon corpus, and used exactly as I have used it here. I must however claim credit for combining hár with hiȝe-fród and, I had thought, even for the manufacture of hiȝe-fród. I needed a reim-formula with h-alliteration and hit upon hiȝe-fród by following that rule-of-thumb I spoke of earlier. Only afterwards I discovered Genesis 1953, háliȝ and hiȝe-fród, along with mar-ginal notes indicating that I had been reading this portion of that poem not very long ago.

I don't like my poem nearly so much as I like the singer's.[10] Yet my poem is composed of the same formulas out of which this singer and other Anglo-Saxon singers of ability created their poems. The diction of my poem is schematized to no greater

370

degree than the diction of most other surviving old English poems. What my experiment helps to prove, then, is that the simple use of formulaic diction is no guarantee of aesthetic success. Conversely, the use of a formulaic diction does not make such success impossible. Beowulf, with its highly schematized diction yet continually marvelous subtlety, is sufficient proof to the contrary.

If my feeble attempt to compose formulaic poetry only serves to demonstrate once again the subtle art of the singer of Beowulf I shall be satisfied. I should be more than satisfied if the experiment should serve also to remind the reader that this subtle art is a traditional and formulaic art, and that it is possible to praise the four lines of Beowulf I have chosen to examine as, for their purposes, the best of all possible combinations of formulas.

NOTES

1 The evidence for this statement is contained in Appendix A, "Supporting Evidence," of my "Studies in the Technique of Composition of the Beowulf Poetry . . . ," Harvard University (unpublished doctoral dissertation), 1955, 200–385.

2 Milman Parry, "Studies in the Epic Technique of Oral Verse-Making. I. Homer and Homeric Style," Harvard Studies in Classical Philology, XLI (1930), 85.

3 Parry uses the term system to designate a group of formulas of similar construction (pp. 85–89). For a discussion of certain systems of formulas in Anglo-Saxon poetry, see Francis P. Magoun, Jr., "Oral-Formulaic Character of Anglo-Saxon Narrative Poetry," Speculum, XXVIII (1953), especially 450–453, and also my "The andswarode-System in Old English Poetry," Speculum, XXXII (1957), 523–528.

4 As opposed to that portion of the measure accounted for by a rest or harp-substitution. See John Collins Pope, The Rhythm of Beowulf (New Haven, 1942).

5 See Parry, p. 80.

6 Quotations from Beowulf and other Old English poems are cited in the normalized spelling proposed by Francis P.

Magoun, Jr., in "A Brief Plea for a Normalization of Old-English Poetical Texts," <u>Les Langues Modernes</u>, XLV (1951), 63–69, and adopted in Magoun's own classroom edition of the poem, <u>Beowulf and Judith, Done in a Normalized Orthography</u> . . .(Cambridge, Mass., 1959). [This edition is based primarily upon Charles Leslie Wrenn, <u>Beowulf with the Finnesburg Fragment</u>, London-Boston, 1953.]

7 Quite by accident the study of this passage (which, by the way, I chose at random) led me to what seems to be a rather dramatic demonstration of this principle. In my reflections on what the singer <u>might</u> have said here it seemed to me that, had he chosen not to mention but rather to allude to Hrothgar in his second verse, he might have substituted for Hróþ-gár a vowel-alliterating noun or phrase such as <u>se ealdor</u>. In consequence he would probably have substituted for hrædlíce the adverb ofostlíce in the second measure of the first verse. The point is that the singer is likely to have regarded such synonymous and metrically equivalent polysyllables as interchangeable. As a matter of fact the singer of <u>Beowulf</u> uses at line 3130 ofostlíc[e] exactly as he uses hrædlíce here, that is, as the second measure of a C-verse which begins the line: þæt híe ofostlíc[e] / út ȝeferedon / díere máðmas. . . . But another singer, the singer of <u>Genesis</u>, at one point in his poem appears to have supplied one of these two adverbs where he intended the other. In "Genesis 1316," <u>MLN</u>, LXXIII (1958), 321–325, I discuss this fascinating slip of the singer more fully. Had I not been, in effect, performing the part of the apprentice singer by seeking here for a different polysyllabic adverb than hrædlíce I should not have stumbled so soon across this slip, nor so quickly have grasped what I found in <u>Genesis</u> 1316.

8 Klaeber (Fr. Klaeber, <u>Beowulf</u> . . . , Third Ed. [Boston, 1950]) gives a prominent place to <u>reim</u>-formulas (which he more accurately but also more ponderously calls "copulative alliterative phrases") in his list of "formulas, set combinations of words, phrases of transition, and similar stereotyped elements" (lxvi). John S. P. Tatlock, in "Laȝamon's Poetic Style and Its Relations," in <u>The Manly Anniversary Studies in Language and Literature</u> (Chicago, 1923), 7,

calls attention to these formulas in Lawman: "One chief function of his shorter epic formulas was as expletives to fill in a half-line [a whole verse in Old English poetry] for which he had no matter, that he might not be obliged to introduce a new theme." (My italics.)

9 See my "Studies in . . . Beowulf" (note 1, above), Chapter VI, especially 90–94 and the chart which accompanies this chapter on 118–120.

10 A close comparison of my poem with the Beowulf singer's seems to me to show a sharp contrast between the ceremonial slowness with which the Anglo-Saxon gets Wulfgar in the D-verse éode ellen-róf before his lord and the rather discourteous bump with which in the B-verse éode hilde-déor I get him into the royal presence. Nor do I like for describing Hrothgar the jigging rhythm of my hár and hiʒe-fród so well as the singer's eald and unhár. My éode þá is also a vaguer introduction to the passage than the singer's more precise suggestion of Wulfgar's turning away from Beowulf in order to move towards Hrothgar in hwearf þá. But then this is where I've got by trying to be different from a great singer.

THEME AS ORNAMENT IN ANGLO-SAXON POETRY

Robert E. Diamond

It seems now to be generally agreed that Anglo-Saxon poetry
not only is different from modern poetry in verse form and subject matter but is an entirely different kind of poetry. The basic
study in the re-evaluation of Old English poetic technique is
Francis P. Magoun, Jr.'s "Oral-Formulaic Character of Anglo-
Saxon Narrative Poetry,"[1] which applies to Old English poetry
the discoveries of Milman Parry and Albert Lord about formulaic
diction in Homeric poetry and in the oral poetry of Jugoslavia.[2]
Subsequent studies which further explore formulaic diction in
Anglo-Saxon poetry are Magoun's "Bede's Story of Cædman: The
Case History of an Anglo-Saxon Oral Singer"[3] and an earlier
paper of my own, "The Diction of the Signed Poems of Cynewulf."[4]
These articles focus attention chiefly on the formula, which usually
occupies the space of one verse or one measure of a verse.
Professor Magoun also opened up the problem of the theme as a
larger formulaic unit in "The Theme of the Beasts of Battle in
Anglo-Saxon Poetry,"[5] suggesting that the theme is essentially
a convention, which the poet might call upon when he had a battle
to narrate. The wolf, eagle, and raven do not advance the action:
they are essentially ornament. It seems likely that such poets
depended less on what moderns usually think of as inspiration
than on a large stock of formulaic diction and of set pieces or
themes.

Stanley B. Greenfield has also dealt with this matter, refin-
ing analysis further by breaking a theme down into subthemes in
"The Formulaic Expression of the Theme of 'Exile' in Anglo-
Saxon Poetry."[6]

Magoun pointed out that a theme is looser and more flexible
than a formula, varying in length and combining formulaic ele-

Reprinted by permission of the Modern Language Association and the
author from PMLA, Vol. LXXVI (1961), pp. 461–8.

ments in a number of ways.[7] Another important aspect of the
use of the theme is that it may be introduced in a way that seems
to violate modern notions of verisimilitude or decorum. For example, the beasts of battle appear at the beginning of the Finnsburg fragment, although the fighting seems not to have started
yet, and although the battle takes place indoors. This seeming
lack of realism need not strike a jarring note. To say that the
battle birds are singing and that the wolf is howling is just another way of saying that there is a fight either going on or about
to begin. It is a kind of poetic cliché. (It must be borne in mind
that the term "cliché" is not a pejorative one in discussing oral-
formulaic poetry, as it would be in discussing the work of, say,
Tennyson.) It seems likely that much of our misunderstanding
of Old English poetry has been our failure to see that it is different in kind from modern literature. Although inevitably we
see the art of a vanished age through modern eyes, we can make
an effort to discover the conditions of composition of the poetry
of a defunct tradition and to work out the details of how the poets
put their poems together. We are only now on the threshold of a
more scientifically analytical and objective approach to the Anglo-
Saxon poetic tradition. In trying to think our way back into the
minds of these poets, we will surely find that an analysis of the
use of themes is revealing.

In Cynewulf's Elene, the main business of the poem deals
with Constantine's vision on the eve of battle and St. Helena's
Invention of the True Cross. As might be expected, the poet
uses many formulas that appear in other Christian contexts.
But embedded in the poem are two themes that stand out as perfect examples of set pieces. One of these is the theme of battle,
and with it the associated subtheme of the beasts of battle. Although it might be argued that the battle is structurally necessary
in the story of Constantine, it seems clear that the poet has
handled the battle in a manner much more expanded than the
essential story demands. In lines 18b–34, war is declared. Included in this passage is the first of the beasts-of-battle subthemes that Magoun has pointed out (27b–30), although no fighting has yet taken place. In lines 35–42a, the enemy approaches.
In lines 42b–56a, the Roman army advances. In this passage
there is another appearance of the subtheme of the beasts of battle
that can be added to Magoun's catalogue: Hrefen uppe gol, / wan
ond wælfel (52b–53a). Lines 65b–68a are devoted to the encamp-

ment before battle. In lines 105–108, the command to begin the battle is given. The battle itself occurs in lines 109b–143. It is a very fine passage, directly in the Germanic battle tradition. It is detailed, but the details are not the details of Constantine's campaign, but the details that come into any Anglo-Saxon battle poem, including a third appearance of the beasts of battle, as Magoun has indicated (110–114a). It is followed by a short transitional passage which might perhaps be labeled the return from battle (148–152). The battle scene is heavily formulaic. Checking every verse against the entire corpus of Anglo-Saxon poetry reveals that 22 of the 69 verses (or 31.8 percent) are repeated elsewhere, and at least part of another 27 verses is formulaic, i.e., 49 of the 69 verses (or 71 percent) are demonstrably formulaic. It seems clear that although the subthemes of approach, encampment, etc., that surround the central battle passage (themes that might properly be called war themes, as distinct from battle themes) may have some parallel to the story of Constantine, the battle itself is a purely formulaic set piece, an excellent example of a theme. It is reproduced here with the formulas underlined, broken lines used for substitution within formulaic systems. The supporting evidence is assembled from the entire corpus of Old English poetry. All references are to the six-volume Anglo-Saxon Poetic Records, edd. G. P. Krapp and E. V. K. Dobbie (New York, 1931–53). The abbreviations for the titles of poems are those suggested by Magoun in Études Anglaises, VIII (1955), 138–146.

(1)

Formulas in theme

Elene 109b–143

Byman sungon

110 hlude for hergum. Hrefn weorces gefeah,
   urigfeðra, earn sið beheold,
   wælhreowra wig. Wulf sang ahof,
   holtes gehleða. Hildegesa stod.
   þær wæs borda gebrec ond beorna geþrec,
115 heard handgeswing ond herga gring,
   syððan heo earhfære ærest metton.
   On þæt fæge folc flana scuras,
   garas ofer geolorand on gramra gemang,
   hetend heorugrimme, hildenædran,
120 þurh fingra geweald forð onsendan.

Stopon stiðhidige,   stundum wræcon,
bræcon bordhreðan,   bil in dufan,
þrungon þræchearde.   þa wæs þuf hafen,
segn for sweotum,   sigeleoð galen.
125 Gylden grima,   garas lixtan
on herefelda.   Hæðene crungon,
feollon friðelease.   Flugon instæpes
Huna leode,   swa þæt halige treo
aræran heht   Romwara cyning,
130 heaðofremmende.   Wurdon heardingas
wide towrecene.   Sume wig fornam.
Sume unsofte   aldor generedon
on þam heresiðe.   Sume healfcwice
flugon on fæsten   ond feore burgon
135 æfter stanclifum,   stede weardedon
ymb Danubie.   Sume drenc fornam
on lagostreame   lifes æt ende.
Ða wæs modigra   mægen on luste,
ehton elþeoda   oð þæt æfen forð
140 fram dæges orde.   Daroðæsc flugon,
hildenædran.   Heap wæs gescyrded,
laðra lindwered.   Lythwon becwom
Huna herges   ham eft þanon.

Supporting Evidence

109b Exo 159, Dan 192.

110a Ele 406. Cp. Ele 180 ahangen for hergum; Exo 276 Hof ða for hergum; M Bo 26.57 haten for herigum.

110b Cp. DHl 88 Bona weorces gefeah; Bwf 1569 secg weorce gefeh; Bwf 2298 hwæðre wiges gefeh; Ele 247 cwen siðes gefeah.

111a Ele 29 Urigfeðera / earn sang ahof; Jud 210, Sfr 25. Cp. Gen 1984 deawigfeðera; Exo 163 deawigfeðere.

111b Cp. Ele 243 se ðone sið beheold; Phx 90, 114 sið behealdan.

112a Cp. Bwf 629 wælreow wiga.

112b Cp. Ele 29 earn sang ahof; Ele 867, Wds 104, Chr 502 sang ahofon.

113a Cp. Ridl 93.29 wulfes gehleþan.

113b Cp. And 375 Wæteregsa stod.

114a Cp. Mld 295 Ða wearð borda gebræc; Bwf 2259 ofer borda gebræc.

114b Cp. Rdl 35.6 ne þurh þreata geþræcu.

116a Ele 44 under earhfære; And 1048 mid earhfare; Jln 404 þurh eargfare; SnS 129 atole earhfare; Chr 762 eglum earhfarum.

117a Gen 1382 on fæge folc.

117b Jud 221.

118b Cp. Ele 108 on feonda gemang; Jud 193 in sceaðena gemong; Jud 303 þurh laðra gemong; Jud 225 in heardra gemang; Ele 96, Jln 420 on clænra gemang.

119a And 31.

119b Ele 141, Jud 222.

120a Bwf 764 wiste his fingra geweald.

120b Bwf 45. Chr 764 forð onsendeð; And 1506 forð onsende; Bwf 2266 forð onsended.

121b Ele 232.

123b þa wæs is a widespread introduction to C-, B-, and A3-verses. For other C-verses, cp. Ele 138, 229, And 40, 122, 230, 892, 1097, 1116, 1155, 1302, 1394, 1584, Gen 1967. For B-verses, cp. Ele 7, 212, 839, 1131, Jln 140, Chr 527, 550, 738, Bwf 642, 980, 1008, 2580, And 147, 1201, 1274, Gen 78, 2791. For A3-verses, cp. Ele 1, 144, 194, 282, 894, 967, 1043, 1125, Jln 32, 38, 236, 267, 635, Bwf 1288, 1896, 1905, 2821, And 161, 981, 1643, Dan 345.

124a Exo 127 segn ofer sweoton.

124b And 1549 fusleoð golon; Chr 623 fusleoð galan; Exo 578 fyrdleoð golan; Bwf 786 gryreleoð galan; And 1127, 1342 hearmleoð galan; Bwf 2460 sorhleoð gæleð; DrR 67 (hypermetric) Ongunnon him þa sorhleoð galan.

12 b Ele 23. Cp. Exo 125 scyldas lixton; Exo 175 cumbol lixton; Ele 90 gimmas lixtan.

126a And 10, 18. Cp. Ele 269 ofer herefeldas.

126b Cp. Exo 482 fæge crungon; BrB 10 Hettend crungon; Rui 28 Betend crungon.

128a Ele 20. Cp., with substitution of Wedera, Bwf 225, 697, 1894, 2900, 3156; Denia, Bwf 389, 696, 1323, 1712, 2125; Geata, Bwf 205, 260, 362, 1213, 1856, 1930, 2318, 3137, 3178; Geotena, Bwf 443; Sweona, Bwf 2958, 3001.

128b Cp. Ele 107 ond þæt halige treo; Ele 429 hwær þæt halige trio; Ele 442 ymb þæt halige treo; Ele 840 þurh þæt halige treo; Ele 701 Ic þæt halige treo; XSt 415 on þam halgan treo.

129b Ele 62, MBo 9.3.

130a A formulaic system: with substitution of æ-, cp. Jln 648; god-, Bwf 299; man-, Jln 137, Ele 906, Chr 1436, Phx 6, PPs 140.6; naht-, PPs 58.2; riht-, Phx 632, Jln 8, Chr 1655; till-, Rdl 59.7; woh-, MBo 9.36.

130b Cp. Ele 25 þa wæron heardingas; Run 70 ðus heardingas.
131a Chr 258.

131b Wan 80. Cp. Ele 136 Sume drenc fornam; Bwf 1123 þara ðe þær guð fornam; Bwf 1205 hyne wyrd fornam; Bwf 1436 ðe hyne swylt fornam; Bwf 2119 sunu deað fornam; Bwf 2236 Ealle hie deað fornam; Bwf 2772 ac hyne ecg fornam.

132a Cp. Bwf 1655 Ic þæt unsofte / ealdre gedigde; Jud 228 wrehton unsofte.

132b Dan 258 aldre generede. Cp., with substitution, Gen 2526, Rdl 15.19 feorh generigan; Dan 233 (hypermetric) hwæðere heora feorh generede.

133a Cp. Rdl 29.4 of þam heresiþe; Exo 153 on ðam spildsiðe.

134a Mld 194 flugon on þæt fæsten / and hyra feore burgon. Cp. MBo 1.20 foron on ðæt fæsten.

134b Cp. And 1538 woldon feore beorgan; Bwf 1293 feore beorgan.

135a Cp. Bwf 2540 under stancleofu; PPs 135.17 He of stanclife; Phx 22 ne stanclifu.

135b A formulaic system: with substitution of eard, cp. And 176, 599, Chr 772, Jln 20, HbM 18, Pnt 11, PPs 95.12, 132.1; wic, Phx 448, Whl 26, Jln 92; reced, Bwf 1237; sæl, Bwf 2075.

136a Ele 37 on Danubie.

136b See 131b above.

137a Cp. Bwf 297 ofer lagustreamas; PPs 143.8 wið lagustreamum; Dan 387 þa ðe lagostreamas. A formulaic system: with substitution of ea-, cp. And 1261; eg-, Ele 241, Bwf 577; brim-, And 348, 903, Bwf 1910; mere-, Dan 502, Aza 126, Rdl 66.9, MBo 28.34; sæ-, PPs 79.11, 88.23, 92.6; wæter-, PPs 77.44.

137b Bwf 2823. Cp. Bwf 2790 ealdres æt ende. Cp. also Bwf 224 eoletes æt ende; Whl 15 sundes æt ende; Exo 128 landes æt ende; Chr 1029 eardes æt ende; Jud 272 (hypermetric) þa wæs hyra tires æt ende.

138a For the first measure, see 123b above. Cp. And 1571 þær wæs modigra / mægen forbeged; Ele 1293, And 395, Exo 101, 300 modigra mægen.

138b Cp. Ele 261 foron on luste; And 1140 morðres on luste; And 1573 flod wæs on luste; Whl 26 wedres on luste; And 1023 (hypermetric) Nu is þis folc on luste.

139a Jud 237.
139b Glc 1277 oþ æfen forð.
140a And 1535.
140b Cp. Rdl 3.56 stræle fleogan.
141a See 119b above.
142b Jud 310.
143b Ele 148.

There is another clear example of a theme passage in Cynewulf's Elene. When Constantine has ascertained that the mysterious sign is the cross of Christ, his mother sets out to find
the actual True Cross, holiest of relics. To get from where she
is to the Holy Land, she has to lead her followers over the sea.
(2) At this point, Cynewulf enters upon a thirty-one line passage of
conventionalized description of the voyage. He could just as
easily have devoted one or two lines to translating St. Helena
across the Mediterranean, but he chose to launch into a heavily
formulaic sea-voyaging passage. Again, the details are not the
details that a close knowledge of the actual events or of the legend
would call for. They are the same details that would be found in
any sea-voyaging passage in Anglo-Saxon poetry. We are, in
fact, dealing with a formulaic theme. Checking this passage reveals that 45 of the 62 verses (or 72.5 percent) are demonstrably
formulaic, including 20 whole-verse repeats (32.2 percent). The
old familiar kennings are brought out and used again. Since this
theme is native to the Germanic North, the ships are "ring-
prowed," without regard to the actual facts of Roman ship design.
Such facts have little to do with a poetic theme. It is as if the
poet turned it on, and the traditional formulas came tumbling
out, and then he turned it off, and St. Helena, having arrived in
the Holy Land, goes on about the chief business of the poem,
finding the True Cross. The passage is reproduced here.

Elene 225–255

225 Ongan þa ofstlice eorla mengu
  to flote fysan. Fearoðhengestas
  ymb geofenes stæð gearwe stodon,
  sælde sæmearas, sunde getenge.
  Ða wæs orcnæwe idese siðfæt,
230 siððan wæges helm werode gesohte.

þær wlanc manig   æt Wendelsæ
on stæðe stodon.   Stundum wræcon
ofer mearcpaðu,   mægen æfter oðrum,
ond þa gehlodon   hildesercum,
235 bordum ond ordum,   byrnwigendum,
werum ond wifum,   wæghengestas.
Leton þa ofer fifelwæg   famige scriðan
bronte brimþisan.   Bord oft onfeng
ofer earhgeblond   yða swengas;
240 sæ swinsade.   Ne hyrde ic sið ne ær
on egstreame   idese lædan,
on merestræte,   mægen fægerre.
þær meahte gesion,   se ðone sið beheold,
brecan ofer bæðweg,   brimwudu snyrgan
245 under swellingum,   sæmearh plegean,
wadan wægflotan.   Wigan wæron bliðe,
collenferhðe,   cwen siðes gefeah,
syþþan to hyðe   hringedstefnan
ofer lagofæsten   geliden hæfdon
250 on Creca land.   Ceolas leton
æt sæfearoðe,   sande bewrecene,
ald yðhofu,   oncrum fæste
on brime bidan   beorna geþinges,
hwonne heo sio guðcwen   gumena þreate
255 ofer eastwegas   eft gesohte.

Supporting Evidence

225a Glc 1201. Gen 1316 ongann ofostlice. Ongann þa is a
common introduction to B-, C-, and D-verses: for other C-
verses, cp. Ele 827, 900, Jln 270, 536, Glc 1001, Gen 2636, 2902,
DrR 27, Wds 9; B-verses, cp. Ele 198, 286, Glc 1145; D-verses,
cp. Ele 1147, And 1398.
225b Cp. Exo 334 manna menio; Dan 727 gumena mænigeo.
Cp. also XSt 110, 726 deofla menego; Glc 201 feonda mengu; Dan
5 wigena mænieo; SnS 397 cwicra manigo.
226a Cp. And 1698 Ongan hine þa fysan / ond to flote gyrwan.
Cp. also Mld 41 on flot feran.
226b A formulaic system: with substitution of brim-, cp.
And 513; mere-, M Bo 26.25; sæ-, And 488; sund-, Chr 852, 862;
wæg-, Ele 236.

227a Cp. Exo 581 on geofones staðe; Ele 60 ymb þæs wæteres stæð; And 852 on geofones stream; Ele 1200 ofer geofenes stream; Bwf 362 ofer geofenes begang; Phx 118 ofer geofones gong; Bwf 1394 ne on gyfenes grund.

227b Glc 724.

228a. Cp. Whl 15 setlaþ sæmearas; Exo 289 sælde sægrundas.

228b Cp. Ele 1113, Bwf 2758 grunde getenge; Rdl 6.3, 77.2, M Bo 31.7 eorðan getenge; Run 54 lyfte getenge.

229a For the first measure, see Ele 123b above. For the rest, cp. And 770b, of which the MS reading is þær orcnawe; but Krapp emends this verse to þær orcnawe wearð, which is not a particularly good reading from the point of view of scansion; Von der Warth emends it to þær wæs orcnawe, a much better reading.

230b Bwf 2346. Cp. also And 1121 corðre gesohton; Rdl 93.11 duguþe secan.

231a Cp. And 1085 þa wearð forht manig; Gen 1969 Sceolde forht monig; Chr 801 þær sceal forht manig. Cp. also, with a noun substituted, Bwf 399 ymb hine rinc manig; And 1116 þa wæs rinc manig; Deo 24 Sæt secg monig; And 1225 þær wæs sec[g] manig; Bwf 918 Eode scealc monig; Bwf 3077 Oft sceall eorl monig; Bwf 2762 þær wæs helm monig; Chr 1174 Ða wearð beam monig.

231b SnS 204, M Bo 26.31 on Wendelsæ.

232a Cp. Rdl 2.6 streamas staþu beatað, / stundum weorpaþ; M Bo 6.15 on staðu beateð; Mld 25 þa stod on stæðe.

232b Ele 121.

233a And 788. And 1061 be mearcpaðe.

233b Cp. Bwf 2908, Wds 12 eorl æfter oðrum; Wld I.5 secg æfter oðrum; XSt 26 an æfter oðrum; Phx 343 worn æfter oþrum; Rui 10 rice æfter oþrum; Rsg 31 lif æfter oþrum; Exo 347 þa þær folcmægen / for æfter oðrum.

235a And 1205 ordum and bordum. Cp. Ele 24 Wordum ond bordum.

235b Ele 224 byrnwiggendra. A formulaic system: with substitution of burg-, cp. Ele 34; lind-, Ele 270, Jud 42, M Bo 1.13; rand-, Jud 188, Exo 436; sweord-, Exo 260.

236a Ele 1221, Chr 101, Gen 1574. Bwf 993 wera ond wifa.

238b Cp. Mld 110 bord ord onfeng.

239a And 383, M Bo 8.30. Brb 26 ofer æra gebland.

239b Cp. Bwf 2386 sweordes swengum.

240a Cp. Rim 29 sweglrad swinsade; Wds 105 hleoþor swinsade; Bwf 611 hlyn swynsode; And 453 sæ sessade.

240b For the first measure, cp. Mnl 101 Ne hyrde ic guman a fyrn; Bwf 38 ne hyrde ic cymlicor; Bwf 1842 ne hyrde ic snotorlicor. For the second measure, cp. Chr 602 þe us sið ond ær; Gen 2935 þe he him sið and ær; Ele 974, Mnl 200 þara þe sið oððe ær; Jln 710 þe ic siþ oþþe ær. Cp. also, with the order reversed, Ele 572 ne ær ne sið; Jln 548 þæt ic ær ne sið; Ele 74 þonne he ær oððe sið; Chr 893 þara þe ær oþþe sið; Chr 1052 þæt hi ær oþþe sið; Rdl 60.8 æt ic æt oþþe sið; Glc 369 ær oþþe sið; Jln 496 þe ic ær ond siþ; Bwf 2500 þæt mec ær ond sið.

241a See Ele 137a above.

241b Gen 1774 idesa lædan. Cp. Gen 1720 idese brohte; Gen 1875 idese feredon.

242a A formulaic system: cp. And 311 on faroðstræte; And 898 þæt ðu on faroðstræte; Bwf 239 ofer lagustræte. Cp. also Jln 480, Gen 145 on mereflode.

243a A metrically defective verse. All the evidence indicates that the verse ought to read þær gesion meahte. Cp. Bwf 571, 1078, Glc 486 geseon meahte; Exo 83, And 1714 geseon meahton; Bwf 648 geseon ne meahton. Cp. also Bwf 961, 1998, DHl 43 geseon moste; Bwf 1628, 1875 geseon moston; Chr 1348 geseon mosten; M Bo 20.273 gesion moten.

243b See Ele 111b above.

244a And 223. And 513 brecað ofer bæðweg. For a formulaic system built of verb, preposition, and weg compound, cp. also HbM 42 faran on flotweg; Sfr 63 hweteð on hwælweg; Glc 257 fleoð on feorweg.

244b Cp. Glc 1332 Lagumearg snyrede.

246a A D-verse. For C-verses, cp. Bwf 1907 No þær wegflotan; And 487 hu ðu wægflotan.

246b Cp. Ele 96 Cyning wæs þy bliðra; Mld 146 Se eorl wæs þe bliþra.

247a Cp. Ele 848 collenferhðe. / Cwen weorces gefeah. Also Ele 378, Jud 134, And 349, Whl 17.

247b See Ele 110b above.

248a Cp. Chr 864 Utan us to þære hyðe; Glc 1333 gehlæsted to hyðe.

248b Bwf 1131. Bwf 32, 1897 hringedstefna.

249a Ele 1016, And 398, 825.

249b Jln 677, Chr 857. Mnl 28 geliden hæfde.

250a <u>Ele</u> 262, 998. Cp. <u>Bwf</u> 580 on Finna land.

251a Cp. <u>Rdl</u> 60.2 æt merefaroþe; <u>And</u> 289, 351 on merefaroðe.

251b Cp. <u>And</u> 269 wære bewrecene; <u>Chr</u> 831 wælmum bewrecene. See also <u>Ele</u> 131a above.

252 Cp. <u>Chr</u> 863 ealde yðmearas, / ancrum fæste.

254b <u>Ele</u> 1095. <u>Jud</u> 62 (hypermetric) galferhð gumena ðreate. For a formulaic system, with substitution of <u>beorna,</u> cp. <u>Ele</u> 872; <u>secga, Ele</u> 271, <u>And</u> 1636; <u>wigena, Ele</u> 217; <u>þegna, Ele</u> 151; <u>folca, Ele</u> 215; <u>sceaþena,</u> Jln 672, <u>Bwf</u> 4.

255a <u>Ele</u> 995. <u>Dan</u> 69 on eastwegas; <u>Phx</u> 113 on eastwegum. Cp. <u>Exo</u> 68 on norðwegas; <u>Exo</u> 155 of suðwegum; <u>PPs</u> 74.6 ne of westwegum. For a formulaic system of C-verses consisting of preposition plus further <u>weg</u>-compounds, cp., with substitution of eorþ-, <u>Ele</u> 735, 1014, <u>PPs</u> 71.11, 73.7, 91.8, 112.5, <u>Phx</u> 178, <u>DrR</u> 120; feor-, <u>Bwf</u> 37, <u>PPs</u> 67.26, <u>FtM</u> 27, <u>And</u> 928; <u>flod,</u> Sfr 52; <u>fold-,</u> <u>And</u> 206, <u>Glc</u> 1250, <u>Chr</u> 1529; <u>forþ-,</u> <u>Exo</u> 32, 350; <u>holm-,</u> <u>And</u> 382; <u>mold-,</u> <u>Ele</u> 467, <u>Jln</u> 334, <u>Glc</u> 1039; <u>wid-,</u> <u>Bwf</u> 840, 1704, <u>Chr</u> 482, <u>PPs</u> 105.36, 144.20.

255b <u>Chr</u> 626 eft gesecan; <u>XSt</u> 211 eft geseceð.

The theme of sea voyaging in <u>Beowulf</u> is introduced, as one might expect, at the points in the narrative where the poet has to move the hero from his homeland to Denmark and from Denmark back home. The voyage is announced (198b–200); the voyagers go to the shore (208–209); the ship is loaded and launched (210–216); 15 verses are devoted to the voyage itself (217–224a); the voyagers moor their ship and go ashore (224b–228). This passage describes Beowulf's journey to Denmark in the most general traditional terms. Of the 47 verses devoted to the voyage, 27 are demonstrably formulaic (57.4 percent), including 10 whole-verse repeats (20.8 percent). The return voyage also breaks down into subthemes: the ship is readied (1896–1903a); 18 verses are devoted to the voyage itself (1903b–1912a); the ship lands (1912b–1913); the harbor guard moors the ship (1914–1919). Of these 48 verses, 38 are demonstrably formulaic (79.1 percent), including 10 whole-verse repeats (20.8 percent). In the hero's long recapitulation of his Danish adventures (2000–2151), he passes over the voyages without a word. The poet was no doubt reluctant to turn the sea-voyaging theme back on, having turned it off only eighty lines before. Instead, the poet has his hero launch into the digression of the Heathobard feud, which

has not even happened at the time of Beowulf's triumphant return.

An interesting variation on the sea-voyaging theme is Cynewulf's use of it as a simile at the end of Christ II (850–863).
The poet compares the difficulties of the soul in traversing this
world to the difficulties encountered on a stormy voyage at sea;
the haven of safety at the end of the voyage is salvation. This
passage is also clearly a set piece, studded with traditional sea-
voyaging formulas. Of the 28 verses in the passage, 21 are
demonstrably formulaic (75 percent), including 12 whole-verse
repeats (42.8 percent). The passage is reproduced here.

Christ II 850–863

850   Nu is þon gelicost   swa we on laguflode
      ofer cald wæter   ceolum liðan
      geond sidne sæ,   sundhengestum
      flodwudu fergen.   Is þæt frecne stream
      yða ofermæta   þe we her on lacað
855   geond þas wacan woruld,   windge holmas
      ofer deop gelad.   Wæs se drohtað strong
      ærþon we to lande   geliden hæfdon
      ofer hreone hrycg.   þa us help bicwom,
      þæt us to hælo   hyþe gelædde,
860   godes gæstsunu,   ond us giefe sealde
      þæt we oncnawan magun   ofer ceoles bord
      hwær we sælan sceolon   sundhengestas,
      ealde yðmearas,   ancrum fæste.

Supporting Evidence

850a And 501, Phx 424 Is þon gelicost.

850b Cp. Gen 127 ofer laguflode; And 244 ofer lagoflodas;
Jln 480 on mereflode; Sfr 59 mid mereflode; PPs 62.3 and on
wæterflodum.

851a And 201, Mld 91. And 222 ond on cald wæter; And 253
on cald wæter. A formulaic system consisting of preposition,
adjective, wæter: with substitution of deop, cp. Brb 55, Bwf 509,
Gen 1331, 2876, SnS 225; heah, Gen 1451; brad, SnS 276; wid,
Bwf 2473.

851b And 256. M Bo 26.60 ceole liðan.

852a Cp. Phx 103 ofer sidne sæ; Bwf 507 on sidne sæ; PPs 145.5 and sidne sæ. Cp. also Chr 677 ofer sealtne sæ; M Bo 19.16 on sealtne sæ; PPs 76.16 on widne sæ.

852b See Ele 226b above.

853b Cp. Jln 481 under reone stream; And 1538 fleon fealone stream.

855a Cp. M Bo 8.41, 13.65 geond þas widan weoruld; M Bo 9.58 geond þas lænan worold.

855b Cp. Bwf 572, And 843 windige weallas; Bwf 1358 windige næssas.

856a And 190, Glc 1292.

856b And 313 Is se drohtað strang. Cp. Bwf 756 ne wæs his drohtoð þær.

857 Jln 677 ærþon hy to lande / geliden hæfdon. For other A-verses ending in the phrase to lande, cp. And 398, Bwf 1623, Run 47, Rdl 22.12, 33.2. For the off-verse, see also Ele 249b above.

858a Cp. Bwf 471 ofer wæteres hrycg; SnS 19 on wæteres hrigc.

859 Cp. PPs 106.29 And he hi on hælo / hyþe gelædde. Cp. also SnS 246 hælo hyðe: PPs 117.27 wis to hælu.

860 Chr 660. For the on-verse, also Ele 673. Cp. further Ele 182, Glc 357 ond him giefe sealde; Dan 199 ðe him gife sealde; Dan 420 hwa þa gyfe sealde.

861b Cp. Gen 1433 ofer nægledbord; Gen 1333, 1357 under earce bord; Gen 1481 under salwed bord.

862b See Ele 226b above.

863 Cp. Ele 252 ald yðhofu, / oncrum fæste.

There are a number of sententious passages of general wisdom throughout Anglo-Saxon poetry. Some of these take the form of lists of the various talents and fates which the Lord metes out to mankind. The theme of sea voyaging turns up briefly in two of these gnomic passages, one in Christ II (676b–678a) and one in The Gifts of Men (53b–57). These seem to be clear cases of a familiar theme introduced in telescoped form into a long catalogue of parallels. These two passages belong more specifically to the subtheme of the mariner, as distinct from the actual voyage theme. Again, the passages are formulaic in diction: of the 13 verses, 9 are demonstrably formulaic (69 percent), including 2 whole-verse repeats (15 percent).

THEME AS ORNAMENT IN ANGLO-SAXON POETRY

In the Anglo-Saxon Chronicle poem on The Death of Edgar, there is an interesting passage which may serve to illustrate the use of themes. This rather prosy and rambling poem relates all the most important events of the year 975. Although the poem is for the most part factual and relatively straightforward in style, the passage on the expulsion of Oslac, earl of Northumbria (24–28), is heavily ornamented. The factual substance of the passage could be reduced to verses 24a and 25a: And þa wearð eac adræfed . . . / Oslac, of earde. . . . All the rest is decoration. It might have been expected that the poet, wishing to enrich the texture, would naturally be attracted in the context to the ample stock of formulas associated with the theme of exile, and in verse 28b there is indeed an echo of this theme: hama bereafod. Since Oslac was exiled overseas, however, the poet launches into an abbreviated sea-voyage passage, using no fewer than 4 whole-verse formulas meaning "the sea." Of the 10 verses, 7 are demonstrably formulaic, including 4 whole-verse repeats. The passage is reproduced here.

The Death of Edgar 24–28

And þa wearð eac adræfed   deormod hæleð,
Oslac, of earde   ofer yða gewealc,
ofer ganotes bæð,   gamolfeax hæleð,
wis and wordsnotor,   ofer wætera geðring,
ofer hwæles eðel,   hama bereafod.

Supporting Evidence

24b Fin 23, Psm 50.1.

25a Cp. Gen 2806 idese of earde; Rdl 73.5 wegedon mec of earde; Rdl 83.8 eall of earde.

25b Bwf 464, And 259. Cp. Sfr 46 nefne ymb yða gewealc; Sfr 6, Exo 456 atol yða gewealc.

26a Bwf 1861, Run 79. Cp. And 293, Run 46 ofer fisces bæð.

26b Cp. Brb 45 beorn blandenfeax.

27a Cp. Dan 417 wis and wordgleaw. Cp. also And 473b–474a rædsnotterran, / wordes wisran.

27b Cp. OrW 79 under wætra geþring; And 368 ofer yða geþring; Bwf 2132 þæt ic on holma geþring.

28a And 274, Sfr 60.

DIAMOND

not

Of all Anglo-Saxon poems, the one we might expect to make the most extensive use of the theme of sea voyaging is probably The Seafarer. But that is to be misled by the title given it in modern times. Some of the sea-voyaging formulas do come into the poem, but for the most part not united in any single set-piece passage. The reason is not far to seek: this is not truly a poem about sea voyaging. It is an elegy, a conventionalized handling of spiritual suffering. In conveying his ideas, the poet makes tangential use of such themes as cold weather, exile, and sea voyaging, but he shapes them to his purpose and is never carried away by them. The sea-voyaging formulas are scattered (5a, 6a, 7b, 14b, 18b, 19a, 34b, 35a, 46b, 52, 59b, 60a, 63a, 64a), with the exception of a very interesting passage on the subtheme of sea birds (19b–25a). This sea-bird passage ought perhaps to be compared to the appearance of the sea gull in Andreas 371b–372a. It seems quite likely that the sea birds in these two passages are somehow related to the theme of the beasts of battle, for the gull that appears in Andreas is not just establishing a salty seascape atmosphere: it is searching for corpses to prey upon (ond se græge mæw / wælgifre wand). And, in the Seafarer passage, the screaming, dewy-feathered eagle (24b–25a ful oft þæt earn bigeal, / urigfeþra) is surely the same bird that figures among the beasts of battle. The only other eagles at sea in Anglo-Saxon poetry are the eagles in Andreas 863, which also appear in the Latin and Greek analogues of the passage and are not mere ornamentation.

Although much of Andreas tells the story of a sea voyage and there are many sea-voyaging formulas scattered throughout the first third of the poem, there is no single passage where the theme is developed as a set piece. There seems to be no instance where the poet turns on the theme and cannot turn it off again until he has produced a description that is pure decoration, for its own sake. The Andreas poet seems instead to have been in control of his material and to have expanded the sea-voyage theme into a long passage, like the Seafarer poet, shaping it to his own purpose. This may well be due to the source he was translating, which would give him less freedom to introduce themes at will, although, of course, he used traditional oral-formulaic diction in translating the narrative. There are, however, two striking examples of other themes in Andreas. One of these occurs in a ten-line address by Andreas' followers to

388

(4)

the saint, in which they profess their loyalty to him and beg him not to leave them. In this passage, the Old Germanic comitatus loyalty is given eloquent expression. This heroic theme, closely related to the themes of exile and of battle, is found in such poems as Beowulf and The Battle of Maldon, but seems strangely out of place in a saint's legend. The comitatus theme also appears in many passages throughout Old English poetry in abbreviated form in gnomic tags concerning the duties of a warrior or of a lord. Of the 20 verses of this passage, 15 are demonstrably formulaic (75 percent), including 9 whole-verse repeats (45 percent). The passage is reproduced here.

Andreas 405–414

405   "Hwider hweorfað we   hlafordlease,
     geomormode,   gode orfeorme,
     synnum wunde,   gif we swicað þe?
     We bioð laðe   on landa gehwam,
     folcum fracoðe,   þonne fira bearn,
410   ellenrofe,   æht besittaþ,
     hwylc hira selost   symle gelæste
     hlaforde æt hilde,   þonne hand ond rond
     on beaduwange   billum forgrunden
     æt niðplegan   nearu þrowedon."

Supporting Evidence

405b Bwf 2935.

406a Ele 413, 555, Phx 353, 412, Chr 535, Gen 858, 2270. Jud 144 geomormodum; Glc 1060 geomormodes.

406b And 1617, Jud 271. Vgl 49 gode orfeormne.

407a Chr 1313, Ele 514, Jln 710 synna wunde; Jln 355 synna wundum. Cp. Bwf 565 mecum wunde; Bwf 1075 gare wunde.

408b Rdl 33.13 on ealra londa gehwam. Cp. And 935 on landa gehwylc; Dan 408 ofer landa gehwilc; Dan 375 and þec landa gehwilc.

409a Cp. Chr 195 fracoð in folcum.

409b Cp. Phx 396 þone fira bearn; Jud 24 þæt mihten fira bearn; Gen 408 (hypermetric) fira bearn on þissum fæstum clomme.

410a And 350, 1141, Gen 2036, Rdl 22.20. Bwf 1787 ellenrofum; And 1392 ellenrofes; Jln 382 ellenrofne.

410b And 608, Ele 473 æht besæton.

411b LPr II.75 symle gelæstað.

412a For other A-verses ending in the phrase æt hilde, cp. Bwf 1659, 2575, 2684, Mld 55, 123, 223, 288.

412b Cp. Bwf 656 siþðan ic hond ond rond. Cp. also, with the word order reversed, And 9 þonne rond ond hand.

413a A formulaic system with substitution: cp. And 1226 on þam wælwange; Glc 921 on þam sigewonge.

413b Cp. Brb 18 (B.MS) garum forgrunden; Brb 43 wundum forgrunden; Bwf 2335, 2677 gledum forgrunden; Phx 227 bæle forgrunden.

414a A formulaic system with substitution: cp. Jud 217 æt ðam æscplegan; Bwf 1073 æt þam lindplegan; Wld I.13 æt ðam sweordplegan; Mld 268 æt þam wigplegan; Chr 573, F Ap 22 æfter guðplegan; And 1369 to þam guðplegan; Bwf 2039 to ðam lindplegan; Mld 316 se ðe nu fram þis wigplegan.

414b Bwf 2594 nearo ðrowode.

(5) The other set piece in Andreas is the short passage (1255b–1262a) in which the poet develops the theme of cold weather. Although in some versions of the legend, St. Andrew's cannibals dwelt in Scythia, a relatively northern country, in the Old English poetic version, Mermedonia seems to be identified with Ethiopia. A moment's reflection would surely indicate that Ethiopia is not a place where snow binds the earth, icicles hang, and the streams freeze over. It seems likely that the poet, in detailing the sufferings of the imprisoned saint, added cold to the list of torments and was carried away by the theme. The result is a striking passage of description, heavily studded with formulas native to northern Europe. Of the 14 verses, 10 are demonstrably formulaic (71.4 percent), including 3 whole-verse repeats (21.4 percent). The passage is reproduced here.

Andreas 1255b–1262a

Snaw eorðan band
wintergeworpum.   Weder coledon
heardum hægelscurum,   swylce hrim ond forst,
hare hildstapan,   hæleða eðel
lucon, leoda gesetu.   Land wæron freorig
cealdum cylegicelum,   clang wæteres þrym

> ofer eastreamas,   is brycgade
> blæce brimrade.

Supporting Evidence

1255b Cp. Sfr 32 hrim hrusan bond.

1256b Cp. DrR 72 Hræw colode; Run 92 hraw colian; Ele 882 Leomu colodon; Glc 1307 lic colode.

1257b Cp. M Bo 29.62 swylce hagal and snaw; Phx 248 þonne forst ond snaw; Aza 104 fæder, forst ond snaw; Wan 48 hreosan hrim ond snaw; Phx 14 Ne mæg þær ren ne snaw.

1258a Cp. Bwf 1678 harum hildfruman; FtM 13 har hæðstapa. Cp. also Bwf 103 mære mearcstapa; Bwf 1348 micle mearcstapan; Run 6 mære morstapa.

1258b And 21.

1259a Cp. DHl 115 eal folca gesetu.

1260a Phx 59.

1260b Cp. And 1536 Weox wæteres þrym; Phx 41 Swa iu wætres þrym.

1261a Cp. Bwf 1910, And 348 ofer brimstreamas. See also Ele 137a above.

1261b Mxm I.72 is brycgian.

If more Anglo-Saxon poetry had survived, we might be able to work out in more detail how the various themes are related to each other. For example, ceremonious greetings and reception of strangers in Beowulf (so strongly reminiscent of The Odyssey) seem to be a subtheme of the greater theme of court scenes. Related to this is the business of the coast-guard in Beowulf, which is in one sense a subtheme of the sea-voyage theme. Let us hypothesize that this voyage subtheme is here expanded by transferring the ceremonious greeting to the shore. This may perhaps be analogous to the relationship between the subtheme of rough seas and the theme of the storm at sea. The more fully developed theme of the storm at sea is found in passages in Andreas, in the swimming contest with Breca in Beowulf, and in the second and third Riddles.

Similarly, the celebrated Red Sea passage in Exodus 44–500, in which the Egyptian army is destroyed by the waves, may throw some light on the problem. The passage, which is an expanded paraphrase of the Bible passage, seems to be essentially

DIAMOND

the blend of two themes, battle and storm at sea. The way in
which the battle formulas and the sea-storm formulas are combined suggests that two larger units of poetic construction—the
two themes—have been joined together to embellish this scene.
The interpenetration of the two themes is strikingly represented
by such a line as, for instance, Exodus 482, in which the on-
verse (flod famigode) describes the action of the sea, and the
off-verse (fæge crungon) might be found in any battle passage.

Theme-splicing of this kind would seem to be a much more
likely explanation of the bloody waters in the Red Sea scene than
any echo of Beowulf. Recent studies of Old English poetry tend
to discount the likelihood that any one Anglo-Saxon poem consciously echoes any other. The more we find out about formulaic diction, the stronger the assumption that all the poets drew
on the same stock of traditional diction. The paradox is that
the more we understand about the way these poems were put together, the less certainly we can pronounce on the relationships
of the poems to each other.

NOTES

1 Speculum, XXVIII (1953), 446–467.

2 Magoun includes a selected bibliography of the work of
   Parry and Lord.

3 Speculum, XXX (1955), 49–63.

4 PQ, XXXVIII (1959), 228–241.

5 Bulletin de la Société Néophilologique de Helsinki, LVI
   (1955), 82–90.

6 Speculum, XXX (1955), 200–206.

7 "Beasts of Battle," p. 90.

THE ORAL-FORMULAIC ANALYSES OF OLD ENGLISH VERSE

Robert D. Stevick

The scant remains of Old English verse provide only a thin and uneven fossil record for the palaeontologist of literature. Interpretations of that record, of course, have never been lacking. In the earliest stages of Old English study they seemed to require only the taxonomist's inspection and classification or the trained judge's identification of the hybrid characteristics of, say, the Germanic burh and the Christian monastery. For the most part, however, the nature and development of poetry of the Anglo-Saxons neither appear in the certitude of self evidence nor sustain a simplicity of analysis. If our present understanding of the nature and history of this body of verse is more complex, more tentative, but presumably more accurate, it has become so through the ingenuity of scholars in erecting upon that meager record some remarkably cogent accounts of literary evolution. Without an appreciable increase in the fossil record, this scholarly achievement has been primarily the result of resourcefulness in seeking new methodology for dealing with historical data.

The methodological breakthrough identified with Francis P. Magoun, Jr., is a prominent current example of scholarly resourcefulness. Applying the methodology developed by Milman Parry and Albert B. Lord in the study of a living oral poetry, he was able to discern the pervasiveness of the oral-formulaic character of Old English verse. In the few years since he published "The Oral-Formulaic Character of Anglo-Saxon Poetry"[1] and "Bede's Story of Caedmon: The Case History of an Anglo-Saxon Oral Singer"[2] several things have happened to his discovery. None of them should surprise us if we recall the history of almost any major breakthrough in knowledge; nor should their diverse and random character necessarily be distressing.

Reprinted from Speculum, Vol. 37 (1952), pp. 382–9, by permission of the author and the publisher.

One of the most engaging applications of oral-formulaic analysis of Old English verse is Robert P. Creed's attempt to reconstruct the process of composition of a passage from Beowulf.[3] Enacting the process in slow motion, he unmakes and then makes anew the verses according to the inferred rules of the game. To test the process, furthermore, he remakes the same passage using different formulas, producing his own version of that portion of the poem. In so doing he purports to offer an illustration of how the formulaic diction does the poetizing for the Anglo-Saxon singer, how, in fact, the rapid and extempore composition before an audience was accomplished.

A deliberate narrowing of the field of investigation is undertaken in Robert Diamond's analysis of the diction in the four signed poems of Cynewulf.[4] His procedure, he says, is to apply Magoun's ideas to Cynewulf's poems "just as he [Magoun] takes the ideas of Parry and Lord on formulaic poetry in general and applies them to Anglo-Saxon poetry." The results of this analysis show us several aspects of the scope, the grammatical structure, and the metrical forms of formulaic phrases and formula systems; the conclusions to be drawn are that Cynewulf composed in the traditional formulaic style — since the poems are, by Diamond's analysis, about 63 percent demonstrably formulaic — though it is not easy to make precise distinctions between oral poems set down, poems composed "in the ordinary modern way," and poems composed by learned poets using traditional (i.e., oral) formulas.

Inevitably there have been reservations expressed with respect to Magoun's theory or parts of it, for the most part in the form of suggestions for modification and refinement. The tendency of these reservations is generally consistent. Claes Schaar, for example, points out the error of equating the two propositions "all oral poetry is formulaic" and "all formulaic poetry is oral."[5] It may well be, he argues, that the surviving texts may be the products of a transitional period, when there were written texts and lettered poets were using and modifying the oral-formulaic materials; there may indeed be influence, in the common literary sense, of one poet drawing on the text of another rather than drawing solely from the common formula stock. Jackson J. Campbell, applying the "touchstone" for oral verse, finds that The Seafarer is neither plainly oral nor plainly lettered.[6] Rather, he infers from oral-formulaic tests together with tests for poetic diction that an older poem full of the older (oral) conventions has been remembered and reworked by a lettered homilist-poet—a man with full knowledge of the style of oral poetry and even a certain reduced command of its formulas. Once again, the existence of a transitional period is insisted upon; the records we have are, thus, more likely to be the works of English monks and churchmen rather than scops; they were educated in Christian Latin literature, and were in practice carrying over oral traditions into lettered poetry, not merely transcribing performances of oral singers.

Further reservation is expressed by A. G. Brodeur in context of his discussion of the diction of Beowulf.[7] By questioning Magoun's assumption that a lettered poet would be incapable of composing in the formulaic manner, he attempts to establish the Beowulf poet as a trained scop, who at the same time is literate and cultivated. The richness of his diction, the prominence of unique compounds and kennings, the style and structure of the poem, he asserts, point to a man we must again place in a transitional poetic milieu, when the ability to read, to invent new diction, and to compose with deliberation were not inconsistent with a man's training as a professional scop.[8]

These several examples define, I believe, the direction of the applications and modifications offered for Magoun's oral-formulaic theory of Old English verse. In the meantime, application and extension of the theory have produced important reinterpretation of several poems. Stanley Greenfield's exploration of "The Formulaic Expression of the Theme of 'Exile' in Anglo-Saxon Poetry"[9] is one of the best, particularly for its inclusion of aesthetic considerations of the advantages and disadvantages of formulaic composition and of the nature of originality within this tradition.

In this cursory review of publications dealing with a new phase of Old English literary study two things are prominent. First, the amount and ingenuity of the scholarly activity are impressive: the new methodology applied to several segments of the extant Old English verse is rapidly producing results whose security and significance are noteworthy. Second, however, the total character of these investigations is disappointing. We may begin obliquely by saying that, if we consider the contributors as a group working on a single problem, their metaphysics are muddled. It is unfair, of course, to the individuals to impute to them the faults of the group. Yet, without clearly formulated and mutually shared postulates, without regular comparison and scrutiny of methodologies, without sufficient scope or clarity of purpose, the laborers in this literary museum may be thought of as assembling some quite startling palaeontological exhibits, possibly as unhistorical as they are ingenious.

Singer vs poet

On the one hand, for instance, there is strict adherence by some to the postulate of the "singer" and avoidance of the concept "poet." The text, if it is heavily formulaic, is then a "performance" (perhaps modified a little in the process of being captured in writing) rather than a poem composed by a poet. On the other hand, others talk of the "poet" and his "poem," of writers working within a tradition, with traditional materials, as they compose poems and, at times, put the traditional materials to uses quite foreign to the source of their formulas.

Crit.

As a specific case we may consider Magoun's inferences from his analysis of Caedmon's Hymn about the history of Old English Christian verse and its distinctive formulas. His argument, replete with charts and lists of evidence, is that the poem is formulaic, its language quite traditional, inasmuch as 83 percent of its diction is demonstrably formulaic — i.e., the dictional elements appear elsewhere in the corpus of Old English verse. Now, he says, the eight references to the Deity compose 44 percent of this formulaic poem; and since, if Caedmon was a "singer" it is unlikely that he would compose new such a proportion of his poem, we may conclude that there was a Christian formulaic vocabulary for verse developing before Caedmon. (And, we should add, developing for some considerable time, if we consistently maintain that singers learned and preserved traditional formulas to a far greater extent than they invented new ones.)

To call Caedmon's Hymn "formulaic" may mean either of two things: (a) that it is made up of formulas, that it uses ready-made poetic components — "formulaic" in a substantive sense; or (b) that it is made in the manner of formulaic verse, that it somehow resembles it (perhaps even using some traditional formulas) — "formulaic" in an attributive sense. In the first case, however, he needs either to adduce instances of formulas from earlier texts or to present an independent body of evidence confirming the hypothesis that there were earlier instances of these formulas. The first alternative we may write off for absence of records; the second, besides straining the earlier limit of Anglo-Saxon Christianity, requires convincing reason to reject the opposite assumption that other occurrences of these formulas are borrowings, directly or indirectly, from Caedmon or his imitators and successors. Unless this reason appears, we have no substantial warrant to accept the inference of a body of Christian formulas available to Caedmon. And this reason has not yet appeared. Moreover, to call the Hymn formulaic in the attributive sense permits no inference at all about prior development of a Christian poetic vocabulary.

We may feel it in our hearts that Magoun's assertions concerning Caedmon's Hymn in particular and the history of Christian poetic formulas generally may be substantially accurate; but empathy has always been an untrustworthy historical prop, however valuable it may be heuristically. The networks of inferences and their postulates still must appear in sound historical array.

Let us consider one more instance. Creed's slow-motion enactment of the process of composition of the Beowulf passage is performed on the postulate of a singer (not a poet) putting together verses rapidly in accordance with rules of measure, verse, and alliteration, under the requirements of his narrative, and with respect to aesthetic effect. It implicitly discounts any possible differences between the "text" of a live performance and a written text (in an age neither skilled nor motivated to capture pure examples of traditional art) and any possible differences between the neat extant text and earlier manuscripts by which the poem was transmitted. The process described is essentially that of commencing with a common formula, then adding a measure or verse at a time, hardly looking farther ahead than the next alliterative stave. Now, while the psychology of poetic improvisation still lies in the limbo of guesswork, we may take some clues from an analogous process — musical improvisation. Perhaps the nearest parallel among familiar forms is jazz. We may affirm immediately the position that, in the process of improvisation, each successive phrase or formula is to some extent determined by its immediately preceding context, as well as by the cumulative effect of all that goes before it. This is about as far as Creed's analysis goes, and it is certainly the process most susceptible to simple explanation. But if there are similiarities between poetic and musical improvisation beyond this — and I am convinced there are[10] — then much more needs to be said if we are to understand the methods, stages, and accomplishments of formulaic composition. For example, the performer of jazz will employ anticipations, larger as well as smaller structural patterns, overlapping patterns, contrapuntal movements—will, in short (if he is a good musician), deliver a highly complex performance, an adequate description of which would be exceedingly long and, in the present state of musical terminology, surpassingly difficult. Moreover, in a traditional oral (or musical) art form—as opposed to a tradition perpetuated in writing or notation—memory of past performances will have a very large effect on any further performance; any familiarity at all with successive jazz performances suggests strongly that performers (and particularly professional ones) repeat earlier performances as entities, subject only to such changes as faulty memory, momentary experiments, or effects of audience reaction may produce. They do not build each performance merely a phrase at a time. Composition, in this respect, represents relatively slight modifications within an entire "piece" or a substantial stretch of the selection being presented. But composition in improvisational art, for traditional themes handled repreatedly by professional performers, can hardly be conceived of entirely as fresh creation measure-by-measure, phrase-by-phrase, line-by-line, as Creed has represented it. In fact, Creed's reconstruction equally suits the procedure of a lettered poet composing pen-in-hand in a formulaic manner.

The problem inherent in Creed's reconstruction of the making of a formulaic poem can be restated as follows. There is an ambiguity in the concepts of "composition," "singer," "poem," and "performance." What Creed has apparently given us is a rational, analytic reconstruction of the cumulative effects on some verses of a large number of performances and the tradition in which they participate—effects, moreover, possessing a more complex and fortuitous history than his analysis allows us to conceive. Reconstruction of the process of composing— of putting together—a performance-text is not identical to reconstruction of the history of modifications of a traditional, repeated "piece" when that history is terminated in a stipulated text; yet the two in traditional art are inseparable. Composition, in other words, is a process of both singer and tradition. This is the ambiguity of "composition." It is inseparable from the ambiguity of "singer" as one who "sings," as those singers who

398

have contributed to the surviving shape of a piece of verse, and as that one who produced a given text (or performance). It is the ambiguity of the "poem" as an evolving archetype ever represented anew and as a designated member in a series of successive modifications of a whole piece within a body of tradition. It is the ambiguity of "performance" as act and as object.

Now if we inquire into causes of these difficulties in oral-formulaic analyses of Old English verse, we may be able to discover some obstructions to refinement of the oral-theory for Old English; we may be able to recognize and remove some limitations to its utility. Inquiry is facilitated by recent publication of Albert B. Lord's The Singer of Tales, embodying the acknowledged base for the oral-theory in Old English studies; a systematic inquiry may be preferable to an historical one.

The cogency of the Parry-Lord theory is maintained for the oral epic song—a narrative in verse, developed and perpetuated within an unlettered tradition, manifested in traditional formulas and themes, and distinct from "ballads and comparatively short epics." The definitions and restrictions for "oral song" are explicit, and the theory limited to that specific art form. Nevertheless, oral-formulaic analyses for Old English verse take their evidence from all poetic forms—from Caedmon's Hymn to Beowulf. It is possible, of course, that in Old English verse the distinction between The Seafarer, say, and Beowulf is unimportant in this respect. Yet Lord's book would not lead us to expect this.[11] Moreover, these analyses for Old English regularly recapitulate the Parry-Lord postulates about rapid, extempore composition (performance) of extended narrative songs, thereby putting the hymns, lyric-elegies, and moral and homiletic pieces in the appearance of anomalies as sources of data or topics of generalization for the oral-theory.[12] It may be that these non-narrative poems in Old English are of a different order from the epic oral narratives, and may prove intractable—even disruptive—to the narrative-based theory.

Over-extension of the oral-theory may be in itself sufficient cause for some difficulties we have described. It may also be a contributing cause to difficulties over the question of transitional aspects of Old English verse. In Lord's analysis the most careful distinctions between oral and literary texts of epic songs precede the assertion that the relationship between the two types, or styles, is not only one of either-or, but also one of not both.

While a period, a career, or a repertory may be termed "transitional," in combining oral and literary techniques, the categories are held to be exclusive for individual texts or for individual singers at a particular time. In reaching the decision that in all his data there is no such thing as a transitional text, Lord insistently confines his argument to the traditional epic song form and to the technical requirements of a performer within the tradition of oral epic song.

Faced with the contradiction between denial of the possibility of transitional texts and the conviction that, in Old English verse at least, some texts must be transitional, we may seek the resolving distinction in the nature of the evidence on both sides. Whether there is a relevant distinction between epic song and other, especially non-narrative, verse becomes a crucial question. If the distinction is significant, then transitional texts (for non-epic songs) can perhaps be described more directly than as products of a transitional period. If it is not significant, then the Parry-Lord theory has only analogical, suggestive value for Old English studies, requiring thorough re-examination and reconstruction of concepts and inferences regarding oral-formulaic aspects of Old English poetry.

That the contributions to study of the oral-formulaic character of Old English verse have been random and diverse, I shall re-affirm, should not necessarily be distressing. That the total product of contributors to this study has been fragmentary, piecemeal, and not entirely consistent is less tnan we might have hoped for. But that, as a result of these conditions, even some of the contributions[13] turn out upon inspection to lack historical rigor or conceptual clarity is a clear sign (tacen sweotol) that all is not well.

A remedy is more easily urged than prescribed. Perhaps the over-all requirement is that of unified and systematic procedures, together with stipulation of specific purposes; these purposes, I assume, are primarily (not exclusively) those of accurate literary history. Instead of random methods, there is need for a self-corrective methodology. Instead of merely techniques of investigation, techniques oriented to comprehensive theories. In ultimate terms: instead of loosely related experiments, a science. Or, from the scholar-teacher's point of view, rather than ask "Who is the best judge?" ask "How is the best judgment to be made?"

ORAL-FORMULAIC ANALYSES OF OLD ENGLISH VERSE

The practical problem of how to achieve more unified and systematic procedures can be solved only in practice itself, of course. Some areas of endeavor may be more promising than others for the inevitable trial and error attempts at progress. Some have already been implied. Distinctions need to be made in order to remove ambiguities and bring the terminology under control: whether "formulaic" is used in a substantive or attributive sense, whether "performance" denotes an act or an object, whether "singer" is particular or generic, whether "composition" is process or product, of an individual or a tradition or both, whether a "poem" is a text or an abstraction—these are some immediate problems of definition. Further, since we have established a time in which poetry was oral and formulaic and a somewhat later time in which poetry was composed in writing, and the evidence indicates a material continuity between those times, we infer, with Schaar, Campbell, Brodeur, and others, that there was a gradual transition. The need now is to establish the stages of that transition—at least in schematic form—so that a particular poem, or section of one, can be placed in the historical continuum and interpreted according to its context. We need, in other words, a denser historical record. But this in turn requires careful delimitation of oral texts and styles together with distinctions, probably, between the styles and techniques of oral epic narrative and shorter, non-narrative verse.

Beyond these "internal" areas, there are others that may provide useful resources for continued progress. Historiography, for instance, seems to have advanced rapidly (for some time now without the help of literary historians) and may well save the historian of literature much of the effort of discovery or the frustration of fruitless speculations. The history of physical anthropology may yield a lesson that endless fact listing and classification, without orientation to a comprehensive theory, produces only facts and groups of facts whose significance is open only to speculation—that the gathering of facts produces problems but does not solve them. Magoun's "supporting evidence" for his analysis of Caedmon's Hymn, in relation to his assertions about Old English Christian poetic vocabulary, is a case in point. Other art forms, like jazz, may provide suggestive analogies for investigation of the nature of a popular form of art, of its performers, of its history, and of its methods.

From such a variety of fields of knowledge may come models
or patterns — at least experience — on the basis of which to
develop investigative patterns and integrate them into a comprehensive schema.

Investigations of Old English literary history, obviously,
could also profit by taking a larger scope: indeed, this may be
the most likely method for achieving through practice those
unified, systematic procedures which, at a certain stage of development, begin to operate in a self-corrective manner. In
the continuing effort to expand and correct the accounts of
literary evolution in the Anglo-Saxon period, we may recall the
history of the theory of organic evolution and conclude with the
kind of praise known where knowledge has progressed conspicuously: the major trouble with the methodological breakthrough
embodied in the oral-formulaic analyses of Old English verse
is that it needs to be succeeded by refinements and still further
breakthroughs and ultimately assimilated into a comprehensive
literary history.

NOTES

1 Speculum, XXVIII (1953), 446–467.

2 Speculum, XXX (1955), 49–63.

3 "The Making of an Anglo-Saxon Poem," ELH, XXVI (1959),
445–454.

4 "The Diction of the Signed Poems of Cynewulf," PQ, XXXVIII
(1959), 228–241.

5 "On a New Theory of Old English Poetic Diction," Neophilologus, XL (1956), 301–305.

6 "Oral Poetry in The Seafarer," Speculum, XXXV (1960),
87–96; still further, Wayne A. O'Neil, "Another Look at
Oral Poetry in The Seafarer," Speculum, XXXV (1960),
596–600.

7 The Art of Beowulf, Ch. I. (Berkeley and Los Angeles, 1959).

8 It may strengthen Brodeur's case for the poet's training
and method of composition to consider the factor of length
of the poem. So long a poem — even if conceived of as re-

cited in three sittings (or singings)—if composed in a purely oral way from the common formula stock, would in all probability have more frequent repetitions or "favorite" formulas, fewer unique compounds, and more frequent lapses or other flaws in structure and style.

9 Speculum, XXX (1955), 200–206.

10 There is hardly a flaw in the parallel between Albert B. Lord's description of oral-epic improvisation, in The Singer of Tales (Cambridge, Massachusetts: Harvard University Press, 1960), and the nature and history of improvisational (traditional) jazz.

11 This is the tenor of the exposition of the oral-theory and the analysis of Beowulf, including its supporting evidence.

12 Looking back at my analysis of "Formal Aspects of The Wife's Lament," JEGP, LIX (1960), convinces me that, whatever the proportion of formula-content of The Wife's Lament, its close, intricate, symmetrical patterns together with its brevity are incompatible with extempore oral composition. This is one poem, for a start, that I believe should be excluded from oral-formulaic analyses.

13 I have deliberately selected, for extended analysis, essays by Magoun, as the originator of this special area of study, and by Creed, as a highly productive contributor to its development.

VI. PARTICULAR POETS AND POEMS

THE POETRY OF CÆDMON

C. L. Wrenn

The authentic Cædmon, as distinct from the expansive poet
of Junius, has attracted explorers and speculators from the
time when Hickes first doubted the authenticity of the "Cædmon
poems" of the Junius MS. and Wanley discovered the Moore MS.
version of "Cædmon's Hymn" till now: and Gollancz, naturally,
in seeking to provide the necessary background to his reproduction of MS. Junius 11, could not resist the fascination of once
more trying to relate Cædmon—"the morning star of English
poetry" as he calls him—to the poetry he was reproducing. I
have therefore thought it appropriate to take the poetry of the
authentic Cædmon for my subject.

What impressions and inferences may profitably be drawn
from a study of Cædmon's <u>Hymn</u> in the light of all of its background that we can recover, concerning the poet himself and
his poetry? I shall generally confine myself to this limited field,
because this poem is the one piece which by all but universal
agreement may be studied as the authentic work of Cædmon himself: and I am not enough of a speculator to venture further at
present.

1. The Canon

In presenting my ideas of the poetry of Cædmon, I shall take
the extreme course of confining myself to the nine lines of the
<u>Hymn</u>. For this is the only work of this poet which can be ac-
cepted as his with something approaching certainty, and the only
one which we can hope to study with the aid of something like an
appropriate background. Of the mass of Anglo-Saxon poetry
which was once attributed to Cædmon, only parts or substrata

Reprinted from <u>Proceedings of the British Academy</u>, XXXII (1946), pp.
277–95, by permission of the author and the publisher.

of Genesis and parts of The Dream of the Rood—apart from the Hymn—are still likely to find any serious defenders. Elsewhere[1] I have given my reasons for regarding the Ruthwell Cross inscription (which is all that can be implied by any attribution of The Dream of the Rood to Cædmon) as too late in time—apart from difficulties of style and dialect—for our poet. But I reject with more reluctance the possibilities of Cædmonian elements in the Genesis because of the attractive arguments put forward by Gollancz himself in his introduction to his facsimile of the Junius MS. Indeed, his conclusion, after a lengthy survey of all the poems in the manuscript in possible relation to Cædmon, was curiously emphatic. His final words were these: "Genesis A may, I think, have the same ascription as the Hymn. 'PRIMO CANTAVIT CÆDMON ISTUD CARMEN.'"[2]

Now that there may be evidence of a more scientific character for the work of Cædmon in the Genesis is suggested by the careful and ingenious application by Sievers of his own methods of Schallanalyse in the article "Cædmon und Genesis" which he published in the Max Förster Festschrift in 1929.[3] Here he demonstrated, as he thought, that fifty-four lines or half-lines from the earlier part of Genesis not only may be, but must be, the work (basically) of Cædmon. He applied with its full scientific technique the tests of Schallanalyse, and found that the fifty-four lines or parts of lines showed the Personalkurve of Cædmon, as well as requiring that special kind of voice which must have been his. Thus, for instance, Sievers freely admits that the striking resemblance between Genesis, lines 112, 113, and 116a with lines 5 ff. of the Hymn may be easily otherwise accounted for. What is important and utterly decisive, he says, is rather that the Genesis lines have the Personalkurve and the Stimmart of the Hymn. Here are the two passages:

Genesis:
    Her ærest gesceop ece drihten,
    helm ealwihta, heofon and eorðan,
    . . . .
    . . . .
    frea ælmihtig.

THE POETRY OF CÆDMON

The <u>Hymn</u>:
  He ærist scop ælda bar<u>num</u>
  heben til hrofe haleg scepen.
  . . . .
  . . . .
  . . . . frea allmectig.

The resemblance is a good deal closer if Sievers' own reconstructed earliest Northumbrian of Cædmon's actual speech is
substituted in both passages for the usual authorities: but I have
quoted them respectively from the Moore MS. of the <u>Hymn</u> and
the Junius MS. The method employed by Sievers for the recovery
of the authentic pieces of Cædmon in the <u>Genesis</u> — separated
and intercalated, like the above example, by the products of a
<u>Redactor</u> — is that set forth most clearly by him in his lectures
on <u>Ziele und Wege der Schallanalyse</u> published in 1924. But it
is made very clear at the outset of this exposition of <u>Schallan-
alyse</u> that only those who possess certain qualities in their motor
nerves can participate in such experiments or judge of their effects. One must be a <u>Motoriker</u>, as he says, be conscious of a
kind of motoric invitation, "eine motorische Einladung," to be
able to respond effectively to what one hears. To quote Sievers'
words:[4] "Only such people as possess more than a certain minimum of motor responsiveness ("ein gewisser Mindestgrad von
sog. motorischer Veranlagung") can at once and without difficulty
take in the distinctions under consideration, while all those who
lack this minimum of motor responsiveness and must rely in the
main on their acoustic and visual powers . . . lack the power to
perceive consciously any such reactions in themselves or in
other people." Now Sievers himself seems to have stood alone
in fully possessing the above qualities — in being in fact a <u>Motor-
iker</u>. While it would be presumptuous to disparage the <u>soi-
disant</u> scientific work of one of the very greatest of philologists,
it would be equally unscientific to seek to use Sievers' results
without being oneself <u>motorisch</u>: and I can lay no claim to receiving any motoric summons when I hear poetry recited. Indeed, left to myself, I should have been tempted to think the nine
lines of Cædmon's <u>Hymn</u> both too remote and too brief for the
establishment with any degree of sureness of a Becking <u>Personal-
kurve</u>, or the kind of voice and dialect which it originally had.
I am therefore constrained, as I have said, to confining myself

to a consideration of the Hymn alone. For the other recent
scientific method of establishing canonicity, that which works
by statistics of vocabulary, must clearly be inapplicable to so
small a piece.[5] As I propose to speculate somewhat in what
follows on Cædmon and his poetry, it is all the more necessary
that I should make it clear at the outset that my Cædmon canon
is limited to the established fact of the authenticity of the Hymn.
But how vast is the historical and literary significance of this
little poem it will now be my main purpose to show.

2. The Tradition

I am not prepared, without a great deal of discussion for
which this is not the place, to accept Gollancz's defence of parts
of the Genesis as basically the work of the authentic Cædmon,
since the scientific aids touched upon above are not applicable.
Junius' assumption that the whole contents of his manuscript
was the work of the first Northumbrian poet, resting on the apparent correspondence between the subject-matter of the poems
and Bede's account of Cædmon's compositions, does, however—
though rightly rejected by everyone now—remind one of the
possibility that the compiler of the Junius MS. was directed in
his choice of texts by Bede's statement. I think, too, that he
may have been partly influenced in this by the fact of a strong
tradition of the great importance and significance of Cædmon.
That there was an Alfredian tradition independent of anything
derivable from Bede was first vaguely implied by Hickes, who
was the first to cast doubt on the authenticity of the contents of
the Junius MS. in his Institutiones Grammaticae Anglo-Saxonicae
et Moeso-Gothicae printed with the special type left by Junius
in 1689,[6] and strengthened this doubt in his great Thesaurus.
But it was Humphrey Wanley who first definitely proved the
genuineness of the Moore MS. version of the Hymn as of the
year 737; and it was too in his great companion to Hickes's
Thesaurus[7] that this manuscript—ever since forming the basic
text—was first printed. But in fact, two years before his printed
work, Humphrey Wanley had given the now familiar information
fixing the date of the Moore MS. by means of its chronological
notes in an unpublished letter to Dr. J. Smith dated 28 August
1703. I quote a part of this pioneer letter now, because it makes
it quite clear that Wanley was the real discoverer, alike of the

importance of the Moore MS. of the <u>Hymn</u> and of the Alfredian independent tradition of Cædmon.

This Book [the Moore MS. of Bede's <u>Historia Ecclesiastica</u>] confirms a most ingenious Conjec-ture of Dr Hickes, who reading over the Saxon Version (or Paraphrase) of Bede, in Lib. IV, Cap. 24, observed the Song of Cædmon to be in <u>Verse</u>, and answering to Bede's <u>Latin</u> words, which made him guess, that K. Ælfred when he came to that place, did not translate Bede, but put in Cædmon's own Words, which were then extant. And from this, he was induced to believe, that the printed book ascribed by Mr Junius to Cædmon, is not his, but a later composition. So, the Dr has printed this Song in his Grammar now in the Press, mending some faults therein: and I in this MS upon the same leaf of Parchment with the above written List and Notes [the chronological data] <u>but before them</u> and (I verily think) by the same hand, tho' in lesser characters, was glad to find the same, with Cædmon's name to it, in the following words, which being, as the rest, written A.D. 737 I take to be one of the most antient Specimens of our language any where extant. [Here follows a transcript of the Moore MS. version of Cædmon's <u>Hymn</u> written as prose.][8]

Wanley's discovery of the Alfredian tradition of Cædmon was somewhat amplified by Bishop Percy in his <u>Reliques</u> in an addendum to the "Essay" which he prefixed to the collection of poems. After quoting in parallel Bede's Latin and Alfred's Anglo-Saxon to bring out what the English version has seemed to add, Percy comments thus: "In this version of Alfred's it is observable, (1) that he has expressed the Latin word <u>cantare</u>, by the Anglo-Saxon words <u>be hearpan singan</u>, 'sing to the harp'; (2) that when Bede simply says, <u>surgebat a media cæna</u>; he as-signs a motive, <u>aras for sceome</u>, 'arose for shame': that is, either from an austerity of manners; or from his being deficient in an accomplishment, which so generally prevailed among his countrymen."[9] Now while the expansion of the Latin <u>cantare</u> into <u>be hearpan singan</u> may have no special significance and

411

accords with Alfred's sometimes explicative method of rendering, the addition of the words for sceome does, I suggest, imply that the king had some more vivid knowledge of the story of Cædmon's miracle than the text of Bede's Latin: and this I take to have been a distinctive English tradition. That the text of the Hymn was held in special reverence and preserved with wide-spread and con- scious care, seems beyond doubt in view of the fact that there are known to-day—apart from possible losses yet to be discovered in libraries—no less than seventeen copies of the Anglo-Saxon version; four in Northumbrian dialect copied into the manuscripts of the Latin text of Bede's Historia Ecclesiastica, eight in forms of Late West-Saxon inserted into other Latin copies of the same, and five in Late West-Saxon included at the appropriate place in manuscripts of King Alfred's translation of Bede.[10] One manu- script, one poem, is the usual rule for extant Anglo-Saxon verse. The apparent parallel of Bede's Death-song, with its twenty- seven manuscript copies, stands quite alone, and is to be ex- plained on similar, if more obvious lines.

Let me now read you the earliest datable Northumbrian version of Cædmon's Hymn (the Moore MS. of A.D. 737 written within sixty years of the poet's death), with a rough translation for convenience, and then ask you to consider whether compari- son of outstanding features seen in the grouping of this and the other versions does not further confirm the existence in the time of King Alfred of a still living oral tradition of the Hymn.

> Nu scylun hergan hefaenricaes uard
> metudaes maecti end his modgidanc
> uerc uuldurfadur sue he uundra gihuaes
> eci dryctin or astelidæ
> he aerist scop aelda barnum
> heben til hrofe haleg scepen.
> tha middungeard moncynnæs uard
> eci dryctin æfter tiadæ
> firum foldu frea allmectig
> primo cantauit Caedmon istud carmen.

(Now ought we to praise heaven's kingdom's guard- ian, the might of the Creator and the thought of his mind, the works of the Father of glory. How he the Eternal Lord set up a beginning for every wondrous

thing. He who is the Holy Creator designed heaven
as a roof for the children of men. Then mankind's
guardian, Eternal Lord, All-mighty ruler, afterwards
made the earth for men.)

The seventeen copies of this Hymn have been grouped in
various ways—those written into Latin MSS. of Bede as against
those naturally falling in their proper place in manuscripts of
the Alfredian Bede; Northumbrian versions as against those in
Late West-Saxon; those which seem to be copies from other
versions; and those which may be thought to have resulted from
more or less uncertain attempts at reproduction from memory.
But throughout all versions the reading of the latter half of line
five shews two groups which cover all. For Bede's filiis hominum, nine manuscripts have the sense "for children of earth,"
and eight "for children of men." That is, all versions may be
classified as having either eordu bearnum (Northumbrian) corresponding to the Late West-Saxon eorðan bearnum, or Anglian
aelda barnum (with the corresponding Late West-Saxon equivalent ylda bearnum). The Dijon and Paris MSS. are late copies
of a specifically Northumbrian version which had eordu bearnum,
followed by the five Alfredian MSS. (which read eorþan bearnum)
and the copies entered in two late Latin Bede MSS., those of
Hereford Cathedral Library and Bodley Laud 243, which have
eorðe bearnum. The form eordu must at least go back to Northumbrian of the later eighth century. The two Northumbrian
datable MSS., the Moore of A.D. 737 and the Leningrad of 746,
give the reading aelda barnum (Leningrad actually ældu barnum)[11]
which is the basis for what may be called the "children of men"
group and is followed by the Late West-Saxon ylda bearnum in
six Latin manuscripts of the Historia Ecclesiastica which include
the Anglo-Saxon Hymn as against the two (Hereford and Laud
243) already mentioned. It has been usual—and it is natural—
to assume that the reading of the two oldest Northumbrian versions, Moore and Leningrad, aelda barnum, must be the right
one since it agrees so markedly with Bede's filiis hominum, is
what must have seemed a familiar Biblical phrase, and occurs
not infrequently in Anglo-Saxon poetry, as for instance in Beowulf 70. The expression "for children of earth," eordu bearnum,
on the other hand, is not, I believe, to be found anywhere outside
Cædmon's Hymn. Now I cannot help feeling that if one were try-

ing to remember the Hymn without a copy to refer to, one might
easily retain the general sense of the passage in question while
not being able to recall just the exact phrasing. In this situation,
is it not natural to recall the familiar "for children of men,"
aelda barnum, rather than an original eordu bearnum? For the
one sounds Biblical and is common in poetry, as well as being
what one would have read in Bede's Latin: while the other would
have no associations outside its own original context. I therefore would propose that more attention should be given to the
possibility of taking the basic eordu bearnum from the Dijon and
Paris versions as the original difficilior lectio, and the Moore
and Leningrad aelda or ældu barnum as the unconscious substitution from associations with Bede, the Bible, and with other
poetry. But in any case, without at all pressing this hypothesis
(since it can be nothing more), I think the occurrence of the alternative readings eordu and aelda in Northumbrian versions of
the Hymn of the eighth century, each supported by a continuing
later West-Saxon correspondence of eorðan and ylda, does imply
the preservation of the Hymn at an early stage by the process
of oral rather than written tradition. It must be remembered
too that Bede deliberately made a freer rendering in Latin, as
he explains, because "neque enim possunt carmina, quamuis
optime composita, ex alia in aliam linguam ad uerbum sine
detrimento sui decoris ac dignitatis transferri."

Bede gave the sense, not ordo ipse uerborum: and it was
Alfred who, omitting Bede's explanation of his freedom of rendering, carefully substituted for Bede's quorum iste est sensus
the clear expression "of which this is the order," þara endebyrdnes
þis is.[12] The conscious verbal accuracy implied in the Alfredian
statement, if we remember that all the Alfredian versions have
the "children of earth" reading eorðan bearnum, suggests the
possession of an oral tradition: and that this was ultimately from
Northumbria is indicated by the eordu bearnum which lies behind the Dijon and Paris versions. For eordu is a specifically
early Northumbrian form. It is also to be considered whether
the rendering in the Alfredian versions of Bede's mihi cantare
habes in the speech of the being who spoke with Cædmon in his
dream by þu meaht me singan, does not imply some corroboration of a separate English tradition independent of Bede: for habes
does not seem to have had the meaning of the Anglo-Saxon meaht.
Other less significant differences between groups of versions of

the Hymn might be cited in favour of the theory that it had its earlier transmission through oral tradition very carefully sought after. But enough has been said to show the very great importance which must have been attached to Cædmon's Hymn by the Anglo-Saxons quite apart from the influence of Bede's famous chapter setting forth the miracle. Even in the nine lines of the Hymn, too, I think we can feel something of that "Cædmonian style" which came to be characteristic of so much Anglo-Saxon Biblical poetry and is not entirely to be divorced from the influence of Cædmon himself. Indeed this style was carried over into the lands of the "Old Saxons" who, with their Anglo-Saxon Christian culture, received the tradition and the manner of Cædmonian Christian heroic poetry. As Humphrey Wanley said of the Heliand: "Grandiloquo modo stylo cædmoniano conscripta sunt omnia." What then was the nature of the miracle so movingly narrated by Bede in the twenty-fourth chapter of his fourth book?

3. The Miracle

Perhaps to some, at first, the miraculous tale told by Bede of Cædmon's first obtaining the power of song may seem just a piece of folk-lore easily to be paralleled elsewhere in the Germanic world and not to be taken too seriously by the literary historian. It would be natural, they might think, to idealize the first Anglo-Saxon Christian poet for Bede and his readers, and the same or similar tales are told of the nameless poet of the Old Saxon Heliand and of the Old Icelandic skald Hallbjörn Hali. The story is narrated in the Praefatio to the Heliand and more especially in the Versus de Poeta et Interprete hujus Codicis.[13] But these are later by far than the poem itself, and the remarkable line in the latter which says of the Heliand-poet

Qui prius agricola mox et fuit ille Poeta,

merely shows the strength of the Anglo-Saxon tradition of Cædmon which is here being imitated quite naturally among the "Old Saxons" who had received the "Cædmonian poetry" from the English missionaries. As for Hallbjörn Hali, the account in the þorleifs þáttr of how the poet was helped in a dream to compose a drápa on his patron has only the most general resemblance to the Cædmon story.[14] Moreover, Iceland, too, received much of its early Christian culture at least indirectly from England.

Again, one versed in the current psychology or in its vul-garisation might explain the "miracle" as just an interesting example of "inferiority complex"—especially in view of the amplification "for shame" which the Alfredian version adds to Bede's account of the poet's leaving the convivium. But miracles have, in fact, seemed so often to be wrought through the ordinary human instruments and processes: and the resulting Hymn is no whit explained away by a psychological explanation of the form and subject-matter of Cædmon's dream and vision. The dreams of the inferiority complexed do not necessarily fructify in mira-cles: and this poem was, in the view both of the monks of the monastery where it was first heard and of Bede, a clear miracle. Bede, also, was a careful and scrupulous historian, though he had not the modern limitation which would have precluded him from recording what he had received without seeking to offer a purely rational explanation. At first the Hymn may seem to have little intrinsic worth as poetry. Yet the more one reads it and allows it be become assimilated in one's mind, the more one feels it has qualities of balanced and rhythmic grandeur which still have some poetic appeal. But I do not think it was because they felt it to be a piece of great poetry in itself that the monks instantly recognized its production by the herdsman as miraculous. It is evident from the account of the doings of Cædmon and his com-panions at their convivia that at least the recitation—if not the actual composition—of poetry, was to be expected among the Anglo-Saxon peasants of late-seventh-century Northumbria. Like some parts of North Wales, Iceland, and the Faroe Islands, the Anglo-Saxon agricultural folk had their own forms of cul-ture independent and far antecedent to books. St. Aldhelm found an appreciative audience when he sang poetry on the bridge. As I have said, I think Percy was right in his Essay on the Ancient English Minstrels to imply that the story of Cædmon has signifi-cance in the history of the ballad. Though in general only the poetry of aristocratic origin has been preserved in writing by the Anglo-Saxons, there must have been a native peasant poetry with which Cædmon's companions were familiar, which he was ashamed he could not recite or compose. The miracle, then, I would propose, which instantly struck the monks and was so piously recorded by Bede was not that a herdsman attached to a monastery recited a poem of his own composition merely: but rather that one obviously quite untrained in the aristocratic heroic tradition of the Anglo-Saxon poetic manner — its highly technical diction, style, and metre — suddenly showed that in a night, as it were, he had acquired the mastery over this long and specialized discipline.

Perhaps, too, Cædmon's Hymn, and the series of full Biblical poetic paraphrases which he afterwards was able to make on hearing the Sacred subject-matter repeated and explained, seemed a miracle in another sense as well. For if this poet was, in fact, the very first to apply the Germanic heroic poetic discipline of vocabulary, style, and general technique to Christian story and Christian edification, then, indeed, the Hymn must be regarded (as it must have been at the time of its original recitation) as a great document of poetic revolution in early Anglo-Saxon England. Whoever first applied pagan traditional poetic discipline to Christian matter set the whole tone and method of subsequent Anglo-Saxon poetry. He preserved for Christian art the great verbal inheritance of Germanic culture. The nameless Roman poet who complained at the Gothic feast of the barbarians "eating and drinking and making poetry" reminds us poignantly — as the late R. W. Chambers remarked in his edition of Widsith — of how great is our loss in having nothing but this odd reference of the great poetic culture of the Goths. As the Roman poetaster says in the Latin Anthology:

> Inter eils Gothicum matian ia drincan ia scapian;
> Non audet quisquam dignos edicere versus.

> (Amid the health-drinkings of the Goths, they eat and
> drink and make poetry; no one dares recite worthy verses.)

Yet some of us would willingly give the whole Anthology for a a piece of real Gothic poetry of the size even of Cædmon's Hymn. But for all this loss, the nine lines of the Anglo-Saxon Cædmon do make some reparation. For they mark the beginning of that union of Latin Christendom with what remained of a Germanic cultural set of linguistic values, which was to make for the greatness of Beowulf and what is of most worth in Anglo-Saxon poetry.

Looking at the Hymn, one is struck by the fact that in its nine short lines there seem to be at least nine words which must have then belonged to the aristocratic heroic-poetic tradition —

417

words of a diction which would not be in use among the peasants
who had shared the poetic evenings at the convivia with Cædmon:
words which were to become part of the ordinary tradition of
Anglo-Saxon Christian poetry. These words are: Metod 'creator,'
with its suggestions of measurement, fate, and vastness; modgidanc
'mind-thought,' Bede's consilium, calling up a vista of poetic
compounds which was to run through Anglo-Saxon poetic literature; wuldurfæder 'father of glory,' of which the first element
wuldor is poetical in its own right; ælda, in the phrase aelda
barnum 'for the children of men,' which was part of the common
Germanic poetic vocabulary (as witness the exactly parallel
usages in Old Norse and Old High German), an expression which
Beowulf and many another poem were to make familiar (or, as
I have already suggested, the alternative and apparently unique
eordu, in the phrase eordu bearnum 'children of earth'); mid-
dungeard 'the middle enclosure' or 'world,' almost better remembered from the part played by its equivalent in Old Norse
mythology; tiadæ 'made,' or 'created'; firum 'for men,' a poetic
expression well used in its Old Saxon form in the Heliand; folde
'earth,' in its Northumbrian oblique case form foldu; frea 'ruler,'
or 'king,' the word chosen by Wulfila as Gothic frauja, for the
regular title of the Lord in his Bible translation, probably because of its more poetic and dignified associations.

All of these once formed part of the common Germanic poetic
vocabulary in the aristocratic heroic diction which Christianity,
along with the great traditional Germanic metre, took over into
a new—and yet never fully interrupted—heroic poetry of new
values blended with still living Germanic sentiments and symbols.
The voices of Christ's disciples, rising up as they sing His dirge
in what is implied in the Ruthwell Cross inscription remind us
of those similar voices of the warriors of Finn and Hengest who
in Beowulf walked round the funeral pyre builded for the slain on
both sides—for Finn's sons and Hengest's lord Hnæf.

So far as our surviving records go, these traditional poetic
words of Cædmon's Hymn appeared for the first time, used with
propriety and in the right technique of metre, applied to Christian sacred story, on that morning when the Northumbrian herdsman recited the fruits of his dream to the amazed monastic
brethren. Each of them, no doubt, had its wealth of poetic and
traditional associations, its delicate suggestiveness. The metre,
too, unlike the usual peasant verse with its rougher and probably

freer alliterative rhythm, perhaps astoundingly conformed to
the true heroic aristocratic pattern. Cædmon had shown them
what could be done with the best of the traditional art applied
now for the first time to the new truth. If Northumbrian monks
later sometimes were to relapse into a preference for poetic
lays of Ingeld—as Alcuin's famous letter suggests—Cædmon
had suddenly shown them in this blend of pagan word and rhythm
with new Christian truth, that there was a legitimate answer to
the rhetorical question "Quid Hinieldus cum Christo?" Though
the poem was indeed good, the miracle was, I believe, primarily
a technical one—a miracle, in fact, of language.

4. The Poet Cædmon

What may we know or infer concerning the poet himself?
To the relatively full account of Bede in the familiar chapter xxiv
of his fourth book, little can be added beyond those small points
which a study of the Alfredian tradition, as already suggested,
may bring out. To these latter, as discussed above, one may
perhaps add the possible difference between Bede's statement
that Cædmon was at the time of his miracle provectioris aetatis
and the Alfredian rendering gelyfedre yldo 'of infirm old age,'
or at least 'of weakened old age.' For while the Latin expression
implies advancement in age, the Anglo-Saxon participle gelyfed
should mean literally 'weakened.' But this is a small and doubtful point. We know that this state of the poet was reached at a
date between A.D. 658 and 680, since these were the limits of
the rule of the Abbess St. Hild over the monastery of Streones
Healh (Northumbrian Streunaes Halch, as in Leningrad MS., etc.).
But whether Cædmon's monastery was at Whitby, as is generally
accepted, or Strensall, as the formal purely linguistic evidence
might suggest, we have as yet no means of finally deciding.[15]
Either place would put the poet and his dialect in the present
North Riding of Yorkshire, but there would be considerable dialectal differences in the language spoken in places some thirty
miles apart, such as Whitby and Strensall.

Nor do we know just what methods of writing from dictation
were likely to have been employed by him who first wrote down
Cædmon's Hymn from the poet's mouth. He could not have been
an ideal—still less a consistently phonetic scribe: and Sievers'
means of determining Cædmon's actual type of voice, his Stim-

<u>mart</u>, are denied to us who are not "motoric." Sievers' own
reconstruction of the actual <u>Hymn</u> seems to rest largely on the
so-called "Y" version—that which lies behind the Dijon and
Paris copies.[16] But while, as I have said, there is much to be
said for the <u>eordu bearnum</u> 'children of earth' reading as against
the <u>aelda barnum</u> 'children of men' of the two earliest Northumbrian manuscripts (which Sievers does not accept), I cannot see
how his <u>hebunricæs weard</u> in the first line, and <u>hebun</u> in line six,
should be preferred to the <u>hefenricæs</u> and <u>heben</u> in which Moore
and Leningrad practically agree. For the <u>hefen</u> type must be
quite as old as the <u>hefun</u> form with different grade of vowel: and
the fact that the Ruthwell Cross inscription has the <u>hefun</u> type in
its <u>heafunæs</u> seems evidence against <u>hefun</u> for the <u>Hymn</u>, since
the Runic inscription probably came from the North of the Northumbrian area where a distinctly different dialect from that of Cædmon is to be looked for.[17] The argument that the version which
lies behind the Dijon and Paris MSS. and contained the definitely
eighth-century Northumbrian reading <u>eordu bearnum</u> (for which
I have offered support as the original wording) must be nearer
to Cædmon than the common text of Moore and Leningrad has
been rejected often because that <u>eordu</u> version must have used
the runic symbol ᚹ (<u>wynn</u>) for <u>w</u> instead of the earlier <u>u</u> or <u>uu</u>.
Wynn must lie behind such spellings as <u>þue</u> (<u>we</u>) and <u>þueard</u>
(<u>weard</u>) which are common to both Dijon and Paris: and <u>wynn</u>,
we are told, did not come into use till late in the eighth century.
But the fact is that charters are found sporadically using <u>wynn</u>
as early as the last quarter of the seventh century as well as
in the earlier eighth century. Anderson has sought to show that
the English material in the Leningrad MS. represents a dialect
probably that of Bede himself in the monastery of Wearmouth;[18]
and that of the Moore version is certainly different from this in
some respects. But we do not know whether the Moore MS. scribe
in the year 737 was writing as he then habitually did, or was striv-
ing faithfully to reproduce the very sounds of Cædmon's <u>Hymn</u>
which had been handed down in oral tradition as a sacred text
in a manner comparable to the transmission and preservation
over more than two millennia of even the accent-marks in the
hymns of the <u>Rigveda</u>. The unparalleled and possibly archaic
forms of the Moore MS. version, like <u>haleg</u> (cf. the Gothic Runic
inscription at Pietroasa with its <u>hailag</u>) and <u>scepen</u> in line six,
might strengthen this latter hypothesis. One might note, too,

the form hrofe in the same line, where the scribe might be
thought to have inadvertently omitted to put the older hrofæ,
just as the carver of the Ruthwell Cross inscription cut walde
for waldæ.[19] The fact that the Leningrad MS. here has the expected early form hrofæ supports this view. But I do not propose here to offer any detailed examination of the text of the
Hymn: but merely to show that—while conclusive evidence is
yet wanting, scholars are probably right in following Wanley
and Hickes of long ago by taking the Moore MS. as the nearest
to the authentic Cædmon that we are able to get, despite the discovery of so many manuscripts in the last half-century. The
one exception I would make to this generalization is the doubt
in favour of the eordu bearnum 'children of earth' reading so
often mentioned before. To the facts about the poet Cædmon so
far recalled, then, we may add the Moore MS. version as being,
on the whole, probably a careful reproduction from a sound local
tradition of the very words and forms of Cædmon himself at a
time not more than sixty years after his death.

There is no need to elaborate on the character of the poet
himself. Bede has told his story simply and clearly. I shall
not attempt a modern interpretation of Bede's statements, which
can add no facts save those I have touched upon—the existence
of an independent Alfredian tradition going back to at least eighth-
century Northumbria, the widespread care bestowed upon the
preserving of this text, and the probability that we may study
the Moore MS. version as something very near to the actual forms
used by the poet himself when he first dictated the Hymn. It is,
indeed, an astonishing fact that among so large a number as
seventeen copies of the Hymn there should throughout be an almost complete agreement as to the words used by Cædmon.
Spelling, dialect, date of copying, scribal convention—these
things account for almost all the divergences among the copies,
with the one remarkable exception of the "children of earth" and
"children of men" difference, which points to a period of oral
transmission as distinct from copying. This oral transmission,
then, may be added to our collection of probabilities, if not actually
of facts. By putting in the historical background to Bede's description, we could further picture the environment in which our poet
grew up, created poetry, and died. But I am not qualified to do
this, nor is the material as abundant as one might expect.[20]

Nor is anything of value to be had for the appreciation of
Cædmon the poet by an etymological speculation upon his name.
It may well be of ultimately Celtic origin, parallel with the
Primitive Celtic Catumanus,[21] where the element Katu corresponds with the Welsh cad 'battle,' and has been found in a number of other Anglo-Saxon names such as that of St. Chad. But
this does not help us to explain the genius of Cædmon; and certainly there is nothing individual in our nine lines of the Hymn
which could be linked with any inference of Celtic ancestry.
The name is not peculiar to the poet, moreover. The Kadmon
of the Ruthwell Cross inscription, if still admissible as part of
the Runic statement, would merely be the name—not of the poet
of the verses—but of the rune-carver.

The style, tone, and diction of the Hymn do not, in fact, show
anything that can be made to suggest the individuality of its
author. But they are in the Anglo-Saxon equivalent of Matthew
Arnold's "grand style," if they have not quite the Aristotelian
$\sigma\pi o\upsilon\delta\alpha\iota\acute{o}\tau\eta\varsigma$. Their literary or poetic qualities are those of
their kind—those of that stylus Cædmonianus which was to be
the characteristic quality of Anglo-Saxon Christian heroic verse.
What is, I believe, the true significance of the Hymn is not anything which we can re-picture in the mind of the poet himself,
but rather the fact that it is a miraculous revolutionary docu-
ment which was one of the greatest landmarks in the history of
our English poetry. When the poet of Beowulf made Hrothgar's
scop sing of the creation—whatever may have been the actual
source of the passage, he was using the stylus Caedmonianus—
whether consciously or not:

> þær wæs hearpan sweg,
> swutol sang scopes, sægde se þe cuþe
> frumsceaft fira feorran reccan,
> cwæð þæt se ælmihtiga eorðan worhte,
> wlitebeorhtne wang, swa wæter bebugeð,
> gesette sigehreþig sunnan ond monan,
> leoman to leohte landbuendum,
> ond gefrætwade foldan sceatas
> leomum ond leafum, lif eac gesceop
> cynna gehwylcum þara ðe cwice hwyrfaþ.[22]

THE POETRY OF CÆDMON

The genius of Cædmon, if the word is at all to be used, was the fact that he was the vehicle through whom a particular art-form was first employed—a "form and pressure" which was to rule not only the Biblical poems of the Junius MS. but in some sense the whole of Anglo-Saxon heroic poetry, and to impart something by way of inheritance to the great aristocratic four-teenth-century romance of Sir Gawain and the Green Knight. No doubt, it may be said truly that the need to preserve the traditional Anglo-Saxon metre dictated unconsciously the sur-vival of the traditional heroic vocabulary: for without this wealth of words how could the alliterative rhythm have continued? But it is also true that it was the first-fruits of the poet Cædmon's vision that showed by example and model how this inheritance of language and metre was to be applied to what must have seemed at first an entirely alien matter and thought. Though we may not with sureness ascribe any of the "Cædmonian poems" to the herdsman of Streones Healh, the great tradition of style and diction of which his Hymn was the first exemplar is, indeed, most properly to be associated with his name. The language of the old Ingeld and much of the heroic sentiment and symbolism which it implied joined the new Gospel—if I may apply in a new context the words of Bede—"sine detrimento sui decoris ac dignitatis." The example and impelling tradition created through the miracle described by Bede were the vehicles of this union.

Of the importance of Cædmon's Hymn as a linguistic docu-ment, I do not think this is the occasion to speak in any detail. This is, in fact, the one aspect of the text that has so far general-ly received full and careful attention. The scholarly presenta-tion of the whole apparatus of the textual evidence by Dobbie in America (see note 10), and the philological study (in condensed form) by A. H. Smith (see note 16), have well covered much of the ground in this field. The comparatively recently discovered Leningrad MS. has, after a not very satisfying first detailed presentation of the Hymn in Speculum of 1928,[23] now received fairly full treatment—including its other Anglo-Saxon material— by O. S. Anderson in Sweden (see note 11).

A text which is extant in seventeen copies, ranging from the eighth to the fifteenth centuries (the extreme limits being repre-sented by the Moore and the Paris MSS.), cannot but supply heter-ogeneous and significant philological material. Besides being in itself the outstanding piece of Early-Northumbrian in our language,

Cædmon's Hymn thus affords a wealth of forms and spellings, of dialectal characters, and examples of insular and continental scribal methods, which can scarcely be paralleled. But it is just because all this linguistic evidence—by no means yet fully sifted—is now available in convenient form to the researcher that I have preferred here to emphasize rather those aspects of the poet Cædmon's importance which the enthusiasm of the philologist is apt to pass by or to take for granted. If Gollancz's appellation of "the morning star of English poetry" be thought fanciful or mere sentiment, it is certainly true that Cædmon was the first vehicle of good Anglo-Saxon poetry as we know it, and of a new method of Germanic poetry of great power, which was not only to revolutionize our poetic history, but was to spread with almost equal poetic power far over the continent of Europe. For the Heliand, the Old Saxon poem of the Gospel-harmony— whose later-added Praefatio and introductory verses apply the Cædmon-story to its nameless author—is indeed a Cædmonian poem in the widest sense. Nor could the Old-Saxon Genesis, whose fragments still survive, have come into existence without the impulse of a new poetic culture which the Anglo-Saxon missionaries carried with them into Germany from England in the eighth century. Cædmon was at once an Anglo-Saxon scop and a Christian maker: and it is the blending of these two functions in one man hitherto unable even to use the peasant oral poetry of his native environment, that is commemorated by Bede in his account of the miracle.

NOTES

1   "The Value of Spelling as Evidence," Transactions of the Philological Society for 1943, pp. 19–22. Cf. W. G. Collingwood, Northumbrian Crosses of the Pre-Norman Age (London, 1927), pp. 112 ff. Collingwood's "Typological theory" does not seem to have been taken seriously enough by the philologists, who must, it seems to me, accept it as unanswerable from the point of view of the history of art, and re-think their linguistic assumptions accordingly.

2   The Caedmon MS. of Anglo-Saxon Biblical Poetry, Junius XI [the figure should strictly have been Arabic] in the Bodleian Library, with Introduction by Sir Israel Gollancz; published for the British Academy (Oxford, 1927), p. cvi. For Gol-

lancz's full view of Genesis and Cædmon, see ibid., pp. xlviii-lxviii.

3 Britannia, Max Förster zum sechzigsten Geburtstage (Leipzig, 1929), pp. 57–84.

4 Ziele und Wege der Schallanalyse; Sonderdruck aus der Festschrift für Wilhelm Streitberg, Stand und Aufgaben der Sprachwissenschaft (Heidelberg, 1924), p. 66.

5 Udney Yule, Statistical Study of Literary Vocabulary (Cambridge, 1944).

6 Institutiones Grammaticae Anglo-Saxonicae et Moeso-Gothicae Auctore Georgio Hickesio Ecclesiae Anglicanae Presbytero . . . Oxoniae, e Theatro Sheldoniano, 1689. Typis Junianis, 4to.

7 Antiquae Literaturae Septentrionalis Liber Alter, seu Humphredi Wanleii Librorum vett. Septentrionalium, qui in Angliae Bibliothecis extant . . . Catalogus Historicocriticus [book ii or vol. iii of George Hickes' Thesaurus], (Oxoniae, 1705).

8 MS. Bodley, Eng. Hist. C vi, fol. 40. My attention was kindly drawn to this important letter of Wanley by Mr. J. A. W. Bennett of Magdalen College, Oxford.

9 Reliques of Ancient English Poetry: consisting of Old Heroic Ballads Songs, and other pieces of our Earlier Poets, together with some few of later date, 3rd ed. (London, 1775), Vol. I. An Essay on the Ancient English Minstrels, pp. li-lii. It is interesting to note that Bishop Percy evidently regarded the poems recited at the convivia of Cædmon and his companions as described by Bede as the precursors of the English ballads.

10 For a full account of all these seventeen versions of the Hymn and of the literature on the subject, see The Manuscripts of Cædmon's Hymn and Bede's Death Song with a Critical Text of the Epistola Cuthberti de Obitu Bedæ, Elliott Van Kirk Dobbie (New York, 1937).

11 Since Dobbie surveyed the whole subject with full bibliographical apparatus (see note 10), O. S. Anderson of Lund

has made a special study of the Leningrad MS. of the Historia
Ecclesiastica in which chapters on Cædmon's Hymn are included. See Old English Material in the Leningrad MS. of
Bede's Ecclesiastical History (Lund, 1941). He gives a new
facsimile of the Leningrad Hymn, and defends the reading
ældu as being not necessarily an error for ælda, but a genuine
Northumbrian form comparable to the yldo (gen. pl.) of Beowulf 70.

12 I do not accept the view put forward by T. Miller in his edition
of the Alfredian Bede for the Early English Text Society and
commonly followed, that the Anglian forms in the manuscripts
imply Anglian origin for the archetypal text. So many manuscripts were copied in the West Midlands in the tenth and
eleventh centuries that it is common to find "Late West-
Saxon" works showing Anglian forms — often of a demonstrably Western type. King Alfred's Bede was doubtless
copied much; and for historical reasons the late survivors
seem to have been copied in the West for the most part. But
the linguistic evidence based on supposed dialect characters
seems to me quite insufficient to prove a non-Alfredian
authorship of the lost original, but merely to show the place
of origin of some scribes of later copies.

13 See Eduard Sievers' edition of the Heliand (Halle, 1878),
pp. 3–6.

14 For an account of Hallbjörn Hali in this connexion, cf. Finnur
Jónsson, Den Oldnorske og Oldislendske Litteraturs Historie
(Copenhagen, 1923), II, pp. 75–76.

15 Cf. A. H. Smith, The Place-names of the North Riding of
Yorkshire, in the Place-Name Society's series (Cambridge,
1928), s.v. Whitby and Strensall.

16 Eduard Sievers in Britannica, loc. cit., pp. 72–73. For the
"Y" version see P. Wuest, "Zwei neue Handschriften von
Cædmon's Hymnus," ZDA, XLVIII (1906), 205–226. Here
the Dijon and Paris MSS. are fully treated. Cf. Frampton's
somewhat sweeping article "Cædmon's Hymn," MP, XXI
(1924), and A. H. Smith's Three Northumbrian Poems (London, 1933).

17 Both the Dijon and Paris MSS. have hefunricæs in the first line, which Sievers seems to follow: but both manuscripts have efen (presumably a Continental spelling of hefen) in the sixth—thereby agreeing in this latter with Moore and Leningrad against Sievers.

18 O. S. Anderson, op. cit., pp. 137–145.

19 See Transactions of the Philological Society for 1943, loc. cit.

20 The late Wilhelm Levison's Ford Lectures for 1943, though they treat of the century which followed Cædmon, make some valuable additions to our impressions on this subject. See England and the Continent in the Eighth Century, by Wilhelm Levison (Oxford, 1946).

21 Cf. the Caturiges of Caesar's Commentarii.

22 Beowulf, lines 90 ff.

23 Olga Dobiache-Rojdestvensky, "Un Manuscrit de Bède à Leningrad," Speculum, III (1928), 314–321. For the slight earlier descriptions of this manuscript see the references in Dobbie, op. cit., p. 16.

THE DREAM OF THE ROOD AS PROSOPOPOEIA

Margaret Schlauch

As succeeding generations of scholars have studied the body of Old English lyric poetry and given tribute to its enduring literary qualities, an almost incredulous amazement has been expressed repeatedly concerning the originality of form and the extraordinary emotional intensity manifested in it. These qualities are particularly striking in the anonymous verse monologues which make up a considerable part of the whole lyrical offering. It is generally admitted that these poems show exceptional skill and mastery of technique; they are not the fumbling efforts of untaught beginners. For poems such as Wanderer, Seafarer, and Banished Wife's Lament, classical models have been suggested more than once. These lyrics represent persons as speakers. As partial explanation of their genesis, it has been pointed out that any cultivated Englishman of the time would have known and admired such declamatory passages as the speech of Æneas (most famous of exiles) to Dido and Dido's own lament at the involuntary perfidy of her guest in Vergil,[1] and the more lachrymose epistolary monologues in Ovid's Heroides. Hilda Reuschel has recently suggested that Ovid's personal expressions of an exile's woe in the Tristia and Epistolae ex Ponto may have contributed to the very wording of Old English lyrics.[2] The originality of treatment by Anglo-Saxon writers is generally conceded,[3] but it is undisputed that Latin models were near at hand and well-loved.

As a literary type, the Dream of the Rood stands somewhat apart from the other elegiac monologues in Old English. Here for the major part of the poem the speaker is an inanimate object, not a person. The discourse of the Rood is enclosed in another one, that of the dreamer who heard it speak; but the inner monologue is the essence of the poem. To endow the Cross with

Reprinted from Essays and Studies in Honor of Carleton Brown (New York University Press, 1940), pp. 23−34, by permission of the author and the publisher.

power of locution was to use a device of unexampled effectiveness in making vivid an event about which, for all devout Christians, the entire history of the world revolved. The object most
intimately associated with that breath-taking moment when "the
veil of the temple was rent in twain from the top to the bottom;
and the earth did quake, and the rocks were rent" might well be
given speech with profound literary effectiveness. Yet this was
not commonly done at the time. The Old English poet was not
following a literary tradition concerning the Rood; he was making an innovation with the originality of genius.

Concerning the independence of models manifested by this
author, A. S. Cook remarks in his introduction to the poem:

> The second part, the address of the cross, is unique
> in its composition. The notion of representing an
> inanimate object as speaking to him who stands in
> its presence, and communicating information or
> counsel, is as old as the Greek epigram. This was
> originally an inscription on a monument, a statue,
> or a votive offering preserved in a temple, and not
> seldom represented the work of art, or the dead who
> reposed beneath the monument, as addressing the
> passer-by.[4]

As literary analogues Professor Cook cites some of the Greek
epigrams from the Anthology and several in Latin in which a
dead person, or the statue of a dead person, speaks briefly from
the tomb. He also refers to an epigram which Ovid puts into
the mouth of a parrot (Amores, II, 6) and another, perhaps spurious, at the beginning of Heroides, IX. Such simple statements
in the first person singular were inscribed on bells, swords,
and house fronts. Beyond these, however, he offers no literary
parallels before the Old English period. If this were all, the
originality shown by the author of the Dream of the Rood would
indeed be all but unbelievable.

Now I have no desire to diminish the glory of the Old English
poet, whose literary gifts remain beyond dispute no matter how
many models he may have had. But I do wish to point out that
Professor Cook has neglected to consider a number of poems in
Latin which bridge the period from the Greek Anthology to eighth-
century England and perceptibly diminish the appropriateness of

the term "unique" as applied to the speech of an inanimate object—even if it is to be the Rood—in the literature still extant in the eighth century. Moreover, I should like to point out that even without any models in Latin, a gifted writer might have found the suggestion for such a poem as the Dream of the Rood in Latin rhetorical texts of the time which discussed prosopopoeia, or discourse by inanimate objects. The poems suggested so far as direct sources or models for the Dream differ from it most conspicuously in being third person narratives instead of monologues. Thus Ebert[5] proposed a fourth-century poem De Cruce by Cyprian, also called De Pascha,[6] as a direct inspiration for the Old English poem; but this is allegorical exposition with but a slight modicum of narrative in the third person. Such texts are pertinent in a general way, since they exemplify interest in the Cross as a theme, but they leave out of account the interesting aesthetic problem of the innovation in Rood literature: the use of elegiac monologue.

In the golden age of Latin literature there was already a marked development of imaginary discourses by inanimate objects. This was a device particularly favored by the elegiac poets. Among the better known examples of this and later ages are: the discourse of the Tress of Berenice by Catullus; the apologia or exculpatio of a courtesan's doorpost in a dialogue also written by Catullus;[7] a similar theme, Verba Januae conquerentis by Propertius;[8] the discourse attributed to his book of Tristia by Ovid;[9] a panegyric on the emperor composed by Ausonius and put into the mouth of the Danube River;[10] a discourse delivered by a statue of Dido and another by the petrified Niobe, also by Ausonius.[11] An anonymous writer of the days of decline and fall represents the City of Rome itself speaking in its desolation:

> Vix scio quae fueram, vix Romae Roma recordor,
>   Quae populo, regnis, moenibus alta fui.
> Cesserunt arces, cecidere palatia Divum,
>   Jam servit populus, degeneravit eques.
> Quae fueram totum quondam celebrata per orbem,
>   Vix sinor occasus vel miminisse mei.[12]

Elizabeth Hazelton Haight has pointed out the popularity of this literary device among the Roman elegiac poets. Speaking of The Lock of Berenice by Catullus, she says:

THE <u>DREAM OF THE ROOD</u> AS PROSOPOPOEIA

The fact that the speaker in this elegy is a Talking
Tress associates it with all those poems in which
inanimate objects (tombstones, statues, doors) are
given voice. The common device of the Speaking
Door Catullus uses in another poem, which is not
a monologue, but a dialogue, between House Door
and Poet Catullus. . . . The House Door poem [of
Propertius, she continues later] (I, 16) may have
been suggested by Catullus LXVII. It is not specifically stated to be the door of Cynthia's house, but
may be the door of any courtesan. . . . House Door
speaks a monologue about its disgrace in having
sunk from the portal of a consul whither triumphal
cars drove, to the barred door of a Light o' Love
where all night excluded lovers chant their lamentation.[13]

Of such themes the speaking tree, or the wooden statue
which recalls that it was once a tree, presents the closest classical parallel to the monologue passage in the <u>Dream of the Rood</u>.
A poem long attributed to Ovid, <u>De Nuce</u>, represents a nut tree
as complaining about the hurts and indignities to which it is exposed because passers-by shake it and throw stones at it in order
to obtain the ripened nuts.[14] The tree protests its innocence,
and laments the failure of the gods to act as husbandmen and
protect the trees which were formerly in their charge.

1 Nux ego iuncta viae, cum sim sine crimine vitae,
     a populo saxis praetereunte petor.
  obruere ista solet manifesta poena nocentes,
     publica cum lentam non capit ira moram.
  nil ego peccavi: nisi si peccare vocetur
     annua cultori poma referre suo.

Fertility is a curse, not a blessing; if it were sterile it would
be unmolested: "Certe ego, si numquam peperissem tutior
essem." It has suffered mutilation not because of hatred but
because of desire for the booty:

37 at mihi saeva nocent mutilatis vulnera ramis,
     nudaque deiecto cortice ligna patent.

> non odium facit hoc, sed spes inducta rapinae.
> sustineant aliae poma: querentur idem.

The tree also laments because it is suffering from thirst, because it is not permitted to bring its fruit to maturity, because winter, hated by most creatures, is necessarily welcome to it on account of the peace it brings, and because it cannot escape from threatened wounds ("nec vitare licet mihi moto vulnera trunco"). These manifold ills cause it to desire death:

> 159 o! ego, cum longae venerunt taedia vitae,
>   optavi quotiens arida facta mori!
>   optavi quotiens aut caeco turbine verti
>   aut valido missi fulminis igni peti!
>   atque utinam subitae raperent mea poma procellae,
>   vel possem fructus excutere ipsa meos!

The poem ends with a direct exhortation to the traveler by the wayside: if I have deserved this punishment or been harmful in any way, burn me or cut me down at once; if not, leave me in peace and pass on!

The resemblances of this poem to the Dream of the Rood are largely generic, because both are laments and both are spoken by trees. The chief difference lies in the important circumstance that Nux complains of its own misfortunes, whereas the Rood solicits pity for the crucified Christ whom it bore. Certain verbal parallelisms result from the similarity of theme: "ac ic sceolde fæste standan" and "hyldan me ne dorste" (ll. 43b and 45b) recall "nec vitare licet mihi moto vulnera trunco, / quem sub humo radix vinclaque firma tenent?" (ll. 169 f.). The general statements "Feala ic on þam beorȝe ȝebiden hæbbe / wraða wyrda" (ll. 50 f.) and "Sare ic wæs mid sorȝum ȝedrefed" (l. 59a) seem to echo the equally general sentiments of Nux such as "sic ego sola petor, soli quia causa petendi est: / frondibus intactis cetera turba viret" (ll. 45 f.). There are specific references in both poems to the wounds suffered by the tree. Rood says: "eall ic wæs mid strælum forwundod" (l. 62b), and Nux refers to its "mutilatis vulnera ramis" (l. 37). Nux protests its innocence: "nil ego peccavi: nisi si peccare vocetur / annua cultori poma referre suo" (ll. 5 f.). There is at least an implied protestation of innocence in the Rood's repeated emphasis on its

inability to do otherwise than carry out the Lord's will (ll. 35
and 42) even though its part in the crucifixion made it seem for
a time most loathsome to men ("leodum laðost," l. 88a).

In the Dream of the Rood a few lines are devoted to a description of the tree's life in the forest, and an account of the day
when men came and bore it away on their shoulders (ll. 28–33).
In Latin literature too the wooden statue of a god sometimes refers to the time when it was transformed from a block of wood
into an image. The most conspicuous examples are to be found
in the group of poems giving speech to the god Priapus, of which
Horace's satire (I, 8) Canidia is probably most famous:

I   Olim truncus eram ficulnus, inutile lignum;
    Cum faber, incertus scamnum faceretne Priapum,
    Maluit esse deum. Deus inde ego, furum aviumque
    Maxima formido. . . .

Not all of the Latin Priapea are composed in the first person,
but many which are contain a few lines on the transformation
from tree to image,[15] and many stress its tutelary function.

Familiarity with the Ovidian De Nuce on the part of the
author of the Dream of the Rood is by no means improbable.
The poem was commonly included among the authentic works
of Ovid. The earliest English manuscripts known to contain it
postdate the Norman Conquest,[16] but this does not preclude
knowledge of it in England at an earlier date, since collections
of the Ovidian poems are extant in continental manuscripts from
the eleventh and twelfth centuries.[17] The collection of Priapea
was not lost in the Middle Ages; it was preserved partly, no
doubt, because the poems were attributed to Vergil. A ninth-
century manuscript of Murbach, Germany, contains these poems
together with other short ones traditionally ascribed to Vergil.[18]
The text of Horace's Canidia was also known in Europe before
the time of the Conquest, though there is no record of an 'Oratius
totus' in England before 1170.[19]

Besides these Latin discourses by trees or wooden images,
there are, as Professor Cook has pointed out, a few riddles
which bear a remote resemblance to the Dream of the Rood.
Number 17 by Eusebius (eighth century) represents the Cross
as speaking briefly in the first person, but the discourse is a

form of enigmatic definition, entirely lacking in the narrative element so conspicuous in the Dream:

> Per me mors adquiritur, et bona vita tenetur;
> Me multi fugiunt, multique frequenter adorant;
> Sumque timenda malis, non sum tamen horrida justis;
> Damnavique virum, sic multos carcere solvi.[20]

It is because of their continuity with this distinctly classical tradition that some of the Old English riddles composed in the first person singular show similarity of phraseology with the Dream of the Rood; for instance, number 72, which concerns a spear, begins "I grew in the mead, and dwelt where earth and sky fed me, until those who were fierce against me overthrew me when advanced in years." (Compare this with "me vilem et e rude fuste / Manus sine arte rusticae dolaverunt" in number 63 of the Priapea.) The riddles are not, however, the sole or nearest source of inspiration available. Discourse by an inanimate object, making use of narrative, was a form known and practised according to the precepts of mediaeval rhetoric.

That form was known as prosopopoeia, and was usually discussed in conjunction with ethopoeia, or imaginary monologue attributed to a human but fictitious character. The two cannot be very well separated, since prosopopoeia assumes that an object feels and speaks like a person.

Priscian, following his source Hermogenes, gives the following brief description of the two germane forms under the heading of adlocutio, which is the ninth of his topics:

> Adlocutio est imitatio sermonis ad mores et suppositas personas accommodata, ut quibus verbis uti potuisset Andromache Hectore mortuo: conformatio vero, quam Graeci προσωποποιίαν nominant, est, quando rei alicui contra naturam datur persona loquendi, ut Cicero patriae reique publicae in invectivis dat verba.[21]

The example from Homer—the discourse of Andromache—had been used by Hermogenes; the Ciceronian instance of prosopopoeia —the discourse by the City of Rome to Cicero—was Priscian's substitute for a similar but less familiar instance from Greek oratory in which the sea is made to speak.[22] After a brief definition of simulacri factio (εἰδωλοποιία), or the attribution of speech to the dead, Priscian makes some general remarks on the appropriateness of certain types of speeches to certain circumstances and individuals. He classifies all monologues into three groups according to their style or emotional tone: orationes morales, passionales, and mixtae.

> Passionales sunt, in quibus passio, id est commiseratio perpetua inducitur, ut quibus verbis uti potuisset Andromache mortuo Hectore; morales vero, in quibus obtinent mores, ut quibus verbis uti potuisset rusticus, cum primum aspexerit navem; mixtae, quae utrumque habent, ut quibus verbis uti potuisset Achilles interfecto Patroclo; habet enim et passionem funeris amici et morem de bello cogitantis. Sed operatio procedit per tria tempora, et incipit a praesentibus, recurrit ad praeterita et transit ad futura: habeat autem stilum suppositis aptum personis.

As prosopopoeia the Dream of the Rood appears to be an oratio passionalis (a specific Cross speaks, not one of a class; moreover, the aim is certainly to evoke "commiseratio perpetua"). Emporius used the term pathopoeia for such impassioned fictitious orations.[23] The Dream observes the suggested time sequence of present-past-future by means of the introduction in which a dreamer recounts his vision of the Cross as an event in the present time, by the Rood's narrative account of the Crucifixion in the past, and by the closing references to a future life. The Rood says:

> 119 Ac ðurh ða rode sceal   rice ʒesecan
>   of eorðweʒe   æʒhwylc sawl,
>   seo þe mid Wealdende   wunian þenceð.

The dreamer adds:

> 135   7 ic wene me
>   daʒa ʒehwylce   hwænne me Dryhtnes ród,
>   þe ic her on eorðan   ær sceawode,
>   on þysson lænan   life ʒefetiʒe,

> 7 me þonne ȝebrinȝe   þær is blis mycel,
> dream on heofonum, . . .

In discussing imaginary monologues, some writers like Emporius limited themselves to ethopoeia, stressing the general advice that discourse must be made to harmonize with the characteristics (mores; the ἦθος of Hermogenes) of the type of person being presented. Isidore of Seville echoes Priscian in his definition of prosopopoeia; he quotes the same example from Cicero's speeches: "Etenim si mecum patria mea . . . loqueretur. . . ."[24]

Another type of Latin discourse may be found represented in the Dream of the Rood, subordinate to the narrative embodied in prosopopoeia. Although not intended as an exculpation or speech of defense from an implied charge, the Rood's narrative contains certain phrases suggesting a desire to dissociate itself from the cruel tragedy to which it served as instrument. For a time it suffered reproach for this:

> 87   Iu ic wæs ȝeworden   wita heardost,
> leodum laðost,   ærþan ic him lifes weȝ
> rihtne ȝerymde,   reordberendum.

But throughout the narrative the Rood's helplessness has been emphasized. Just as the voluntary character of Christ's sacrifice is underscored in certain locutions,[25] so the involuntary function of the Cross appears in such phrases as: "þær ic þa ne dorste ofer Dryhtnes word / buȝan oððe berstan" (ll. 35 f.); "Bifode ic þa me se Beorn ymbclypte; ne dorste ic hwæðre buȝan to eorðan" (l. 42); "Ac ic sceolde fæste standan" (l. 43b); ". . . hyldan me ne dorste" (l. 45) and "Ic þæt eall beheold. / Sare ic wæs mid sorȝum ȝedrefed" (ll. 58 f.).

Literary defense from a charge, whether overt or implied, was known as purgatio. All of the longer mediaeval rhetorics discussed it. Cassiodorus, for instance, shows it graphically charted as a subdivision of a technique of defense known as concessio ("I admit that I did this, but . . ."), which in its turn is a subdivision of qualitas assumptiva in the class known as iuridicalis. His definition is:

> Purgatio est, cum factum quidem conceditur, sed
> culpa removetur. Haec partes habet tres: inpruden-
> tiam, casum, necessitatem.[26]

This definition of purgatio is to be found with but slight verbal changes in Martianus Capella[27] and Isidore of Seville.[28] Alcuin elaborates it by presenting hypothetical cases:

> Purgatio est, per quam eius qui accusatur non factum
> ipsum, sed voluntas defenditur: ea habet partes tres,
> inprudentiam, casum, necessitudinem. Inprudentia
> est, cum scisse aliquid is, qui arguitur, negatur, ut
> . . . [an example follows taken from a typical contro-
> versia]. Casus autem infertur in concessionem, cum
> demonstratur aliqua fortunae vis voluntati obstitisse,
> ut . . . [example follows]. Necessitudo autem infertur,
> cum vi quadam reus id quod fecerit fecisse defenditur,
> hoc modo . . . [an example of shipwrecked persons who
> involuntarily violated the law of Rhodes about its harbor:
> "vi et necessitate sumus in portum coacti"].[29]

The Cross indicates repeatedly that it performed its dolor-
ous function "vi et necessitate"; it is for this reason that parts
of its speech sound like a purgatio using the technical plea of
necessitudo. The approximation to this particular form of concessio or defensive pleading also explains the resemblance to
Middle English and other poems in which the Cross tells of its
unwanted function as part of its defense in a disputation with
Mary. Professor H. R. Patch has already called attention to the
slightly argumentative tone which anticipates the disputes between Mary and the Cross.[30] Mary is mentioned in the Old English poem, but the defense, if such it may be called, is directed
not to her but to the dreamer. The epithet reus is probably more
appropriately applied to the Cross in the later disputation than
in the Dream of the Rood, but a knowledge of rhetoric may have
caused the author to bring out the element of concessio in its
speech.

The Latin poems and rhetorical theory here presented are
intended to illuminate the literary genesis of the Dream of the
Rood rather than to supply specific sources for lines and phrases.
Its relationship to the general body of literature of devotion to
the Cross, as demonstrated by Ebert, Stevens, Patch, and Williams, is not to be doubted. But if Cyprian's allegorical exposition De Cruce, the hymns of Fortunatus and acrostic poems
glorifying the Cross give important evidence for the prevalent

appeal of the theme, its poignant effectiveness of form can be
better accounted for by pagan theory and practice of prosopopoeia.
The Ovidian De Nuce is not in any sense a source for the Dream
of the Rood, but its existence helps us to understand the element
of tradition which shapes the work of even a great innovator like
the Old English author. After all, his greatest innovation was in
the style and intensity which made of his poem an oratio passionalis
(pathopoeia) in every sense of the word. Emporius had said that
there were three levels of discourse possible in the composing of
this (as any other) type of speech; "vasta, humilis, temperata."
These three, as he was well aware, were but three variant terms
for the ancient Greek schools of oratory: Asiatic, Attic, and
Rhodian.[31] The English poet chose and successfully handled an
oratio vasta, the only appropriate one for a monologue by the
Rood. That he did this is truly his chief literary glory. No amount
of defining of rhetorical tradition, and no number of literary analogues on any level, can lessen that great distinction.[32]

NOTES

1 Rudolf Imelmann, Forschungen zur altenglischen Elegie
(Berlin, 1920), especially pp. 188 ff. and 225 ff.

2 "Ovid und die ags. Elegien," BGDSL, LXII (1938), 132 ff.

3 Ernst Sieper, in Die altenglische Elegie (Strassburg, 1915),
stresses the Germanic tone and content of the poems, and
argues for kinship with Celtic (Welsh) poetry (pp. 55 ff.).

4 The Dream of the Rood (Oxford, 1905), p. xliii. Citations
from the poem follow the edition by Bruce Dickins and Alan
S. C. Ross (London, 1934).

5 Adolf Ebert, Allgemeine Geschichte der Literatur des
Mittelalters im Abendlande (Leipzig, 1887), III, 70–72; also
in Sächsische Gesellschaft der Wissenschaften, Berichte,
Phil. -hist. Classe, XXXVI (1884), 81–93.

6 S. Thasci Caecili Cypriani Opera Omnia, ed. G. Hartel,
Part 3, in Corpus Scriptorum eccl. Lat. (Vienna, 1868–1871),
III, 305 f.

7 Carmina, 46 and 67.

8   Elegiae, I, 16.

9   Tristia, III, 1.

10 Epigrammata, 3.

11 Ibid., 118 and 27.

12 N. E. Lemaire, Poetae Latini Minores ex recensione Werns-
    dorfiana (Paris, 1825), IV, 536.

13 Romance in the Latin Elegiac Poets (New York, 1932), pp.
    22 and 102.

14 P. Ovidii Nasonis Carmina, ed. A. Riese (Leipzig, 1871), I,
    220–224 (Poetae Ovidiani: Nux).

15 See Priapea in Catulli Tibvlli Propertii Carmina, ed. L.
    Moeller (Leipzig, 1901), pp. 95–119. There are 85 poems
    in this collection. Only those representing the image as
    speaking are in any way pertinent. Number 10 is typical:
    "Insulsissima quid puella rides? / Non me Praxitiles
    Scopasve fecit, / Nec sum Phidiaca manu politus. / Sed
    lignum rude vilicus dolavit / Et dixit mihi: tu Priapus
    esto! . . ." In number 63 the image recounts the history
    of its origin, his sufferings, and the final insult put upon
    him: "Parumst, quod hic cum fixerint mihi sedem, / Agente
    terra per caniculam rimas / Siticulosam sustinemus
    aestatem? / Parum, quod imos perfluunt sinus imbres, /
    Et in capillos grandines cadunt nostros / Rigetque duro
    barba vineta crystallo; / Parum, quod acta sub laboribus
    luce / Parem diebus pervigil traho noctem. / Huc adde,
    quod me vilem et a rude fuste / Manus sine arte rusticae
    dolaverunt, / Interque cunctos ultimum deos numen / Cucur-
    bitarum ligneus vocor custos . . . ." In number 85, written
    by Catullus, the speaker stresses his role of guardian:
    "Quercus arida, rustica fabricata secure, / Nutrivi ut magis
    et magis sit beata quotannis / Huius nam domini colunt me
    deumque salutant . . . ." Cf. also number 84, likewise by
    Catullus. In an elegy by Tibullus (I, 4), Priapus makes a
    reply to a speech addressed to him.

16 Canterbury, Christ Church (dated 1170); Durham (twelfth
    century). See Max Manitius, Handschriften antiker Autoren
    in mittelalterlichen Bibliothekskatalogen (Leipzig, 1935)

(= <u>Zentralblatt für Bibliothekswesen</u>, Beiheft 67), pp. 62 ff. De Nuce is specifically mentioned as part of both of these MSS.

17 Ibid., p. 67.

18 Ibid., p. 47. See Moeller's edition of the Priapea, p. xlvi, for reference to a fragmentary codex of the eighth or ninth century containing a few of the poems.

19 Ibid., pp. 55 ff. The earliest surviving mediaeval MSS of Horace were done in France and Germany in the ninth and tenth centuries.

20 Quoted by Cook, op. cit., pp. xlix.

21 Prisciani Praeexercitamina ex Hermogene versa, ed. Carolus. Halm in Rhetores Latini Minores (Leipzig, 1863), pp. 557 f.

22 The text of Hermogenes is to be found in his Προγυ'μνάσματα, ? ed. Hugo Rabe (Leipzig, 1913), p. 20: 'Ηθοποιία ἐστί μίμησις ἤθους ὑποκειμένου προσώπου, οἷον τινας ἄν εἴποι λόγους 'Ανδρομάχη ἐπὶ ῞Εκτορι. Προσωποποιία δὲ, ὅταν πράγματι περιτιθῶμεν πρόσωπον, ὥσπερ δ ῎Ελεγχος παρὰ Μενάνδρῳ, καὶ ὥσπερ παρὰ τῷ 'Αριστείδη ἡ θάλασσα ποιεῖται τοὺς λόγους πρὸς τοὺς 'Αθηναίους . . . .

23 Ed. Halm, Rhet. Lat. Min., pp. 561 ff.

24 Origines, "Capita quae sunt de Rhetorica," in Halm, Rhet. Lat. Min., pp. 507–522, § xiii.

25 See William O. Stevens, The Cross in the Life and Literature of the Anglo-Saxons, Yale Studies in English, XXIII (New York, 1904), p. 74

26 "De Rhetorica" in the Humanae Institutiones, ed. Halm, Rhet. Lat. Min., pp. 495 and 497.

27 "De Rhetorica" in his De Nuptiis Philologiae et Mercurii, V, ed. A. Dick (Leipzig, 1925), p. 227.

28 Op. cit., p. 509.

29 Disputatio de Rhetorica, ch. 15, in Halm, Rhet. Lat. Min., p. 532.

30 "Liturgical Influence in the Dream of the Rood," PMLA, XXIV (1919), 233.

31 Halm, Rhet. Lat. Min., p. 561.

32 It is significant that a later rhetorician, Geoffrey Vinsauf, proceeds from a brief definition of prosopopoeia to a discourse by the Cross as his most ambitious example of the type: "Vocis in hac forma sanctae Crucis ecce querela. / Crux ego rapta queror, vi rapta manuque canina / Et tactu polluta canum. . . ." The speech is interspersed with frequent addresses to man (homo). See Geoffrey's "Poetria Nova" in Edmond Faral, Les Arts poétiques du xiie et du xiiie Siècle (Paris, 1924), p. 211.

THE INTERPRETATION OF THE SEAFARER[1]

Dorothy Whitelock

This paper does not set out to solve the individual cruces of the Exeter Book poem known as The Seafarer, nor does it claim to be an exhaustive survey of the views of former scholars. O. S. Anderson's careful study, "The Seafarer: An Interpretation,"[2] has rendered such a survey unnecessary. In spite of the long preoccupation of scholars with this poem, there is still no agreement on its meaning, and it is perhaps worth while to suggest a solution along different lines. It will be enough for my purpose to outline briefly the main positions taken up by others.

There have been two main difficulties in the way of the general interpretation of this poem: the one is the apparent vacillation in the author's attitude to sea travel in the first part of the poem, the other the complete absence of any reference to the sea in the latter part,[3] which consists of moralizing reflections. The first difficulty led Rieger in 1869[4] to formulate his theory that the first part is a dialogue in which an old man speaks of the hardships and a young man of the attractions of seafaring. This view won considerable support, though there has been difference of opinion as to the allotment of lines to the postulated speakers. Strong arguments against it were brought forward by Lawrence,[5] who held that the poem indicates the shifting moods of a sailor, for whom the sea, in spite of its dangers and hardships, has an irresistible appeal. Schücking[6] has demonstrated that such an attitude would be anachronistic in these early times, and Anderson agrees with him.

Both of these interpretations left the second difficulty unsolved. The second part of the poem seemed to have no connection with what had gone before, and so the exponents of either opinion accepted the theory, first advocated by Kluge,[7] that the

Reprinted from Chadwick Memorial Studies, Early Cultures of North West Europe, edited by Sir Cyril Fox and Bruce Dickens (Cambridge University Press, 1950), pp. 261–72, by permission of the publisher.

second part does not belong to the original poem, but is a later addition. This type of criticism of Old English poetry is less fashionable than it used to be,[8] and Anderson performs a useful service in demonstrating the weaknesses of the various attempts to divide the poem.[9] It is needless to re-examine such theories here, for all are based on the alleged lack of connection between the first and the second parts of the poem. If it can be established that a connected line of thought runs through the poem, the reason for dismembering it vanishes.

I share Anderson's conviction that the general reflections of the second part rise naturally from the references to sea travel in the first part, but not his belief that these references are to be interpreted allegorically. His view is, as he says, based in part on a suggestion of Ehrismann's[10] that the dangerous voyage is an allegorical representation of the afflictions of life, but he rejects Ehrismann's opinion that a contrast is being drawn between a winter and a summer voyage and that a materialistic view of life, represented by the nobleman living in luxury, is being opposed to the ascetic view of a monk, to whom the pleasures of the world are in themselves sinful. Anderson follows Schücking[11] in taking the voyage mentioned in l. 42, for which the Seafarer is longing, not only as "the life of the pious on earth" but as "life on the road to Eternity, and in this sense also death." While the hardships of the sea represent human life in the world, the poet "is longing to leave the cliffs and rocks of time and set out for the distant glories of eternity." This interpretation is worked out in detail with an ingenuity to which a brief summary cannot do justice. Either of these allegorical interpretations has the merit of establishing a sequence of thought between the references to sea travel and the remainder of the poem. I am not concerned to weigh their comparative merits as I do not think that the poem is an allegory. I shall try to defend its unity while clinging to a literal interpretation.

In passing, it may be noted that the theory that it is an allegory has failed to convince others. Doubt is implied by C. L. Wrenn[12] and clearly stated by S. B. Liljegren.[13] The main difficulty is that we are given no hint of any kind that the beginning of the poem is anything other than a realistic description. There is nothing equivalent to the expression "my life's bark" with which Anderson, though translating only the simple ceol 'ship,' warns us early on to be on our guard. It may be, as Anderson says, that "many of his phrases vividly recall venerable sentences used in every homily book; the rocks of life, the fetters of existence, the hunger for the life to come, the coldness and loneliness of life, etc.," but, unlike the homilists, the poet fails to give the slightest clue that he is using the terms rocks, fetters, etc. as images. The strongest argument brought forward against the dialogue theory, namely the absence of any indication in the text, seems to apply with equal force to the theory of allegorical interpretation.

I doubt whether a pious Englishman of the age of Bede and Boniface, or indeed much later, would have seen, as modern scholars have done, any inconsistency in a man's determination, or even eagerness, to venture forth on a journey whose perils and hardships he fully understands from his previous experience, in order to "seek the land of foreigners afar off." After all, was not this one of the recognized ways in which a man who did not "believe that earthly prosperity will last for ever" might earn his right to inherit the eternal joys?[14] It may be worth while to examine the poem with the thought of the voluntary exile, the peregrinus, in mind.

The poet declares that he will tell a true lay about himself, about his frequent sufferings at sea. With great vividness he describes the storm and the cold, the hunger, exhaustion and loneliness, pausing twice to point out that his sufferings lie beyond the conception of the happy dweller on land, of the man who, "proud and flushed with wine," knows the joy of life in the great houses. He contrasts the cry of the sea-birds with the sounds of revelry in the hall and he paints one of those winter scenes so dear to the Anglo-Saxon poet: "The shadow of night darkened, snow came from the north, frost bound the earth, hail, coldest of grains, fell on the ground." Then he continues:

> Forþon cnyssað nu
> heortan geþohtas, þæt ic hean streamas,
> sealtyþa gelac sylf cunnige;
> monað modes lust mæla gehwylce
> ferð to feran, þæt ic feor heonan
> elþeodigra eard gesece;
> forþon nis þæs modwlonc mon ofer eorþan
> ne his gifena þæs god, ne in geoguþe to þæs hwæt,
> ne in his dædum to þæs deor, ne him his dryhten to þæs hold,

> þæt he a his sæfore sorge næbbe,
> to hwon hine dryhten gedon wille.
> Ne biþ him to hearpan hyge, ne to hringþege,
> ne to wife wyn, ne to worulde hyht,
> ne ymbe owiht elles, nefne ymb yða gewealc,
> ac a hafað longunge se þe on lagu fundað.   (33b–47)

[(Therefore)[15] my heart's thoughts constrain me to
venture on the deep seas, the tumult of the salt waves;
at all times my heart's desire urges my spirit to
travel, that I may seek the land of foreigners afar off;
because there is no man on earth so high-hearted,
nor so liberal with his gifts, nor so bold in his youth,
nor so daring in his deeds, nor having so gracious a
lord, that he will not always feel anxiety over his
voyage, as to what is the Lord's purpose for him.[16]
He will have no mind for the harp, nor for the receiving of rings, no pleasure in woman nor delight
in the world, nor mind for anything else, except the
tossing of the waves, but he who puts out to sea has
always yearning.[17]]

In other words, while earthly success may cause a man to
forget the purpose of his being in the world, may lull him to a
trust in material things,[18] the man at sea will be in no such
danger, and the poet's heart urges him to leave his native land
to seek a foreign country across the sea for this very reason.
The coming of spring intensifies this impluse:

> Bearwas blostmum nimað, byrig fægriað,
> wongas wlitigað,[19] woruld onetteð;
> ealle þa gemoniað modes fusne,
> sefan to siþe, þam þe swa þenceð
> on flodwegas feor gewitan.[20]   (48–52)

[The groves blossom, cities grow fair, the fields become beautiful, the world's astir. All these things
urge on to his journey the man eager of heart, urge
on the spirit of him who thus intends to depart far on
the paths of the sea.]

Since he must leave all for dangerous paths, the cuckoo, though it is the herald of summer, can to him foretell nothing but sorrow. Once again he reiterates that a man who lives in luxury cannot even imagine the sufferings of an exile:

> Swylce geac monað geomran reorde,
> singeð sumeres weard, sorge beodeð
> bitter in breosthord. þæt se beorn ne wat,
> esteadig secg, hwæt þa sume dreogað
> þe þa wræclastas widost lecgað.   (53–57)

[Likewise the cuckoo with its mournful note[21] urges him, the herald of summer sings, forebodes bitter sorrow in his heart. The man living happily in luxury[22] does not know what some endure, those who journey furthest on the paths of exile.]

The forþon that introduces the next sentence could refer, not only to this last idea—the blind complacency of the prosperous man as a state of mind to be avoided—but also to the whole of the previous argument—but I prefer to take it as correlative with forþon of l. 64. The passage runs:

> Forþon nu min hyge hweorfeð ofer hreþerlocan;
> min modsefa mid mereflode
> ofer hwæles eþel hweorfeð wide
> eorþan sceatas, cymeð eft to me
> gifre ond grædig; gielleð anfloga,
> hweteð on hwælweg hreþer unwearnum
> ofer holma gelagu; forþon me hatran sind
> dryhtnes dreamas þonne þis deade lif,
> læne on londe: ic gelyfe no
> þæt him eorðwelan ece stondað.   (58–67)

[(Therefore) my thoughts are now roaming beyond the confines of my breast; with the ocean flood my spirit roams widely over the surface of the earth, over the whale's domain, and comes back to me eager and hungry; in its solitary flight it calls urgently, irresistibly impels my heart on the whale's path across the expanse of the seas; because dearer to me are the

joys of the Lord than this dead life, transitory on
earth: I do not believe that earthly happiness will
endure for ever.]

unity

Far from thinking that with l. 64b we begin the work of a
continuator, I do not believe, with Anderson and others, that a
new section commences here, nor even a new sentence.[23] The
three and a half lines that begin here seem to me the culmination of what has gone before; for the first time the poet states
unequivocally what it is that makes his restless spirit eager to
embrace again the hardships he has described so forcibly. In
my opinion these lines are the central lines of the poem, and all
that follows is an elaboration of their theme. The mortality of
man, the need to live so as to merit eternal life, the decay of the
glory of mighty civilizations, in which each man can see a parallel to his own inescapable fate, the uselessness of hoarded wealth
to the soul, the folly of forgetting the fear of the Lord—all are
topics closely related to the theme of the first part of the poem
as I interpret it. In the last twenty lines or so there are difficulties of interpretation which I do not propose to discuss here;[24]
they do not affect materially my main thesis. The poem ends
with a normal homiletic conclusion, on the note "Let us strive
to reach our heavenly home," and I contend that the poet has
shown us that for him the way lies through pilgrimage, with re-
nunciation of worldly pleasures. He is not going seafaring for
its own sake, but, as an islander, he cannot reach the land of
foreigners except across the sea, and when we remember the
conditions of early voyaging we need not wonder that this part
of his journey should occupy so much of his thought.[25]

References to voluntary exile are common in historical
sources of the early Anglo-Saxon period. We are told in the
anonymous Vita Ceolfridi Abbatis that Ceolfrith's elder brother,
Cynefrith, abbot of Gilling, withdrew to Ireland to study the scriptures and to serve the Lord more freely in tears and prayers,[26]
and Bede's Historia Ecclesiastica has many such references.
For example, Ecgberht, "qui in Hibernia diutius exulauerat pro
Christo,"[27] or "quem in Hibernia insula peregrinam ducere
uitam pro adipiscenda in caelis patria retulimus,"[28] had made
a vow, "quia adeo peregrinus uiuere uellet, ut numquam in in-
sulam, in qua natus est, id est Brittaniam, rediret,"[29] which
the Old English translation renders: "þæt he â wolde for Gôde

447

his lîf on elðeodiȝnesse libban 7 næfre to Brytene ealonde hweorfan,
þær he acenned wæs."30

Peregrinus had a wider meaning than our 'pilgrim,' often referring, to quote J. F. Kenney, to "the man who, for his soul's good,
departed from his homeland to dwell for a space of years, or for
the rest of his life, in strange countries."31 Bede speaks in
similar terms of Willibrord,32 Wihtberht33 and the two Hewalds,34
all Englishmen living in Ireland. The presence of two Anglian
runic inscriptions on the Isle of Man suggests that English peregrini went there also.35 The Old English version normally renders Bede's various phrases "on elþeodignesse lifian." The Irish-
man Fursey came to England because "he wolde for Godes lufon
on elþiodignesse lifian."36 Many sought the Continent: Hild
wished to lead the life of a pilgrim in the monastery of Chelles,
"quo facilius perpetuam in caelis patriam posset mereri"37; but
Rome was naturally the chief resort. Commenting on Ine of
Wessex, who retired there "cupiens in uicinia sanctorum locorum
ad tempus peregrinari in terris, quo familiarius a sanctis recipi
mereretur in caelis," Bede adds that many of the English race,
"nobiles, ignobiles, laici, clerici, uiri ac feminae," went to Rome
for this end,38 and when he records the similar act of Coenred
of Mercia and Offa of Essex he tells how the latter "reliquit
uxorem, agros, cognatos et patriam propter Christum et propter
euangelium, ut in hac uita centuplum acciperet et in saeculo
uenturo uitam aeternum."39

There is also no lack of references to pilgrimages in the
normal modern sense; the visiting of the shrines of the apostles
and martyrs was not the least important of the motives that took
Benedict Biscop, like our Seafarer, many times across the sea;40
on his first journey he was accompanied by the young Wilfrid,
whose biographer Eddi makes him refer to the example of Abraham in order to explain his journey abroad and quote, in an abbreviated form, Matthew xix. 29.41 Many other examples of
pilgrimages across the sea could be drawn from the writings
of Bede, the correspondence of Boniface and Lul and other
sources. It is unnecessary to attempt an exhaustive list.42 The
frequency of pilgrimages is shown not only by the well-known
letter in which Boniface reveals his anxiety on account of the
moral dangers to which the pilgrims may be exposed,43 and by
the arrangements made at Rome and elsewhere for their reception, but also incidentally by letters such as that in which between

719 and 722 the Abbess Eangyth, herself wishing to journey to
Rome "like most of her kindred and friends," complains of the
unprotected position in which she has been left by lack of kinsmen, many of whom have departed to visit the shrines of the
Apostles Peter and Paul and of the martyrs, virgins and con-
fessors.[44] The Vita Willibaldi affords another example of several members of one family becoming peregrini, and it is interesting to note that Willibald's father was at first reluctant, fore-
seeing the type of situation of which the abbess complains.[45]
Lul in one of his letters speaks of leaving Britain with almost
all his kindred when he crossed "the threatening masses of the
raging sea" in his longing to visit the shrines of the Apostles.[46]

Pilgrimages are frequently mentioned in later records,
though the motive and purpose are not so fully stated and it is
not always clear whether what is intended is a visit to a shrine
or a permanent exile from one's native land. There is Continental evidence for an English colony in Rome in the ninth century
and later,[47] and several English documents imply that there
was a practice of retiring to Rome or other Continental shrines
late in life, in order to end one's life there. Thus between 805
and 807, the reeve Æthelnoth and his wife make arrangements
for the permanent disposal of their estate in the event of either
or both of them going south,[48] and Abba, about 835, gives instructions for the disposal of land left to his wife, if after his death
she should enter a nunnery or go south.[49] The ealdorman Alfred
(871–889) similarly envisaged the possibility of his widow's
journeying to Rome after his death,[50] and about the same period
the widow of a Mercian thane, desiring to go to Rome, sold an
estate to a kinsman of her husband.[51] Again, between 929 and
939, a certain Weohstan sold an estate before going to Rome
with his wife and son.[52] These may have been sales to raise
money for the pilgrimage. Several wills have survived from the
eleventh century made by persons about to "go over the sea"[53]
or go to Rome,[54] or in one case to Jerusalem,[55] and the Exeter
guild statutes suggest that pilgrimages were common, for they
state what each member is to contribute "æt suþfore."[56] Flo-
doard's Annales record under 921 and 923 the slaughter by the
Saracens of a great number of Anglo-Saxon pilgrims on the way
to Rome.[57] In 1027, Cnut secured freedom from toll for his
subjects travelling to Rome, whether merchants or "orandi causa
viatores."[58] Whether for a brief visit or a permanent stay, there

is no doubt that pilgrimages across the sea were common throughout the Saxon period, and it would be possible to compile a fairsized list of personages, from kings like Æthelwulf and Cnut downwards, who journeyed abroad for this purpose.

From their correspondence and the statements of their biographers, it is abundantly clear that the Anglo-Saxon missionaries to the Continent regarded their mission as a pilgrimage and trusted to win a heavenly home by relinquishing their native land. Boniface calls himself "exulem Germanicum"[59] and gives "timor Christi et amor peregrinationis" as the cause of his separation from his friends,[60] and Archbishop Cuthberht uses the phrase "in tam periculosa ac ferocitate plena peregrinatione pro amore aeternae patriae" with reference to his mission.[61] The biographers refer frequently to the disregard for worldly goods and the contempt for transitory pleasures of this world, often quoting the promise of Matthew xix. 29. A few quotations will suffice: of Wynnebald we are told that, "propinquorum amicorumque suorum carnalium affectum postponens, presertimque propria hereditatis patriam cum noverca, fratrum sororumque suorum clientello contempnens, ignotas peregrinationis, predas probare penetrareque malluit quam presentis vitae huius falsis divitiarum florere prosperibus"[62]; and Alcuin says of Willibrord: "patriam, cognationem et amicos, fervente fide, pro amore Dei dereliquit; terrena contempsit, ut caelestia adquireret."[63] According to her life by Rudolf, Leoba was enjoined by Boniface before his last journey never to desert the land of her <u>peregrinatio</u>: "praesertim cum huius temporis spatia ad aeternitatem comparata brevia sint et non condignae passiones praesentis saeculi ad futuram gloriam quae revelabitur in sanctis."[64] Instances could easily be multiplied, but enough have been given to show the prevalence of the desire for pilgrimage and exile as a means of obtaining eternal life.[65]

The "peregrinatio pro amore Dei," or "propter nomen Domini," or "ob amorem Christi," plays, as is well known, a very important part in the Irish Church,[66] and it occurs also in the lives of Welsh saints.[67] In one of these Tatheus journeys from Ireland to Wales with eight companions in a ship "sine instrumentis naualibus,"[68] which at once reminds us of the three Irishmen who, according to annal 891 of the Anglo-Saxon Chronicle, came to King Alfred in a boat without any steering gear, "because they wished for the love of God to be on pilgrim-

age, they cared not where." The wording "hi woldon for Godes
lufan on elþiodignesse beon" is almost identical with phrases in
the Old English translation of Bede. I submit that the poet of
The Seafarer meant the same thing by "elþeodigra eard gesecan"
and that he has given poetic expression to the impulse that sent
numbers of his countrymen to the schools of Ireland, to the mission fields of Germany, and to the shrines of distant saints.[69]

NOTES

1 This paper owes much to the encouragement and helpful
   criticism of Professor Dickins, Dr K. Sisam and Miss F. E.
   Harmer. I do not, however, wish to imply that they are in
   complete agreement with the conclusions reached.

2 Kungl. Humanistiska Vetenskapssamfundets i Lund Årsberättelse (1937–38), I.

3 Usually assumed to begin at l. 64b.

4 "Der Seefahrer als Dialog hergestellt," ZDP, I (1869), 334–
   339.

5 "The Wanderer and the Seafarer," JEGP, IV (1902), 460–
   471.

6 Review of Sieper, Die altenglische Elegie, in Englische Studien,
   LI (1917), 107. Lawrence's view is defended briefly by E.
   Blackman, MLR, XXXIV (1939), 254 f.

7 "Zu altenglischen Dichtungen: I. Der Seefahrer," Englische
   Studien, VI (1883), 322–327. See other literature cited by
   Anderson, op. cit., p. 2, note.

8 See e.g. B. F. Huppé's defence of the unity of The Wanderer
   in "The Wanderer: Theme and Structure," JEGP, XLII (1943),
   516–538.

9 Op. cit., pp. 2–6.

10 "Religionsgeschichtliche Beiträge zum germanischen
   Frühchristentum," Beiträge zur Geschichte der deutschen
   Sprache und Literatur, XXXV (1909), 209–239. Kluge had
   in 1883 considered and rejected the possibility of allegorical
   interpretation (Englische Studien, VI, 324) and Sweet, in the
   seventh edition of his Anglo-Saxon Reader (1894), speaks

of "a parallel between a seafarer's contempt for the luxuries of life on land . . . and the aspirations of a spiritual nature."

11 Op. cit., p. 109.

12 YWES, XIX (1938 [1940]), 48.

13 "Some notes on the O.E. poem The Seafarer," SN, XIV (1941–42), 145–159.

14 See below, pp. 447 ff. A tenth-century Old English penitential includes among the twelve means of obtaining forgiveness of sins: "þæt gehwa his æhta 7 his bearn 7 his eard forlæte for Godes lufon, 7 on ælþeodignysse fare, 7 þær hys lif geendige" (B. Thorpe, Ancient Laws and Institutes of England (London, 1840), II, 224; R. Spindler, Das altenglische Bussbuch (Leipzig, 1934), p. 175). There is nothing to correspond to this passage in the Latin sources of this penitential.

15 I think it possible that forþon here is correlative with the forþon of l. 39 and redundant in a modern rendering, though S. O. Andrew (Syntax and Style in Old English [Cambridge, 1940], p. 33), who shares my belief that the instances at ll. 58 and 64 are correlative, suggests that when the principal sentence comes first the stress "is laid not so much on the action predicated by the verb as on the reason for it." My general argument does not, however, depend on this interpretation of forþon, which is often rendered "assuredly" or some other vague word. For discussion see Lawrence, op. cit., pp. 463–466; M. Daunt in MLR,XIII (1918), 474–478; E. A. Kock, Lunds Universitets Årsskrift, N.F.Avd. I, Bd. 14, Nr. 26, p. 75; Anderson, op. cit., pp. 7–9; L. L. Schücking, Anglia-Beiblatt, XLIX (1938), 301 f.; Liljegren, op. cit., pp. 152–155.

16 This passage has difficulties. Sisam doubts whether the to hwon clause can be taken as an indirect question and points out that dryhten is used in two different senses within three lines. He suggests that the line is interpolated, comparing the almost identical line Exhortation to Christian Living, l. 61 (E. van K. Dobbie, The Anglo-Saxon Minor Poems [New York, 1942], p. 69; Grein-Wülker, Bibliotek der angelsächsischen Poesie [Kassel, 1883–98], II, 276). In this context the reference is undoubtedly to the fate of the soul after

death, and I interpret similarly the line in The Seafarer.
A man crossing the dangerous seas will have the thought
of death constantly in his mind. What the poet wishes to
shun is the state of the man described in the Judgement
Day poem in the Exeter Book:

> Lyt þæt geþenceð,
> se þe him wines glæd wilna bruceð,
> siteð him symbelgal, siþ ne bemurneð,
> hu him æfter þisse worulde weorðan mote. (77—80)

17 It is frequently assumed that longung means a longing to be
at sea, but the word in Old English often means grief and
could here apply to the voyager's misery, which yet is safer
for the soul than the life of pleasure on land. Kershaw translates "there is never any peace of mind for him who goes to
sea." Or the "yearning" may refer to the longing for the
security which only "the joys of the Lord" can give.

18 This is also the theme of Hrothgar's advice to Beowulf,
ll. 1724—1752. See also note 16 above.

19 MS. wlitigað is usually emended to wlitigiað, but -ig- is a
perfectly defensible late tenth-century spelling for [iji].

20 Reading, with most editors, gewitan for MS. gewitað.

21 Anderson has a long discussion (pp. 22—26) on the cuckoo
and its mournful note and concludes that the poet has in
mind the cuckoo as the announcer of death, in accordance
with his theory that the desired sea journey signifies death.
This is, of course, unnecessary, and the similar reference
to the mournful cuckoo in a happy context in The Husband's
Message shows that the choice of the epithet need have no
connection with the poet's mood.

22 Accepting est- for the manuscript efteadig. The sense
deliciae for est is well evidenced. B. Thorpe's "favoured
mortal," with est in a different sense, comes to much the
same thing. But the emendation seft- improves the alliteration.

23 Judged by his punctuation, Sweet, op. cit., shared my view.
See also S. O. Andrew, op. cit., p. 33.

24 Reference must, however, be made to K. Sisam's note, "Seafarer, Lines 97–102," in RES, XXI (1945), 316–317, in which he shows that this much-disputed passage, at one time supposed to contain heathen reminiscences, is based on certain verses of Psalm XLVIII. The Psalter was, of course, one of the books most familiar to Irish and Anglo-Saxon peregrini.

25 The dangers of sea travel are mentioned many times in the correspondence of Boniface and Lul and also in other literature concerned with peregrini. See e.g. Bede, H.E. I, 33; III, 15; V, 1; Eddius, Vita Wilfridi, cap. 13; Vita Willibrordi, p. 125; Vita Willibaldi, p. 90; and the Latin poem by Aedilwald in MGH Auct. Antiq. XV, 528 ff., and also in MGH Epistolae, III, 242 ff.

26 Cap. 2. C. Plummer, Baedae Opera Historica (Oxford, 1896), I, 388.

27 H.E. III, 4. See also IV, 3: "ipse peregrinus pro Domino usque ad finem uitae permansit."

28 H.E. V, 9. The Old English version is: "he in Hibernia þam ealonde in elþeodignesse lifde for þæm ecean eðle in heofenum to begytenne" (ed. J. Schipper, Bibliothek der angelsächsischen Prosa, IV [Cassel-Goettingen, 1899], 589).

29 H.E. III, 27.

30 Ed. J. Schipper, p. 320 (Corpus Christi College, Cambridge, MS. 41).

31 James F. Kenney, Sources for the Early History of Ireland (New York, 1929), vol. I: Ecclesiastical, p. 488. See also W. Levison, England and the Continent in the Eighth Century, pp. 36, 44, 52, 55; Dom Louis Gougaud, Christianity in Celtic Lands (London, 1932), pp. 129–131.

32 H.E. III, 13: "peregrinam pro aeterna patria duceret uitam."

33 H.E. V, 9: "peregrinus anchoreticam in magna perfectione uitam egerat."

34 H.E. V, 10: "multo tempore pro aeterna patria exulauerant."

35 P. M. C. Kermode, Manx Crosses (London, 1907), nos. 25, 117, a reference which I owe to Professor Dickins.

36 Ed. J. Schipper, p. 276, translating H.E. III, 19: "cupiens pro Domino . . . peregrinam ducere uitam."

37 H.E. IV, 23.

38 H.E. V, 7.

39 H. E. V, 19. This is based on Matthew xix. 29, Mark x. 29–30, Luke xviii. 29–30. Cf. Historia Abbatum, §1, and Sermo in Natale S. Benedicti Abbatis, §1.

40 Bede tells us in his Sermo in Natale S. Benedicti Abbatis, loc. cit., that Benedict at one time intended to spend his whole life abroad, but that the Pope forbade this and ordered him to escort Archbishop Theodore to England.

41 Eddius, Vita Wilfridi, cap. 4. Matthew xix. 29, had also been used by Bede (n. 39, above).

42 See e.g. Levison, op. cit., pp. 36–44; Gougaud, op. cit., pp. 167–169.

43 Letter 78. M. Tangl, Die Briefe des heiligen Bonifatius und Lullus (MGH Epistolae Selectae, I), p. 169.

44 Letter 14. Tangl, op. cit., p. 24.

45 Vitae Willibaldi et Wynnebaldi (MGH Scriptores, XV, I), p. 90. This work, written by an Anglo-Saxon nun of Heidenheim, called Hugeburc (Hygeburh) towards the end of the eighth century, includes a most interesting account of Willibald's pilgrimage to the Holy Land. See Levison, op. cit., pp. 43 f., 294.

46 Letter 98. Tangl, op. cit., p. 219.

47 See Cardinal F. A. Gasquet, A History of the Venerable English College, Rome (London, 1920), pp. 11–19.

48 A. J. Robertson, Anglo-Saxon Charters (Cambridge, 1939), p. 6, l. 2: "gif hiora oðrum oððe bæm suðfor gelimpe." The term was borrowed into Old Norse as suðrfǫr 'pilgrimage.'

49 F. E. Harmer, Select English Historical Documents of the Ninth and Tenth Centuries (Cambridge, 1914), p. 3, l. 20: "suð to faranne."

50 Ibid., p. 13, ll. 21 f.

51 Birch, Cartularium Saxonicum, no. 537.

52 Ibid., no. 640. Cf. also nos. 192, 293, 313.

53 Whitelock, Anglo-Saxon Wills, nos. XXVIII, XXXVIII.

54 Ibid., no. XXXIV.

55 Ibid., no. XXXIX.

56 B. Thorpe, Diplomatarium Anglicum Ævi Saxonici, p. 614.

57 MGH Scriptores, III, pp. 369, 373.

58 F. Liebermann, Die Gesetze der Angelsachsen, I, 276.

59 E.g. Letter 30. Tangl, op. cit., p. 54.

60 Letter 94. Tangl, op. cit., p. 214.

61 Letter 111. Tangl, op. cit., p. 239.

62 Vitae Willibaldi et Wynnebaldi, p. 107.

63 Vita Willibrordi (MGH Scriptores rer. Merov. VII), p. 140.

64 Vita Leobae (MGH Scriptores, XV, I), p. 129. Cf. Romans viii. 18.

65 See also S. J. Crawford, Anglo-Saxon Influence on Western Christendom, 600–800 (London, 1933), pp. 32 f., 64–71.

66 See Kenney, op. cit., pp. 487 ff.; Plummer, op. cit., II, 170 f.

67 E. G. A. W. Wade-Evans, Vitae Sanctorum Britanniae (Cardiff, 1944), pp. 2 f., where St Brynach, "extra patriam se portans, patriam uoluit adquirere peregrinando"; or pp. 24 f., where Petrocus began "mundana pro celestibus uilipendere," and became a peregrinus in Cornwall.

68 Ibid., pp. 272 f. With this should also be compared the tradition related of the English peregrinus Bertuinus, that he crossed the Channel "sine remigandi auxilio." See Vita Bertuini (MGH Scriptores rer. Merov. VII), p. 180.

69 Only after this article was complete did I have access to J. A. W. Rosteutscher, "Germanischer Schicksalsglaube und angelsächsische Elegiendichtung," Englische Studien, LXXIII (1938–39), 17–19. He realizes that the life of loneliness is

regarded as having a positive value for the Christian, and he refers briefly in a footnote to the voluntary exiles mentioned by Bede, but, as he does not develop this thought nor draw the conclusions that I do, and as he takes the voyage in the first part of the poem merely to symbolize the sorrows of a life of loneliness, it seems best to let what I have written stand.

OLD ENGLISH POETIC DICTION AND THE INTERPRETATION OF THE WANDERER, THE SEAFARER AND THE PENITENT'S PRAYER

E. G. Stanley

The Wanderer and The Seafarer deal with the miseries of exile, and if the Christian moral ending is ignored they provide stirring evidence for a view of Germanic heroes as men who willingly bore the hardships that were their lot, and exulted in them. The endings of the poems are not now looked upon as "spurious," but rather as the culmination of the poems. The exiles no longer exult in their miseries but are miserable. The OE wrecca is no longer the cognate Recke but the "wretch" of which he was the etymon. The Wanderer and the Seafarer are no longer Teutonic heroes hedged about with pietistic innovations but a part of mediæval Christian literature. That was the view of Ehrismann in 1909 and of Dr. Dorothy Whitelock quite recently.[1] Ehrismann took The Seafarer to be allegorical, and Dr. Whitelock takes him to be a voluntary exile, who has laid upon himself the hardships of exile as a penitential discipline.

The connexion of The Seafarer with penitential discipline has been placed beyond doubt by Dr. Whitelock's study. It seems possible to extend this connexion to The Wanderer, though not if her very literal interpretation of the poems is maintained. In support of the view that both poems are connected with penitential discipline a third poem in the Exeter Book may be adduced. It has been called The Exile's Prayer, Klage eines Vertriebenen, and Resignation. Wülker simply called it Gebet, and since the long opening is without doubt penitential it may be called The Penitent's Prayer.[2]

Three things relevant to the interpretation of The Wanderer and The Seafarer are to be found in The Penitent's Prayer, and

Reprinted from Anglia, Vol. 73 (1955), pp. 413–66, by permission of the author and the publisher.

all three have a direct bearing on OE poetic diction and rhetorical devices. First, there is mention of a journey or journeys, perhaps an example of OE symbolic poetic diction; secondly, it shows confusion of the first and third person singular, perhaps the result of the rhetorical device of ethopoeia; and thirdly it is penitential, and therefore perhaps governed by the traditions of penitential prayer. The first point is the most controversial and will be dealt with at some length.

I

Some Aspects of Old English Poetic Diction

With some OE figurative diction to be discussed later it is not possible to be sure if the figure was not as real to the Anglo-Saxons as the reality that gave rise to the figure. Since similes consist in acknowledged comparison no such doubt arises with them; though both sides of the comparison may have been felt as having existence, only one side of the comparison is part of the discourse, the other merely explains, illustrates, or adorns the discourse at that point; and it is acknowledged formally by the syntax that that is the function of the simile. It is, therefore, in the nature of the device of simile that it prevents the intermingling of the symbol and the thing symbolized which, as Wyld says, is characteristic of OE poetry.[3] Comparison is a mode of thought which in simile becomes acknowledged as an explicit literary mode of expression. The extensive use of simile shows the Anglo-Saxons to have been accustomed to figurative thought, and this gives some justification to the belief that much of what might appear realistic in their poems was capable of figurative interpretation. The following brief survey aims at an appraisal of the range and nature of OE similes.[4]

There are the brief comparisons of one thing with another: the boat moving like the foamy-necked bird (Beowulf 217–218, Andreas 496–498); the sword melting like battle-icicles when the Father unleashes the fetters of frost (Beowulf 1605–11); the weapons melting like wax (Andreas 1145–48); blood shall flow like water (Andreas 952–954); the Whale's form is like a rough stone, like a floating reed-bed surrounded by sand-dunes (The Whale 8–10); the wicked stand like stone (Judgment Day II 174–175).

Some similes are more complicated, depicting whole scenes, and relying considerably on the device of variation: the Panther's coat is like Joseph's tunic (The Panther 19–30); the dying Saint's breath is like the smell of honey-flowing herbs in summer (Guthlac 1271–78); the Israelites are to multiply so that they shall be as numerous as stars and ocean-sands (Daniel 315–324; cf. Azarias 32–41); the three holy children and the angel in the furnace meet with weather like a mild summer's day (Daniel 273–277; 345–351; cf. Azarias 61–66).

Some of the OE similes involve long comparisons, in which the whole as well as the part is compared: the earth firmly established with seas, stars and air in movement about it is like the yolk within the egg (The Metres of Boethius 20, 161–175); the flesh of the Phoenix is renewed as fruit gathered in at harvest-time produces, through the nature of the seed, the new life in spring (The Phoenix 240–259).

Some of the similes have abstract themes. They may be simple: Satan's words flying in sparks are like poison (Christ and Satan 161–162); good deeds shine like the sun (The Phoenix 598–601); life useless and without wisdom is like cattle roaming without sense (Solomon and Saturn 21–24). Others are more complex, either in expression or in thought: the soul is purged by fire as gold is purified (Elene 1308–14); alms disperse the wounds of sin and heal the soul as water puts out fire (Alms-Giving 5–9); life is like a perilous journey upon the seas with salvation the haven (Christ 847–866); the ornaments of life pass away as does the wind which roars and then grows calm, the old days, the joys of life, are departed as water glides away (Elene 1266–81); the Day of Judgment comes like a thief in the night (Christ 867–877); the sinful mind that speaks fair words is like the bee bearing sweet sustenance and a poisonous tail behind (Homiletic Fragment I 15–30).

In addition to these similes there is the allegory of The Phoenix culminating in the long simile towards the end of the poem. In it the allegory of the Phoenix is explained.

Some of the similes are obviously not original. Thus the Day of Judgment coming like a thief in the night goes back to 1 Thessalonians 5,2; 2 Peter 3,10; Revelation 3,3 and 16,15. The comparison of the soul being purged by fire, as gold is refined, is a common-place. The three holy children and the angel in the furnace meet with gentle weather in Daniel 3,50 (= A. V.

The Song of the Three Children 27): "et [angelus] fecit medium fornacis quasi ventum roris flantem, et non tetigit eos omnino ignis, neque contristavit, nec quidquam molestiae intulit." In the context God's promise to make the Israelites as innumerable as the stars of heaven and as the sand that lieth upon the sea-shore is derived from Daniel 3,36 (= The Song of the Three Children 13): "Quibus locutus es, pollicens quod multiplicares semen eorum sicut stellas coeli, et sicut arenam quae est in littore maris."

On the other hand, even in verse which has on the whole the character of a free translation the OE version may at times contain similes not found in the original. Thus the appearance of the Whale like a reed-bed surrounded by sand-dunes is not in any known Latin version, though the comparison of the coat of the Panther with Joseph's tunic is.[5] Similarly the comparison of the earth with the yolk of an egg is an addition to The Metres of Boethius.[6]

These similes show that the Anglo-Saxons understood the meaning and function of the device of simile, so that they could take over similes found in their source. They could amplify the similes of the original (as the poet of Daniel does, for example) in exactly the same manner as they amplified their source elsewhere; they could adorn it, as they adorned all poetry, by the device of variation. They understood the device of simile so well that they could invent similes of their own, and all the more complex similes referred to appear to owe little, if anything, to a source. They could superimpose on the device of simile the device of the kenning, as Cynewulf does in the second part of Christ (847—866). In short, the OE poets knew how to handle similes with ease, and in doing so they show that they were accustomed to figurative thought as well as to figurative diction.

Allegory was probably not indigenous with the Anglo-Saxons, but the extent of originality is irrelevant here. Many of the allegories were borrowed. The Phoenix, the longest example of sustained allegory in OE poetry, is based on De ave Phoenice ascribed to Lactantius. The whole poem is, of course, allegorical, though it is only at the end that the allegory is resolved. The poet fully understood the allegory of the original and skilfully amplified it. So did Cynewulf when in the second section of Christ he amplified Gregory's homily on the Ascension.[7]

The literary techniques of amplification and variation are not relevant to the present discussion: the nature of OE figurative thought is. The modern reader attempts to segregate the factual from the allegorical, and finds it difficult. In the Middle Ages the attempt would not have been made with didactic writings, and almost all OE poetry is didactic.

alleg.

The Scriptures recorded historical facts which are the means of Christian teaching through the method of allegorical, analogical, and tropological exegesis.[8] The OE biblical poems are for the most part little more than the biblical narrative, paraphrased and amplified to fit the requirements of metre, alliteration and variation. No attempt is made to provide, as Otfrid did for example, formal exegesis. Like an unglossed bible the OE biblical paraphrases supply the text only: they are factual. In the non-biblical didactic poems, however, the didactic purpose comes first and bodies forth the fact: suitable facts must be introduced to enshroud the doctrine, as the body does the soul. Of the two sides, fact and allegory, it is not possible to say which is the obverse and which the reverse. The Phoenix, the Bee, the Panther, and Fastitocalon, the Whale, in short all observable nature is what it is so that and because it enables that which is taught by it to be taught by it. The created universe is the work of a master rhetorician.

A very common image is that of the castle of the soul, the wounds of sin, and the arrows of the devil. The three are related.

The wounds of sin are referred to in the second section of Christ:

> Forþon we a sculon   idle lustas,
> synwunde forseon,   ond þæs sellran gefeon.
> Habbað we us to frofre   fæder on roderum
> ælmeahtigne.   He his aras þonan,
> 760 halig of heahðu,   hider onsendeð,
> þa us gescildaþ   wið sceþþendra
> eglum earhfarum,   þi læs unholdan
> wunde gewyrcen,   þonne wrohtbora
> in folc godes   forð onsendeð
> 765 of his brægdbogan   biterne stræl.
> Forþon we fæste sculon   wið þam færscyte
> symle wærlice   wearde healdan,

þy læs se attres ord   in gebuge,
biter bordgelac,   under banlocan,
770 feonda færsearo.   þæt bið frecne wund,
blatast benna.   Utan us beorgan þa,
þenden we on eorðan   eard weardien;
utan us to fæder   freoþa wilnian,
biddan bearn godes   ond þone bliðan gæst
775 þæt he us gescilde   wið sceaþan wæpnum,
laþra lygesearwum.

The passage is related to another by Cynewulf:

Ic [the devil] þe, ead mæg,   yfla gehwylces
or gecyðe   oð ende forð
þara þe ic gefremede,   nalæs feam siðum,
synna wundum.   (Juliana 352–355)

The devil then goes on to say how he had hoped to turn Juliana
from salvation, and how he leads astray the righteous by sweet
temptations; but he does not always succeed:

Gif ic ænigne   ellenrofne
gemete modigne   metodes cempan
wið flanþræce,   nele feor þonan
385 bugan from beaduwe,   ac he bord ongean
hefeð hygesnottor,   haligne scyld,
gæstlic guðreaf,   nele gode swican,
ac he beald in gebede   bidsteal gifeð
fæste on feðan,   ic sceal feor þonan
390 heanmod hweorfan,   hroþra bidæled,
in gleda gripe,   gehðu mænan,
þæt ic ne meahte   mægnes cræfte
guðe wiðgongan,   ac ic geomor sceal
secan oþerne   ellenleasran,
395 under cumbolhagan,   cempan sænran,
þe ic onbryrdan mæge   beorman mine,
agælan æt guþe.   þeah he godes hwæt
onginne gæstlice,   ic beo gearo sona,
þæt ic ingehygd   eal geondwlite,
400 hu gefæstnad sy   ferð innanweard,
wiðsteall geworht.   Ic þæs wealles geat

ontyne þurh teonan;   bið se torr þyrel,
ingong geopenad,   þonne ic ærest him
þurh eargfare   in onsende
405   in breostsefan   bitre geþoncas
þurh mislice   modes willan,
þæt him sylfum   selle þynceð
leahtras to fremman   ofer lof godes,
lices lustas.

In the poem <u>Vainglory</u> in the <u>Exeter Book</u> the devil's arrows are associated with Envy:

Bið þæt æfþonca   eal gefylled
feondes fligepilum,   facensearwum;
breodað he ond bælceð,   boð his sylfes
swiþor micle   þonne se sella mon,
30   þenceð þæt his wise   welhwam þince
eal unforcuþ.   Biþ þæs oþer swice,
þonne he þæs facnes   fintan sceawað.
Wrenceþ he ond blenceþ,   worn geþenceþ
hinderhoca,   hygegar leteð,
35   scurum sceoteþ.   He þa scylde ne wat
fæhþe gefremede,   feoþ his betran
eorl fore æfstum,   læteð inwitflan
brecan þone burgweal,   þe him bebead meotud
þæt he þæt wigsteal   wergan sceolde.

Part of Hrothgar's sermon in <u>Beowulf</u> is on the same theme:

1735   Wunað he on wiste;   no hine wiht dweleð
adl ne yldo,   ne him inwitsorh
on sefan sweorceð,   ne gesacu ohwær
ecghete eoweð,   ac him eal worold
wendeð on willan   (he þæt wyrse ne con),
1740   oðþæt him on innan   oferhygda dæl
weaxeð ond wridað.   þonne se weard swefeð,
sawele hyrde;   bið se slæp to fæst,
bisgum gebunden,   bona swiðe neah,
se þe of flanbogan   fyrenum sceoteð;
1745   þonne bið on hreþre   under helm drepen
biteran stræle   (him bebeorgan ne con),
wom wundorbebodum   wergan gastes.

464

There are two further references in Juliana to the devil's
arrows and the figure of the castle of the soul:

> Oft ic [the devil] syne ofteah,
> ablende bealoþoncum   beorna unrim
> monna cynnes,   misthelme forbrægd
> þurh attres ord   eagna leoman
> sweartum scurum.   (468–472)

> Forþon ic [Juliana], leof weorud,   læran wille,
> æfremmende,   þæt ge eower hus
> gefæstnige,   þy læs hit ferblædum
> windas toweorpan.   Weal sceal þy trumra
> strong wiþstondan   storma scurum,
> leahtra gehygdum.   (647–652)[9]

To understand the figure of the castle of the soul and the
wounds of sin it is essential to understand the nature of the
devil's arrows that cause the wounds of sin to break open the
castle of the soul. The arrows of the devil are at once allegorical and real; they form part of the Anglo-Saxon theory of disease,
for the devil afflicts mankind by means of his shafts with sinful
thoughts and physical illness. In the source the devil strikes
his victims with blindness, in Cynewulf's Juliana the devil's
weapons are stated in expansion of the source: the venomous
point and black showers. The belief that diseases are the work
of demons is, of course, not peculiar to the Germanic tribes,
but it seems that the belief in the demonic origin of diseases
coalesced with the particularly Germanic doctrine of elf-shot.[10]
In the charm against ælfsogoða ('hiccough or heartburn due to
elves'? or perhaps less precisely 'elf-disease'), extant in the
tenth century Leechbook, it is stated that if a man has ælfsogoða
his eyes are yellow where they should be red.[11] The charm is
entirely Christian and sufficiently learned to require the leech
to be able to write as well as to sing Latin. It involves the brew-
ing of a potion containing a multitude of herbs as well as baptis-
mal water, and the oil of extreme unction is used for writing
three crosses. As regards the present discussion the most important statement in the charm is the last: "þes cræft mæg wiþ
ælcre feondes costunge." A Christian charm against an elvish
disease, the first symptom of which is that the eyes grow yellow,

has power against every temptation of the devil. How elves send diseases is well-known through the metrical charm Wiþ Færstice:[12] they shoot their victims with spears or arrows.

There is, therefore, a close, factual connexion in practical medicine between disease shot by elves and the temptations of the devil. The powers of darkness of whatever origin, Christian or pagan, use the same weapons to afflict mankind; the skill that has virtue against the elvish sickness will banish the temptations of the devil too.

But poems are not written as manuals of therapeutics. Except in the devil's speech in Juliana where Cynewulf (like his source) dwells on bodily afflictions, the emphasis is on the trials of the mind and of the body through sin. The wounds that are to be despised in Christ 757–758 are the wounds of sin, vain lusts. The weapons of the devil are lygesearo. In Beowulf 1746–47 it is with wom wunderbebodum (which are his bitter arrows) that the devil afflicts mankind. The diseases of the body are directly related to the sins of the flesh. In the medical allegory by which the arrows of the devil can blind the eye, pierce the body, and torment the spirit, there is no scientific neatness; and the modern reader accustomed to scientific precision is in danger of importing the neat distinction of fact and figure into an age that did not know it or need it.

The devil's arrows, the wounds of sin, and the castle of the soul are at once fact and figure. The emblem of the cup of death starts as an allegory.[13] There is no need to reprint here the various passages where the image occurs in OE verse, for the Anglo-Saxon poetic treatment of the theme is best illustrated by the fullest example, from Guthlac B:[14]

> Ða wæs Guðlace on þa geocran tid
> mægen gemeðgad, mod swiþe heard,
> elnes anhydig. Wæs seo adl þearl,
> hat ond heorogrim. Hreþer innan weol,
> 980 born banloca. Bryþen wæs ongunnen
> þætte Adame Eue gebyrmde
> æt fruman worulde. Feond byrlade
> ærest þære idese, ond heo Adame,
> hyre swæsum were, siþþan scencte
> 985 bittor bædeweg. þæs þa byre siþþan
> grimme onguldon gafulrædenne

þurh ærgewyrht,   þætte ænig ne wæs
fyra cynnes   from fruman siððan
mon on moldan,   þætte meahte him
990   gebeorgan ond bibugan   þone bleatan dryne,
deopan deaðweges,   ac him duru sylfa
on þa sliðnan tid   sona ontyneð,
ingong geopenað.

    The poet of <u>Guthlac B</u> must have understood that the emblem
of the drink of death, of which he makes such full use, was not
to be taken literally; the same is presumably true of the poet of
<u>Andreas</u>, yet in the long passage that includes the word "meo-
duscerwen" (1522–54) he extends the emblem of the drink of
death, allowing it to merge with the description of the actual
death by drowning. In the context it is quite clear that <u>meoduscer-</u>
<u>wen</u> is ironical,[15] and has some such meaning as "the dispensing
of mead"; this is amplified by the passage that follows (1532–46),
in which is described the bitter draught, the mighty flood that
brought death to the Mermedonians. Few passages show more
clearly how concretely the Anglo-Saxons interpreted allegory
at times. The poet of <u>Andreas</u> admits of no dividing line between allegory and reality.
    This merging of fact and figure must be considered in re-
lation to the examples of allegorical writing in which there is
no doubt that the poet was quite clear that he was writing allegory.
The following are such examples:

Ðu eart se weallstan   þe ða wyrhtan iu
wiðwurpon to weorce.   Wel þe geriseð
þæt þu heafod sie   healle mærre,
5   ond gesomnige   side weallas
fæste gefoge,   flint unbræcne,
þæt geond eorðb[yr]g eall   eagna gesihþe
wundrien to worlde   wuldres ealdor.   (<u>Christ</u>)

        Bi þon se witga cwæð
þæt ahæfen wæren   halge gimmas,
hædre heofontungel,   healice upp,
sunne ond mona.   Hwæt sindan þa
695   gimmas swa scyne   buton god sylfa?
He is se soðfæsta   sunnan leoma,

englum ond eorðwarum æþele scima.
Ofer middangeard mona lixeð,
gæstlic tungol, swa seo godes circe
700 þurh gesomninga soðes ond ryhtes
beorhte bliceð. (Christ)

Gylden is se godes cwide, gimmum astæned,
hafað sylfren leaf; sundor mæg æghwylc
65 ðurh gastes gife godspel secgan.
He bið seofan snytro and saule hunig
[and modes meolc, mærþa gesælgost].
. . . .
Lamena he is læce, leoht wincendra,
swilce he is deafra duru, dumbra tunge,
scyldigra scyld, scyppendes seld,
80 flodes ferigend, folces nerigend,
yða yrfeweard, earmra fisca
and wyrma welm, wildeora holt,
on westenne weard, weorðmynta geard.
(Solomon and Saturn)

A further reference to God as physician is to be found in
Judgment Day II 43–81, ending with the words:

Hwi ne bidst þu þe beþunga and plaster,
lifes læcedomes æt lifes frean?

God as physician is the counterpart to the devil as origin of disease.

The purpose in quoting these passages is not to demonstrate the degree of originality to be found in them. They form
part of the varied allegory in which religious teaching was expressed; their originality is of no importance, but the range of
allegorical thought and the means of expression is. Christ 699
contains the word swa giving proof that the poet knew that the
imagery he was using was in the nature of a simile. In Vainglory 34 the allegory is (as far as it is not factual) resolved by
the use of the word hygegar. Gæstlic guðreaf in Juliana 387 is
used similarly, and in the same passage (line 400) it is made
clear that the castle is the mind. In most cases, however, the
allegory is not explicit, and in some cases it is possible that

what seems figure to us was fact to the Anglo-Saxons. In other cases, particularly in the last examples quoted, the assumption must have been made by the poet that the audience was familiar with allegory, and he need not explain it.

Similarly there is no explanation by the poet in the following example of a different type of parabolical diction, though there are no grounds for believing that this type of imagery was common with the Anglo-Saxons:

> "Hu mæg þæm geweorðan   þe on westenne
> meðe ond meteleas   morland trydeð,
> hungre gehæfted,   ond him hlaf ond stan
> on gesihðe bu   [samod] geweorðað,
> streac ond hnesce,   þæt he þone stan nime
> wið hungres hleo,   hlafes ne gime,
> gewende to wædle,   ond þa wiste wiðsæce,
> beteran wiðhyccge,   þonne he bega beneah?"
>   (Elene 611–618)[16]

In the symbolic parallelism of the bread and the stone the audience, steeped like the poet in biblical imagery, especially of the Psalms and the Gospels, may be assumed to have caught the biblical echo, and the same is true of the figure of the cornerstone of the church. There is no such echo in the case of the parallelism of the Exeter Book Maxims 25–29:

>   Beam sceal on eorðan
> leafum liþan,   leomu gnornian.
> Fus sceal feran,   fæge sweltan
> ond dogra gehwam   ymb gedal sacan
> middangeardes.[17]

OE verse, balancing phrase against phrase, varying noun with noun in parallel sentence structure, lends an air of continuity and junction to what is often discontinuous and disjunct in sense. The Maxims in particular exploit this balance, so that the juxtaposition of the tree and the dying man was probably symbolic by design. This interpretation receives further support from the use of the same symbolism in The Penitent's Prayer:

> Nu ic me sylf ne mæg
> fore minum wonæhtum   willan adreogan.
> 105 Wudu mot him weaxan,   wyrde bidan,
> tanum lædan;   ic for tæle ne mæg
> ænigne moncynnes   mode gelufian
> eorl on eþle.   Eala dryhten min,
> meahtig mundbora,   þæt ic eom mode [s]eoc,
> 110 bittre abolgen.   Is seo bot æt þe
> gelong æfter [l]ife.

Here the tree and the forest are symbolic of divine law irrevocable, by which the new life of spring must give way to the
decay of autumn.

Possibly because there still lingered on in the present
century the notion that the OE poets were "sons of nature," a
part of the "Gothick" conception of the Dark Ages, some philologists singled out symbolism such as this, though they failed to
realize the degree of poetic art to be found in a multitude of
figurative devices which they largely ignored. As a result there
emerge generalizations such as that of H. C. Wyld's:[18]

> The old poets are fond of using the processes of
> nature as symbols of moods; it might indeed al-
> most be said that for them
> the meanest flower that blows can give
> Thoughts that do often lie too deep for tears.

Few will deny that with the old poets the processes of nature may
be symbols of their moods: but it is not the flower that gives the
thought; with the OE poets it is the thought that gives the flower.
And the flower that is born of the mood may take on sufficient
concreteness to appear capable of existence without and outside
the mood.

In some examples of OE allegory it has proved difficult to
be sure if what seems allegory to us was not fact to the Anglo-
Saxons. In others, what may have been both fact and figure to
them seems only fact to us. The only certainty is that the OE
poets could take over figures of speech from their sources: they
understood the nature of the imagery of the source, and could
rely on their audience to understand their adaptation and amplification.

It is the purpose of the present section of this article to show how much in OE verse was part of a wide and elaborate poetic diction, the expression of a mode of complex, figurative thought. Metaphors have an important place in poetic diction. Again it is difficult to be sure of the division between figure and fact. There is the further difficulty that it is not always possible to distinguish the living from the dead metaphor, alive only to the philologist, at all times conscious of the origins. Dead metaphors can have no place in this discussion of the living mode of OE figurative thought. It must begin with the literalness of devices like the very common poetic circumlocution describing advancing warriors as bearing forward their arms or armour.[19] This circumlocution is not so much the result of figurative thought as of the requirements of the metre; for the metre depends on nouns rather than verbs for stress. The lack of directness based on heavily stressed nouns gives great dignity to the advance of the warriors. The circumlocution produces such kennings as garberend, helmberend, and lindhæbbend for "warrior."

Somewhat less literal are the very common phrases at the beginning of speeches of which the following are some examples: "wordhord onleac" (Andreas 601); "hordlocan onspeon" (Andreas 671); "modhord onleac" (Andreas 172); "hreðerlocan onspeon" (Elene 86); "wordhord onwreah" (Vainglory 3). Again, these phrases were introduced partly to fulfil the requirements of the metre, based on nouns. They do, however, retain some of their figurative nature in spite of their frequent use, and they must be considered as a part of the general figure that thought is secure in the mind, a figure underlying the idea of binding fast a man's thought within his mind:

> Heald hordlocan,   hyge fæste bind
> mid modsefan.
> (Homiletic Fragment II 3–4)

> Ic to soþe wat
> þæt biþ in eorle   indryhten þeaw,
> þæt he his ferðlocan   fæste binde,
> healde his hordcofan,   hycge swa he wille.
> 15 Ne mæg werig mod   wyrde wiðstondan,
> ne se hreo hyge   helpe gefremman.
> Forðon domgeorne   dreorigne oft

STANLEY

in hyra breostcofan   bindað fæste;
    swa ic modsefan   minne sceolde,
20 oft earmcearig,   eðle bidæled,
    freomægum feor   feterum sælan.
          (The Wanderer[20])

In such phrases as "wroht webbian" (cf. Andreas 672, Elene 309), and in the kennings for women (cf. Marquardt, p. 265) freoðuwebbe (Beowulf 1942, Widsith 6), the use of "weaving" may well no longer have been felt as a metaphor. Andreas 63–64, "elþeodige inwitwrasne searonet seowað" (MS. seoðað), seems, however, to have preserved all the original liveliness of the image. Weallan is often used figuratively. Beowulf alone contains five examples: "weallað wælniðas" (2065), "hreðer inne weoll" (2113), "breost innan weoll" (2331), "heortan sorge weallinde wæg" (2463–64), "weoll sefa wið sorgum" (2599 f.). Among the numerous instances in the rest of OE poetry Andreas 767–770 is particularly instructive in showing the associations invoked by the figure:

Man wridode
geond beorna breost,   brandhata nið
weoll on gewitte,   weorm blædum fag,
attor ælfæle.[21]

The figurative use of weallan is closely related to the figurative use of wylm, its derivative noun:

oððæt deaðes wylm
hran æt heortan.   (Beowulf 2269–70)

Yrre ne læt þe   æfre gewealdan,
heah in hreþre,   heoroworda grund
wylme bismitan.   (Precepts 83–85)

þonne hi gebolgene weorðað, him wyrð on breostum inne beswungen sefa on hraðre mid ðæm swiðan welme hatheortnesse.   (The Metres of Boethius 25, 45–47[22])

472

Mostly when <u>wylm</u> is used figuratively it is compounded:

> Wæs him se man to þon leof
> þæt he þone breostwylm   forberan ne mehte,
> ac him on hreþre   hygebendum fæst
> æfter deorum men   dyrne langað
> beorn wið blode.   (<u>Beowulf</u> 1876–80)

> ond þa cearwylmas   colran wurðaþ.
>   (<u>Beowulf</u> 282)

> ond him wiflufan
> æfter cearwælmum   colran weorðað.
>   (<u>Beowulf</u> 2065–66)

"cnyssed cearwelmum" (<u>Elene</u> 1257); "wæron heaðowylmas heortan getenge" (<u>Exodus</u> 148); "hat heafodwylm" (<u>Elene</u> 1132); "soden sarwylmum"[23] (<u>Guthlac</u> 1150). Except in <u>Beowulf</u> 904–905, "hine sorhwylmas lemede to lange," the compound <u>sorhwylm</u> is always found together with the verb <u>seoþan</u>, as in <u>Beowulf</u> 1993, <u>Guthlac</u> 1073 and 1262.

The word <u>weallan</u> and the related <u>wylm</u> usefully illustrate the nature of some **OE** metaphorical diction. The words used literally can refer to either water or fire, the surge of the ocean or the surge of flames. Both meanings can be used figuratively, and they are often combined. <u>Weallan</u> and <u>seoþan</u> are very similar in meaning and usage. Since the surging blood of wounds or flood of tears are literal, it is not always possible to estimate the extent of fact and figure in what may at first sight appear a figurative use; often, however, the device of variation makes it certain that the OE poet felt that he was using an image.

A very vivid metaphor seems to underlie "morþorbed stred" (<u>Beowulf</u> 2436), and, assuming it to be a corruption of the same phrase, "hildbedd styred" (<u>Andreas</u> 1092). The metaphor seems to be related to the common figure of the sleep of death, as for example in <u>Beowulf</u> 1007–08:

> þær his lichoma   legerbedde fæst
> swefeþ æfter symle.

A striking figure of speech often used in OE verse gives life to expressions of feelings: "gryreleoð galan" (Beowulf 786); "fusleoð galan" (Christ 623, Andreas 1549, Guthlac 1346); "hearmleoð galan" (Andreas 1127, 1342); "sigeleoð galen" (Elene 124); "sorhleoð gæleð" (Beowulf 2460), etc. Closely related to this figure is: "forþon wæs in wicum wop up ahafen, atol æfenleoð" (Exodus 200–201). It was still a living figure, capable of some originality of treatment, as in "horn stundum song fuslic f[yrd]-leoð" (Beowulf 1423–24); "hringmæl agol grædig guðleoð" (Beowulf 1521–22). Here the figure is combined with the device of personification.

Most of the remaining metaphors occur once only in OE verse. Some of them are found also in prose, and not a few have parallels in mediæval Latin. Once again, the present article is intended to show how much OE poetry required more than literal understanding. The source of the figures is irrelevant.

Among the simplest metaphors is the use of goldhord and earcnanstan (Christ 787 and 1195) to describe Christ. Christ 328–329 says of the Virgin:

þu eart þæs wealldor,　þurh þe wealdend frea
æne on þas eorðan　ut siðade.

The Kentish Hymn 19 speaks of the joys "on ðære upplican æðelan ceastre."

In a number of cases a basically simple figure is expanded into a more elaborate conceit: in The Rune Poem (66) it is said of a ship on the high seas, "se brimhengest bridles ne gymeð"; i.e. the simple metaphor of "ocean steed," so common in OE,[24] is expanded into a steed that fails to respond to the bridle.

A passage which is obviously metaphorical, in that the sun moving across the heavens is called a "sail," is the much disputed Exodus 80–90.[25] The OE poet is imagining the pillar of cloud and fire as a veil or cloud of the sun by day, and sunlike by night. The importance of the metaphor lies in the elaboration: the sail is provided with invisible riggings.

A good example of the difficulty the modern reader has in evaluating the extent of OE poetic diction is provided by "the fetters of frost." He has no means of establishing if what seems to him so imaginative an example of imagery was not a scientific fact to the Anglo-Saxons; for how else is the solidifying of water to be explained? Maxims I 74–75 has "An sceal inbindan forstes fetre felameahtig god." Beowulf 1132–33 has "winter yþe beleac isgebinde," and in 1607–10 it is said of the melting sword:

þæt wæs wundra sum,
þæt hit eal gemealt   ise gelicost,
ðonne forstes bend   fæder onlæteð,
onwindeð wælrapas.

The idea of the fetters of ice almost certainly gave rise to the kenning "waþema gebind" (The Wanderer 24 and 57; cf. H. Marquardt, op. cit., pp. 176–177). At the centre of the present discussion lie the metaphors for moods and abstract ideas. But before these can be discussed the smallest units of OE poetic diction, the poetic compounds, must be considered. They will illustrate further how much of what appears factual in OE verse is not truly factual.

The reason why it was possible for the Germanic compounds to contain a first element which was not given the full extent of its individual meaning, but was used rather to give colour to the second, the more important element, is probably to be found in the grammatical nature of the compound. The second element was the more important because it determined the gender of the compound as a whole and took the inflexional ending. The second element, therefore, determined the function of the compound within the sentence. In OE verse (as in the Gmc. alliterative verse in general) the first element, being formally dependent on the second, added to the meaning of the second element and gave weight to it in the metrical system, thus resulting in the substantival solidity which is a marked feature of the alliterative metre, and the direct consequence of its rules.

OE poetic diction was particularly rich in compounds the first element of which gives colour to the second. Hoops (Beowulfstudien, pp. 20–24) has discussed in some detail the fact that in such compounds as ærgod (Beowulf 130, 989, 1329, 2342, 2586) and ærglæd (Exodus 293), though ær- preserves some of its temporal force, the principal meaning is one endowing the second element of the compound with the noble qualities that were associated with a glorious past. Similarly, in the case of nominal compounds with a first element meaning "war, battle, sword," etc., the second element is merely coloured by the first, which imparts to it a strong martial flavour. This is too obvious to need amplification at length. Examples are heorugrim, heorogifre (probably heorogeong, The Battle of Finnsburh 2), æscrof, and the host of beadu- and heaþo- compounds. With this type might be compared such words as gealgmod.

Dr. B. M. White says, "The finest nature poetry in OE was incidental, the setting for an action, or the symbol of a state of mind or moral concept."[26] She might have gone further and added that even where it provides the setting for an action the so-called OE nature poetry seems to provide the symbol of a state of mind. The view advanced in this article requires the opposite statement, a statement not so much at variance with Dr. White's analysis of the nature of OE nature poetry as at variance with the view implicit in her statement, that the natural phenomenon came before the mood. This opposite statement is: the finest OE figurative diction is that in which a state of mind or moral concept evokes in the poem the description of a natural phenomenon, associated by the Anglo-Saxons with that mood or moral concept; once again, it is the thought that gives the flower, not the flower that gives the thought.

Thus it appears that with the Anglo-Saxons morning was a time of special misery; at that time of day battles began, and the warriors stirred with difficulty from the heavy sleep in the mead-hall. It is a far cry from the time of day when Emilie or Corinna go a-maying. In Beowulf 3022 warriors must grip the morning-cold spear: in ME the Franklin's girdle and the soft skin of the Fair Maid of Ribblesdale are as white, or whiter even than the morning-milk, not because the cows yield particularly white milk in the morning, but because to the thirteenth and fourteenth centuries the morning was the time when all things were at their freshest, whitest, purest.

The exact time of day or night which the Anglo-Saxons described as uht(a) is not easily determined.[27] But the mood is clear. The early morning is a time of terror without solace. It is the time when the Wife in her Lament (7) feels all the poignancy of sorrow, uhtcearu:

> þonne ic on uhtan   ana gonge
> under actreo   geond þas eorðscrafu.   (35–36)

In <u>Beowulf</u> 2450 the Father calls to mind "morna gehwylce" his
son that rides the gallows; and the Wanderer says:

> Oft ic sceolde ana   uhtna gehwylce
> mine ceare cwiþan.   (8–9)

Usages such as these may help to explain the phrase
"morgenlongne dæg" (<u>Beowulf</u> 2894). It is a phrase that cannot
be taken literally: the parallel "sumorlang dæg" (<u>The Wife's</u>
<u>Lament</u> 37) can. The mood implied by the word <u>morgenlong</u>
is that of <u>morgenceald</u> (<u>Beowulf</u> 3022), <u>morgencolla</u> (<u>Judith</u> 245),
and especially "ond him biõ a sefa geomor, mod morgenseoc"
(<u>The Penitent's Prayer</u> 95–96). The words "morgenlongne dæg"
form an illogical combination that conveys with great economy
how the lonely fear of early morning is extended into the day
as the band of nobles sat, grieving in their hearts, waiting for
news of Beowulf, his death or safe return.

The cold misery of the morning is a continuation of the
"nearwe geþancas þe on niht becumaõ" (<u>An Exhortation to Christian Living</u> 53). The OE poets had developed an efficient vocabulary for describing night-fall and shadow, and they made use
of it for factual descriptions, as night falling on Heorot before
the attacks by Grendel and his dam, or Andreas returning to
prison after a day of torment (1245–50, 1303–10). Night and
shadow is also used with obvious symbolism. <u>The Kentish Hymn</u>
(28) speaks of "dark sins," and in <u>The Judgment Day II</u> (135–
140) all the evil done by man "on þystrum scræfum . . . on eorõan"
is made manifest by day; <u>Beowulf</u> (119–120) equates sorrow with
"wonsceaft wera"; Grendel (as an aspect of the devil[28]) is described by the demonic "deorc deaþscua" (160), the battle with
him is "nihtbealwa mæst" (193); he is a "sceadugenga" (703) who,
like the dragon in the second half of the poem, shows his hatred
in the dark of night. Christ is endowed with all the attributes of
light and glory to contrast with the dark surroundings of man,
and in <u>Christ</u> 113–118 he is asked in prayer:

> þæt þu þa beorhtan us
> sunnan onsende,   ond þe sylf cyme
> þæt õu inleohte   þa þe longe ær,
> þrosme beþeahte   ond in þeostrum her,
> sæton sinneahtes;   synnum bifealdne
> deorc deaþes sceadu   dreogan sceoldan.

Such obvious figurative uses show the Anglo-Saxons to be familiar with the interpretation of darkness as an aspect of evil, gloom and terror.

The OE poets treated cold similarly. As was "morning," so "cold, frost and winter" are used for their associations with misery. They too, often lack factual precision. The alliterative phrase "cold care" survives into late ME, and has often been commented on.[29] Darkness and winter are frequently combined in OE poetry, for they combine to assail man in his misery.[30] The idea of "cold care" leads to the compound wintercearig (The Wanderer 24), which therefore cannot mean "sad with old age," a translation given in the glossary of Sweet's Reader as an alternative to "sad with the gloom of winter." Guthlac, though pierced with hot, feverish arrows (1143), is freorig ond ferð-werig (1157). In the Vercelli Soul and Body (15–16) the spirit speaks to the dust "swa cearful, cealdan reorde." In Andreas (138) the Mermedonians are described as caldheorte. In Deor (4) Welund endured wintercealde wræce, in Beowulf (3022) the spear is described as morgenceald; and Beowulf supports the son of Ohthere over the wide sea with warfare and weapons: "he gewræc syððan cealdum cearsiðum, cyning ealdre bineat" (2395–96).

Cold and misery are especially associated with the sea. Examples are to be found in Beowulf, cealde streamas (of the dwelling of Grendel's race, 1261); in Andreas, cald wæter (201, 222, 253), and transferred to the cliffs, caldcleofu (310); cf. Christ 847–866. Whatever the interpretation of The Wanderer and The Seafarer, it is certain that much of the feeling of misery and desolation that gives them their peculiar effectiveness is due to such passages as:

> Ond þas stanhleoþu   stormas cnyssað,
> hrið hreosende   hrusan bindeð,
> wintres woma,   þonne won cymeð,
> nipeð nihtscua,   norþan onsendeð
> hreo hæglfare   hæleþum on andan.
>
> (The Wanderer 101–105)

>   þær mec oft bigeat
> nearo nihtwaco   æt nacan stefnan,
> þonne he be clifum cnossað.   Calde geþrungen

> wæron mine fet,   forste gebunden,
> caldum clommum,   þær þa ceare seofedun
> hat ymb heortan.   (The Seafarer 6–11)

Fetters are described as cold on earth and in hell.[31] In both prisoners are held bound, and are described in similar terms. The cold fetters of hell are mentioned in Christ 1629, and in Christ and Satan 635 we hear of "clom and carcern and þone caldan grund" as a description of hell. Imprisonment on earth is described similarly in Andreas 1212. The Seafarer is held prisoner by the fetters of frost (8–10).

In the description of hell in Genesis B 313–317 many of the poetic devices that have been discussed are to be found together:

> þær hæbbað heo on æfyn   ungemet lange
> ealra feonda gehwilc   fyr edneowe;
> þonne cymð on uhtan   easterne wind,
> forst fyrnum cald,   symble fyr oððe gar:[32]
> sum heard geswinc   habban sceoldon.

In this description of hell, besides frost and early morning, there is the eastern wind. The wind-swept headlands and wind-swept halls were the scenes of exile and misery: in Beowulf (2455–57) the Father lamenting for his son sees with sorrow in his son's dwelling the deserted wine-hall, "windge reste reote berofene." A scene of cold fear is imagined by Adam in that part of Genesis B which corresponds to Fragment I of the OS Genesis (here quoted):

> Hu sculun uuit nu libbian,   efto hu sculun uuit an
>   thesum liatha uuesan,
> nu hier huuilum uuind kumit   uuestan efto ostan,
> suðan efto norðan,   gisuuerek upp dribit,
> kumit haglas skion   himile bitengi,
> ferið forð an gimang   (that is firinum kald).
>   (Fragment I 14–18 = Genesis B 805–809)

In Christ and Satan 384–385 the devils lament full of fear "wide geond windsele" and speak of the Harrowing as a storm. In Andreas the Saint knew the land of the Mermedonians when he saw before the city gates:

Beorgas steape,
hleoðu hlifodon, ymbe harne stan
tigelfagan trafu, torras stodon,
windige weallas. (840–843)

The Wife in her <u>Lament</u> thinks of her disconsolate lord sitting
in a scene of sorrow:

under stanhliþe storme behrimed,
wine werigmod, wætre beflowen
on dreorsele. (48–50)

In all these examples of desolate scenes the effect of misery seems to be foremost in the poet's mind, not realism. Similar descriptions are, of course, used factually, e.g. to describe
the storm at sea in <u>Andreas</u> 369–376, or the Breca episode in
<u>Beowulf</u> (especially 544–548).

On the other hand there are occasions when the situation
seems to demand a scene of sorrow, and all the poet supplies
is factual discourse. Though sad at heart and bereft of courage
the messenger in <u>Guthlac</u> 1326–47 crosses the sea, the scene
is described by the poet without any attempt at portraying the
messenger's state of mind in terms of the factual description:
it was not in his source.[33]

In a number of cases the symbolic is so closely interwoven
with the factual element in the description that it is not possible
to say which is foremost in the poet's mind: the narrative calls
for a description of scenery, and the conventions of OE poetic
diction enable the poet to advance out of it and by means of it
the symbolic description of a state of mind. An example of this
type of extension of a factual description is that of darkness
descending on the eve of the saint's death in <u>Guthlac</u>:

þa se æþela glæm
setlgong sohte, swearc norðrodor
1280 won under wolcnum, woruld miste oferteah,
þystrum biþeahte, þrong niht ofer tiht
londes frætwa. Ða cwom leohta mæst,
halig of heofonum hædre scinan,
beorhte ofer burgsalu. Bad se þe sceolde
1285 eadig on elne endedogor,

480

awrecen wælstrælum.   Wuldres scima,
æþele ymb æþelne,   ondlonge niht
scan scirwered.   Scadu sweþredon,
tolysed under lyfte.   Wæs se leohta glæm
1290 ymb þæt halge hus,   heofonlic condel,
from æfenglome   oþþæt eastan cwom
ofer deop gelad   dægredwoma,
wedertacen wearm.³⁴

Another example of extension of the factual description required
by the narrative into a symbolic description (mirroring Hengest's
mood) is perhaps to be found in Beowulf 1131–37:

Holm storme weol,
won wið winde,   winter yþe beleac
isgebinde,   oþðæt oþer com
gear in geardas,   swa nu gyt deð,
þa ðe syngales   sele bewitiað,
wuldortorhtan weder.   Ða wæs winter scacen,
fæger foldan bearm.

In one case symbolism is so strong that a poet forgets that
the description he is producing conflicts factually with the narrative. The poet of Andreas writes:

þa se halga wæs   under heolstorscuwan,
eorl ellenheard,   ondlange niht
1255 searoþancum beseted.   Snaw eorðan band
wintergeworpum.   Weder coledon
heardum hægelscurum,   swylce hrim ond forst,
hare hildstapan,   hæleða eðel
lucon, leoda gesetu.   Land wæron freorig
1260 cealdum cylegicelum,   clang wæteres þrym
ofer eastreamas,   is brycgade
blæce brimrade.   Bliðheort wunode
eorl unforcuð,   elnes gemyndig,
þrist ond þrohtheard   in þreanedum
1265 wintercealdan niht.   No on gewitte blon,
acol for þy egesan,   þæs þe he ær ongann,
þæt he a domlicost   dryhten herede,
weorðade wordum,   oððæt wuldres gim
heofontorht onhlad.

481

The OE prose legend of St. Andreas and the known Latin and Greek sources provide no indication of this wintery scene, which is no more than anticipatory variation and expansion of the word winterceald in line 1265. To the poet steeped in the traditions of OE poetic diction and technique, "snaw eorðan band wintergeworpum" merely amplifies the night of winter-cold torments, and the rest follows naturally. That there is no indication of winter otherwise, and that snow is rare in Asia Minor is quite irrelevant.

It is perhaps permissible to see a means of explaining "isig ond utfus" (Beowulf 33) along similar lines. The current explanation is that isig means "icy" which, because it does not fit, is weakened to "gleaming like ice," though no parallel semantic development is adduced. W. Krogmann rightly suggests that the wintery scene is factually at variance with the context.[35] But if it is possible for an OE poet to use warmth and cold as expressions of solace and misery[36] the word isig may mean no more than winterceald, a word evocative of sorrow: the factual meaning does not matter. The word hrimgeat (The Ruin 4[37]) may be the result of a similar symbolism. Hoar-frost is mentioned later in the line, and it seems to have been introduced there only to evoke regret. There is nothing in the context to indicate that the season is winter.

Winter is the season of cold terror. To wander alone in a scene of wintery desolation is to feel all the misery there can be on earth. Whoever finds himself there, cold and without shelter against the blasts of wind, may well remember the joyous feasting in the wine-hall and the king, the gold-giving friend of men, sharing out treasure by the hearth, while he must dwell in the grove, an "earm anhaga," the companion of the wolf in the Cotton Maxims (18-19): "wulf sceal on bearowe, earm anhaga"; for the wolf infests the slopes where only the powers of darkness go gladly. The wolf-infested slopes and the hart pursued by hounds distinguish the famous description of the way to Grendel's lair from the sources and analogues. Nowhere else are the standard OE poetic phrases combined to such effect. It is a scene of moors, of paths of exile, wolf-infested slopes, wind-swept headlands, perilous tracts of fenland where the mountain-stream goes down under the gloom of mountain-sides, a flood under the earth; the pool stands overhung by groves covered with hoar-frost, a wood held by its roots overhangs the water (Beowulf

1351–76). Factually the scenery could hardly exist. The combination of fenland and mountains, of wind-swept headlands and woods overhanging the pool is not possible: it is a gallimaufry of devices, each of which is horrific in its associations. One of these devices must be discussed further, the wolf, the symbol of slaughter. Once again the compounds provide some of the evidence. The warriors in Exodus 181 are described as "hare heoruwulfas" (MS heora wulfas); in Daniel wulfheort is three times used to describe the enemies; the Mermedonians are called wælwulfas in Andreas 149, as are the Vikings in The Battle of Maldon 96. The poet of Deor (21–22) speaks of "Eormanrices wylfenne geþoht." Whatever the background of Wulf and Eadwacer, it is certain that neither the word wulf nor hwelp refers to animals. Wulf may refer to an outlaw, or it may be a name simply, and his son is punningly described as hwelp. The clearest indication of what the associations of the word wulf were, is to be found in the Exeter Maxims 146–151:

> Wineleas, wonsælig mon   genimeð him wulfas to geferan,
> felafæcne deor.   Ful oft hine se gefera sliteð;
> gryre sceal for greggum,   græf deadum men;
> hungre heofeð,   nales þæt heafe bewindeð,
> ne huru wæl wepeð   wulf se græga,
> morþorcwealm mæcga,   ac hit a mare wille.

Here the cruelty of the wolf seems to be combined with the associations of the cry of wolf's head.[38] It is possible that the reference to the wolf in the Cotton Maxims 18–19, "wulf sceal on bearowe, earm anhaga" is primarily associated with the symbol of outlaws. That is certainly the aspect of wulf which underlies the reference to the devil in Christ 256 as "se awyrgda wulf."

Most frequently the wolf is found in the company of the eagle and the raven as satellites of battle. There is little point in quoting at length the passages where the beasts of battle are to be found.[39] The theme, which admits of some variation in treatment, is obviously a part of traditional descriptions of battle. In Beowulf 3024–27 the treatment of the theme is perhaps the most striking, but it is, as far as one can tell, within the traditional pattern, unlike the treatment in The Wanderer 80–84, which is only slightly related to a scene of battle, and The Fortunes of Men 10–14, where there is no explicit connexion with battle, and the beasts are merely a means of disposing of corpses. The original audience may, of course, have supplied the connexion with battle, seeing that the association was so common. Originally the beasts may well have been factual, but in OE verse they are called in by the poets when they describe carnage, because they feel such descriptions to be incomplete without them. Together they circle about the dead: the gray wolf has his fill, the dark raven croaks, and the eagle greedily feasts on the carrion, in competition with the wolf. To mention any one of the beasts is like speaking of worms and epitaphs in Modern English, to speak of more than one is to call up all that is most abhorrent to warriors.

The raven on the battle-field is closely related to the raven feeding on gallows (e.g. The Fortunes of Men 33–42; Beowulf 2448, and [if the emendation is correct] 2941). Unconnected with these is the description of the raven announcing the new day (Beowulf 1801–02), which is similar to the cuckoo as harbinger of spring and the new year in The Seafarer 53–55, The Husband's Message 20–23, and Guthlac 744. These examples are part fact and part symbol. They are more closely related to the type of symbolism of the decay of autumn for the dying man than to the symbolism of the wolf's head for outlaws.

This survey of OE poetic diction has shown that the Anglo-Saxons were not reluctant to introduce figurative diction in their poetry. Many of the devices they used may not have been indigenous; but they used them, and understood that what was expressed as a figure was not necessarily capable of factual interpretation too. That is made explicit in Christ (1327–31):

> Nu we sceolon georne   gleawlice þurhseon
> usse hreþercofan   heortan eagum,
> innan uncyste.   We mid þam oðrum ne magun,
> heafodgimmum,   hygeþonces ferð
> eagum þurhwlitan   ænge þinga.

The eyes of the mind may achieve what the eyes of the head will not.

The OE poets here and there introduce similes and allegories of their own in poems based on Latin sources. The author of the OE Phoenix adds much to his source and thus proves that he has understood the nature of the allegory. And yet the distinction between factual and figurative speech cannot always be maintained. The allegory of the devil's arrows merges and coalesces with diseases sent like wicked thoughts by poisonous darts of elves and demons. In other cases, as so often in verse of all ages, the facts only exist as symbols of moods. The Anglo-Saxons have no difficulty in expressing abstract thought in their language; they do so often enough in prose. But in verse they achieve their effects by concrete imagery. An excellent example, in which the figurative nature of the diction is explicit, is the description of the strong mind in terms of tempestuous seas (Exeter Maxims 50-58):

Styran sceal mon strongum mode. Storm oft holm gebringeþ,
geofen in grimmum sælum;   onginnað grome fundian
fealwe on feorran to londe, hwæþer he fæste stonde.
Weallas him wiþre healdað, him biþ wind gemæne.
Swa biþ sæ smilte,
þonne hy wind ne weceð:
swa beoþ þeoda geþwære, þonne hy geþingad habbað,
gesittað him on gesundum þingum, ond þonne mid gesiþum
healdaþ
cene men gecynde rice.

This passage has a close bearing on the interpretation of The Wanderer and The Seafarer. The first four lines show exactly the same kind of parallel symbolism found in these Maxims 25-29. It is an example of the processes of nature being used as the symbols of moods, and the simile contained in the passage makes it certain that the processes of nature are to be interpreted symbolically.

In their concrete imagery the OE poets are helped by the nature of their language, in which it was possible to compound words in such a way that the literal meaning of the elements of the compound might be fused, and the full force of the first element lost. Much has been made of the originality of the compounds in the so-called elegies of the Exeter Book, and this originality has been used as evidence for the dating of the poems. Many of them occur once only, and their precise suitability seems to indicate that they are nonce-formations. Yet if more poetry on the themes of the "elegies" had survived many of these compounds might be found more than once. There is no evidence to suggest that late OE verse was less fertile in imaginative compounds than the verse of any other period.[40]

One theme, that of mutability, deserves special mention, first, on account of the prominent place it holds in the "elegies," and secondly, because its treatment provides an excellent instance of the difficulty of establishing which comes first, the symbol or the mood. The theme of mutability and the hope in the stability of the life to come shapes much of the poetry of the Anglo-Saxons, not only the "elegies" of the Exeter Book, but also poems as diverse as Beowulf, Widsith, The Fortunes of Men, and the Vercelli Homiletic Fragment. The manner of treating the theme is also diverse. Some poems stress the hope more than the regret, others single out one aspect of mutability, as for example the mutability of royal grandeur in Hrothgar's sermon in Beowulf; in some of the "elegies," however, the theme of mutability encompasses all things on earth. In part of The Wanderer and the whole of The Ruin the mutability of worldly glory is symbolized by a city once glorious and now seen crumbling in decay[41]:

>
> Ongietan sceal gleaw hæle hu gæstlic bi∂,
> þonne ealre þisse worulde wela weste stonde∂,
> 75 swa nu missenlice geond þisne middangeard
> winde biwaune weallas stondaþ,
> hrime bihrorene, hry∂ge þa ederas.
> Woria∂ þa winsalo, waldend licga∂
> dreame bidrorene, duguþ eal gecrong,
> 80 wlonc bi wealle. Sume wig fornom,
> ferede in for∂wege, sumne fugel oþbær
> ofer heanne holm, sumne se hara wulf
> dea∂e gedælde, sumne dreorighleor
> in eor∂scræfe eorl gehydde.
> 85 Yþde swa þisne eardgeard ælda scyppend
> oþþæt burgwara breahtma lease
> eald enta geweorc idlu stodon.
>
> (The Wanderer)

What came first, the sight of the ruin or the mood of regret at the passing of worldly glory? Only a subjective answer can be given; in the case of The Ruin it may well be that the sight of decay came before the mood; in The Wanderer, however, the description of the ruin seems only one strand in the composite of concrete instances of mutability. As in The Ruin, the treatment of the buildings leads to the treatment of its erstwhile inhabitants. In The Wanderer the transition from the ruin to the inhabitants is made by way of a catalogue of the fates of men. These catalogues are common in OE verse. In them the method of providing concrete instances to make palpable a doctrine is employed with the greatest economy; the instances are shorn of all that is not essential to the doctrine. Examples of such catalogues are: Christ 664–681 (how God has given to each of mankind his particular skill); Juliana 472–494 (how the devil sends sinners to death); Elene 131–137 (of various deaths); The Gifts of Men 30–96, 106–109 (of the various endowments of mankind); The Fortunes of Men 10–92 (the various fortunes, bad and good, that may be the lot of men).

Such catalogues impart illustrative variety to the doctrine or mood that forms the subject of the poems or of part of the poems. A somewhat different type of catalogue of instances, used for a similar purpose, is exemplified by:

Hwær cwom mearg? Hwær cwom mago?   Hwær cwom
                                        maþþumgyfa?
Hwær cwom symbla gesetu?   Hwær sindon seledreamas?
Eala beorht bune!   Eala byrnwiga!
Eala þeodnes þrym!   (The Wanderer 92–95)

Her bið feoh læne,   her bið freond læne,
her bið mon læne,   her bið mæg læne.
                       (The Wanderer 108–109)

Similar lists occur in: Christ and Satan 163–171 (list of regrets similar to The Wanderer 94–95); Christ 590–598 (aspects of hell and heaven); Hrothgar's sermon, Beowulf 1762–68 (the ills of old age and means of death); The Judgment Day II 254–267 (the various afflictions that are not in heaven); Beowulf 2260–66 (the joys that are no more).

II

The Use of the First Person Singular

What distinguishes The Wanderer and The Seafarer as well as The Penitent's Prayer from such concrete instances as were listed in the poetic catalogues is the use of the first person singular, by means of which the mood of the poems is brought closer to the audience than would be possible by an entirely impersonal treatment. The use of the first person singular is the rule in the "elegies."[42] It is also the rule in the Riddles, though there are exceptions. The frequency with which the first person was introduced without any personal feeling, and the occasional interchange of the first and third person singular indicate that the convention of the first person could be used without the poet's feeling personal attachment to the first person in his poems. It is, however, difficult to assess the degree of this personal attachment in individual cases, especially in the "elegies."

F. Tupper in his edition of the Riddles[43] has discussed how in the English as well as in the Latin Riddles of the Anglo-Saxons the themes are brought to life by making their subjects speak in the first person. There are two kinds of uses of the first person: first, the poet may relate what strange wonder he saw or overheard[44]; secondly, the subject of the Riddle speaks, usually relating its history or attributes, asking the audience at the end to name it, "Saga hwæt ic hatte!"[45] This use is relevant to the interpretation of The Wanderer and The Seafarer in that it exemplifies a non-literal, conventional use of the first person.

Two of the Riddles of this type are of slightly more interest because of their unusual treatment of the first person. Riddle 33 combines a description of its subject (ice, iceberg) in the third person with an autobiographical account spoken by the ice or iceberg in the first person. The words linking the two halves are:

> sægde searocræftig   ymb hyre sylfre gesceaft:
> "Is min modor   etc. etc."   (8–9)

No doubt the reason for this combination of two distinct methods of telling a riddle was to give variety; it is an example of the combination of passages describing one particular thing from the slightly differing point of view of varied grammatical persons. The use of the first person in this poem, like that in the "elegies," results in a more direct effect.

Riddle 86 also combines the third with the first person, yet it does so by what to modern ears appears to be merely an end-formula that has been added anacoluthically. Again there is a descriptive passage in the third person, and only at the end (instead of asking for the solution with the words "Saga hwæt hio [seo wiht] hatte!") the subject itself speaks in the first person, saying, "Saga hwæt ic hatte!" We may assume that the scribe merely blundered, that he still has Riddle 83 in his mind which has this particular ending; or we may feel that the blunder arose because of the greater frequency of the formula in the first person. In either case we may feel justified in emending to establish, or perhaps to reestablish, concord. On the other hand, in view of the common mixture of grammatical person in the "elegies" and elsewhere, we may feel less certain about our ability to detect with the ears of the twentieth the solecisms of the eighth or ninth or tenth centuries. To the Anglo-Saxons the passage may have seemed to contain nothing that was disturbing. It is alogical rather than illogical, and may be justified by reference to such examples of similar constructions as that of the opening of Alfred's "Preface" to the Pastoral Care, in which the opening formula of a royal writ continues anacoluthically with the king's personal statement: "Ælfred kyning hateð gretan Wærferð biscep his wordum luflice and freondlice; ond ðe cyðan hate ðæt me com swiðe oft on gemynd . . . ."46

As Professor Margaret Schlauch has shown, the treatment of the first person in the Riddles is closely related to the Cross speaking in The Dream of the Rood.47 It is possible that in The Husband's Message the message itself, and not a living messenger, is speaking, though the MS is too damaged to allow of certainty. The device is prosopopoeia, by which an object is made to feel and speak like a person. As Dr. Schlauch says, prosopopoeia was usually discussed in conjunction with ethopoeia, by which an imaginary monologue is attributed to a human but fictitious character.

B. F. Huppé is right when he says that it seems likely that the use of the first person in the "elegies" was ethopoeic.48 The Wife's Lament is a straightforward example of ethopoeia. It begins by emphasizing that the Wife is speaking about her own misfortune:

> Ic þis giedd wrece   bi me ful geomorre,
> minre sylfre sið.

The ethopoeic opening formula is almost the same as that of The Seafarer:

> Mæg ic be me sylfum soðgied wrecan,
> siþas secgan.

III

The Penitential Tradition

The Seafarer is a Christian poem: The Wife's Lament is not.[49] The Seafarer is a penitent; his theme is, as Dr. Whitelock says,[50] "me hatran sind dryhtnes dreamas, þonne þis deade lif, læne on londe" (64–66). In The Seafarer the use of ethopoeia is part of the conventions of penitential literature, especially of the informal confessional. Ethopoeia is similarly used in conjunction with the conventions of informal confessionals in The Wanderer and The Penitent's Prayer, poems with which The Seafarer is, therefore, closely related. In The Wanderer and The Seafarer the theme of the mutability of this dead life is emphasized, so that these poems are related to The Ruin and The Rhyming Poem.

The conventions of informal confessional verse must be discussed, as far as they are relevant, before the interpretation of the poems as a whole is attempted. No direct Latin source has been found for any of the ME informal penitential hymns,[51] and similarly there appears to be no direct source for The Penitent's Prayer, and that in spite of the great number of Latin penitential hymns extant. The vernacular informal penitential hymns, and their Latin counterparts, go back to the same liturgical traditions. Prayers of the type underlying them are to be found, for example, in The Book of Cerne[52] prayers Nos. 8 and 10, of which Kuypers says (p. xxiv), "In both there is a minute enumeration of all possible sins, even of crimes the most heinous and unlikely. The penitent speaks as though he had been guilty of them all." In confessions such as these the penitent lays upon himself a load of sins no one man, though the worst of sinners, can have committed.[53] Although they cannot be the true confessions of an individual sinner these prayers are in the first person singular, so that, when they are read by another or to another sinner, he may feel his sins to be included in the prayer he is

saying or hearing, and he will thus feel himself directly impli-
cated in the prayer.

These prayers gave rise to an English tradition of informal
confessionals of which one example of a later period is of interest on account of the acknowledgment it makes that the imaginary
situation, though it is recounted in the first person singular, is
not to be interpreted autobiographically:

> To mete murþes ich wes wel fous,
> ant comely mon ta calle—
> y sugge by oþer ase bi ous—
> alse ys hirmon halt in hous,
> ase heued-hount in halle.
>
> (Heȝe Louerd, þou here my bone [MS
> Harley 2253], lines 81–85)[54]

Line 83 states clearly that the poet is speaking of others as well
as of himself. Confessions tell in the first person singular of
sins committed by others as well as by the speaker. They lead
to the looser, informal penitential verse in which the speaker
assumes, ethopoeically, various roles of typical sinners.

IV

The Interpretation of The Wanderer,
The Seafarer and The Penitent's Prayer

The results of the three preceding sections lead to an interpretation of The Wanderer, The Seafarer and The Penitent's
Prayer largely different from existing interpretations, yet based
on conventions found elsewhere in OE poetry. The survey of OE
poetic diction has shown that the Anglo-Saxons were fully conversant with figurative thought and diction. They treated allegory
in a manner revealing a relationship of fact to figure so close
that the figure was only an aspect of the fact, and not separable
from it. They used metaphor at times so vividly that its use may
seem illogical. With them the processes of nature do not, as a
rule, lead to thoughts, but rather they use the processes as symbols of moods: a concrete scene may be little more than a description of a mood. The nature of their language allowed them to compound in such a way that the elements that form the compounds

may have a meaning individually different from the meaning which the element contributes to the total meaning of the compound. To understand the OE poets we must give up the attempt to distinguish precisely between fact and figure; levels of meaning have no place in interpreting OE poetry, for the word "levels" assumes a definite relationship of higher and lower meanings of a word or figure. OE verse has no levels of meaning; words and figures are more like nodes of meaning.

A literal interpretation of these poems must fail, for they are not exercises in realism. Those who seek to find in the pious Wanderer or Seafarer heroes of old, contending with the fretful elements, do not usually succeed without lopping and polling the received text—a method of criticism which is, as Dr. Whitelock reminds us, less fashionable than it used to be.

Dr. Whitelock herself has advanced a solution which explains The Seafarer within the firm framework of what is known of Anglo-Saxon society. If, however, the poem is looked upon as poetic embroidery of biographical facts it seems doubtful if one important contradiction within these facts can be explained. The poet describes a winter journey on the sea such as he has often experienced (lines 1–33). Then we find him at home, waiting for the cuckoo's song to harbinger a milder season, more favourable to seafaring. It seems that he has returned at the very time when he would have been best able to prove his willingness to embrace the hardships of wintery exile. If he has returned he cannot be a true penitent, who must for the love of God leave all he holds dear, and "on ælþeodignysse far[an], & þær hys lif geendige[an]."[55] Dr. Whitelock suggests that the description of wintery seafaring that opens the poem is a factual account of the experiences the man often had, before he decided to go into exile. If this view is accepted, the poem is the soðgied of the intending exile.

Dr. Whitelock rejects the allegorical interpretation (in the manner of Ehrismann and Anderson) because the allegory is not explicit. In this, I think, she is right. Dr. Whitelock as well as Ehrismann and Anderson ask the question: Is the description and situation in The Seafarer factual or figurative? Her interpretation is entirely factual, theirs figurative. But it is a question to which no satisfactory answer can be found: the poem is neither realism nor allegory. It is an imagined situation, invented to

give force to the doctrine which forms the end of the poem and
is its purpose.
The poem opens:

> Mæg ic be me sylfum   soðgied wrecan,
> siþas secgan,   hu ic geswincdagum
> earfoðhwile   oft þrowade,
> bitre breostceare   gebiden hæbbe.

When a speaker assumes a role, and wishes to convey clearly
that he is no longer what we know him to be, he stresses his
role by insistent use of the first person. The insistent use of
the first person in the opening line of The Seafarer has the ring
of Costard's "I Pompey am"; and we should do him wrong to
cry, "You lie, you are not he."

The Seafarer's opening words of identification are followed
by a long speech, also in the first person, giving the experiences
and feelings of a man in the typical situation of seafaring, an example of ethopoeia. The contention of the present article is that
exile combines within its natural situation all the misery which
OE poetry expressed by the anguish of solitude, darkness, cold.
The nature of OE poetry is such that there is no means of separ-
ating fact from figure. Factually or figuratively, it is miseries
such as these that a man must flee to, if he sees no lasting hope
in this dead life of worldly joys. For that reason voluntary exile
was a penitential discipline in Anglo-Saxon society; and in Anglo-
Saxon poetry the most effective way of inducing contempt of the
world is to tell ethopoeically of the miseries that are in this
world, and how much more gladly and readily they are to be em-
braced than the false joys of this dead life.

O. S. Anderson says of the dialogue theory which assumes
that there are two speakers in The Seafarer, both using the first
person singular, that "it may now safely be left out of the discussion."[56] Perhaps it may be resurrected in a modified form:
there are two speakers speaking in the first person, the ethopoeic
exile (lines 1–33a), and the wise, pious man eager to go on pilgrimage (33b–end). The break comes (as it does in all the various dialogue theories) in line 33; for the speaker who says (33b–
35b) that he himself is now eager to make trial of seafaring cannot be the man who has just told of the hardships he has experienced in seafaring. The dialogue theories were advanced in the

first place to overcome this difficulty, which is not explained
satisfactorily by any of the later theories. The ethopoeic opening is the speech of a man whose imaginary exploits have led
to a true view of this world; the poet has chosen this manner of
conveying his message because it is the most vivid method of
conveying it. The poet then expresses his wish to follow a way
of life as contemptuous of the world as that of the ethopoeic Seafarer; he is speaking of himself, but he hopes to urge others to
follow the same way of life, for his poem is didactic.

Within the wise man's speech in the first person there is a
long passage in the third person (39–57) in which is painted a
picture of false happiness, such as one may imagine to be the
happiness enjoyed by the intended audience. Others (in the third
person) have joy in vanities; the poet (speaking in the first person) has seen through these false joys, and urges them to aban-
don the world, telling them how he himself now is eager to depart over the seas. The proud man in the hall lives in vanity,
the wise man follows the Seafarer, however hard his lot. The
change of person underlines the didacticism: "y sugge by oþer
ase bi ous."

From line 58 the intending exile speaks again in the first
person, applying to himself what he has said: because he loves
the joys of the Lord more dearly than this dead life, transitory
on earth, he is filled with longing to make his pilgrimage.[57]
The rest of the poem expresses in the form of a homily (ending
in a prayer) the teaching that underlies the whole poem: how
recognition of the vanity of worldly wealth and wordly aspirations
leads to more lasting gain.[58]

The Penitent's Prayer is closely related to The Seafarer
both in manner of expression and in subject-matter. The greater
part of the poem is in the form of a penitential prayer, beginning
with an informal confession. Then it introduces the theme of
exile, and finally there is a message of resignation. Unlike The
Seafarer, the manner of exposition in The Penitent's Prayer is
confused.

The long prayer which begins the poem contains some features which seem to foreshadow the more specifically personal
second half of the poem. Immediately after the opening invoca-
tion the subject of the poem is stated:

5   Ic þe, mære god,
        mine sawle bebeode   ond mines sylfes lic,
        ond min word ond min weorc,   witig dryhten,
        ond eal min leoþo,   leohtes hyrde,
        ond þa manigfealdan   mine geþohtas.
10   Getacna me,   tungla hyrde,
        þær selast sy   sawle minre
        to gemearcenne   meotudes willan,
        þæt ic þe geþeo   þinga gehwylce,
        ond on me sylfum,   soðfæst cyning,
15   ræd arære.

The Penitent is here not merely asking, as he did in line 1, to be taken into the presence of God. He is asking to be shown where, i.e. in what manner of life, it is best for him to observe the will of God. The rest of the poem is about this life. The Penitent is aware that change in his manner of life is required of him if he is to be saved:

        Hæbbe ic þonne þearfe   þæt ic þine seþeah,
30   halges heofoncyninges,   hyldo getilge
        leorendum dagum,   lif æfter oþruni
        geseo ond gesece,   þæt me siþþan þær
        unne arfæst god   ecan dreames,
        lif alyfe,   þeah þe lætlicor
35   bette bealodæde   þonne bibodu wæron
        halgan heofonmægnes.

"Lif æfter oþrum" means "a new way of life on earth after the former way of life," rather than "life eternal." Only thus is the full significance of siþþan 'the life hereafter,' brought out: it stands in opposition to the new way of life on earth.[59] A somewhat similar ambiguity arises with the phrase "frætwian mec on ferðweg" (72). Thorpe followed by Grein's Bibliothek emended to forðweg, so that neither Bosworth-Toller nor Grein-Köhler records ferðweg at all. Wülker (following Grein in Germania, X [1865], 427) restored the MS reading, translating it lebensweg — "ein wort, das allerdings sonst nicht belegt ist, aber in bildung richtig und leicht verständlich ist." In the context (cf. especially "gæst gearwian" (74), however, "via animae" seems a more likely rendering, and that is, no doubt, what Mackie intended to convey by "my pilgrimage" in his translation.

With "Huru me frea witeð" (76b) a new part of the poem begins. Up to this point the prayer was very general. The next seven lines, though still not absolutely specific, contain a less general revelation of the Penitent's guilt and of his punishment, the suffering he has endured for the sins he has committed without always understanding them. Among these sufferings is the wretchedness of exile. Thus is introduced an account in the third person of the state of exile of a "wineleas wræcca," an account very similar to that given by the Seafarer, ll. 39–57. The Penitent tells of the miseries of exile, ending his account in the third person with the words:

> Ic bi me tylgust
> secge þis sarspel   ond ymb siþ spræce,
> longunge fus,   ond on lagu þence.   (96–98)

Bi in "bi me tylgust" is ambiguous. It might mean "about," i.e. he is telling a tale from experience of exiles in general, though for the most part he draws on his own experience. The device of litotes is so common in OE verse (not, however, in the "elegies") that it might be possible for tylgust to have the force of "entirely." This interpretation makes "Ic bi me tylgust secge þis sarspel" exactly parallel to the opening words of The Seafarer: "Mæg ic be me sylfum soðgied wrecan." The context, however, is not exactly parallel. The Seafarer continues his story in the first person, a straightforward example of ethopoeia, while in The Penitent's Prayer these words conclude an account of exile given in the third person. This change of person might be an example of the anacoluthic use of the ethopoeic formula, similar to the examples quoted on pp. 448 ff. above. A more likely explanation is that bi does not mean "about," but "for my sake, in connexion with me." This meaning is rare. It is found in Beowulf, where Hrothgar after telling his tale about Heremod says to Beowulf, "Ic þis gid be þe awræc" (1723–24), and be is recognized by the editors as having that meaning, and not the normal meaning. Another instance is quoted by Bosworth-Toller, Supplement, s.v. be III (17).[60]

If bi in line 96b of The Penitent's Prayer means "for the sake of" the change of person presents no difficulty. The account (given in the third person) of the exile is connected with the Penitent's own plight by the words, "I tell this tale of misery

mainly for my own sake, and urged on by longing I speak of a
journey and think of the sea." The phrase "longunge fus" (98)
echoes the last words before the sarspel: "forþon ic afysed
eom earm of minum eþle" (88-89).[61]
Line 99 is obviously incomplete both in sense and metre.
The editors rightly supply a word meaning "mind," e.g. "Nat
min [sefa] hwy ic gehycge." From what follows it becomes
clear that the Penitent, eager to go on pilgrimage, has not the
means to buy a boat, nor has he any friends to help him to go
on his journey.

Lines 103-111 have been discussed above. The passage is
about the irrevocable destiny of the Penitent: "Is seo bot æt þe
gelong æfter life"; the divine law is symbolized by the new life
of spring giving way to the decay of autumn.

It is difficult to understand why this passage introduces so
specific a cause of misery as calumny, tæle. It may have been
this that led Schücking to believe that the Penitent was a specific
person whose story was known to the original audience.[62] Though
he himself calls the poem Klage eines Vertriebenen he would have
preferred an actual name in the title: X. Y.'s Klage. Yet surely,
Schücking has himself given the reason for the introduction of
calumny when he says that the poet introduces "das Gefühl der
Enttäuschung und Verbitterung im Abrechnen mit der Unge-
rechtigkeit der Menschen." Calumny is typical of the injustice
of the world, as is the sorrow the Penitent gained at all times
in return for love. Calumny is now felt to be a specific injustice,
but that it was treated as an example of what is general in penitential literature is shown by the penitential Psalm 101.9 (= A. V.
102.8): "Tota die exprobrabant mihi inimici mei; et qui laudabant
me adversum me jurabant"; and similarly the penitential Psalm
37.12-13 (= A. V. 38.11-12): "Amici mei, et proximi mei adversum
me appropinquaverunt, et steterunt. Et qui juxta me erant, de
longe steterunt, et vim faciebant qui quaerebant animam meam.
Et qui inquirebant mala mihi, locuti sunt vanitates; et dolos tota
die meditabantur."

The rest of the poem is a straightforward lament of the
Penitent in his misery, ending on a note of resignation, which
provided the title given by Dobbie to the poem as a whole.

It is a muddled poem. Confession of sins committed is at
its centre:

STANLEY

> Nu þu const on mec
> firendæda fela,   feorma mec hwæþre,
> meotod, for þinre miltse,   þeah þe ic ma fremede
> grimra gylta   þonne me god lyfde.   (25–28)

The sense of guilt makes the Penitent seek another way of life
on earth, so that God may hereafter allow him to share in the
eternal bliss. The thought of the life to come makes death seem
imminent: the penitential journey away from the joys of the
world is as the first step towards the bliss he hopes to enjoy:

> Nu ic fundige to þe,   fæder moncynnes,
> of þisse worulde,   nu ic wat þæt ic sceal,
> ful unfyr faca;   feorma me þonne,
> wyrda waldend,   in þinne wuldordream,
> ond mec geleoran læt,   leofra dryhten,
> geoca mines gæstes.   (41–46)

He must prepare his soul for its pilgrimage (70–74). Endurance
of hardships here is the best preparation for the journey the soul
is to undertake. He must

> gæst gearwian,   ond me þæt eal for gode þolian
> bliþe mode,   nu ic gebunden eom
> fæste in minum ferþe.   (74–76)

These hardships are best endured in penitential exile. In this
poem it is once again impossible to say what is allegory, what
is fact. The division is too precise; the ferðweg, the journey
of the soul towards God, begins as a penitential journey away
from the joys of the world. Three times the Penitent repeats
that he is eager to depart, "fus on ferþe" (84), "ic afysed eom"
(88), and "longunge fus" (98). The Penitent tells for his own
sake chiefly the tale of the friendless exile, who must bear, as
must all penitents, the anger of the Lord, and then goes on,
autobiographically as it seems, to speak of his own poverty
which prevents him from becoming an exile.

The value of The Penitent's Prayer for the interpretation
of The Seafarer lies in the combination of confession and exile.
The Penitent is not himself able to go on pilgrimage, he is too
poor; but he introduces the subject of exile for his instruction

and example in words reminiscent of The Wanderer and The Seafarer:

> Ne mæg þæs anhoga,
> 90 leodwynna leas,   leng drohtian,
> wineleas wræcca,   (is him wrað meotud),
> gnornað on his geoguþe,
> ond him ælce mæle   men fullestað,
> ycað his yrmþu,   ond he þæt eal þolað,
> 95 sarcwide secga,   ond him bið a sefa geomor,
> mod morgenseoc.

The central theme of The Wanderer is:

> Ongietan sceal gleaw hæle   hu gæstlic bið,
> þonne ealre þisse worulde wela   weste stondeð.
>
> (73–74)

The poem is not merely about the mutability of all things on earth, but transcends the mutability of this world to state the permanence of what is spiritual, gæstlic. B. T. Huppé has emphasized the formal and thematic importance of the beginning and end of the poem;[63] the poet starts from and returns to the hope of God's Grace and Mercy, and he contrasts the security, fæstnung (line 115), of heaven with the mutability of the world.

That is the theme of the poem. Of the two sides of this theme, the hope of heaven and the misery and mutability of this world, only one is treated fully, for the poet refers only briefly to the hope of heaven, expending the whole of his art on the description of misery and mutability, making full use of the resources of OE poetic diction.

The Wanderer is directly related to informal penitential poetry, though, of course, not as closely as The Penitent's Prayer, and probably not even quite as closely as The Seafarer. The poet imparts directness to his teaching by the use of "oratio recta" in the speech of the Wanderer and the speech of the Wise Man, who may be the same as the Wanderer. With this poem, as with The Seafarer, much energy has been spent in the attempt to determine where to place the inverted commas required by modern editors. Syntactic justification may be found for look-

ing upon the first five lines of the poem as either a part of the
Wanderer's speech or as outside the Wanderer's speech.[64] The
Wise Man who speaks towards the end of the poem may or may
not be the same as the Wanderer who speaks at the beginning.
The second may even be a speech within the first. All this is
too precise. The poet is writing on the subjects of mutability
and misery, and there are two ways open to him: direct moralizing or the use of imagery. He uses both in this poem, and he uses
them in such a way that monotony is avoided. The Wanderer and
the Wise Man are introduced because they suitably embody aspects of his teaching, so that much of the direct moralizing is
made part of their speeches, especially of the speech of the Wise
Man. Since these fictitious characters were introduced by the
poet as a variation in the means of expression, so that what they
say is not their own speech as living individuals but remains the
poet's teaching, it is not easy to tell where the fictitious characters
take over from the poet, where they take over from each other,
and where the poet takes over from them; and that in spite of the
use of the "swa cwæð" formula. It is the poet's teaching, whoever may be speaking.

Like the Seafarer, the Wanderer is introduced because his
experiences as an exile call for the very phrases which form
the OE stock poetic expressions of misery: the loneliness of the
morning, the icy sea, frost, snow and hail, all the ingredients
of cold care.[65] More clearly even than the Seafarer, the Wanderer
remembers his former joys, the memory of which seems all the
more bitter to him in his present misery. But the way in which
they remember their former happiness is different. The Seafarer left the joys of the world and knew them to be false joys;
the Wanderer, however, relates how he buried his lord (lines
22–23a) and how he then sought another court, to regain his former happiness. The fall of princes may bring about the dispersal
and exile of retainers, but that is not the voluntary exile of penitence. The fall of princes, the ruin of courts and the dispersal
of the comitatus, these are the most potent symbols of the mutability of worldy glory; they taught the Wanderer a truer sense of
values:

> Forþon ic geþencan ne mæg   geond þas woruld
> for hwan modsefa   min ne gesweorce,
> 60   þonne ic eorla lif   eal geondþence,

> hu hi færlice   flet ofgeafon,
> modge maguþegnas.   Swa þes middangeard
> ealra dogra gehwam   dresoseð ond fealleþ,
> forþon ne mæg wearþan wis   wer, ær he age
> 65   wintra dæl in woruldrice.

It is difficult to relate the preceding passage, telling in the third
person of the miseries of exile, to the speech of the Wanderer
who tells his own experiences in the first person. It is the same
type of change of grammatical person as is found in The Seafarer.
In The Wanderer the change is introduced by:

> Wat se þe cunnað,
> hu sliþen bið   sorg to geferan,
> þam þe him lyt hafað   leofra geholena.   (29–31)

This seems very similar to two passages in The Seafarer:

> þæt se mon ne wat
> þe him on foldan   fægrost limpeð,
> hu ic earmcearig   etc.   (12–14)

and:

> Forþon him gelyfeð lyt,   se þe ah lifes wyn
> gebiden in burgum,   bealosiþa hwon,
> wlonc ond wingal,   hu ic werig oft
> in brimlade   bidan sceolde.   (27–30)

The Wanderer differs from The Seafarer in these similar constructions in that the positive "wat se þe cunnað" introduces experiences related in the third person, whereas in The Seafarer
the negative "þæt se mon ne wat" and "him gelyfeð lyt" introduce
the Seafarer's own experiences told in the first person. The Seafarer tells of his own particular experiences which are beyond
the knowledge and belief of the prosperous man. The Wanderer
in his speech seems concerned to establish as fact experiences
of exile, such as are known to all seafaring men. The account
of the events at sea, told in the third person, are the Wanderer's
tale of a typical wanderer. Looked at from the point of view of
the poet, who is using various means of expressing his teaching

poetically, the situation is this: to give force to the teaching of
how mutable and miserable this world is a Wanderer is introduced who has memories of hardships, battles, and the fall of
kinsmen and of princes; he relates his miseries in the first
person and then stresses the universality of his experiences by
saying that they are such as all seafarers know; the Wanderer,
who had been introduced by the poet as best exemplifying typical miseries, tells now of typical miseries of wanderers. The
Wanderer uses this technique not only to lend universality to
his experiences at sea, but also to lend universality to his experience as a lordless retainer:

> Forþon wat se þe sceal   his winedryhtnes
> leofes larcwidum   longe forþolian,
> ðonne sorg ond slæp   somod ætgædre
> earmne anhogan   oft gebindað.   (37–40)

Such miseries as the Wanderer has experienced are known to
all men who have had a similar fate, and such miseries lead to
wisdom.

Among the passages of direct moral instruction expressed
in gnomes are two definitions, the Wanderer in lines 11b–18 defines reticence as the practice of nobles and then applies his
definition to himself, and in lines 62b–72 a wise man is defined.
This definition introduces the statement of the theme of the poem
in lines 73–74, and what follows makes it clear that only a wise
man can draw the lesson from the ruins around him. The ruin
is the stock figure expressing mutability in OE poetic diction.
The way in which the poet of The Ruin gives directness to the
teaching of mutability is to begin with the sight of a real ruin
and to give the appearance of drawing the moral from the sight
of that ruin. The poet of The Wanderer cannot do that, there is
no ruin for him to begin with. Yet he too has found a method of
endowing the stock image with life, by associating it closely with
his definition of a wise man. The argument is this: wisdom is
founded on experience; no one can be wise before he is old; an
old man will live to see ravaged the scenes of his youthful happiness; in the contemplation of these ruins he shows his wisdom
by moralizing "ubi sunt qui ante nos fuerunt." It is a wise man
who understands how spiritual all things shall be when the prosperity of all this world stands deserted as now here and there

ruins stand, wind-swept and rime-covered, throughout this earth;
for he has drawn the full lesson from the scattered ruins around
him, and that lesson is the theme of the poem:

> Ongietan sceal gleaw hæle   hu gæstlic bið,
> þonne ealre þisse worulde wela   weste stondeð,
> 75   swa nu missenlice   geond þisne middangeard
> winde biwaune   weallas stondaþ,
> hrime bihrorene,   hryðge þa ederas.
> Woriað þa winsalo,   waldend licgað
> dreame bidrorene,   duguþ eal gecrong
> 80   wlonc bi wealle.

Then follows the "sum" catalogue on the manner of dying, which
includes birds—not necessarily the eagle and the raven—and the
gray wolf, as well as a brief allusion to burial rites. This leads
to the introduction of the Wise Man's speech which begins with
"ubi sunt," followed by regret and sorrow as he beholds the sad
remnants of former pomp and glory; but on earth all things are
transitory. The entire speech is gnomic. The Wise Man was
created by the poet because it is typical for wise men to speak
in gnomes, and gnomes express moral teaching with the greatest directness and force. The end of the poem seems to stand
outside the direct speech. In it the poet once more sums up the
teaching of the whole.

Figures of a Wanderer and a Seafarer are created by the
poets because they best embody contempt of the world, for by
their way of life they have experience of miseries gladly endured in preference to vanities and false joys. When they speak
of these experiences they teach the poets' theme. The Wanderer
and the Seafarer themselves are not the theme of the poems, but
the best means of expressing it. OE poetic diction provides the
key to an understanding of OE didactic poetry.[66]

NOTES

1 G. Ehrismann, "Religionsgeschichtliche Beiträge zum germanischen Frühchristentum," Beiträge zur Geschichte der
deutschen Sprache und Literatur, XXXV (1909), 213–218;
D. Whitelock, "The Interpretation of 'The Seafarer,'" in The
Early Cultures of North-West Europe (H. M. Chadwick Memo-

<u>rial Studies</u>), eds. Sir Cyril Fox and Bruce Dickins (Cambridge, 1950), pp. 259–272. No attempt will be made in this article to discuss the various interpretations of the poems.

2 Each of these names sums up an editor's or commentator's interpretation of the poem; and I am well aware that in giving the poem a new title I too am assuming at the outset what I set out to show. But to call it merely <u>Prayer</u> is too vague, and none of the other titles fits.

3 "Diction and Imagery in Anglo-Saxon Poetry," <u>Essays and Studies</u>, XI (1925), 83.

4 The survey is not complete. Among the similes omitted are some where the interpretation of the text, or the text itself, is in dispute, and some which, though formally similes, are of little interest as regards poetic imagery.

5 Cf. A. Ebert, "Der angelsächsische Physiologus," <u>Anglia</u>, VI (1883), pp. 243–245.

6 Cf. G. P. Krapp, <u>The Anglo-Saxon Poetic Records</u>, V (New York, 1932), xlviii.

7 Cf. O. F. Emerson, "Originality in Old English Poetry," <u>RES</u>, II (1926), 18–31; A. S. Cook, <u>The Christ of Cynewulf</u> (Boston, 1909), xliii–xlv; C. Schaar, "Critical Studies in the Cynewulf Group," <u>Lund Studies in English</u>, XVII (1949), 31–34, 42–43.

8 Cf. C. Spicq, "Esquisse d'une histoire de l'exégèse latine au Moyen Age," <u>Bibliothèque Thomiste</u>, XXVI (1944), pp. 98–99.

9 It should be noted that though Cynewulf follows his source, <u>Acta Julianae Virginis Martyris</u>, quite closely at times, the use of the figure of the devil's arrows is his addition. (O. Glöde, "Cynewulf's Juliana und ihre Quelle," <u>Anglia</u>, XI [1889], 146–158, gives an excellent account of Cynewulf's use of the source.) The last quotation renders the injunction, "aedificate domos vestras super firmam petram, ne venientibus ventris validis disrumpamini" (quoted from W. Strunk, <u>The Juliana of Cynewulf</u> [Boston, 1904], p. 48). It seems likely that the connecting link between the two aspects of this figure represented by these two passages is to be found in the word <u>scur</u>, which means in the first place 'a shower, a storm of rain, snow or hail,' and secondly 'a shower of missiles.'

The phrase flana scuras is found in Judith 221 and Elene 117; a similar use has been quoted above from Vainglory 35.

10 Cf. J. H. G. Grattan and C. Singer, Anglo-Saxon Magic and Medicine (Oxford, 1952), p. 60; and C. Singer, "Early English Magic and Medicine," Proceedings of the British Academy, IX (for 1919–20), 353–360.

11 The charm is reprinted (as Charm 17D) in G. Storm's, Anglo-Saxon Magic (The Hague, 1948), pp. 224–233.

12 G. Storm, op. cit., pp. 140–151 (Charm 2); cf. W. Horn, "Der altenglische Zauberspruch gegen den Hexenschuss," Probleme der englischen Sprache und Kultur (Festschrift for J. Hoops), ed. W. Keller (Heidelberg, 1925), pp. 88–104.

13 Carleton Brown, "Poculum Mortis in Old English," Speculum, XV (1940), 389–399, has discussed the emblem with great learning, and more recently G. V. Smithers, English and Germanic Studies IV (1952), 67–75, has presented an even wider survey of the use of the emblem in medieval literature. They have established beyond all doubt that the Anglo-Saxons were fully conversant with it. Among the poetic uses of the emblem are Guthlac 863–871 (as well as 976–993 quoted above), Juliana 483–490, and as C. Brown convincingly suggests, Maxims I 78 (emending deada to deaða and translating "the deep cup of death is the secret longest hidden"). (In Genesis B 717–723 the fruit which Eve gave to Adam is hell and death, but it is not called "drink.")

14 The source, Felix's Vita S. Guthlaci (ed. P. Gonser, Das angelsächsische Prosa-Leben des hl. Guthlac, AF, XXVII [1909]) does not contain this figure.

15 Cf. R. M. Lumiansky, "The Contexts of OE 'ealuscerwen' and 'meoduscerwen,'" JEGP, XLVIII (1949), 116–126, and Smithers, op. cit.

16 Judas's reply to Elene. The source has: "[Helena] dixit ad illum, 'Vita et mors propositae sunt tibi: elige tibi quod vis, vitam an mortem.' Judas dixit, 'Et quis in solitudine constitutus, panibus sibi appositis, lapides manducat?'" (Quoted from C. W. Kent's edition of the poem [Boston, 1889], p. 41.)

17 This type of parallelism may well be indigenous with the
    Anglo-Saxons. A similar figure occurs in the Hávamál 50:

> Hrǫrnar þǫll,
> sús stęndr þorpi á,
> hlýrat hęnni bǫrkr ne barr;
> svá 's maðr,
> sás mangi ann,
> hvat skal hann lęngi lifa.
>   (ed. F. Jónsson [Copenhagen, 1924],
>   pp. 56–57)

Wülker, Krapp-Dobbie and Mackie (in his translation) all
begin a fresh sentence with fus (Maxims I 27). This might be
interpreted as indicating that the two statements are not connected. It is, however, in the nature of the Maxims to combine things in contrast: lines 39–44 connect the innocent at
heart in his happiness with the misery of the blind man pun-
ished by God; lines 45–49 juxtapose the infirm man in need
of the physician with the young man who must be taught.
More commonly comparison and contrast join things custom-
arily compared and contrasted, frost and fire (71), the man
of shame and the man pure in heart (66). In the Cotton Maxims
similarly, the thief must go about in murky weather, the
demon must dwell alone in the fenland (42–43); cattle must
procreate and teem on earth, in heaven the star must shine
bright as the Lord commanded (47–49); good must strive
with evil, light with darkness, hostile armies must fight each
other, foe against foe contesting about land, and sins must
be laid to the sinners charge (50–54). It is possible that the
compiler of the Cotton Maxims thought of some of them as
no more than disjointed truths.

18 E&S, XI, 69.

19 Cf. R. Heinzel, QF, X (1875), 24, who refers to Beowulf
    291–292, 333–335, 2539–40.

20 An excellent account of the kennings describing thought and
    speech is to be found in H. Marquardt, "Die altenglischen
    Kenningar," Schriften der Königsberger Gelehrten Gesell-
    schaft (Geisteswissenschaftliche Klasse), 14 (1938), pp. 199–
    200.

21 OS. wallan is also used figuratively in much the same way.
(Cf. E. Sievers' Heliand [Halle, 1878], p. 407, s.v. erregt
and n. 9.) Cf. Genesis B 353–354 and 589–590.

22 In this particular case it is possible that the source suggested
the image: "Hinc flagellat ira mentem fluctus turbida tollens"
(Philosophiae Consolationis, Lib. iv, Met. ii, 7).

23 The meaning is "tormented by surging wounds," the metaphor
being directly related to that in such phrases as "benne
weallað" (Andreas 1405); "weollon wælbenna" (Exodus 492);
"sarbennum soden" (Andreas 1239).

24 Cf. H. Marquardt, op. cit., p. 228.

25 The metaphor segl may well have been inspired by the fact
that in OE the word could mean either "sail" or "sun." The
gender of segl = 'sail' was masc. or neut., that of segl =
'sun' probably neut.

26 Essays by Divers Hands, N.S., XXV (1950), 13.

27 F. Tupper, in "Anglo-Saxon Dæg-Mæl," PMLA, X (1895),
111–241, has shown that uhtsang 'nocturns,' formerly only
'vigils,' became a separate canonical hour in the Anglo-
Saxon Church, and uhta might include both "nocturns" and
"matins." Uht(a) and its compounds usually glosses "tempus
matutinum," but at times it stands for "the middle of the
night"; Bosworth-Toller quotes from De Officiis Diurnalium
et Nocturnalium Horarum: "De nocturna celebratione. On
uhtan we sculon God herian, ealswa Dauid cwæð: 'Media
nocte surgebam ad confitendum tibi.'" The matter is further complicated by seasonal changes, as the Ancren Riwle
says (EETS, CCXXV [London, 1952], p. 9): "vhtsong bi nihte
ine winter, ine sumer iþe dawunge." In Beowulf 2271–73
the dragon is called "eald uhtsceaða . . . se ðe . . . nihtes
fleogeð"; uhtfloga (2760); and the time is stated with greater
precision as middelnihtum (2782, 2833). The general impression given by the account of the fight with Grendel (702 ff.)
is that it took place when darkness fell, and this is confirmed
by the description of Grendel as "eatol æfengrom" (2074), yet
this last account of the battle describes it as uhthlem (2007).
It is "on uhtan ær dægrede" that the Harrowing of Hell takes
place according to Christ and Satan 402, 404, and 463–464.

28 Cf. J. R. R. Tolkien, "Beowulf: The Monsters and the Critics," Proceedings of the British Academy, XXII (1936), 278–280.

29 Especially by L. Whitbread, PQ, XVII (1938), 365–370; and cf. L. L. Schücking, Untersuchungen zur Bedeutungslehre der ags. Dichtersprache (Heidelberg, 1915), p. 10.

30 Winter and darkness can also be used as the basis for moralizing. An example is to be found in Solomon and Saturn (in Robert J. Menner's edition for the MLA [New York, 1941] = 293–313), 302–322. The imagery is far from original (cf. Menner, pp. 130–131), but it is used effectively, as far as one can tell from a difficult and incomplete text.

31 That the Anglo-Saxons visualized hell with hot and cold alternating has often been commented on. The idea goes back i.a. to The Book of Enoch. Cf. E. J. Becker, The Medieval Visions of Heaven and Hell (Baltimore, 1899), pp. 58–60.

32 F. Klaeber (The Later Genesis [Heidelberg, 1931], p. 50) relates "fyr oððe gar" to Genesis A (43) where "fyre ond færcyle" describes the torments of hell. B. J. Timmer (in his edition of the poem [Oxford, 1948], p. 102) refers to the charm Against a Sudden Stitch, where spere is used of a sudden pain. Similarly gar may well refer to the elvish nature of devilish torments.

33 Cf. P. Gonser, "Das angelsächsische Prosa-Leven des hl. Guthlac," AF, XXVII (1909), 167.

34 Felix's Vita merely has a factual reference to the night (cf. Gonser, op. cit., p. 166).

35 "AE. 'isig,'" Anglia, LVI (1932), 438–439.

36 In the Exeter Book Judgment Day 106–107 "hot and cold" are used in variation of "good and evil," i.e. still metaphorically though quite differently from the usual metaphor.

37 In so difficult a context it is impossible to be certain. With "hrim on lime" later in the line it may well be that the first hrim is merely written in anticipation of the second, as the emendators suggest. Cf. J. Nenninger, Die altenglische "Ruine," (Limburg, 1938), pp. 10–11.

38 Cf. The Laws of Edward the Confessor VI, "Lupinum enim gerit caput a die utlagationis sue, quod ab Anglis 'uulfesheued' nominatur." F. Liebermann, Die Gesetzte der Angelsachsen, I (1903), 631. Also cf. OIcel. vargr = (1) 'wolf,' (2) 'outlaw.'

39 They are referred to individually or together in: Genesis 1983–85, 2157–61; Exodus 161–169; Elene 27–30, 52–53, 110–116; Judith 205–212, 292–296; The Wanderer 80–84; The Battle of Maldon 106–107; The Battle of Brunanburh 60–65; The Battle of Finnsburh 5–6, 34–35; Beowulf 3024–27; The Fortunes of Men 10–14, 33–42.

40 E. D. Grubl in her Studien zu den angelsächsischen Elegien (Marburg, 1948), p. 29, says: "Es ist allgemein bekannt, dass in der späteren Epoche der angelsächsischen Literatur die sprachschöpferische Kraft nachliess, während sie in der frühangelsächsischen Zeit stark an den Tag trat. Wir können also auf Grund des häufigen Auftretens von Hapaxlegomena in den Elegien sagen, dass diese Gedichte früh entstanden sein müssen." It is difficult to establish what is "allgemein bekannt" in OE studies: that Dr. Grubl's statement is wrong is easily demonstrated. The datable late poems, i.e. the Chronicle Poems and The Battle of Maldon, show much originality in their compounds, and even when A. Campbell's reservation (in his edition of The Battle of Brunanburh [London, 1938], p. 41) is heeded, that "No doubt, if more OE poetry were preserved, many of these words would be found to be common," the list remains impressively long: ealdor-lang, heaþolind, scipflota, hereflema, mylenscearp, bilgesleht, cumbolgehnast, garmitting, wælfeld, hasewanpada, guðhafoc, arhwæt from The Battle of Brunanburh; hæfteclomm from The Capture of the Five Baroughs; wintergetel (cf. OS wintargital), niþweorc from The Coronation of Edgar; cræftgleaw from The Death of Edgar; æschere (cf. the proper name in Beowulf), beaduræs, bricgweard, færsceaða, fealohilte, feolheard, feorh-hus, forþgeorn, garræs, gryreleoð, hringlocan, wihaga, woruldgesælig from The Battle of Maldon. Obviously the compounds in these poems convey a sentiment different from that of the compounds in the Exeter "elegies." This difference is not a matter of date but of poetic "genre."

41 Cf. Nenninger, Die ae. "Ruine," pp. 34–41, where the theme is discussed.

42 E. Sieper, Die ae. Elegie (Strassburg, 1915), pp. 13 f.: "Die Ich-Form war für diese Gattung die Regel, und die Sänger fühlten sich gebunden, sie zu beachten. Eingangs, oder auch im weiteren Verlaufe des Gedichts, wird hervorgehoben, dass das leidvolle Schicksal vom Betroffenen selbst erzählt wird." He refers to The Seafarer, Deor, The Penitent's Prayer, and the elegies appended to Cynewulf's poems. Cf. K. Sisam, "Cynewulf and his Poetry," Proceedings of the British Academy, XVIII (1932), 320 f.; reprinted in Studies in the History of OE Literature (Oxford, 1953), pp. 23 f.

43 The Riddles of the Exeter Book (New York, 1910).

44 Riddles 13, 19, 29, 31, 32, 34, 36, 37, 38, 42, 43, 45, 47, 48, 49, 51, 52, 53, 55, 56, 58, 59, 64, 67, 68, 75, 76, 87, and the Latin Riddle 90. This use of the first person is autobiographical only in the sense in which a "chanson d'aventure" is autobiographical. It is hardly related to the use of the first person in the "elegies."

45 Riddles 1, 2, 3, 4, 5, 6, 7, 8, 9, 10, 11, 12, 14, 15, 16, 17, 18, 20, 21, 23, 24, 25, 26, 27, 30, 33, 35, 40, 60, 61, 62, 63, 65, 66, 71, 72, 73, 74, 77, 78, 79, 80, 81, 83, 85, 86, 88, 91, 92, 93, 95.

46 Cf. F. E. Harmer, Anglo-Saxon Writs (Manchester, 1952), p. 11.

47 "The 'Dream of the Rood' as Prosopopoeia," Essays and Studies in Honor of Carleton Brown (New York, 1940), p. 30.

48 "The Wanderer: Theme and Structure," JEGP, XLII (1943), 517–518.

49 It is not impossible that The Wife's Lament (like the other non-Christian "elegies") is to some extent inspired by the example of Ovid; cf. H. Reuschel, "Ovid und die ags. Elegien," Beiträge zur Geschichte der deutschen Sprache und Literatur, LXII (1938), 132–142. (The Ovidian echoes Dr. Reuschel hears in The Wanderer and The Seafarer are altogether too vague.)

50 "The Interpretation of 'The Seafarer,'" p. 266.

51 Cf. F. A. Patterson, The Middle English Penitential Lyric (New York, 1911), p. 25.

52 Ed. A. B. Kuypers (Cambridge, 1902).

53 Similar confessions are to be found, for example, in Precum
    Libelli Quattuor Ævi Karolini, ed. André Wilmart (1940),
    pp. 21–24, 56–57, 73–75, 89–90.

54 "I was very ready to meet pleasures, and to be called a
    handsome man—I speak of others as well as of ourselves—
    as is the retainer of high rank in the house, as [is] the chief
    huntsman in the hall."

55 Quoted by Dr. Whitelock, "The Interpretation of 'The Sea-
    farer,' "p. 263, n. 3, from a tenth-century penitential frag-
    ment.

56 The Seafarer, An Interpretation, Kungl. Humanistiska Veten-
    skapssamfundets i Lund Årsberättelse (1937–38), I, 1.

57 Dr. Whitelock's punctuation of this passage, op. cit., p. 266,
    provides the only satisfactory interpretation.

58 After the analysis of the nature of OE rhythmic prose and
    its relationship to verse made by Angus McIntosh in his lec-
    ture on Wulfstan's Prose (Proceedings of the British Academy,
    XXXV [1949]) modern critics will no longer feel inclined to
    hack off lines 109–end from the supposedly heroic beginning,
    merely on account of irregularities in the metre, however
    violent and inconsonant with the beginning it may appear.
    Lines 109–115a have always been marked with dots, stars,
    and obelisks, or heavily supplied with words and phrases.
    Thorpe's emendation of mod to mon is probably essential:

    Stieran mon sceal strongum mode   ond þæt on staþelum
                                            healdan,
    ond gewis werum,   wisum clæne,
    scyle monna gehwylc   mid gemete healdan
    wiþ leofne, ond wiþ laþne bealo.   (109–112)

    "One must restrain a headstrong mind and hold it within
    bounds; and in pure ways constant towards men everyone
    shall bear himself with moderation towards a friend, and
    keep malice in moderation towards a foe." The emendation
    (Holthausen, Anglia Beiblatt, XIX [1908], 248), "wiþ leofne

511

[lufan] ond wiþ laþne bealo," provides a smoother reading, though it is perhaps not strictly necessary.

The interpretation of lines 113–116 becomes clear if it is considered in conjunction with the parallel passage of lines 97–102:

> þeah þe græf wille   golde stregan
> broþor his geborenum,   byrgan be deadum,
> maþmum mislicum   þæt hine mid wille,
> ne mæg þære sawle   þe biþ synna ful
> gold to geoce   for godes egsan,
> þonne he hit ær hydeð   þenden he her leofað
>   (97–102)

> þeah þe he hine wille   fyres fulne
> oþþe on bæle   forbærnedne,
> his geworhtne wine,   wyrd biþ swiþre,
> meotud meahtigra   þonne ænges monnes gehygd.
>   (113–116)

"Though a brother desires to strew with gold his brother's grave, to bury him among the dead with divers treasures which he (the survivor) wishes to go with him (the dead), before the terror of God gold cannot be of avail to the soul that is full of sin, when he had been keeping it in a hiding-place during his lifetime here."

"Though a man wishes the friend whom he has gained to be full of fire [i.e. fully consumed by fire] or burnt up on the pyre, fate is stronger (than his wish), the Lord more mighty than any man's thought."

Both passages refer to traditional Anglo-Saxon last rites, either burial with treasure in a grave, or cremation on a pyre. It may well be that some significance attaches to the fact that the brother buries, the friend cremates the dead. What the significance is I do not know. The poet stresses in these two passages that, though a man is buried with his kin, though the rites of burial are performed in accordance with ancient custom, God determines the fate of the soul, and the funeral rites are ineffectual. Line 102 reinforces this meaning by stressing the antithesis of burying the treasure of the man who has hoarded it all his life. Dr. Sisam has drawn attention to the connexion between lines 97–102 and Psalm 48 (A. V. 49) (RES, XXI [1945], 316–317). It seem possible that the indifference to burial and crematory rites shown by the poet is partly based on the injunction to leave the dead to bury their own dead, and partly on a Christian's dislike of what may have originated in pagan practices.

59 This interpretation is also implicit in W. S. Mackie's translation in his edition of The Exeter Book, Pt. 2, EETS, CXCIV (London, 1934), 165.

60 "Nis þis gewrit be anum men awriten ac ys be eallum" follows the AMEN at the end of the Anglo-Saxon Heptateuch, MS Laud Misc. 509, fol. 115vo in the Bodleian Library. E. Thwaites in his edition of 1698, p. 163, printed the words at the end of the Heptateuch; B. Assmann is, however, undoubtedly right in taking the words as the heading of the Epistle to Wulfget (Grein-Wülker, Bibliothek der angelsächsischen Prosa, III [Cassel + Goettingen, 1889], p. 1). The meaning of be is "concerning," i.e. Ælfric's Epistle concerns not only Wulfget, to whom it is written, but all other men also. This is borne out by the "Incipit" of the Epistle to Sigefyrð which immediately follows that to Wulfget (fol. 120vo): "Incipit libellus de ueteri testamento et nouo. Ðis gewrit wæs to anum men gediht, ac hit mæg swa ðeah manegum fremian. Ælfric abbod gret freondlice Sigferd," etc. (cf. Assmann, p. 13).

61 It seems unlikely that "ic afysed eom" means "I have been driven" (thus Mackie); the meaning is probably "I am inspired with longing." Bosworth-Toller, Suppl., s.v. afysan, cites another example which combines afysan and longung from the Blickling Homilies (EETS, OS, LVIII [Oxford, 1874], p. 131); Toller translates afysan here "to make eager, to inspire with longing": "þonne hwylcum men gelimpeþ þæt his ful leof fæder gefærþ, ne mæg þæt na beon þæt þa bearn þe unbliþran ne syn, & langunga nabban æfter þæm freondum?

Swa gemunde & wiste ure se heofonlica Fæder his þa leofan
& þa gestreonfullan bearn afysed & on myclum ymbhygdum
wæron æfter him."

62 L. L. Schücking, Kleines ags. Dichterbuch (Leipzig, 1919),
p. 21.

63 JEGP, XLII (1943), 516–538. His critics (led by S. B. Greenfield, "The Wanderer: A Reconsideration of Theme and Structure," JEGP, L [1951], 451–465) are probably right when they
suggest that some of his structural analysis represents too
refined a reading of the poem; even so, his article marks
the most significant recent advance in the interpretation of
the poem, and the present contribution is heavily indebted
to it, especially as regards the ethopoeic use of the first
person.

64 Cf. Sir William Craigie, Philologica, II (1923), 9; W. S.
Mackie, "Notes on Old English Poetry," MLN, XL (1925),
92.

65 Cf. S. B. Greenfield's excellent article, "The Formulaic
Expression of the Theme of 'Exile' in Anglo-Saxon Poetry,"
Speculum, XXX (1955), 200–206, which appeared when the
present contribution was at press.

66 I wish to thank Mr. D. S. Brewer of Birmingham, Mr. R. W.
Burchfield of Christ Church, Oxford, and Mr. G. T. Shepherd
of Birmingham for a multitude of valuable suggestions in connexion with this article. Many of them I have silently accepted; some I rejected at my peril. I also wish to thank
Mr. K. W. Humphreys, the University Librarian, and his
staff for their help at all times, and finally I wish to thank
Professor and Mrs. Roy Pascal in whose hospitable house
parts of this article were read in November 1954 to the
Literary Circle in the University of Birmingham.

ON THE GENRE OF THE WANDERER

J. E. Cross

The poem known as The Wanderer, like its protagonist, is
anonymous and solitary. When problems of structure are apparent in such a poem it is natural to relate it to a background of
life and ideas. The major problems have been the lack of a
clear sequence of thought throughout the poem[1] and especially
the "incongruity"[2] between the body of the poem which could be
mainly pagan lament and its specifically Christian conclusion.
To solve these problems research has, at times, proceeded
like a game of snap in the matching of Germanic pagan sources
with those from the Bible and patristic Christian writings. I too
have isolated themes in order to eliminate improbable connections, but fortunately my findings have suggested an approach
which may obviate previous concern to distinguish Germanic
pagan or patristic Christian and may alleviate difficulties of
the poem's structure and meaning.

The approach is opened by one fact, two near-facts or
"reasonable assumptions," and a recurrent opinion in recent
criticism based on the expressed sentiments of the poem.

The fact is the undoubted and accepted Christian consolation at the end of the poem. No pagan could have stated such a
clear acceptance of the next life in the terms of the last two
lines. The "reasonable assumptions" from presented evidence
are the presence of two figures of rhetoric, one the figure of interrogatio in the ubi sunt passage[3] and the other the figure of
repetitio (the repetition of the initial word in successive phrases)
in the OE sum-series (ll. 80–84).[4] This suggests that the poet
had a knowledge either of rhetoric, or of those writings where
rhetorical figures abound. The recurrent opinion is in such
papers as that of Professor Greenfield who speaks of "a negative

Reprinted from Neophilologus, Vol. 45 (1961), pp. 63–75, by permission
of the author and the publisher.

de consolatione,"[5] of Professor Lumiansky who saw influence
from Boethius's Consolation of Philosophy and wished to rename
the poem "The Exile's Consolation,"[6] and of Miss Tucker who
demonstrated the consolatory value of the poem to the modern
reader — "at times of loss and loneliness The Wanderer can
come unmistakeably alive."[7]

    I hope it is clear that I shall consider the relationship of
the OE poem to a genre within epideictic oratory, the Greek
paramythia, the Latin consolatio, of which Boethius's "Golden
Book" is only one example.[8] The customs of the genre were
known to theoretical rhetoricians and practising writers from
the time of Crantor (c. 235–c. 275 B.C.)[9] at least to Erasmus
and the Elizabethan rhetoricians Henry Peacham and Thomas
Wilson.[10] Famous practitioners include Plutarch, Pliny, Cicero,
Seneca, Cyprian, Basil the Great, Gregory of Nyssa, Gregory
Nazianzen, John Chrysostom, Ambrose, Jerome, and Paulinus
of Nola within the period prior to the writing of The Wanderer.[11]
Clearly the genre flourished — in poems, treatises, letters, and
homiletic addresses — and earlier examples were known and
used by later writers. Cicero and Plutarch knew the lost treatise
of Crantor;[12] Augustine and Jerome referred to the lost consolatio of Cicero on the death of his daughter Tullia,[13] and Ambrose imitated an effective argument initiated by Servius Sulpicius Rufus[14] to console his friend Cicero on the same occasion.
In effect, a Christian or a late pagan writer who had received a
normal education was amply equipped with arguments to console
for death, exile, or any other misfortune of this world.

    Owing to its personal adaptation for different mourners and
different occasions[15] the genre did not have a rigid pattern. It
might or might not contain encomium or praise of the dead, but
it usually included some lament and, obviously, themes of consolation.[16] These latter were gathered from poets, dramatists
and philosophers who often had offered consolation before the
genre of paramythia/consolatio had been formalised. Such solacia
are the topoi, the loci communes, the commonplaces, which were
available for selection by later pagan and earlier Christian writers,
and a writer was expected to know them. The Emperor Julian
(the Apostate) writes to a fellow rhetorician Himerius on the
death of his wife: "If it were any other man to whom I had to
write about this, I should certainly have had to use more words
in dealing with it; for instance I should have said that such an

event is the common lot, that we must needs submit, that nothing
is gained by excessive grief, and I should have uttered all the
other commonplaces considered appropriate for the alleviation
of suffering, that is if I were exhorting one who did not know them.
But since I think it unbecoming to offer to a man who well knows
how to instruct others . . . I will forbear all such phrases."[17]

In a consolatio, one would expect to find a situation calling
for consolation, usually some lament, and identifiable solacia,
the consolatory commonplaces of the genre.

The anhaga in The Wanderer is in a most desperate situation.
He is alone, he suffers, and we hear of it in his opening lament.
Yet the 115 lines of the poem include more than a dozen themes
used by pagan and Christian writers of consolatio, one used only
by Christians. For the sake of brevity I shall consider the general structure of the poem while identifying the themes.

The opening lament is poignant enough without historical
knowledge of rhetorical genres but its anguish is deepened with
the realisation of consolations denied, either at the outset by
the situation, or after abortive attempts to obtain them. Here
is a man whose kinsmen are denied to him by death ("winemæga
hryre," l. 7) or by distance ("freomægum feor," l. 21). Unlike
Cicero he cannot reflect:[18] "I but shared these misfortunes with
yourself and certain others . . . and I always had a sanctuary
to flee to and a haven of rest." Nor can he accept the advice of
Seneca to Polybius:[19] "Do you turn, rather from the thoughts
that torture you to the many and great sources of consolation
you have, and look upon your admirable brothers, look upon
your wife, look upon your son . . ." or of Jerome who reminds
Salvina that her two children remain to console her for the loss
of her husband.[20] He cannot be consoled as Basil consoled the
wife of Briso:[21] "Let your sons stand as living images, giving
consolation for the absence of him for whom you yearn."

There are no kinsmen, no friends, since in this general
context "lyt . . . leofra geholena" (l. 31) is probably a litotes,
and his generous lord (goldwine) is covered by the darkness of
the earth (ll. 22–23). What can this man do and what does he
attempt?

He recalls the manly precept of controlling and keeping his
plaintive thoughts within himself (ll. 12–14, 17–19), knowing that
those who are eager for glory do this. Such rule of conduct is
expected from the Stoics, and Seneca rebukes Marullus who "was

reported to be rather womanish in his grief"[22] and tells Lucilius:[23] "Our forefathers have enacted that, in the case of women, a year should be the limit for mourning . . . In the case of men, no rules are laid down because to mourn at all is not regarded as honourable." But the Christian Theodoret of Cyrus implores the deaconess Casiana[24] "to remember those words that charge us to master our feelings," and a consolatory sermon (attributed to Augustine, but probably by John Chrysostom) counsels that a man must restrain his grief in silence and not publish it by outward show.[25] Ambrose in the two remarkable sermons (De Excessu Fratris Satyris) to console others on the death of his own brother first quotes the apocryphal 4th Book of Esdras X.15: "Now . . . keep thy sorrow to thyself and bear with good courage the things which have befallen thee"[26] and later orders: "Put aside your grief if you can; if you cannot, keep it to yourself."[27]

The precept may have called the anhaga to his task of self-consolation, for, with such as Augustine who says on the duties of a consoler:[28] "His acts should be characterized by a tranquillity of mind." He recognises:

> Ne mæg werigmod   wyrde wið-stondan
> Ne se hreo hyge   helpe gefremman (ll. 15–16).

We have been reminded recently that hreo is cognate with a noun meaning "stormy weather"[29] and carried powerful associations which lead far from the required tranquillity.

Yet control of feelings does little for the Wanderer, who remains full of care and misery (earmcearig l. 20). He therefore seeks another lord (sinces brytta l. 24) who:

> . . . mec freondleasne   frefran wolde (l. 28)

and it is worth noting that frefran, usually translated "comfort," of course can mean "console." Seneca had told Lucilius:[30] "You have buried one whom you loved; look about for someone to love." But in the generalisation which follows, and through the antitheses of ll. 31–32, we know that he is unsuccessful. Still:

> warað hine wræclast   nales wunden gold
> ferð-loca freorig   nalæs foldan blæd

where wunden gold is a metonymy for the protective generosity
of a lord.

He is alone with his memory, and there could be solace in
the remembrance of past delights. To Seneca,[31] "the thought
of my dead friends is sweet and appealing." Plutarch consoles
his wife at the loss of her two-year-old daughter:[32] "But rather,
just as she was the most delightful thing in the world to embrace,
to see, to hear, so too must the thought of her live with us and
be our companion, bringing with it joy in greater measure, nay
in many times greater measure than it brings sorrow . . . and
we must not sit idle and shut ourselves in, paying for those
pleasures with sorrows many times as great."

Ambrose addresses his dead brother in an emotional passage:[33] "Thou art present, I say, and art always brought before
me, and with my whole mind and soul I embrace thee, gaze upon
thee, address thee, kiss thee; I grasp thee whether in the gloomy
night or in the clear light when thou vouchsafest to revisit and
console me sorrowing."

He welcomes sleep which had separated him from his brother
in life but now in death allows a consolation in reminiscence.
But "sorg and slæp somod ætgædre" hold the Wanderer in empty
consolation. For him "sleep is not the balm of hurt minds: it is
the twin of sorrow."[34] He awakes with the sea-birds, with frost
and snow mingled with hail (ll. 47–48). He is still alone. For
him remembrance increases sorrow—"wyn eal gedreas (l. 36)."

No one misses the anguish of lament in the first section of
the poem, yet six loci communes, precepts for behaviour or
solacia, found in examples of consolatio, have been distinguished
and seen denied to the mourner. The second section of the poem,
the general moralising, however, has appeared to lack contact
with the first part and in itself to be a patchwork of abrupt transi-
tions. Here identification with the genre is illuminating.

For, if personal consolations are denied to an individual,
at least, said the old writers, he should take consolation from
the common condition of men. Ambrose affirms:[35] "Wherefore
we propose, dearest brethren, to console ourselves with the
common course of nature, and not to think anything hard which
awaits all." Plutarch praises the "manly" words of Merope:[36]
"Others as well as I have drunk life's dregs." "No man should
make a special grievance of what happens to all alike" warns
Cicero.[37]

The Wanderer considers other men, the proud noblemen who have suddenly died, and to me it seems that the unusual (and possibly ambiguous)[38] manner of expressing his sadness indicates that the poet knew of the consolation in the common lot of man. Adapting Mrs. Gordon's explanatory translation:[39]

"Truly I cannot imagine (any reason) in the world why my mind should not be saddened when I fully consider the lives of men," etc. (ll. 58–61).

The phrasing of this statement suggests that it is a doubting answer to the consolation which is in his mind. His mind is sad, I take it, and both Cicero and Seneca would have sympathised. In his treatise on consolation Cicero notes:[40] "Not even the comforting effect of the phrase 'You are not the only one' in spite of its constant use and frequent benefit, is perfectly reliable. It is beneficial, as I have said, but not always and not in all cases." And to A. Torquatus:[41] ". . . it is but a poor consolation that is based on the miseries of others," while Seneca speaks more strongly:[42] "The solace that comes from having company in misery smacks of illwill." Yet the personal lament is over. The significant verbs of the first section are in the past tense. His "frustrated expectation has long since been given up," now it is not an uncontrollable anguish over his fate . . . it is a sadness caused by contemplation.[43] The ancients knew that to draw a man away from himself was to open the way to consolation. No longer does the Wanderer speak in the first person. He now considers other men and other events.

If we can accept the idea that the lessening of grief by generalisation is an indication of some consolation, we may now see a selection of consolatory topoi. The passage of time (ll. 62–63), though presented as the decay of the world (see below for this topic), allows its consolation of wisdom with age (ll. 64–65).[44] This leads to a definition of wisdom as the quality of control and moderation in conduct, which at all times has been a defence against the whimsicalities of Fate. In pagan times, as Plutarch remarks, a wise man's code derived from two of the inscriptions at Delphi:[45] "These are: 'Know thyself' and 'Avoid extremes,' on these two commandments hang all the rest."

He elaborates the second, that a man should be "heedful, in whatever may befall him, not to go beyond the limit of propriety, either in being elated to boastfulness, or in being humbled and cast down to wailings and lamentations. . . ." Christians such as Ambrose and Jerome accepted this ethic for secular life.

"Let there be that moderation in adversity which is required in prosperity," Ambrose commands,[46] while Jerome[47] quoted the saying of the Seven Wise Men of Greece: "Nothing in excess." These statements are in consolationes, and OE homiletic illustrations to these OE poetic lines show that moderation in conduct was required of a native Christian.[48]

Such "wise" men could gain and offer consolation from sources which appear strange to the modern reader. Basil, Cyprian, Seneca and Pseudo-Ovid (Consolatio ad Liviam), regarded the collapse of the world as a consolation. Basil urges the wife of Nectarius:[49] "Look about you at the whole universe . . . and reflect that all the visible world is mortal . . . the beauties of the earth, the earth itself — all are doomed to perish, all in a little while will not be. Let the thought of these things be a consolation for what has befallen you."

Seneca, who subscribes to the Stoic doctrine of cyclic conflagrations, by which the existing universe was destroyed and the process of creation renewed, exhorts Marcia:[50] "For if the common fate can be a solace for your yearning, know that nothing will abide where it is now placed, that time will lay all things low and take all things with it. . . . It will cover with floods the face of the inhabited world, and, deluging the earth, will kill every living creature, and in huge conflagration it will scorch and burn all mortal things."

Cyprian expresses the commonplace more urgently. So does the poet of The Wanderer:

> Ongietan sceal gleaw hæle   hu gæstlic biðonne eall þisse worulde wela   weste stondeð
> (ll. 73–74).

Gæstlic has the strength of its root in agæstan "to strike fear into,"[51] and a wise man will realise the horror of the event, which to all Christians was only a little time away. Cyprian could speak of the last days in A.D. 252 as he consoled and exhorted the faithful during the terrors of a plague then sweeping the civilised world. His consolation is the common one that death is a release from the evils of the times:[52] ". . . now that the world is collapsing and is oppressed with the tempests of mischievous ills; in order that we who see that terrible things have begun, and know that still more terrible things are imminent, may regard it as the greatest advantage to depart from it as quickly as possible."

The visible sign of the decay of the world and the impending doom is the ruins everywhere (ll. 74–77). Seneca, Cicero's friend Servius Sulpicius Rufus (in a passage known to Byron), and Ambrose took consolation in the ruins of great cities: ". . . towns at one time most flourishing, now lying prostrate and demolished before one's very eyes. I began to think to myself 'So! we puny mortals resent it, do we, if one of us . . . has died . . . when . . . there lie flung down before us the corpses of so many towns.' Take my word for it, I was not a little fortified by that reflexion."[53]

Even Theseus in The Knight's Tale could console the lovers at the death of Arcite with: "The grete tounes se we wane and wende" (CT A. 3025), an idea not in either of Chaucer's main sources for the speech.[54]

All things made by man and even God's earthly creation will pass. Take consolation in this, the ancients could have said, and Christians could also have seen the congruity of apparently the most unconsolatory line in the poem:

yþde swa þisne eardgeard   ælda scyppend (l. 85).

On a similar occasion Augustine explained:[55] "By the destruction of Rome God is correcting his people in order to console them." The precept though not the application relies on such Biblical admonitions as this is the Book of Job: "Blessed is the man whom God correcteth therefore refuse thou not the chastening of the Almightie for he maketh the wound and bindeth it up, he smiteth and his hand maketh whole" — quoted in the words of Henry Peacham from his chapter on Paramythia.[56]

Now the man who considers the ruin and the dark life (ll. 88 ff.) recalls fatal battles and the loss of earthly delights with the rhetorical figure of interrogatio: "Hwær cwom mearg?" (ll. 92 ff.). Plutarch used the same figure to express solace in the universality of earthly transience. He has praised Merope's words quoted above and continues:[57] "With this the following might appropriately be combined:

> Where are now all these things magnificent?
> Great Croesus, Lord of Lydia? Xerxes too
> Who yoked the sullen neck of Hellespont?
> Gone to Hades and Oblivion's house

and their wealth perished with their bodies."
The OE duguþ, anonymous but loved, have also perished but
the brief comment

> wyrd seo mære (1. 99)

—the glorious fate—reminds us that for heroes "their renown
will be a consolation to the mourners," as Demosthenes puts it.[58]
Finally the word lǣne in the last comment on earthly transience—"her bið feoh lǣne," etc. (1. 108)—suggests a contact
with the topos "life is a loan," for lǣne (adj.) is cognate with lǣn
(sb.) 'loan.' The commonplace occurs regularly in consolationes;
for example,[59] Euripides: "Death is a debt which all mortals
owe"; Cicero: "Nature granted the use of life like a loan without
fixing any day for repayment"; Ambrose: "Now, He who deposited
the pledge has taken it back"; the perfunctory consolation of the
hypocritical Friar in Chaucer's Summoner's Tale: "God be
thanked of his loone"; and others.

This section of the poem clearly uses topics of consolatio
but as clearly they console only in so far as a wise man recognises what life is and braces himself against it. The tone is
contemplative but sad. Regret for past glories breaks through
what could have been consolation in the ubi sunt passage. The
description of the harshness of nature (ll. 101–106) in the present cancels the brief consolation from the glory of the dead heroes.
The wise man's last thoughts are on the power of fate and the
hardships of the earth.

Secular consolation, known to both pagans and Christians,
is "poor consolation" as Cicero said, and it is worth noting pagan
and Christian attitudes to this kind of consolation within the Christian period. When Basil consoled Bishop Elpidius[60] on the death
of his grandchild, he used no topics from pre-Christian consolation. Nor did Theodoret of Cyrus when writing to the bishop
Irenæus.[61] There was clearly no need to point out to these
ecclesiastics, confirmed in their faith, that things of the earth
offer no real consolation. The pagan, Pliny the Younger (second

to first centuries A.D.), who consoled others with rhetorical and philosophical commonplaces, cannot himself be consoled by them, as he says in a letter to Calestrius Tiro on the death of a mutual friend:[62]

"Speak comfort to me therefore I entreat you . . . by supplying me with some arguments, that are uncommon and resistless, that neither the writings nor the discourses of philosophers can teach me. For all that I have heard and all that I have read occur to me of themselves; but all these are by far too weak to support me under so heavy an affliction."

The Christians however had for themselves a "resistless" argument and the OE Christian poet concludes:

Til biþ se þe his treowe gehealdeþ   (l. 112)

which in a general context may be glossed by the words of Paul, I Thessalonians IV.13, quoted regularly in Christian consolations:[63] "We would not, brethren, have you ignorant concerning those who are asleep, lest you should grieve even as others who have no hope."

The OE Christian poet concludes: "Well it is with him who seeks grace, consolation (frofor) in the Father in heaven, where all the security awaits us."

To my mind the progress of the poem is best explained in terms of a consolatio where topics of the genre are used first to intensify the lament, then to attempt some measure of secular consolation by generalisation which is yet unsatisfactory, in order to emphasise the supreme consolation of security in the next life.

This general survey does not preclude the possibility of other more direct influences for shorter sequences and links within the poem. As I have explained elsewhere the sequence of examples within the OE sum-series suggests strongly that this is an echo of the heretical objection to the dogma of resurrection of the flesh which was quoted and rejected time and again by Christian apologists.[64] The figure of interrogatio was often chosen by Christian homilists to admonish their listeners on the transience of life[65] and it is likely that the ubi sunt passage was modelled on these, though there is no note of admonition in the poem. The phrasing of precepts of a man's conduct is too close to OE examples in sermons to look for a source

524

other than in Christian writings.[66] And the statement that ruins exemplify the coming doom looks very like a link suggested by the typological explanations favoured by Biblical commentators. Gregory the Great, for example, preaches a sermon on Luke XXI. 25–32 where Christ recounts the signs of the end of the world and states: ". . . ex ruina mundi prope esse agnoscitur regnum Dei."[67]

Such hints as these foreshadow the conclusion for the aware reader, others may progress with the surface sequence of thought to the only real consolation for the Christian.

In a series of powerful scholarly essays[68] Mr. Smithers has recently re-emphasised the similarities between The Wanderer and The Seafarer. Both to him are allegories and the protagonist in each case represents a Christian in exile in this world who desires to return to his patria in heaven. There is however, to my mind, a basic error in Mr. Smithers' thinking about the relationship of the two poems. It is that if two poets draw on the same or similar sources they necessarily write exactly the same kind of poem. No one I think would doubt that the two poets wrote out of a similar background. In this sense the poems are "companion-pieces" and the identification of a source or a figure in a passage of one may be regarded as evidence of a similar source in the other. Yet there are differences of detail and of structure which may allow The Wanderer to be interpreted quite differently from The Seafarer. I see no objection to the proposed allegory being applied to The Seafarer. It was a common topos for Christians, as well attested by Ehrismann[69] and even more fully by Mr. Smithers. Now that elþeodigra eard[70] has been re-translated as "fatherland of the peregrini," with good philological reason, the significant facts of the poem agree with the necessary details of the topos. A Christian of this period could easily accept The Seafarer as yet another illustration. But if he attempted to do this for The Wanderer he would be stopped abruptly by the lines:

> siþþan geara iu   goldwine min(n)e
> hrusan heolster biwrah   and ic hean þonan
> . . . .
> sohte sele dreorig   sinces bryttan (ll. 22–23, 25),

o⁴⁄₇   for he would realise that the <u>anhaga</u> is in exile for another reason than that which causes the Christian's exile in this world. No reason is given for the seafarer's exile in the other poem, nor is it very often in Latin and Greek examples of the common allegory. But, as Mr. Smithers has shown, a Christian has no abiding city in this world as a son of Adam and because of Adam's sin.[71] This difference between the situations in the two OE poems is important, for if <u>The Wanderer</u> is to be interpreted as an allegory, we might reasonably assume that the dead lord was also a type, and the other lord, so desperately sought, should also have an allegorical application. Clearly this leads to absurdity, for a Christian's lord is Christ whose death is not the cause of a Christian's exile in the world, and what Christian would seek another lord if his lord Christ were dead? On such basic details as this theories of implied allegory stand or fall.

NOTES

1 N. Kershaw, <u>Anglo-Saxon and Norse Poems</u> (Cambridge, 1922), p. 1.

2 I. L. Gordon, "Traditional Themes in <u>The Wanderer</u> and <u>The Seafarer</u>," <u>RES</u>, N.S., V (1954), 6.
   T. C. Rumble, "From <u>Eardstapa</u> to <u>Snottor on Mode</u>," <u>MLQ</u>, XIX (1958), attempts to explain "the somewhat illogical continuity of thought" (p. 229) as typical of a reverie (pp. 229–230).

3 See J. E. Cross, "<u>Ubi Sunt</u> Passages in Old English," <u>Vetenskaps-societetens i Lund Årsbok</u> (1956), pp. 25–44.

4 See Cross, "<u>The Wanderer</u> lines 80–84—A Study of a Figure and a Theme," <u>Vetenskaps-societetens i Lund Årsbok</u> (1958–1959), pp. 77–110, especially pp. 83–84.

5 S. B. Greenfield, "<u>The Wanderer</u>: A Reconsideration of Theme and Structure," <u>JEGP</u>, L (1951), 462.

6 R. M. Lumiansky, "The Dramatic Structure of the Old English <u>Wanderer</u>," <u>Neophil</u>, XXXIV (1950), 104–111.

7 S. I. Tucker, "Return to <u>The Wanderer</u>," <u>EIC</u>, VIII (1958), 231.

8 Although Lumiansky made a case for the knowledge of De consolatione Philosophiae in the early OE period, the contacts he cites between The Wanderer and Boethius are not distinctive enough to convince us that our poet knew the book. By broadening the issue to consolatio in general, the parallel ideas increase and the probability of the poet's knowing either the principles or examples of consolatio grows.

9 On the early history of the genre see: Sister M. M. Beyenka, Consolation in Saint Augustine (Washington, D.C., 1950), pp. 1–30; and The Oxford Classical Dictionary s.v. consolatio.

   For discussion of examples see: Sister M. E. Moran, Consolation in Ancient Greek Literature (Washington, D.C., 1917); C. Favez, La Consolation Latine Chrétienne (Paris, 1937); and Sister M. E. Fern, The Latin Consolatio as a Literary Type (Saint Louis, Missouri, 1941).

   I am indebted to my colleague Ian Bishop who recommended Favez and Fern and thus started this investigation.

10 See B. Boyce, "The Stoic consolatio in Shakespeare," PMLA, LXIV (1949), 771–778.

11 Beyenka, loc. cit.

12 Cicero, Tusculan Disputations, trans. J. E. King (London, New York, 1927), I. xlviii. Plutarch (pseudo?), to Apollonius, passim, in Moralia, vol. II, trans. F. C. Babbitt (London, New York, 1928).

13 Augustine, De Civitate Dei XIX. 4.2.; Jerome, Ep. LX. 5.

14 Compare Ambrose to Faustinus Ep. XXXIX. 3 with Servius Sulpicius Rufus to Cicero in Cicero, The Letters to his Friends, trans. W. G. Williams (London, New York, 1952), I, 270 ff. Latin, p. 271 ff. English.

15 Cicero, Tusculan Disputations, III. xxxiii, ed. cit., 320 Latin, p. 321 English. Seneca, Moral Essays, trans. J. W. Basore (London, New York, 1932), Vol. II, to Marcia II. 1., p. 8.

16 Fern, op. cit., p. 7, does not include encomium in what she regards as a typical structure. Beyenka, op. cit., p. 2, em-

phasises that for Christians form plays a less important part and ideas become paramount. On the occasional use of eulogy see Oxf. Class. Dictionary s.v. consolatio.

17 The Works of the Emperor Julian, trans. W. C. Wright (London, New York, 1923), Vol. III, Ep. LXIX, p. 228 Latin, p. 229 English.

18 Cicero, to his Friends, ed. cit., I, 278 Latin, 279 English.

19 Seneca, Moral Essays, ed. cit., Vol. II, to Polybius xii. 1, p. 390 Latin, p. 391 English.

20 St. Jerome, Works, in Nicene and Post-Nicene Fathers (Oxford, New York, 1893), Vol. VI, Ep. LXXIX. 7, pp. 165–166.

21 St. Basil, the Letters, trans. R. J. Deferrari, 4 Vols. (London, New York, 1926–40), Vol. IV, Letter CCCII, p. 232 Greek, p. 233 English.

22 Seneca, Epistulae Morales, 3 Vols., trans. R. M. Gummere (London, Camb., Mass., 1925–34), Vol. III, Ep. XCIX. 1, p. 128 Latin, p. 129 English.

23 Ibid., Vol. I, Ep. LXIII. 13, p. 434 Latin, p. 435 English.

24 In Nicene and Post-Nicene Fathers (Oxford, New York, 1892), Vol. III, 256, col. 2.

25 Noted by Beyenka, op. cit., p. 85. The ascription is discussed on p. 81, note 58.

26 St. Ambrose, Select works and letters, in Nicene and Post-Nicene Fathers (Oxford, New York, 1896), Vol. X, On the Decease of Satyrus, I. 68, p. 171.

27 Ibid., II. 7, p. 175.

28 PL 32. 1333 cited by Beyenka op. cit. p. 44. Cf. Jerome, Ep. XXXIX, ed. cit., p. 49: "But he is a poor comforter who is overcome by his own sighs, and from whose afflicted heart tears are wrung as well as words."

29 R. W. V. Elliot, "The Wanderer's Conscience," ES, XXXIX (1958), 194.

30 Seneca, Epist. Moral., ed. cit., Vol. I, Ep. LXIII. 11, p. 434 Latin, p. 435 English.

31 Ibid. Vol. I, Ep. LXIII. 7, p. 432 Latin, p. 433 English.

32 Plutarch, To his wife. 3, in Moralia, Vol. VII trans. P. H. de Lacy and B. Einarson (London, Camb., Mass., 1959), p. 584 Greek, p. 585 English.

33 Ambrose, Satyrus I. 72, ed. cit., p. 172.

34 Tucker, op. cit., p. 234.

35 Ambrose, Satyrus II. 3, ed. cit., p. 174.

36 Plutarch (pseudo?), Vol. II, to Apollonius 110 D, ed. cit., p. 152 Greek, p. 153 English.

37 Cicero, to his Friends, ed. cit., I, p. 436 Latin, p. 437 English.

38 Lumiansky, op. cit., p. 106.

39 Gordon, op. cit., p. 6.

40 Cicero, Tusculan Disputations, III. xxxiii. 79, ed. cit., p. 318 Latin, p. 319 English.

41 Cicero, to his Friends, ed. cit., I, 440 Latin, 441 English.

42 Seneca, Moral Essays, ed. cit., Vol. II, to Marcia XII. 5, p. 40 Latin, p. 41 English.

43 Greenfield, op. cit., pp. 454 and 458.

44 Cicero, Tusculan Disputations, I. xxxix. 94, ed. cit., p. 112 Latin, p. 113 English; and Book of Wisdom IV. 9.

45 Plutarch (pseudo?), Vol. II, to Apollonius 116 C.D., ed. cit., p. 182 Greek, p. 183 English, and 116 E, p. 184 Greek, p. 185 English.

46 Ambrose, Satyrus, II. 11, ed. cit., p. 175.

47 Jerome, Ep. LX. 7., ed. cit., p. 126.

48 F. Klæber, "Notes on Old English Poems," JEGP, XII (1913), 259.

49 St. Basil, The Letters, ed. cit., Vol. I, Letter VI, To the wife of Nectarius in Consolation, p. 42 Greek, p. 43 English. The same topos is used in Vol. IV, Letter CCCI, To Maximus Consolatory, pp. 228, 229; and Vol. IV, CCLXIX, pp. 138, 139.

50 Seneca, Moral Essays, ed. cit., Vol. II, to Marcia XXVI. 6., p. 94 Latin, p. 95 English.

51 G. V. Smithers, "The Meaning of The Seafarer and The Wanderer," Medium Ævum, XXVI (1957), 141.

52 Cyprian, On the Mortality, 25, quoted from translation in The Ante-Nicene Christian Library, Vol. VIII, The Writings of Cyprian (Edinburgh, 1868), p. 467. For the topos see also Pseudo-Ovid, Consolatio ad Liviam.

53 Servius Sulpicius Rufus in Cicero, to his Friends, IV. v. 4., ed. cit., Vol. I, p. 272 Latin, p. 273 English. Compare Ambrose, Ep. XXXIX.3. To Faustinus.

54 I hope to consider Chaucer's knowledge and use of the genre of consolatio in a future paper.

55 Quoted by Beyenka, op. cit., p. 56.

56 The Garden of Eloquence by Henry Peacham, facsimile reproduction, W. G. Crane (Gainesville, Florida, 1954), p. 100.

57 Plutarch (pseudo?), Vol. II, to Apollonius. 110 D, ed. cit., p. 154 Greek, p. 155 English.

58 See Moran, op. cit., chap. VI for this topos.

59 Euripides Alcestis 782, quoted by Moran, chap. II, where classical examples of the topos are cited or quoted. Cicero, Tusculan Disputations I. xxxix, ed. cit., p. 111; Ambrose, Satyrus I. 3., ed. cit., p. 161; Chaucer, Canterbury Tales, D. 1861.

60 Basil, The Letters, ed. cit., Vol. III, Ep. CCVI.

61 Theodoret, Ep. XII, ed. cit., p. 253.

62 Pliny, Letters, trans. W. Melmoth, revised W. M. L. Hutchinson (London, New York, 1915), I xii, p. 44 Latin, p. 45 English.

63 E.g. Jerome, Ep. XXXIX. 3., ed. cit., p. 51; Ambrose, Satyrus I. 9, ed. cit., p. 162; Augustine, who preaches two consolatory sermons on the text in PL 38, 935–939; Basil, Letters, ed. cit., Vol. I, Letter XXVIII, pp. 162, 163; Vol. II, Letter CI, pp. 188, 189.

64 Cross, "On The Wanderer," lines 80–84, pp. 85–95.

65 Cross, "Ubi Sunt Passages in Old English," passim.

66 Klæber, ibid.

67 PL 76, 1080 A.

68 Medium Ævum, XXVI (1957), XXVIII (1959).

69 Paul und Braunes Beiträge, 35 (1909), pp. 209–239.

70 Until G. V. Smithers ("The Meaning of 'The Seafarer' and 'The Wanderer,'" Medium Ævum, XXVI [1957], 145–147) re-interpreted elþeodigra eard, the situation in The Seafarer could not be equated with that in the Christian allegory. Heaven is always the Christian's patria in the examples of the allegory and the older interpretation would have the seafarer moving in a different direction. There were attempts to get over the difficulty. O. S. Anderson (The Seafarer, an Interpretation [Lund, 1937], p. 30) referred to "the unknown country" as the seafarer's destination, and Claes Schaar (Cynewulf Group [Lund, 1949], pp. 95–96) used this suggestion to illustrate discussion on eardes uncyðöu, Juliana 701a. But the situations are different. In Juliana, and in Fates of the Apostles 91–95, 109–114, Cynewulf is speaking of the unknown home of the soul after death; no man is certain whether he will go to Heaven or Hell because he does not know how his deeds will be assessed (cf. Blickling Homily II). The seafarer however desires to go to elþeodigra eard and every man is certain about his desired destination. If he desires to go to an "unknown country, land of foreigners" or anything other than patria it cannot be to the Christian's heaven.

I abstract from the history of criticism of this poem firstly to emphasise the importance of Smithers' re-interpretation and secondly to stress the necessity of agreement in basic details before a poetic situation can be equated with that in a common allegory.

71 Smithers, Medium Ævum, XXVI, pp. 145 ff. Another important example of the theme illustrated by Smithers occurs in the unpublished Vercelli Homily XIV, the relevant part of which is transcribed below from the facsimile reproduction in M. Förster, Il Codice Vercellese (Rome, 1913), with extra readings from N. Ker, "C. Maier's transcript of the Vercelli

Book," Medium Ævum, XIX (1950), 23–24; and from Maier's transcript by kind permission of the Master of the Library, Lincoln's Inn. A diagonal smear over the lower half of fol. 77r makes the text partly illegible. fol. 77r l. 3: "ðurh diofles facen and þurh his inwit we wurdon on frymþe beswicene. And for Adames gewyrhtum we wæron of ðam . . . . setl neorxnawanges gefean ut ascofene and on þas wræc sende þysse worulde þe we nu on lyfiað forþan we nabbað her nanne fæstlicne staðol ne langsum [cf. Paul Heb. XIII. 14] ne eðel ac we gelomlice geseoð to hwan se eorðlica dæl and sio mennisce gecynd wiorðan sceal. Cwæð se apostol be ðan Sanctus Paulus: Dum sumus in corpore peregrinamur a domino [II. Cor. V. 6]. Swa lange swa we bioð on þyssum deadlicum life and on þyssum menn[iscum] gecynde swa lange we bioð elðeodige from ussum dryhtn[e]." In this extract may be noted:

i. the historical reason for the Christian's exile in this world.
ii. the interlacing of Biblical echo and quotation which gave Paul's authority for belief in the exile.
iii. another figurative use of elþeodig unrecorded in OE dictionaries.

The sermon continues with other ideas which are relevant to an understanding of the structure of The Seafarer:

i. fol. 77r ll. 12–13 ". . . . is deadlice lif [cf. Seafarer 65b] elcor nymþe hit is se weg."
ii. emphasis on man's own deeds to win eternal reward or punishment fol. 77r ll. 14–16. Cf. Seafarer 72–80a, the exhortation to bold deeds against the devil to win eternal reward.

DRAMATIC VOICES IN THE WANDERER AND THE SEAFARER

John C. Pope

In this article I propose to reconsider the structure and certain aspects of the meaning of The Wanderer and The Seafarer. The Seafarer even more than The Wanderer has been the subject of a great deal of interpretation, and much of it has enduring value; but certain very basic issues are still in doubt—largely, I believe, because we have not reached a full understanding of its structure. My view of the structure is only a little different from some others that have been advanced both long ago and recently; yet I think the difference makes the basic idea more acceptable, and this idea itself needs to be brought into relation with what other critics have had to say about the probable meaning of certain passages. The Wanderer, by contrast, has seemed a relatively clear and well-organized poem and the usual view of its structure, though in my opinion incorrect, has had only a few undernourished rivals. Hence my interpretation is novel enough to need careful demonstration. But it is not entirely without antecedents, and is really more obvious than the interpretation of The Seafarer. Certain parallel features of the two poems strongly suggest the same basic structure, and certain features peculiar to The Wanderer seem to point the way to a fuller understanding of that structure. For the sake of clarity, therefore, I shall begin with The Wanderer.

I

The prevailing view of The Wanderer in its formal aspect has been that it consists principally of a long dramatic monologue, lines 8–110, spoken by a man who is introduced in line 6 as an eardstapa or wanderer. This monologue is enclosed by a

Reprinted from Francis P. Magoun, Jr., Franciplegius (New York University Press, 1965), pp. 164–93, by permission of the author and the publisher.

seven-line introduction and a five-line epilogue spoken imper-
sonally by the poet, and it contains within itself a subordinate
speech by a purely hypothetical person, introduced as se . . .
þisne wealsteal . . . deope geondþenceð, he who deeply considers
this foundation.[1] The hypothetical speech, coming at the end of
the monologue, is a lament for all that men care for on earth
and for the earth itself. It puts what the principal speaker has
to say in a grandly objective way. When it is finished the wanderer himself stops talking and the poet adds the epilogue.

But now, at the head of the epilogue, we read,

Swa cwæð snottor on mode,   gesæt him sundor æt rune.

That is, "So spoke one wise in spirit, sat by himself at counsel."
To whom is the poet referring? Those who take lines 8–110 as
the wanderer's speech generally assume, as surely they must,
that the poet is referring by this new epithet to the wanderer
himself. He can hardly mean the speaker of the closing lament
in lines 92–110, for that indefinite person is merely a rhetorical
figment, and his speech is introduced by the present-future acwið
'will say,' to which the preterite cwæð here does not properly
correspond. It is plausibly argued that the wanderer has spoken
not only of his personal sufferings (ll. 8–57) but with philosophical breadth of the losses all men must sustain in this unstable
world (ll. 58–110). Hence, having appeared to us at first as
merely an eardstapa, he has earned by his discourse the epithet
of a wise man, a snottor on mode.

This is roughly the view set forth by Max Rieger in 1869,[2]
and very ably reasserted by S. B. Greenfield in 1951.[3] There
are some variations of it that are of interest though they do not
change the basic conception of the structure. Thus it was assumed by Thorpe in the first modern edition of the poem, and
later by Gollancz and others, that the wanderer rather than the
poet spoke the first five lines—a very probable inference which
will prove to be of some importance.[4] A logical extension, though
somewhat less inviting, is a recent suggestion that the last four
lines also are spoken by the wanderer, so that only the lines describing the speaker, 6–7 and 111, are the poet's.[5] Real dissent
from the prevailing view has been rare,[6] though it should be remembered that some of the most reputable editors have been
unwilling to commit themselves as to where the wanderer's speech

ends. They put a quotation mark before line 8 for the beginning
(or resumption) of his speech, but one looks in vain for a corresponding mark of conclusion.[7]

If one is to object to the prevailing interpretation it must *Divisions?*
be rather for what it leaves unexplained than for any demonstra- *Speakers?*
ble error. It does not openly conflict with the development of
meaning in the poem, and it explains plausibly what the poem
itself says, in lines 6 and 111, about who is talking. But this explanation is not inevitable, and there are other points at which
we may wonder whether we are on the right track. Most notably,
there is a sharp cleavage between the first half of the poem,
lines 1–57, and the second, lines 58–115.[8] In the first half the
wanderer is dwelling on the sorrows he himself has endured,
generalizing them only enough to include others whose lot closely
resembles his own. A cold and desolate sea provides the setting
for poignant descriptions of the loneliness that attends a friendless and lordless retainer. In the second half he seems to have
put aside his personal sorrows, indeed all his past experience
with its desolate seascapes, in exchange for thoughts about mankind at large, for images of walls and cities in ruin, for the
sweep of history and the awesome prospect of the end of the
world. And the change comes, not gradually, but all at once.
We may easily begin to wonder whether the speaker is really
the same, whether it is advisable to identify the eardstapa with
the snottor on mode.

An unsuccessful but nevertheless significant effort to separ-
Cit. ate the two characters was made some twenty years ago by Ber-
1943 nard F. Huppé.[9] His basic feeling, that the poet was making a
distinction between a man hemmed in by his own bitter experience
and a man whose mind could range freely over the universe with
philosophic detachment, was grounded in the contrast to which I
have already alluded. Unfortunately a slip in reasoning caused
him to ignore the natural division between lines 57 and 58 and to
assert that the eardstapa's speech extended to line 62a. His reason was that the pronoun ic, after giving way to the third person
in lines 30–57, had reappeared in the sentence at 58–62a and
that therefore the eardstapa must still be speaking. This was
a fatal deduction, for lines 58–62a are lines that introduce a
broad consideration of human life and if they are spoken by the
eardstapa they mark him as a philosopher, so that there is no
reason to deny him any of the ideas that follow. Mr. Greenfield,

in the article cited above, accepting as an obvious truth the fallacy in Mr. Huppé's reasoning about the pronoun, had no difficulty in showing that the latter's analysis of the structure was inconsistent in itself and much less satisfactory than the traditional view. Additional trouble was created by Mr. Huppé's effort to identify the wise man's speech with the concluding lament, lines 92–110, so that he was obliged to designate the lines between speeches, 62b–91, as a bridge passage spoken by the poet. The result of this analysis could only be general confusion. The important perception at the root of it was nearly obliterated.

What did not occur to Mr. Huppé, probably because he had already assigned lines 92–110 to the snottor on mode, was that if there are two speakers in a poem they can both use the pronoun of the first person. Suppose we start with the possibility that the eardstapa and the snottor on mode are different characters, as the different epithets suggest, and ask ourselves how much of the poem, in that event, is appropriate to each. The answer is very clear: Lines 1–5 and 8–57 are appropriate to the eardstapa; lines 58–110 (including the imaginary lament, 92–110) are appropriate to the snottor on mode. Lines 6–7, identifying the first speaker, line 111, identifying the second, and lines 112–115, bringing down the curtain with a combination of gnomic wisdom and pious reassurance, may best be left to the poet. The hypermetric form of the last five lines helps to set them off as an epilogue.

If now we look more narrowly at the two speeches thus distinguished we shall find that we have replaced one vaguely inclusive character with two firmly defined ones. The wanderer's speech becomes the perfectly rounded utterance of a person whose own bitter experience has made him an authority. Having achieved some measure of resignation to his lot, he is expressing for all who have suffered similar losses just what this kind of sorrow is made of. His concluding generalization,

> Cearo bið geniwad
> þam þe sendan sceal   swiþe geneahhe
> ofer waþema gebind   werigne sefan,

should not be taken primarily as an appeal for sympathy. It is concurrently, and more importantly, a truth gleaned by suffering. From beginning to end he is telling us what he has learned about life. His personal history gives him the right to speak.

And since we have thus limited his speech, it is important
to make sure that it has a proper beginning. The first five lines
do not say anything that is beyond the range of such a character,
and they say much that is appropriate to him:

> Oft him anhaga   are gebideð,
> metudes miltse,   þeah þe he modcearig
> geond lagulade   longe sceolde
> hreran mid hondum   hrimcealde sæ,
> wadan wræclastas.   Wyrd bið ful aræd!

The opening clause keeps the consoling possibility of God's ultimate mercy in view without assuring us that the speaker has already obtained mercy. He does seem to have reached a state of
comparative tranquillity, but his past sorrows are still vivid in
his mind, and they form the substance of what he has to communi-
cate. As he begins to recall them he thinks of the inexorable
power of fate. It is characteristic of him to generalize out of
his own experience, so that his hypothetical characters are but
projections of himself. Thus the word anhaga (repeated in line
40) sums up his own loneliness. (We may remember that it is
used of Beowulf in a similar situation, when he swims back to
his country alone after having witnessed the death of Hygelac
and all the Geatish host.) And the image of one stirring the rime-
cold sea anticipates the climactic seascapes of lines 37–57. So
long as the wanderer is thought to be responsible for speaking
most of the poem one may toy with the idea that the poet speaks
the opening lines in such a way as to anticipate the wanderer's
own point of view while he adds a bit of piety. But if the bulk of
the poem consists of two complementary speeches, this kind of
introduction is less appropriate. Besides, the wanderer's speech
needs some sort of generalization at the start to hold it together.
His words at line 8 are not a beginning but a development proceeding out of what has been said in lines 1–5. Thus, although
the pronoun of the first person appears in line 8 for the first
time, the sentence is not otherwise comparable to the sentences
with which The Seafarer and The Wife's Lament begin. And the
Swa cwæð eardstapa at line 6, though there is precedent for such
an expression (under somewhat different circumstances) as an
introduction to a speech, is much more likely to refer to something already said.[10]

In the second speech we find just as consistent a characterization as in the first. The snottor on mode proclaims himself at
once as a person who relies, not on direct experience, but on the
wide reach of his thought:

> Forþon ic geþencan ne mæg   geond þas woruld
> for hwan modsefa   min ne gesweorce,
> þonne ic eorla lif   eal geondþence,
> hu hi færlice   flet ofgeafon,
> modge maguþegnas.   Swa þes middangeard
> ealra dogra gehwam   dreoseð ond fealleð.

Verily[11] I cannot think, within the range of this
world, why my mind should not grow dark, when I
consider all the life of highborn men, how of a sudden they have relinquished the hall-floor, proud
young retainers. So this world, each and every day,
droops and falls.

There are several ways in which this passage gains by being
attributed to the second speaker. It was always a little puzzling
to find the wanderer giving reasons for the darkening of his mind,
as if it had not been darkened long ago by the death of his kinsmen.
But the thinker, if he is to feel an answering sadness, must explain the ground for it. In the second line the possessive min now
takes on the extra meaning that explains why it is carrying the
alliteration: "why my mind should not grow dark," that is, "my
mind also, like the wanderer's." But what chiefly strikes our
attention is the sweeping generalization, so much greater in range
and abstraction than the wanderer's, and so objective, as having
nothing to do with the speaker's personal losses: "all the life of
highborn men" (where, as the modge maguþegnas more clearly
shows, it is men like the wanderer and his fellow-retainers that
are in view, but collectively and by implication as representatives
of mankind). And immediately after we encounter the image of
the drooping and declining world, suggesting on the one hand that
men are continually dying and disappearing from the world like
leaves from some continually decadent tree, and on the other
that the world is now in its sixth and final age, and resembles
an old man on the brink of the grave.
We come next to some lines often blamed for irrelevance:

Forþon ne mæg weorþan wis   wer, ær he age
wintra dæl in woruldrice.   Wita sceal geþyldig,
ne sceal no to hatheort   ne to hrædwyrde,
ne to wac wiga   ne to wanhydig,
ne to forht ne to fægen,   ne to feohgifre,
ne næfre gielpes to georn,   ær he geare cunne.
Beorn sceal gebidan,   þonne he beot spriceð,
oþþæt collenferð   cunne gearwe
hwider hreþra gehygd   hweorfan wille.

Verily [or therefore?] a man cannot become wise
before he has a share of winters in the world. A wise
man must be patient, must not be too hot of heart or
too hasty of speech, nor too weak a fighter nor too
reckless, nor too fearful nor too sanguine, nor too
greedy for money, nor ever too eager to boast before
he knows for certain. A fighting man must wait, when
he is to speak his vow, until bold of spirit, he knows
for certain whither the purpose of (men's) breasts
will turn.

Surely this passage, though it is still a digression from the main
course of the argument, looks a good deal more pertinent when it
is recognized as part of the characterization of the second speaker.
He is no modig maguþegn himself, though he may well belong to
the warrior class for whose benefit he speaks, but a man schooled
in prudential wisdom, and he seems to exhibit this practical aspect of his training at a point where his meditation brings it to
mind, partly to show that he knows what is expected of a coun-
selor.[12]
    As now his thought carries him forward to the general doom,
to its miniature yet impressive prototypes in the ruins that
darken the landscape, and to his mournful realization that nothing earthly can endure, he reminds us further of the value he
attaches to the intellect. Thus at line 73 he says it is the gleaw
hæle who must know how terrible it will be when the world is
destroyed, and when he introduces his hypothetical elegist in
lines 88–90 he defines him as one frod in ferðe and requires him
to think deeply before uttering his lament. But I need not continue. From first to last he answers to the definition: he is snottor
on mode.

Once we have made this distinction between the speakers it is difficult to resist it, for it so obviously matches the pattern of theme and image in the poem, and is so direct and simple an explanation for the poet's own words, the swa cwæð eardstapa and swa cwæð snottor on mode. But we may well hesitate momentarily in the face of the unfamiliarity of the form. Here we have two speeches complementing one another, the second a challenging extension of the first, yet the speakers are apparently not disputing with one another and the only direct indication that the second has been listening to the first is the vague implication of his opening forþon and the comparison implicit in his first sentence. This is certainly not an ordinary dialogue in which the speakers are addressing each other. What is the fundamental conception that can render such a juxtaposition of two speeches intelligible?

For a time I was inclined to believe that the poem was a meditative monologue by the thinker in which, after speaking lines 1–5 in his own character, he introduced the wanderer and quoted his words. Then, at line 58, the thinker resumed his meditation and proceeded to the end of it at line 110, after which the poet identified him as the principal speaker. This notion may need passing attention, because something very like it has already been suggested for The Seafarer; but it is surely mistaken. Once we recognize that the first five lines are much more appropriate to the wanderer than to the thinker, we are confronted by two consecutive speeches of almost the same length, and although the second is more inclusive tnan the first and comprehends it intellectually, there is no good reason why the second speaker should be made to quote the first. It is much simpler and more intelligible, as well as fairer, for the poet to quote each of them in turn, acting as a neutral reporter and letting us make up our own minds about the importance of each.

A much more satisfactory answer to the problem of the two speakers is suggested by the poet himself when he describes his second speaker, the snottor on mode, and says he was sitting apart at counsel, gesæt him sundor æt rune. Even if we take this expression with Bosworth-Toller as meaning primarily "sat apart communing with himself," it suggests that he would normally have been expected to be communing with others, taking his place æt rune. For example, in Beowulf, lines 171–172, we are told that many a man among the Danes gesæt rice to rune, and (or even at us) in the manner of a philosopher or a preacher, as if to inculcate a contempt for the world. Rather he assimilates his mood to the other's and seems, as the poet tells us, to be communing with himself though at counsel. He has been following a train of thought and it has ended in a bleak though strangely sublime vision of destruction. If we choose to find it instructive or consoling that is our affair.

Clearly our modern title for the poem does it less than justice. I shall not try to supplant it after more than a century of use, but perhaps I may be allowed to invent, for the sake of summary, one of those generous Elizabethan titles, borrowing a contradiction or two from Peter Quince: "The Wanderer's Lament and the Wise Man's Meditation: Being a Double Elegy and Most Doleful Consolation in Two Voices and an Epilogue, Wherein They that have Lost what they have Loved may Behold the Image of their Sorrow and may Feelingly Know that All Things Earthly Vanish into Night."

II

The idea that there are two speakers in The Seafarer emerged early in the modern criticism of the poem and has recently, after a period of disfavor, been put forward again in a significantly modified form. It will appear once more in these pages, this time in a form strongly resembling that which has just been ascribed to The Wanderer. But along with many resemblances to The Wanderer, The Seafarer exhibits some important differences. It is a much harder poem to follow from passage to passage, so that the question of its dramatic form is seriously entangled with other problems of interpretation. We may profitably begin, therefore, by reminding ourselves of certain peculiarities of the poem and of some notable efforts to deal with them.

Under the scrutiny of two sharply opposed interpreters, Kluge and Anderson, who in this one matter agreed, the poem seemed to fall into three unequal sections, with one point of division after the first quarter and another in the middle.[15] I shall follow Anderson in calling the sections A1, A2, and B, although these symbols do not express the relationship that will ultimately emerge. The division in the middle between A and B (l. 64 or 66) is determined by a contrast in ostensible subject matter and style. The first half, A, is lyric and dramatic and

in Andreas, line 1161, that the counselors of the famished Mermedonians gesæton sundor to rune. The association of the word run with the consultations in hall by a king's trusted advisers is otherwise illustrated by the description in Beowulf, 1325, of the dead Æschere as having been Hrothgar's runwita. It seems possible, then, that the poet is not only describing the isolation of the thinker but at the same time implying that the scene is a nobleman's hall where a number of men are assembled to share experiences and ideas. The topic this time is bereavement, or more broadly, mutability, and two men of vastly different experience and training speak in turn. They are not disputing with one another but making their separate contributions to the discussion, the second, of course, speaking with full awareness of what the first has said and building upon it, but addressing himself, as the other had done, to the group.

Such, I believe, may well be the dramatic assumption behind these partly corroborative, partly antithetic speeches, though certainly the hall was not the only place where, in everyday life, men might have spoken successively on a topic without directly addressing one another, and it must be admitted that the poet has withheld all but the barest hint of a stage setting. The emphasis, beyond question, is on the speeches themselves, and whatever may be their relation to the patterns of actual discourse, it is clear that these dramatic voices are put in sequence for us in order that the poet may do justice to two different aspects of his theme.

At bottom, in fact, the poet reveals by the contrasting elements in these speeches his consciousness of the rival claims of two schools of thought, almost of two cultures. His love for the old Germanic poetical traditions and his mastery of them are amply revealed in the speech of the wanderer and are not altogether hidden in the speech of the wise man. The opposition between the two characters is by no means absolute. But some of the thinker's ideas in this speech and its whole purport reflect the influence of the Mediterrranean learning that became available in the wake of the conversion. The fact that the poet preserves so much of the feeling of tradition in his imagery and his expressions suggests not only his unusual skill but the labor of predecessors in making poetry out of these new ideas and modes of feeling. The author of The Wanderer, in a more radical way than the author of Beowulf, seems deliberately to juxtapose the new mode and the old, to exhibit both the strength and the limitations of the old, and to suggest a synthesis dominated by the new.

As for the poem itself, it seems to me to gain greatly in precision and richness of meaning by the recognition of its duality. When we consider the relations of the two speeches we see that both characterization and theme have become sharper and have developed additional significance by their interaction in our minds. And the poet himself, in comprehending both his characters and the range of their thought and feeling, has displayed a breadth of understanding far beyond what we could see in the monologue we have grown accustomed to reading.

We must beware of oversimplifying the contrast between the two speakers. Both, we should assume, are nominally Christian, both preserve elements of old traditions, both show some interest in the world and its values. But the wanderer, as a typically loyal retainer, belongs to the conservative aristocratic world in both life and poetry; the thinker, though he recognizes a native tradition of wisdom, has moved into the sphere of Biblical and patristic learning, with some flavor of classical philosophy. And the darkness of spirit that has come over both these characters has different roots and leads to different conclusions. The wanderer's whole-souled devotion to his lord and his fellows of the comitatus is at once the sign of his nobility and the cause of his sorrow. This all-absorbing passion has been turned by the death of those he loves into the cold fetters of his loneliness. As the recurring images of confinement in the first half of the poem suggest, the wanderer is imprisoned by the sheer unchanging emptiness of his lordless, friendless environment. If he has found some alleviation of his misery it is not because he has learned to see it in a different light.

The thinker, in contrast, is not thus confined, nor has he suffered so personal a loss. His pensive melancholy, beautifully balanced against the other's sorrow, comes from the knowledge of other people's losses and the prospect of the general doom. His mind is constantly moving outward to survey men's history, to look on a landscape sprinkled with ruins, to look through life and the world. It is remarkable how often he uses geond, meaning variously "over, through, throughout," both as preposition and verbal prefix; it helps to emphasize the notions of penetration and range. The whole oppressive extent of the wanderer's

suffering is diminished by his comprehensive view into the image of one disconsolate survivor of a battle saving a dead comrade from the birds and beasts of prey by burying him in the earth— quite uselessly, of course.[13] Thus, although he very movingly laments the passing of all things that seem of value in the world, there is a certain coolness in his attitude toward individual things and persons. His aloofness, as he sits apart, carries very different implications from the other's loneliness. For there is a balance in his thinking between sadness at the instability and waste of the world and the liberating energy of his thought. The elegy with which he concludes his speech expresses this balance with remarkable clarity and power. By its succession of images of good things that have perished it moves from a beginning full of regret and longing to deepening gloom and total disaster. But when, in the closing line, we find it said that "all this foundation of earth shall become void," we can hardly help recognizing that in the relentless completion of his thought the thinker has annihilated the very ground that breeds these vanishing satisfactions. Any expression of grief involves some release, but there is something almost triumphant in the sweep of this vision of dissolution.

Thus I am persuaded that there is more reason than ever to look upon this elegiac poem as having strong affinities with the literary consolation, as has recently been maintained afresh and very ably by J. E. Cross.[14] As Mr. Cross shows, the main reason for listing the poem as a member of this genre is not the brief acknowledgment of God's mercy at the beginning nor the assurance of steadfastness in heaven at the end, though certainly the latter is a significant way of closing the frame. The main reason is that the grounds for lamentation in the second half of the poem are also familiar medicines for a personal grief: in general, the contemplation of other people's distress tends to mitigate our own, and a panorama diminishes the importance of the foreground. With the separation of characters, it becomes evident that the entire speech of the thinker is at one and the same time a lament and an antidote against the sort of misery that had so long engulfed the wanderer. We need not be surprised at the bitterness of the medicine if we remember the methods of Dame Philosophy in Boethius, nor at the tendency toward consolation in a lament if we remember the funeral elegies of the poets.

But certainly what we have in The Wanderer is no reversal of mood, nor does the second speaker aim his speech at the first

contains frequent references to the sea, whereas the second, B, starts with a reasoned attack on the world and its values, ends with precepts and a sermon-like exhortation, and does not mention the sea. There is a transitional sentence (ll. 64b–66a) that preserves a bit of the imagery of A (the reference to land in contrast to sea) while it introduces the main theme of B, but otherwise the contrast is clearly marked. The division after the first quarter is determined by what has been interpreted by some as a change of speaker, by others as a shift to a new aspect of the same speaker's character, and to his present purposes as opposed to his past experience. The beginning, A1 (ll. 1–33a), tells in the first person of the hardships endured by a man who has made numerous voyages and remembers the wintry ones with particular vividness. He contrasts his misery with the satisfactions of a landsman, his own knowledge of pain and anxiety and loneliness with the landsman's cheerful ignorance. The remainder of the first half, A2 (ll. 33b–64a), also predominantly in the first person, tells of the speaker's desire to make a voyage to a far country, denies that the satisfactions on land can distract a man from his voyage, and says that all the adornments of the land in its blossoming season urge a man to set out if he means to go far. The cuckoo urges him too and bodes sorrow. In confirmation of this note of sorrow and in accord with the earlier section, the speaker says that the prosperous man cannot know what is suffered by those who go farthest on the paths of exile. Yet the speaker is irresistibly impelled to set forth.

Before Kluge had distinguished these three sections Max Rieger had noted the signs of a change in line 33 and had concluded that there must be two speakers. He regarded the poem as a dialogue between an old man, full of bitter experience, and a young man who longed to make a voyage in spite of the other's warnings. The young man's first reply came at the beginning of A2 and there were further exchanges in the course of which no distinction was recognized between A and B.[16] Kluge, in the article already mentioned, accepted the dialogue theory but pointed out the weakness of the evidence for all the changes of speaker after the first and held that there were only two speeches, the old man's in A1 and the young man's after it. But he limited the young man's speech, as a significant piece of characterization, to A2, because he regarded B as a rather bungling addition to the original poem and was not concerned to reconcile it with A.

To Kluge himself and to other critics the separation of A
and B seemed even more important than the question of dialogue
within A. According to Kluge, if one accepted B as an integral
part of the poem one might feel obligated to read A as an allegory, a reading that he thought incompatible with the internal
evidence. By isolating A one could look on it as a purely imita-
tive and secular piece, a lyric and dramatic treatment of men's
relations with the sea. On this matter he won the support of W.
W. Lawrence, who was concurrently unwilling to accept the notion of a dialogue and tried to show that the contrast between A1
and A2 could be reconciled with the assumption that there was
only one speaker.[17]

But Kluge's argument in dismissing B pointed to the means
by which it was soon to be defended. Gustav Ehrismann was the
first to present an allegorical interpretation.[18] He maintained
that the poem was a loosely organized monologue setting forth
the nature and claims of the monastic ideal of life. One set of
symbols represented ascetic rigor and otherworldly aspiration
in terms of a seafarer's life of toil and trouble on the sea and
his concern to reach a far country, while another contrasting
set represented the aristocratic ideal of worldly success and
pleasure in terms of the prosperous landsman and all the cher-
ished satisfactions of life in the hall. In B the worldly satisfactions were disparaged as perishable, and the true end of a good
Christian's endeavor was seen to be the attainment of the Lord's
joys in heaven. There is no doubt that the contrasting images
of A, when isolated, can be thus simply related to the main thesis
of B; but if one considers them in the whole context provided by
the formal elaboration of the poem a number of complications
arise. Ehrismann made no attempt to explain the sequence of
thought from passage to passage. He seems to have considered
this a hopeless enterprise, for he described the author as a mere
compilator, a clumsy arranger of appropriate passages out of the
work of his predecessors, some of whom were skillful poets.

Thus it was left for O. S. Anderson, in the article cited above,
to try to read the poem as a coherent and consistent allegory.
Since he had followed a number of critics in rejecting the dialogue theories of Rieger and Kluge, he was obliged to explain the
supposed allegory in A with respect to the life of its one speaker.
He tried (as unsuccessfully, I think, as everyone else) to avoid
the implication of a change of speakers at the start of A2, but in

other respects he admitted a contrast between A1 and A2. A1, he maintained, was a presentation of the speaker's past life under the figure of voyaging along a dangerous coast in the winter. A2, then, presented the same speaker's longing to set out on a long summer voyage across the deep sea to a far distant country; that is, to take leave of this world altogether and make for the heavenly home.

There are several objections to this interpretation. For one thing, the meaning of the symbols shifts disconcertingly. In A1 the sea represents the vicissitudes of the world; in A2 it represents a passage to the hereafter at the point of death. If the shift were from literal to figurative meanings there would be no difficulty, but the literal meanings of sea and land are (for Anderson) an unregarded element in both sections: and shift is from one figurative meaning to another. Again, there is nothing in A1 to suggest that the speaker means anything beyond what he says. The account he gives of his sufferings at sea, though partly conventional, has seemed to contain so many imaginative touches and to mean so much when taken at face value that many readers are reluctant to take it otherwise. Unless as a secondary interpretation made in retrospect, an allegorical interpretation, having no power to make any of it more intelligible, is merely a nuisance.

It was this last objection that Dorothy Whitelock stressed when she proposed her ingenious and in many ways persuasive interpretation.[19] By assuming with her that the speaker is both a sailor and a religious zealot, a peregrinus pro amore Dei, we can come very close to accepting everything in the poem at face value as spoken in character. For such a person would have had firsthand acquaintance with the actual sea (A1), would have reason to plan another voyage, longer and more strenuous, perhaps, for religious ends (A2), and would be ready enough to philosophize and preach (B).

Certainly this interpretation much surpasses its predecessors in refinement and judgment. It does not foist allegory or religious overtones on verses that do not invite them, and yet it permits the positively religious implications of A2 and B to be recognized freely without the suspicion that they are the work of an interpolator. It also provides a historical context within which not only the seafaring peregrini but the age in which they flourished can be more clearly understood.

Yet it does not solve quite all the problems. For one thing it does not explain or condone (in terms of dramatic or poetic propriety) the absence of sea imagery in B. A pilgrim who was so deeply aware of the actual sea as to be capable of making the words of A1 his own might, in ordinary life, indulge in moral reflections such as we find in B without once mentioning the sea— in fact if the poem has one author, it is clear, no matter how we interpret it, that he has displayed this versatility. But a poetically conceived pilgrim ought not so to violate dramatic probability. For another thing, though as I have said this interpretation permits the religious implications of A2 and B to be recognized, its literalness nevertheless limits the meaning of A2. For, whereas A1 seems to gain by a literal interpretation, A2 seems to gain by an allegorical one. This peculiarity of A2 has been emphasized by studies more recent than Miss Whitelock's and will be considered in due course.[20]

Above all there is a stubbornly particular difficulty. Like all the theories that have treated the poem as a simple monologue, this theory does not give a satisfactory explanation for the language of the first sentence of A2:

Forþon cnyssað nu
heortan geþohtas   þæt ic hean streamas,
sealtyþa gelac   sylf cunnige.[21]

If one gives sylf the emphasis that its position in the verse demands, there is no good way to avoid the implication that the speaker has not been to sea before. This was pointed out specifically by Wülker,[22] and it was the one firm piece of evidence for the dialogue theories of Rieger and Kluge. If the experienced seafarer of A1 is still talking, why does he not say eft cunnige instead of sylf cunnige? In so crucial a matter the poet would hardly have sacrificed sense to a convenient alliteration. Those who have regarded the poem as a monologue have been obliged to believe that the poet was using sylf in a vacuous way and to find translations that would rob it of meaning. Lawrence, who made the first attempt to get around the difficulty, altered and weakened the sylf by a free paraphrase in which he inserted "again" for an eft that is not in the manuscript: "Even I myself, who have endured so much hardship, am impelled to make trial of the waves again."[23] Miss Whitelock, dealing more exactly with

the rest of the sentence, simply leaves sylf untranslated: "Therefore my heart's thoughts constrain me to venture on the deep seas,
the tumult of the salt waves."[24] One has only to reread the original after any of the translations given by the proponents of the
monologue theory in order to feel that the evidence of the text
at this point is flatly against them.[25] Yet if they found the older
dialogue theories unsatisfactory on other grounds, what were
they to do?

An answer of great interest, constituting what seems to me a
signal advance, was made a few years ago by E. G. Stanley in the
course of his article, "Old English Poetic Diction and the Interpretation of The Wanderer, The Seafarer, and The Penitent's
Prayer."[26] He suggested that the poem, though not a dialogue,
does in fact have two speakers, one of whom is quoting the other
at the beginning. He regards A1 as a speech attributed to a typically conceived seafarer and quoted by the principal speaker as
a basis and point of departure for his own discourse, which fills
the rest of the poem. In order to emphasize the limited reality
attributed to the person whose speech is quoted, and perhaps to
suggest the direct influence of the rhetoricians, Mr. Stanley bor-
rows the term ethopoeia from Mr. Huppé and gives it a more
specialized sense than it normally conveyed:[27]

> There are two speakers speaking in the first per-
> son, the ethopoeic exile (lines 1–33a), and the wise,
> pious man eager to go on pilgrimage (33b to the end).
> The break comes (as it does in the various dialogue
> theories) in line 33; for the speaker who says (33b–
> 35b) that he himself is now eager to make trial of sea-
> faring cannot be the man who has just told of the hard-
> ships he has experienced in seafaring. The dialogue
> theories were advanced in the first place to overcome
> this difficulty, which is not explained satisfactorily by
> any of the later theories. The ethopoeic opening is
> the speech of a man whose imaginary exploits have
> led to a true view of this world; the poet has chosen
> this manner of conveying his message because it is the
> most vivid method of conveying it. The poet then ex-
> presses his wish to follow a way of life as contemptu-
> ous of the world as that of the ethopoeic Seafarer; he
> is speaking of himself, but he hopes to urge others to
> follow the same way of life, for his poem is didactic.

In spite of some dubious features that will be questioned
presently, this interpretation marks a real advance because it
deals more justly than previous interpretations with the natural
implications and relationships of the text. The return to a strict
interpretation of <u>sylf</u> is only one of its merits. Even if Mr. Stanley is wrong, as I believe he is, in thinking that one speaker is
quoting the other, he is right in feeling that the relation between
the speakers is not that of an ordinary dialogue. The second
speech is not so much a reply to the first as a major declara-
tion of purpose and belief for which the first speech has given
the stimulus. There are elements of contrast suggesting rejoinder as the second speech opens, but its main effect is to add
another dimension to the imagery and transfer the discussion to
another realm. Thus the notion that the second speaker quotes
the first (however unsatisfactory in some respects) more nearly
accords with the content of the speeches than would the notion
of an ordinary balanced conversation or debate such as we usually find in a dialogue. More important, however, is Mr. Stanley's
perception that if A1 is set apart, A2 and B can easily be joined
together as the speech of a consistent character. For the talk
of voyaging in A2 does not, like the talk in A1, reveal any direct
experience of the sea, much less any deep subjection to its physical being. Even if we take the voyage literally, as Mr. Stanley,
following Miss Whitelock, seems inclined to do, it is a voyage
undertaken by the speaker as a part of his effort to disengage himself from the grip of the phenomenal world. With full dramatic
propriety, therefore, though still perhaps to our regret, his
thoughts move beyond images of the sea to their real center.

Kluge's version of the dialogue theory insisted on a completely secular and realistic interpretation of both A1 and A2, and
treated B as essentially a separate, not properly relevant poem.
But the allegorists and Miss Whitelock, defending the relevance
of B, showed that A2 had strong signs of spiritual if not fully
allegorical implications. Since they did not distinguish between
the speakers of A1 and A2 they did not see the significance of
what they nevertheless helped to establish, that A2 and B have
much more in common than A1 and B. Hence Mr. Stanley's return to the notion of two speakers is not a return to Kluge's kind
of poem. It involves the acceptance, with Kluge, of a literal and
secular A1, but also, with the allegorists and Miss Whitelock, of
a religious, possibly allegorical A2 and of a firm union between

A2 and the thematically dominant B. In consequence there is opportunity for a more complete release of meaning in the various parts, and a more intelligible relationship between them than ever before.

Yet I think we can profitably modify Mr. Stanley's account of the structure and also his interpretation of the meaning. I shall begin with the structure, and first with the problem already mentioned, Mr. Stanley's notion that one speaker is quoting the other. An obvious objection is that the man alleged to be quoting does not say so. How can we understand what he is doing unless he introduces the other speaker with a swa cwæð? If the poem gives us two dramatic characters speaking in turn we can understand the omission of stage directions even if we have been sadly bewildered by their absence; but Mr. Stanley assumes a more or less autobiographical speech made by the poet himself in his own substantial character, at the start of which, without warning, he imitates a seafarer. It does not seem at all likely that the poet, in such a case, would not identify the subordinate speaker. Furthermore, the shadowy character attributed to the imaginary seafarer in contrast to the substantial poet is really not fair to the vividness and power of the speech. Why not accept the simpler view of the old dialogue theory and assume that the two speakers belong to the same plane of dramatic reality: that is, that they are equally fictitious and are speaking in turn? The second speech will still take the first as its point of departure, still overbalance it in length and scope, but will not disparage its authority in its own sphere.

Here at last The Wanderer may be called upon to lend its support and at the same time to suggest a further improvement in Mr. Stanley's view of the structure. The Wanderer, as described above, and The Seafarer show several very striking resemblances, some of which have already emerged and need only be called to mind: (1) Both begin with the speech of a fictitious character. (2) Both introduce a second fictitious character who builds on and enlarges what the first has said. (3) Both introduce the second character's speech with forþon.[28] (4) Both make use of the pronoun of the first person at the beginning of the second speech and imply a difference between the "I" now speaking and the "I" who has previously spoken, one of them giving alliterative prominence to min, the other to (ic) sylf. So much the reader will no doubt have observed for himself. But now there is a fur-

ther resemblance, one that has often been noticed elsewhere but
has not yet been brought to attention here: (5) Both have a passage at the end beginning with hypermetric verses. In The Wanderer this passage has already been taken to be an epilogue
spoken by the poet. In The Seafarer the corresponding passage,
though much longer, is probably the same thing.

Hitherto we have not paid attention to the internal structure
of the second half of the poem, called B, since most of the problems could be treated by assuming its homogeneity. But in fact
there is a noticeable difference between the part that extends to
line 102 and the remainder, lines 103–124. As it happens, these
verses begin a new page (actually a new gathering) in the Exeter
Book, and Thorpe, the first editor of The Seafarer, suspected
that a leaf was wanting and they were the end of another poem.[29]
There is no supporting evidence for this conjecture and there
are signs of relevance in the lines; but there is excellent reason for believing that they are not a part of the second speaker's
discourse. In lines 66b–102 this speaker is explaining why he
has said (64b–66a) that he prefers the joys of the Lord to this
dead, transitory life on land, and parenthetically (72–80) main-
taining the worth of virtuous action. He shows the instability of
the world and the ultimate worthlessness of earthly satisfactions,
ending at line 102 with the worthlessness of gold. Then in lines
103–106 we encounter a series of precepts and gnomic observations that are vaguely pertinent but do not continue the argument.
Six of the first eight of these lines are hypermetric, then the normal form returns. Finally, in lines 117–124, we have a lucid
passage beginning like the closing exhortation of a sermon and
ending with Amen.

> Utan we hycgan   hwær we ham agen,
> ond þonne geþencan   hu we þider cumen. . . .

Now the sermonizing conclusion, unlike the gnomic passage,
is obviously relevant to the poem, but neither of them sounds
like the second speaker. He impresses us in the early part of
his speech as a man of intense feeling and compulsive purpose,
full of the excitement attending a great personal decision. His
reasoned pronouncements from 64b to 102 can readily be understood as his effort to justify the way of life he is choosing. The
generality and loose sequence of the strongly worded gnomes

form a contrasting boundary beyond which can follow the sermonizing conclusion with its gentle admonition and encouragement.

It is best, then, to take the precepts with their hypermetric
opening and the cheerfully pious exhortation as an epilogue spoken
by the poet as master of ceremonies. And this view is corrobo-
rated by the epilogue of The Wanderer, greatly though it differs
in length. The first of its five neatly balanced hypermetric lines
has no counterpart in The Seafarer, being an identification of the
second speaker. But its next three and a half lines correspond
in their gnomic style to the first fourteen of The Seafarer, and
its last half-line, þær us eal seo fæstnung stondeð, corresponds
in the use of the first person plural and in the blend of admonition and reassurance to the last eight of The Seafarer.

Thus it appears that in The Seafarer, as in The Wanderer,
there are two complementary speeches by sharply differentiated
persons, and that the poet, having presented these speeches, adds
a conventional epilogue. This conception of the structure differs
from Mr. Stanley's in that it sees both the persons who make
use of the pronoun ic as dramatic characters clearly distinguished
from the poet, and puts both speeches in the same plane of reality.
This conception also entails a different analysis of the parts of
the poem from that which is implied by the symbols A1, A2, and
B. The first speech corresponds to A1, but the second, containing within itself the transition from talk of voyaging to ratiocina-
tion, combines A2 with two-thirds of B (ll. 33b–102), and leaves
the end of B (ll. 103–124) to be set firmly apart as a mere epilogue to the poet's dramatic vision.

The main structural differences from The Wanderer are the
absence of swa cwæð to identify either of the speakers and the
different proportions of the speeches. The first difference may
be due to faulty transmission of The Seafarer (though it is hard
to find a good place in the first speech for an identifying aside),
or, more probably, to an attempt to move one step closer to
drama. The difference in proportion, however, is closely associated with the radical difference in theme and genre (as Mr.
Cross has insisted)[30] between the two poems. For The Seafarer
presents, in the central character of its second speaker, a man
about to commit himself to a fateful course of action. In the
early part of his speech he talks of his purpose and reveals the
turbulent emotions that impel him toward it; in the later part,
after stating the values that govern his choice, he defends it by

a reasoned attack on the values he plans to reject. The first speech, insofar as it exists for a purpose beyond itself, is not something to be extended and counterbalanced like the speech of the wanderer, but something whose sensory vitality is to be transferred by the second speaker's thoughts to a different realm of meaning.

That the voyage this speaker contemplates has a spiritual end cannot well be doubted, since he says so clearly that the joys of the Lord are hotter to him than this dead, transitory life on land. And certainly his comparison invests the expression lif on lande with a figurative meaning, so that it comes to stand for the life of the worldling. I am not sure, even so, that there is a way to distinguish between the literal voyage that might be contemplated for spiritual ends by the sort of man Miss Whitelock has imagined and the allegorical voyage that might stand generally for the devout life amid the turbulent seas of the world. Yet for a number of reasons I am strongly inclined, now that the first speech in the poem does not have to be included in the same figurative pattern, to regard the voyage as allegorical.

Thus, for one thing, if the voyage is allegorical, the speaker becomes more centrally representative of the religious life, so that both his voyage and his later rejection of worldly values acquire greater scope. Again, if he is not literally concerned with the sea, even as an instrument of purification, it is easier to understand why he never mentions it in the discursive part of his speech. His purpose, which demands a repudiation of the sensory world, merely declares itself openly after the images put into his mind by the vivid discourse of the veteran Seafarer have served their turn. And finally, I think the descriptive part of his speech has the character of the best allegorical composition, in that while it is lifelike and vivid and seems almost right as an imitation of a young man's eagerness for a voyage of ordinary adventure, it suggests, both by its extraordinary intensity and by certain expressions, that it ought to have some deeper import and a more general application. The prospective voyager, when he mentions the anxiety a man must have for his voyage, talks (though not quite explicitly in the negative sentence, ll. 39–43) as if every man that amounted to anything had a voyage to make. And at one or two points I am inclined to accept as secondary implications the meanings that have been proposed by a recent advocate of Anderson's theory.

One of these is elþeodigra eard, the destination of the prospective voyage according to line 38. This has usually been interpreted as "the land of foreigners (or strangers)" and taken
as a description of a normal seafarer's destination abroad. But
G. V. Smithers, in the first part of his study of The Seafarer and
The Wanderer,[31] has argued that the word elþeodig here is used
with reference to the idea that good Christians are exiles and
aliens on earth, destined to travel as peregrini toward their
patria in heaven (as in Hebrews 11:13–16, and in many passages
in the church fathers) and that elþeodigra eard should therefore
be taken as a reference to heaven, the future dwelling place of
those who are now strangers on earth. So interpreted, elþeodigra
eard anticipates and partially explains the speaker's enthusiasm
for the joys of the Lord in lines 64b–66a, as Mrs. Gordon points
out in accepting it in her edition (p. 9). It helps to explain, too,
the ravenous hunger of the speaker's soul (as described in lines
61–64a, a controversial passage of which I shall have more to
say in a moment) at the sight of the far-off destination it has
scouted on its preliminary flight. I think, therefore, that Mr.
Smithers' interpretation, in spite of its riddle-like treatment of
the expression, is probably correct. Yet I should prefer to regard elþeodigra eard as deliberately ambiguous, like certain expressions that have been pointed out elsewhere in the same
speech.[32] The word eðel 'homeland' is the usual and less equiv-
ocal term for the heavenly home when it is looked upon as the
proper dwelling place of sojourners on earth, whereas eard is
more neutrally taken as whatever country one lives in or is heading for.[33] Hence the ordinary translation, "land of foreigners,"
will naturally come to mind first, and it should be allowed to do
so, for it fits the ordinary idea of a voyage that gives the figure
its initial interest. But eard is also used for a dwelling place
in heaven, and in one of Ælfric's homilies it is used pointedly in
that sense, because Ælfric is developing the comparison between
the promised land of the Israelites, þone behatenan eard, and the
heavenly destination of the Christian journey.[34]

A second expression, less central but corroborative, occurs
in the lines that describe the approach of summer, enumerating
the signs that, as we learn immediately after, admonish the man
who plans a long voyage to set forth:

> Bearwas blostmum nimað,   byrig fægriað,
> wongas wlitigað,   woruld onetteð.

The image of the hastening world can be explained, perhaps, as
a mere reminder of the swift passage of the seasons provoked
by the thought of the earth's activity and change as it bursts into
bloom; and once again, as with elþeodigra eard, we can welcome
this superficial meaning for its relevance to the figure of the
voyage. But there seems to be an almost ominous urgency in
the expression as it follows upon words so cheerfully evocative
of springtime beauty, and the impression is strengthened when
we find the cuckoo, as warden of summer, seconding the admonition with mournful speech and foreboding sorrow. The ominous urgency is very well explained if we accept the suggestion,
made briefly by Mr. Smithers and more elaborately by Mr. Cross,
that woruld onetteð is primarily an allusion to the impending though
unpredictable end of this world.[35] Not only does the word onettan
occur in several sermons with reference to the haste with which
the world approaches its end, but Mr. Cross shows in detail how
Gregory the Great, commenting on the image of the fig tree in
Christ's prediction of the end of the world (Luke 21.29 ff.), turns
a simple comparison into a paradox by leaving out the middle
terms, making earth's fertility and growth into a direct prognosti-
cation of its ruin. Ælfric quotes the whole passage from Gregory
in his sermon for the second Sunday in Advent,[36] stating the paradox as follows:

> Soðlice mid þisum wordum is geswutelod þæt ðises
> middangeardes wæstm is hryre. To ðam he wext þæt
> he fealle; to ðy he sprytt þæt he mid cwyldum fornyme
> swa hwæt swa he ær sprytte.

Immediately afterwards Gregory and Ælfric remind us that the
world, having reached its sixth and last age, is like an old man
about to die, and the same reminder occurs in lines 81b–90 of
The Seafarer. I find it hard, therefore, to resist Mr. Cross's
conclusion that woruld onetteð involves the threat of doom. Thus
the prospective voyager has a reason beyond what is usual for
setting out while the weather is propitious. No man can know
whether there will be other summers after this one, and the voyage means the difference between life and death.

By no means, however, does my acceptance of these secondary meanings involve a commitment to the Andersonian view,
now elaborated by Mr. Smithers, that the voyage represents

merely the speaker's passage, at death, into the next world. Nor do I agree with Mr. Smithers' suggestion that we should return to the wælweg of the manuscript in line 63, with or without the extreme interpretation he has put upon the passage in which it occurs. The passage has caused trouble, however, and must receive some comment before I take up the larger problem of the speaker's death.

The six and a half lines beginning at line 58 form the climactic ending of the descriptive section of the speech. The speaker's soul leaves his breast, goes out over the sea, and comes back to him gifre ond grædig, as if hungering for what it has seen across the water.[37] The passage concludes as follows according to the manuscript:

> gielleð anfloga,
> hweteð on wælweg   hreþer unwearnum
> ofer holma gelagu.

In the first of his articles Mr. Smithers argues strongly for wælweg as "way to the abode of the dead" instead of Thorpe's almost universally accepted emendation, hwælweg. Neither compound occurs anywhere else in Old English, but hwælweg has the advantage of conforming to normal alliterative practice and of being obviously pertinent to the context. To make wælweg into a durior lectio instead of a simple piece of carelessness on the part of the scribe requires too great a strain on both versification and meaning—for although the notion of a violent death as a possible element in the voyage is not necessarily to be excluded even from my own reading of the passage, we must keep pagan associations with Valhalla very far in the background if we are to accept such a word as a description of a devout Christian's transit to heaven. There is an artistic difficulty, too, for such a blunt disclosure of the underlying meaning would shatter the illusion created by the richly figurative language of the passage. The time for disclosure is a moment later, when the images have done their work. Thus I think Mrs. Gordon has made the right choice in preferring the emendation.[38]

Still more emphatically I must protest against a subordinate interpretation by which Mr. Smithers has sought to strengthen the idea that the speaker is about to die. He suggests that the anfloga of line 62b, instead of being the bird-like soul (hyge) that has been the subject of the preceding verbs, and can very appropriately be described as a "lone flier" (ānfloga), is a disease (*andfloga) ready to give the speaker a quick release into the next world.[39]

This last interpretation represents the extreme to which the Andersonian allegory has been pressed; but even the moderate interpretation of Anderson himself, by taking the prospective voyage as a voyage of death, runs counter to many of the implications of the poem even for those who, like Mrs. Gordon, take it as a monologue. Actually, as Mr. Smithers' own examples from the Bible, the fathers, and the Old English homilists abundantly demonstrate, the usual assumption about the return of the pilgrim to his heavenly home is that it is to be accomplished by a toilsome journey on earth in which death figures merely as a limit; and when the sea is introduced it is primarily associated with the tribulations of the world. Hence the closing sentences of Mrs. Gordon's rejoinder seem to me essentially right:

> The vain and fleeting pleasures and comforts of
> this world ("life on land")are to be left behind, and
> the suffering exacted by God from his followers (the
> sorge of the sea-journey) is to be undertaken with
> eagerness in the quest for eternity. The Seafarer
> [meaning the speaker of the whole poem, but we may
> aptly think of the second speaker only] does not
> choose death; he responds with eager longing to the
> challenge of that suffering.[40]

An argument for this interpretation within the poem is the passage (ll. 72–80) in which the second speaker concludes that a man should earn the praise not only of those who live after him on earth but of heavenly spirits by fighting against the devil before he dies. This argument is all the stronger if we do not regard lines 1–33a as an account of the prospective voyager's earlier life. By giving these lines to a different person we convert the voyage contemplated in lines 33b–64a into the major adventure of the second speaker's life. We need not insist, with Rieger and Kluge, that he is a very young man, but it is at least appropriate to think that he has not passed the period of manly vigor. This accords well with the imagery of the summer voyage as well as with his ardor, and likewise with his rejection

(implicit in ll. 39–47, explicit in ll. 64b–102) of the world and
its satisfactions. An old man gains little credit by renouncing
what he is obliged to leave. The reasoning here is calculated
to persuade those who can still make a choice, and the speaker
ought to be such a one himself. He must still earn the joys of
the Lord, however vividly he imagines them in advance.

The poem that has now taken shape is more complex than
The Wanderer in spite of the close similarity in structure. By
its use of two speakers it sets up a comparison between two kinds
of seafaring and so not only shifts the focus from the natural to
the supernatural order but transfers the poignant immediacy of
the poetry of sense to the realm of spiritual action. This aspect
of the design seems basic enough to justify such a modified title
as The Two Seafarers. But the second seafarer is the principal
character and the essential conflict in the poem is the conflict
that Ehrismann imperfectly discerned between two ideals of conduct. It begins in the first speech as a mere contrast between
life on land and life at sea. It is transformed in the second speech
into a conflict between the secular ideal as defined by aristocratic
standards and the religious, not exclusively monastic, ideals of a
servant of God.

When we look at the second seafarer's speech as now established we see that it means most at several places if we assume
that he himself, like many a man who took up the cross in those
days, is a man of noble birth who can look forward to the successes and rewards of the comitatus, the blæd and dream of the
dugup with which he contrasts the heavenly counterparts in lines
79–80. When he says in the sentence starting at line 39 that no
man on earth is so proud, so liberal (or so talented?), so youth-
fully keen, so valiant in his deeds, or so graciously treated by
his lord that he will not always have anxiety for his voyage, as
to what the Lord will bring him to, he is indirectly explaining
his own anxiety and, therefore, implying that he himself has
some share of the endowments he describes. The lures of life
on land that he mentions in line 44, the harp and the receiving
of rings, are foremost among the joys of the hall. He says they
cannot keep a man from thinking about the surge of the waves,
but later (ll. 80b–90) he encourages himself to forsake all such
noble satisfactions by reflecting that the world is getting old and
the glories of the heroic past have grown dim. It is relatively
easy to scorn the soft and sheltered prosperity of the sefteadig

secg of line 56 (according to Grein's emendation, which Mrs.
Gordon accepts), but the aristocratic ideal includes heroic action as well, and this secular heroism must also be rejected or
at least surpassed. That is what the speaker is trying to accomplish in lines 72–80. As we know from Beowulf, the military argument was very similar to the religious one: Since death
is inevitable, its hazards must be ignored. Dom ær deaðe is all
a man can hope to attain. The second seafarer does not deny
this argument, but carries it a step farther in his effort to establish a new and superior heroism. By fighting against the devil
instead of ordinary enemies he can hope to receive both the secular hero's reward, the praise of his successors on earth, and
something much more valuable, because permanent, the praise
of the angels.

Concl. I have tried to show that, by attending to the slight indications of the language and the major implications of the content,
we can find ample evidence for repunctuating The Wanderer and
The Seafarer and treating them as consisting, each in its way,
of two dramatic speeches and an epilogue. The proof, as it seems
to me, rests largely on the increased clarity, dramatic consistency, and richness of meaning in the poems when thus read.
But I must not leave wholly unanswered the objection that was
often made to the old proponents of dialogue in The Seafarer.
Why is the point of change in The Wanderer so weakly marked?
Why has the change in The Seafarer, though not quite so unobtru-
sive in itself, been left so entirely without the aid of stage directions? And why is the epilogue marked by so slight a hint as a
group of hypermetric lines and a change of tone? How could any
reader of the Exeter Book when it was new have understood the
form any better than a reader of today? To this objection I can
only say that I think there has indeed been a mechanical failure
in the written presentation of the poems. So many scholars
would not have gone wrong for such a long time if there had been
due warning of the changes I have mentioned. But this is an easy
mistake for a poet or an anthologist to make when he is recording poems in an age that is accustomed to oral delivery. I do not
think, as the dual performance of Widsith and his fellow Scilling
might suggest, and as Rieger imagined for The Seafarer, that
there would normally have been two performers: the epilogues
of both poems render this doubtful, and the swa cwæð's of The
Wanderer preclude it. But before an audience a single performer

might have indicated the change by shifting his position or by a change of tone after a pause, and he might also have given warning of what was coming by a revealing title and a few words of explanation before he began. In the Edda we find dialogue poems introduced by explanations in prose, and it seems as if something of the sort might have been general when poems were recited, though rarely included when they were put on parchment. It is as if The Wanderer and The Seafarer had been recorded in too nakedly poetical a form with only such explanations (namely, the swa cwæð lines in The Wanderer) as had all too inadequately been incorporated as orthodox verses. In the dialogue of Solomon and Saturn the speakers are identified, but by formulas that stand outside the verse. In the dialogue of Joseph and Mary in the Christ there are no explicit identifications, and we must judge, as in The Seafarer, entirely by what the speakers say (that is, until Mary's carefully introduced speech at the end), though I must add that I do not myself believe in the rapid interchange of speeches ascribed to Joseph and Mary in our editions.

The form I have attributed to The Wanderer and The Seafarer has no exact parallel either in Old English or elsewhere, so far as I know; but the sharply differentiated dramatic speeches I have outlined, in contrast to the loose and often inconsistent monologues we have been accustomed to reading, are of a sort that is by no means unusual in Old English poetry. From Beowulf to the Exeter Book Riddles there is abundant evidence that Old English poets took delight in inventing speeches for clearly imagined characters. We have wholly dramatic monologues in The Wife's Lament, The Husband's Message, the passionate little lyric Wulf and Eadwacer, and the brilliant Deor. All these poems have their obscurities, to be sure, but not in their dramatic aspect. We have a carefully framed dramatic monologue in Widsith. And in what is probably the finest of all the dramatically conceived poems, The Dream of the Rood, we have a speech within a speech; for the dreamer is as carefully conceived a character as the rood itself. Thus The Wanderer and The Seafarer, if we can attribute to them the form I have described, take their places even more securely than before as members of a vigorous dramatic tradition.

One may naturally ask whether these two poems are the work of the same poet or merely closely related products of the same poetic circle. The extraordinarily close resemblances in style, structure, and underlying ideas make it hard for me to resist the

POPE

conclusion that they belong to the same poet, and the differences
I have noted, important though they are, need not be considered
an obstacle. Still, there is probably room for doubt. What appears certain is that each of these poems is the work of an accomplished and original poet, one who had full command of the
traditional poetic idiom in combination with unusual powers of
invention,[41] who understood the ancient feelings and attitudes
of his people and also the intellectual and spiritual claims of
the new age. If there were two such poets, the age was the richer.

NOTES

1 Quotations are from The Exeter Book, edd. G. P. Krapp and
E. V. K. Dobbie (New York, 1936), pp. 134–137. Once or twice
I have altered the punctuation.

2 "Über Cynewulf," ZDP, I (1869), 313 ff.; on The Wanderer,
324–330.

3 "The Wanderer: A Reconsideration of Theme and Structure,"
JEGP, L (1951), 451–465. Greenfield's analysis has recently
been elaborated by Willi Erzgräber, "Der Wanderer, Eine
Interpretation von Aufbau und Gehalt," Festschrift zum 75.
Geburtstag von Theodor Spira, edd. H. Viebrock and W. Erz-
gräber (Heidelberg, 1961), pp. 57–85.

4 Codex Exoniensis, ed. B. Thorpe (London, 1842), p. 286; The
Exeter Book, Part I, ed. I. Gollancz, EETS, 104, (London,
1895), p. 287. Their punctuation is briefly supported by W.
S. Mackie, MLN, XL (1925), 92.

5 T. C. Rumble, "From Eardstapa to Snottor on Mode: The
Structural Principle of 'The Wanderer,'" MLQ, XIX (1958),
225–230.

6 For example, Norah Kershaw (Mrs. Chadwick), in Anglo-
Saxon and Norse Poems (Cambridge, 1922), pp. 8 ff., limits
the wanderer's speech to lines 8–29a, after which the first
person gives way to the third; but in her introductory remarks
on p. 6 she expresses uncertainty. Emily Doris Grubl, in her
Studien zu den angelsächsischen Elegien (Marburg, 1948),
pp. 15 ff., limits the wanderer's speech to lines 8–57, attri-
buting all else to the poet himself until the conclusion, 112–

115, which she attributes to the snottor on mode. Her analysis on p. 31, however, disregards speakers and treats the poem as consisting of prologue (ll. 1–5), Part I (ll. 6–57), Part II (ll. 58–110), and conclusion (ll. 111–115).

7 The list includes Sweet, Gollancz, Bright, Kluge, and (perhaps unintentionally) Krapp and Dobbie. See Huppé's article, cited below in n. 9, pp. 518 f.

8 Fernand Mossé prints the poem with an extra space between lines 57 and 58, and in his notes calls lines 58–115 the "seconde partie de la poème" (Manuel de l'Anglais du Moyen Âge, I, Vieil-Anglais [Paris, 1945], pp. 290 and 404). F. P. Magoun, Jr., setting off the introduction and conclusion, divides the middle section into Part I (ll. 8–57) and Part II (ll. 58–110) of the wanderer's speech (Anglo-Saxon Poems . . . Normalized [Second Corrected Printing, Dept. of English, Harvard Univ., 1961], pp. 18–21). Earlier Ernst Sieper had tried to show that lines 58–110, along with the prologue and epilogue, were not part of the original poem. (Die altenglische Elegie [Strassburg, 1915], pp. 197 ff.) Grubl (above, n. 6) and Erzgräber (above, n. 3) observe the same division into two parts between lines 57 and 58 but treat these parts (with prologue and epilogue) as members of a carefully unified whole.

9 "The Wanderer: Theme and Structure," JEGP, XLII (1943), 516–538.

10 This was Mackie's opinion in the article cited above, n. 4. Greenfield (op. cit., supra, n. 3, pp. 455 f.) cited two examples in which swa cwæð precedes a quotation and held that Mackie's argument was therefore inconclusive. He chose to attribute lines 1–5 to the poet for the sake of what he thought was the most satisfactory structure. His view is supported by Erzgräber (op. cit., supra, n. 3, pp. 77 f.), who nevertheless calls attention (p. 75) to the link between anhaga, line 1, and anhogan, line 40.

11 This meaning of forþon was ably discussed by W. W. Lawrence in his influential though now largely superseded article, "The Wanderer and The Seafarer," JEGP, IV (1902), 460–480; on forþon, pp. 463 ff. Fundamentally the word asserts that there is some sort of connection between what has been said and

what follows. "As for that" is perhaps as close as one can
come to the vague meaning paraphrased here by "verily."
I find this vague meaning earlier in the poem at line 37 and
probably also at line 64, though this last may be "therefore."
The meaning is certainly "therefore" at line 17. The same
meanings and another "because" or "for," appear in The
Seafarer. The case for an adversative sense, first suggested
by Rieger for The Seafarer, is strongly supported by Marjorie
Daunt, "Some Difficulties of The Seafarer Reconsidered,"
MLR, XIII (1918), 474 ff. Some of her examples are persuasive but a clearly adversative sense does not seem to be demanded in either of these poems. See further n. 28 below.

12 A rhetorically similar passage in Blickling Homily X (ed.
Morris, p. 109, ll. 26–30), to which G. V. Smithers has called
attention (Medium Ævum, XXVI [1957], 140), is by contrast
one-sidedly clerical in content.

13 Ll. 80–84. J. E. Cross has shown that at least the sum-formu-
la of this passage, and possibly the enumeration of different
ways by which the body may be destroyed, can be attributed
to the influence of patristic writings. ("On The Wanderer
Lines 80–84: A Study of a Figure and a Theme," Vetenskaps-
Societetens i Lund Årsbok [1958–59], pp. 75–110.) Yet
whether this influence is admitted or not, I think we must
recognize the basic sense of the passage as something rather
different from what the fathers were concerned about. Here
the distinction between the accusative plural in Sume wig
fornam and the following instances of the accusative singular sumne should be observed. The thinker has just pictured
a military host lying dead by a wall. He says, with understatement, that "some," meaning "many," had been carried
off by war, and he now mentions what happened to the corpses:
"One a bird carried off over the high sea, one the grey wolf
shared with death, one a sad-faced earl hid in an earth-pit."
A very similar interpretation is set forth by Erzgräber, op.
cit., supra, n. 3, p. 69.

14 "On the Genre of The Wanderer," Neophilologus, XLV (1961),
63–75. The idea was suggested earlier, with apt comparison
to Boethius, by R. M. Lumiansky, "The Dramatic Structure
of the Old English Wanderer," Neophilologus, XXXIV (1950),

104–112. Erzgräber (above, n. 3) presses still further the argument for Boethian influence.

15 F. Kluge, "Zu altenglischen Dichtungen, I, Der Seefahrer," Englische Studien, VI (1883), 322–327; O. S. Anderson, "The Seafarer: An Interpretation," K. Humanistiska Vetenskapssamfundets i Lund Årsberättelse (1937), pp. 1–49.

16 Rieger's brief exposition forms part of the article cited above, n. 2, ZDP, I (1869), 330–332. On pp. 334–339 he printed the entire poem as a dialogue according to his theory. The old man speaks ll. 1–33a, 39–47, 53–57, 72–124; the young man, ll. 33b–38, 48–52, 58–71.

17 Op. cit., supra, n. 11. Lawrence's opinion has sometimes been misrepresented, as if he had accepted as original all but lines 103–124. On p. 462 he says, "I believe with Kluge that 64b–124 is an addition," and it is to this entire half of the poem (which Kluge had called homiletic) that he must be referring in his conclusion, p. 480: "There seems no reason to assume that the Wanderer and the Seafarer are not preserved in essentially their original form, with the exception of the homiletic addition to the latter poem." Doubting the originality of such a large part of The Seafarer could seem a small matter to Lawrence because his article was aimed chiefly at the fantastically disintegrative theory of R. C. Boer. It is a wholly different and subordinate problem that Lawrence takes up on p. 471, where he agrees with Thorpe that lines 103–124 may be, not an addition, but the end of another poem. See below, n. 29.

18 "Religionsgeschichtliche Beiträge zum germanischen Frühchristentum, II, Das Gedicht vom Seefahrer," Beiträge zur Geschichte der deutschen Sprache und Literatur, XXXV (1909), 213–218.

19 "The Interpretation of The Seafarer," in Early Cultures of North-West Europe: H. M. Chadwick Memorial Studies (Cambridge, 1950), pp. 261–272.

20 Mrs. Gordon advances another objection in her excellent edition (London, 1960), p. 6. I do not make use of it here because (properly enough for Mrs. Gordon but disconcertingly here) it draws evidence for the speaker's character indiscriminately from A1 and A2.

21 Ll. 33b–35. My quotations are from Mrs. Gordon's text, though I have sometimes altered the punctuation, and for consistency I spell forþon as one word.

22 Richard Wülker, Grundriss zur Geschichte der angelsächsischen Literatur (Leipzig, 1885), p. 210.

23 Op. cit., supra, n. 11, p. 467.

24 Op. cit., supra, n. 19, p. 264.

25 Mrs. Gordon weakens sylf partly by a shift of emphasis and partly by a different interpretation of the clause in lines 34b and 35: "And so the thoughts trouble my heart now that I myself am to venture on the deep (or towering) seas." Here she gives partial recognition to sylf ("I in person" rather than "I also") but argues that the saving distinction is to be found in the emphasis on the deep seas, as if the speaker had made only coastal voyages before—a distinction that would be much clearer if only sylf were omitted. Her "now that" further weakens the effect. But this interpretation of nu . . . þæt is abnormal (the ordinary idiom being nu . . . nu) and is rendered very improbable by the seeming parallelism of the clause of purpose in the next sentence. (She is probably right, however, though this does not affect the argument, in taking heortan as object of cnyssað.)

26 Anglia, LXXII (1955), 413–466; esp. 454 f.

27 Huppé discusses ethopoeia in the article cited above (n. 9), pp. 517 f. He took the term from Margaret Schlauch, "Prosopopoeia in The Dream of the Rood," in Essays and Studies in Honor of Carleton Brown (New York, 1940), pp. 30 f., who found it mentioned several times in Rhetores Latini Minores, ed. C. Halm. See especially the accounts of it by Emporius (Halm, pp. 561 ff.) and Isidore (Halm, p. 514). It applies properly to any imaginary speech so devised as to characterize the speaker, and therefore to almost all speeches in poetry, to which the rhetoricians resort for models. It seems hardly worth reviving, but it may have served as a catalyst for some good ideas of Mr. Stanley's.

28 At line 33b in The Seafarer the meaning of forþon may be exactly like that at line 58 in The Wanderer, an "as for that"

which we may render as "verily" or "truly," or it may be
"therefore," referring to the seafarer's statement that the
landsman cannot believe what he has endured at sea: therefore the second speaker is impelled to make trial for himself. On the whole I prefer the vaguer sense. I also prefer
not be take the forþon's at lines 33 and 39, or those at 58
and 64, as correlatives, as Miss Whitelock suggested in the
article cited, pp. 264, 266, because the suspension created
by the first forþon in the pair weakens the force of the sentence it introduces. Elaborate logical structures are usually hostile to poetry. In both instances the first forþon (ll.
33 and 58) can be "verily" or "truly," the second (ll. 39 and
64) "for." See above n. 11.

29 Codex Exoniensis, p. 312, n. The idea was mentioned with
at least tentative approval by others, e.g., Lawrence, op. cit.,
supra (n. 11); N. Kershaw, Anglo-Saxon and Norse Poems,
p. 18; Krapp and Dobbie, The Exeter Book, p. xxxviii. W. J.
Sedgefield omitted these lines from his Anglo-Saxon Verse-
Book, saying (p. 32), "We have omitted 22 or 23 lines with
which the poem ends in the MS, as they are definitely religious rather than moralizing. It is possible that the latter
part of this poem and of The Wanderer may have been later
'tailpieces' added by some monk for purposes of edification."
Sweet, who first included the poem (as a monologue) in the
seventh edition of his Anglo-Saxon Reader in 1894, accepted
lines 103–108 as comparable to the last four lines of The
Wanderer but relegated the rest to his notes. The problem
is reviewed by Mrs. Gordon on p. 11 of her edition.

30 Op. cit., supra, n. 14.

31 "The Meaning of The Seafarer and The Wanderer," Medium
Ævum, XXVI (1957), 137–153; continued in XXVIII (1959),
1–22; Appendix, 99–104; the discussion of elþeodigra eard
is in XXVI, 147–151.

32 Earthly and heavenly meanings of dryhten in lines 41 and
43; dream in 65, 80, and 85; blæd, 79 and 88; duguþ, 80 and
85. See S. B. Greenfield, "Attitudes and Values in The Seafarer," SP, LI (1954), 15–20; also Mrs. Gordon's edition,
pp. 26 f., and her discussion of "life on land," pp. 4 ff. and
42.

33　See the references under these words in Joseph Bosworth–
　　T. N. Toller, An Anglo-Saxon Dictionary and Supplement
　　(Oxford, 1898 and 1921). Mr. Smithers' most persuasive
　　Old English illustration, from Blickling Homily II (ed. Morris,
　　p. 23, ll. 1–7) has eþel: ". . . we synd on þisse worlde ælþeodige,
　　. . . and nu eft sceolon oþerne eþel secan, swa wite, swa wuldor,
　　swe we nu geearnian willaþ." Cf. also Ælfric, Catholic Homilies,
　　ed. Thorpe, I, 162, ll. 16–20: "Nis ðeos woruld na ure eðel, ac
　　is ure wræcsið; forði . . . we . . . sceolon efstan mid godum
　　geearnungum to urum eðele, þær we to gesceapene wæron, þæt
　　is to heofenan rice."

34　Catholic Homilies, ed. Thorpe, II, 214, ll. 25–27: "He gehælð
　　his folc fram heora synnum, and gelæt to ðam ecan earde
　　heofenan rices, swa swa se heretoga Iesus gelædde þone ealdan
　　Israhel to ðam earde þe him behaten wæs." The word eard is
　　repeated in the same sense at p. 222, lines 11 and 12; but at
　　line 25 heaven is "ðone ecan eðel." I must add that the in-
　　terpreters of the Bible did not feel obliged to adopt the same
　　allegory for every mention of foreign travel. Thus Ælfric,
　　expounding the parable of the talents (Matt. 24:14 ff.) trans-
　　lates "Homo quidam peregre proficiscens" as "sum rice man
　　wolde faran on ælðeodigne eard" or, a little later, "on ælðeo-
　　dignysse," and then cites Gregory for the interpretation:
　　"Hwæt is se man þe ferde on ælðeodignysse buton ure Drihten,
　　seðe, mid þam lichaman ðe he on eorðan underfeng, ferde to
　　heofenum? Witodlice flæsces wunung is eorðe, and Cristes
　　lichama wæs gelæd swilce to ælðeodignysse ða ða he wæs
　　ahafen to ðære heofenlican wununge, þær ðær næfre ær nan
　　lichama ne becom." (Thorpe, II, 548, 550. Max Förster,
　　Anglia, XVI (1894), 3, identifies Gregory's homily as the
　　ninth of the series on the Gospel.) By this line of reasoning
　　we could take elþeodigra eard as heaven because it is the
　　land of spirits, who are strangers to the flesh; but certainly
　　the interpretation offered by Mr. Smithers rests on a much
　　more basic and widely diffused concept of the Christian's
　　status on earth.

35　Smithers, Medium Ævum, XXVIII, 7; Cross, "On the Allegory
　　in The Seafarer—Illustrative Notes," same volume, pp. 104–
　　106.

36 Catholic Homilies, ed. Thorpe, I, 614.

37 In his second article, Medium Ævum, XXVIII, 14 ff., Mr.
Smithers cites evidence to show that behind this vivid passage is the widespread superstition that a man can send his
soul out of his body and that it may appear to others in the
form of an animal, often a bird. The same point has been
made independently by Vivian Salmon, "The Wanderer and
The Seafarer, and the Old English Conception of the Soul,"
MLR, LV (1960), 1–10. These illustrations seem decidedly
pertinent, though there is no need to insist on taking the
superstition literally here: it gives imaginative form to a
universal psychological experience. Miss Salmon, however,
has made it appear likely that related superstitions are responsible for some of the expressions in The Wanderer, ll.
52–55, notably the otherwise puzzlingly redundant combination, secga geseldan.

38 E. G. Stanley has renewed the plea for wælweg in his review
of Mrs. Gordon's edition, Medium Ævum, XXXI (1962), 54–
60. He proposes (p. 58) a double meaning, both wælweg 'oceanway,' first adopted by Grein, and Mr. Smithers' wǣlweg. The
meaning "oceanway" would certainly be acceptable if the al-
liance of wæl and weg could be shown to be probable (as I
think it cannot), but the demands of alliteration would not be
served, for crossed alliteration on h and w does not seem at
all probable with this particular grammatical pattern. Mr.
Stanley urges that a scribe would not be likely to change an
easily understood compound such as hwælweg to anything so
difficult as wælweg; but a scribe might very well drop an h
without intending to change a meaning. The scribe of the
Exeter Book has omitted initial h before a consonant at Christ
783 (leotan corrected to hleotan); Azarias 22 (to worfne corrected to tohworfne); Phoenix 126 (remig), 137 (-leoþres),
197 (gewæs corrected to gehwæs); Juliana 577 (bi lænan);
Widsith 14 (wala); Riddle 15, 4 (leorum); 33, 3 (leahtor); 54,
5 (rand). Before vowels he has added it wrongly or omitted
it on numerous occasions: e.g., Christ 615 (is for his), 885
(healle for ealle), 1412 (ingonge for hingonge); Guthlac 271
(hus for us), 950 (hælmihtiga), 1215 (onhæfen for on æfen);
Azarias 61 (hofne corrected to ofne); Phoenix 477 (eortan
for heortan), 650 (elpe for helpe); etc. My attention was

called to this phenomenon by Miss Whitelock, to whom I am indebted for some very helpful criticism both at this point and elsewhere. I must add that Mr. Stanley says nothing in this review of his earlier interpretation of The Seafarer and seems inclined to favor that of Mr. Smithers.

39 Medium Ævum, XXVIII, 20–22. Mrs. Gordon's desire to identify the ānfloga with the cuckoo (geac) of line 53 (edition, p. 9) seems ill advised as soon as we are willing to grant that the soul itself resembles a bird in flight. The epithets of line 62a, gifre ond grǣdig, accord with the verb gielleð of 62b and should refer to the same creature. There is no need to identify the hyge with any particular bird, but these words would suit a bird of prey (ful oft þæt earn begeal, 24; [ic] gielle swa hafoc, Riddle 24, 3) at least as well as a sea gull, a bird that Mrs. Gordon understandably thinks inappropriate. Perhaps in the whole context the eagle supplies the greatest number of relevant characteristics, since he not only flies alone, screams, and has a voracious appetite, but is noted for his powerful flight and his sharp eyes. As a type of St. John the Evangelist he can look at the divine radiance by which others are blinded. But of course the speaker would hardly wish to claim for his soul more than a distant resemblance to so exalted a symbol.

40 Mrs. Gordon's edition, p. 10.

41 The traditional attitudes and expressions are naturally most abundant in the speeches of the two traditional characters, the wanderer and the veteran seafarer. That is probably the main reason for what J. J. Campbell has noted in his study of the distribution of verse formulas and poetic diction in The Seafarer: "Oral Poetry in The Seafarer," Speculum, XXXV (1960), 87–96. That there is a distinction between oral and written composition in different parts of the poem is unlikely on general grounds and is rendered still more unlikely by W. A. O'Neil, "Another Look at Oral Poetry in The Seafarer," Speculum, XXXV (1960), 596–600.